The European Marketplace

The European Marketplace

James Hogan

M

First edition published 1991 by
THE MACMILLAN PRESS LTD
London and Basingstoke

Associated companies in Auckland, Delhi, Dublin,
Gaborone, Hamburg, Harare, Hong Kong, Johannesburg,
Kuala Lumpur, Lagos, Manzini, Melbourne, Mexico City,
Nairobi, New York, Singapore, Tokyo.

British Library Cataloguing in Publication Data

The European Marketplace.
   1. European Community countries. Economic
integration
   I. Hogan, James
   337. 1'432

   ISBN 0-333-51858-6

Typeset and printed in Great Britain

For

WILLIAM POETON

and

THE UNION OF INDEPENDENT COMPANIES

Contents

Contents

PART SEVEN: THE INFORMATION NETWORK

Foreword

Europe is in a state of profound change. Within the European Community we have the creation of a genuine Single Market, with closer economic and political ties between the member countries. In the East we are witnessing the total reshaping of almost all those countries which have lived so long in the shadow of occupation, war and repression. I see this new decade as having special significance for Europe.

The Single European Market has developed a dynamic of its own. The 1992 process has become everbody's property, not just the preserve of bureaucrats and politicians. People throughout the Community expect the Single Market to affect their lives and they expect it to benefit them both in their work and as consumers. Business decisions in all forward-looking companies are being taken in a European context, while existing investment activity reflects the new confidence which commerce and industry have in the Community's future.

As our economies come closer together, we will also see progress in the economic and monetary field and a strong commitment to an open Community which does not shut itself off from the outside world. This is all the more important at a time when the political and economic character of the East European countries is changing so fast. Their renaissance will be long and at times painful, but the Community's political and economic stability is going to prove an invaluable support for them. Indeed, I would expect the Community to become an increasingly effective and positive influence in world affairs during the 1990's.

In the face of all these changes, business and industry must think in strategic terms. The home market is now the Single European Market, extending to the European Free Trade Area countries and perhaps beyond. It is a time to look ahead and adapt to the new landscape of Europe which is in the making.

SIR LEON BRITTAN
Commissioner for Competition
Commission of the European Communities
Brussels

Acknowledgements

The Editor is grateful to hundreds of organisations and people throughout Europe, too numerous to mention individually, for the information and advice they have provided during the preparation of this book. The European Commission in London has been particularly helpful in providing research facilities. Many of those who have assisted have gone to considerable lengths to provide extensive briefing, background material and factual information. Special thanks are also due to Walter Allan, Andrea Hartill and Penny Allport at Macmillan Publishing for their advice, support and patience during the time it has taken to complete the work. James Haywood has gallantly read the proofs.

Contributors

GEORGE BAIN is the Principal of the London Business School, Chairman of the Council of University Management Schools and a member of the National Forum of Management Education and Development.

BARRY BALDWIN is Director of Independent Business Services for Price Waterhouse Europe and Co-ordinator of Price Waterhouse's 1992 Services in the UK. He was seconded to the Conservative Research Department from 1980-82 to advise on smaller business policy.

BARCLAYS BANK PLC

CAROLINE BENTLEY is a principal with Goodall Alexander O'Hare & Company, business strategy consultants. She has developed growth and acquisition strategies for many leading European companies and has worked for Price Waterhouse and the European Parliament.

MISHKA BIENKOWSKI is a Project Director in EPRC Ltd, a company associated with the University of Strathclyde. She is co-author of EPRC's regular publication *Government Support for British Business* and runs EPRC's on-line financial incentives database, AIMS.

BIRD SEMPLE FYFE IRELAND WS is the Scottish member firm of the Eu-Lex European law network.

JOHN BREBNER is the principal of the City firm of solicitors, Brebner & Co., specialising in continental European laws. He is the author of *Setting Up a Business in the European Community*, published by Kogan Page.

MONICA BREBNER is a legal researcher with Brebner & Co. and is reading languages at Exeter University.

MARGUERITE-MARIE BRENCHLEY has worked for the London office of the European Commission since 1973. As Librarian she has acquired extensive knowledge of sources of European information.

BRITISH TECHNOLOGY GROUP is a self-financing public organisation licensing new scientific and engineering products to industry and providing finance for the development of new technology.

COMMITTEE OF DIRECTORS OF POLYTECHNICS

CONFEDERATION OF BRITISH INDUSTRY

DEPARTMENT OF TRADE AND INDUSTRY

EDWARD DOLLING is the Director of Operations in Coopers and Lybrand Deloitte for Eastern Europe and the Soviet Union.

KELLY DOW is Chairman of International Software Marketing, East Grinstead and a former winner of the Institute of Directors Salesman of the Year Award.

TED ETTERSHANK is Managing Director of Hill Samuel Commercial Finance.

SUSAN FOREMAN is a chartered librarian (Reading University and Department of Trade and Industry) and is responsible for setting up the library of the Office of Fair Trading. For nine years she edited the books page of *British Business*, formerly published by the DTI.

PHILIP GOLDENBERG is a partner in City solicitors, S. J. Berwin & Co, and specialises in UK corporate finance. He is a member of the CBI's London Regional Council and his firm is a founder member of the CBI's 1992 Initiative.

TERRY HANSON is Social Sciences and Official Publications Librarian at Portsmouth Polytechnic library.

TIMOTHY F. BEYER HELM is founder of the London School of Economics European Society and press spokesman for the European movement.

JAMES HOGAN is the author of several business guides including *The Export Guide to Europe* (Macmillan, and Gale Research, USA). He has served for fifteen years in the overseas trade-related divisions of the Department of Trade and Industry, including five years as the EC News Editor of *British Business*. As a journalist he has written extensively in the business press.

SIR DEREK HORNBY is Chairman of the British Overseas Trade Board, Chairman of the National Accreditation Council for Certification Bodies (NACCB) and Chairman of the British Institute of Management.

ROLAND KING has had 33 years experience with Price Waterhouse and is now Director of the firm's European Community services consultancy in Brussels. Previous assignments include 16 years service in Paris where he was appointed Senior Partner in the French firm.

LEATHES PRIOR is the English member firm of the Eu-Lex European law network.

CHARLES McCARTAN is an Associate Director of Trade Indemnity Plc. He is also a member of the Institute of Credit Management and is a frequent lecturer on risk management.

PETER MORGAN is the Director-General of the Institute of the Directors.

ANTHONY NOLAN is the Contracts Director for a multi-million pound British company, and is responsible for contracts in operation throughout Europe. He is also consultant to a design corporation specialising in developments in the USA.

NEIL PAYNE is the Executive Partner in Coopers and Lybrand Deloitte for Eastern Europe and the Soviet Union.

ANTHONY PIERCE is Managing Director of Export Control Ltd, an export payment and risk company. Former positions include Group Export Finance Manager and Treasury Operations Manager for BICC, and group Export Credit Manager for The Plessey Company.

EDWARD PITT is a Partner in Clifford Chance, the London-based international law firm. He practices in EC law, in particular EC competition (anti-trust) law and international trade law (anti-dumping). He has practised in Brussels for ten years.

WILLIAM POETON is President of the Union of Independent Companies, Chairman of Poeton Industries Ltd and a former Vice-President of the Economic and Social Committee in Brussels.

NIGEL REEVES is the Professor of German and Head of the Department of Modern Language at Aston University, Birmingham. He is published extensively on foreign language proficiency for overseas trade and won the 1990 Goethe Medal for his contribution to fostering the use of the German language abroad.

MIKE ROSSER is Managing Director of J. Walter Thompson Plc. He has held senior management posts in several prominent companies including Allen Brady & Marsh, Dorland, and Ogilvy and Mather.

ANTHONY SAXTON is Chairman of the London recruitment consultancy, Saxton Bampfylde International and founder Chairman of the British Association of Executive Search Consultants (BAESC).

SUSANNE SCHALK is a Senior Consultant with Coopers and Lybrand, Frankfurt.

IAN STARR is a partner in the international law firm, Clifford Chance, where he specialises in intellectual property rights and EC law relating to such rights

JANET TEMPLE is the Administrator of the Council of University Management Schools.

CRAIG THOMSON is a member of the European editorial team of the Economist Intelligence Unit.

HUGH THOMSON is the Director of Research and Development Services at the University of Strathclyde. Formerly, he has been Managing Director of Integrated Micro Applications Ltd and held a senior position at the Production Engineering Research Association.

RICHARD WAKERLEY is a senior consultant with the EDI (Electronic Data Interchange) and DIP (Document Image Processing) Group of the National Computing Centre (NCC)

PETER WEBSTER is a former head of publicity at the British Overseas Trade Board. He has attended more than 40 trade fairs throughout the world and has contributed features on overseas trade and trade promotion in numerous newspapers and trade periodicals.

MACMILLAN/PICKUP

National Training Directory 1991

The PICKUP initiative is run by the Department of Education and Science. The information in this directory is compiled by Guildford Educational Services Ltd.

October 1990
ISBN 0 333 53913 3
£75.00

Table of Contents

■ Order Form ■ ■ ■ ■ ■ ■ ■ ■ ■ ■ ■

To: Globe Book Services Ltd
   Macmillan Publishers
   Stockton House
   1 Melbourne Place
   London WC2B 4LF
   Tel: 071-379 4687

Please send me
_____ copy/copies of
Macmillan/PICKUP National Training Directory 1991
at £75 per copy (plus £2 postage)
ISBN 0 333 53913 3

For priority service, please 'phone with your order:
071-379 4687

Please allow 28 days for delivery

☐ I enclose my cheque payable to
Globe Book Services for £_____

☐ Please invoice me (Companies and Libraries only)

☐ Please charge my credit card for £_____

   ☐ Access   _____
   ☐ Visa   _____
   ☐ American Express _____

Card No _____

Expiry Date _____

Signature _____

(Orders cannot be accepted without a signature)

Name _____

Address _____
_____
_____
_____

Telephone _____

1   2   3   4   5   6   7   8   9

Introduction

This book is unashamedly pragmatic in focusing on information which independent businesses and their advisers can exploit for profit. Speculation on the merits or otherwise of European integration takes second pace, though several contributors have raised important, if not urgent, questions which they believe must be answered if British industry is to become a more productive and competitive force in the European marketplace. Commentary in the key-note articles is often forthright, since this is a book which speaks *for* business, not *at* business. This is no time, as we approach the completion of the Single Market and observe the European Economic Space widening every day, to mince words about the need to strengthen Britain's manufacturing base. Put simply, the country cannot sell what it does not make. But there are fears that industry is under-prepared for the much publicised 'challenge of Europe', and there are fears, too, that smaller companies, in particular, will be vulnerable to the activities of the larger corporations in Europe, some of which may face radical reorganisation and, possibly, relocation.

For the determined information seeker, facts and analysis on all aspects of doing business in Europe are in abundant supply. If anything, there is an information glut. The network of widely dispersed sources includes government departments, trade organisations, universities and colleges, on-line databases, libraries, publishing houses, management consultancies and the European Community's institutions. A problem many people encounter, however, is difficulty in gaining access to facts which can advance them in their pursuit of new business. The passive nature of the information network is such that a kind of 'black hole' phenomenon has appeared into which valuable information disappears, unread, without trace.

The contributors are highly knowledgeable in their respective fields and all have something important, if not urgent, to say. And some, such as the law firms Clifford Chance and Brebner & Co. provide business information and services of an order which might surprise many businesses. The Lawlink system developed by Brebner & Co., in association with the London Chamber of Commerce and Industry, foreshadows the day in which company managers will 'travel' to see their customers by interactive video. Clifford Chance publishes detailed reports on aspects of European Community law and business which would be difficult to surpass. None of the contributors are cheer-leaders for the British government or the European Community and some, despite their true blue credentials, are distinctly opposed to certain aspects of Conservative economic and industrial policy and the manner in which policy is conducted. If nothing else, the creation of the Single Market is a catalyst for debate on the future of industry, for we have entered an era in which politics and business have become inextricably entwined. We all now see that the European marketplace is the foundation for European political and social cohesion and lasting peace. Events in Eastern Europe and the end of the

Cold War have brought lasting peace within our grasp. Lasting prosperity, however, has yet to come.

Certain subject areas have been played down in this guide, partly for lack of space to do justice to them and partly because business is already familiar with them. Complying with technical standards, for example, is a complex issue and deserves close attention on the part of exporting companies. But such companies do not need to be told in a guide of this kind that their products must conform to the technical and safety standard requirements in force in the countries into which they intend to sell. In such cases, basic sources are listed to provide a way into the information network. If a subject is not covered directly, there will probably be a bibliographical or database source listed. Therefore, in using this guide, there is an advantage in becoming acquainted with the contents of the extensive bibliographical chapters and the coverage of on-line databases in Part Eight. Many of the available publications and hand-outs available provide sources of further information.

Other areas covered in the guide, such as workforce and management training, executive recruitment, EC grants and loans, export finance, legal requirements when setting up a business and major EC policy areas such as competition policy have been covered at length because they present fresh practical challenges to business when studied in a pan-European context. The prospect of 'selling' through technology transfer methods, such as the licensing of patents and technical know-how, for example, takes on a conspicuous European dimension when seen in the context of the competition rules, intellectual property, contract law and practice, finance for development, or the interaction between EC law and national law in the countries in which licencees are based.

For those company managers and business advisers who have been satiated with propaganda and slogans extolling the benefits of the Single Market, or the warnings against lack of action, this book may come as a refreshing change, it predicts no economic miracle. Its premise echoes Francis Bacon's dictum that 'opportunities are made and not found', as indeed they always will be.

JAMES HOGAN
London

PART ONE

THE EUROPEAN DIMENSION

1 People and Products

Cultural differences within a united Europe

Mike Rosser

Britain was the last of the major Community powers to make a public issue of the EC's Single Market programme. Many British companies are only just awakening to the potential changes being orchestrated in Brussels; changes which may not only vastly alter the way businesses are conducted, but also affect our daily lives. The proposed new order is bound to become increasingly controversial as the 'Committee', consisting of Britain and eleven foreign partners, votes each step into implementation while attempting to satisfy local needs in their respective countries.

Many believe that Britain's 'island' mentality poses a challenge to a truly integrated market in Europe. Despite the building of the Channel tunnel, the British may for a long time continue to regard Britain as separate from the Continent they call Europe. Some of these attitudes are rooted in outdated fears and prejudices, often second-hand when adopted by the younger generation. But, overall, our fears are the product of ingrained thinking habits. Margaret Thatcher's visit to a number of European capitals and her controversial comments then and recently, have done nothing to help achieve the reality of the Single Market. But Britain is no different from many of the other EC member states who, despite their perceived attitudes, also put the needs and requirements of their own countries before those of Europe.

Despite these negative attitudes, the Single Market programme goes ahead. It is Europe's best plan for halting the slide in economic growth by tackling the problem at its root — the weaknesses of companies, protected for too long in small and comfortable home markets. Better management will be forced on Europe's businesses which will put the EC economy on a stronger footing to face the biggest economic threat of the 21st Century — that is, living in the shadow of USA and Japanese economic power.

Will Europe be one market after 1992?

The birth of the Single European Market will be attended by midwives representing salesmanship, industry, international politics and high-flying finance, but as we tire of celebrating the birth of the new Europe, what can we expect to see on the continental shelf once the barriers are down? In the interests of better European understanding, a leading British research company, Mintel, has published one of the most comprehensive studies ever into European lives, loves, leisure and spending habits. From Stuttgart to Seville and from Brussels to Birmingham, financial nosey parkers from Mintel peered into the bank balances, bedrooms and boozing habits of adults in France, Belgium, Germany, Italy, Spain, Britain and the Netherlands. Although the report weighs in at 10,000 pages and is eight volumes in total, one will not have to read far before seeing that the facts cancel any fear of creeping Europeanisation in our lifestyles and outlooks. Harmonised we might well be, but the only thing these seven countries (and probably the other five) really have in common are the Eurovision Song Contest and a profound dislike of Belgian food. In short, says Mintel, the picture postcard stereotypes of the bossy German, the stuffy Englishman, the pasta-touting Italian, the chauvinistic Frenchman and the boring Belgian, still hold true. In their view, the economic barriers may be being broken down, but we have perhaps never been more divided.

Cultural differences

We can see how Europe remains fragmented as a market in many ways by, first, looking at some of the major differences in the people within some of the European countries; and, second, by looking at major differences in marketing approaches country by country. Once we start to research European markets in detail, looking beyond the legislative changes in order to grasp the facts about the people, the communities and townships to which we hope to direct sales, we see that the changes in the Single Market are primarily a matter of improved access, and do not necessarily in themselves create opportunities. In many instances real opportunities will be created where new businesses are established as part of economic development programmes, just as some existing opportunities will be lost when businesses relocate and rationalise their operations. In principle, however, the task of marketing and selling is not made easier by changes in the Single Market, since once the changes are made, they benefit every supplier in the field. This places everyone on a level playing field in terms of access, though not, of course, in terms of the many other factors in competitiveness which apply. Recognising and adapting to cultural differences is a fundamental factor in competitiveness, as most regular exporters understand. Sometimes we see our "different" European neighbours as amusing caricatures, but there is often enough truth in national stereotypes to interest market researchers.

According to the Mintel study mentioned earlier, West Germany with its preponderance of wealthy widows, should prove something of a happy hunting ground for international toy boys. The Germans are the wealthiest of all the European people and stay that way with high levels of savings, little borrowing and a racial fear of inflation dating back to the Weimar Republic. German men find themselves outnumbered and outmanoeuvered by their highly assertive women-folk, but the vast majority (88 per cent) insist on choosing the family car. Although the growth in income of the Germans has outstripped that of any country in Europe, the German economic miracle could be in decline.

Turning to the French, most Europeans envy their relaxed lifestyle, their fertile countryside and their gourmet food and wine. Flying the flag is second nature to the chauvinistic French; so enamoured are they with France that holidays abroad are rated low. Two-day breaks in France, however, are a must. Rates of marriage and divorce are increasing in the rest of Europe, but the French do not seem to be the marrying kind. If the Frenchman had more money to spend he would opt for more weekend and day trips but failing that, he would plump for a new stereo. Do not, however, try to interest him in a new kitchen or a high-powered saving plan. These do not figure on a Frenchman's list of priorities.

We, the British, on the other hand (according to the research), are debtors and unrepentant users of hire purchase, credit cards, overdrafts and mortgage facilities. While 34 per cent of the British use debit or credit cards, only per cent of canny Germans feel a similar need. The British use of loans for house purchase is also unusually high. Jingoism does not greatly impress the average "Brit". The "I'm backing Britain" slogans of the '70s would not appeal today, though the British are by no means ashamed of their country. Britain remains a largely conservative (with a small "c") country in its attitudes and lifestyle and we tend not to trust "flashy foreigners".

The Belgians are Mr and Mrs Average. Average in their birthrate, their spending habits and even in their leisure pursuits. They would save any cash that came their way or, equally boringly, spend it on home decoration. What they would not dream of spending any extra money on is holidays or a new car. In addition, they are among the least nationalistic folk in Europe and are happy to buy foreign cars and household items such as fridges and washing machines without a second thought for the health of the Belgian economy.

Now the Italians; they love cars in general, and Italian cars in particular. They love women in general but are not particular which country they come from. No less than 84 per cent of Italian households boast a set of wheels — the figure for Britain is 65 per cent — and 33 per cent of Italians have back-up transport in the form of scooters or motorcycles. Italians rate a better house above a candlelit meal for two, unlike the French. For so long the "sick man" of Europe, Italy is now engaged in rapid recovery.

Moving West, we come to Spain where the Spanish male can look macho when strutting around a Benidorm beach dressed in posing pouch and weighty gold medallions. But he can afford to, thanks to major improvements in the Spanish economy over the last few years. Spain now has a middle class and it is buying environmental-friendly flysprays to prove it. Despite these improvements however, Spain is still the poorest of the seven nations covered by the research. For every pound earned and spent by the Germans, the Spanish earn and spend just 63p.

The final country covered by the Mintel research is The Netherlands who for so long have been the butt of the Euro joke — tulips, and "nil points" in the Eurovision Song Contest. The Dutch are cosmopolitan, adventurous and a lot more financially profligate than you might expect. They are big debtors, second only to Britain, and if extra cash came their way, they would spend it on meals out and bathroom improvements. With a large student population, the Dutch are not interested in buying cars — most of them cycle to work — and less than 50 per cent of them own their own homes, which bucks a very marked European trend.

Mintel's research covering these seven of the twelve EC countries, shows how different each of them and their peoples are and there is no doubt that had the research covered the other five countries — Ireland, Portugal, Greece, Denmark and Luxembourg — a similar pattern of differences would have emerged; differences that will be hard to overcome in a Single Market. Clearly, such conspicuous differences in tastes and buying patterns occur throughout the wider European marketplace, which now includes Eastern Europe. The Norwegians, for example, with their moralistic attitude to alcohol and early nights, could hardly be more different in temperament and lifestyle than the Slavs, Poles and Moldavians whose capacity for enjoying life to the full has not been dampened by decades of political oppression and economic austerity. Going further East to Moscow, already we see that the MacDonald's burger has hit town, even if the Muscovites still have to queue for hours on end for a loaf of bread.

Marketing approaches

The rules and regulations relating to business practices which are legal, decent and honest vary a great deal from country to country. One has only to view tapes of TV commercials from countries such as France, Germany, Denmark and Italy to see that a large number would not have been allowed on the air in the UK. The Independent Television Authority in the UK takes many knocks from "do-gooders". Their rules and regulations with regard to what is allowed to be aired, both in terms of programmes and advertising, are stricter than anywhere in the world. Despite having some problems with the authority most advertising agencies and clients are happy to concur with the IBA's principles and code of ethics.

Europe, seen in the light of these differences, is hardly the Single Market, with a consistent legalised set of rules to cover marketing and advertising across Europe that Brussels and Whitehall would have us believe. We have enough trouble getting everyone to agree to the same rules in the UK. And we have seen in nearly twenty years of EC membership how difficult it has been to achieve a consensus in the Council of Ministers in Brussels in order to adopt new EC Directives and Regulations. With the introduction of the majority voting procedure, however, plus the political impetus provided by the Single Market programme, the legislative process is speeding up. Yet, even with these efforts to impose uniformity across a wide field of legislation, we will still have to produce different styles of advertising for the same product across most countries of Europe. Some clients, for example, still need different commercials to cover North America and Canada where everyone speaks English. Uniform laws and a common language do not guarantee uniformity of tastes and preferences.

One example of this situation occurs with J. Walter Thompson's (JWT) worldwide assignments for Warner Lambert's Clorets product (a mouth freshner). Commercials work differently in the USA from those in Canada whilst different ideas work in Spain and in the UK. The UK advertisement utilises the comedians Hale and Pace who threaten people about having "their head chopped off" if they do not use the product. But, imagine the negative impact of using this idea, based on characteristic British humour, in France — especially in 1989, the 200th anniversary of the storming of the Bastille.

So, in answering the question — "Will Europe be a truly Single Market from 1993 onwards?" — whilst we may believe that the Single Market will eventually exist, it may well not be completed in every sense before the year 2000. Many of the proposals and economic, cultural and legal differences will certainly not be resolved by the end of 1992. Companies cannot expect to be able to treat Europe as a total Single Market for many years.

Europe and the rest of the world

Having discussed the differences in people and marketing approaches within the EC countries which could seriously affect the successful introduction of the Single Market, there are two other factors which could equally affect Europe in the post-1993 period. One is "The Other Europe" — the Eastern bloc; the other is that part of Western Europe which is still not part of the EC — the European Free

Trade Association group of countries, consisting of Scandinavia, Finland, Iceland, Austria and Switzerland.

Although Western Europe is poised for momentous changes in the post-1993 period, political and commercial upheavals now surging through "The Other Europe" — the Eastern Bloc — have proved to be much more dramatic and far-reaching in their effects on business and trade than we could have suspected. Western European governments have never quite known what to do about trade opportunities within Eastern Europe. The policy has been erratic, oscillating between the "soft man" and the "hard man" approach. That is, alternately lending extravagantly in the hope that a taste for capitalist baubles will eventually make the communists go soft enough to melt into democracy, and squeezing hard enough to make them tighten their belts until they scream and force a popular uprising. Neither technique has ever worked of course. Those countries in Eastern Europe who are emerging into a more liberal economic and political mould are doing so largely under their own momentum, now that Moscow's "dead hand" is perceived to have been lifted. If the changes that are currently occurring in the Eastern Bloc continue to build momentum, as seems likely, and if the West spends enough money in helping Eastern European governments to develop their economies, then over the next decade, former Iron Curtain countries could become a shop counter in a way that only four years ago seemed a far-fetched fantasy.

As for the major players outside the EC, the creation of the Single Market may present problems for us in Europe, but at least Britain has the advantage of being on the inside! The reverberations seem ominous in Washington and Tokyo, both anxious about what they see as the creation of a "Fortress Europe". So, with suspicion growing more intense around the world, each trading country outside Europe is ready to hit back at the first sign of protectionism, real or imagined. The free trade forces had hoped for the opposite signal from the General Agreement on Tariffs and Trade (GATT) negotiations which took place recently in Montreal. But the talks failed to progress and a slide backwards to more insidious forms of protectionism is likely to occur.

In much of the world, particularly in the booming export-led economies of East Asia, there is growing concern that the Americans and Europeans might form defensive regional blocs. One instance which provoked worries in Japan about a Fortress Europe occured in 1988 when a Vice President of the European Commission, suggested that Japan pay retrospective compensation to European exporters for having kept them out of its markets for so many years. Although these comments were disowned in Brussels, they provoked an outcry among the Japanese. To counter the threat, large American and Japanese companies are building massive bases in all the major European countries to ensure that, where possible, they too are established inside Fortress Europe before the end of 1992.

Unfortunately, in Britain we do not try so hard to break into large non-EC markets. We stand and admire the competitive vigour of Japan's domestic marketplace, but have still not solved the riddle of how to break into it. Fortress Japan has resisted imports for decades. As Michael Heseltine has pointed out: "In matters of free trade everyone sins, while all proclaim their virtue." Already, the progress to a Single European Market has problems aplenty from within. The current and anticipated future activities in the Eastern European bloc, and the activity of American and Japanese companies and governments, could make this progress even tougher than the creators of the Single Market have foreseen.

Opportunities and problems

When the barriers eventualy come down, there will be the opportunity of reaching a potential market of 320 million consumers. This fact is well known, and for many, though not all, companies it is a realistic assessment of the marketing opportunities. It is vital that, despite all the potential problems there will be, companies do not ignore this opportunity. Dependent upon the size of the company, a senior person, or a team of people, reporting directly to the Board, should examine all future opportunities to ensure that, when the time comes, their company is prepared to take full advantage. The most suitable products or services must be found and researched to ensure they meet the European Standards of quality and safety. Following this, professional methods of selling and marketing must be planned in finite detail. Nothing ever sells itself.

Turning from opportunities to dangers, the team within each company should also consider the potential threat of competition in the home market from other European companies. Surprisingly, many British companies are still not taking this threat seriously. But it cannot be ignored, especially since mainland European companies do not have to overcome the language barrier, most of their senior personnel speaking fluent English as a second language.

Those managers who keep on saying about the Europeans that "they all speak English" or "we can always get it translated", could be uttering their own famous last words. The question of language learning is covered in detail in *Languages and Business*, Part Three, Chapter 6. One can but stress the obvious, that Continental buyers will judge products and companies very much by how well they communicate. Many of them speak English because they take their customers seriously, and they expect to be taken seriously in return. This means that an effort must be made to communicate with customers on their own terms. If you are bidding for an Italian contract against a French company, which handles telephone calls in fluent Italian, it is obvious that your French competitor is in with a head start. So, whatever one thinks about relying on the use of English, one way to appreciate the benefit of learning foreign languages is to look ahead and imagine how you would fare against competitors who can communicate easily with your potential Continental customer.

The role of advertising agencies

The whole area of opportunities and potential threats is one that we at JWT, as an international advertising agency, have become heavily involved with for a number of our clients. Our planning personnel sit on our clients' Single Market teams and contribute to the creation of their future business plans. Therefore, in talking to an advertising agency, select one which is capable of offering sound professional advice and is prepared to become involved in your future business planning. So who should you talk to? According to a recent report published by Databank, the type of agencies most likely to offer a professional service relating to the Single Market are those which:

☐ Have a well-developed European attitude and are outward looking, intellectually equipped, and determined to apply the widest strategies.

☐ Recognise the significant changes that are about to transform the media scene both in European and global terms, and have established media teams to take advantage of these opportunities, especially in areas of Satellite and Cable television.

☐   Have a talent for creative work based on a common language across television, press, posters, packaging, point of sale, mail shots and exhibitions.

☐   Can offer a total communications-related service, not purely an advertising service.

☐   Have clients in the financial, insurance and other "invisible" businesses or with products or services well-known across Europe.

The Databank report stated that, at the time the study was carried out, only four of the UK's 3000 plus advertising agencies were properly prepared for 1992. JWT was among them. This surprised the many agencies that have been boasting of the development of European networks, but as Databank suggests, the secret of future success is flexibility in business, and not merely a string of European addresses at the bottom of an agency's letterhead. Databank's study showed that the best prepared advertising agencies were in the large groups, and all could offer a wide range of communication-related services, not just advertising. They were the only agencies offering total service.

Developing a European attitude

Using JWT as an example, since the early 1980's, JWT has recognised the growing importance of international business and has organised itself to handle this business professionally. The process began before the Single Market was first considered, since a very high percentage of the agency's clients are international. In addition to a European network of well- respected JWT agencies, the agency ensured that, through its personnel, it was intellectually equipped to handle this type of business.

In 1982 JWT Europe media directors held a conference to discuss the agency's attitude to media for the rest of the twentieth century to ensure that the agency stayed ahead of competitors in this area. Decisions taken at the conference, fully supported by senior management of the agency, laid down a blueprint which the agency has been working to and updating since. In the following year a similar conference was held, including senior media personnel from JWT's North America, South America and Australasia agencies. The result was a global blueprint which has helped JWT remain one of the most professional global agencies for media. A further major development in 1984 was the agency's global media hotline which enables client and agency personnel to obtain updated information and facts relating to the media scene from any market. Co-ordinated by four major regional agencies in Manchester, Chicago, Sydney and Buenos Aires, this is a sophisticated system for supply of media information.

Since becoming part of the WPP Group in 1987, JWT has been able to develop closer working relations with specialist communications companies within the group, covering strategic marketing services, public relations, market research, graphics and design, sales promotion, incentive and motivation, and audio, visual and video communications. The latest company to join WPP has been The Henley Centre for Forecasting.

It is important to build clients in the financial and insurance arena, specifically those with products or services that are well-known in Europe. A client list such as JWT's which includes National Westminster Bank, Yorkshire Building Society, Swinton Insurance Brokers, Kellogg's, Ford and Warner Lambert is a firm base.

9

CONTACTS

The Institute of Practitioners in Advertising and the Market Research Society supply information to their members and to companies seeking to contact an advertising agency or market research consultancy. The European organisations listed below provide contacts in advertising and research in other European countries.

Institute of Practitioners in Advertising
44 Belgrave Square
London SW1X 8QS
Tel: (071) 235 7020
Fax: (071) 245 9904

Market Research Society
15 Northburgh Street
London EC1V 0AH
Tel: (071) 490 4911
Fax: (071) 490 0608

European Association of Advertising Agencies(EAAA)
Avenue du Barbeau 28
B-1160 Brussels
Tel: (32) 2 672 4336
Fax: (32) 2 672 0014

European Society for Opinion and Marketing Research (ESOMAR)
JJ Viottastraat 29
NL-1071 JP Amsterdam
Tel: (31) 20 664 2141
Fax: (31) 20 664 2922

2 The New Europeans

Business people at the forefront of change

James Hogan

Fifty years after Jean Monnet penned in 1943 his ideas for a united states of Europe the Single Market will formally, if not in every detail, have been completed. Many British managers and sales executives, however, will be 'newcomers' to the Single Market and the wider European marketplace, having lived apart from Europe in body and in spirit all their lives. Others may have travelled to and from the Continent several times, though without absorbing much of the business atmosphere. There are those, too, who do not even think about European unity, and doubt that it will have any noticeable bearing on their lives. Recent political developments in Europe, however, have been of epic dimensions and must have convinced at least some of the sceptics of the reality of European unity. The sheer force of events has compelled everyone to look beyond British shores to witness the political map of Europe being redrawn. The dismantling of the Berlin wall, the re-unification of the two Germanies, the disintegration of the Warsaw Pact, and the Russian-German co-operation pact of 1990 were events of monumental importance, resulting from a new mood of conciliation which had swept through Europe, taking millions of citizens by surprise. These events have clarified modern aims and values which the peoples of Europe are, in the main, determined to share. The reluctant British, it seems, and the newly liberated East Europeans, are also ready to become members of the international business community.

Business people, in particular, find themselves in the vanguard of change, since it is they who, amidst an encircling atmosphere of legal, administrative and political upheaval, must bring the fact of economic growth into being. Without an active, indeed dynamic, business sector, Europe's economy will stagnate, and individual countries will lapse, once again, into protectionism, introspection and isolation. A great many British business people, however, still lack first hand experience of research, marketing and distribution in the open European marketplace, which is gradually and systematically being cleared of barriers to the free flow of goods, services, capital and people. Not all the barriers have been removed but, long before the process of removing them began, the French, the Germans and other Europeans were thinking and behaving as internationals, sometimes ahead of formal developments. In stark contrast, however, the British have waited for proof. And there could be no more convincing proof than the lifting of the iron curtain, or the demolition of the Berlin wall.

The eruption of popular free market politics in Eastern Europe, brought about by a string of revolutions, in which the old Communist ideologues were overthrown, has made it easier for company managers in Britain at last, to disentangle facts from values in European affairs. The values are peace, prosperity, free trade, and fair competition. The facts are the creation of a European marketplace, increasing political, economic and social cohesion within Europe and, above all, freedom to make money. These facts and values, in proving irresistable to East Europeans, now seeking to participate in the European marketplace, are reaffirmed in the minds of complacent Britons, many of whom, it seemed, were in danger of becoming prisoners on their own island.

In receiving the message so loudly and clearly, we are indebted to television. There could hardly have been a better way of seeing history in the making than watching live transmission of the astonishing exodus of East Germans, many of them scrambling over the Berlin wall in a state of delirium, when a few days earlier they would have been shot. Some were determined to cross into the West, if only for a few hours, to breathe the fresh air of democracy. Until that moment, in the minds of a great many ordinary people in Britain, European politics, national sovereignty, and the Single Market, were merely subjects for discussion which had coalesced into an indistinguishable and unexciting whole.

British 'insularity'

British so-called insularity has been a standing joke in Brussels circles since the UK's accession to the EC in 1973. An outdated colonial outlook, preoccupation with the balance of power, inborn dislike of foreigners, an exaggerated sense of national pride, and staunch opposition to intrusions into British affairs — these are commonly quoted reasons for Britain's reluctance to fully immerse itself as a nation into European political and economic life. But Britain is not alone in Europe in its sense of national pride, in its pursuit of its national interests or in its dislike of outside interference in domestic affairs. Other European countries are equally concerned with the preservation of sovereignty and national identity. Yet they still manage to cultivate a European economic dimension.

On the trade front, it is obvious that there is no tradition of insularity in larger UK companies, since Britain has been a great international trading nation for centuries. And if smaller businesses are finding it difficult to transform themselves into internationally-minded companies overnight, they are no different to the countless smaller companies in, say, the USA which can hardly bring themselves to send goods to a neighbouring state, let alone another country. So it is not realistic to suppose that smaller companies in other European countries automatically see themselves as pan-European operations simply because their geographical and cultural position is convenient. As every company manager knows it takes more than mere location to make a company competitive.

The cause of Britain's insularity is not, therefore, some negative quirk in the British national character. It is poor husbandry of the country's economic assets, undermining business confidence. If company managers thought there were real marketing opportunities in Europe, they would sieze them. Economic factors, however, have stood in the way and it is common knowledge that, in comparison with France and Germany, the British economy is productively and competitively weak. It is now being publicly argued that the weakness in the economy stems from long-term industrial decline and is exacerbated by lack of effective policies to reverse the downward trend. The reluctance to ensure a flow of investment capital into manufacturing industry on the part of the Conservative government between 1979 and 1990 forced the economic debate into an odd display of political posturing during 1990. The Conservative government appeared to be evading the call to back industrial regeneration, a cause to which it is ideologically well disposed, while the Labour Party was arguing for policies to strengthen the manufacturing base (privately owned), a cause to which it is not ideologically committed. Indeed, Clause 4 of the Labour Party's constitution concerning nationalisation of industry remains to be reactivated at any such time as the Party chooses to 'revert to type'. The irony of this situation is obvious.

One immediate explanation for the 'recession' of 1990 was the earlier decision to relax lending controls on the banks, a measure which precipitated a credit boom and a demand for goods which British industry could no longer supply. Something had to be done to curb spending and control inflation and the blunt instrument of high interest rates was thought to be the answer. Of course, it had an inflationary impact on the cost of living, mainly through interest rates on mortgages, but high interest rate also hit smaller, independent manufacturers in various ways. Most notably, the cost of investment capital became too high. The raising of interest rates was a measure aimed at the symptom, rather than the cause of the economic sickness. Shadow Chancellor, John Smith wasted no time in rounding on the government in a TV interview for concentrating on the cost of credit to the consumer and to business, rather than on the behaviour of lending institutions who had been all too eager to sell credit at the expense of the country's balance of payments position.

Seen in the context of the run up to the completion of the Single Market, this slow-down in the economy and the simultaneous loss of business confidence meant that the impact of government initiatives, such as the Enterprise Initiative, the Export Initiative and the *Europe Open for Business* publicity campaign was seriously impaired. The more discouraged industry became, the more desperate the government's propaganda machine became. Hence the spectacle of a beleaguered government claiming that awareness of the Single Market among managers had risen from 16 per cent to over 90 per cent in the course of one year, a statistic which had no meaning in terms of preparedness for doing business in the Single Market in any sense, let alone taking advantage of any marketing opportunities that the Single Market would bring.

Once we begin to recognise that British attitudes to European integration are influenced by economic factors, we see that slowness in becoming active participants in the building of the new Europe is not entirely the fault of the British individual. Many in the British business community, who had not been active in Europe, also perceived the changes taking place through a miasma of verbal confusion, public relations gimmickry and dire election propaganda emanating chiefly from Whitehall. Things reached an all time low when, in the run up to the 1989 European election, posters appeared bearing a Government-inspired jibe about living on a 'diet of Brussels'! The British European Democrats (Conservative) paid a high price for this juvenile waggery. They lost their majority in the British contingent at the European Parliament, a slump in their fortunes which leaves them outnumbered by Socialists during the crucial period covering the rest of the programme to complete the Single Market.

Verbal ineptitude had previously got the better of Whitehall when, in 1988, the Department of Trade and Industry (DTI) launched its multi-million pound campaign to publicise the Single Market. Company managers were assured, for example, that Europe was already 'open for business', when it was clearly apparent to many people that Europe was still closed. Later a weary audience was offered another inferior slogan, 'The Single Market is here now: Where are you?', an exhortation which had an unfortunate ring of desperation about it. No-one is more conscious of the fact that opportunities are made, and not found, than an exporter. But the overwhelming impression created by this bland publicity was that tangible marketing opportunities were being created by the programme to complete the Single Market, and that early preparation would provide the key to success. Not surprisingly this expensive exercise failed to release the energy that would take British business deeper into the European marketplace.

Taken together, the wavering commitment in government, the delinquent streak in its political strategists, and the over-reliance on glib advertising slogans have emphasised the shortcomings in the Government's and the Civil Service's conduct of European policy in the UK. This makes it all the more difficult to foster a commitment in industry. The captains of industry, many of whom can be relied on to toe the line, may affirm the commitment of their own organisations to European economic and monetary union, but they do not speak for the millions of individuals in business who have no regular contact with trade and industry organisations, professional bodies, chambers of commerce and quangos; people who we expect to send out as an advance party to do business with other Europeans and show us, by their example, how we can adapt to conditions in many different markets and how we may broaden our outlook.

Origins of European unity

The events in Eastern Europe during 1989-90 appeared to erupt spontaneously and, for many people, the Single Market is also a 'new' development, even though it is the Common Market (Mark II), which Britain has been a member of since 1973. But the causes of the acceleration of the process of European integration, and the creation of a vast free market, are not of some mysterious origin. Historians may trace the origins of European unity to distant eras, perhaps as far back as Caesar's campaigns, but the precise, identifiable causes of present day developments date back to World War II. After a violent and frequently tragic history, culminating in the horrors of that war, Europe has come of age. We live in a mature society in which war is regarded as an aberration, something to read about, though redundant, like colonialism. We now prefer to see wealth creation, not as a matter of plundering other people's resources, but of competing to the best of our own ability. The creation of the new European marketplace is intended to ensure that everyone competes on an equal basis, but it may surprise people of the younger generation that the seeds were sown in 1940 when Britain and France proposed the Franco-British Union. The unfulfilled alliance embodied, in principle, joint responsibility in defence, foreign affairs, and financial and economic policies. After the war, devastated by Hitler's excesses, other European countries also discovered their common interest in collective responsibility for economic recovery and political stability.

There have, of course, been many formal steps in creating European unity since World War II, and there are many enlightened and far-sighted individuals who have contributed to Europe's good fortune. However, the ideas of French Planning Commissioner in De Gaulle's government, Jean Monnet, must be singled out as forming the conceptual basis of what followed in the process of European integration. Monnet was dedicated to the cause of European unity and world peace, and became the principal architect of most of the early European initiatives and Treaties. His forecast for Europe was accurate. In 1943, while working with the French provisional government based in Algiers, he noted:

> *'There will be no peace in Europe if States are reconstituted on a basis of national sovereignty with all that that implies in terms of prestige politics and economic protectionism. If the nations of Europe adopt defensive positions again, huge armies will be necessary again. Under the future peace treaty, some nations will be allowed to re-arm; others will not. That was tried in 1919; we all know the result. Intra-European alliances will be formed; we know what they are worth. Social reform will be impeded or blocked by the sheer weight of military budgets. Europe will be reborn in fear'[1].*

Europe was indeed reborn in fear but, since then, with the help of Marshall Plan funds, West Germany emerged economically triumphant from the ashes of the war. West Germany has husbanded its financial and industrial resources to the full to become the most powerful economic force in modern Europe, but in a different atmosphere to that which prevailed immediately prior to World War II. The Europe of today is not the Europe of the 1930s. It is becoming increasingly united and balanced. Monnet, backed by French minister, Robert Schuman, among others, succeeded in launching his plans with the crucial, if prosaic sounding European Coal and Steel Community, established under the Treaty of Paris, 1951. The original six members, Belgium, France, Italy, the Netherlands, Luxembourg and West Germany established the European Economic Community under the Treaty of Rome in 1957.

Half a century after Monnet sketched out his ideas for a united states of Europe, the Soviet Union's Mikhail Gorbachev has begun in the East a process of conciliation and economic recovery on a comparable scale. Gorbachev acted to end the cold war and sought to free Russia from the stranglehold of self-defeating Communist dogma. If his vision comes to full fruition, then the picture of the whole European continent, united in its pursuit of prosperity, will be complete. However, a great deal of mistrust of the Soviet Union has to be dispelled, though Gorbachev's consent to a reunified Germany remaining within the NATO alliance and the Soviet Union's support of United Nations economic sanctions against Iraq in 1990 have helped. A larger, stronger Germany is also a source of anxiety, particularly among people who suffered German occupation and the systematic savagery with which the Nazis dispatched real and imagined enemies. Doubts of this order cannot be resolved overnight. But, if the threat of any recurrence of such a tragedy is to be permanently removed, we must make our own, individual contribution to the cause of peace by accepting and enjoying our European status.

The Single Market

The European Community's Single Market initiative is, so far, the culminating achievement in the grand design to unite Europe. It occupies most of the European marketplace and its twelve member states have a combined population of 334 million (including East Germany). More European countries have applied to join the EC, though no new admissions are imminent, except for East Germany which automatically became a member on reunification with West Germany. Hungary has been quick to signal its impending application and join the queue of applicant countries. The European Free Trade Association (EFTA) countries are also seeking to strengthen their trading links with the Single Market countries in order to create a European Economic Space .

Positive and inspiring those these initiatives are, they create uncertainty in the marketplace for many companies, particularly smaller and medium-sized companies of up to 500 employees. These companies are, at all times, vulnerable to erratic fluctuations in the trading environment. Business orthodoxy dictates that decisions are based on certainties; certainty of economic stability, certainty of available finance for investment, certainty of skilled labour, and the certainties of demand, distribution and payment. The Single Market programme offers only one guarantee — free and fair access to the European marketplace. The makers of the new Europe, however, envisage an economic miracle, but individual managers must make their own decisions as to whether it is wise to attempt to amplify any success in local markets and repeat it on a European scale.

Although the Single Market comprises the larger, and most accessible part of the European marketplace, it is not wise to treat it in isolation of the rest of Europe, particularly in the light of the political developments in Eastern Europe and the degree to which EC countries trade with other Western European countries outside of the Community, notably the EFTA countries. There is still a danger, however, that the enormous emphasis given to the completion of the Single Market, the EC's internal market or common market, as it is sometimes described, will divert attention from any marketing opportunities, investment prospects or the threat of new competition now gathering momentum in countries as diverse as Norway and Hungary. Indeed, one of the declared aims of the Single Market is that it should strengthen European industries to enable them to compete in world markets. The Single European Act of 1986 introduced much needed procedures to speed up the process.

Key events in uniting Europe

The following chronological list of events and initiatives in the evolution of the new Europe draws from *Steps to European Unity*, published by the European Commission[2].

1940: Proposed Franco-British Union
Britain and France propose that they act as "one nation" to fight a common enemy, Germany. The proposal embodied notions of joint responsibility in defence, foreign affairs, and financial and economic policies. Monnet is involved in the abortive negotiations.

1943: Monnet proposes the end of national sovereignty
French planning Commissioner, Jean Monnet, while in Algiers, expresses ideas which are to change the face of Europe. Monnet's greatness, however, lies in his dedication to action, not words, and in his ability to influence and persuade European leaders to take the far-reaching political initiatives to unite Europe.

1946: United States of Europe
British Prime Minister, Winston Churchill, calls for a United States of Europe in a speech at Zurich.

1947: Organisation for European Economic Co-operation (OEEC)
The OEEC is set up, originally to regulate the flow of aid to Europe under the US Marshall Plan. The organisation extended its terms of reference to embrace

economic co-operation between all Western European countries and, eventually, to include other Western developed countries under its present name, the Organisation for Economic Co-operation and Development (OECD).

1948: Western European Union (WEU)

The Treaty of Brussels establishes the WEU, consisting at first of five member countries — Belgium, France, Luxembourg, the Netherlands and the United Kingdom. The Union, essentially a forum for ideas promoting economic and defence co-operation between its members, plays only a supporting role in European developments. West Germany and Italy join the Union in 1954, but its defence role is overtaken by NATO (North Atlantic Treaty Organisation). Britain's commitment to the WEU was weak.

1948: Benelux

Belgium, the Netherlands, and Luxembourg establish the Benelux union, essentially a customs union, significant as a modern precedent for European economic union. In the 19th century, the Zollverein, a customs union formed between autonomous German states is an historic precedent, interesting in that it can be seen as a step towards the unification of Germany.

1950: The Schuman Plan

French Foreign Minister, Robert Schuman, proposes a political initiative under which the coal and steel production and consumption in West Germany and France, are to be pooled. The architect of the plan is Jean Monnet . The plan specifically reconciles France and West Germany by establishing joint control of vital coal and steel resources, thus removing any further threat of West German domination over Europe. The memorandum embodying the plan states eloquently that "world peace cannot be safeguarded without the making of creative efforts proportionate to the dangers which threaten it"; and that "Europe will not be made all at once, or according to a single plan. It will be built through concrete achievements which first create a de facto solidarity"[1].

1951: Treaty of Paris

The Treaty establishes the European Coal and Steel Community , of six countries (Belgium, France, Italy, Luxembourg, Netherlands, West Germany), based on the Schuman Plan. Production and consumption of coal and steel is supervised by the High Authority . The Council comprises ministers of The Six. An Assembly and a Court of Justice are also established. Monnet's grand vision of a powerful, but peaceful Europe begins to take shape. He is appointed President of the ECSC's High Authority, based in Luxembourg in 1952.

1952: European Defence Community

A treaty intended to establish a European Defence Community and a European Political Community, proposed under the Plevan Plan is signed, but not implemented. Monnet recommends to the French Prime Minister, Rene Plevan, that a European Defence Community could be established along similar lines to that of the European Coal and Steel Community. The proposal collapses two years later when it is rejected by the French Government. A simultaneous proposal for a European Political Community (EPC) dies with it. The question of whether European "federalists" are trying to do too much too soon enters the debate, an argument which has remained with us ever since.

1955: Action Committee for the United States of Europe (ACUSE)

This Committee is formed under the guidance of Jean Monnet. A key meeting, chaired by Belgian minister, Paul-Henri Spaak , adopts proposals in 1956 which form the basis for the Treaty of Rome establishing the European Economic Community (EEC), and a second Treaty of Rome establishing the European Atomic Energy Community (EURATOM).

1957: European Economic Community (EEC)
The momentous step is taken to establish the EEC between the existing member states of the European Coal and Steel Community, set up in 1951 (see above). The Treaty of Rome lays down the legal structure of the EEC and remains as the basis of European Community law as we know it today.

1957: European Atomic Energy Community (EURATOM)
The European Atomic Energy Community is established simultaneously with the EEC under a separate Treaty of Rome, comprising the six EEC/ECSC member countries.

1958: European Free Trade Association (EFTA)
Seven European countries outside the EEC establish the European Free Trade Association. The EFTA members are Austria, Denmark, Norway, Portugal, Sweden, Switzerland and the United Kingdom. Free trade agreements are negotiated between EFTA countries and the EEC.

1961: The Fouchet Plan
A proposal by Christian Fouchet for political union fails.

1963: Franco-German Co-operation Agreement
A new Franco-German pact is agreed, to some extent alienating other member states, but strengthening the Franco-German axis. The pivotal relationship between France and West Germany is, to this day, a source of distrust of French and German ambitions in Europe.

1964: Common Agricultural Market
Formally set up under the European Agricultural Guidance and Guarantee Fund (EAGGF), this becomes the contentious Common Agricultural Policy (CAP) of later years, producing in the 1970s and 1980s the notorious food mountains and wine lakes at great cost. Much of the subsidised produce has been sold cheaply on world markets to the dissatisfaction of some of the EEC's major trading partners, notably the USA, itself a large agricultural exporter. British housewives lament the loss of cheap imported butter and lamb from New Zealand . The growing unpopularity of this aspect of the CAP culminated in the early 1980s in confrontation between the British government and the Community, exacerbated by protracted wrangles over the size of Britain's contribution to the EC budget.

1965: The Empty Chair
France boycotts meetings in protest against proposals for an "own resources" system of financing EEC policies.

1966: The Luxembourg Compromise
The crisis is resolved by a compromise agreed in Luxembourg which affords consideration and protection of any member's vital national interests. France ends its boycott.

1969: The Hague Summit
A crucial summit held at The Hague agrees bold Community policies to consolidate European unity. These include enlargement, the creation of the EC budget from own resources levies, and political co-operation in external relations.

The summit gives a much needed boost to the political will of member states to act in the direction of closer integration.

1970: Monetary Union
A step is taken towards European monetary union as central banks of The Six agree a monetary support mechanism.

1970: The Luxembourg Report
This report presented by EEC Commissioner, Viscount Davignon, is approved by The Six and the principle of political co-operation on foreign affairs is established. Europe aims to speak with one voice in international affairs. In practice, however, political co-operation between member states is achieved at sporadic intervals, usually at times of political crisis. There is no guarantee that member states will act in concert.

1973: First EC enlargement
The United Kingdom, Ireland and Denmark leave EFTA to join the EEC. The free trade agreements between the EFTA countries and the EEC come into force.

1975: Agreement on European Elections to introduce direct elections to the European Parliament is reached.

1979: European Monetary System (EMS)
The EMS becomes a reality. An exchange rate mechanism is established. The European Currency Unit (ECU) is proposed. Britain declines to join the exchange rate mechanism.

1979: First European Parliament Elections
The inaugural direct European elections to the European Parliament are held. The new parliament of 410 Euro-MPs represents constituencies in the nine member states.

1981: Second EEC enlargement
Greece joins the European Community.

1981: European Currency Unit (ECU)
The ECU replaces the European Unit Account, bringing the EC a step nearer to creating a single European currency and complete monetary union. Britain's reluctance to participate in the EMS or to endorse the principle of a single European currency later prompts French President, Francois Mitterand, to propose a two-speed Community in which those members who wish to move quickly towards total European economic, political and monetary union may do so by agreement between themselves under a new treaty.

1982: Greenland withdraws
Greenland, an autonomous part of Denmark, holds a referendum and withdraws from the EEC.

1984: Second European Parliament Elections
A European Parliament of 434 members is elected.

1985: Third EC enlargement
Spain and Portugal join the European Community.

1986: The Single European Act (SEA)
The Act marks radical steps forward in accelerating the process of integration. It augments the Treaty of Rome in many areas, but two practical innovations assist

the development of the Single Market. First, it introduces the Co-operation Procedure which, in effect, means majority voting in the Council of Ministers where all new Directives must be adopted; and it establishes the New Approach whereby the hitherto laborious process of matching the product technical and safety standards of the twelve member countries is replaced by a system of reciprocity. All being well, this means that standards acceptable in one EC country will eventually be acceptable throughout the EC as a whole.

1989: Third European Parliament Elections
A European Parliament of 481 Euro-MP's representing constituencies in the twelve member states is installed at Strasbourg.

1989: Berlin wall breached
This signals the eventual reunification of Germany and an end to the cold war, as well as causing disquiet about the economic and military strength of a reunified Germany in Europe.

1989/90: Soviet domination ends
Eastern European Communities break free of Soviet control. They begin to establish market economies and closer links with Western Europe.

1990: NATO realignment
The reshuffling of NATO policies paves the way for improved relations with the Soviet Union.

1990: German/Russian entente
Russia agrees to a reunified Germany remaining in NATO. Under this co-operation pact Russia is to receive financial aid to assist in the regeneration of the Soviet economy and the process of democratisation.

1990: Soviet Union backs NATO sanctions against Iraq
Soviet Union support for American and European opposition to Iraq's invasion of Kuwait heralds a new era in international co-operation.

1 *Jean Monnet, a Grand Design for Europe*, published by the Office for Official Publications of the European Communities, Periodical 5/1988, *European Documentation* series, 50pp, free, ISBN 9 789282 589205.

2 *Steps to European Unity — Community Progress to Date: a Chronology*, published by the Office for Official Publications of the European Communities, 100pp, free, ISBN 92-825-7346-X.

3 Corporate Strategy

Preparing for the Single Market

Caroline Bentley

*'The process of 1992 won't stabilise until after 2000, but no-one
can stop it any more'.*
Sir John Harvey-Jones

'A collectivised, protectionist, over-regulated Utopia'.
Sir John Hoskyns

Proponents claim that the Single Market will fundamentally change business in the European Community, while critics argue its importance is grossly exaggerated, a product of clever hype. Whichever is the case, understanding the impact of the creation of the Single Market is now firmly on the management agenda for the 1990s. But many executives remain perplexed. What is the right view to take? What actions are needed? Can a company develop a "strategic" view of Europe?

This chapter discusses the Single Market in the context of developing a corporate strategy. Correctly anticipating the changes that the Single Market brings is fundamental to future success in Europe. But many companies have approached Europe narrowly, resulting in misguided management decisions. The chapter also discusses the likely impact of the Single Market on business. Although the impact on each sector will be specific, involving a mix of industry and individual company factors, some general conclusions and pointers emerge. The second section of this chapter, *Preparing for the Single Market*, covers the strategic approach to Europe as part of a wider process of strategy development. Finally, the chapter explores certain aspects of acquisitions.

Single Market implications for corporate strategy

The following examples, all based on real situations, are typical of how UK companies are responding to the creation of the Single Market and related strategic issues. As case histories, they illustrate the importance of forecasting the direct impact the Single Market may have on an industry sector and the company's operation, highlighting the need to assess possible indirect implications.

Threat to existing markets: A UK machine tool manufacturer is under threat in the home market from a German competitor. Previously inactive, the competitor has recently purchased a small, ailing company in the UK in addition to operations in France and Benelux, gaining an opportunity to build a comprehensive product range and to reduce production costs. How should the threatened UK manufacturer respond?

A manufacturer of public transportation equipment knows that the opening up of public procurement as part of the Single Market programme will lead to increased competition in a hitherto protected market. Here the decision is whether to attempt to become an aggressive European player or to accept a limited decline in market share.

Adapting to European standards: A DIY manufacturer faces significant retooling costs in order to survive in Europe, when new European standards come into force. The company's current range will be obsolete as the products do not conform to the new standards which apply in the UK as much as in any other EC market. The German producers lobbied for their standards — the British did not. Needless to say the new CENELEC standard bears an uncanny resemblance to existing German regulations. The company wants to ensure that no further unpleasant surprises lurk in the Brussels woodpile.

Sharpening the competitive edge: A UK-based wines and spirits merchant was already active, but not particularly profitable throughout Europe. The company revised its logistics strategy, reducing the number of warehouses from forty to twelve, increasing the availability of products to the customer by 15 per cent and reducing costs by over £2m. The company is now exploring opportunities for increasing its competitive edge that this move has made possible.

1992: A catalyst of change

The advantages of preparing for Europe ahead of, or more thoroughly than, competitors — whether they be in the UK, mainland Europe, the United States or Japan — cannot be overstated. The Department of Trade and Industry's 1992 publicity campaign, *Europe Open for Business*, dubbed "the most successful marketing campaign of the 1980s", ensured that most companies became aware of the Single Market programme, and that some took steps to prepare. Yet, in reality, the impact of the publicity campaign, though welcome, was not as impressive as it first seemed. Many companies, in taking so-called action to prepare for the open market, did little more than request a board paper on the impact of Single Market legislation.

Understanding the legislative implications is, of course, an important element of preparation, provided a company is prepared to take action, once the likely impact of new regulations has been assessed. In some industries, such as financial services and telecommunications, the process of deregulation is already having a profound effect on industry structure. For many companies, the prospect of lower transport costs, mutual recognition and changes in indirect taxation, all need to be planned for but, at first sight, do not change the basis of competition.

The real significance of the accelerated programme of measures to complete the Single Market, however, has been as a catalyst of industry change. The primary drivers of change are global: typically the need to compete effectively against American or Japanese companies, as well as European, to gain adequate market share to achieve profitability. Shrinking product life cycles combined with the mounting investment levels needed to develop new products, in sectors as diverse as electronics and pharmaceuticals, have led companies to seek a global market for their products.

While there is little evidence of "global" markets developing as heralded in the 1970s, global "segments" are becoming apparent. Companies such as Suchard and BMW have identified different categories of consumer behaviour and preferences. They now develop products to appeal to those consumers, irrespective of whether they live in Italy, Denmark or the UK. The retail sector also provide examples here. Benetton and Stefanel have both adopted a clear niche positioning, appealing to highly targeted customer groups within each market, but developing a retail concept and formula which, with only minor modifications, can succeed in a number of European countries.

Massive restructuring has already occurred in many European industries. This process of concentration has in most cases been accompanied by severe rationalisation of production facilities, distribution and marketing, with the aim of driving down the cost base. For example, in white goods, the number of European competitors has declined from fifteen to five since 1979 leaving Maytag, Electrolux, Whirlpool, GEC and Bosch Siemens. Electrolux has expanded aggressively, successfully managing the post-acquisition transition and accepting plant closures to ensure that production and logistics synergies are fully utilised. Over a similar period, the number of competitors in coffee has fallen from eighteen to just four. Jacob Suchard, one of the survivors, is implementing an extensive programme of production rationalisation and concentration to take full advantage of the benefits of the scale it has acquired.

Against this background, Sir John Harvey-Jones' prediction that only half the number of current companies will survive into the next century seems cautious! In both examples cited, however, industry change gathered pace throughout the 1980s. The same applies to almost all other industry sectors. So what has been the significance of 1992 in this process?

The 1992 programme has had an impact on how competition is waged. 1992 means deregulation. Deregulation, in every industry in the world, has meant lower profitability. Convergence of national price levels and pressure on profit margins will result in the shake-out of weaker firms. So 1992 means that industry structures are set to change further.

Developing a competitive strategy that protects the company from these threats is critical. Two generic options are available: the first seeks to ensure a position as lowest cost producer, the second to add value by differentiation, either in the product or in service. These are often but not always mutually exclusive routes. The pursuit of a successful competitive strategy will lead to new ways of competing. How to develop a successful competitive strategy for Europe is examined in more detail in the next section of this chapter. Some of these trends are already evident, but can be expected to increase: companies will aggressively rationalise, adopting both a greater specialisation and concentration in production; they will seek to develop distinctive positions in product markets across Europe, leading to increased cross-border investment, often through mergers, acquisitions and alliances.

Market share is often regarded as a major determinant of profitability. It is this belief that, at least in part, lies behind the wave of acquisitions spreading through Europe. In redefining the "home market" to cover the EC member states' territories, many companies have discovered their position to be weak. Defining in which market the company competes is critical. Moreover, the close trading links between the EC countries and the rest of Europe, including, in time, the newly opened markets in Eastern Europe may further extend the boundaries of a company's European market.

Building a strong position in a small, clearly defined market can be highly successful. For example, BSN's target is to be either number one or two in each specific market segment targeted, whether this be yoghurt, beer or noodles. As a strategy it is more effective than aiming to be number one or two in the prepared food market. Acquisition is one means of strengthening a company's position rapidly. It also brings some defensive gains by removing potential targets from competitors' grasp. Another major reason given for acquisition is the potential that synergies offer — whether in R & D, in production, marketing, or logistics — for reducing the overall cost base. In practice, synergies often prove elusive. But when these objectives have been realised, the benefits are considerable. Electrolux offers a good example of how acquisitions have led to synergies being achieved.

The growth of acquisition activity is related to but not dependent on 1992. New EC competition policy rules governing large scale mergers and acquisitions will simplify the regulatory aspects of acquisitions — but many other factors are important in determining whether to proceed with an acquisition. These are examined in the third section of this chapter.

In summary 1992 is an enabling device, serving to accelerate the process, but not, in itself, sufficient to cause significant change. The pace and extent of industry change will vary across sectors. In some, where regulation and national protection are rife, 1992 will be a significant factor. In many, the global competitive environment is likely to provide more impetus. The implication for companies is that the Single Market cannot effectively be addressed as a stand alone issue. Planning a Single Market strategy requires the company to assess its own position, and evaluate opportunities within the broader patterns of global competition and change.

Preparing for the Single Market

What are the implications of the structural change discussed in the previous section? How can companies prepare to compete effectively in Europe post-1992? There is no single answer.

Size and type of company will be one factor. Multinationals have long looked at the total European market when planning their operations. It could be argued that US corporations may even be at an advantage as they have no 'national' axe to grind and have often already established a European headquarters. This breadth of vision gives an advantage over a company used to operating only in a single culture. Multinationals are likely to remain in the vanguard of further changes. A number of opportunities are becoming available to enable multinationals to integrate their pan-European operations more effectively. 3M is just one example, among many, of a company introducing European wide product management for certain products.

A key question for multinationals will be how best to manage the organisation in changing market conditions. Highly decentralised structures may prove inefficient, but many companies are loath to return to highly centralised organisations. The answer may lie in centralising certain functions where clear benefits can be identified: R&D, production and purchasing are all contenders. Against this, other functions, notably sales and marketing, may require central co-ordination but great flexibility in their application at local level. The key to success is seen by one American executive based in Europe as the ability to "think global but act local" — not always the easiest feat for multinationals to achieve!

In contrast, smaller, national businesses face a different set of issues. Here the key question is likely to concern the desirability and pace of expansion into Europe. A number of options exist. Evaluating the risks and benefits of each is the major challenge for companies seeking European growth.

First, the company can appoint a local agent or distributor. Low investment and comparatively low risk must be balanced against the lack of control that such arrangements typically involve. The next step down the spectrum of risk, return and commitment is to contemplate licensing, or some other form of contractual agreement. The third option is to start a greenfield operation, but the risk and investment required rarely make this financially attractive unless the company has a key advantage, either in cost or differentiation.

Alliance or joint venture is the fourth option. Alliances in various guises are becoming a popular way of entering Europe. Although risks are lower than with acquisition, experience indicates pitfalls are common. Short term alliances set up to achieve specific objectives where both partners share common aims, where there is clear management control and, in case of disaster, clear break-up provisions are agreed in advance can be successful. ICI's link with Enichem in PVC and EVC is one example. Quick hamburgers in France, a joint venture between Casino and KBB is another. The financial services sector has rushed to form alliances and cross shareholdings in anticipation of an open European market. Yet already there is evidence that some are not fulfilling expectations. Amro Bank in the Netherlands and Societe Generale in Belgium, for example, recently announced the dilution of their alliance into a joint marketing agreement.

Cross-shareholding is already widespread in continental Europe but relatively uncommon in the UK. Changing the corporate culture to accept cross shareholdings as a means of forging alliances may prove to be a major stumbling block for some traditional UK firms. Companies with greater flexibility towards ownership structure may have an advantage in building a strong European network.

A fifth option is acquisition. The risks and returns are potentially greater than with the other options. It is however a route that many companies embrace, often without fully thinking through the consequences and implications. In the third section of this chapter, we examine some of these issues in more depth.

The above list of options indicates the complexity of the choices available to companies who are considering expansion into Europe. How can they start to evaluate these various approaches to develop a strategy that will be successful for their particular firm in a specific industry?

As indicated earlier, 1992 cannot be separated from the overall process of strategy formulation. The checklist below gives some generic questions which any company needs to be able to answer in developing a successful European strategy. Beyond these broad indicators are a number of issues specific to the company and industry which should be addressed. The outcome of going through this process is likely to vary enormously between companies. A small number of companies may conclude that no change is required. For others, the initial reaction may be one of near panic at the enormity of the challenges ahead. But in each case, management will have a clear and well reasoned case for a plan of action.

Checklist

Changes in the industry sector
What is the pace of change? Is it quickening?
If so, what or who is driving that process?
Are supplies or customers becoming more powerful?
Is there a threat from new technologies, substitute products or new competitors?
What is the implication of the regulatory and economic environment?
Who are the major competitors and what are they doing?

Impact of the Single Market
What specific proposals will have a direct impact on:
    the industry?
    the company?
    customers?
    suppliers?
What actions are required to respond?
What indirect consequences can be anticipated?

Ability to respond
What are the best and worst case scenarios?
How does my position compare with competitors?

Improving competitiveness
Objectives: what are they?
Strategy: is expansion required or is there an attractive niche?
R & D: are there economies of scale?
Production: are there cost savings through rationalisation?
Logistics: can costs be cut?
Marketing: are there benefits from greater co-ordination?
Sales: do we have the right structure and people?
Finance: are there cheaper sources of finance?
Human resources: do we have the right people?
Organisation: do we have the right structure?

Resources required
Capital
Human resources
Commitment

Acquisitions and alliances

Although an effective European strategy does not automatically imply growth, the statistics indicate that an increasing number of companies are looking to expand their operations in Europe through acquisitions or alliances Yet research (Porter et al) indicates that up to 50% of acquisitions fail.

Inability to merge the corporate cultures of the two companies is frequently a major, if unquantifiable, factor in this failure rate. These risks can be heightened if the acquisition is in Europe, if the country and business culture are not well understood. Significant cultural differences between European firms remain and are likely to persist well beyond 1992. Many UK firms seeking to expand into Europe have, to their cost, underestimated the difficulties of integrating and managing Continental acquisitions.

For the unwary then, the Single Market programme, with its tempting lure of an enormous 'home market', freed from irritating and costly barriers, could prove a trap. Successful acquisition in Europe is by no means guaranteed by 1992. Indeed, one can anticipate that the current wave of acquisitions will be followed by a corresponding wave of closures and disposals.

So smart chief executives will be pondering on how they can ensure their companies make successful acquisitions. A number of pointers can be offered, based on experience in dealing with European acquisitions. The process of acquiring in Europe is not inherently different from other markets, but ensuring familiarity with local conditions accompanied by thorough planning are both essential to success. The following five golden rules indicate the range and complexity of issues involved in a successful acquisition.

Know what you want to achieve
Acquisition for acquisition's sake will achieve nothing. Going through the process outlined in the previous section is one approach to clarify the rationale to expand into Europe. The next question is whether acquisition is the right route. Acquisition offers a means of establishing a position in a new market rapidly, often with added benefit of denying a competitor access, though the competition policy implications must be watched (see *The Competition Rules*, Part Six, Chapter 3). Yet the risks of failure are high. The basic question is: does acquisition offer significant advantages over other routes into Europe? For many it will but for some, alliances with clearly set objectives may offer an attractive alternative.

Plan the acquisition carefully
Thorough screening of targets is essential to identify companies that match your objectives. The search should concentrate on two aspects:

☐ Attractiveness

☐ Availability

Too many companies react to opportunities offered, instead of shaping and pursuing targets that match pre-selected criteria. Finding an ideal company is, in itself, not easy an easy goal to achieve, but settling for second best will rarely result in success. A strategy may not fall into place immediately. Some targets may need to be stalked for years, rather than months before becoming available. At that point, their attractiveness needs to be thoroughly reassessed.

Two further points apply. First, industry and company information is not uniformly available in European markets. This issue is being specifically addressed by the Single Market programme, since not every EC country currently has such stringent legal requirements as the UK does for disclosure of financial information. The difficulty of obtaining reliable financial data is compounded by the permitted variations in the handling of tax and accounting measures. Expert advice, covering the market position of the target company, as well as its financial position, is invaluable.

Second, ownership structures in Europe mean that friendly takeovers are the order of the day. Relatively few publicly quoted companies are available compared with the UK and US markets. This dictates how an approach should be made; an initially aggressive approach can sour any potential deal. Many companies are turning to respected third parties, whether consultants, bankers, lawyers or accountants to effect introductions.

Know the value of an acquisition

Many companies pay over the odds for synergies that are never realised. Yet, given the difficulties in obtaining accurate information, it may be impossible to place an accurate value on the company from an external review alone. Assuming that initial negotiations have commenced, an effective way of gaining further information is to suggest the appointment of an independent third party to carry out a valuation exercise.

The value of the company may be much higher or lower than the value to the present owner or to other potential purchasers. Whatever happens in the negotiations, the value of the target company to the aquiror will be unchanged. do not go above this ceiling. In the thrill of the chase, this simple principle is often forgotten!

Build an acquisition team

Recent research by Price Waterhouse indicates that the experience curve applies to acquisitions. Identifying, negotiating and implementing an acquisition demands specific skills. For a company fresh to acquisitions to attempt a complex deal in an unknown market is to court disaster. It is sensible to establish an acquisitions team, drawing in one or two managers who may subsequently be involved in managing the acquisition, plus others to cover the financial and strategic implications. A pool of outside advisors can also play a useful role. Consultants can help develop the strategy, identify and approach targets. Bankers, lawyers and accountants all play their role in the deal. Sometimes they can be critical to its success. In an acquisition of a French beauty product company by a UK conglomerate, the viability of the deal turned on the ability of the local French lawyer retained by the acquiror to draw up a tight contract linking payment to overall performance. The final price paid was much less than originally envisaged by the seller — or it must be admitted — by the acquiror as many hidden problems emerged post-acquisition.

Price Waterhouse recently carried out some research into factors leading to success or failure of acquisitions. The role of advisors was one aspect covered. One, not untypical response, is illuminating. 'Merchant bankers are parasites, but facilitators…and passable document writers. Lawyers are vital; accountants relatively useless, but necessary, to do the numbers'.

Plan ahead to implementation

Knowing what you want to do with the company once the deal is signed is also critical. Some conglomerates such as Hanson have a specialist 'post acquisition' audit team to look into each new acquisition and determine further action.

Within weeks, a clear plan is drawn up, refining the pre-acquisition expectations. More importantly, decisions and changes are made and implemented rapidly, partly to signal the intentions of the new owners. Acquiring in Europe can add severely to the usual problems of post-acquisition integration. Do you have local management to put in? Do you want to retain the existing management team? If so, bear in mind statistics confirming that up to 50 per cent of senior managers in acquired companies leave (voluntarily or involuntarily) within twelve months. Identifying and involving key management figures in the acquired company from an early stage could prevent unnecessary loss, particularly if local market knowledge was one asset you wanted to acquire.

As well as the usual unexpected problems and, occasional, bonuses that emerge post acquisition, it is important to have, or to develop rapidly, a clear picture of how the company will compete in the market.

European acquisitions also raise questions about reporting and organisational structures which must be settled at an early stage to avoid future conflicts. Again pre-planning is invaluable.

4 Winners and Losers

Restructuring major corporations
The risks for smaller businesses

Barry Baldwin

It has been predicted that only 50 per cent of European business will survive increased competition stimulated by the completion of the Single Market. The remaining 50 per cent will disappear over the next five to seven years, as a result of mergers, acquisitions or simply going bust. Although this is a broad brush forecast, no-one has disputed it, and there is certainly evidence to show that corporations with a pan-European strategy are successful. Most multinational corporations, American, Japanese and European, have been developing their pan-European strategies over recent years and are now well placed to respond to 1992 and the development of the Single Market. Not far behind, efficient major national companies are also developing plans for 1992, but a significant number have yet to put in place a realistic strategy, hence the thrust of the poor forecast for survival.

Restructuring is not, of course, a new phenomenon. What is new in Europe is the scale on which restructuring is to take place. Smaller businesses have always been vulnerable to big business strategies. But, as the completion of the Single Market progresses and competition intensifies, the implications of big business strategies for smaller businesses become profound. As traditional major suppliers and customers change their pattern of trading, smaller businesses will be denied opportunities for supply and purchase which hitherto existed. Difficulties will be compounded by an additional loss of big customers and suppliers which go out of business, having failed to respond to the increased competitive environment.

Many owners of small businesses, and even managers of some largers ones, have consoled themselves with the thought that the world will not turn upside down on 31 December, 1992, concluding wrongly that the completion of the Single Market will not affect them. They have correctly surmised that it will be well into the 1990s before all the proposed changes are introduced, implemented and take effect. But what they are failing to recognise is that 1992 is only shorthand for a gradual process that has already begun. It has been said many times by many people that the time to act is now, when plans can be developed which will keep pace with the Single Market as it evolves. The message is no less important simply because it is no longer new, or being shouted from the rooftops, the initial 1992 euphoria having passed. The risk for companies remains. A last minute response to 1992 will result in desperate measures being taken from a position of weakness. This chapter highlights problems smaller companies face as larger companies implement radical restructuring plans, and suggests practical steps which companies can take now, within their resources, to preserve their markets. Ultimately, however, any determined company can extend its activities beyond its home base into the wider European marketplace.

The first step — assess the impact of the Single Market

All businesses, irrespective of size and whether or not they export, should carry out an 'audit' to assess the impact of Single Market measures on their activities. As this book shows, the scope of Single Market developments is vast. But, if nothing else, company managers should isolate the details given in the European Commission's White Paper, *Completing the Internal Market*[1]. The legal measures proposed in the White Paper are being gradually adopted and implemented throughout the European Community and, together with subsequent legislation, are bound to affect a great many, if not all, business operations in some way.

Simultaneously, changes that are already taking place can be monitored. The Single Market programme has set in motion radical structural changes in certain industry sectors and in individual company plans and strategies. By observing these changes now, smaller businesses can see the direction in which European industry is moving in the longer term. There are, however, six major factors which, it is already known, will substantially affect business activity:

- □ Harmonisation of technical standards and certification procedures: this stimulates additional product development to meet any new requirements, and inevitably involves extra time and cost.

- □ Price cutting: Foreign-based competitors will enter the home market of passive businesses, intensifying competition and putting existing price levels under pressure.

- □ Market shares: Foreign companies will take up agencies and distributorships to market complementary products in the UK; or, European principals may abandon agencies and distributorships in the UK and start dealing direct.

- □ Public procurement : EC-wide access to tendering for public sector contracts will increase competition, putting pressure on prices and margins, and placing unprepared contractors and sub-contractors at risk, while encouraging the more efficient ones.

- □ Health and safety: Under more demanding regulations some working environments could be classed as substandard, requiring significant and costly improvement.

- □ Loss of business: If customers are adversely affected by changes in their industries and markets, their smaller, perhaps local suppliers will also lose out.

Options for major companies

The vulnerability of major corporations and the accompanying implications for smaller businesses may be difficult to perceive in detail. Therefore, a planned approach, anticipating and preparing for any setbacks, is needed. To survive, major companies are likely to adopt one or more of the following strategies which could injure smaller suppliers:

Cheaper sources of supply
Large corporations will seek new, cheaper sources of supply or sub-contract, linked to a supplier reduction programme. This will occur as harmonised technical standards in the EC and the expansion of the larger 'home market' encourage longer, cost cutting production runs, supported by cheaper, faster, more efficient distribution.

Rationalising production
Production will focus on the more profitable items as manufacturers exploit market niches across the EC, targeting specific customer types, in preference to supplying a bigger range of products to a wider range of customers in the smaller home market.

Disposal of non-core activities
Some companies will opt for simple cost-cutting measures, such as the disposal of non-core, less profitable or loss making activities. In other words, an entire subsidiary of a large corporation could be closed down, damaging local suppliers and sub-contractors.

Relocation
The geographical spread of markets across Europe will result in the relocation of manufacturing plants and distribution warehouses to reduce delays and maximise the benefits of cheaper, faster transport.

Reductions in inventory levels
Inventory levels will be cut as a result of faster delivery and longer production runs, with greater emphasis on 'Just in Time' methods of supply. Orders placed by large corporations with smaller suppliers will, therefore, be smaller and more frequent; an advantage to smaller suppliers located close to the major manufacturer, but a disadvantage to smaller suppliers operating from a distance. To some extent, this problem may be overcome, if the product supplied is uniquely in demand, or if speedy transport is arranged. However, the extra cost, or drain on cashflow, of buying from a distance in bulk (to secure plentiful supplies and avoid gaps in production) is usually the main factor in deciding to buy locally.

Acquisitions
Many companies will favour growth by aquisitions, as an alternative to organic growth, to develop new markets. There may be more emphasis on pan-European purchasing, plus disruption of existing supply patterns to businesses acquired. The impetus for acquisition will come not only from expansion-minded European companies, but more particularly from non-EC groups intent on establishing or expanding their presence in the Single Market. Investing in an EC-based operation is one way of overcoming the so-called 'Fortress Europe' problem, or protectionism in the form of high tariffs on imported goods.

Action for smaller businesses

The first question smaller company managers must explore as a matter of urgency is: 'What happens if I do nothing?' The question cannot be answered unless a senior executive is entrusted to review the potential position in depth. It is important to understand that, however academic the review may appear to be, the process of carrying it out will, in itself, reveal much that the company should know and attend to. A review will identify strengths and weaknesses in the business; in particular, highlighting any threats that 1992 has already introduced, and will continue to exascerbate. It follows that the report should be acted on immediately, not filed for later use. Everyone in the business should be involved in the review process and be briefed on the implications for the future as the action plan is drawn up. Such a plan may include the following elements:

Talk to major suppliers

Find out what suppliers' plans are and ensure that they too are aware and up-to-date on 1992 developments, especially any changes in technical standards. Ascertain whether existing patterns of distribution will continue; if not, determine the impact on your business. Try to reach an initial conclusion about the ability of your suppliers to remain in business, or whether they are vulnerable to a takeover, or are seeking to be acquired by a major company. If so, what type of company will it be? What are its plans?

Consider alternative suppliers

Assuming that no alternative suppliers exist in the home market, visit trade fairs in other EC member states to source comparable and competitive supplies. Consider any new supplier's response to technological advances and the extent to which a new source of supply might provide a more competitive edge to your own end product. Obviously, price, delivery and especially quality require careful review, as well as technical back-up and after sales service. A review of this type, if it does not lead to a more competitive source of supply, may unearth an opportunity to market a foreign product at home, as an agent-distributor, to complement your existing range. This will strengthen your position at home against incoming competition.

Talk to major customers

Hopefully, major customers will have made their own plans for 1992 involving a survival strategy. In particular, you will want to know if your customers are considering alternative suppliers, or whether they will be affected by the impact of changing technical or safety standards so that you can adapt your product in time. You will need to be satisfied that your business can respond, within its existing resources, to the cost and timescale of any changes. As is the case with suppliers, take a view on the vulnerability of major customers to more intensive competition or acquisition, and likely impact this will have on your own business. Choosing customers is a matter of picking winners in the European marketplace. In short, your own future is only as safe as theirs.

Seek alternative major customers

Identify existing suppliers of potential new customers in the home market. Pinpoint reasons why you have not already supplied the potential customers. What chance is there of reversing the position? Assuming a reasonably solid home base, opportunities to sell in other EC member states should be explored, taking advantage of the so-called enlarged 'home market'. Visit trade fairs in the target market to check out the competition, taking the opportunity to meet potential customers and agents. The visit also helps to identify any need for product development and to alter pricing structure.

Exporting

Although smaller business need not be afraid of exporting, it is not a one-way track to success. Despite the view held by some that exporting to Europe is no different to selling at home, there are many unknown elements and risks involved, as well as unfamiliar business practices. Penetrating new markets demands persistence and hard work, with the ability to absorb up-front costs, and probable early losses, until a new market is established. It will be more competitive than the home market and, therefore, the product must be better than competing products — at least at its own technical level — preferably with a quality standard which matches the Euro-standard. It is important not to spread the marketing effort too thinly, initially confining it to one or two markets, possibly even part of one market.

The experience of other smaller exporters will be useful in shortening the inevitable learning curve. Joining a local export club, small business club or a chamber of commerce , active in export promotion, is a recognised way of familiarising oneself with exporting techniques plus, of course, getting to know the sources of information, advice and practical help. The trade representation movement, though patchy, is an important channel of knowledge for smaller businesses. Trade associations and others in the information network, such as the Euro-information centres (see *The Brussels Connection*, Part Seven, Chapter 1) provide valuable contacts and briefing material.

Joint ventures offer an alternative, possibly more economical means of entering new markets, though reaching a working agreement with a prospective partner can be a lengthy process. The EC's BC-Net is a source of information for link-up with like-minded companies (see *The Brussels Connection*, Part Seven, Chapter 1). Care should be taken to vet any agreements with Euro-partners, possibly licencees, to ensure that they are compatible with the law in the jurisdiction/s in which the agreement takes effect.

Researching foreign markets

Treat each European market as a separate local market, recognising local tastes, culture and tradition. Claims that Europe is like one big home market are attractive, but premature. The product must be right for the target market. Quality standard, design, packaging, pricing and promotion must be modified, if necessary. Otherwise, competitors will spot any drawbacks and work to eliminate your product, with the added advantage that you have already done the spadework to develop the market. With this in mind, the exporter should evaluate his own and his competitor's technology. The cost and timescale for any product development or innovation must be considered before going ahead. There may also be a need for customer training and technical back-up in a foreign language, plus the all-important after sales service. Language labelling and modified packaging design may be mandatory. Much of the information you need can be gathered by market research organisations. A great deal of information is already available, often free of charge, from government agencies, chambers of commerce and trade associations . However, there is no substitute for a visit to the foreign market to see it at first hand, preferably taking in a trade fair.

Accessing new customers in Europe

If there are no plans to set up a branch or subsidiary in another EC member state (for which expert taxation and legal advice is essential), the choice is between using a direct salesforce and an intermediary, usually an agent or distributor.

Undoubtedly the exporter has greater control over a direct salesforce, but the cost may be too high to justify the result, especially in the early stages of entering a new market. Local employment laws may also be too onerous for a smaller business. Being paid on results, agents still offer the most economical means of operating in markets in which the exporter has no direct presence. Agents do, of course, speak the local language and many have a ready-made circle of customers with whom they are held in esteem and enjoy trust. Customers always prefer to buy in their own language and, even though they may not expect a supplier to speak the local language fluently, they expect some effort to be made to speak it reasonably well. Imagine how you would feel if a potential foreign supplier had to speak to you through an interpreter! Using a local agent, however, relieves exporters of some of the pressure to communicate in local languages, though anyone acting as export marketing director in an EC member state ought to be able to speak the local language as a mark of commitment, if nothing else (see *Languages and Business*, Part Three, Chapter 6).

Agents can be located in several ways:

☐ Trade publications

☐ Advertisements

☐ Trade fairs and exhibitions

☐ Government agencies

☐ Chambers of commerce

☐ Trade associations

☐ On-line databases, such as *Export Network*

☐ Directories and word of mouth

Having located and appointed an agent, however, the smaller export cannot afford to sit back and expect the agent to go it alone. Keeping in touch with agents is vital to support and motivate them, and meet important customers.

Streamline export administration

Export paperwork has been greatly reduced in recent years, notably with the introduction of the Single Administrative Document , removing much of the burden of red tape for smaller exporters. The elimination of border controls between Single Market countries, when fully implemented, will also ease administrative burdens and speed up the flow of goods, helping to ensure that they reach the customer in good condition. In themselves, however, these advances do not clear the field of bureaucratic problems for exporters. Much still depends on how efficiently the exporter handles documentation and administration. Mistakes can be costly. Prices should normally be quoted CIF (Cost, Insurance, Freight) and invoiced in the customer's own currency. The European Currency Unit (Ecu) is also being used increasingly, though not yet on a large scale. Exporters and customers alike understand, think and plan naturally in their own currency. Most customers do not want to bear any exchange risk. Therefore, a good freight forwarder can ease export administration and, if required, arrange transportation and delivery (See also *Maximising Profits — I*, Part Four, Chapter 1).

Incorrectly processed documentation is a major cause of delay in delivery, and sometimes in payment if export credit insurance is involved. Computerisation has provided many of the answers in processing documentation.

Finance: a critical factor

The initial impact of exporting on cashflow should be recognised in advance and planned for. The outgoings can extend over two years, perhaps even more, before profits are realised. Initial outgoings cover:

☐ Market research

☐ Visits to the marketplace

☐ Product development and design

☐ Packaging and labelling

☐ Translation and preparation of trade literature and technical manuals

☐ Language training

☐ Sales training

☐ Documentation processing and transfer systems

☐ Order processing and price quoting systems

☐ Export administration training and staff

☐ Exhibiting at European trade fairs

☐ Export finance

Any increase in turnover, plus the standard rate of VAT, has to be funded in the short term, along with any increase in inventory levels, recognising longer credit terms than those which apply in the home market. It may also take longer to collect outstanding billings in a foreign market. Invoicing in currency, which is attractive to the customer, means that the exchange risk is borne by the exporter. Most banks provide export finance packages and many provide expert advice to their account holders. The object is to ensure that the cost of finance does not erode profits. High interest rates and a strong pound do not help UK exporters, but it is still possible to minimise the effects of such economic disadvantages. One interesting possibility is a currency loan, if the export market is a country with a lower rate of interest than the home market, and when there is a reasonable prospect of a steady stream of currency income. Explore the different forms of finance available. Leaning on your friendly bank manager is not always the cheapest, or most efficient means of securing finance (see Part Four, *Cashflow and Profits*).

Seeking help

The 1992 message for smaller businesses, particularly those at risk from the vulnerability of major corporations, is not to sit back and wait for the competition to arrive, as it surely will. There is plenty of free, or low-cost advice available to whet the appetite for action. For first-time exporters, the comprehensive marketing plan — albeit a bland, forgettable phrase — is, nevertheless, indispensable. If the expertise for constructing the plan is not available in-house, external advice should be sought. The Department of Trade and Industry (DTI) *Enterprise Initiative* offers a starting point. Within the DTI scheme, individual initiatives cover marketing, business planning, financial and information systems, quality, design, manufacturing systems and exporting (see *UK Official Sources of*

Information, Part Seven, Chapter 2). The DTI also publishes a range of 1992 booklets under the auspices of its *Europe Open for Business* publicity campaign.

Much of the advice and assistance available has been on offer, in some form or other, for a long time. This should not deter businesses from obtaining the new crop of publications, or approaching present sources of advice. The point is that 1992 and the Single Market add fresh urgency and depth to many of the facts and principles we already know and accept in general. Amidst this mass of general information, facts essential to winning new business or complying with new regulations emerge with daunting regularity, and will continue to do so until the Single Market programme is complete, a goal which is still a long way off. Only by keeping up to date with developments will smaller companies be in a position to adapt to profound, possibly even traumatic, changes in the marketplace, involving, as outlined above, the streamlining, restructuring and relocation of major corporations on which so many smaller businesses depend for survival.

1 *Completing the Internal Market*, European Commission White Paper to the European Council, preceding the Single European Act. Original text published as COM(85)310 final, later reproduced in the *Document* series ISBN 92-825-5436-8, Price 3.90.

5 The National Wealth

Independent companies and economic policy

William Poeton

It is impossible to predict success for businesses in a highly competitive European marketplace without taking into account the impact of national economic, industrial and financial policies. The European economies differ greatly in character and efficiency from one country to another, and there are, in particular, fundamental differences in attitudes to the provision of finance for investment. Therefore, businesses in some countries, notably France and Germany, enjoy very significant advantages over businesses in other countries, such as Britain. The smaller, independent business is particularly vulnerable to these long-established differences, as well as to temporary fluctuations in economic and industrial policies, whether they occur across the international marketplace, or as a result of adverse factors arising out of the conduct of national policies.

In France and Germany there has, since World War II, been an organised system for channelling resources into industry, particularly independent companies in the manufacturing sector. Fundamental to the success of such a system is the belief in the special importance of industry for the attainment of national economic objectives; a belief which ought to be shared by government, banks and the business community as a whole.

The economic objective must be wealth creation plus policies to support and encourage the manufacturing sector. But since the war, in contrast with some of Britain's major trading partners, Britain has seen a decline in manufacturing output and a sharp fall in the numbers employed in manufacturing. More recently, Britain's trade deficit in manufactured goods has reached record proportions, due to the increasing availability of consumer credit and the resulting surge in demand. British manufacturing industry did not have enough independent businesses left to meet such a sudden increase in demand. Therefore, the gap was filled by overseas competitors. Many in the British business community now believe that Britain's national heritage — economic viability, based on the ability to create wealth through manufacturing — has been neglected. There are many problems, but the most acute is the lack of affordable investment finance.

The nature of Britain's industrial revolution, which foreshadowed similar revolutions in other developed countries, was such that there was originally no need to provide organised finance for industry. Yet, despite the development of many other industrial powers, the picture has hardly changed. No tradition has been built up for an organised system of finance in Britain, as it has elsewhere, although there is some evidence that the pattern is slowly changing. The pressures on companies to compete in Europe's free market, however, are unprecedented in their urgency, and this means that we must measure the speed of change against the challenges that face smaller, independent businesses in an increasingly competitive environment in Europe.

Historically, the banking tradition in Britain has been one of a mercantile and financial nature, and the industrial enterprises, spawned by the original industrial revolution, were established and financed, in the main, by private individuals, largely out of their personal fortunes which were amassed from trade, shipping and the colonies. Recently, however, seeing the decreasing availability of investment finance, the Union of Independent Companies has proposed a radical change in the British banking tradition — the creation of a Business Development Fund — which will channel funds to worthwhile investment projects through the normal banking network. Essentially, the proposal is to create an industrial banking system, similar to that which is proven in Germany, so that the provision of finance for industry can be dealt with as a separate issue, no longer part of the "system" which does not discriminate between the needs of the industrial sector and consumers in the conduct of economic policy. Government backed export initiatives, management initiatives or training initiatives are not, in themselves, a sufficient guarantee of a healthy independent business sector. Business needs finance for investment, first and foremost, as a foundation for a healthy, growing manufacturing sector.

After the devastation of World War II, Germany had no special class of wealthy people when it developed the urgent national commitment to creating industrial power, and was faced with a situation in which, unlike in Britain, enterprises could not afford to wait to grow from small beginnings, on the basis of retained earnings. Germany had to match Britain's then industrial supremacy, hence large amounts of capital were needed to establish industrial enterprises, which only organised finance could provide. German banks were led to a position in which they could transform deposits into long term funds for industry. Without such a bold initiative, Germany could not have achieved such rapid, spectacular post-war growth.

The remarkable factor is that German banks were prepared to take the risks that they took in the beginning of post-war German industrialisation, helped of course by the inflow of Marshall Aid funds. These funds were never spent, but invested to provide long term loans for industry at subsidised interest rates. Such a commitment could still only come about through a deep appreciation of the vital role of industry in national economic development. The German government also helped to finance reconstruction, but it did so through the banks, or by helping banks to finance their clients. In allocating the Marshall Aid funds, and channelling those funds through banks, the choice of investment projects were made by the banks and passed on to an administering board, which provided the necessary finance. The wise use of these funds played a major part in the post-war reconstruction of the German economy and, in 1953, a law was introduced to keep these funds separate from other government funds, to preserve their integrity and also to be certain that industrial loans were used to finance fixed investment in the private sector. Thus, the banks were prepared to depart from conventional lending rules, at considerable risk to themselves, to assist in the process of reconstruction. By contrast, banking in Britain is based on the pawnbroking principle, demanding that borrowers provide collateral; and, all too often, ceilings on loans are decided by the value of the company's disposable assets, not on the intangible assets which often provide a more realistic assessment of a company's worth.

The German attitude to smaller businesses is, fortunately, substantially reflected in the European Community's enterprise policy; a policy in which the interdependence between the smaller business sector and the European economy is recognised and encouraged. More businesses means more competition and, therefore, greater commercial, social and economic benefits.

The Treaty of Rome has provided the Community with its own business forum in Brussels, the 189-strong Economic and Social Committee (ESC) (see *The Brussels Connection*, Part Seven, Chapter 1), in which industry can express its views. The ESC has a legal right to opine on the content of proposals and its members' views bring home to Community officials much detail of the day-to-day running of the economies of member states. Unfortunately, in the UK, the initial impetus to raise the status of the smaller business sector, which began promisingly with the 1983 European Year of Small and Medium-Sized Enterprises, has begun to wane. Only the government's 1992 advertising campaign, commendable as far as it goes, is filling the void. The network of small business information contacts and counsellors of one sort or another, is also helpful, but none of these contacts can tackle the root of manufacturing industry's problems in order to arrest the decline in manufacturing output that has beset the British economy since the 1950s.

The German experience

In a paper on the contribution of small businesses to the German economic miracle[1], Willibord Sauer, Secretary-General of the Union of Craft Industries and Trades of the EEC (UAEEC), has recorded the German experience in which the German small businesses sector was nurtured under the guidance of Chancellor Adenauer's Minister for Economics, Professor Erhard. Sauer highlights two key aspects of Erhard's plan which focus on the role of smaller enterprises:

☐ "Professor Erhard's first aim was to encourage as many people as possible to start up a business. Trade restrictions were abolished and the general freedom to engage in business was established. A strict anti-trust policy followed. The funds of the European Recovery Program were used for a general cheap credit programme bent upon establishing the conditions of fair and efficient competition.

☐ All this meant ignoring demands for policies favouring the big industries in which pre-war Germany had excelled, whilst the needs and scarcity problems of the worse-off sections of industry were recognised. This led to the creation of the maximum number of new, mostly small firms".

Although, pre-war, small and medium-sized enterprises made up more than 95 per cent of Germany's businesses, their contribution had been overlooked: Sauer reminds us that the astonishing German recovery is generally attributed to the re-emergence of big business. But the success of big business alone did not provide Germany's economic miracle, and it will probably not produce it in East Germany once the reunification of Germany is fully accomplished unless the pattern of organised finance in West Germany is repeated in the East. As Sauer says: 'The importance of small businesses in (West) Germany was not only to be measured in their output and direct contribution to the GNP, but also by their direct and indirect contribution to the productive efficiency of bigger firms, via competition, sub-contracting, and maintenance. Small firms contributed to the overall efficiency of the German economy and played a 'profound stabilising role in German post-war society, dependent, as it has been, on a free market economy'.

Whether or not one sees much relevance in the German experience to the state of British industry, the truth of the basic argument — that a healthy independent manufacturing sector is essential to a healthy economy — is confirmed by the German results. As Sauer explains in his paper, Erhard was convinced that competition would achieve the best results in terms of economic progress and profits, and so he concentrated on implementing competition as the most efficient means of achieving and maintaining prosperity for all. His ideas did not entail a policy of protection for smaller firms from the rigours of competition. Outright protection would only have led to inefficiency, but he recognised the need to avoid taking measures which would directly or indirectly favour big business. In the UK, big companies have depended on a protected business environment and, when the barriers in Europe finally come down, 1992 could be their Waterloo.

The economy and business confidence

In recent years, Whitehall's concern for other people's good housekeeping has acquired a more painful edge. Government has increased its dependence on random manipulation of monetary and fiscal measures in order to prop up its economic strategies. The result for business is the reverse of what it should be in a healthy economy. Instead of government supporting the business sector by providing a sound economic base, we have a situation in which the business sector is supporting the government in keeping economic policy on the rails. In such an atmosphere, little priority is attached to strengthening the smaller business sector, in preparation for the changes that the Single Market will bring, despite what ministers may say.

Time is now short. The government's Single Market publicity campaign has entered its second phase; consisting of more advertising, a new slogan — 'The Single Market is here now. Where are you?' — and the publication of another glossy booklet listing well-known trade contacts for yet more advice. The first stage of the campaign, lasting nearly two years, concentrated and succeeded in increasing awareness of the Single Market. Rightly we are being informed that awareness is one thing, and action is another. But this second stage of the campaign, concentrating on preparedness, seems only to be increasing awareness of the need to prepare, but no action. Real preparedness may not come until real changes are made in the working environment for business.

Independent companies in the United Kingdom exist in an unsettling atmosphere of hope, mingled with disappointment, in which enlightened policies are glimpsed from afar, but rarely penetrate the veil of punitive economic and monetary dogma which characterised the conduct and style of economic policy through 1980s. In a balanced, orderly administration, economic measures and industrial policy are not conceived in isolation. The two are inter-related. This point is axiomatic to any enterprise policy or initiative in Europe if we are to prevent the benefits of the Single Market programme being cancelled out by other factors. We know from past experience that the opening up of the European marketplace has not been the primary cause of Britain's growing deficit in trade in manufactures with EC partners. Indeed the pattern of Britain's trade has shifted substantially towards Western Europe since Britain joined the EC in 1973.

The root cause, as stated earlier, is the decline in manufacturing output (not to be confused with increased productivity) and the shedding of manufacturing labour, while in Germany, for example, Britain's strongest competitor in Europe, the number employed in manufacturing has remained at a constant level. In the USA, Britain's biggest overseas market, the number employed in manufacturing has actually risen, during the same period.

In the run up to the completion of the Single Market, the pundits tell us that only 50 per cent of British companies have taken steps to prepare for business in the European marketplace. Even among those businesses which have taken action, the degree of meaningful action — that is, action which advances a company in the pursuit of real business — is unknown. Some companies are, of course, taking the Single Market seriously, and looking at the question of import substitution as well as exporting to other European markets. But many such companies have to content themselves with entering into the spirit of 1992, perhaps by doing little more than obtaining government literature, employing bilingual switchboard operators, or commissioning a report on the impact of 1992 on their business operation. One senses that many such reports could not be translated into action in the present economic climate.

Given the difficulties which affected the UK economy during late 1980s and into the turn of the decade, it should come as no surprise that the level of preparedness for the early 1990s is disappointing. Against the bleak economic landscape of the moment, measures which are being taken to remove barriers some years hence fail to ignite entrepreneurial ambitions. More likely, managers are looking over their shoulder for the next 'blip' in the economy, or the next intrusion by Brussels into their business life. For example, there are elements of the European Commission's proposed Social Charter which would, if implemented, entitle the workforce in smaller companies to veto company decisions, or outnumber the directors on the board. Such fears, accompanied by adverse economic factors, blunt the will to compete.

The crux of the matter for independent businesses is that the European marketplace is not opened up solely by the removal of trade barriers, except in theory. In practice, many other obstacles lie between smaller companies and success in the European marketplace. Some problems persist at national level and bear no relation to the Single Market programme, except to take the edge of its benefits. An end in the UK to mandatory disclosure of sensitive financial information, technically required, but not enforced, in other Community countries, is an example of just one improvement, to which Whitehall could readily agree. This requirement compels companies to make known to potential predators financial information which could transform a flourishing independent company into liquidation fodder overnight. An aggressive customer has only to spot that it provides the bulk of a small supplier's business, by comparing the value of its orders to the supplier's turnover, before putting the squeeze on prices and profits. Such tactics may precede a purely opportunistic bid for acquisition at a favourable price. The enforcement of this rule exposes a worrying lack of concern which makes repeated reassurances that Whitehall attaches high priority to the well-being of the smaller company sector ring hollow.

Looking at the detail of the Single Market programme itself, still outstanding is the full harmonsation of national tax systems in the EC, without which the existence of a truly European company, operating across borders without physical hindrance or fiscal disincentives, has no great meaning. Even where existing reciprocal tax arrangements apply, tax collection procedures are complicated enough, without having to master half a dozen different ways of routing tax to avoid paying twice. The European Commission reminds us in an issue of its monthly newsletter *Target 92* that it has submitted various proposals to the Council of Ministers and states that new "measures must be introduced if all forms of double taxation are to be eliminated". Appropriately in the same issue the Commission reasserts that "one must never lose sight of the fact that Europe cannot be built without its business and industrial enterprises".

With so many examples at hand of obstacles to growth, observers can easily disprove the convenient, indeed fashionable, counter-theory that high interest rates and other economic factors feature only marginally in company plans. This may be the case in the new technology field where high added value assures a company of healthy profits. Outside of this modern scenario, however, the idea that canny, 'salt of the earth' entrepreneurs always save up for a rainy day is a folk myth.

Response to the Single Market programme

Curiously, the warning signs of difficulty in Europe for independent British companies have come from the Government itself. Announcing stage two of the Department of Trade and Industry's *Europe Open for Business* campaign in January 1990, Trade Minister, Lord Trefgarne, stated that he was 'concerned about the many firms, particularly the smaller ones, who still have to act', believing that the Single Market is of little or no relevance to them. As a nation, whenever we worry about industry's alleged disappointing response to the momentous changes in Europe, the question which springs most easily to mind is: 'Why are British companies slow to respond to opportunities in Europe?' The question we should really be asking is more direct: What is *preventing* so many UK companies from looking for new business in Europe?

A timely foretaste of today's lack preparedness for the Single Market came in 1983, three years before the signing by member states of the Single European Act, in a report on UK/EC trade[2], prepared by the House of Lords Select Committee on the European Communities. The report highlights the fact that the initial reaction of much of British industry to opportunities of EC membership was 'sluggish because of misunderstanding and ignorance of European conditions; and ill-founded enthusiasm was often dissipated when the real problems of trading in Europe were encountered'. This view of British industry's response to EC membership is accepted throughout Europe. The Lords put their finger on the cause, however, by stating: 'the adverse balance of United Kingdom trade in manufactures with the rest of the Community is not primarily due to membership; other causes are responsible for the decline, which is in line with a similar decline in trade with other industrialised nations'. The Lords referred specifically to disincentives to tackle European markets arising from high inflation, and 'violently fluctuating exchange rates'. It was clear, the report stated, that 'the rise in sterling from 1979 on, coming on top of rapid cost and price inflation, was such as to wipe out almost all actual and potential benefits from membership of the Community'.

On the credit side, the government has, to a considerable extent, lived up to another conclusion which the Lords set down in their report: 'The British Government should in particular work for the removal of non-tariff barriers to trade within the Community and should provide information and assistance to industry in developing markets there'. In this respect, the Government has achieved impressive results in increasing awareness of the Single Market and awareness of the need for companies to adapt to changes in the trading environment, and all that the changes imply, by the end of 1992. Whitehall has, for many years, vigorously advocated the removal of non-tariff barriers to trade within the Community. But the lifeblood of business is the availability of finance and cashflow, not good intentions. The measures being taken to complete the Single Market and remove barriers to trade are fired by highly credible intentions. But the tangible benefits for business, in the form of profits, is for many smaller companies entirely a matter of speculation. In short, what companies have to go on is boundless encouragement but only a modicum of support. As the Lords report unreservedly maintains: 'ill-founded enthusiasm was often dissipated when the real problems of trading in Europe were encountered'. The real problems are, as the report confirms, the adverse economic conditions.

The report also concluded that UK companies had not responded enthusiastically enough to opportunities in Europe, while conceding that economic factors mitigated against their efforts; conclusions which would fit the present difficult climate. We know from the Lords report that the problem has been aired before and that the way in which economic factors detract from the benefits of easier access to the European marketplace are not new. More and more government money and effort is injected into the 1992 awareness campaign, commendable government initiatives to advise smaller businesses on all manner of management, exporting and technical matters abound; but the underlying problem — the health of the industrial sector — is largely by-passed on grounds that market forces will sort the wheat from the chaff, or that no price is too high to bring inflation down — hence the continuing high cost of finance for business when the bank rate soars.

Representative organisations in the private sector, such as the Union of Independent Companies, believe that the Government has the will, but not the power, due to the civil service's vested interest in maintaining the present system, to reduce the impact of economic and other difficulties on the independent business sector. Out of the three million or so enterprises in the UK, the majority are classified as smaller or medium-sized enterprises; a disadvantaged majority. Under a system so dominated by the Treasury, the fortunes of the health of the smaller companies sector still rest ultimately with monetary theorists in Whitehall. Businesses are reduced to clamouring for fairer treatment in order to fulfill the promise which Whitehall says is expected of them.

1 *The Contribution of Small Units of Enterprise to the German Economic Miracle*, Willibord Sauer, Acton Society Occasional Papers (Siena Series No. 13), available from the Acton Society Trust, 5 Addison Bridge Place, London W14, Tel: (071) 603 2444.
2 *Trade Patterns: The United Kingdom's Changing Trade Patterns subsequent to Membership of the European Community*, report by the House of Lords Select Committee on the European Communities, 1983, HMSO ISBN 0-10-404184-6.

CONTACTS

Broadly speaking, the definition of a small firm is one with up to 50 employees. The definition of a medium-sized company is one with 50 to 500 employees. There are a great many organisations representing industries throughout Europe, many of them with listening posts in Brussels which keep them in touch with the EC's institutions. The EC's own business forum is the Economic and Social Committee (ESC) (see *The Brussels Connection*, Part Seven, Chapter 1). However, a small number of umbrella organisations receive support from the European Commission and are concerned primarily with the impact of developments in Europe on the smaller company sector. They fall into two groups, one of which has a co-ordinating office, Eurogroup, in Brussels.

The grouping arrangement developed out of the European Community's Small and Medium-Sized Enterprises Task Force initiative which began in 1984, and enables the organisations involved to obtain financial support from the Commission. The Task Force's function has since been taken over by the Commission's Directorate General for Enterprise Policy, Commerce, Tourism and Social Economy (DGXXIII). The interests of larger businesses are mainly represented in Brussels by UNICE (Union of Industries of the European Community) (also a member of a Eurogroup), to which Britain's Confederation of British Industry is affiliated (see *Representing Industry*, Part Seven, Chapter 3).

In Britain, the Union of Independent Companies (UIC) has been extremely active and insistent in drawing the attention of Brussels and Whitehall to the problems which the independent manufacturing sector has to overcome, and regularly attends meetings organised by EUROPMI (see below). Its president has had the responsibility of representing in Brussels all UK manufacturing industry in his capacity as Vice-President and member of the ESC. The UIC's newsletter *Common Sense*, which takes its name from the treatise of the same name by the American pamphleteer, Thomas Paine, has regularly set out detailed problems in the conduct of economic policy as they affect independent manufacturing companies, and has suggested practical measures and changes in policy to reduce burdens and constraints on investment.

Acronyms
Confusion may arise when small business organisation acronyms vary according to the language in which the names appear, or on which version of the acronym is commonly accepted; ie. the acronym, EIBC (European Independent Business Confederation) changes to AECM when the organisation's French title (Association Europeenne des Classes Moyennes) is used.

European Community

European Commission
Directorate-General for Enterprise Policy,
Commerce,
Tourism and Social Economy (DGXXIII)
Rue de la Loi 200
B-1040 Brussels
Tel: (32) 2 235 3168/7014/1111
Telex: 21877 COMEU B

Economic and Social Committee (ESC)
Industry Section
Rue Ravenstein 2
1000-Brussels
Tel: (32) 2 519 9011
Fax: (32) 2 513 4893
Telex: 25983 CESEUR
May also be referred to as the European Economic and Social Committee (ECOSOC).

Small and medium-sized enterprise representative organisations

Eurogroup

European Group for Small Business and Crafts (EUROGROUP)
Place d'Albertine 2
100-Brussels
Tel: (32) 2 511 8623
Fax: (32) 2 219 4250

Membership

European Committee of Small and Medium-Sized Independent Enterprises (EUROPMI)
Rue de Stalle 90
B-1180 Brussels
Tel: (32) 2 376 8557
Fax: (32) 2 376 0171
Telex: 64496

European Medium and Small Business Union (EMSU)
PO Box 12 04 43
D-5300 Bonn
Tel: (49) 228 167654
Fax: (49) 228 163273
Telex: 886529

European Independent Business Confederation (EIBC)
Rue Victoire 16
1060-Brussels
Tel: (32) 2 537 2589
Fax: (32) 2 537 9348
Telex: 63685

Other representative organisations

Confederation of European Industries (UNICE)
Rue Joseph II 40
1040-Brussels
Tel: (32) 2 237 6511
Fax: (32) 2 231 1445

Union of Craft Industries and Trades of the EEC (UEAPME)
Rue de Spa 8
1040-Brussels
Tel: (32) 2 238 0671
Fax: (32) 2 230 9354

Federation of European Wholesale and International Trade Associations (FEWITA)
Ave d'Auderghem 33-35
3rd Floor
1040-Brussels
Tel: (32) 2 231 0799
Fax: (32) 2 230 0078
Telex: 26946

Confederation of European Retail Trades (CECD)
(Address as for FEWITA above)

UK representative organisations

UK organisations representing smaller, medium-sized and independent businesses have links with, or are affiliated to, the European organisations listed above.

Union of Independent Companies
Bradfield Road, Silvertown
London E16 2AY
Tel: (071) 476 3171
Fax: (071) 474 0098

CBI Small Firms Council
Confederation of British Industry
Centre Point, 103 New Oxford Street
London WC1A 1DU
Tel: (071) 379 7400
Fax: (071) 240 1578
Telex: 21332

Forum of Private Business
Ruskin Chambers
Drury Lane
Knutsford
Cheshire WA16 6HA
Tel: (0565) 4467
Fax: (0565) 50059

Association of Independent Businesses
133 Copeland Street
London SE15 3SP
Tel: (071) 277 5158
Fax: (071) 277 7717

National Federation of Self Employed and Small Business Ltd
140 Lower Marsh
London SE1 7AE
Tel: (071) 928 9272
Fax: (071) 401 2544

PART TWO

SELLING
FROM
THE UK

1 The European Sales Team

Streamlining the sales and exporting operation

Kelly Dow

In making a study of the Single Market concept and taking the trouble to plough through the mountains of paperwork intended to persuade companies to take full advantage of new marketing opportunities in Europe, it became clear to me that most small and medium-sized companies would soon be running for the hills. The larger corporations are being given the chance to achieve a rapid market spread through mergers and acquisitions, but the smaller manufacturers can only guess at how the historic developments in the European marketplace will affect the day-to-day running of their business. Unable to judge whether the experts are right or wrong about the future, many company managers feel that they have little choice but to continue as they are for the time being. There is, however, much that they can do to improve the likelihood of success.

Starting with the broad view of events in Europe, peace has broken out everywhere and, if the predictions are accurate, we will see the European economy boom, stimulating demand across a market of 350 million or so consumers. Specifically, exporting to other European countries and import substitution in the home market will be on everyone's mind. Import substitution, replacing imported goods with domestically manufactured items, is as much a challenge as exporting to new markets, since it often entails competing with established lines of supply from low-cost Far Eastern countries. Adapting and developing products for distant regional markets is a long term process. So, in the immediate future, many companies are going to have to continue to make do with their existing product range. This means that companies will want to begin selling from their home base right away. Many will certainly attempt to do so, and their first task will be to adapt and improve their salesforce and build in support procedures in their marketing and export departments which will assist sales personnel out in the field in achieving a higher standard of performance.

The scale of the anticipated upheaval in the European marketplace must now be apparent to anyone who has ever read a newspaper or a free hand-out on the Single Market. Indeed, the questions which come to mind can be overwhelming, causing many company managers to switch off and adopt a 'take each day as it comes' attitude. What I have tried to do over the last few years is to strip away the verbiage and get down to the basic requirements of selling in the new Europe. Simplification is the name of the game, and I can confirm that the so-called 'challenge of Europe' boils down to the fact that the problems of the future will be the same problems that face most managers today, if on a somewhat magnified scale. If the methods seem all too familar — ongoing training in a broader range of skills, communications, motivation and field support — the means of achieving them on a European scale are not. Until now, we have only had to deal with one European country at a time. But, in future, our salesforce must be capable of operating with equal competence in regions as distant and diverse as Southern Spain and Lapland. We must not forget that a large part of the EC's trade is with the neighbouring countries in the European Free Trade Association (EFTA), currently seeking to strengthen links with the EC countries in what is known as the European Economic Space.

The attractions of a bigger, more open market in Europe can be deceptive, perhaps encouraging the belief that, if demand is going to boom, then the selling opportunities will be self-evident and all we need do is sit back and wait for it to happen. We may also become too anxious to learn about the workings of the EC in its entirety. But, no matter how accomplished we may become at dealing with the EC institutions or understanding the workings of the European marketplace, including the Single Market, it continues to be the case that nothing is ever achieved unless we have highly trained sales people out in the field facing customers and closing deals. We must continue pushing hard for our market share while passing through the learning curve to become Europeanised. We cannot afford to drop everything while we study the European way.

All this may be self evident to many people, even too obvious to mention. But how many companies have yet to review closely the level of specialised export sales training they have implemented in their companies? And what courses in market familiarisation have they run to ensure that everyone in the company has a clear idea of the habits and customs of our new European partners? The gulf which exists in many people's experience between knowing what to do and actually doing it is still very wide. Many company directors exist in a curious state of limbo. They accept that they have to remotivate and re-orientate their salesforce, but they are not sufficiently motivated themselves to put any plans into action. Admittedly, they may be inhibited by costs and other factors which need to be taken into account when contemplating investment in expanding sales. But, sooner or later, any serious exporter is going to have to review standards of practice in the export marketing department. Selling in Europe is on the boardroom agenda, and managers know that, to succeed, requires a higher degree of control and more sophisticated communications systems than they have been used to. It will also require a marked change in attitude towards customer support in today's market culture.

As always, product credibility, or positioning, say, a cheaper range properly in the market, will continue to be standard aims. But the credibility and adaptability of the salesforce and support staff is just as important in a multi-lingual, multi-faceted marketplace where standards of business performance will be as much a competitive advantage as any competitive edge in the product itself. For instance, the practice of quoting ex-works prices in Sterling is going to become a thing of the past. Remember, Sterling is a foreign currency to everyone else in the Single Market. Joining the Exchange Rate Mechanism is not changing everything to the extent many assume it will, since there will still be fluctuations in the value of Sterling. The main consideration for the salesteam, of course, is that the customer is not deterred by the uncertainty created in the mind when one has to convert currency on paper. Buyers are not bankers.

Another elementary mistake, admittedly made by would-be exporters, is making cold calls on potential customers on holiday, perhaps even depositing the company literature (in English) at the reception desk. With all due credit to the many highly professional companies now selling in Europe, these things still happen. I have even come across a situation where a bright, young salesman has had to suffer the indignity of tracking down his boss on the golf course on a Friday afternoon, in order to get permission to close a deal. Nothing demotivates staff in the field more than discovering that people back home are taking it easy; and sales executives who are not given authority to close a deal lose standing with their customers. An even bigger danger, of course, is that any delay in obtaining the go-ahead leaves time for an aggressive competitor to jump in and win the business.

One market, many facets

Although many aspects of the sales function will not change fundamentally in the Single Market, or in the wider European marketplace, they may become more difficult to accomplish in a more intensely competitive atmosphere. Our success will depend as much on our individual abilities to act quickly and confidently, adapting to and, indeed enjoying the different characteristics and customs which continue to flourish all over Europe. This will require a fundamental change in attitude on the part of a lot of sales managers. Above all, however, we should be aware that, as Europe becomes a Single Market, while in sales and marketing we must start to think in the singular, we will still have to act in the plural. The barriers may be coming down, and there will be greater freedom of movement of the goods and services we sell, but we should not forget that we will still be selling to numerous other countries and regions, all with different habits, cultures, attitudes and social levels of development and expectancy, not to mention at least another ten languages. This scenario will not change fundamentally, and so it is in these circumstances — one market with many facets — that we are all going to have to learn to do business.

Of course, experienced sales executives do not believe that European unity leads to drastic loss of national identity or national characteristics. The French and German customers they meet today are the same as the French and German customers they met years ago. But there may well be greater uniformity in certain lines of merchandise; partly because new laws to harmonise standards will enable companies to concentrate on bigger production runs, and partly because of the way that the retail trade has been going in recent years, with chainstores and franchise operators establishing identical outlets, selling identical products across Europe. The Big Mac you eat in Red Square will be identical to the Big Mac you eat in Oxford Street. So, throughout the European continent, there will be increasing similarities in the 'identity' of High Streets, if not in the people and their ways. Marks & Spencer, Macdonalds, and even our own banks are familiar names everywhere Europe. Yet, although we may be selling to different branches of the same 'Euro-business', we will find that a buyer in Munich thinks and acts differently to a buyer in Madrid.

Outside of the retail trade, in the highly competitive market for industrial goods, it will be a case of *exporting* as usual to European markets, again within a more competitive atmosphere than we have ever experienced before. Sales to other EC countries from the UK are rather diplomatically categorised by HM Customs & Excise as "outgoing sales". Yet, to all intents and purposes, they are still export sales. The new, trendy definition of the Single Market as the UK's Home Market is misleading, though it is convenient shorthand for getting across to the public the European idea. Fortunately, now that the initial impact of the public relations exercise in increasing awareness of the Single Market is wearing off, more people are beginning to understand that there will be no conspicuous benefits for them in Europe that will not be available to every other company in Europe, and available to non-European competitors seeking to get on the 'inside' by setting up their own operation, possibly by means of takeovers and acquisitions. The homogeneous laws being adopted in the EC, and the harmonisation of standards and business practices, plus cross-border activity in financial and other services, will benefit *every* company in Europe on one simple level — on the level of access. In terms of the approach to marketing and selling, however, Europe remains as fragmented and diverse as we have always known it to be. There are few, if any, companies in the UK, for example, that would be willing to place sales to the Single Market under the control of the UK Sales Director, even if this would be a logical, though impractical extension of the Single Market theory.

Higher standards of selling practice

As far the vital frontline activity of selling is concerned, in addition to language barriers, there are going to be problems of styles of selling and different levels of after sales service requirements to be met that will, in many cases, be far higher than is generally required in the home market, in circumstances in which suppliers enjoy long-standing relationships with customers. So when trying to motivate and lead a sales team over great distances, most companies will have to implement much higher levels of support and training than have been the norm in the past.

Once we accept, however, that there is no Single Market dimension, as such, for the salesforce, the first point to get clear in our minds is that freedom of movement of goods and services, and the simplification of the paperwork, will have little effect on basic selling practice. It will be no different to having your Head Office in Cornwall with your nearest market in the Highlands of Scotland, as far as communications and control are concerned. Add to this the problems of different customs and languages and you have the measure of the task before you. There may be additional difficulties resulting from the ever increasing use of manufacturing methods like 'Just in Time'. Nothing in the creation of the Single Market alters the fact that buyers of machinery components, for example, prefer not to tie up cash flow in bulk orders. Distance will also continue to be a problem, since a reliable source of replacements and after sales service must be on hand in large manufacturing plants where, if one part of the production line breaks down, it may effect the entire plant if repairs are not carried out instantly. This is not to say that foreign suppliers are less reliable. It is a matter of breaking ingrained habits and well-established supply patterns. Large manufacturing companies, in particular, will buy only from locally established — therefore, usually indigenous — suppliers. A walk round the gigantic ZF automatic transmission plant near Saarbrücken can be a chastening experience. The logos on the machines read like a *Who's Who* of German big business. There are, of course, other classic problems, such as being taken over by one's biggest customer, as part of a ruthless corporate cost-cutting exercise. But this is not a theme for this chapter.

The general assumption is that the completion of the Single Market in Europe presents a marketing imperative, if not actually a ready-made marketing opportunity. But there is an additional imperative — to strengthen sales performance in the existing home market to ward off incoming competition. So higher standards of selling will also be required in the home market. By strengthening the home performance many companies will find themselves better placed to make the most of marketing opportunities arising elsewhere in Europe. Insular attitudes among many smaller and medium-sized companies may, therefore, only be short-lived, as companies take stock of their position and begin to contemplate the long-term planning and investment needed to launch a European sales and marketing drive. In any event, companies should be in a position to respond quickly to product changes and market demands from a variety of sources, and be familiar with the different product standards required in different markets, also taking into account the anomalies which will continue to be present in packaging and presentation across Europe. Even if the standards to which one's own product conform are acceptable in another EC country under the 'new approach' system of reciprocity, one still has to determine what customers and dealers in other markets are used to. There may well be commercial 'norms' involved with are not primarily a question of applying legal norms.

Computerising export sales

The enormous advances in computer technology mean that, within a short space of time, sales people in Europe will be linked on a modem line, available in an increasing number of hotels today, with the office, enabling them to place direct their orders and update their management reports at any time of the day or night. It is, therefore, of great importance to ensure that the export department is computerised. With these changes, and a flourishing commitment, we can win large slices of new prosperous markets. Computerisation must now be an integral part of overcoming traditional problems of communication.

As a practical example of how a European sales operation can be set up using computerised methods, the following case study may be helpful to companies of all sizes. We decided to recruit the computer into the export department and to make use of some of the excellent low cost software packages now on the market. We were unable to tackle all the markets within Europe from a standing start and, therefore, chose four prime markets to attack in the first phase of our European operations. The next step was to appoint agents throughout the EC and set up an effective distribution system to supply the agents.

We then had the problem of recruiting sales people and training them to service the markets. Many companies that I have talked to naturally assume that it is best to recruit local sales people for each market, in order to overcome the problems of language and unfamiliarity with the markets. This is a policy that one should be very careful in adopting. Unless you are prepared to actually set up offices in the countries concerned, what you will, in effect, be recruiting are "front room" sales people — people who use their own house as a sales office. This is not an uncommon practice in the UK, for example, where one finds that some fairly large companies have sales representatives in, say, Scotland and Ireland or even Manchester working out of their front rooms. My own experience in this type of operation is that it leads to de-motivation of sales people, poor communications and the general loss of a working team spirit.

It is my firm belief that the best way to start sales operations in Europe is to recruit people from the home market and have them operate out of Head Office, as if they were in any other sales territory. In our case we chose this route as the easiest to implement and control. We had chosen four prime markets in which to launch our European operation. We then initiated a recruitment campaign to find four suitable people who possessed knowledge of the local language or were familiar with market in which they were going to sell.

We were, in fact, able to recruit two people — one who spoke fluent Spanish, the other a French speaker. The Spanish speaker was also experienced in selling in Spain, whilst the French speaker had not worked commercially in France. The other two people we recruited had appropriate export experience, but could not speak the languages required. We sent the foreign language speakers to refresher courses and the two other sales people attended a four week intensive commercial language course. Next, the company put together a library of books, magazines and video films from each of the countries covering a wide range of subjects and had newspapers from each country delivered on a daily basis. In other words, we implemented a total immersion course for the sales team which, incidentally, also encouraged other people in the company to become interested in the international dimension we were bringing into the company.

The effectiveness of this course of action was quickly proven. We now have people who are rapidly becoming specialists in their chosen markets, but who also understand the company and its requirements. They are able to operate out of the Head Office, knowing the kind of information required, and they are confident in the support services the rest of the company provides.

Management quickly recognised that sales people operating on the European mainland would need a greater degree of freedom to negotiate than was normal policy. They were going to need as many advantages as possible to compete, and win, in highly competitive markets. We began to quote fully delivered prices in the local currency and, in order to do this effectively, we bought an export management software system that not only allows the company to make these calculations, but also to determine exactly the gross profit from each delivery, thus allowing a margin for negotiation, whilst knowing the bottom line effect. Broadly speaking, this means not randomly pricing a consignment but being able to calculate in a few seconds the profit income from each individual product within the consignment. The system also helps the company to monitor the entire complex export sequence from quotation to documentation.

The next step was to ensure that deliveries were never held up by the complications of export documentation. This was achieved through the use of the Spex export documentation system created for this purpose by SITPRO (Simplification of Trade Procedures Board — see page 413), the Government agency. We can now produce our own SAD (Single Administrative Document) documents within minutes.

The overall benefit to us is tight control on costs and profits, plus highly efficient support procedures, allowing our salesteam to be able to compete confidently. We have as much control over sales activity in other European markets as we do in the UK. New problems do arise from time to time, but with the ongoing training programme and management commitment the company feel capable of meeting and overcoming them.

With the sales team operating and achieving encouraging results, the company is already planning the second phase of the operation. This will be to set up two or three strategically situated sales and marketing centres within the mainland of Europe. The centres will be manned and computerised operation bases, from which our mainland sales team of between eight and ten people will be able to work out of during their time in the field, and which will serve as customer liaison centres.

Logic dictates that the final phase of integration would be to place the sales and marketing activity closer to the centre of the market, say in Northern France. This is not, in my opinion, feasible or desirable. Europeanising an operation essentially means handling sales on a bigger geographical scale and responding to different local requirements, for the reasons explained in this chapter and elsewhere in this book. It does not mean, however, that every company will seek to become a kind of Euro-company, divorced from its national origins. In our case, we feel that there is a uniqueness to both the company and its products which should remain linked to our British origin. Therefore, it is important to us to preserve both our company and national identities. Tight management control, the comprehensive use of computers and an active commitment to Europe will enable us to overcome many of the problems of distance.

2 A Shop Window in Europe

Exhibiting at trade fairs

Peter Webster

Participation in European trade fairs should be an essential element of any marketing strategy for Europe. Already, every year, some 5,000 British exhibitors from large and small companies selling consumer products, capital goods and services take space in European exhibitions, a large majority attending the same event year after year. At present most trade fairs take place in West Germany and France, although virtually all countries in the European Community host some events. Eastern Europe too — notably Poland, East Germany, Hungary and Czechoslovakia — also stage important international trade fairs. Potential exhibitors should consider the following:

Testing the market: Discovering from face-to-face contact with European buyers and agents the virtues and shortcomings of your product or service. Its acceptability in terms of design, price, packaging, delivery dates and specifications.

Attracting customers: Although generally most potential buyers will come from the country hosting the fairs, buyers from all over the world visit European events — ranging from the Hanover International Trade Fair to the International Food Exhibition in Paris. Although some fairs only admit bona-fide buyers and agents, many also admit other visitors

Meeting agents and distributors: Being an exhibitor provides an unrivalled opportunity to meet existing and potential agents from the host country and elsewhere. This means a substantial saving in time and money for the exhibitor: agents are coming to you rather than you travelling to individual agents spread over cities throughout the world.

Making Sales: At the great majority of exhibitions, substantial hard orders are signed on the stands. Real business is done and real profits made. This is true across the whole spectrum of industry from food and furniture to medical equipment and machinery. Trade fairs are not only showcases but market places.

Evaluating the competition: Trade fairs provide a unique opportunity to evaluate your competitors — and all under one roof. In a single day you can see more of your rival's products, their literature and the interest in their goods than on any other single occasion. Invaluable on-the-spot information.

Launch pad for new products: A European trade fair is an ideal launch pad for a new product or service. The potential buyers are there, consumer reaction can be assessed and widespread publicity achieved. Many British companies regularly use trade fairs for unveiling their latest products.

Maximising results

To achieve the maximum results, and to make your investment in a trade fair as cost effective as possible, requires three essential commitments — money, manpower, and long term planning. To decide to be at a trade fair a couple of months before opening day or put the responsibility of organising a stand on the newest member of staff is a waste of company time and money. Senior staff with enough resources and time — six months to a year — need to be allocated. The major questions and decisions to be fixed before the exhibition are:-

Choice of event: Every year there are hundreds of trade fairs throughout Europe. Many of them overlap and seek exhibitors from the same industry. Some have a much better track record than others in attracting potential buyers. Choosing the right fair is critical to success. Space at these premier fairs must be booked early, often a year or more in advance.

Managing your stand: How many staff are needed to man the stand? — at least two for even the smallest display. Which staff? Sales, technical or both and have they any experience in manning a stand and dealing with a wide range of enquiries?

Language: Are the staff to man the stand fluent in at least the vernacular of the host country? Do you need an interpreter, if so, for your sole use or can you share one — and the cost — with other British exhibitors?

Stand location: Do you want your stand with other British participants or by itself among foreign exhibitors?

Dressing the stand: — What is going to be displayed — is it static or working and how are you going to get your display to the stand?

Literature and printed material: What literature are you going to have available? Where is it going to be printed and in what quantity and how much will it cost? How many languages will it be printed in — at least that of the host country? Who is going to do the translation and check it?

Attracting visitors: How are you going to get the right visitors to your stand — those who can influence buying decisions. A mail shot to a targeted audience? Paid advertising? Editorial publicity? Through your existing agents and distributors? These are prime questions to be answered. There is no point in having a stand that does not receive the quality of visitor, and in the numbers, to justify your investment in the event.

Meeting increased demand: If you get new businesses from the fair, can you guarantee realistic delivery dates. On what basis are you prepared to accept orders — CIF, FOB or both? Are you pricing in sterling or the buyer's currency?

Publicity: Don't hide your light under a bushel. Put out press material in Britain and the host country about your participation. During and after the event, publicise orders gained, new products shown, extra distributors and new markets achieved. Make contact with the trade and specialist press and the local press in the host country. Use the services of the Central Office of Information in the U.K., the press facilities at the fair ground and any help the British Embassy or Consulate can provide, especially in the way of contacts in the country.

59

Venue Accommodation: At most of the major trade fairs in European cities accommodation reasonably near the fair ground is booked early. So a British company needs to decide well in advance how many rooms are required and whether hotel facilities for entertainment will be wanted.

Finally, there is the assessment of total cost pre, during, and post event. Resources need to be allocated and after the fair an analysis needs to be done on the cost effectiveness of the entire operation.

Thousands of British companies have already discovered that exhibiting in Europe can be a profitable exercise. The key to success is commitment and planning: either do it thoroughly or not at all.

Practical advice and assistance

Every British company contemplating exhibiting in Europe can get practical help and objective advice before making a decision. The main sources are the Department of Trade and Industry (DTI), (regional offices are listed on page 425) chambers of commerce and trade associations.

For the past 20 years the DTI, under British Overseas Trade Board export promotion programmes, has helped British firms to exhibit in Europe and throughout the world. Currently, the DTI assists some 3,000 British exhibitors at European events alone. For first time participants the DTI provides reduced rates for a stand and allied support services through its joint venture scheme (where British companies exhibit as a group). The Department helps with:

☐   Advice about the stand

☐   Finding agents and distributors

☐   Meeting technical requirements

☐   Translation

☐   Shipping

☐   Publicity

Above all, the DTI removes the burden of dealing with overseas exhibition organisers and booking space at the fair.

Many chambers of commerce and trade associations are approved by the DTI as sponsors for joint ventures. These are listed on pages 62-80. These organisations are able to provide detailed guidance about the opportunities — and problems — of being in a trade fair.

CONTACTS

The DTI's *Promotion Guide* lists the main events world-wide and is available from all DTI regional offices. The *Exhibition Bulletin* from the London Bureau, 266-272 Kirkdale, Sydenham, London SE26 4RZ (Tel: 081-778 2288) lists fair organisers in Europe and world-wide.

Selected DTI approved sponsors for overseas trade fairs and outward missions

Agriculture, farming, horticulture, commercial fishing and forestry including related machinery and technology

The Agricultural Engineers Association Ltd
Samuelson House
Paxton Road
Orton Centre
Peterborough
Cambs PE2 0LT
Tel: (0733) 371381

Association for the Advancement of British Biotechnology
1 Queen Anne's Gate
London SW1H 9BT
Tel: (071) 222 2809

British Poultry Federation Ltd
High Holborn House
52-54 High Holborn
London WC1V 6SX
Tel: (071) 242 4683

Commercial Horticultural Association
CHA Secretariat
96 Church Street
Great Bedwyn, Marlborough
Wiltshire SN8 3PF
Tel: (0672) 870392

The Federation of Garden & Leisure Equipment Exporters Ltd
96 Church Street
Great Bedwyn, Marlborough
Wiltshire SN8 3PF
Tel: (0672) 870392

Sea Fish Industry Authority
Sea Fisheries House
10 Young Street
Edinburgh EH2 4JQ
Tel: (031) 225 2515

Aircraft, aerospace and aeronautical equipment

Society of British Aerospace Companies
29 King Street
St James's
London SW1Y 6RD
Tel: (071) 839 3231

Antiques and fine arts

The Fine Art Trade Guild
16-18 Empress Place
London SW6 1TT
Tel: (071) 381 6616

Fine Arts & Antiques Export Committee
144 New Bond Street
London W1V 0LY
Tel: (071) 629 0834

Audio-visual products, films, radio and television broadcast and sound recording equipment, videotext and teletext

Association of Professional Recording Services Ltd
2 Windsor Square
Silver Street
Reading RG1 2TH
Tel: (0734) 756218

Producers Association Ltd
162-170 Wardour Street
London W1V 4LA
Tel: (071) 437 7700

The British Phonographic Industry Ltd
Roxburgh House
273/287 Regent Street
London W1R 7PB
Tel: (071) 629 8642

Federation of British Audio
Landseer House
19 Charing Cross Road
London WC2H 0ES
Tel: (071) 930 3206

Professional Lighting & Sound Association
7 Highlight House, St Leonards Road
Eastbourne, East Sussex BN21 3UH
Tel: (323) 410335

Radio and Electronic Equipment Manufacturers Association (British)
4th Floor,
Landseer House
19 Charing Cross Road
London WC2H 0ES
Tel: (071) 930 3206

Videotext Industry Association
Preview House
Boundary Road
Loudwater
High Wycombe
Buckinghamshire HP10 9QT
Tel: (06285) 29213

Banking and finance

British Invisible Exports Council
Windsor House
39 King Street
London EC2V 8DQ
Tel: (071) 600 1198

Scottish Financial Enterprise
PO Box 183
91 George Street
Edinburgh EH2 3ES
Tel: (031) 225 6990

Books and periodicals including Publishing

The Publishers Association
19 Bedford Square
London WC1B 3HJ
Tel: (071) 580 6321

Building, building services, public works, construction equipment and materials

British Blind and Shutter Association
Heath Street
Tamworth
Staffordshire B79 7JH
Tel: (0827) 52337

British Precast Concrete Federation Ltd
60 Charles Street
Leicester LE1 1FB
Tel: (0533) 536161

Building Centre Group
Building Exhibitions Management Division
George House
George Road
Edgbaston
Birmingham B15 1PG
Tel: (021) 455 9600

The Concrete Society
Framewood Road
Wexham
Slough SL3 6PJ
Tel: (0753) 662226

Federation of Manufacturers of Construction Equipment & Cranes
Carolyn House
22-26 Dingwall Road
Croydon
Surrey CR0 9XF
Tel: (081) 688 2727

Ceramics, refractories, pottery and glassware

British Ceramic Confederation
Federation House
Station Road
Stoke-on-Trent ST4 2SA
Tel: (0782) 744631

British Ceramic Plant & Machinery Manufacturers Association
PO Box 107
Broadstone
Dorset BH18 8LQ
Tel: (0202) 695566

British Glass Manufacturers Confederation
Northumberland Road
Sheffield S10 2UA
Tel: (0742) 686201

Glass & Glazing Federation
44-48 Borough High Street
London SE1 1XP
Tel: (071) 403 7177

Chemicals and allied industries including cosmetics and pharmaceuticals

Association of British Pharmaceutical Industry
12 Whitehall
London SW1A 2DY
Tel: (071) 930 3477

British Aerosol Manufacturers Association
Kings Buildings
16 Smith Square
London SW1P 3JJ
Tel: (071) 828 5111

British Plastics Federation
5 Belgrave Square
London SW1X 8PH
Tel: (071) 235 9483

Chemical Industries Assocaition
Kings Building
Dean Stanley Street
London SW1P 3JJ
Tel: (071) 834 3399

The Cosmetic Toiletry & Perfumery Association
35 Dover Street
London W1X 3RA
Tel: (071) 491 8891

Plastics and Rubber Institute
11 Hobart Place
London SW1W 0HL
Tel: (071) 245 9555

Clothing and fashion design

British Knitting & Clothing Export Council
British Apparel Centre
7 Swallow Place
Oxford Circus
London W1R 7AA
Tel: (071) 493 6622

British Menswear Guild
Wool House
Carlton Gardens
London SW1Y 5AE
Tel: (071) 839 2620

Clothing & Footwear Institute
Suite 105/106
Butler's Wharf Business Centre
45 Curlew
London SE1 2ND
Tel: (071) 403 9926

National Childrens Wear Association of Great Britain
40 Oxford Street
London W1N 9FJ
Tel: (071) 636 1833/4

Computers (hardware and software) and office machinery and equipment (except Stationery)

British Office Technology Manufacturers Alliance
Owles Hall
Buntingford
Hertfordshire SG9 9PL
Tel: (0763) 73475

Business Equipment & Information Technology Trade Association
Leicester House
8 Leicester Street
London WC2H 7BN
Tel: (071) 437 0678

Computing Services Association
5th Floor
Hanover House
73/74 High Holborn
London WC1V 6LE
Tel: (071) 405 2171/3161

Confederation of Information Communication Industries
19 Bedford Square
London WC1B 3HJ
Tel: (071) 580 6321

Display and shop equipment

Shop & Display Equipment Association
24 Croydon Road
Caterham
Surrey CR3 6YR
Tel: (0883) 348911/2

Education and training

The British Council
Education Counselling Service
10 Spring Gardens
London SW1A 2BN
Tel: (071) 930 8466

Committee of Directors of Polytechnics
Kirkman House
12-14 Whitfield Street
London W1P 6AX
Tel: (071) 637 9939

Engineering — electronic, electrical and nuclear

Association of Manufacturers of Domestic Electrical Appliances
Leicester House
8 Leicester Street
London WC2H 7BN
Tel: (071) 437 0678

BEAMA Ltd
Leicester House
8 Leicester Street
London WC2H 7BN
Tel: (071) 437 0678

Circuit Equipment and Materials Association
10B Boundary Road
Brackley
Northamptonshire NN13 5ES
Tel: (0280) 705045

Electronic and Business Equipment Association
Leicester House
8 Leicester Street
London WC2H 7BN
Tel: (071) 437 0678

**The Electronic Components Industry
Federation**
Romaro House
399-401 Strand
London WC2R 0LT
Tel: (071) 497 2311

Engineering — mechanical including metals and metal working, woodworking, machine tools, design control and productivity

British Compressed Air Society
Leicester House
8 Leicester Street
London WC2H 7BN
Tel: (071) 437 0678

British Fluid Power Association
Carlyle House
235-237 Vauxhall Bridge Road
London SW1V 1EJH
Tel: (071) 233 7044

**British Metallurgical Plant Constructors'
Association**
Room 629
162-168 Regent Street
London W1R 5TB
Tel: (071) 734 3031

British Pump Manufacturers Association
Carlyle House
235 Vauxhall Bridge Road
London SW1V 1EJ
Tel: (071) 931 0476

British Robot Association
Aston Science Park
Love Lane
Aston Triangle
Birmingham B7 4BJ
Tel: (021) 359 0981

Engineering Industries Association
16 Dartmouth Street
Westminster
London SW1H 9BL
Tel: (071) 222 2367

**Federation of British Hand Tool
Manufacturers**
Light Trades House
Melbourne Avenue
Sheffield S10 2QJ
Tel: (0742) 663084

Gauge & Tool Makers Association
3 Forge House
Summerleys Road
Princes Risborough
Buckinghamshire HP17 9DT
Tel: (0844) 274222

**International Wire & Machinery
Association**
PO Box 84
Leamington Spa
Warwickshire CV31 1FX
Tel: (0926) 334137

Machine Tool Technologies Association
62 Bayswater Road
London W2 3PH
Tel: (071) 402 6671

Mechanical Handling Engineers Association
Bridge House
Smallbrook Queensway
Birmingham B5 4JP
Tel: (021) 643 3377

Metal Trades Organisation (METCON)
Carlyle House
235-237 Vauxhall Bridge Road
London SW1V 1EJ
Tel: (071) 233 7011

Institute of Metals
1 Carlton House Terrace
London SW1Y 5DB
Tel: 071-839 4071

Process Plant Association
Graiseley
11 Brook Street
Leighton Buzzard
Bedfordshire LU7 8LQ
Tel: 0525 374386

65

The Production Engineering Research Association of GB
Nottingham Road
Melton Mowbray
Leicestershire LE13 0PB
Tel: (0664) 501501

Woodworking Machinery Supplies Association Ltd.
PO Box 10
Epping
Essex CM16 7RR
Tel: (0378) 78873

Food and drink, food machinery, hotel and catering equipment

The Allied Brewery Traders' Association
85 Tettenhall Road
Wolverhampton WV3 9NF
Tel: (0902) 22303

The Brewers Society
42 Portman Square
London W1H 0BB
Tel: (071) 486 4831

British Food Export Council
301-344 Market Towers
1 Nine Elms Lane
New Covent Garden Market
London SW8 5NQ
Tel: (071) 622 0188

Small Independent Brewers Association
2 Balfour Road
London N5 2HB
Tel: (071) 359 8323

Footwear

British Footwear Manufacturers Federation
Royalty House
72 Dean Street
London W1V 5HB
Tel: (071) 734 8901

Satra Footwear Technology Centre
Satra House
Rockingham Road
Kettering
Northamptonshire NN16 9JH
Tel: (0536) 410000

Furniture, furnishings, lighting, floor and wall coverings, interior design, household equipment, hardware and DIY

Association of Suppliers to the Furniture Industry Ltd
PO Box 10
Epping
Essex
Tel: (0378) 78873

The British Contract Furnishing Association
PO Box 384
London N12 8HF
Tel: (081) 445 8694

British Furniture Manufacturers Federation
30 Harcourt Street
London W1H 2AA
Tel: (071) 724 0857/8

The British Hardware & Housewares Manufacturers Association
35 Billing Road
Northampton NN1 5DD
Tel: (0604) 22023

Cutlery & Silverware Association of the United Kingdom
Light Trades House
Melbourne Avenue
Sheffield S10 2QJ
Tel: (0742) 663084

Decorative Lighting Association
Bryn House
Bishop's Castle
Shropshire SY9 5LF
Tel: (05884) 658

**Home & Contract Furnishing Textiles
Association**
Reedham House
31 King Street West
Manchester M3 2PF
Tel: (061) 832 8684

**Leisure & Outdoor Furniture
Association Ltd**
60 Claremont Road
Surbiton
Surrey KT6 4RH
Tel: (081) 390 2022/2027

Lighting Industry Federation
Swan House
207 Balham High Road
London SW17 7BQ
Tel: (081) 675 5432

**Wallcovering Manufacturers Association of
Great Britain**
Alembic House
93 Albert Embankment
London SE1 7TY
Tel: (071) 582 1185

Hospital, medical, surgical, optical and dental equipment including associated laboratoryware

Association of British Healthcare Industries
Consort House
26-28 Queensway
London W2 3RX
Tel: (071) 221 4612

British Dental Trade Association
Hill House
Hill Avenue
Amersham
Buckinghamshire HP6 5BQ
Tel: (0494) 431010

Federation of Manufacturing Opticians
37-41 Bedford Row
London WC1R 4JH
Tel: (071) 405 8101

Jewellery, giftware, clocks and watches

**British Clock & Watch Manufacturers
Association**
British Horological Institute
Upton Hall
Upton
Newark
Nottinghamshire NG23 5TE
Tel: (0636) 813795

**The British Jewellery & Giftware
Federation**
27 Frederick Street
Birmingham B1 3HJ
Tel: (021) 236 2657

Leather, leather goods and fur

The British Leather Confederation
Leather Trade House
Kings Park Road
Moulton Park
Northampton NN3 1JD
Tel: (0604) 494131

**British Leathergoods Manufacturers
Association**
27 Frederick Street
Birmingham B1 3HJ
Tel: (021) 236 2657

Skin Hide & Leather Traders Association
20-21 Tooks Court
London EC4A 1LB
Tel: (071) 831 7581

Offshore industries

Association of British Offshore Industries
4th Floor
30 Great Guildford Street
London SE1 0HS
Tel: (071) 928 9199

British Oil Spill Control Association
4th Floor
30 Great Guildford Street
London SE1 0HS
Tel: (071) 928 9199

Energy Industries Council
9th Floor Newcombe House
45 Notting Hill Gate
London W11 3LQ
Tel: (071) 221 2043

Institution of Mining & Metallurgy
44 Portland Place
London W1N 4BR
Tel: (071) 580 3802

Motor vehicles, motor cycles and bicycles and their accessories

The Bicycle Association of Great Britain Ltd
Starley House
Eaton Road
Coventry CV1 2FH
Tel: (0203) 553838/9

**The Motor Cycle Association of
Great Britain Ltd**
Starley House
Eaton Road
Coventry CV1 2FH
Tel: (0203) 553838/9

**Society of Motor Manufacturers &
Traders Ltd**
Forbes House
Halkin Street
London SW1X 7DS
Tel: (071) 235 7000

Music and musical instruments

Music Industries Association Ltd
7 The Avenue
Datchet
Slough SL3 9DH
Tel: (0753) 41963

The Music Publishers Association Ltd
7th Floor
Kingsway House
103 Kingsway
London WC2B 6QX
Tel: (071) 831 7591/2/3

Packaging materials and machinery, handling and storage

British Paper & Board Industry Federation
Papermakers House
Rivenhall Road
West Lea
Swindon SN5 7BE
Tel: (0793) 886086

The Institute of Materials Management
Cranfield Institute of Technology
Cranfield
Bedford MK43 0AL
Tel: (0234) 750662

Institute of Packaging
Sysonby Lodge
Nottingham Road
Melton Mowbray
Leicestershire LE13 0NU
Tel: (0664) 500055

Processing & Packaging Machinery Association
Progress House
404 Brighton Road
South Croydon
Surrey CR2 6AN
Tel: (081) 681 8226

Research Association for the Paper & Board, Printing & Packaging Industry
Randalls Road
Leatherhead
Surrey KT22 7RU
Tel: (0372) 376161

Philately

Philatelic Traders Society
27 John Adam Street
London WC2N 6HZ
Tel: (071) 930 6465/6

Photographic equipment

British Photographic Association Ltd
Carolyn House
22-26 Dingwall Road
Croydon
Surrey CR0 9XF
Tel: (081) 681 1680

Printing, printing machinery and stationery

British Federation of Printing Machinery & Supplies
Queens House
55-56 Lincolns Inn Fields
London WC2A 3LJ
Tel: (071) 831 3303

British Office Systems & Stationery Federation
6 Wimpole Street
London W1M 8AS
Tel: (071) 637 7692

British Printing Industries Federation
11 Bedford Row
London WC1R 4DX
Tel: (071) 242 6904

Safety, fire and security and associated equipment including civil defence

Council of British Fire Protection
Equipment Manufacturers
48A Eden Street
Kingston upon Thames
Surrey KT1 1EE
Tel: (081) 549 8839

Scientific and laboratory equipment (excluding medical)

British Laboratory Ware Association Ltd
Guild House
30-32 Worple Road
London SW19 4EF
Tel: (081) 947 5733

The Gambica Association Ltd
Leicester House
8 Leicester Street
London WC2H 7BN
Tel: (071) 437 0678

SIRA Ltd
Technology Services Division
South Hill
Chiselhurst
Kent BR7 5EH
Tel: (081) 467 2636

Ships and boats, shipbuilding, ports and marine equipment

British Marine Equipment Council
4th Floor
30 Great Guildford Street
London SE1 0HS
Tel: (071) 928 9199

British Marine Equipment Association
4th Floor
30 Great Guildford Street
London SE1 0HS
Tel: (071) 928 9199

British Naval Equipment Association
4th Floor
30 Great Guildford Street
London SE1 0HS
Tel: (071) 928 9199

The British Marine Industries Federation
Boating Industry House
Vale Road
Weybridge
Surrey KT13 9NS
Tel: (0932) 854511

British Naval Equipment Shipping
4th Floor
30 Great Guildford Street
London SE1 0HS
Tel: (071) 928 6599

General Council of British Shipping
30-32 St Mary Axe
London EC3A 8ET
Tel: (071) 283 2922/626 8131

Ship Repairers & Shipbuilders Independent Association
33 Catherine Place
London SE1E 6DY
Tel: (071) 828 0933

Sports and leisure activities and goods, including caravans, camping equipment, recreation facilities and equestrian

British Sports & Allied Industries Federation Ltd
23 Brighton Road
South Croydon
Surrey CR2 6EA
Tel: (081) 681 1242

British Photographers Association
1 West Ruislip Station
Ruislip
Middlesex HA4 7DW
Tel: (0895) 634191

Telecommunications, telephones and associated equipment

Sound and Communications Industries Federation
4B High Street
Burnham
Slough SL1 7JH
Tel: (06286) 67633

Textiles and textile machinery including fabrics, fibres, yarns and knitting equipment

British Carpet Manufacturers Association
Fourth Floor
Royalty House
72 Dean Street
London W1V 5HB
Tel: (071) 734 9853

British Needlecrafts Council
The Old Vicarage
Hayley Hill
Halifax HX6 6DR
Tel: (0422) 351215

British Textile Confederation
British Apparel and Textile Centre
7 Swallow Place
London W1R 7AA
Tel: (071) 491 9702

British Textile Machinery Association
20 Ralli Courts
West Riverside
Manchester M3 5FL
Tel: (061) 834 2991

The Irish Linen Guild
Lambeg Road
Lisburn
Co Antrim BT27 4RL
Northern Ireland
Tel: (0846) 677377

National Wool Textile Export Corporation
Lloyds Bank Chambers
43 Hustlergate
Bradford BD1 1PE
Tel: (0274) 724235/6

Transport and transport systems

Railway Industry Association
6 Buckingham Gate
London SW1E 6AE
Tel: (071) 834 1426

Toys, hobbies, crafts, games and amusements

**British Amusement Catering Trades
Association**
122 Clapham Common
North Side
London SW4
Tel: (071) 228 4107

**British Toy & Hobby Manufacturers
Association Ltd**
80 Camberwell Road
London SE5 0EG
Tel: (071) 701 7271

Crafts Council
12 Waterloo Place
London SW1Y 4AU
Tel: (071) 930 4811

Water effluent and air treatment plant including anti-pollution, cleaning and refuse disposal equipment

British Water Industries Group
9 Harley Street
London W1N 2AL
Tel: (071) 436 7541

National Society of Clean Air
136 North Street
Brighton
Sussex BN1 1RG
Tel: (0273) 26313

**Society of Laundry Engineers &
Allied Trades Ltd**
78-80 Borough High Street
London SE1 1XG
Tel: (071) 403 2300

Other specialised trade fairs

British Anaerobic & Biomass Association Ltd
PO Box 7
Southend
Reading RG7 6AZ
Tel: (0635) 62131

Other specialised trade associations

British Baby Products Association
60 Claremont Road
Surbiton
Surrey KT6 4RH
Tel: (081) 390 2022

British Consultants Bureau
Westminster Palace Gardens
1-7 Artillery Row
London SW1P 1RJ
Tel: (071) 222 3651

The British Direct Marketing Association
Grosvenor Gardens House
35 Grosvenor Gardens
London SW1W 0BS
Tel: (071) 630 7322

British Franchise Association
75A Bell Street
Henley-on-Thames
Oxfordshire RG9 2DB
Tel: (0491) 578049/50

**British Promotional Merchandise
Association**
Suite 12
4th Floor
Parkway House
Parkway
East Cheam
London SW14 8LS
Tel: (081) 878 0738

British Tourist Authority
Thames Tower
Black's Road
Hammersmith
London W6 9EL
Tel: (081) 846 9000

The Defence Manufacturers Association
Park House
Broadford
Shalford
Guildford
Surrey GU4 8DW
Tel: (0483) 579333

**The Hairdressing Manufacturers and
Wholesalers Association Ltd**
Clare Cottage
Oakbank
Haywards Heath
West Sussex RH16 1RR
Tel: (0444) 452580

The Pet Trade & Industry Association Ltd
103 High Street
Bedford MK40 1NE
Tel: (0234) 273933

**The British Institute of Non-Destructive
Testing**
1 Spencer Parade
Northampton NN1 5AA
Tel: (0604) 30124/5

3 The Market for Inventions and Ideas

Technology transfer in Europe

British Technology Group

Innovative British companies and research and development establishments are renowned for their inventions and know-how. The commercial application of innovations in Europe is made easier by National Research Development Organisations (NRDOs) which may assist with funding of technological developments and then licence them to industry. In the UK the NRDO is the British Technology Group (BTG) which is a member of the EUROTECH network of NRDO's (see below). BTG works extensively with research institutions, university research establishments and polytechnics to licence new products and processes to industry, and financially assists companies to develop new, innovative technologies. BTG's activities, and its links with other NRDOs through the EUROTECH network, serve as an illustration of the way in which the marketing of know-how has become a source of major international business.

Third parties (ie. private companies) may become involved with BTG, either indirectly through participation in collaborative research and development projects undertaken with universities and other R & D institutions, or directly through BTG's funding activities. University-industry collaboration is covered in *Universities and Industry*, Part Three, Chapter 3. For business/polytechnic joint activities see *Polytechnics and Business*, Part Three, Chapter 4. Information on specific EC research and development programmes is given in *EC Grants and Loans*, Part Four, Chapter 7. The legal aspects of licensing know-how are outlined in *European Community Law*, Part Six, Chapter 1 and in *Corporate Structures*, Part Five, Chapter 1.

EUROTECH[1]

EUROTECH is a unique network in which a group of NRDOs have agreed to act locally on each other's behalf in sourcing and licensing selected technologies. This approach takes advantage of local market knowledge, language fluency and business culture, as well as bringing international licensing within reach of a wide range of universities, research institutes, small and medium-sized enterprises and private inventors.

The primary objective of EUROTECH is to assist with the commercial exploitation of the vast fund of technology in Europe's many universities, technological institutes, research laboratories and small and medium-sized enterprises and private inventors.

The primary objective of EUROTECH is to assist with the commercial exploitation of the vast fund of technology in Europe's many universities, technological institutes, research laboratories and small and medium-sized enterprises which are continually creating innovative technology, but often lack the means to exploit it. Commercial exploitation of technology through EUROTECH and its membership of NRDOs benefits both the sources of technology and European industry by means of transnational licensing, recognising that technology transfer is a long-term risk business.

The network operates on the basis that each member appoints a EUROTECH executive to act as a focal point for communication with the member organisation and as a gateway to local sources and companies. Technologies received from sources of invention by a EUROTECH executive may be offered to other EUROTECH executives in one or more target countries of the EC. These offers are then assessed and, if accepted, are offered to potential licencees in the target countries. The market is approached according to guidelines agreed between the executives involved who exchange information on marketing activities and results. Experience exchange includes technology selection, based on needs and interests; formulation of offers for technology transfer; exchange of assessment experience; intellectual property rights; exploitation of licence offers. Members have also adopted common procedures and methods of communication which inlcude:

☐ Standardised formats to describe offers

☐ Established methods for assessment and exploitation planning

☐ Rules governing exchange of information between members

☐ A comprehensive database for monitoring international licensing operations

The EUROTECH project is supported by the EC's SPRINT programme and comprises the following NRDOs, one from each member state of the European Community:-

Belgium (IRSIA-IWONL)
Denmark (DIC)
France (ANVAR)
Germany (FhG)
Greece (ITE)
Ireland (EOLAS)
Italy (GNR)
Luxembourg (LUXINNOVATION)

Netherlands (TNO)
Portugal (JNICT)
Spain (IMPI)
United Kingdom (BTG)

British Technology Group

BTG undertakes two complementary types of activity: the transfer of technology
— prospective new products and processes — from public sector and other
sources to industrial manufacturers under licence; and the provision of funding on
commercial terms for UK companies undertaking development projects involving
a significant degree of technical innovation. Since a substantial industrial
development effort may be required to transform promising research findings into
a commercial product, BTG may combine its roles as licensor and source of
development funding to give a new technology the best possible chance of
ultimate success.

BTG's licensing and funding activities are spearheaded by four technology-
based operating divisions working in the areas of science, pharmaceuticals,
electronics and information technology. These are backed by patent, legal,
finance and business development divisions. The organisation is large enough to
retain these specialist skills as an in-house asset, yet small enough to ensure short
lines of communication and a minimum of bureacracy. It has the resources not
only to protect and develop inventions, but also to tackle infringements of its
intellectual property. Technology is transferred to industry in return for agreed
downpayments and sales-related royalties from the licensee. BTG monitors
licensees' performance and makes periodic audits of their royalty payments.
BTG's own income is derived from successful licensing. When income begins to
flow from successful licensing, BTG channels the early rewards to the inventive
source. Ultimately, the net licence income is shared between BTG and the source
on a 50:50 basis. Some of BTG's major recent industrial project earners include:

Amphibious hovercraft (Hovertravel)
Digital control and data systems (Babcock Bristol)
Synthesised signal generators (Racal Dana)
Alkali-resistant glass fibre (Pilkington)
Personal pagers (Multitone)
Visual display system controller (Rediffusion Simulation)
Pyrethrin analogues (Wellcome, ICI)

Recent licensing successes include:

□ **Diagnostic imaging:** Johnson & Johnson have assigned a major portfolio of
patents on diagnostic imaging technology to BTG to license worldwide.

□ **Glass ionomer cement:** Licence agreement signed with G-C Dental Industrial
Corporation (Japan) under BTG's patents on glass ionomer cement invented
at the Laboratory of the Government Chemist.

□ **Magnetic resonance imaging:** Licence agreements reached with Siemens
(Germany) Toshiba, and Hitachi (Japan).

□ **BTG 1501**: Potential anti-anxiety drug licensed to G. D. Searle and Co
(USA).

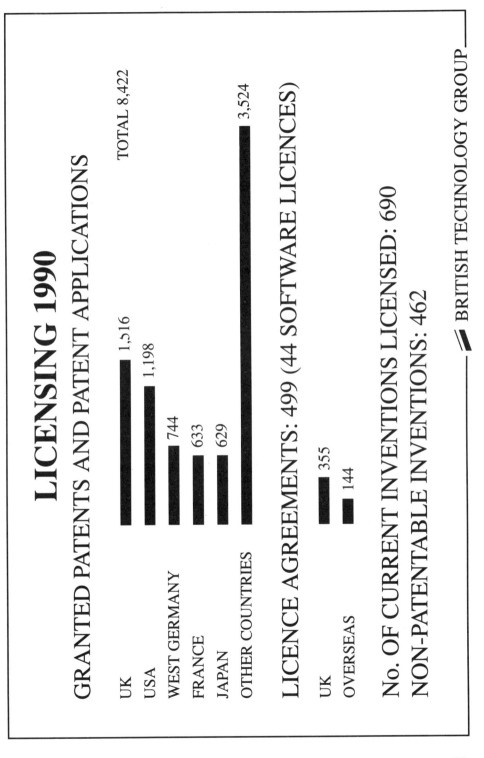

LICENSING 1990

GRANTED PATENTS AND PATENT APPLICATIONS

TOTAL 8,422

UK — 1,516
USA — 1,198
WEST GERMANY — 744
FRANCE — 633
JAPAN — 629
OTHER COUNTRIES — 3,524

LICENCE AGREEMENTS: 499 (44 SOFTWARE LICENCES)

UK — 355
OVERSEAS — 144

No. OF CURRENT INVENTIONS LICENSED: 690
NON-PATENTABLE INVENTIONS: 462

BRITISH TECHNOLOGY GROUP

BTG is also involved in the development and exploitation of inventions arising from cancer research, a licensing drive within the aerosol industry to promote the Atmosol environmentally acceptable aerosol system, and the sub-licensing of BTG patents on spray forming of metals.

Finance for industrial innovation

BTG provides finance on commercial terms for companies carrying out development work in the UK involving a significant degree of technological innovation. There are no formal upper or lower limits to the sums BTG can provide, but they are generally in the range of 50k to £1m. Participation by other investors and eligibility for government grants are not precluded. Equity participation is the perferred method if a technology is best developed by creating a new company or expanding an existing one, or if the successful growth of a company is critically dependent on the technical innovation. BTG will also work alongside venture capitalists and other investors as part of a syndicate in which the Group's ability to assess the commercial prospects of complex technologies may be crucial to other participants. Finance is also available from BTG for academic researchers or institutions who seek to set up their own companies to commercialise the results of their research activity. Further details of BTG activities and funding facilities can be obtained from BTG offices in London, Manchester and Edinburgh (see below).

Technology transfer in the European Community[2]

Agreements on technology transfer may contain provisions protecting the parties involved which could infringe the competition rules of the EC (see *The Competition Rules*, Part Six, Chapter 3). A licensor transferring technology creates a competitor who is capable of producing identical products of the same quality and technology standard. Therefore, the licensor naturally seeks to protect legitimate licensing interests. The licensee, on the other hand, will only agree to take the licence and to undertake the necessary investment if there is reasonable protection from competition from the licensor and other licencees. The European Commission, which has the power to enforce the competition rules directly from Brussels, generally regards such licensing agreements as pro-competitive in that they promote technical and economic progress, and has show a favourable attitude to technology transfer in research and development, patent licensing, and know-how licensing. The group exemptions adopted by the Commission under Council Regulation 19/65 are:

Regulation 2349/84 on patent licensing agreements

Regulation 418/85 on research and development

Regulation (draft) on know-how licensing

---

1 Source: Dr. Mike Knight, Chairman of EUROTECH
2 Source: Brebner & Co, London (solicitors).

CONTACTS

British Technology Group
101 Newington Causeway
London SE1 6BU
Tel: (071) 403 6666
Fax: (071) 403 7586

British Technology Group Northern Office
Enterprise House
Manchester Science Park
Lloyd Street North
Manchester M15 4EN
Tel: (061) 226 2811

British Technology Group Scotland Office
23 Chester Street
Edinburgh EH3 7ET
Tel: (031) 220 2860

4 Electronic Data Interchange

The modern trade route

Richard Wakerley

EDI is a term which sounds like yet another of those three letter acronyms, beloved by the computer industry, to describe some esoteric technology for computer buffs. This paper sets out to evaporate the mists of mystique hanging over EDI by explaining how EDI is transforming the way we do business and its strategic significance with respect to the European market.

EDI is of strategic importance, fundamentally altering the manner in which trading is undertaken and giving rise to significant changes in trading relationships and patterns. It provides the only feasible basis on which a unified market can operate effectively within Europe. Progressive firms who are actively developing and incorporating EDI within their business are gaining a competitive advantage but as EDI based trading becomes the norm those companies who are without such systems may find themselves at a considerable disadvantage.

EDI stands for 'Electronic Data Interchange' and, very simply, means the transfer of structured data held on one computer directly to another. Looking at the three terms in more detail:

☐ The term 'Electronic' refers to the manner in which the data is held and transferred in an electronic form. Typically this is directly across some form of communications network or physically on some form of electronic medium such as magnetic tape or disc.

☐ The 'Data' is typically trade documents such as invoices, orders, shipping notes and customs data. When used for such trade documents EDI is often referred to as TDI, or trade data interchange, on which this paper concentrates. However the scope of EDI is much wider and extends to the exchange of technical data such as product specifications and technical drawings, financial data, ie payments by electronic funds transfer and enquiry/reservations data used in interactive bookings systems.

☐ The 'Interchange' usually takes place between the computer applications of two companies. This contrasts with similar technologies such as electronic mail which operates between people, and on-line database access operating between a person and a computer.

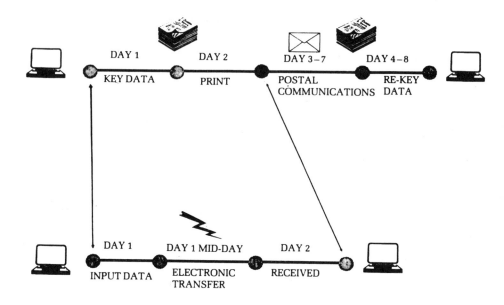

Figure 1: Reduction in length of trading cycle

EDI is not a new technology but a new way of doing business and, as such, represents a natural progression in the application of information technology (IT) within business. In the past companies have sought to become more efficient by applying IT to automate their internal clerical procedures. With most data now held electronically on computer systems and the scope for further internal efficiencies clearly limited, the advantages of trading electronically have become apparent. Since it is estimated that some 70% of computer output is subsequently being re-input to other computers, the scope is considerable. Some enterprising companies have been operating direct trading links with one or two large trading partners for many years. A key advantage of EDI is the use of agreed message standards so that it can be applied easily and efficiently to all trading links. A more formal definition of EDI is:

'The transfer of structured data, by agreed message standards, between business applications on two computers, by electronic means.'

Benefits of EDI

The benefits of adopting EDI accrue at both the operational and strategic level. Currently the cost savings arising from the operational benefits are most apparent and having typically formed the cost basis for justifying the uptake of EDI. In the longer term, however, the strategic benefits will become both more apparent and more significant.

Benefits

What are the main benefits
you expect from EDI

■ Now

▨ In 5 Years

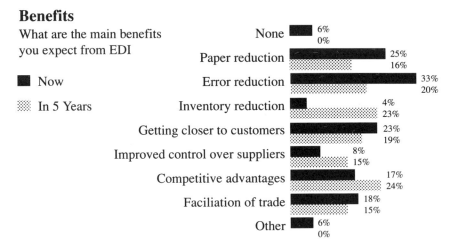

Figure 2: The Benefits of using EDI
(Courtesy of Price Waterhouse Management Consultants)

Operational benefits

EDI is often referred to as paperless trading since it eliminates the printing, posting and data entry phases associated with paper based transactions. Savings immediately accrue from the reduction in paper, postage and more significantly from a reduction in administrative overheads. A Yankee Group report estimates that over half of all order entries made manually are incorrect in some way. Consequently by eliminating the manual re-entry of data where most errors occur this produces a significant increase in accuracy with an associated reduction in costs. The savings are therefore greatest on the processing of incoming invoices and orders but as figure 3 illustrates the savings on the outgoing side are still significant.

Incoming Messages (Per 1000)

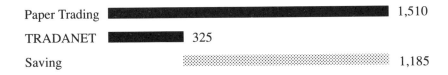

Outgoing Messages (Per 1000)

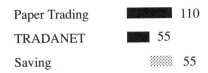

Figure 3: Cost savings using Tradanet

Strategic benefits

The testament to EDI being a business issue and not merely a technological issue lies in the longer term strategic benefits that accrue. Effectively EDI reduces the length of the trading cycle and brings trading partners much closer together in their trading relationship. In the future the use of EDI, particularly when driven from a customer perspective, is going to alter the fundamental trading patterns within industries.

A major benefit is an improved level of customer service. The reduction in the length of the trading cycle, typically from 4-8 days to 2 days, or less, is a major contributing factor (see Fig. 1). Increased levels of speed and accuracy enable the supplier to provide the customer with the right product at the right time and where problems do arise staff, freed from clerical duties, can concentrate on providing a higher level of service to customers. Alternatively, customers themselves are able to receive up-to-date electronic status information on the progress of their orders.

Undertaking EDI inevitably requires increased co-operation between trading partners to resolve issues such as the timing and frequency of transfers, the use of common communication protocols and standardised messages. During this process companies develop a better understanding of the manner in which their trading partners operate and of their requirements. Provision of stabilised order schedules and longer term forecasts by customers allow suppliers to tailor production rates so minimising stock levels. As the trading relationship develops the degree of trust and openness will increase, encouraging for example joint development projects. The supplier gains a competitive edge and the customer benefits through an improved level of service.

In a time when markets are fluctuating and shifting rapidly companies must be both flexible and efficient, yet these demands are often in direct competitition. New management techniques and technologies, such as just-in-time and computer integrated manufacturing coupled with computer aided design, automatic warehousing schemes and bar coding, etc, must be applied in order to compete in this market. Within this scenario, EDI is an integral component underpinning techniques such as just-in-time manufacturing by providing fast and accurate trading systems.

The uptake of EDI is both speeding up the trading cycle and reducing its length by bringing a degree of integration between trading partners in the supply chain. Smaller but more frequent orders are being made with a subsequent rise in transactions that can only be handled cost effectively by using EDI based systems. With reduced inventory levels and more effective systems, falling production costs result in more competitive products and greater total sales. This trend is particularly pronounced in America where end-customer demand is being used to drive the supply chain. Quick Response systems, as they are termed, rely heavily on EDI to underpin the adoption of responsive manufacturing techniques, streamlined distribution processes and the identification and analysis of sales trends.

Undertaking EDI

In order to undetake EDI, transactions held in an in-house message format must first be extracted from the end application, such as the purchasing system. Conversion software maps the in-house message formats to those of the standard being used and a communications interface transmits them over some form of network. The reverse process is applied to incoming messages from the network. The standards place no restrictions on how the components should be implemented. Often the conversion and communicatons software are placed on a front end processor but equally all three components may be integrated into the host system. At its simplest, EDI can be undertaken with a PC, modem and EDI software package so making it feasible for all but the smallest firms.

The standards are totally independent of the communication carrier. In the past magnetic tape has been a popular option and is still in common use for bulk data transfer. In order to derive the benefits from a reduced trading cycle more direct links have become popular utilising leased lines, the public switched telephone network, and the packet switched data service. A particularly popular option in the UK is the use of Value Added and Data Services, or VADS. These provide a store and forward network across which EDI messages can be sent and received with other trading partners subscribing to the service.

EDI standards

The key to EDI is in agreed standards. Transactions held in an in-house format need only be converted into one standard format in order to undertake trading with many other partners. An EDI standard is defined by a number of components.

□ Data element directory

□ Syntax

□ Message and Message Design Guidelines

A data element directory is equivalent to a dictionary defining the vocabulary of the EDI language. Data elements are items such as order number, product code, despatch date, etc and the syntax governs how these may be combined to form messages, in other words an EDI grammar. The messages relate to the type of transaction being undertaken and a standard will often define the more common types such as invoices, orders, despatch advice notes, credit notes, etc while message design guidelines provide assistance on the design of more specialised messages.

In Europe work on standards was originally undertaken by SITPRO in the early 1970's and has since been developed by the United Nations giving rise to the UN/TDI syntax and UN/TDED directory. In the UK retail sector the TRADACOMS standard evolved based on the UN/TDI syntax but its own directory and message formats. The scope of the TRADACOMS standard has now grown well beyond the retail sector finding widespread application across many sectors in the UK.

In America EDI standards have developed in parallel under the auspices of the ANSI X.12 committee. America leads the world in EDI and the ANSI X.12 standard is well established. In an attempt to harmonise the European and American standards the UN set up a joint committee on EDI to develop an international standard for EDI called EDIFACT, or *EDI For Administration, Commerce and Transport*. Using the UN/TDED directory and a syntax derived from the ANSI X.12 and UN/TDI syntaxes, the EDIFACT standard is gaining rapid acceptance, particularly for international trade.

Significance of EDI in the Single Market

The challenge of the Single Market is to break down national barriers to trade and create one Europen market in which goods and services flow easily between member states. Competition, undertaken on an equal basis, will result in a highly competitive market in which prices and costs fall. This is estimated to yield an overall 5% rise in Europe's GDP together with the creation of some 5 million jobs.

Fundamental to this vision is the creation of a marketplace in which all partners can trade on an equal basis. This requires a harmonised legal, fiscal and technical framework which the European Commission is seeking to create by trying to implement legislative measures contained within the Single European Act. However to create a truly competitive market within Europe, demographic barriers must also be eliminated or minimised.

In practice this means that, when trading, a European supplier must be as accessible as a local supplier. Demographic considerations give rise to two main problems. Firstly, distance creates barriers due to the increased time and cost of communicating. Secondly, language can also present a considerable barrier and is often symptomatic of more subtle social and cultural differences that make trading more difficult and costly. EDI, supported by good European telecommunications networks, can act as a European business language largely eliminating these demographic barriers. With EDI, trading with different companies, whether national or European, is reduced ultimately to the specification of different electronic addresses.

The European Commission is well aware of the significance of IT, telecommunications and EDI to the development of the Single Market. The 'Framework Programme' co-ordinates research within the European Community, and the information society stream accounts for some 42% of the budget, encompassing the ESPRIT and RACE programmes into information technology and telecommunications. Of particular note in this context is the TEDIS programme which supports the development and application of EDI within the Community, particularly by small and medium-sized companies. In addition, the Commission's EDI/Unite program aims to overcome the problems caused by the immaturity of EDI standards. That the efforts of the Commission with respect to the Single Market are having an effect, is evidenced by a Yankee Group report in which a quarter of the European companies surveyed stated that they are planning to change their information systems and computer networking strategies to make ready for the Single Market. The significance of EDI within this can be appreciated by the anticipated growth in the European EDI products and services market at a rate of 20% from some $110 million in 1989 to over $400 million by 1994, according to a recent Frost & Sullivan study.

EDI and international trade

At present EDI tends to be undertaken primarily on a national basis, with fax, telex and telephone used for international communications. Large multi-national companies with private data networks are the main exception to this. The development of the EDIFACT standard coupled with the deregulation and commercialisation of telecommunications networks and the pressure for international trade from the Single Market are set to change this scenario. There are already a number of international trading groups using EDI such as the

EFIC project in the chemical industry, ODETTE in the European motor industry and European re-insurance companies using RINET.

Trading in the Single Market should be eased by the elimination of cross border fiscal controls eliminating the need for customs declarations. Some information will still need to be submitted for the regulation of hazardous, restricted or prohibited goods, VAT declarations and the collection of statistics. EDI messages will no doubt be developed to cater for this while for international trade the United Nations CUSDEC message, based on EDIFACT, provides an international method for electronic customs declarations. The legal status of electronic trading is still unclear and this is further complicated when trading between different countries. In practice many EDI users enter into interchange agreements which define the legal responsibilities and liabilities of each trading partner. In many ways however electronic trading is much more reliable and accurate than traditional mechanisms, as witnessed by the lower premiums insurance brokers are likely to offer on trading liability insurance. The application of various security techniques such as encryption, sequences checks, control fields, passwords, etc when combined can provide a very secure trading mechanism and it is the validity of these measures and algorithms upon which the legal status issue will eventually be determined.

European network services

Access to networks and VADS on a European wide basis is clearly fundamental to supporting EDI in 1992. The Commission of the European Communities was trying to establish a managed data network service across Europe based on the services of 22 nations' PTTs. This approach has now been dropped in favour of establishing a deregulatory environment similar to that operating in the UK whereby the basic PTT services can be used by third parties to provide value added services across Europe.

Several service providers already operate European and World wide network services including GEIS, INFONET and IBM. In addition British Telecom, through its Tymet acquisition and AT&T, who recently acquired Istel, clearly aim to build their own global networks. The Commission's 'Open Network Provision' (ONP) initiative however will greatly simplify the regulatory environment particularly with respect to the provision of harmonised terminal equipment certification. Consequently European VADS, similar to INS and Istel in the UK, look likely to appear in the future and the increased competition should ensure competitive services. By using international standards, such as X.25 and X400, VADS should be made to interwork and provide users with services suitable for EDI trading across Europe.

CONTACTS

National Computing Centre
The NCC is a membership organisation run on a commercial basis. There are over 2,500 members, of which most are users of information systems. The NCC offers public and in-house training courses, training materials, software, standards conformance testing services and conformance testing software, consultancy services and publications.

National Computing Centre
Oxford House
Oxford Road
Manchester M1 7ED
Tel: (061) 228 6333
Fax: (061) 228 2579

(Head office)

National Computing Centre
Ground Floor
Cowcross Court
77 Cowcross Street
London EC1M 6BP
Tel: (071) 490 5828
Fax: (071) 490 8628

Simplication of Trade Procedures Board

SITPRO leads in developing techniques for transmitting documents via Electronic Data Interchange (EDI), or paperless trading. EDI methods are available to anyone with an ordinary desk-top micro-computer and a telephone connection, or access to a dedicated computer link or value-added network. The principal SITPRO products are:

Interbridge software (EDI)
EDIFACT Service (EDI)
Export Stationery (Exportsets, Postpacks)
Copier systems (overlays)
Spex software (document processing)

Simplification of Trade Procedures Board
Venture House
29 Glasshouse Street
London W1R 5RG
Tel: (071) 287 3525
Fax: (071) 287 5751

(For SITPRO distributors see page 413)

The EDI Association (EDIA)

EDIA develops the use of paperless trading by promoting the understanding and implementation of EDIFACT based EDI (see above) in international trade and transport within the UK. There are over 170 UK member companies and the association has close links with European EDI bodies. It provides a forum for response to trading initiatives such as TEDIS and COST 306.

Cleeve Cottage
Cobham Way
East Horsley
Surrey KT24 5BH
Tel: (04865) 5834
Fax: (04865) 5838

5 The Mark of Quality

A key to competitiveness in Europe

Sir Derek Hornby

The date for the completion of the Single Market is partly symbolic. Changes and harmonisation leading to market opportunities have been in progress for some time and will continue long after 1992. These opportunites are not being ignored by Britain's European partners, and even a company which has no intention of selling outside its own country must protect its market from those who enjoy new freedom to enter it. Since the Single Market will place firms in a more competitive environment, prices will necessarily be more competitive and, increasingly, the customer, both corporate and individual, will look more closely at other factors which improve competitiveness Quality of product and quality of service will be foremost amongst these and this is why quality has become a major issue in British industry. Already, more than 12,000 firms are stealing the limelight and lucrative contracts, by winning certificates of quality which show they are fit and efficient. These firms are able to display symbols which indicate that their management systems meet with the widely recognised and respected standard, having been assessed against the British Standard 5750/EN 29000. The standard is recognised across all European borders. There is no limit to the activity or size of company which can be assesed to BS 5750 – EN 29000/ISO 9000. From one-man band to multi-national, this ubiquitous standard marks the path for the quality system. Just as important as product specification is delivery on time, maintenance of performance, traceability of faults and quality of service. The message is deliver value for money and profits will follow, especially after 1992.

Companies who commit themselves to a quality programme are making a statement about themselves in the Single Market and the importance they place in giving their customers value for money and reliability, whether they are selling goods or services.

Quality assurance is an international language which, across borders, facilitates a mutual understanding between industries, suppliers and contractors, of all nationalities. It will remain the hallmark of good faith and trust, within and across borders, between purchaser and supplier in the Single Market. Assessment systems standardised on EN 29000 will be of great benefit in intra-community trading — and export outside of the European Community.

Role of certification bodies

Certification bodies are independent organisations which carry out assessments of a company's quality management systems and, when they are satisfied, issue a certificate indicating conformance to the British Standard BS 5750, which has been harmonised with the European EN 29000 and the international ISO 9000.

Assessment by a third party certification body is carried out by a team of independent assessors knowledgeable in the field of activity of the company seeking assessment. This is to ensure that contractors at home and abroad can have confidence in a supplier and be assured that he runs an efficient operation and produces reliable goods and services.

Certification may go further and indicate that particular products themselves conform with their own specification. In this case, the certification body's symbol may be displayed on the goods themselves.

Role of the NACCB

Many firms are now seeking third party certification from bodies which themselves have been approved by independent expert assessors from the National Accreditation Council for Certification Bodies.

The NACCB is a national statutory body set up by the Department of Trade and Industry (DTI) in 1984 to uphold the standards of certification bodies operating in UK industry. It deploys teams of experienced assessors who examine the fitness of certification bodies for accreditation under a set of published criteria. These include an assessment of the independence, integrity and technical competence and subsequent accreditation awarded by the Secretary of State for Trade and Industry on the recommendation of the NACCB. The certification bodies accredited have the right to use the National Accreditation Mark, a gold tick and crown. The companies they certificate also receive the right to use the Mark indicating the status of the body which certificated them.

Fifteen certfication bodies in the UK have so far been accredited and there are many more applications for accreditation in the pipeline. The NACCB regularly receives enquiries from a growing number of industrial sectors.

Gold tick and crown

The NACCB's gold tick and crown symbol is an important initiative which aims to help firms from the UK and overseas demonstrate their achievements to a worldwide audience, and to show their commitment to maintaining the quality of goods and services they supply.

The Council plays an active part in negotiations in Europe aimed at Community-wide recognition of accredited bodies' certificates. The objective is to avoid requirements for re-testing and re-certification in other countries.

Now, a growing number of European countries are working hard to set up their own certification bodies and to publicise to businesses in their own countries the merits of assessment and certification to the European Standard EN 29000.

When companies obtain certification from these accredited certification bodies they too win the right to use the gold tick and crown symbol combined with the logo of the certification body on their letterheads and promotional literature.

Efficiency

Assurance of efficiency for managers

Apart from providing evidence of efficiency to customers, there are further clear incentives to companies to seek accredited certification. Company directors or managers receive assurance that the company system can be relied on, that competitiveness and profits are being maximised, internal wastage and re-work reduces. They are assured that product developments and marketing initiatives will not be frustrated by shortcomings in the support systems — from development and design through contract negotiation to production and despatch. Of course, no quality system can replace marketing flair and good product design but a bad system can ruin the best ideas and waste a lot of money.

Assurance of reliability to contractors
Quality management certification indicates that a firm has the capability to manufacture or provide services to a specification set by its customers. And it provides independent verification of capability, of sound quality management and reliable customer service, vital to customer confidence. Nowadays, fitness for purpose is expected by everyone — by public bodies and private individuals, and by industry, ever more concerned to control the quality of its products and services.

Quality assurance helps firms in all sectors
Certificated companies come from all sectors of British industry. They include manufacturers of textiles, engineering machinery, glass, furniture, chemicals, freight forwarders, manufacturers of pressure vessels, suppliers of construction materials, toy manufacturers through to service sectors firms such as shipping consultants, environmental engineers, financial services, leisure, architecture and public administration.

UK awareness of quality

In the UK, an increasing number of companies and institutions are taking a keen interest in quality for products, services, marketing, production, management and customer after-care. Quality will be the key to competitiveness and is likely to be the single most important factor in determining how effectively British companies meet the challenge of Europe.

The trend is led in the UK, in part, by the fact that, increasingly, public and private sector purchasers are specifying accredited certification in their tender lists. This removes the need for individual assessment by each purchaser — since suppliers have been examined by experts in that field. The drive for quality is gaining momentum as businesses realise that it will affect their operations in the Single Market and that, in order to ensure their market share, they must set out to prove the quality of their goods and services.

The development of national accreditation systems leading to bilateral, and ultimately, multilateral agreements on equivalence has a crucial role to play in building that confidence which is essential to growth in trade.

The Department of Trade and Industry consultancy service

Through its Enterprise Initiative the DTI offers to meet half or more of the cost of 5 to 15 days' consultancy advice for firms or groups employing fewer than 500 people. With such help, certification of your system by an accredited body should follow as a test of your achievement and evidence of it for your customers to see.

CONTACTS

Free leaflets and brochures are available from the NACCB at the address given below. The White Paper of 1982 "Standards, Quality and International Competitiveness" is available from HMSO Cmnd No 8621.

National Accreditation Council for
Certification Bodies
3 Birdcage Walk
London W1 9JH
Tel: (071) 222 5374
Fax: (071) 222 0197
Telex: 9413487 UK SERV G

The fifteen certification bodies accredited by the NACCS to date are:-

Loss Prevention Certification Board
Melrose Avenue
Boreham Wood
Hertfordshire WD6 2BS
Tel: (081) 207 2345
Fax: (081) 207 6305
Telex: 291 835

LRQA
Norfolk House
Wellesley Road
Croydon CR9 2DT
Tel: (081) 688 6883
Fax: (081) 681 8146
Telex: 28636

Yarsley Quality Assured Firms Ltd
Trowers Way, Redhill
Surrey RH1 2JN
Tel: (0737) 765070
Fax: (0737) 768445
Telex: 8951511

UK Certification Authority for Reinforcing
Steels Ltd
Oak House, Tubs Hill
Sevenoaks
Kent TN13 1BL
Tel: (0732) 450000
Fax: (0732) 450 571
Telex: 95407

BASEC
PO Box 390, Breckland
Linford Woods
Milton Keynes MK14 6LN
Tel: (0908) 220908
Fax: (0908) 320856
Telex: 825777

BSIQA
Linford Woods
Milton Keynes MK14 6LN
Tel: (0908) 220908
Fax: (0908) 220671
Telex: 82126

BVQI
3rd Floor
70 Borough High Street
London SE1 1XF
Tel: (071) 378 8113
Fax: (071) 378 8014
Telex: 918989

QSRMC
Wolsey House
High Street
Hampton
Middlesex TW12 2FQ
Tel: (081) 941 0273
Fax: (081) 979 4558

ASTA
Credential Chamber
23-24 Market Place
Rugby
Warwickshire CV21 3DU
Tel: (0788) 78435
Fax: (0788) 73605

Sira Certification Services Ltd
Saighton Lane
Saighton
Chester CH3 6EG
Tel: (0244) 332200
Fax: (0244) 332112
Telex: 61441

Det Norske Veritas
Veritas House
112 Station Road
Sidcup
Kent DA15 7BU
Tel: (081) 309 7477
Fax: (081) 309 1834
Telex: 896526

CQA
Arcade Chambers
The Arcade
Market Place
Newark
Nottinghamshire NG24 1UD
Tel: (0636) 708700
Fax: (0636) 708766

CICS
Queen's Road
Penkhull
Stoke on Trent ST4 7LQ
Tel: (0782) 411008
Fax: (0782) 412331
Telex: 36228

Another useful organisation is:
NAMAS
National Physical Laboratory
Teddington
TW11 0LW
Tel: (081) 977 3222
Fax: (081) 943 2155
Telex: 262344

Associated Offices Quality Certification Ltd
Longridge House
Longridge Place
Manchester M60 4DT
Tel: (061) 833 2295
Fax: (061) 833 9965

NICQA
National Information Council for Quality
Assurance Ltd
112 Midland Road
Luton
Bedfordshire LU2 0BL
Tel: (0582) 482783
Fax: (0582) 27553

PART THREE

MANAGEMENT WORKFORCE AND COMPANY SKILLS

1 A New Breed of Bosses

The search for the Euro-executive

Anthony Saxton

A new breed of manager is emerging in Europe. Dubbed "the Euro-executives", the new managers feel at home in any European country, speak two or three languages with enviable fluency, and bask in the certainty of heading the shortlists for the most influential jobs. Cuckoo-like in their rapid ascendancy, they are pushing out the older breed of executives who know how to manage in only one or two countries, speak only their native tongue, and prefer to work for one company for most of their working lives.

The hallmark of true Euro-executives is adaptability, enabling them to blend easily into the local culture of different European territories. These skills are not easy for others to emulate. Unlike languages, cultural adaptability cannot be learned at night school. Aspiring Euro-executives who, through hard work, become proficient in two or three European languages still do not equal born Euro-executives who have been listening and thinking in several languages for most of their lives.

Companies seeking to expand into Europe now realise that macro-structures make more sense. But they need a management organisation which fits the new regime, replacing the practice of running separate companies in each country with a single pan-European entity. It is in this new macro-structure for Europe that Euro-executives flourish. Indeed, they will be the only kind of executive qualified to run a pan-European operation. The old-style single country manager is thus becoming vulnerable, restricted by a lack of experience in European markets.

The search for the Euro-executive

As the traditional single territory manager becomes redundant, Euro-executives will become the most valued management species, with major companies competing for their services. Initially, they will be in short supply, however, as a market research report *The Search for the Euro-Executive*[1], prepared by SRU and published in 1989 by headhunters, Saxton Bampfylde International, shows. The report highlights the difficulties which some companies seeking to expand into Europe will face in recruiting top managers. In the UK, for example, there may be problems at middle-management level in companies with newly Europeanised horizons.

The smaller European countries produce a higher proportion of executives in relation to their population size. The Danes, Dutch, Swiss and Scandinavians are accomplished linguists and find it easy to settle and succeed in widely differing countries. Other factors which make a successful Europeanist may not appear on an individual's CV, but are revealed in the Saxton Bampfylde study. The influencing factors include:

☐ Parents of different nationalities

☐ Education and residence in several countries

☐ Changes of jobs to widen experience

The actionable point for the recruiter is that the best Euro-managers are not too tightly emotionally wedded to their present company. A life-time of international service within one large company may serve to blunt sensitivity to local culture, such is the company-cultural potency of some of the world's largest organisations, insulating executives from the mores of their host country.

On gender, the study found that few experienced Euro-executives were female. It is not difficult to see how the colonial attitude to hiring management and development in many international companies tends to favour selection criteria which relate more to an executive's ability to thrive in Africa and the locker-room, rather than in the more subtle milieux of top European boardrooms. But women not only represent the majority of modern language graduates, they are also widely thought to have the edge on men in sensitivity, another hallmark of the Euro-executive. It therefore makes sense to look for female candidates for important European positions.

Recruiting Euro-executives

Although it is clear that ideal Euro-executives are in short supply and much sought after, it will not be easy to track them down and attract them. The Euro-executive phenomenon will, therefore, make good business for the better headhunters with good European facilities. Recruiting first class candidates is a skill which demands patient stalking, skilled advocacy, as well as money, if potential recruits are to be persuaded to change company.

Broad-scale recruitment methods are unlikely to be effective or economic in attracting this class of managers for two reasons:

☐ They do not read job ads: They already work in good companies, holding down excellent jobs, and have no need to job hunt.

☐ There are few pan-European media through which to reach them[2].

The wise recruiter will pre-empt the difficulty and the high cost of locating and attracting targets by recruiting them at an early stage in their careers; for example, at those business schools which offer **MBA** courses with a specific European content. A selection of leading schools with a strong European business content are listed at the end of this chapter, though many more business schools are offering Euro-options and subsidiary language courses.

The executive search consultant thrives on an upper management skill shortage. It must come as no surprise, therefore, to learn that the emergence of Euro-executives and the value placed on them by European-based business are major factors in accelerating the headhunters' efforts to themselves adapt to the new demands of the Single Market and the ever widening European marketplace. The key to successful headhunting lies in an ability to carry out research in several different European countries simultaneously, in the appropriate languages, and to co-ordinate the findings into one actionable plan, so that the most promising candidates can be interviewed promptly in their different locations. From these candidates the consultant distills a shortlist of three or four of the most promising new recruits.

After the client has held first interviews with shortlisted candidates, further help is needed from the recruitment consultant, who nowadays should be able to carry out further references and qualification checks in as many countries and languages as the candidates may represent.

While several search firms maintain networks of European offices, not all of them are proficient in multicultural searches. The gap is being filled by newer independent search firms banding together, combining their abilities to create systems for carrying out searches in several countries simultaneously, while relating and reporting to the client in a single format at one location. Such services cost a little more than a traditional one-country search, but the little extra is little grudged by the employers who want to attract and keep the pick of the new breed of Euro-executives.

The Saxton Bampfylde report is based on a survey carried out by SRU among Chief Executives in top UK companies, interviews with commercial managers with a European dimension to their jobs, interviews with executives with responsibility for their company's Europeanisation, soundings from European Commission officials who have first-hand experience of being lobbied by European businessmen, and research with business school professors and administrators concerned with the formation of the Euro-executive group. Views expressed at several Single Market-related conferences, covering human resources questions, were also taken into account. The following is a summary of the report's main conclusions:

Qualities of the Euro-executive

☐ The ideal Euro-manager comes from smaller countries like the Netherlands and Denmark and has experience in:
Another culture (at an early stage)
Another language (at an early stage)
A multinational company
Financial services
Consultancy/marketing

plus

A flexible cast of mind
Social skills to match
Sensitivity to local mores

Four types of Euro-executive are currently on offer in the European management market:
Senior statesmen in multinationals
Expatriates with experience of a foreign posting
Journeymen with Europe-wide experience in a narrow specialism.
Euro-yuppies; up and coming Euro-executives

☐ Near Euro-executives exist in major multinationals, businesses which are already global. But the overwhelming corporate cultures of these businesses often make their executives less truly international, and less transferable than their emerging juniors.

☐ Overall, the serious senior, say, 45 plus board-level Euro-executive, barely exists in most UK companies. This responsibility is usually taken by managers with ongoing responsibilities, rather than dedicated and experienced Europeanists.

☐ There is a developing younger generation which will soon qualify and will have to be accommodated at the top. Otherwise they will go elsewhere and be lost to British business.

☐ Recruitment definitions among companies, however, remain inconsistent and imprecise, leading to the possibility of seriously mistaken appointments. The criteria for Euro-competence are not yet clearly established.

Demand for Euro-executives

☐ The demand for Euro-executives in Europe will outstrip supply well before the Single Market is completed. The relative job immobility of many potential Europeanists will lead to aggressive solicitations of the available talent.

☐ This imbalance will significantly affect international recruitment and salary relativities. UK companies will need to make considerable efforts both to recruit new Europeans and to retain any existing Euro-competent managers.

☐ Strategic and structural readiness for Europe management practice varies enormously between UK businesses. Some businesses are already "living" in the Single Market, for example, while others have merely flagged up the issue without taking action. The key factors in variations in company readiness are:

Business sector
Extent of multinational activities
Corporate culture/history

1 *The Search for the Euro-executive*, Saxton Bampfylde International Plc, 35 Old Queen Street, London SW1H 9JD. Tel: (071) 799 1433.
2 *Financial Times* (Frankfurt), *The Economist, New York Herald Tribune* (Paris).

CONTACTS

Universities, business schools and colleges supply training for the skills needed by the new breed of Euro-Executives. The business schools listed below are among the leading European business schools offering MBA courses with a specific European content. However, universities, university management schools and business colleges in the UK, between them, also offer a wide of language and business-related courses with a European content. For information on university management schools see *The Making of Managers*, Part Three, Chapter 2. For university language courses and other business related activities, including collaboration in research and development, see *Universities and Industry*, Part Three, Chapter 3. For information on polytechnics see *Polytechnics and Business*,

Part Three, Chapter 4. Student exchange and European education programmes are described in *The European Student*, Part Three, Chapter 5. For specific information on language training see *Languages and Business*, Part Three, Chapter 6.

European Business School
Regents College
Inner Circle
Regent's Park
London NW1 4NF
Tel: (071) 486 0141
Fax: (071) 487 7456

Instituto de Estudios Superiores de la Empresa (IESE)
Avenida Pearson 21
08034 Barcelona
Tel: (34) 3 204 4000
Fax: (34) 3 205 4564
Telex: 50924 IESB E

Institut Europeen d'Administration des Affaires (INSEAD)
Boulevard de Constance
77305 Fontainebleau Cedex
France
Tel: (33) 1 6072 4000
Fax: (33) 1 6072 4242
Telex: 690389 F

IMEDE
PO Box 915
CH 1001 Lausanne
Switzerland
Tel: (41) 21 267112
Fax: (41) 21 266725
Telex: 25871

Institut Superieur des Affaires (ISA)
1 rue de la Liberation
78350 Jouy-en-Josas
France
Tel: (33) 1 3956 7000
Fax: (33) 1 3956 7430
Telex: 600325 F

London Business School
Sussex Place
Regent's Park
London NW1 4SA
Tel: (071) 262 5050
Fax: (071) 724 7875
Telex: 27461

Manchester Business School
Booth Street West
Manchester M15 6PB
Tel: (061) 275 6333
Fax: (061) 273 7732
Telex: 668354

Rotterdam School of Management
Faculteit Bedrijfskunde
Erasmus University
Burgemeester Oudlaan 50
3000 DR Rotterdam
The Netherlands
Tel: (31) 10 408 1927
Fax: (31) 10 452 0204
Telex: UBRT 24421

Scuola di Direzione Aziendale (SDA)
Universita L. Bocconi
Via Bocconi 8
20136 Milan
Italy
Tel: (39) 2 8384 6622
Fax: (39) 2 8384 6300
Telex: 316003 SDABOC I

2 The Making of Managers

A role for business schools

George Bain and Janet Temple

British business is beginning to realise that for too long managers have been an underdeveloped resource. This recognition, occuring against the background of accelerating economic, social and technological change and increasingly fierce competition in Europe, has led to demands for a new professionalism among managers. Employing organisations are placing new emphasis on management education and development since, in such a highly competitive marketplace, it is no longer sufficient for managers to have "learned it the hard way". The depth and complexity of knowledge required is too great to continue to rely on management by instinct; and it is not enough for managers to take a short crash course, which may suit them merely because it does not take them away from the "real job" for long. Given the rapid rate of environmental change, management education and development must be a career-long process.

Large sections of the business community now appreciate that the key to corporate success in Europe is effective management. It may even seem obvious to say so. But appreciating the principle and taking action are two different things. The expectation of fierce incoming competition when all the barriers to trade come down in Europe has meant that more companies are aware that the businesses which will survive this competition will be those whose managers have the right education, experience, expertise and professional skills. What is now needed to support changing attitudes and to meet heightened expectations is a creative partnership between managers, employers and the providers of management education and development. The 34 university management schools represented by the Council of University Management Schools (CUMS) are working to foster this creative partnership.

Management development is a complex process. It involves giving managers conceptual frameworks for understanding the broader business environment; providing training in specific skills; and cultivating those personal qualities and competences which mark out the really successful manager. It is a continuing process, not a once-and-for-all experience. Most importantly, it enables individual managers to achieve personal career objectives which also satisfy the corporate requirement for a highly professional management cadre. Seen in this light, it becomes clear that the drive to achieve a high standard of management education which addresses the specific needs of business, calls for a collaborative approach. But, despite the growing appreciation of the need for management education, many companies have still not built management education into their

forward plans for Europe. Hard-pressed directors, absorbed by day-to-day problems in running a business, often demand results which the skills of their management team may not be able to produce. So, if companies are to succeed in Europe, they must provide a framework for their employees, within which patterns of career development and opportunities for varied and challenging practical experience can be integrated at appropriate stages, plus opportunities for more formal education and training.

It is at this point that university management schools can make their most effective input. Increasingly the schools are adopting a more flexible approach to the delivery of their education products, both to individuals and organisations. Most schools now offer part-time courses to enable managers to continue in employment while studying. Distance learning degrees are now part of the mainstream curriculum in several management schools. Other schools are now working in collaboration with business organisations, either individually or in consortia, to design programmes which complement and are integrated into a company's in-house development schemes.

The resources and products of university management schools are available to business and industry to support their strategies for doing business in Europe. They offer courses leading to degrees, diplomas and other recognised qualifications plus non-award bearing short courses, either bespoke or off-the-peg, on specialist topics. They also provide training in specific skills, consultancy advice on business practice, as well as research across a wide range of management-related skills.

University management schools now conduct all their course work in an international or European context. Some offer special emphasis on European issues, either in the core subjects or in opportunities for in-company projects. Some recruit students or members of their staff from overseas to enable them to conduct class discussions with a European viewpoint. Language training is, of course, another important aspect of management education (See *Languages and Business*, Part Three, Chapter 6).

University management school courses

Master of Business Administration (MBA) programmes
MBA courses are available at most university management schools in full-time, part-time, distance learning and consortium formats. These programmes provide prospective general managers with a rigorous challenging and practical education relevant to all areas of commerce, industry and the public sector.

Specialist Masters and Diploma programmes
These are designed to provide a strong professional grounding in one of the many sub-disciplines of management. Courses are often operated in conjunction with the relevant professional bodies.

Undergraduate programmes
Programmes in business administration and related topics provide the requisite knowledge base for a career in management. They offer structured analytical training in highly relevant subject areas.

Short courses

Short courses are available across a wide range of specialist topics, and are designed either for specific employing organisations or available on an open basis. Tailored where appropriate to meet the differing needs of senior managers or young high-flyers, short courses are a flexible and well-targeted medium for management development.

CONTACTS

For further information and advice on the range of courses available, research capabilities of university management schools and consultancy services, contact your local university management school or the Council of University Management Schools.

Council of University Management Schools
Warwick Business School
University of Warwick
Coventry CV4 7AL
Tel: (0203) 523523 ext. 2834
Fax: (0203) 523719

University management schools

The following business schools are members of the Council of University Management Schools.

Ashbridge Management College
Berkamsted
Hertfordshire HP4 1NS
Tel: (044) 284 3491
Fax: (044) 284 2382

Aston Business School
Aston University
Nelson Building
Gosta Green
Birmingham B4 7DU
Tel: (021) 359 3011
Fax: (021) 359 7358

University of Bath
School of Management
Claverton Down
Bath
Somerset BA2 7AY
Tel: (0255) 826826
Fax: (0255) 826473

Birmingham Business School
University of Birmingham
PO Box 363
Birmingham B15 2TT
Tel: (021) 414 6689
Fax: (021) 414 6707

University of Bradford
Management Centre
Emm Lane, Bradford
Yorkshire BD9 4JL
Tel: (0274) 542299
Fax: (0274) 305340

University of Cambridge
Institute of Management Studies
Cambridge CB2 1RX
Tel: (0223) 338171
Fax: (0223) 338076

Canterbury Business School
University of Kent
Faculty of Social Sciences
Keynes College
Canterbury
Kent CT2 7NP
Tel: (0227) 764000
Fax: (0227) 459025

Cardiff Business School
UWIST
Colum Drive
Cardiff CF1 3EU
Tel: (0222) 874000
Fax: (0222) 874419

City University Business School
Frobisher Crescent
Barbican Centre
London EC2Y 8HB
Tel: (071) 920 0111
Fax: (071) 588 2756

Cranfield School of Management
Cranfield
Bedfordshire MK43 0AL
Tel: (0234) 751122
Fax: (0234) 751806

Durham University Business School
Mill Hill Lane
Durham DH1 3LB
Tel: (091) 374 2211
Fax: (091) 374 3748

University of Edinburgh
Department of Business Studies
50 George Street
Edinburgh EH8 9JY
Tel: (031) 667 1011
Fax: (031) 667 7938

Glasgow Business School
Department of Management Studies
University of Glasgow
53-59 Southpark Avenue
Glasgow G12 8LF
Tel: (041) 339 8855
Fax: (041) 330 5669

Henley Management College
Greenlands
Henley-on-Thames
Oxfordshire RG9 3AU
Tel: (0491) 571454
Fax: (0491) 571635

Heriot-Watt Business School
PO Box 807
Riccarton
Edinburgh
Tel: (031) 225 6465
Fax: (031) 449 5153

University of Hull
School of Management
Hull HU6 7RX
Tel: (0482) 466236
Fax: (0482) 466205

Imperial College
The Management School
53 Prince's Gate
Exhibition Road
London SW7 2PG
Tel: (071) 589 5111
Fax: (071) 823 7685

University of Lancaster
The Management School
Gillow House
Lancaster LA1 4YX
Tel: (0524) 65201
Fax: (0524) 63806

University of Leeds
School of Business and Economic Studies
Leeds LS2 9JT
Tel: (0532) 431751
Fax: (0532) 332640

London Business School
Sussex Place
Regent's Park
London NW1 4SA
Tel: (071) 262 5050
Fax: (071) 724 7875

London School of Economics
Department of Accounting and Finance
Houghton Street
London WC2A 2AE
Tel: (071) 405 7686
Fax: (071) 242 0392

Loughborough University of Technology
Department of Management Studies
Loughborough
Leicestershire LE11 3TU
Tel: (0509) 263171
Fax: (0509) 610724

Manchester Business School
Booth Street West
Manchester M15 6PB
Tel: (061) 275 6333
Fax: (061) 273 7732

Manchester School of Management
UMIST
PO Box 88
Sackville Street
Manchester M60 1QD
Tel: (061) 236 3311
Fax: (061) 228 7040

University of Newcastle-upon-Tyne
Management Division
Department of Accountancy and
Management
13 Windsor Terrace
Newcastle-upon-Tyne NE1 7RU
Tel: (091) 222 6188
Fax: (091) 222 8131

University of Nottingham
Institute of Management Studies
University Park
Nottingham NG7 2RD
Tel: (0602) 484848
Fax: (0602) 420825

Open Business School
Walton Hall
Bletchley
Buckinghamshire MK7 6AA
Tel: (0908) 274066
Fax: (0908) 655802/655815

Templeton College
University of Oxford
Kennington
Oxford OX1 5NY
Tel: (0865) 735422
Fax: (0865) 736374

University of Sheffield
School of Management and Economic
Studies
Sheffield S10 2TN
Tel: (0742) 768555
Fax: (0742) 739826

**Southampton University Management
School**
Enterprise Road
Chilworth
Southampton SO1 7NS
Tel: (0703) 233331
Fax: (0703) 593939

University of Stirling
School of Accountancy, Business,
Computing and Economics
Stirling FK9 4LA
Tel: (0786) 73171
Fax: (0786) 63000

Strathclyde Business School
University of Strathclyde
Sir William Duncan Building
130 Rottenrow
Glasgow G4 0GE
Tel: (041) 552 7214
Fax: (041) 552 2501

University of Ulster
Faculty of Business and Management
Shore Road
Newton Abbey
County Antrim
Northern Ireland BT37 0QB
Tel: (0232) 365131
Fax: (0232) 852926

Warwick Business School
University of Warwick
Coventry CV4 7AL
Tel: (0203) 523523
Fax: (0203) 523719

3 Universities and Industry

Hugh Thomson

Access to the research facilities of universities and their highly-motivated academic staff and researchers is relatively inexpensive, and is often the best way of developing technology, acquiring skills and introducing expert training facilities into a company's operation. Much more expensive for companies is investment in their own in-house research facilities and manpower. It may be even more costly to exit from one such area of activity after a few years and invest in something new. Technology is best transferred through people, and such people, suitably educated, are a university's prime business. This chapter introduces companies to the benefits of collaboration with universities on research projects, and the use of university consultancy and advisory services. Companies envisaging collaboration on research and development with a university should also refer to *EC Grants and Loans*, Part Four, Chapter 7 for details of available grants in certain areas of technology.

University-industry collaboration is not a recent innovation. At the turn of the century, some UK universities and colleges formed working relationships with local industries. It has taken the best part of the century, however, for the mutual need for collaboration to re-emerge because of financial pressures and skill shortages. Some companies still believe that university-industry collaboration is solely about access to advanced programmes of science and technology, which may prove expensive to translate into commercial form. Increasingly it is to do with the provision of new knowledge and skills of direct benefit to companies. The range of activities is wider than most companies appreciate. Everything from advanced technology to market research, management training and language learning now falls within the scope of a broad-based university-industry partnership. Some of the main activities are:

☐   Collaborative research

☐   Contract research and development

☐   Technological training

☐   Consultancy and problem solving

☐   Business and commercial studies

☐   Market research

☐   Management training

☐   Technology transfer

☐   Contract laboratory services

- □ Industrial placements
- □ Language training
- □ Translation services
- □ European studies
- □ European Documentation Centres
- □ Business information

In the late 1980's, university-industry collaboration became a regular conference topic, as newcomers to the concept began to explore the apparent complexities involved. Since then all universities in the UK have engaged in collaboration or liaison with industry, though some universities are not yet as fully committed to collaboration as they might be. On industry's side, there are still too many companies who have not experienced a working relationship with a university, or who have not even assessed what the benefits might be. Nevertheless, collaboration is a firmly established feature of industrial and university life. Increasingly, it will become a matter of joint policy between universities and industry; a symbiosis to be supported, refined and enlarged, since the benefits to both sides are substantial.

Despite long-standing recognition in principle of the benefits of collaboration, the question remains as to *why* it has taken so long for the relationship to be recognised as important to the health of both parties. Two primary factors have undoubtedly hastened the trend towards collaboration in recent years — financial pressures on both sides, and the availability to industry of skills. Universities have experienced financial pressures in their funding from government. For industry, financial pressure comes with the high costs of maintaining an adequate in-house research and development base. The shortage of skilled, well-educated graduates has also been identified as one of the major problems facing industry now and in the future.

These substantial forces have still been slow to make their impact on new working relationships between universities and industry, but now a new encouraging factor in the need for collaboration is gaining ground. Rapid developments in Europe have brought into sharp focus the need for industry to perform as well as, if not better than, competitors. The completion of the Single Market, occuring simultaneously with newfound access to East European markets, compels industry to look for ways of improving quality, efficiency and expertise, as well as minimising costs. Developments in university and industry-relationships so far demonstrate that companies can achieve better, quicker results through collaboration, thus giving companies additional advantages in the challenge of introducing newer and better products and processes at an ever accelerating rate.

The real difficulty in making progress has always centred on the fact that universities and industry are large complex communities, differently motivated, having different objectives, and with widely differing management styles. Nevertheless, substantial common interest exists and companies and universities have worked hard to understand each other's needs, to engage in dialogue, and to establish an interface at which working arrangements can be negotiated. There are now substantial opportunities for more companies to work with universities. The university movement is itself actively 'marketing' and publicising its services to industry.

Benefits of collaboration

To outline the benefits, collaboration offers a company the opportunity to invest at relatively low cost, perhaps even speculatively, in strategic research. In some instances, the availability of university facilities may be a decisive factor in whether or not companies embark on new or advanced development. The speculative nature of such research, however, is often acknowledged by the provision of government or EC grants. At a commercial level, companies can purchase access to technology for use in their business via licences, contracts for research and development , or by investing in start-up companies and joint ventures with universities. Research at a university is a dynamic activity, dependent on a ready mobility of staff and a flow of students and graduates, and so the cost of change is not as great as in companies.

A university gains from industrial collaboration not merely from the finance it receives for research, but also from relations with companies which broaden the university's knowledge and the skills and perceptions of its staff, all of which are communicated directly to students. Universities fostering fruitful relationships with industry attract the best students, and will be well placed to retrain and re-educate existing staff in companies. Thus the two-way flow of knowledge and experience, vital to healthy competing industries, is nourished.

Any company which forms collaboration relationships with universities gains contacts with academic staff who, through consultancy arrangements, provide advice as well as solutions to problems in technological and business areas. Such collaboration also offers early sight of research results, which may offer new businesses opportunities. These can be translated into commercial activity through contract work with the university. The company can involve its own staff in these projects by negotiating collaborative arrangements with the university, possibly with grant support. These staff become the technology transfer vehicle for the company, becoming retrained in the process. This can be followed up by more broadly based training schemes in the company. As a 'by-product' of this kind of collaboration, but of great importance, is the chance for an early sight of promising under-graduates and post-graduates working in universities. At the moment, far too few companies invest in training at universities and further work on the part of both sides is required to develop training methods which are both more attractive to companies and more accessible to their employees.

Pre-competitive research

In the area of pre-competitive research the UK government and the European Commission have introduced schemes whereby project teams comprised of university and industrial partners receive grant-aided support for carrying out programmes of research in specific areas of technology. Initially, in the UK these were the ALVEY and JOERS schemes. Now the IED and LINK schemes are currently active. The European Commission introduced ESPRIT to support research in information technology, and this scheme has been followed by many other programmes supporting a wide range of technologies. The basic objective of research and development schemes is to promote relevant research through the provision of financial support. An important benefit, however, is that through such schemes university researchers and industry have recognised that they are partners of equal standing, competence, and motivation in the important and sensitive area of pre-competitive and strategic research.

Research institutes

As their relationships with companies develop, some universities are harnessing the benefits of regrouping otherwise dispersed academic strengths to form new research institutes and centres. Government departments, companies and other sources of investment or grant support participate alongside the university to become the founder members, laying the ground for other companies to join as associates. These multidisciplinary institutes provide contract services to companies, undertake collaborative research projects with grant support, and engage in longer term strategic research. Activities are market-led, and companies have the opportunity to influence the direction and scope of the institute's business.

Intellectual property

A large part of university research is funded by the UK Research Councils and the intellectual property rights resulting from this and some other forms of funding usually remain the property of the university. Universities are aware of the value of their intellectual property and recognise the need to seek out industrial partners if such intellectual property is to be effectively exploited. The results of a university's research seldom take the form of a finished product for immediate manufacture and sale by a company. Therefore the industrial partner must recognise that universities usually provide enabling technologies which require a further period of applied research and development before they can be successfully exploited. Universities and their partners work together during this period, the university providing a licence to permit the use of intellectual property which is otherwise protected or kept secret.

UDIL (University Directors of Industrial Liaison)

Companies wishing to explore these possibilities can contact any university for help and advice, Each university has an initial point of contact which is listed in the UDIL handbook. The booklet is obtainable from universities throughout the UK.

The UDIL representative at a university will discuss a company's overall needs and offer introductions to appropriate members of a university's academic staff. If a suitable project can be identified, and falls within the scope of the grant funding schemes, the university will assist companies to draw up specifications for the project and make an application. Some universities have sufficient experience and resources to become project leaders and to take on the project management and administrative tasks. Collaboration need not end with the completion of a programme of strategic research. Successful strategic research leads on to applied research, product and process development, and the manufacture of new products. Universities support their industrial partners throughout each stage. In the context of the European Market, UDIL has formed links with institutions elsewhere in Europe. Companies planning to form joint ventures or set up manufacturing operations in other European countries may want to locate operations close to universities working in the same technological field. The availability of research and industrial collaboration facilities is often promoted by economic development organisations as a key incentive to incoming investment. To quote from the UDIL handbook: 'UDIL is also concerned with the development of professional standards and good practice in the industrial liaison field. For example, it has recently published a widely quoted report on the management of intellectual property in universities. UDIL makes representations on behalf of its members to a variety of policy-making bodies in government, industry and the university system'. UDIL is also the first point of contact for companies seeking advice through consultancy arrangements.

BEST database

The Carter-Longmans database, BEST, lists the skills and experience of individual university staff members. The database assists companies to identify appropriate strengths in one or more universities, as need be. Entries give details of research interests, current projects, grants obtained, area of knowledge and available equipment. For information contact:

Longman Cartermill
Technology Centre
St Andrews
Fife KY16 9EA
Tel: (0334) 77660
Fax: (0334) 77180

CONTACTS

Information on all university business-related activities is available from university information offices. Details of collaborative research facilities can be obtained from the research units within universities or from the directors of industrial liaison (their precise titles may vary from university to university). For information on university management schools see *The Making of Managers*, Part Three, Chapter 2. General information on university activities of interest to industry and exporters can be obtained from the Universities Unformation Unit of the Committee of Vice-Chancellors and Principals.

Universities Information Unit
Committee of Vice-Chancellors and
Principals
29 Tavistock Square
London WC1H 9EZ
Tel: (071) 387 9231
Fax: (071) 388 8649

University Directors of Industrial Liaison (UDIL)
Bureau of Industrial Liaison
University of Surrey
Guildford
Surrey GU2 5XH
Tel: (0483) 509110
Fax: (0483) 300803
Publishes the UDIL Directory listing university industrial collaboration activities.

UCCA (Universities Central Council on Admissions)
PO Box 28
Cheltenham
Gloucestershire GL50 1HY.
For school leavers and students the *UCCA Handbook*, listing universities and the courses they run, can be obtained (price £2.50 for postage outside the UK).

MACMILLAN/PICKUP

National Training Directory 1991

The PICKUP initiative is run by the Department of Education and Science. The information in this directory is compiled by Guildford Educational Services Ltd.

October 1990
ISBN 0 333 53913 3
£75.00

Table of Contents

◀ Order Form ■■ ■■ ■ ■ ■ ■ ■ ■ ■ ■ ■ ■

To: Globe Book Services Ltd
    Macmillan Publishers
    Stockton House
    1 Melbourne Place
    London WC2B 4LF
    Tel: 071-379 4687

Please send me
_____ copy/copies of
Macmillan/PICKUP National Training Directory 1991
at £75 per copy (plus £2 postage)
ISBN 0 333 53913 3

For priority service, please
'phone with your order:
071-379 4687

Please allow 28 days for delivery

□ I enclose my cheque payable to
Globe Book Services for £_____
□ Please invoice me (Companies and Libraries only)
□ Please charge my credit card for £_____
    □ Access   _____
    □ Visa   _____
    □ American Express _____
Card No _____
Expiry Date _____
Signature _____
(Orders cannot be accepted without a signature)
Name _____
Address _____
_____
_____
_____
Telephone _____

1   2   3   4   5   6   7   8   9

4 Polytechnics and Business

Committee of Directors of Polytechnics

As the process of completing the Single Market accelerates and barrier-free access to all European markets, whether or not in the European Community, encourages companies to look further afield for new business, industry and commerce will increasingly look to polytechnics for help and advice. The thirty polytechnics in England and Wales, along with five associated colleges in Scotland, command a wealth of experience in providing courses and information, which can be tapped by companies. Many of those studying at polytechnics are mature students who have either worked in industry, commerce or the professions, or are taking part in sponsored sandwich courses. Interaction between the industrial and professional communities and polytechnics increases awareness among polytechnic students of the needs of industry. Polytechnics are particularly keen to offer help with courses, seminars and consultancy to local and regional business communities, although their services are available to any interested business or industry, irrespective of location.

The expertise which polytechnics offer covers a wide range of subjects with commercial interest or application, including science and technology, law, economics, and languages. There are many other important areas of polytechnic activity which relate to the changes taking place in the European trading environment. A guide is published by the Committee of Directors of Polytechnics (address below), *Services to Industry and Commerce* and the *Polytechnic Courses Handbook*, describing specific projects in which polytechnics are engaged.

The practical uses of the facilities provided by polytechnics, such as consultancy and technology transfer, save businesses time and money by enabling companies to operate more competitively. Seminars and courses may be vital resources in the preparations begun by any company seeking to increase profitability by expanding further within the European marketplace. However, polytechnics also seek to respond to specific needs of businesses and, with this in mind, companies may find that their local polytechnic is able to tailor existing facilities, or introduce courses to meet specific requirements at a particular time.

European business-related services

A number of polytechnics are already offering a range of services to assist companies to prepare for the Single Market, sometimes in association with local business help organisations, such as the innovation centres and local authorities. The range of services, information and advice include:

- □ Information

- □ European Documentation Centres

- □ Research projects

- □ Language courses

- □ Business courses

- □ Export services

- □ European Community law

- □ European studies

- □ Grants and loans

- □ Seminars and conferences

Business and EC information provided by some polytechnics may also be invaluable to companies developing their business activities in Europe. Leeds Polytechnic, for example, is one of several institutions which have established a Business Information Service. In collaboration with the City Council and local companies the polytechnic offers access to:

- □ Academic contacts involved in a wide range of consultancy expertise

- □ National network of library and information centres

- □ Over 300,000 books, 2,500 periodicals, EC publications

- □ Specialist sources of information

The Leeds Polytechnic service handles requests for details on products and trade names, company profiles, EC Directives among its many enquiries. Information provided ranges from simple responses to requests for urgent information to desk research plus a report. The service is especially useful to organisations which recognise the need for confidential, prompt and cost-effective information.

At the Polytechnic of North London (PNL), a European Documentation Centre (one of 44 in the UK) has been operative for several years and has now been merged with a unit providing short language courses for business, specifically aimed towards the Single Market, resulting in the formation of the Towards Europe Bureau . For details of European Documentation Centres see *Libraries*, Part Eight, Chapter 3. PNL has recently received funding for this project under the PICKUP scheme (see *Training the Workforce*, Part Three, Chapter 8). PNL is also part of the Business Co-operation Network (BC-Net), which offers a specialised telecommunications network designed to facilitate technology transfer between small and medium-sized enterprises, and between companies and educational establishments (See *The Brussels Connection*, Part Seven, Chapter 1). Intermediaries such as PNL are designated Business Advisers and provide a consultancy service to over 300 participants involved in the scheme.

Coventry Polytechnic also provides EC information and, in conjunction with the Information Technology Consultancy Unit (ITCU), has published *The Europe 1992 Directory* of basic Single Market contacts and references[1].

Research projects

Like universities, polytechnics may conduct research projects on specific aspects of the Single Market. These may include initiatives of value to commerce and industry. The Institute of Technology in Aberdeen, for example, has undertaken programmes in various fields of applied research on the implications of the Single Market for the economic future of local industries. Studies produced for use by local industries so far include engineering, paper and food processing. Portsmouth Polytechnic took part in the development of a single-stage purification process, Clariflow, to help bring Britain's beaches up to Eurobeach standards. The level of purity required under the EC Directive on the quality of bathing water for beaches has now been met at Sandown on the Isle of Wight, using the Clariflow process to treat effluent discharged into the sea. The work clearly benefits the local tourist industry.

Seminars and conferences

Many polytechnics are running seminar/conference programmes aimed chiefly at small and medium-sized enterprises, covering general and specific aspects of the Single Market. Brighton and Sheffield City polytechnics are among those which tailor seminar programmes to meet identified local needs. In Edinburgh, Napier Polytechnic has organised a major conference covering Single Market legislation. Staffordshire Polytechnic runs short courses with particular emphasis on the impact of European law, such as equal pay, health and safety and information technology. Nottingham Polytechnic has organised a conference on engineering training. Many activities of this type will be continued by polytechnics. Companies should at least contact their local polytechnic for details of conference programmes, since they offer an opportunity for management to familiarise themselves with developments in Europe and to find out what the implications are for their business.

Courses

Polytechnics nationwide run a range of courses at first degree and other levels to prepare students for employment in Europe. Courses combine European languages with business studies, often in association with other higher education institutions in Europe. Thames Polytechnic runs a BA course in international marketing which involves learning a European language and one year working in Europe. At Leeds Polytechnic, student courses cover European finance and accounting, European languages and business. Middlesex Polytechnic runs courses in European economics and European business administration, to date involving study in France, Spain and Germany. Leicester Polytechnic runs an MA course in international business and a BA course in European law, involving study of two languages. Manchester Polytechnic is launching a new degree in business in Europe. A language course using the latest media technology, such as the Communicative Competence course on compact disc is being developed at Teesside Polytechnic. The development of the European Credit Accumulation and Transfer Scheme is in operation in many Polytechnics for the benefit of business students.

Exchange programmes

Most polytechnics recognise the importance of educational links and have initiated staff and student exchange schemes. Joint validation of courses with European educational institutions has also been established, reflecting the growing emphasis on European business. Portsmouth Polytechnic incorporates language studies in all its engineering courses. The South Bank Polytechnic runs courses in electronic engineering which include a period of study in or work experience in Germany. Bristol Polytechnic specialises in modern languages and information systems in German, French and Spanish. Lancashire Polytechnic students in computing, engineering and business have so far undertaken one year's work experience in France, Germany, the Netherlands and Spain. The Polytechnic of Wales is involved in a collaborative venture with Waterford Regional Technology College in the Irish Republic in the field of biological sciences and process technology. Such courses enable polytechnics to develop the mutual recognition of qualifications and professional status, as well as producing future managers adequately equipped to work in Europe.

Polytechnics have also taken full advantage of the ERASMUS programme. ERASMUS (European Action Scheme for the Mobility of University Students) contributes to the twin overall objective of freedom of movement within the EC and increased co-operation within education (for details see *The European Student*, Part Three, Chapter 5). The Committee of Directors of Polytechnics and the Committee of Vice-Chancellors and Principals share the management of the UK ERASMUS Students Grants Council which handles applications for and the distribution of grants under this programme.

The Inter-university Co-operation Programmes (ICPs) established by polytechnics enable students, supprted by Action 2 grants, to spend three months, or more, in partner institutions in Europe. Polytechnics also participate in the LINGUA programme designed to promote the teaching and learning of EC languages.

COMETT (Community Action Programme for Education and Training for Technology) has also been taken up strongly by polytechnics. In particular, the sandwich pattern of a great many polytechnic courses makes the opportunities for student exchange for periods between six and twelve months very attractive.

The European Social Fund (ESF) is another EC initiative to which polytechnics have responded positively, usually in association with local authorities and other organisations, polytechnics being uniquely placed to assist in training for employment and helping to solve the training problems of particular regions.

1 *Europe 1992 Directory*, ICTU/Coventry Polytechnic (address below).

CONTACTS

Committee of Directors of Polytechnics
Kirkman House
12-14 Whitfield Street
London W1P 6AX
Tel: (071) 637 9939
Fax: (071) 436 4966

Polytechnics

City of Birmingham Polytechnic
Director of External Affairs
Perry Barr
Birmingham B42 2SU
Tel (021) 331 5000
Fax: (021) 356 2875

Brighton Polytechnic
European Business Centre
Mithras House
Lewes Road
Brighton
Sussex BN2 4AT
Tel: (0273) 600900
Fax: (0273) 688917

Bristol Polytechnic
Director of External Affairs
Coldharbour Lane
Frenchay
Bristol BS16 1QY
Tel: (0272) 656261
Fax: (0272) 583758

Coventry Polytechnic
Commercial Development Unit
Priory Street
Coventry CV1 5FB
Tel: (0203) 224166
Fax: (0203) 258597

Hatfield Polytechnic
International Centre
PO Box 109
Hatfield
Hertfordshire AL10 9AB
Tel: (07072) 79000
Fax: (07072) 79670

Huddersfield Polytechnic
1992 Working Party
Queensgate
Huddersfield HD1 3DH
Tel: (0484) 22288 Ext. 2294
Fax: (0484) 516151

Kingston Polytechnic
Director of Academic Affairs
Penrhyn Road
Kingston-upon-Thames
Surrey KT1 2EE
Tel: (081) 549 1366
Fax: (081) 547 2398

Lancashire Polytechnic
Preston
Lancashire PR1 2TQ
Tel: (0772) 201201
Fax: (0772) 202073

Leeds Polytechnic
Director of External Development
Calverley Street
Leeds LS1 3HE
Tel: (0532) 462315
Fax: (0532) 425733

Leeds Polytechnic
Faculty of Business
Department of European Business
18 Queen Square
Leeds LS2 8AJ
Tel: (0532) 462315
Fax: (0532) 425733

Leicester Polytechnic
PO Box 143
Leicester LE1 9BH
Tel: (0533) 551551
Fax: (0533) 550307

Liverpool Polytechnic
Business Liaison Officer
Rodney House
70 Mount Pleasant
Liverpool L3 5UX
Tel: (051) 207 3581
Fax: (051) 709 0172

Polytechnic of Central London
309 Regent Street
London W1R 8AL
Tel: (071) 580 2020
Fax: (071) 436 7367

City of London Polytechnic
31 Jewry Street
London EC3 N2EY
Tel: (071) 283 1030
Fax: (071) 623 2858

Polytechnic of East London
West Ham Precinct
Romford Road
Stratford
London E15 4LZ
Tel: (081) 590 7722
Fax: (081) 519 3740

Polytechnic of North London
Holloway Road
London N7 8DB
Tel: (071) 607 2789
Fax: (071) 700 4272

Polytechnic of the South Bank
European Co-ordinator
103 Borough Road
London SE1 0AA
Tel: (071) 928 8989
Fax: (071) 261 9115

Thames Polytechnic
Dean of Continuing Education
Wellington Street
London SE18 6PF
Tel: (071) 316 8137
Fax: (071) 316 8875

Manchester Polytechnic
Department of Economics
Aytown Building
Aytown Street
Manchester M1 3GH
Tel: (061) 228 6171
Fax: (061) 236 5319

Middlesex Polytechnic
Marketing Director
Bounds Green Site
Bounds Green Road
London N11 2NQ
Tel: (081) 368 1299
Tel: (081) 361 1726

Middlesex Polytechnic
Head of Academic Development
Enfield Site
Queensway
Enfield
Middlesex EN3 4SF
Tel: (081) 368 1299
Fax: (805) 0702

Newcastle-upon-Tyne Polytechnic
Ellison Building
Ellison Place
Newcastle-upon Tyne NE1 8ST
Tel: (091) 2326002
Fax: (091) 2358017

Oxford Polytechnic
Director of Corporate Planning
Headington
Oxford OX3 0BP
Tel: (0865) 819001
Fax: (0865) 819073

Portsmouth Polytechnic
Faculty of Humanities and Social Science
Ravelin House
Museum Road
Portsmouth PO1 2QQ
Tel: (0705) 843012
Fax: (0705) 843335

Sheffield City Polytechnic
Pond Street
Sheffield S1 1WB
Tel: (0742) 720911
Fax: (0742) 758019

Polytechnic Southwest
Drake Circus
Plymouth
Devon PL4 8AA
Tel: (0752) 233980
Fax: (0752) 233984

Staffordshire Polytechnic
Beaconside
Stafford ST18 0AD
Tel: (0785) 52331
Fax: (0785) 51058

Sunderland Polytechnic
Director of Commercial and External
Affairs
High Technology Park
Chester Road
Sunderland
Tel: (091) 5100531
Fax: (091) 5100990

Teesside Polytechnic
Educational Development Unit
Middesborough
Cleveland TS1 3BA
Tel: (0642) 218121
Fax: (0642) 226822

Trent Polytechnic
Faculty of Human Sciences
Burton Street
Nottingham NG1 4BU
Tel: (0602) 418418
Fax: (0602) 484266

Wolverhampton Polytechnic
Molineux Street
Wolverhampton WV1 1SB
Tel: (0902) 313000
Fax: (0902) 25047

Wolverhampton Polytechnic
International Office
Wulfruna Street
Wolverhampton WV1 1SB
Tel: (0902) 313001
Fax: (0902) 25015

Scotland

Robert Gordon's Institute of Technology
Hilton Place
Aberdeen AB9 1FP
Tel: (0224) 482211
Fax: (0224) 488545

Dundee Institute of Technology
Technology Transfer Centre
Bell Street
Dundee DD1 1HG
Tel: (0382) 27225
Fax: (0382) 200782

Napier Polytechnic of Edinburgh
Director (Polyed)
Merchiston Campus
10 Colinton Road
Edinburgh EH10 5DT
Tel: (031) 444 2266
Fax (031) 452 8532

Glasgow College
Department of Communication
Cowcaddens Road
Glasgow G4 0BA
Tel: (041) 332 7090
Fax: (041) 331 1075

Paisley College of Technology
Director of Development and Enterprise
High Street
Paisley
Renfrewshire PA1 2BE
Tel: (041) 887 1241
Fax: (041) 887 0812

Wales

Polytechnic of Wales
Department of Business and
Administration Studies
Llantwit Road
Treforest
Pontupridd
Mid Glamorgan CF37 1DL
Tel: (0443) 480480
Fax (0443) 480558

5 The European Student

Exchange programmes and European youth societies

Timothy F. Beyer Helm

There will soon be over 52 million young people between the ages of 15 and 24 in the European Community. These young men and women form the backbone of an ever closer European union and provide the skilled resources for European Industry and Commerce. For many of these young people, their first experiences of Europe will occur whilst they are taking a higher education course. The student who takes full advantage of the opportunities on offer, such as a sponsored trip in Europe, or debating current European issues with leading opinion formers, gains in both confidence and knowledge. Consequently, young people become 'natural' Europeans and mix better with other European professionals.

University experience also provides an opportunity to meet a wide cross-section of future contacts from many backgrounds, and it offers the chance to discover Europe, both from a social perspective and in a commercial context; therefore, experiencing the EC as not just a dry political formula, but as a social and economic environment in which we all live. One current problem is that, for many young people, the opportunities on offer are obscured by a fear of the unknown. But the various student European societies in higher education colleges play a key role in broadening the student's outlook and scope for first-hand experience.

European student organisations organise a variety of activities which bring their members into contact with the business community. Even the ubiquitous parties and social events nowadays involve a large element of fundraising and commercial sponsorship, all of which contribute to the student's range of experience. European societies organise speaking events and debates, drawing together academics, politicians, and business people to discuss topics of mutual interest. This may inform students of the business opportunities open to them, or furnish practical examples of the European marketplace at work.

There are also a number of national and international bodies which seek to bring students together from colleges across country and continent alike. Many offer their membership subsidised access to seminars and conferences, and to other Eastern and Western European activities. Such events provide a forum for young people to learn how their contemporaries throughout Europe view developments, and they serve as an introduction to larger international conferences at which topics are debated in different languages against a multi-cultural background. This chapter deals specifically with the work of student European societies, the Young European Movement, *Jeunesse Europeenne Federaliste*, the Youth Forum of the European Communities, the ERASMUS and COMETT student exchange programmes, and the *stagiare* scheme.

Student societies

University and polytechnic European societies provide an opportunity for forming student opinion on Europe. In addition, students gain experience of discussing their own ideas with visiting speakers. The main ingredients of the success of European societies are variety in their activities plus an ability to bring the outside world and students together. Often the best attended meetings are those at which leading business figures discuss their companies' futures in the European marketplace and the corresponding outlook for present and future employees. For example, the London School of Economics' European Society holds a number of regular meetings which focus on European business opportunities for various British industrial and commercial companies. Topics range from the future of engineering to the role of banks in the Single Market and the importance of a single currency to industry.

Most university European societies also organise political meetings, debates and social events, which enhance their role as 'information brokers' for European Commission schemes of interest to students. This makes them useful points of contact for other societies interested in European affairs and enables them to work in close collaboration with lecturers. A particularly popular event is the 'European Week' — a full week given to events focusing on European nations and European issues. Most individual college organisations are now members of national groupings which assists them in fundraising, administration and arranging subsidised travel, thus providing essential long term stability.

Young European Movement

With over 1000 members the Young European Movement is the largest, and most rapidly growing, national European youth organisation. The movement comprises a federation of European societies across the UK. A London-based central organisation provides assistance to branches and helps plan the launching of new groups. The movement provides a range of direct membership services, including a regular monthly newsletter plus access to international events via its affiliation to *Jeunesse Europeenne Federaliste*. Membership is open to young people aged between 16 and 35, most of whom join at local branches which are located as far apart as Belfast and Reading, although the largest membership grouping is in the London area. With its branch structure and international links, the movement provides an ideal introduction to European affairs and developments.

The Young European Movement aims to inform and persuade young people that the Single Market programme plays a vital role in their future. To this end, the movement holds two annual national events. One is the London Careers Conference which provides an opportunity to explore employment prospects in Europe. The is the movement's annual Summer School in Europe, run jointly with the Federal Trust for Education and Research, an organisation based at the London office of the Young European Movement. The Summer School offers insight into the political structures which might be adopted by the EC in the future.

Jeunesse Europeenne Federaliste (JEF)

Jeunesse Europeenne Federaliste (Young European Federalists) is a European-wide youth organisation with branches in nineteen countries, including Austria, Hungary, Slovenia and Scandinavian countries). JEF is primarily a political (federalist) organisation with local, regional and national sections. Membership offers exceptional opportunities for young people to experience the multicultural European environment in which they may eventually have to work. Meetings cover a range of topics of interest to young people from the environment to the drugs problem.

Information about the group's international seminars and other activities is published in its monthly magazine, *The New Federalist*. JEF is funded by the European Commission, the Council of Europe, the Belgian Government and membership contributions. The organisation is based in Brussels and many of its activities are heavily subsidised.

Youth Forum of the European Communities

The Youth Forum is an umbrella organisation representing a multitude of EC youth groups, be they political (European Democrat Students) or practical (Federation of Youth Hostels in the European Community). The forum serves as a useful contact point for students wishing to learn more about other European youth groups. It publishes a monthly bulletin which carries details of conferences and meetings held throughout Europe. The forum also actively lobbies the press and the European Parliament to ensure that important issues affecting young people, such as unemployment, are properly noted at European level.

ERASMUS

ERASMUS (European Action Scheme for the Mobility of University Students) encourages the mobility of both students and teachers. By fostering inter-university co-operation and exchanges of teachers and students, the European Commission is helping people to adapt to the reality of the Single Market. ERASMUS has established, through a network of EC higher education institutions, the means to promote the exchanges. Students can now undertake a period of recognised study lasting from between three to twelve months in other member states. Financial assistance is provided in the form of mobility grants.

Nearly 30,000 students took part in the ERASMUS 1989-90 programme, compared to 4,000 in 1987-88. The UK has played a major role in ERASMUS and, in 1989-90, around 150 UK institutions took part in some 750 exchange programmes. In total, about 4,500 British students followed part of their studies in another EC country. The academic disciplines which are particularly well represented are languages, engineering and business studies. As well as benefitting those pursuing specific aims, the programme helps to broaden young people's horizons and to increase awareness of the different markets which make up the Single Market. Eventually it is hoped that 100,000 degree students will each year be able to spend some time in another EC country.

COMETT

The COMETT (Community Programme in Education and Training for Technology) was launched in 1986 and has now been extended until the end of 1994. With a budget of £130 million, it is one of the most conspicuous European Commission initiatives to encourage links between business and academia. Participation in the programme is also open to EFTA (European Free Trade Association) member countries. The scheme promotes co-operation in education and training between higher education institutions and companies (including small and medium-sized enterprises) across the EC. Types of project falling within the scope of the scheme are:

☐ University Enterprise Training Partnerships , based on a region or specific technology sector.

☐ Transitional placements for students, graduates and lecturers in industrial companies and, likewise, places for industrial personnel in higher education institutions.

☐ Transnational training courses

☐ Creation of training materials for improving technological skills.

☐ Preparatory visits

COMETT also helps to introduce specific academic skills to industry and further the training of engineers, technicians and managers, in order to prepare them for the Single Market. The UK has a regional network, sending around 350 students each year to other European countries. This has led to the development of some 40 projects concerned with training courses, as well as UK participation in courses initiated in other countries.

The stagiare scheme

This scheme offers graduates secondment to European Community Institutions, enabling them to gain first-hand experience of the workings of the EC. 'Stages' are temporary postings, lasting between three and five months, alongside a sponsoring official. Some financial assistance is available. The institutions which provide places for Stagiares are:

> The European Parliament
> The European Commission
> The Economic and Social Committee

The Economic and Social Committee is the institution most directly concerned with the business point of view, regularly opining on Commission proposals which affect the business and trading environment in Europe and in individual member states. Placements do not lead to permanent appointments in the administrative grades, but they enable graduates to improve their language skills and further qualify themselves for future employment in Europe. Overall, the Stagiare programme offers a unique insight into, and involvement in, the EC 'system'.

Competition for places is tough, with several thousand applications a year for only 300 or so places. The most positive strategy for gaining a placement is to visit Brussels and establish contact with officials who could act as sponsors. For those with no Brussels contact, the best initial points of contact are the Commission's information offices throughout Europe or the European Parliament.

CONTACTS

Young European Movement
Europe House
1 Whitehall Place
London SW1A 2DA
Tel: (071) 839 6622/3
Fax: (071) 930 9788

The European Movement
(as Young European Movement)

Jeunesse Europeene Federaliste
98 rue du Trone
B-1050 Brussels
Tel: (32) 2 512 0053
Fax: (32) 2 512 6673

Youth Forum of the European Communities
10 rue de la Science
B-1040 Brussels
Tel: (32) 2 230 6490
Fax: (32) 2 230 2123

ERASMUS Information
Department of Education and Science
Further and Higher Education Branch
Elizabeth House
York Road
London SE1 7PH
Tel: (071) 934 9353/9631
Fax: (071) 934 9082/0651

UK ERASMUS
Students Grants Council
C/o University of Kent
Canterbury
Kent CT2 7PD
Tel: (0227) 762712

ERASMUS Bureau
15 rue d'Arlon
B-1040 Brussels
Tel: (32) 2 233 0111
Fax: (32) 2 233 0150

COMETT Liaison Office
Department of Education and Science
Elizabeth House
York Road
London SE1 7PH
Tel: (071) 934 9385
Fax: (071) 934 9082/0651

COMETT Technical Assistance Unit
71 Avenue Cortenberg
B-1040 Brussels
Tel: (32) 2 733 9755/6/7
Fax: (32) 2 734 5641

European Commission
Jean Monnet House
8 Storey's Gate
London SW1P 3AT
Tel: (071) 222 8122
Fax: (071) 222 0900

European Parliament
2 Queen Anne's Gate
London SW1H 9AA
Tel: (071) 222 0411
Fax: (071) 222 2713

6 Languages and Business

A key factor in competitiveness

Nigel Reeves

In mainland Europe over 250 million EC citizens do not speak English as their mother tongue. Yet mainland Europe will become the UK's 'home' market when the Single Market is completed. Likewise, the UK will become part of the home market of the other member states of the Community, where many people speak English as a second language. For example, the UK will be as much a part of Germany's home market as is Bavaria or the City-State of Hamburg. Most, if not all, Germans directly engaged in trade with the UK speak English. But the reverse is not true. The same imbalance in foreign language proficiency applies throughout the Community, with the British trailing behind in their efforts to communicate in a customer's own language. Despite the acceleration in removing barriers to trade between Single Market countries, the dilemma as to whether to learn foreign languages, or simply rely on foreigners speaking English, is far from resolved in the minds of many UK business people. This chapter sets out some of the reasons why it pays to invest in foreign language proficiency.

The importance of foreign language proficiency for successful exporting was a contentious issue through the 1970s, and well into the 1980s, as numerous surveys and reports testified[1]. The debates revealed a clear division of opinion between those who used languages to boost their performance in exporting, and stood up in many conferences and said so, and others who were satisfied with using English.

There were many reasons for the reluctance to invest in foreign language learning: the predominance of English as the international language of business; the disappearance of compulsory language learning in English and Welsh schools with the introduction in 1953 of the GCE, and therefore the inability of many aspiring company managers to offer a foreign language; the long-standing tradition of trading with captive English speaking markets. In retrospect, however, the debate can be seen to have reflected a transition period in the history of British overseas trade and British education.

Even by the late 1970s, the UK trading pattern for the period leading up to 1992 had been established with well over half British exports going to European destinations, and only a quarter to English speaking markets. This shift of trade towards Europe was accompanied by a gradual, yet inexorable decline in the UK's share of world trade in manufactures, falling from 25 per cent in 1950 to under 10 per cent by the end of the 1970s.

In 1978, five years after Britain joined the EC, a Royal Society of Arts survey of some 200 exporting firms already showed a distinct correlation between the employment of export executives equipped with foreign language proficiency to degree standard and success in the Queen's Award for Export[2]. In the most extensive series of language need surveys yet carried out, Stephen Hagen and a team of investigators showed in 1988 that attitudes among exporters towards foreign languages were changing. Covering all the major regions of mainland Britain, and with positive responses from some 1150 firms, these surveys revealed that an average of 44 per cent of companies across the country felt that they could significantly have improved their trade performance with access to language expertise[3]. Yet these results preceded any general awareness or impact of the advent of the Single Market. Indeed, the data reflects the views of companies then exporting only a modest proportion of their output, or only a modest proportion to non-English speaking markets. Today's trading circumstances are already substantially different. The concept of the Single Market rests on three principles:

☐ Free movement of goods and services

☐ Free movement of capital

☐ Free movement of people

The Cecchini Report[4] highlights three consequences: growth of European output, integration of the EC economies, and a radical concentration of the number of companies in business. The driving force behind these developments will be competition. Competition will invade hitherto protected local, regional and national markets, reducing the scope for what is, in a European context, purely provincial trading. Competition will also sharpen the quest for qualified personnel, hastened by the demographic decline in the number of people in their twenties across the whole of the Community (except the Republic of Ireland), and made more acute by the need to employ the well qualified, as industry and commerce alike become more knowledge intensive. At the same time, the shape of the European company is changing through an intensifying stream of mergers, acquisitions and joint ventures. Mobility of capital will, inevitably, accelerate the integration and accompanying concentration of companies. Previously, companies operating internationally were generally of three types:

☐ Companies selling from a home base through foreign agents and distributors.

☐ Larger companies developing their own sophisticated marketing and distribution networks

☐ Multinationals with networks of subsidiaries, manufacturing principally for individual national markets while retaining single national ownership.

We are now seeing the emergence, through mergers and joint ventures, of the trans-national European company, in multiple ownership with a truly European board of directors, frequently manufacturing in several centres divided by product, rather than by market. The European Economic Interest Grouping (EEIG) encourages this trend even among smaller companies.

The category covered by foreign language surveys was the direct exporter, companies of great importance to the UK within the Single Market, since they are often the small to medium-sized companies which may eventually grow to multi-national or transnational size. It is believed that, in the free trading conditions of the new market, companies which 'export' across EC frontiers will be the most likely to survive acquisition or competition from the European mainland.

The reasons given by companies before the Single Market initiative began for using foreign languages in export transactions offer a timely basis on which to consider language proficency in a more competitive European trading environment. In an interview-based survey of companies using college foreign language training facilities that David Liston and I conducted in 1984-85, eight main reasons for language learning were identified[5]:

Administration: At company headquarters and offices for translating, and checking trade literature in translation; translating correspondence and replying in a foreign language; sending telexes (now also fax and document transmission); handling telephone calls.

Sales and marketing: Gathering market intelligence; direct contact with overseas customers, circumventing agents; reviving an ailing market; opening new markets, previously inaccessible because of the language barrier; selling at trade fairs; improving and deepening existing business relationships.

Supply: To establish more satisfactory purchasing arrangements with those suppliers who are located outside the UK.

Negotiations with foreign customers: To carry out more successful negotiations, even where English was the official or accepted medium, ensuring that clear, accurate company policy statements are made; gaining insight into the other party's approach, including observing their asides and exchanges.

Customer services: To improve customer service through better knowledge of their needs, plus training the customer's service engineers, and through equipping UK-based service engineers with language skills.

Company network: Improved communications with a subsidiary, inevitably employing foreign nationals.

Licensing: For entering into licensing agreements with foreign-based manufacturers, and supervising them.

On-site control: Greater ease in controlling on-site construction of plant.

In 1989 Michael Pearson, an executive in a British-based multi-national company, which exported around 25 per cent of its UK production, representing 10 per cent of group sales, and with other manufacturing plants located elsewhere inside and outside Europe, produced a list of functions[6] for foreign language usage remarkably similar to those listed above. His list specified that foreign language capabilities were needed for:

☐ Marketing and selling

☐ Intra-group communication, despite the official use of English as the company language. In particular for:
  Product development
  Computer projects
  Planning and budgeting, including board meetings
  Participating in senior appointments

☐ Communication with associated companies, knowledge of those companies being especially important for reliable planning

☐ Transactions with new acquisitions

☐ Legal agreements, such as licensing

What emerges is evidence that accurate and effective communication is vital between the home company and its partners or subsidiaries, and between executives of all national and linguistic backgrounds. The inadequacy of relying on English as the house language, merely because colleagues from outside the UK may speak it, emerges equally forcefully from other recent testimonies, notably from executives in multi-nationals engaged in the manufacture of widely differing products. Peter Blackburn, Head of the European Division of Rowntree-Mackintosh stresses the value of languages for control and for man management: 'In a situation where you are dealing with foreign daughter companies, you need to know what is going on to maintain control, to assess and develop people, to manage the business and deal with people at all levels'[7].

Mike Smith, former joint managing director of SEMA, the pan-European computing services company, was quoted in the *Financial Times* as saying that 'a commitment to language learning is essential, even though the official language of the group is English, because, on important matters, people have to communicate in their native language'. For Beecham Products, the pharmaceuticals multi-national, the stress is rather on the need for foreign languages for differentiated product development[8], a point also made by Michael Pearson (above).

Cultural divides

The views expressed above underline the cultural and linguistic diversity of the Single Market, a crucial feature which trading companies overlook at their peril. One of the major reasons for the stagnation of the Common Market in the early 1980s was the failure of the harmonisation policy. The apparent desire to standardise and homogenise goods across ancient cultural divides went against the grain. The attack on the British sausage and ice cream, on Italian pasta, German beer and French cassis are just a few of the *causes celebres* which reveal the cultural specificity of European tastes.

Difficulty in producing effective pan-European advertising, currently a threat to the viability of European commercial satellite broadcasting, is a further reflection of deep cultural and linguistic divides. Indeed, it is a matter of debate whether global marketing concepts can be effective in Europe, except for products that appeal to Europeans on a basis of equal familiarity, yet equal exoticism, such as Levi jeans, Marlboro' cigarettes, and Coca Cola from the United States. By contrast, the Swiss product, Nescafe, which, despite its household name, is actually sold across Europe in at least twenty-two different roasts, sporting the same small set of brand labels.

When one considers that 82 per cent of the EC's population does not speak English as a mother tongue, it becomes clear why even multi-national companies must take account of language and cultural diversities when marketing and selling. For the trans-national company in the Single Market, the need to adapt to cultural and linguistic diversity becomes still more pressing, in view of the different management styles deriving from many separate European business cultures. It is especially important in a multi or transnational company, if it is to fully justify its existence, for top management and board members to understand each other. It is not just a matter of receiving facts and information. Empathy and the ability to see developments from another's perspective also matter. Struggling with pidgin German or French is no way to cultivate empathy. The key is thorough knowledge of languages, enabling us to live and experience events as our European partners and colleagues do.

The Euro-executive with this breadth of experience and quality of inter-culturality is already in keen demand. According to the definition of the personnel consultants, Saxton Bampfylde International, the ideal Euro-executive is the manager who is able to operate with equal confidence anywhere in Europe[9] (See *The New Breed of Bosses*, Part Three, Chapter 1). Saxton Bampfylde observe that such Euro-executives are difficult to find, but most frequently originate from the Netherlands, Belgium or Scandinavia. In other words, they are people who, as a result of possessing a minority language as their mother tongue, such as Danish, Swedish or Flemish/Dutch, or through having grown up in a multi-cultural and multi-linguistic society, have evolved a natural sensitivity towards cultural distinctions and others' values and perceptions. Yet, according to another report, even the Swedish company, Electrolux, is encountering great problems in identifying suitable Euro-executives, as the title of Christopher Lorenz's investigation, *The Birth of a Transnational: Desperately Seeking the True International Manager*[10], for the *Financial Times* succinctly suggests.

We are left with one question. Which language, other than English, should a company operating in the Single Market tackle? In many cases the issue will be decided by a company's own strategy, the markets it wishes to open, the partners it possesses. We also know that, currently, two languages are most in demand in the UK — French and German — as equal front runners, followed by Spanish (and then Arabic, Japanese, Italian and Russian)[11]. But events in Eastern Europe seem likely to have a profound effect on European trading in the coming decades; indeed, some might argue, as profound as the advent of the Single Market. The opening of Germany's and Austria's traditional hinterlands will decisively tip the balance of economic power in Europe towards German speaking countries. German will surely be restored as the *lingua franca* of Central Europe and, indeed, will vie with English as the predominant trading language of Europe in the coming century.

1 i *Report on the Market Survey of the Non-Specialist Use of Foreign Languages in Industry and Commerce*, edited by G. V. Lee, London Chamber of Commerce and Industry, Commercial Education Scheme, Sidcup, 1972; 1977.
ii *The Use of Foreign Languages in the Private Sector of Industry and Commerce*, Language Teaching Centre, University of York, 1974.
iii *Does Britain Need Linguists? Language Education and our Trading Future*, Export United conference, British Overseas Trade Board, Royal Society of Arts, University of Surrey, 1978.
iv *Factors for International Success: The Barclays Bank Report on Export Development in France, Germany and the United Kingdom*, research study prepared by ITI Research for the British Overseas Trade Board, London Chamber of Commerce and Industry, and Barclays Bank International, 1979.
v *Foreign Languages for Overseas Trade*, report by the British Overseas Trade Board Study Group on foreign languages, foreword by HRH Duke of Kent, 1979.
vi *Languages and Export Performance*, study prepared for the Betro Trust Committee of the Royal Society of Arts by P. E. Consulting Group, 1979.
vii *The Language Key in Export Strategy*, report of a conference at Aston University, Birmingham, 1981.
viii *Business Studies, Languages and Overseas Trade: A Study of Education and Training*, David Liston and Nigel Reeves, foreword by HRH Duke of Kent, Pitman Publishing and the Institute of Export, 1985, 1986.
ix *Education for Exporting Capability: Languages and Market Penetration* , Nigel Reeves, *The Incoporated Linguist* (No. 24, p147-153, 1985), Royal Society of Arts Journal (No. 134, p182-197, 1986).

2 *Languages and Export Performance*, ref. 1 (vi) above.

3 *Languages in British Business: An Analysis of Current Needs*, Edited by Stephen Hagen, Newcastle-upon-Tyne Polytechnic Products Ltd in association with the Centre for Information on Language Teaching and Research, London, 1988.

4 *The European Challenge 1992: The Benefits of a Single Market*, Paolo Cecchini with Michael Catinat and Alexis Jacquermin, Gower Publishing, 1988.

5 *Languages, Business Studies and Overseas Trade*, ref. 1 (viii) above.

6 'Languages in a Multi-national Company', Michael Pearson, The Linguist (No. 5 p146-7 1989).

7 'Languages in a Multi-national Business', Peter Blackburn, p151 of Hagen, ref. 3 above.

8 'How and Why Beecham Products Want to Recruit Linguists', p59 of *Higher Education for International Careers*, Aston University Modern Languages Club and Centre for Information on Language Teaching and Research, London, 1988.

9 *The Search for the Euro-Executive*, Saxton Bamfylde International, London, 1989.

10 'The Birth of a Transnational: Desperately Seeking the True International Manager', Christopher Lorenz, *Financial Times*, 30 June 1989.

11 *Languages in British Business* (pxxii) of Hagen, ref. 3 above. ·

CONTACTS

Universities, polytechnics and business schools also run language training courses for business (see *Universities and Industry*, Part Three, Chapter 3, and *Polytechnics and Business*, Part Three, Chapter 4). With the assistance of government, a network of language-export consortia has recently been established with regional membership by universities, polytechnics and colleges. These can undertake custom-built business language courses for individual companies. There are also many privately run language schools.

Finding qualified translators and interpreters can be difficult. It is a dangerous practice to employ persons without formal technical business and translator's qualifications. Both the Institute of Linguists and the Institute of Translating and Interpreting can help companies to contact specialist translators (see below).

Companies themselves can set up foreign language resource areas stocked with foreign newspapers, magazines and trade journals, perhaps gathered by export executives on foreign trips. Language learning packs are available, the widest range being sold by Linguaphone (see below) includes a new audio-based series called Visa Languages.

The BBC has a number of courses on general conversational language. The BBC's OU Production Unit, together with the Department of Trade and Pitman Publishing have produced a series of language and business communication packs based on authentic video materials (see BLISS, Business Language Information Services, below).

Professional organisations

Institute of Linguists
24a Highbury Grove
London N5 2EA
Tel: (071) 359 7445
Fax: (071) 354 0202

Institute of Translating and Interpreting
318a Finchley Road
London NW3 5HT
Tel: (071) 794 9331
Fax: (071) 435 2105

Language Export (LX) Centres

National LX Co-ordination Office
C/o CILTS
Regents College
Inner Circle, Regents Park
London NW1 4NJ
General enquiries and updates
Tel: (071) 224 3748
Fax: (071) 224 3518

Local LX Centres

Coventry LX Centre
Coventry Technical College
BUTTS
Coventry CV1 3GD
Tel: (0203) 256793
Fax: (0203) 520164

East Anglian LX Centre
EARBC
2 Looms Lane
Bury St Edmunds
Suffolk IP33 1HE
Tel: (0284) 764977
Fax: (0284) 764147

**East Midlands Language Export Centre
(EMLEX)**
Charlesworth
University of Technology
Loughborough
Leicestershire LE11 3TU
Tel: (0509) 222386
Fax: (0509) 610361

ECOSSE Ltd
5 Lynedoch Place
Glasgow G3 6AB
Tel: (041) 332 9886
Fax: (041) 332 9819

**International Business and Export Services
(IBEX)**
PO Box 64
Winchester
Hampshire SO23 8BG
Tel: (0962) 842533
Fax: (0962) 841920

**IC (Languages and Communications
Services) Ltd**
Aston Science Park
Love Lane
Birmingham B47 4BJ
Tel: (021) 359 0981 ext. 6394
Fax: (021) 359 0433

Kingston Language Export Centre
School of Languages
Kingston Polytechnic
Penrhyn Road
Kingston upon Thames
Surrey KT1 2EE
Tel: (081) 547 2623
Fax: (081) 547 1277

Lancashire and Cumbria LX Centre
Lancashire Polytechnic
Preston
Lancashire PR1 2TQ
Tel: (0772) 262232
Fax: (0772) 202073

Language Consultants for Industry
14 Queen Square, Bath
Somerset BA1 2HN
Tel: (0225) 424929
Fax: (0225) 447163

**London Language Export Centre
(LEXCEL)**
72 Great Portland Street
London W1N 5AL
Tel: (071) 323 4977
Fax: (071) 636 5470

Manchester Language Export Centre
Room 29 Cavendish Building
Manchester Polytechnic
All Saints
Manchester M15 6BG
Tel: (061) 228 6171 ext. 2170
Fax: (061) 236 8624

Merseyside Language Export Centre
Modern Languages Building Room 405
University of Liverpool
Liverpool L69 3BX
Tel: (051) 794 2795/6/7
Fax: (051) 794 2827

North East Export Associates (NEEXA)
Newcastle Polytechnic
Room B218 Ellison Building
Ellison Place
Newcastle-upon-Tyne NE1 8ST
Tel: (091) 261 0190)

Oxford and Thames Valley Export Centre
The Cricket Road Centre
Cricket Road
Oxford OX4 3DW
Tel: (0865) 747221
Fax: (0865) 771067

**London Language Export Centre
(LEXCEL)**
72 Great Portland Street
London W1N 5AL
Tel: (071) 323 4977

Services for Export and Language (SEL)
Room 122 Crescent House
University of Salford
Salford M5 4WT
Tel: (061) 745 7480/736 5843

**Staffordshire and Wolverhampton
Language Export Centre
(North)**
The Management Centre
Staffordshire Polytechnic
College Road
Stoke-on-Trent
Staffordshire ST4 2DE
Tel: (0782) 412143
Fax: (0782) 747006

**Staffordshire and Wolverhampton
Language Export Centre
(South)**
School of Languages and European Studies
Wolverhampton Polytechnic
Stafford Street
Wolverhampton WV1 1SB
Tel: (0902) 313001 Ext. 2450
Fax: (0902) 25015

Sussex and Kent LX Centre
Brighton Polytechnic
Falmer
Brighton BN1 9PH
Tel: (0273) 606622
Fax: (0273) 690710

**Wales Language and Export Training
Centre**
University College of Swansea
Singleton Park
Swansea SA2 8PP
Tel: (0792) 295621

**Wales Language and Export Training
Centre (North)**
Newtech Innovation Centre
Croesnewydd Hall
Wrexham Technology Park
Wrexham
Clwyd LL13 7YP
Tel: (0978) 290694
Fax: (0978) 290705

**Yorkshire and Humberside Export Services
(YES)**
Modern Languages Centre
Leeds Polytechnic
Lawns Lane
Farnley
Leeds LS12 5ET
Tel: (0532) 630505

Lingua programme

The main thrust of the European Community's LINGUA programme is in vocational training to promote language learning throughout the workforce and the general population. Support will be made available for a variety of language learning projects including the development of open learning materials, exchanges, and the development of vocational language qualifications. According to the European Commission, the central aims are to 'increase the capacity of citizens of the Community to communicate with each other by a quantitative and qualitative improvement in the teaching and learning of foreign languages'; and to 'ensure effective measures towards the provision, for the benefit of enterprises in the European Community, of the necessary levels of foreign language expertise in the present and future workforce'.

UK LINGUA Unit
Seymour House
Seymour Mews
London W1H 9PE
Tel: (071) 224 1477
Fax: (071) 224 1906

Edinburgh LINGUA Office
3 Brunsfield Crescent
Edinburgh EH10 4HD
Tel: (031) 447 8024

Belfast LINGUA Office
Central Bureau Office
16 Malone Road
Belfast BT9 5BN
Tel: (0232) 664418

Other contacts

BBC training packs

BLISS (Business Language Information Services)
Silbury Business Centre
Silbury Court
356 Silbury Boulevard
Central Milton Keynes
MK9 2LR
Tel: (0908) 604848
Fax: (0908) 662615
Telex: 825 264 SILBURY G

Linguaphone

Linguaphone
St. Giles House
50 Poland Street
London W1V 4AX
Tel: (071) 734 9574

7 Bureaucracy Untrained

The missing business-government partnership

James Hogan

In any exporting company there must be two successful teams playing for the same side — the 'away' team operating out in the field and the 'home' team based at company headquarters. Both teams work closely together to achieve a common goal — new or continuing sales — and all that goes with this objective in the way of customer service and efficient back-up for the sales team. If something goes wrong, there is no question that management should concentrate all its forces on putting matters right. But when one applies this metaphor to the relationship between the British civil service and the country's exporters, the partnership between the two sides appears to be fragile, with one side — the bureaucracy — lacking motivation, seemingly oblivious to the fact that its players in the field are often battling against the odds. There are, of course, mechanisms for supporting business, such as the British Overseas Trade Board's export services programme, but these concern relatively few businesses for brief periods, not business as a whole; and they stand apart from, rather than amidst, what ought to be an actively pro-business civil service.

One common complaint in the business community is that when companies succeed, say, in putting an argument to the European Commission for changes in legislative proposals, they do so *despite*, rather than because of the presence of a UK government official. A civil servant is usually orientated towards Departmental policy, while the company's attention is fixed on its profitability. Were there to be such a mismatch in attitudes between the home and away team in a business it would lead to serious problems. The company would begin to fail in the marketplace, sales figures would fall and an atmosphere of conflict would arise between the sales team and the support staff at company headquarters.

Britain Ltd is experiencing a problem of this order at a crucial time in its economic history. While business looks outwards to Europe, the bureaucracy, having employed public relations professionals and propaganda techniques to convey its 1992 message, looks inwards again to the safety and comfort of its own closed world. Government, having erected a signpost pointing to Europe, has swiftly retreated into Whitehall's labyrinthine bureaucracy in which thousands of employees are engaged in unproductive activities which profit no-one and have no impact on the country's economic performance, least of all on the record balance of payments deficit of £25 billion which seriously mars Britain's trade performance at the beginning of the 1990s.

This assessment of the relationship between government and industry is, admittedly, subjective and partisan in tone. But that does not mean that the central argument — that government and business must work much more closely together in the national economic interest — is not valid. Government must take steps to dispel the feeling that business has to defeat opposition at home as well as the competition in the field. Dissatisfaction with the conduct of economic and industrial policy, mentioned in other parts of this book, and anxieties about the comparatively low level of skills among the workforce and management have been well-aired in discussions between industry and government, though often to little avail. But another basic problem is the inability of so many government employees to appreciate and understand the needs of business and the role they themselves should play in helping Britain Ltd to make a profit in Europe. Training in business priorities is an urgent necessity for civil servants, not just for the chosen few to be seconded to companies here and there, but for *all* civil servants, down to the most junior clerical workers who frequently waste business time and sour the atmosphere with indifference and incompetence.

Many of these recurring obstructions to business efficiency could be eliminated by a change in attitude in the ranks in Whitehall. A now standing joke which is circulating throughout the business community is the one that says that everyone thinks a businessman is some kind of rogue "with one hand on the wheel of a Porche and the other hand in the till." The joke would be funnier still it if was not so true. For example, in 1990, during discussions with a group of businessmen lobbying for more availability of subsidised investment capital for the manufacturing sector an official actually did ask why the taxpayer should be expected to pay for a company manager's new car! Such questions, asked freely by officials, reveal a woeful lack of appreciation of the needs and aims of business. No wonder, then, that the business community feels that the critical eye of the average bureaucrat is simply not on the right target. The general pre-occupation is with saving money by not parting with it without a struggle, but there is no corresponding enthusiasm for making money and generating wealth. The fact that there are more business start-ups every year than ever before is misleading. Most of them are one-person exercises in self-employment, adding nothing to the country's wealth generating base.

Another striking example of how government officials think in the wrong direction occured during the research for this book. When asked for information for inclusion in the book, the head of one government department's information division professed to be 'astonished' that information should be requested for a book which would make a profit for the publisher. This same official is overseeing a busy Whitehall press office issuing press releases on a regular basis to the newspapers which, as we know, are among the most profit led enterprises in existence. The sad conclusion we must draw from attitudes like this is that the pursuit of profit is somehow not the government's concern. But there is a powerful argument for saying that it should be and that, in the instance cited here, the information being requested should *only* have been supplied if it would in some way profit the users.

The relationship between business and government also suffers when double standards are applied in dealing with complaints from industry. In 1990, a small publishing house specialising in drama complained to the government that the a major subsidised theatre had formed a joint venture to publish theatre books with a privately-owned publisher which meant that, in a sense, the public sector was going into business, competing against the private sector in an area where there was no gap in the market. When asked to investigate, the Department of Employment, which deals with small firms policy, maintained that the theatre was justified in forming the joint venture so that it could 'realise the market potential of its own name in print'. Since the theatre was said not to be putting money into the project, but only its patronage, it was considered that no disadvantage was being caused to small publishers in the field affected by the joint venture. In other words, the spirit of the competition rules can be disregarded if the letter of the rules can be circumvented by bureaucratic re-interpretation, and this from a government which has sought to privatise anything that could be privatised.

Single Market information

In principle, the government's Single Market information drive may be commendable. There are many publications of use to business, particularly those available from the Department of Industry concerning technical standards and EC research and development programmes. But a better business sense in Whitehall would have avoided wastage caused by the fact that the 1990 edition of the DTI's full colour information pack on research and development programmes was published shortly before a major reorganisation within the department's research and technology-related divisions. Within a matter of a few weeks, the publication was out of date, a substantial number of the contacts listed having been changed.

More fundamentally amiss, however, is the failure to provide a focal point for European business enquiries which the introduction of the 1992 Hotline cannot disguise. In the 1970s the DTI ran an EEC Information Unit which, rather like the Hotline today, was staffed by a team of people answering enquiries from business about the European Community. In attempts to cut the cost of the civil service — on the surface a commendable aim — the incoming Conservative government ordered across-the-board staff cuts in Whitehall. The trouble was that departmental managers were allowed a great deal of discretion as to which parts of their operation would be trimmed down. The EEC Information Unit was effectively disbanded. All the staff were dispersed to other duties but, because it was seen as being politically unacceptable to abolish the unit altogether, the telephone number remained open to callers by means of an answering machine on the desk of the EC news correspondent of the DTI's *British Business* magazine.

The rationale for this decision was that, since the number of calls received had dwindled to only a few each day, business people had learned all they needed to learn about the EC. The idea that government should actually try to further stimulate interest in doing business in Europe did not even enter the discussion. Thus, when the Single Market initiative was launched, the DTI found itself lacking a suitable enquiry service. The 1992 Hotline, staffed mainly by non-civil servants, was introduced and hailed as a triumph, having received some 100,000 calls within a year. The inescapable truth, however, is that, while the privately run

Hotline may reflect current privatisation policy, it deprives the DTI of an opportunity to cultivate an EC business 'intelligence' unit within its own ranks, serving as link between government and industry, a link which would earn the respect of industry and one through which government and business could genuinely work together to make Britain make a profit in Europe.

8 Training the Workforce

Investing in the development of human resources

Peter Morgan

Creating a workforce that is equipped to meet the demands of business and industry will be one of Britain's major challenges throughout the 1990s and into the next century. For the next twenty years the shortage of people with skills will be a key problem in both traditional and modern high technology industries and, if Britain is to compete successfully in the world, it is vital that the problem is recognised by business and attacked with vigour.

The opening of markets across Europe will bring great opportunities for business, but also fierce competition. The Institute of Directors (IOD) sees the development of human resources — both the individual employee and the workforce as a whole — as the key factor in the ability of companies to sieze the opportunities and meet the challenges. We see the whole nation providing the weaponry in the global economic war but, at present, our armies are seriously underequipped.

There are no limitations on armies in this war. There are no restrictions, either on the number of citizens a nation chooses to put into the economic battlefield, or on the training and technology to be given to its economic 'warriors'. How many we have, and how well equipped they are, is up to us. But, in making these decisions, we need a national commitment to improving education, vocational training and the devlopment of skills. Such a commitment requires employers to stop looking at training as a cost and start regarding it as an indispensable investment. It means a commitment to the continuous training and development of employees throughout their working lives. The present sorry state of education and training in Britain, however, leaves us to confront panzer divisions with the home guard.

Some of our competitors are disturbingly professional about these issues. The West Germans in business behave like the East Germans do in sport. They pick their players while they are still at school and coach them meticulously until they are old enough to compete. They concentrate on developing technical skills and every schoolchild gets a good grounding in other languages. Not surprisingly, the West Germans win about as many enterprise medals as the East Germans win Olympic golds. Britain's failure to equip its workforce with vocational skills is highlighted in the conclusions given by Professor Richard Rose in a recent paper on youth training in which he says:

> 'Although millions of Britons are as well qualified for their work as their German counterparts, Germany has more qualified workers today. If one compares the proportion of the workforce with either a vocational or an

educational qualification then, even after accounting for small differences in national populations, Germany has at least six million more qualified workers in its labour force than does Britain. If qualifications are defined in terms of vocational qualifications alone, then Germany has at least ten million more qualified workers than does Britain'.

These startling numbers do not bode well for Britain's success in the global economic war. Therefore, as decision makers, we must consider the strategic technological choices facing UK Plc which have an important bearing on our attitude to employee development and education in a wider sense; and, as business leaders, we must get involved in improving the calibre of the workforce. This means we must become better employers.

Business has two choices. On the one hand, there is the high technology, high added value, high profit margin business, staffed by highly trained and skilled people. On the other hand, there is the lower technology, lower added value, competing on cost, squeezed margin business, staffed by low-skilled people. Business must assess where their products and services fall in this value added train, bearing in mind the fact that the chain will undergo radical shifts of balance as European markets are opened up under the EC's Single Market programme. The differential will always be the quality of workers.

The National Institute of Economic and Social Research has carried out a number of studies to examine the technological alternatives. The studies have shown that the product complexities of French and German businesses are often beyond the skill levels of their British counterparts. In the clothing industry, for example, the higher added value achieved by qualified operators results in an expanding German industry, despite high pay levels. By contrast, the British clothing industry competes with cheap labour in developing countries at a lower technological level — and is still contracting.

In an enterprise culture we look to our Boards of Directors to develop the strategies to ensure that our companies survive, change and grow more profitable. We know that strategic survival requires an aggressive readiness to accept and accelerate technological change and, in parallel with that change, a continuing investment in training and human resource development. Responsible Boards, concerned about survival and growth, need to be prepared for four different investments in training in the 1990s, which are:

☐ Partnerships with schools

☐ Provision of vocational training

☐ Basic adult education for the lost generation in the on-stream workforce

☐ Technological retraining

Partnership with schools

These partnerships are now quite widespread, having been led by Industry Year, with the work shadowing programmes initiated by the IOD and the Department of Trade and Industry (DTI). Since then, they have been maintained formally within TVEI (Training and Vocational Education Initiative), and informally under local arrangements across the country. The important point about employer involvement at school level is that it provides an opportunity to help young people develop their attitudes, aspirations and aptitudes. It also encourages teachers to try and understand and appreciate how business works. School experience is the foundation of everything that follows.

Schoolchildren should be taught to clearly understand that attitudes and aptitudes developed at school provide the basis for their economic performance throughout life. Therefore, in establishing a stronger vocational content in the school curriculum, we should look for two specific effects; first, higher staying-on rates and, second, for those who do leave school earlier, positive decisions to go into jobs with vocational training. If we do not encourage young people at school to aim for vocational qualifications, we will continue to dissipate our human capital, consigning young brains to the scrap heap.

Vocational training

They key initiative in vocational training is the introduction of Training and Enterprise Councils (TECs) which will assume responsibility for delivering local training programmes. TECs are not yet proven, but the movement is gathering momentum. IOD members are enthusiastic TEC supporters and we encourage all businesses to become involved with their local TEC. We believe it will be a worthwhile investment. The function of TECs is described in the *Contacts* section later in this chapter.

Investment in the lost generation
There are workers, already in the workforce, who do not possess either an academic or vocational qualification. Given that eight out of ten members of the workforce in the year 2,000 are already at work now, and given that technology will be two more generations advanced in ten years time, there is an uncontestable case for adult education of the existing workforce, in order to build the base skills sufficient to handle future technology. It will not be possible to fill this gap with new hires alone. Companies should be looking to offer their employees part-time education, not just in areas directly relevant to their particular job, but in basic all-round skills — mathematics, languages, writing capabilities. This will provide a flexible workforce, adaptable to the changing needs of a business.

Workforce training

Logically following on from the need to create an adaptable workforce out of the existing, largely unqualified workforce, there is a need to train our workforce to master new technology and new marketing patterns which, together, sustain a company's ability to add value and maintain profit margins. This means introducing training programmes at all levels and in all areas of a business. It is not simply a question of retraining machine workers to operate new equipment, or educating the workforce to use advanced computer technology. Retraining also involves making the salesforce aware of the different national markets across Europe, as well as ensuring that negotiators are fluent in relevant languages, particular French and German.

Of the four investments mentioned here, this is the easiest to justify and commit to. It also the hardest to achieve, unless the three other investments have been made. Currently, thirty per cent of employees admit to never having had any sort of training at work. Of those who had an induction course on taking up a job, seventy per cent have received no further training.

There is a downward spiral resulting from this lack of training. The UK is in a viscious circle in many, but not all, industry sectors. Low average skills in the workforce encourage the adoption of low-tech production processes which require low levels of training, exacerbating the skills shortage.

There is a simple equation in the end; standard of living expectations in Britain are too high to enable us to compete with the cheap labour of the Pacific Basin countries — and, indeed, Eastern European countries. If we are to maintain our standard of living, we must compete with the higher added value businesses of Germany, France, Scandinavia, the USA and Japan. If we fail, British industry will be squeezed out through the middle. As stated earlier in this chapter, the time has come for boardrooms to stop seeing training as a cost and to start regarding it as a vital investment for the future survival of their businesses, an investment which is indispensable if Britain is to hold its place as a first world industrial power.

CONTACTS

Sources of information on training schemes are widely dispersed throughout the higher education system, schools, industry training organisations, examining bodies, government training agencies and local training contacts, such as chambers of commerce, employer groups, awarding bodies and trade associations. There are also a number of on-line databases offering speedy access to details of the vast number of courses available.

Recent moves to co-ordinate training programmes at local level have led to the introduction of a network of Training Enterprise Councils (TECs) which, when fully established, will assume overall responsibility for delivering local training programmes and disseminating information on local training opportunities. Individual TECs may elect to work in parallel with existing contacts, such as LENs (Local Employer Networks) and TAPS (Training Access Points), or eventually subsume these activities within their own organisation. The largest part of the training budget administered by the Training Agency will go to the TECs. Therefore, other local training support groups may choose to join the TEC, rather than remain self-financing.

At national level, the Department of Employment's Training Agency will continue to act as a focal point for enquiries. Since the range of contacts is so wide, the following list of contacts is intended as a preliminary guide into the complex network of vocational and employment training programmes, individual training courses and the many training bodies. Companies seeking to introduce training in their workforce prior to the establishment of TEC in their locality, are advised to contact the local area office of The Training Agency (formerly the Manpower Services Commission) which will be listed in the local telephone directory. Enquirers can be guided into the training system through any of the following types of organisation:

☐ Training Agency area offices

☐ Skills Training Agency Skillcentres

☐ Industry Training Boards (ITBs)

☐ Non-Statutory Industry Training Organisations (ITOs)

- Awarding bodies or professional examining bodies

- Higher education institutes

- Lead Industry Bodies

- Training and Enterprise Councils (TECs)

- Local Employer Networks (LENs)

- On-line databases (eg. TAP, MARIS-NET, ECCTIS 2000)

- Other advisory bodies

- Training directories

European Centre for the Development of Vocational Training (CEDEFOP)

CEDEFOP is a European Community institution, set up in 1975 to promote the development of vocational training throughout the EC member states, with the overall objective of creating a better European labour force. Its Management Board comprises representatives of the European Commission, workers' organisations, employers' organisations and governments. The organisation's activities are wide-ranging, but basically falling into three main areas — the provision of information on vocational training developments, research and planning for vocational initiatives in member states, and intra-EC consultation. CEDEFOP's regular, free, publications include *CEDEFOP News* and *CEDEFOP-Flash*. However, the organisation publishes a range of publications and documents, free and for sale, as listed in its catalogue. The free periodicals may also be obtained from the European Commission's information offices.

European Centre for the Development of
Vocational Training (CEDEFOP)
Bundesallee 22
1000 Berlin 15
Tel: (49) 30 88 41 20
Fax: (49) 30 884 12 222
Telex: 184163 EUCEN D

The Training Agency

The Training Agency is the national training authority, replacing the Manpower Services Commission, and operating through a network of some 60 area offices throughout the country. The Training Agency's basic aims are:

- To encourage employers to develop the skills and experience of employees of all ages

- To provide and encourage training for school-leavers

- To help the long term unemployed acquire skills and experience to help them to find regular employment

- To help the education system become more relevant to working life and more responsive to changing demands and opportunities in the labour market

☐   To ensure that the distinctive needs of the self-employed and small firms for training, counselling and other support initiatives, are properly met.

Training Agency programmes fall into two groups. First, there are the programmes and awards which will continue to be run on a national basis by the Training Agency. These include the National Training Awards , the Technical and Vocational Education Inititiative (TVEI), and COMPACTS . The COMPACTS scheme is employer linked and takes it name from the "compact" between schools and local employers, guaranteeing school-leavers jobs. Information on Lead Industry Bodies working to establish national workplace standards can also be obtained from the Training Agency. The second group of programmes concentrates on locally delivered training, adapted to local needs. Local schemes include New Youth Training , Employment Training and Business Growth Training .

Information on all Training Agency programmes can be obtained from local Training Agency area offices, listed in telephone directories. The National Training Enquiry Point (see below) also provides details of local Training Agencies and other contacts. Eventually, however, local TECs, when fully operational, will deliver these programmes and provide information.

The Training Agency
National Training Enquiry Point
Moorfoot
Sheffield S1 4PQ
Tel: (0742) 594317/594318

Skills Training Agency (STA)

The Skills Training Agency, a branch of the Training Agency, has established a network of Skillcentres providing technical training for workers. Employees can attend courses at Skillcentres or at their employer's premises, through the STA's Mobile Training service. Information can be obtained by calling Freephone Skills Training Agency or from local Skillcentres, Training Agency area offices, and STA's head office.

Skills Training Agency
Skills House
Moorfoot
Sheffield S1 4PQ
Tel: Freephone Skills Training Agency
Fax: (0742) 597096

Training and Enterprise Councils (TECs)

A network of TECs is being set up over a period of five years. The councils are headed and controlled mainly by senior managers drawn from the private sector, whose task is to encourage private investment in improvements in all aspects of vocational education and training. Sums of public money, plus staff from The Training Agency area offices, will assist the establishment the TECS. As described in the *Training in Britain* series of reports (see below) "TECs will both deliver government training and enterprise initiatives and promote and direct private sector investment in training and enterprise. To support these activities, TECs will need to analyse relevant trends in the local labour market, draw up a plan containing measurable objectives and set about building relationships with key interest groups". Details of TEC locations can be obtained from the National Training Enquiry Point (see under Training Agency, above), or from Training Agency area offices.

Local Employer Networks (LENs)

Over 100 Local Employer Networks have been established throughout the UK, many linked to local Chambers of Commerce. With the introduction of the TEC network, however, LENs may eventually be absorbed and funded by local TECs. Some may choose to remain independent and eventually become self-financing, working in parallel with a TEC. Although initially funded by the Training Agency for two years, LENs must, after the first two years, become self-financing through subscription charges or fees for services provided to local industry, if they are to continue to operate independently.

Specifically, LENs offer advice to employers on local labour market developments and details of available training courses. They may also carry out surveys and training projects for local industries or individual companies. The LENs project was developed jointly by the former Manpower Services Commission (now The Training Agency), the Confederation of British Industry, and the Association of British Chambers of Commerce. The overall aim is to involve employers in the planning and delivery of vocational education and training at local level. For information contact local TEC offices, Training Agency area Offices or:

The Training Agency
Moorfoot
Sheffield S1 4PQ
Tel: (0742) 594205

PICKUP

The Department of Education and Science PICKUP (Professional, Industrial and Commercial Updating) programme of short courses, in-house training, distance learning and modules run by universities, polytechnics and colleges. The scheme, now widely used by employers, was launched in 1982 by the Department of Education and Science (DES) at a time when the connection between training and business success was becoming increasingly apparent. A recent national survey showed that in the UK around 750,000 people boosted their skills in one year through PICKUP training courses at universities, colleges, polytechnics and other bodies, such as Industry Training Boards. The DES aims to increase this number threefold by the end of 1992. Information on local PICKUP training provision can be obtained from:

DES/PICKUP Liaison Office
Department of Education and Science
Elizabeth House
York Road
London SE1 7PH
Tel: (071) 934 9670
Fax: (071) 934 0872

DES/PICKUP North East and Cumbria Office
Council for Further Education
The Old Medical School
University of Newcastle-upon-Tyne
Queen Victoria Road
Newcastle-upon-Tyne NE1 7RU
Tel: (091) 261 0851
Fax: (091) 261 0857

DES/PICKUP North West Regional Office
PICKUP Office
Woodlands Centre
Southport Road
Chorley
Lancashire PR7 1QR
Tel: (02572) 75474
Fax: (02572) 60583

DES/PICKUP Yorkshire and Humberside Regional Office
PICKUP Office
YHAFHE
Bowling Green Terrace
Leeds LS11 9SX
Tel: (0532) 438634
Fax: (0532) 446239

DES/PICKUP West Midlands Regional Office
PICKUP Office
Wolverhampton Polytechnic
Compton Park Site
Compton Road West
Wolverhampton WV5 9DX
Tel: (0902) 714771
Fax: (0902) 23864

DES/PICKUP East Midlands Regional Office
PICKUP Office
EMFEC
Robins Wood House
Robins Wood Road
Aspley
Nottingham NG8 3NH
Tel: (0602) 298298
Fax: (0602) 299698

DES/PICKUP Thames Valley and North West London Regional Office
PICKUP Office
Oxford Polytechnic
Headington
Oxford OX3 0BP
Tel: (0865) 60254
Fax: (0865) 741150

DES/PICKUP Eastern Counties Regional Office
PICKUP Office
Unit 50-51
St John's Innovation Centre
Cowley Road
Cambridge CB4 4WS
Tel: (0223) 421075
Fax: (0223) 420844

DES/PICKUP South West Regional Office
PICKUP Office
Bristol Polytechnic
Coldharbour Lane
Frenchay, Bristol BS16 1QY
Tel: (0272) 659075
Fax: (0272) 652163

DES/PICKUP South East Regional Office
PICKUP Office
Technology Transfer Centre
Silwood Park
Buckhurst Road
Ascot, Berkshire SL5 7PW
Tel: (0990) 27418
Fax: (0990) 27419

DES/PICKUP London Regional Office
Room 1/67
Department of Education and Science
Elizabeth House
York Road
London SE1 7PH
Tel: (071) 934 0838/9429
Fax: (071) 934 1703

PICKUP Office for Wales
Polytechnic of Wales
Pontypridd
Mid Glamorgan CF37 1DL
Tel: (0443) 493696
Fax: (0443) 404495

PICKUP Office for Scotland
PICKUP Operations Unit
Scottish Education Department
43 Jeffrey Street
Edinburgh EH1 1DN
Tel: (031) 244 5426

Macmillan/PICKUP National Training Directory

(See *Major Training Publications*, page 152)

PICKUP Europe Unit
The PICKUP Europe Unit encourages the development of training and updating services by further and higher education institutions in response to new business needs created by the completion of the Single Market. The unit's main objectives are to:

☐ Raise awareness of the training implications of the Single Market.

☐ Encourage the further and higher education sector to deliver appropriate training provision to industry.

☐ Provide information and publicise good practice applicable to the Single Market.

Further information:

Department of Education and Science
Elizabeth House
York Road
London SE1 7PH
Tel: (071) 934 0881/9000
Fax: (071) 934 9082
Telex: 23171 DESLON

Financial support
Employers may qualify for financial support for PICKUP courses. Support is available from various sources, national or local. A guide to the sources of financial assistance, *Paying for Training*, is available from:

The Planning Exchange
CopyCraft
74 York Street
Glasgow G2 8JX
Tel: (041) 332 8541
Fax: (031) 332 8277

Industry Training Organisations (ITOs)
Training organisations in specific industry sectors can advise companies on their training needs and provide details of sector-related training courses. They carry out similar broad functions of the Industry Training Boards (see below), most of which were abolished under the Industrial Training Act 1982. The work of the 120 ITOs in existence covers 100 sectors of the economy and 37 per cent of the civilian workforce, according to the report *Training in Britain* (see page 153). ITOs raise their income by subscription and fees for their services. A booklet listing ITOs which are members of the National Council of Industry Training Organisations (NCITO) is available from:

The Training Agency
IB5/Room E627
Moorfoot
Sheffield S1 4PQ
Tel: (0742) 594205

National Council of Industry Training Organisations (NCITO)
7 Hottles Green, Shepreth
Nr Royston, Hertfordshire SG8 6PR
Tel: (0763) 263060 Fax: (0763) 263074

Industry Training Boards

There are seven statutory Industry Training Boards (ITBs) carrying out similar functions to the Industry Training Organisations (ITOs) above.

Clothing and Allied Products Industry Training Board (CAPITB)
80 Richardshaw Lane
Pudsey
Leeds LS28 6BN
Tel: (0532) 393355
Fax: (0532) 393155

Clothing Industry Training Board (Northern Ireland) (CLITBNI)
Swinson House
Glenmount Road
Newtownabbey BT36 7LH
Tel: (0232) 365171
Fax: (0232) 862912

Construction Industry Training Board (CITB)
Bircham Newton Training Centre
King's Lynn
Norfolk PE31 6RH
Tel: (0553) 776677
Fax: (0533) 692226

Construction Industry Training Board (Northern Ireland) (CITBNI)
17 Dundrod Road
Nutts Corner
Crumlin BT29 4SR
Tel: (0232) 825466
Fax: (0232) 825693

Engineering Industry Training Board (EITB)
PO Box 48
41 Clarendon Road
Watford
Hertfordshire WD1 1HS
Tel: (0923) 38441
Fax: (0923) 56086

Engineering Industry Board (Northern Ireland) (EITBNI)
Swinson House
Glenmount Road
Newtownabbey BT36 7LH
Tel: (0232) 365171
Fax: (0232) 862912

Hotel and Catering Training Board (HCTB)
Hotel and Catering Training Company
International House
High Street
Ealing
London W5 5DB
Tel: (081) 579 2400
Fax: (081) 840 6217

Offshore Petroleum Industry Training Board (OPITB)
Blackness Avenue
Altens
Aberdeen AB1 4PG
Tel: (0224) 895504
Fax: (0224) 837221

Plastics Processing Industry Training Board (PPITB)
Coppice House
Halesfield 7
Telford
Shropshire TF7 4NA
Tel: (0952) 587020
Fax: (0952) 582065

Road Transport Industry Training Board (RTITB)
Capitol House
Empire Way
Wembley
Middlesex HA9 0NG
Tel: (081) 902 8880
Fax: (081) 903 4113

Training and education advisory bodies

There are a great many sector-related advisory and examining bodies which are listed in training directories (see below). Information on the Certificate of Pre-Vocational Education (CPVE) programme can be obtained from the City and Guilds of London Institute and the Business and Technician Education Council. The following is a selection of general advisory bodies in education and training.

It is not exhaustive, but should serve as a useful introduction to the vocational education and training information network.

Association for Education and Training Technology (AETT)
Centre for Continuing Education
City University
Northampton Square
London EC1V 0HB
Tel: (071) 253 4399
Fax: (071) 250 0837

British Association for Commercial and Industrial Education (BACIE)
16 Park Crescent
London W1N 4AP
Tel: (071) 636 5351
Fax: (071) 323 1132
Telex: 268350 ICSA G

British Institute of Management (BIM)
Africa House
64-78 Kingsway
London WC2B 6BL
Tel: (071) 405 3456
Fax: (071) 430 2477

and

Management House
Cottingham Road
Corby
Northamptonshire NN17 1TT
Tel: (0536) 204222
Tel: (0536) 201651

Business and Technician Education Council (BTEC)
Central House
Upper Woburn Place
London WC1H 0HH
Tel: (071) 388 3288
Fax: (071) 387 6068

City and Guilds of London Institute (CGLI)
46 Britannia Street
London WC1X 9RG
Tel: (071) 278 2468
Fax: (071) 278 9460

The Industrial Society
Training and Advisory Services
48 Bryanston Square
London W1H 7LN
Tel: (071) 262 2401
Fax: (071) 405 1790

Institute of Export
Export House
64 Clifton Street
London EC2A 4HB
Tel: (071) 247 9812
Fax: (071) 377 5343

Institute of Personnel Management (IPM)
IPM House
35 Camp Road
Wimbledon
London SW19 4UX
Tel: (081) 946 9100
Fax: (081) 947 2570

Institute of Training and Development
Marlow House
Institute Road
Marlow, Buckinghamshire SL7 1BN
Tel: (0628) 890123
Fax: (0628) 890208

London Chamber of Commerce Examinations Board
Marlowe House
Station Road
Sidcup, Kent DA15 7BJ
Tel: (081) 302 0261
Fax: (081) 302 4169

National Council of Industry Training Organisations (NCITO)
7 Hottles Green
Shepreth, Nr Royston
Hertfordshire SG8 6PR
Tel: (0763) 263060
Fax: (0763) 263074

National Council for Vocational Qualifications (NCVQ)
222 Euston Road
London NW1 2BZ
Tel: (071) 387 9898
Fax: (071) 387 0978

National Institute of Adult Continuing Education (NIACE)
19b De Montford Street
Leicester LE1 7GE
Tel: (0533) 551451
Fax: (0533) 854514

National Institute of Economic and Social Research
2 Dean Trench Street
London SW1P 3HE
Tel: (071) 222 7665
Fax: (071) 222 1435

Royal Society for the Encouragement of Arts, Manufactures and Commerce (RSA)
8 John Adam Street
London WC2N 6EZ
Tel: (071) 930 5115
Fax: (071) 839 5805

Scottish Vocational Educational Council (SCOTVEC)
Hanover House
24 Douglas Street
Glasgow G2 7NQ
Tel: (041) 248 7900
Fax: (041) 242 2244

On-line information services

A number of on-line databases have been developed through which information on training programmes, learning materials and a range of other training-related details can be accessed. General information on training database services can be obtained from:

Association of Database Services in Education and Training
HMS President
Victoria Embankment
Blackfriars, London EC4Y 0HJ

Training Access Points (TAPs)

TAPS is a countrywide system of computerised databases, still under review, through which information on local and national training programmes can be accessed. Databases may also be used to access information on other education and training databases, such as PICKUP, MARIS-NET and ECCTIS 2000 via British Telecom's PRESTEL. Currently TAPs databases may be housed in high street locations such as local libraries and job centres. A network of TAPs International European agents focuses on opportunities to promote British education and training overseas. Management of TAPs may fall to local TECs in due course. Information is also available on CD-ROM compact discs. The range of TAPs information includes:

☐ Details of work-related education and training for all kinds of skills at every level, including full-time, part-time, informal learning at home and at work, local and national.

☐ Access to information through computer-backed TAP information points located in job centres, libraries and other high street locations, plus mobile TAPs which visit employers' premises.

☐ Support in assembling learning programmes which meet individual or company requirements.

The TAP Unit
The Training Agency
Moorfoot, Sheffield S1 4PQ
Tel: (0742) 597347/597344 (TAP locations)
Tel: (0742) 597340 (TAP International)

TAP Computer Development
Learning Systems and Access Branch
St Mary's House,
C/o Moorfoot, Sheffield S1 4PQ
Information on software and TAP delivery systems. Tel: (0742) 597333

MARIS-NET and Directory of Training

MARIS-NET is an on-line, mainly distance learning, information service covering opportunities in vocational training and education operated by Materials and Resources Information Service (MARIS) Net Ely Ltd. Information across a number of databases is available to subscribers and includes facts on open learning materials, management training, training resource materials, self study materials, CBT and IAV, private and public sector short courses, training films and videos, training services, and hotels and conference venues. Hosted databases include the PICKUP directory of short courses (see below) and the Training Agency's Training Development Information Service (TDIS).

> *Directory of Training* publishes training information directories, including:
> *Directory of Computer Training*
> *Directory of Management Training*
> *Directory of Technology Based Training*

A magazine *IT Training* is also published. For further information on MARIS-NET and *Directory of Training* contact:

MARIS On-line Ltd
1 St Mary's Street
Ely
Cambridgeshire CB7 4ER
Tel: (0353) 661284
Fax: (0353) 663279

ECCTIS 2000

ECCTIS is a national computerised service providing information on courses in further and higher education and their entry requirements. The database holds information on around 60,000 courses in over 700 institutions, mainly universities, polytechnics and colleges, throughout the UK at the following levels:

☐ Postgraduate taught courses, first degree courses, and higher national diploma and certificate courses.

☐ Further education courses; eg. City and Guilds, Royal Society of Arts.

The information held covers courses of more than six weeks full-time, or equivalent part-time duration, leading to recognised qualifications (except school-leaving qualifications, such as the GCSE and Scottish Certificate of Education), plus details of vacant places available on degree level courses in universities, polytechnics and colleges (August and September only). ECCTIS information on courses includes the following details:

Course title
Duration
Mode of study (eg. full or part-time)
Any associated professional qualification awarded on completion of the course
Course normal entry requirements
Name, address and telephone number of the institution
Course structure and content

Further information:

ECCTIS 2000 Ltd
Fulton House
Jessop Avenue
Cheltenham
Gloucestershire GL50 3SH
Tel: (0242) 518724
Fax: (0242) 225914
PRESTEL 888292025

National Training Index
National Training Index operates a database and publishes the major directory in the training field, *National Training Index*.

National Training Index
25-26 Poland Street
London W1V 3DB
Tel: (071) 494 0596
Fax: (071) 494 1268

Major training publications

Macmillan/PICKUP National Training Directory
For details of the Department of Education and Science PICKUP scheme see under *PICKUP* in this chapter. The *Macmillan/PICKUP National Training Directory* contains details of over 20,000 work-related training courses and training opportunities available throughout the UK. It also includes details of courses run by private sector organisations. Courses are listed by subject and, within each heading, training venues are listed under fourteen geographical areas. The directory is divided into 18 main categories:

Business, management
Languages
Law, politics, economics
Computers, electrical and electronic engineering
Engineering production, industrial design
Architecture, construction
Minerals, materials, fabrics
Transport services, vehicle engineering
Sciences, mathematics
Agriculture, horticulture, animal care
Health, personal care
Environment security, health and safety
Food, catering, leisure, tourism
Culture, society, education
Arts, crafts
Communication, self help
Music, performing arts
Sports, games, recreation

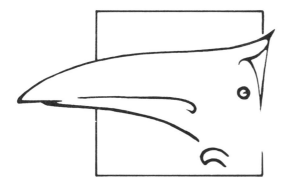

EDDINGTON & POETON PRODUCTIONS Ltd

Specialists in

EC Video Communications

13, Knightsbridge Green, London SW1X 7QL.
Telephone: 071-581 4393 & 071-589 1945   Fax: 071-581 3529
7 Rue Franklin 8-1040 Bruxelles.

The two volume directory (1,500 pp, ISBN 0-333-539133, price £75.00 plus £2.00 postage and packing) is published by Macmillan Publishers Ltd, under licence from Guildford Educational Services Ltd, and the latest information can be accessed via PRESTEL (key in *8881881# or *PICKUP#) and the TAP database (see page 150). To purchase the directory from the distributors contact:

Globe Book Services Ltd
Macmillan Academic and Professional
Reference
Stockton House
1 Melbourne Place, London WC2B 4LF
Tel: (071) 379 4687
Fax: (071) 379 4980

Training in Britain survey

Training in Britain is a survey of funding, activities and attitudes in training, prepared for The Training Agency in 1989 and published by Her Majesty's Stationery Office. The main report and a set of four studies can be purchased at government bookshops. The main report (99pp, ISBN 0-11-361280-X, price £10.00) gives a broad overview. A series of research reports (ISBN 0-11-361279-6, price £20) includes:

Training in Britain: Employers Activities
> Information on the extent to which employers train, and why they train.
> Deloitte/IFF Research Ltd

Training in Britain: Employers Perspectives on Human Resources
> A study of how employers reach decisions on training
> studies (see also Industrial Training Organisations, above). Coopers & Lybrand/Professor Pettigrew, Dr Hendry and Dr Sparrow of the University of Warwick.

Training in Britain: Market Perspectives
> How employers and providers of training interact at a local level
> The Training Agency/Institute of Manpower Studies/Research Surveys of Great Britain and others.

Training in Britain: Individuals' Perspectives
> Individual adults' experience of and attitudes towards training
> Malcolm Rigg of the Policy Studies Institute.

Other reports in the series available on request from ISCO 5 (ISB), The Paddock, Frizinghall BD9 4HD are:

Training in Britain: Providers' Perspectives
Training in Britain: Private Providers
Training in Britain: Market Perspectives — the London Case Study
Training in Britain: Employers' Perspectives Case Studies
Training in Britain: The Benefits of Training
Training in Britain: An Overview of the Evaluation of the Net Benefits of Training
Training in Britain: Funding for Young People — a Literature Review
The Costs and Benefits of Training: An Annotated Bibliography
The Funding of Vocational Education and Training — a Consultation Document
Background Note No. 1
> About the funding study
Background Note No. 2
> Some early research findings.

National Training Index

The National Training Index (price £650.00 annual subscription, including updates) provides information and advice on business training courses (external and in-company), speakers, correspondence courses, training films, open learning and CBT packages. The Index is financed and supported by over 1,000 industrial and commercial companies in the UK, as well as by government departments, local government and government corporations. Information contained in the directory includes:

Details of over 9,000 business courses in the UK
Correspondence courses
Company training schemes
Training films
Open learning packages
CBT packages
Course organisers

National Training Index
25-26 Poland Street, London W1V 3DB
Tel: (071) 494 0596
Fax: (071) 494 1268

The Training Directory

Published by Kogan Page in association with the British Association for Commercial and Industrial Education (BACIE), the 450-page directory reviews all training initiatives and lists contacts in all areas of training provision in the UK. At the relatively low price of £20.00 it offers employers an easy-to-read survey of the complex and diffuse training network, and an economical route to training providers. The main contents cover:

Providers of training courses and consultancy
Government training initiatives
Suppliers of training materials
Training information sources
Training organisations and institutions
Conference venues

Kogan Page Ltd
120 Pentonville Road
London N1 9JN
Tel: (071) 278 0433
Fax: (071) 837 6348

International Yearbook of Educational and Training Technology

Published by Kogan Page (above) in association with the Association for Education and Training Technology (AETT).

Directory of Training

This is a 4-volume directory covering computer training, technology-based training and management training, published by Training Information Network Ltd (price £135.000 plus £5.00 postage and packing).

Training Information Network Ltd
51 High Street
Ruislip
Middlesex HA4 7BG
Tel: (0895) 622112
Fax: (0895) 621582

CBI 1992 Initiative

Employment and Training is a study of human resources which the Confederation of British Industry (CBI) emphasises are crucial to successful corporate planning for doing business in the Single Market. Prepared by Blue Arrow Plc as part of a major series of publications commissioned by the CBI under its 1992 Initiative. The book covers employment conditions, skills and qualifications, transferring skills from country to country, and ways of ensuring consistency of skills standards and quality control of the workforce. Published by Gold Arrow Publications (price £17.95 plus £1.95 postage and packing).

Gold Arrow Publications Limited
862 Garratt Lane
London SW17 0NB
Tel: (081) 682 3858
Fax: (081) 682 3859

PART FOUR

CASH FLOW
AND
PROFITS

1 Maximising Profits — I

Export risks and hidden costs

Anthony Pierce

It is now known that a high proportion of exporting companies are unaware of, or unconcerned about, the financial risks associated with exporting. Even among those companies which have built some measure of risk control into their exporting activity, the perception of the risks involved can be narrow. A CBI survey in May 1989 revealed, for example, that most smaller companies thought that currency risks were the main problem. Payment risks were hardly mentioned. General lack of concern about the financial risks inherent in exporting was also confirmed recently by the low response to attempts by the Institute of Directors and the British Institute of Management to draw members' attention to the problem. A few years ago, Midland Bank and the Simpler Trade Procedures Board quantified the losses which exporting companies incur when payment is delayed by faulty documentation. When payment delays occur, export credit insurance may expire, leaving the exporter open to an even greater risk — non-payment.

Another aspect of the risk perception problem is that risks are thought to exist only when selling in markets which are politically unstable. This is a myth. Losses associated with inadequate cost control can occur at any time, in connection with any kind of business in any market. In the Single Market, the publicity given to the removal of barriers to trade is creating a false sense of security. The Single Market programme will, of course, bring advantages to companies trading across EC frontiers, but the financial risks and hidden costs will not disappear with the abolition of legal and procedural barriers. If anything, the problem could get worse as companies scramble for position in the European marketplace. They may take with them management weaknesses which, though tolerated in the domestic market, create serious problems when competing from a distance. Poor risk and cost control is one such weakness.

The 1992 publicity has emphasised two fundamental changes which will take place in the European trading environment:

☐ Free movement of goods, services and capital

☐ Intensified competition

Meeting intensified competition in Europe is projected as the greatest overall challenge of 1992. If this is so, then the problem of hidden costs could assume major proportions. The added costs of transport, packaging and marketing in Europe need no elaboration here. Price competition is another obvious factor in the squeeze on profits. Everyone intends to confront these cost factors with determination and many companies will succeed in establishing a presence in

159

Europe. But the joy of success could be marred by unidentified costs. The key to avoiding extra costs rests with management, whether a company is large or small. Larger and expanding companies are just as vulnerable as smaller companies and managers in any size of operation experience difficulty in identifying hidden risks and costs. Many have got by so far because profits have been sufficiently high to absorb unhedged risks, with associated costs remaining hidden. But if no effort is made to identify these hidden costs, systems will not be introduced to control them.

Cost control systems are not usually precise enough to pick up differences between estimated costs and actuals. Even when controls exist, there is rarely a meaningful post mortem on anything but conspicuous differences. Inconspicuous cost variations are often overlooked, even though the cumulative effect can result in significant losses. For companies trading in the Single Market this problem could get worse, rather than better. As increased competition squeezes margins, lack of cost control, born of complacency, results in further profit erosion. Obviously, the company with a low cost base and tight controls has the best chance of surviving in the deregulated international, and intensely competitive marketplace created by the completion of the Single Market.

In risk terms, however, the EC is not a single market. It consists of a group of sovereign states, each at different stages of economic development, a Europe of diverse tastes, customs, languages, cultures, currency and geographical differences. Whatever the political pundits may say about an emergent United States of Europe or Federal Europe, full European politicial union could be a long way off. For now, and perhaps for a long time yet, every member state retains its own political, legal, and financial system. At this level, the term Single Market is misleading on three basic counts which fragment, rather than unite markets:

□ Cultural barriers

□ Competitive pressures

□ Financial risks.

These non-integrated dimensions of the Single Market are reflected in the way a customer buys, and in the way competitors sell. Britain's European competitors already appreciate these differences, having had longer experience of selling in the Single Market countries. They are already familiar with the risks, or have developed firm lines of business with known customers where the risks are minimal. But for British companies, urged by the 1992 publicity to look towards Europe, exporting to Europe for the first time can be like stepping into the unknown. Many companies will succeed, but there will be losers as well as winners. The aim of this Chapter is to alert companies to the risks.

Cultural barriers

A study carried out by Hill Samuel, the London merchant bank, for the CBI's 1992 initiative identified ways in which markets are fragmented by cultural differences. The study points out that the French, for example, want their washing machines to load from the top, while the British prefer loading from the front. Germans want high-powered machines that spin most of the dampness out of the clothes, while Italians prefer low powered machines and let the sun do the drying.

The pattern of food distribution in Germany is radically different from that in the UK because of the continuing prevalence of home deliveries in markets such as frozen foods. For this reason freezer centres have never taken off. To meet different local tastes, Nescafe markets 20 different brands of coffee under the same label. In Germany, unlike the UK, low blood pressure is regarded as a condition requiring extensive medication. In France, doctors regularly prescribe drugs for a heart/digestive condition known as "spasmophilia", the existence of which UK doctors do not even recognise. There is a multitude of such differences in culturally based local tastes and preferences which fragment the European market.

The study argues that cultural barriers will persist long after other forms of invisible trade walls have been demolished, although the gap narrows where people are most mobile and wealthy, and where business is increasingly international. As the Single Market progresses, and as the political momentum gathers to liberate East and West Europe from economic constraints, there will be little or no change in regional or national cultures. If anything, the instinct for preserving national and cultural identities will grow stronger, even though in some ways we will be functioning in a European, rather than a national context. This two-tier approach demands greater acceptance of cultural differences. Language capability is not, in itself, the be all and end all of communication in business. Succeeding in the Single European Market is as much a question of attitude as simply directing textbook, marketing skills towards Europe.

In European culture there is a strong emphasis on class distinction which influences the way business is done. The production of high quality hand made products for individual customers, rather than mass production, is one expression of class distinction in society. However, as we have seen in the past, exclusivity aimed at the top end of the market leaves the door open for companies born of low cost, mass production cultures such as Japan. Industry already fears the progress that 'newcomers' are making in expansion and greenfield sectors in the UK, ever strengthening their position in the market. These foreign-based companies are also capable of quickly moving up into the higher value added, lower volume, quality end of a market. In other words, if we do not consciously adapt products and services to diverse European cultural tastes, others will. So the company which builds cultural factors into its products, selling across a range of European cultures, against the background of legal and procedural homogeneity, may withstand competitive pressures from foreign-based competitors, characteristically skilled as they are in low-cost production and financial discipline. Viewed like this, Europe becomes a market in which controlling, or avoiding hidden costs and risks becomes a priority, not an afterthought.

Competitive pressures

Completion of the Single Market involves dismantling all technical, procedural and administrative barriers, a process which, the publicists say, heralds a golden age of opportunity as Europe unleashes its latent productive powers. Many companies, however, would prefer to forego the promise of opportunity, content with the comfortable level of business they already have. The non-tariff barriers to intra-European trade remained precisely because they made life comfortable for 'protected' companies which have grown up behind them. But the irony is, that the barriers which have protected companies in domestic markets within the EC, will not provide the same degree of protection for the same companies operating within the so-called enlarged European domestic market. The enlarged homogenous market is too big and too lucrative for foreign-based competitors to ignore. Clearly for some UK companies, ill-equipped to expand into the wider European market, demolition of the barriers will be painful as they face an onslaught from competitors both from within and outside the EC.

In the UK, the engineering sector, for example, views the removal of trade barriers as distinctly more of a threat than a challenge. A survey conducted by *The Engineer* magazine shows that many of Britain's engineers and engineering managers lack confidence in the UK's manufacturing prospects in the Single Market. More than half of those canvassed judged that French and West German companies would benefit most. A third agreed that the Single Market was more of a threat than an opportunity. Nearly half of the respondents (44 per cent) believed that other EC countries had more trade barriers to remove than Britain. So British engineering companies would not be competing with mainland European companies on a level playing field. If this is so, and it seems that it will be so in some sectors, then the argument for identifying hidden costs and risks at an early stage becomes virtually unchallengable.

Changing distribution patterns will also intensify competition in the European marketplace. Closer to home, the double edged benefit of the Channel Tunnel underlines the case for early preparation to meet competition from incoming continental suppliers. The Single Market will unite Britain and the rest of the European Community in common laws, commercial practices and trade procedures, but it is the tunnel which will cement the bond physically. It is feared, however, that the opening of the tunnel will unleash a sustained attack by continental companies on markets in the UK. The threat is particularly strong in the perishable products category, such as food or other commodities where speed of delivery is a vital competitive factor. Continental suppliers will clearly benefit from improved delivery times. So great is the advantage to continental rivals, they may even begin to service regional markets which local UK companies have traditionally regarded as being safe. This means that identifying hidden costs of financial indiscipline in the local market could be crucial. Companies can no longer afford to assume that such losses can be tolerated and unquestionably absorbed by comfortable profit margins.

Although it is widely recognised that the threat posed by increased competition does not come solely from within the Single Market, British industry has not yet reacted as positively to 1992 as their foreign-based competitors have. In another poll, this time conducted by Peat Marwick McKinlock, a majority of US executives were convinced that free trade within the European Community will present significant trade barriers to non-EC countries after 1992. Many US companies are now formulating and implementing strategies to deal with what they see as a 'fortress Europe'. There is near consensus that strategic alliances between US and EC companies will provide an answer and that, by such means, US companies must increase their manufacturing presence in Europe. US companies also believe that, to succeed in the Single Market, a pan-European strategy is needed, with investment concentrating mainly in West Germany, France and the UK; Italy, Spain and Netherlands attracting only minor investments. So smaller British companies are among those which are particularly vulnerable to market 'poaching' by aggressive foreign-based competitors.

Another method of circumventing barriers to imports from non-EC countries, favoured particularly by Japanese companies, is to transfer technology. Japanese companies will respond to 1992 and economic integration within the EC by transferring technology to their European operations in a bid to avoid international trade friction, says the Industrial Bank of Japan Review. This is achieved by shifting core production processes, design and research and development centres and nurturing local suppliers. The greatest transfers will be in the mass production industries (cars, consumer electronics, electronic parts and office equipment) where the gap between Japan and Europe is greatest. No doubt the welcome to Japanese companies in the EC will be in direct proportion to the size of their technology transfers. When the frontiers fall, some companies will get hurt. Competition will force prices down. Rationalisation across frontiers will close factories. Capital investment will migrate away from its traditional centres. Peripheral regions will atrophy. This is the scenario which is foreseen by those who stand for and promote the Single Market ideal.

At the same time, the EC states will strive to protect through various barriers their weakest industries, mainly mass-production industries, which have in the past been nurtured by national governments in monopolistic market structures. The clamour for protective quota restrictions against imports still echoes throughout Europe, even though the blunt instrument of quotas is politically unacceptable in international trade. In practical terms, however, the desire to protect national industries has resulted in the suppression of market forces which leads to an overcrowding of companies in threatened sectors.

For example, the EC's principal 1992 study group, the Cecchini committee, estimates that about 80 per cent of the EC's boilermaking capacity is surplus to requirements and that, given free competition, the number of firms could fall from 15 to four while prices fell by 20 per cent. The number of electric-locomotive makers could fall from 16 to three, with a 13 per cent price reduction. Surplus boilermakers' and locomotive-makers' jobs would vanish. Some other employment would migrate, typically to lower-wage Mediterranean countries. One economic argument which says that we should welcome such a shake-out in industry is that general consumption will rise. 'New' industrial resources which will be released by the concentration of production in cost effective locations can be diverted to meet demand currently being met by imports. The European Commission is confident that the Single Market will indeed stimulate economic growth, hold down inflation and prove a net creator of jobs. But as Cecchini puts it, the benefits can be realised only at the expense of "protected positions, be they those of companies, industries, regions or nations." While the broad economic theory may be laudable, individual companies finding themselves under threat will be fighting to stay in business. Identifying the risks and hidden costs in advance again becomes an important factor in preparing to meet competition from whichever direction and in whatever form it may come.

Economic factors

Companies will seek to analyse their strengths and weaknesses in the intensified competitive environment. Officials in the Community and the UK Government, along with the press have continually drawn attention to imperatives which companies are now beginning to seriously address. However, it is not all bad news. Some commentators maintain that medium-sized companies, for example, will not necessarily suffer at the hands of European giants, better able to operate economies of scale. Smaller companies may find the promised opportunities rather easier to come by than they first imagined. They still face increased competition but, as we are so often reminded, opportunities will increase naturally because the EC market is made up of 320 million consumers. This massive European market can be dissected into dozens of different markets. They are distinguishable for cultural reasons, as discussed above. Small and medium-sized companies can, therefore, look for what, in Euro-jargon, is their 'niche market'. Indeed some have already tried and succeeded.

Ultimately, whatever the prospects are going to be in the Single Market, company decisions will be influenced by macro-economic considerations which the Single Market programme brings into sharper focus. It is generally agreed that the main macro-economic factors are:

☐ Cost of labour.

☐ Collective bargaining: At European level this works to the disadvantage of less developed, less efficient member states which often need lower wages to offset higher productivity of richer rivals.

☐ Political attitudes: Northern Europe maintains its free-trade outlook. Southern Europe has protectionist inclinations.

In practical terms, cost control decisions are influenced by more mundane factors. They have been identified by the Department of Trade and Industry in its *Action Checklist for Business* as:

☐ Effects of competing in the wider market on the profit and loss account.

☐ Fluctuation in revenues arising from sales expansion/contraction.

☐ Increased operating costs in the Single Market: transport, distribution, rationalisation of production, certification procedures.

☐ Higher costs arising from expansion/rationalisation plans: Market protection/expansion initiatives, sales promotion, product redesign/ development.

☐ Cost of adopting different sales terms in Europe, such as 60 or 90 day open account payment.

☐ Adequacy of the balance sheet for competing in the wider market.

☐ Additional capital expenditure requirements arising from expansion of production/rationalisation and redundancies.

☐ Impact on cashflow and working capital requirements due to changes in productivity and sales patterns.

☐ Ability and cost of raising new financing, including local financing.

☐ Effectiveness of existing resources and procedures, notably existing risk and financial management.

☐ Suitability of existing systems to handle altered demand, such as foreign transactions, currency dealings and risk management, debt collection and larger volumes.

☐ Adequacy of existing risk and cost control systems.

The risks

An example of a contract in which specific risks and hidden costs have been identified is given below. However, a primary risk is incurred when management remains complacement and underestimates the strength of the forces which are coming to bear in the Single Market. Companies should be in no doubt about the revolution in internal company administration which must take place if risk and cost control is to be inculcated at every level of management.

Summary of risk background: Risks associated with trading in the Single Market are greater than companies are accustomed to on the home front. Formal corporate policies and procedures need to be established to identify and control risks and associated hidden costs which undermine profitability. Companies with a low cost base and tighter control procedures will improve their chances of survival and success. No-one can afford to ignore increased risks arising from the additional competition in their domestic market. Even when sales are confined to the home market, companies face competition from foreign-based competitors. The need to adopt suitable competitive strategies, and not just defensive strategies, to continue to trade profitably is clear.

Summary of management priorities: Management must identify risks and attach high priority to risk and associated cost control. This is hard to achieve while margins remain comfortable and risks carried are unseen or appear to be tolerable. It is wise to take action before a crisis occurs. No export contract is entirely risk free. As a matter of common sense companies rarely 'bank' all their forecast export profits. But in the Single Market, as trade barriers are eliminated, managers are beginning to recognise that the risk threshold is increasing

Risks can, in a short time, erode up to 50 per cent of export profit margins. Companies should look for ways of controlling risks and costs to maintain competitiveness and profitablity. This requires skills and experience additional to established techniques when negotiating domestic contracts. There are, of course, certain risks which are not met in the home market. But those risks which do occur in the home market may be less readily controlled. Effective financial discipline, especially risk and cost control, is vital when selling in the context of a larger European market since the traditional distinction between domestic and international trade is not so clearly defined.

Penalty of non-effective risk control

The effect on profit margins of typical export risks is illustrated by the following example of a simple, seemingly innocuous contract for a shipment valued at F.Fr2,500,000 (FOB) UK port:

Typical contract features

> Payment in French francs
> French franc foreign exchange sold forward 6-months
> Payment secured by Irrevocable Letter of Credit
> On-demand performance bond agreed
> Non-payment risk insured with ECGD
> Goods tailor-made for buyer

165

There is nothing abnormal about these assumptions. Many exporters would be glad to sign a contract on these terms. However, as few export contracts perform exactly as intended, a risk has been introduced to illustrate its effect on hidden costs and profit erosion. With a contract like this, it only takes a buyer to request a delay in shipment to incur the following risks:

Financial risks

Payment date delayed — cashflow suffers

Working capital absorbed longer until payment received

Obligation to utilise more expensive banking lines

Interest rates may rise and, therefore, the cost of funding production stocks

Cost of funding foreign exchange rollovers could increase if French Franc strengthens and/or Sterling and Fr.Franc interest rates diverge

Irrevocable letter of credit expires — costs incurred for extension

Commercial risks

The FOB (Freight on Board) terms (where buyer responsible for arranging transport) do not permit constructive delivery by exporter into store so a warehouse receipt cannot be substituted for the transport document to obtain payment

No suspension or termination clause applies, so buyer can call goods forward at own convenience

Risk of losing production space

Impact of inflation pushes up production costs, a disadvantage because there is no price escalation clause

Cost of production suspension and re-start up

On-demand bond extension costs

ECGD credit insurance reviewed/extended

Cost of additional handling, protecting, storing and insuring goods already produced, not shipped, are not covered by contract

Risk of performance bond being called in if exporter does not co-operate

Legal risks

Exporter may dispute buyer's right to delay without payment or compensation

Disputes clause could be weak

Contract subject to buyer's laws and courts as there is no independent arbitration clause.

The direct financial consequences of a number of these risks can be estimated per 3-months as follows:

Cost of shortfall in cashflow 3-months at 15 per cent p.a. £9,000

Extension of bond £50

Foreign exchange rollover financing cost £100

Cost of protecting, handling, storing and insuring £250

Telexes and other communications £100

Possible legal fees in UK and buyer's country £500

Lost purchasing power on delayed payment £1,700

Cost of suspending production £2,000

Additional production start up costs £2,000

Additional costs due to inflation £1,250

TOTAL ADDITIONAL COST: £16,950.

At 10.40 francs to the pound, this is equivalent to F.Fr176,280, or 7 per cent of the contract price per 3-month delay. In this example the root of the hidden costs was twofold; delay, and the lack of an adequate remedy in the contract to prevent the exporter carrying the full cost. This would have a direct, adverse impact on cashflow, payment security, currency hedging, legal and production costs. There is no mechanism in the contract for any potential disputes to be settled easily and cheaply. The on-demand performance bond puts the buyer in a strong negotiating position.

One solution would be to maintain control of the buyer's obligation to pay for work done by using CIF (Cost, Insurance and Freight) delivery terms. In this way the exporter controls shipment and payment documents. Progress payments to secure cashflow of a tailor-made item is sensible, as are appropriate suspension and termination clauses which ensure payment for work done. Before agreeing to delay production, an agreement requiring the buyer to pick up additional costs, such as storage, protection insurance, production suspension and start up costs, is necessary. This does not normally put the performance bond at risk.

Needless to say, none of these clauses are of value if the exporter is not capable of identifying additional costs incurred by the delay. Since additional costs are incurred in unrelated functions - finance, production, commercial, legal and shipping — the exporter needs systems to identify and collate them. This requires efficient, reliable in-house communications.

Role of management

For many companies solutions to risk and hidden cost problems are not clear cut because there is no corporate policy on the subject. In these circumstances, it is probable that no-one would be given direct responsibility for risk identification and control. Many hidden costs continue to be masked in the general overhead. However, as discussed earlier in this chapter, few companies can afford to ignore the competitive pressures of the Single Market which may render cost savings necessary on all fronts. Leaving everything to the company's financial control is not enough. Management at all levels must be conscious of the risks and extra costs generated by slack procedures or loosely-phrased contracts.

There is a clear need for senior management to take a greater interest in risk control. It is often a subject not taken seriously until there is a crisis and risks become financially damaging. Responsibility for risk control is often tacitly passed down the chain of command to a point where it cannot be recognised or responsibly managed, or taken into account in departmental performance analysis.

A turnover with high risk of loss is never as attractive as a turnover with controlled risks. There is therefore a need for a qualitative assessment of performance as well as quantitative.

Typical questions for management

Competitiveness and profitability is improved with the savings made from well managed risks but, to secure the savings, companies must establish in-house guidelines and controls. They also need to ensure that they employ, or have ready access to, skills and experience needed to identify and control risks and hidden costs. Senior management is the final judge of whether an organisation is appropriately structured, trained and prepared to meet the increasing international competition in the Single Market. Awareness of risks and costs could become a decisive factor in the balance between winning and losing. 'There is no profit without risk' is the maxim we frequently hear. More precisely, there is less profit with risk, since manifested risk nearly always generates additional costs. The questions for management are:

- □ Who in the company should be aware of risks and hidden costs?
- □ What company malfunctions lead to hidden costs?
- □ Who is responsible for identifying these functions and exercising control?
- □ More specifically, whose performance measures suffer as a result of the risk?

The manager who introduces risk and cost control procedures will not only improve the company's financial standing with banks, but will also be in a position to defend the company against international competition. In general, managers who succeed in controlling risks and costs display an attitude which enables a company to enter the Single Market with confidence. As a way of incorporating risk and cost control, managers should:

- □ Clearly communicate corporate objectives, priorities and guidelines on risk identification and control to everyone involved.
- □ Establish acceptable exposure levels in respect of commercial risks and financial risks.
- □ Formulate procedures to manage risks to improve competitiveness by keeping risk contingencies down; protect profits by managing currency risk and avoiding speculation; protect cashflow by securing payment and minimising bad debts.
- □ Establish corporate procedures to identify risks-associated hidden costs in five key areas: financial, legal, political, commercial, and market risk.
- □ Encourage an all-round professional approach to risk and cost control. The trade-off between sales, risk control and profitabilty is a difficult judgement to make.
- □ Review corporate structure to ensure that identified risks and costs are allocated to the appropriate function.
- □ Promote multi-disciplinary training to identify and manage risks and hidden costs.

2 Maximising Profits — II

Contract risks and hidden costs

Anthony Nolan

In stark contrast to the excitement we all feel at the prospect of winning orders in Europe, many of us working in the small to medium-sized sector suffer from a psychological resistance to accepting orders from abroad. The general cause is fear of the unknown, but one specific cause may be fear of losing money on a contract because of the piecemeal erosion of profits which occurs at various stages of obtaining and fulfilling an order. Eliminating these losses is, therefore, a primary objective for companies aiming for substantial sales growth in European markets.

First and foremost, the psychological block has to be overcome. In theory, there is no reason why we should not be as happy to accept an order from, say, a customer in Cologne as we are to accept an order from a customer in Cardiff. This is as much a question of attitude as efficiency, a point which has been made in various ways in other chapters in this book. There is, however, a need for those companies intending to compete more strongly in the European marketplace to pay greater attention to the costs involved when fulfilling orders. In responding enthusiastically and speedily to new orders from European customers we may easily overlook losses we are incurring by lack of financial discipline or, indeed, lack of awareness of scope for making substantial savings. Recently, companies have begun to realise, for example, that there are substantial savings to be made in transport and distribution in Europe.

The broad principle of minimising risks and maximising profits described in relation to exporting in the previous chapter applies equally to the processing of contracts, in that money could already have been lost by the time the goods have left the factory gate, because of lack of tight control on costs. If this is happening within a company as a matter of habit in respect of orders from the home market, the problem will be far greater when supplying customers at a distance. The additional costs involved in exporting create an imperative for greater cost control in *every* function within the company. Therefore, if exporting to European markets is going to become a natural part of a company's overall sales growth, new financial disciplines must be introduced at the earliest stage in negotiation. This chapter offers notes on how to avoid incurring losses unnecessarily when negotiating what ought to be profitable deals. However, in the long run, there is no substitute for in-house performance analysis which should take place after any large contract has been completed, or at least at regular sessions between all those involved in company functions which add to the total costs in meeting an order.

The product

It is doubtful if any other manufacturing country in the world produces better engineers, designers and technicians than the UK. We develop new products, solve problems and originate totally new concepts. This is Britain's forte. But when it comes to translating this ability into commercial production, so often this is undertaken by companies in the USA, Japan or some other competitor nation. Yet, the main opportunity in the wealthy European countries and other developed economies is, and will increasingly be, in supplying capital goods with a high added value. The most successful economy in Europe today is West Germany and its success has primarily been built on quality, design and service, rather than on price competitiveness. Long term success in achieving this level of quality has come from a commitment to research and development. Britain may be lagging behind in reaching these production goals, and Britain's standard of company performance may rise in time. But there is still much that companies can do now to compete better with Continental manufacturers.

One important factor in matching strong competition from German manufacturers with a high reputation in the European marketplace is to make best use of the profit making capabilities we already have, which should not be undermined by inexperience in dealing with Continental customers, used to a high standard of company performance. It is not always a question of matching some ideal in the customer's mind. Customers are, themselves, frequently vague about the detail of their requirements. A competent salesperson, however, will convince buyers of their specific requirements, and these requirements should mirror precisely what the company can supply. Spell out precisely what the company produces and what the product can do. There is little point, say, in offering a machine which can *almost* do what is required. If the machine cannot do the full job required by the purchaser, then one might as well be supplying a square window for a round hole. Promising, but not delivering what has been promised means never getting another contract from that particular buyer and perhaps other buyers in the same locality or sector. Bad news always travels fastest.

Technical back-up

Exporters must also ensure that any technical alteration or sophistication of the basic product — which may have been agreed by technical staff with the buyer — is reflected in the contract price. Do not sell a tailor-made product at the same price as the standard item. If the buyer has a facility to pay £100,000 for an order but, because of his special requirements, the cost rises to, say, £150,000, unless the customer agrees this figure at the outset and arranges the extra finance facility, payment may be difficult to obtain at a later date. As stated in the previous chapter, payment delay is, in itself, resulting in additional, unscheduled cost. Therefore, the client should be made aware at the beginning of negotiations of any additional costs of adapting the product. This avoids disputes and bad feeling at a later stage. Equally important from the supplier's point of view, do not sign any performance warranty, unless you are certain your product can meet it. Otherwise your company may be required to provide replacements — at no charge — wiping out profits.

Technical back-up cost is a key factor in profitability. Efficient technical back-up avoids losses arising from expensive, time consuming deficiencies which impair company prospects in the marketplace. On the whole, it is considered that

170

Continental companies provide better technical training and back-up to their salesforce than British companies. Inadequately trained and insufficiently supported sales staff, unable to provide proper technical back-up, incur unnecessary expenses and, therefore, losses when trying to deal with customer complaints. In providing technical back-up, the salesforce must also be able to cover the market adequately. It is not unusual for British companies to have four or five salespeople operating in the local, home market, but only one or two on the Continent.

The tender

It is vital that news of tenders and all the supporting documentation is obtained at the earliest possible stage. The tender documents will be listed in the invitation to tender which may be published, among many possible sources, in the *Official Journal of the European Communities*. By regularly monitoring sources of tender information there is a better chance of there being sufficient time to collate accurate figures. Having received all the relevant information, allow sufficient time to tender. Understandably, there is a temptation for busy companies not to give serious attention to a tender until a few days before the closing date. Completing a tender in a rush is a recipe for loss, since the figures must be based on facts, not on guess work.

When submitting a tender offer, if there are grey areas in the specifications listed, insert a rider in the offer to the effect that the company is unable to be precise because of the inadequacy of the tender information. In completing a price for the labour element of a tender, for example, ensure that your calculations of the costs of skilled and unskilled labour are accurate. Do not quote a cost of labourers when skilled craftsmen may be needed. Remember, an accepted tender is not a final contract and you can withdraw, if you feel that the proposal has become unprofitable. However, withdrawing from a tender at the last moment can lose your company goodwill, so it is better to avoid this possibility by not undercutting out of fear of losing a contract. If you normally submit tenders which give you the minimum acceptable profit margin, then to cut that margin further may earn you short-term advantage, but, if repeated too often, lead to long term unprofitability. The company's director, not the salesperson, should make any decisions to quote lower prices, in order to get a foot in the door. This may have been a strategy adopted by large players in the market in the past, but smaller companies cannot afford to run such risks.

The contract

Expectations become a reality when the contract is signed. Celebrations can be marred, however, by signing a contract in haste which will be regretted later. One of the main differences between selling in the UK and in other European markets is that, whereas a standard contract may be used in the UK, the contract for a Continental supplier can be a one-off, opening up new areas of risk. The risks are created at an early stage when the salesforce closes deals under pressure of intense competition and out of an instinct to triumph in the marketplace, but without working through all the cost saving implications in detail.

It is self-evident that a company cannot succeed in the European marketplace by accepting unprofitable orders. The financial skill is in *knowing* when and how profits are being shaved. Yet, all too often, salespeople are obsessed with simply winning the orders, leaving others in the company to overcome any cost problems which may be implicit in the terms agreed in the deal. By this time, the company may already be seeing that *company* profitability, as distinct from the calculated profit on the product, is depleted. In the course of the deal, the price of the product itself may have been shaved, unrealistic delivery dates may be set which cannot be met without expensive overtime, and other concessions may have been agreed. Taken together, at the point of completing and fulfilling the order, these concessions can result in the order making little or no net profit. Salespeople closing deals on unprofitable contractual terms, which become loss makers, probably cause as many bankruptcies among small and medium-sized manufacturers as any inefficiency in the production process itself.

The sales person closing the deal should always know from whom in the company to take instructions. Only the person who signs the cheques should be listened to when agreeing any variations in a contract. Otherwise, someone without the authority to agree extra payment may ask for extra work to be done, at extra cost, to be undertaken by the supplier. But, when it comes to payment, the person who has suggested the changes may deny doing so. Signed instructions for extra work are always necessary. The same applies in the case of alterations to specifications, delivery terms and dates, payment terms — indeed any part of the content of a contract.

Many suppliers allow themselves to be intimidated by fear of upsetting customer relations by insisting on written instructions and on formal agreement, particularly when trading with regular, friendly customers on open account terms. But it is always dangerous, particularly should legal action arise over a dispute over a contract, not to be able to produce documentary evidence of any additional work or alterations to specifications which have increased costs over the original agreed price. Only correspondence can be quoted in Court, not telephone conversations.

Customer relations

Customer relations are habitually regarded as a matter of keeping existing customers happy once a product has been delivered. But customer relations begin at the first meeting between customer and supplier. The supplier can influence that meeting by initiating it, for example, and inviting potential customers to visit the company so that the product can be seen in the making. Open factory doors can be a positive incentive to European buyers, especially first-time buyers from your company who will welcome an opportunity to meet the people who are to executive the order and with whom they may be in contact for a long time to come. Inviting potential customers may, therefore, be one of the best investments a supplier can make.

'Entertaining' the customer, however, is not simply a matter of supplying hospitality. It is a way of building confidence. If the customer sees the company's labour force in action, and the contract requires some assembly in the customer's locality, then the customer gains confidence from the knowledge that skilled labour or training facilities can be made available, even if it incurs extra cost. In the end, everyone wants the contract to go well and make a profit. British companies, by adapting to customer needs in such ways, stand a much better chance of success in Europe.

3 Money for Business

Sources of working capital finance for European-bound companies

Ted Ettershank

All companies experience working capital shortages at some time in their development. However no management likes to have its expansion plans confounded as a result of such constraints. This is likely to be particularly true of those who are seeking to compete in the new free market.

Special anxieties can affect both new and prospective exporters, which if unchecked can result in missed opportunities due to excessive caution. The main fears attach to speed and certainty of payment from abroad. Methods for solving these problems are dealt with later in this chapter. It is important that newcomers to exporting should use professional services to provide the necessary financial skills whilst these are being built up within their own organisations. Some of these services are dealt with in the section on Packaged Lending. It should be noted that the benefits of these services offset the cost of the facilities offered. It would clearly be impractical to provide full-time staff to carry out activities which are needed only intermittently in the early stages of export activity.

Working Capital requirements are notoriously difficult to forecast. This is primarily because most economic events impinge on the cash resources of the business, so that any variance between out-turn and budget will cause cash forecasts to prove erroneous.

In times of high interest rates particular strains are suffered by those businesses which normally expect to derive most of their working capital from ploughed back profits. Highly competitive conditions can be expected to exist in the new market, such that margins may be squeezed too low to produce this level of profit. Expansion causes a greater need for working capital than is necessarily obvious. The additional investment needed in stocks and debtors is only partially offset by the amount of additional credit taken from suppliers.

Inflation can also produce additional working capital strains of its own. Even if turnover in volume terms does not increase, the amount tied up in stocks and debtors will again not be fully compensated by the amount of additional credit received from creditors.

The working capital market is a highly competitive one, and expanding rapidly. Innovation is likely to be continuous, but for the moment Packaged Lending represents a major contribution to the needs of rapidly expanding companies.

Bank overdraft

This is the traditional source and is fully capable of supplying the needs of many companies.

Advantages
- Well understood and familiar in operation.
- Flexible in amount.
- Can be available for many years despite its temporary nature.

Disadvantages
- Sometimes subject to hidden charges.
- Temporary nature — may be called in at an inconvenient moment due to a credit squeeze by the government.
- Restricted in amount. Subject to renegotiation.

Venture capital

Many companies obtain part of their finance from venture capitalists, usually merchant banks. The British Venture Capital Association, 1 Surrey Street, London, WC2R 2PS will be pleased to supply a list of members.

Advantages
- Reduction in risk by passsing equity into the hands of the venture capitalists.
- Permanence.
- Obtaining expert advice usually at Board level.

Disadvantages
- Loss of sovereignty/suffering managerial interference.
- Loss of profit share.

Factoring of invoices

This enables companies to enhance their working capital supply by selling their debtors to the factoring company. The cash advance can be up to 80% of the value of the invoices. Additional services include the maintenance of the client's sales ledger accounting service, including debt collection, credit control and credit rating.

Advantages
- Permanence: the usual arrangement is for the service to be continuous.
- Sales ledger accounting professionally carried out.
- Debt collection professionally carried out.
- The facility expands as the amount of debts increase. i.e. expansion is automatically financed to a large degree.

Disadvantages
- Lack of confidentiality leads to a fallacious assumption that the client company is in financial trouble. This stems from an unjustified image of the factor as the lender of the last resort.
- Intervention by factoring company in the relationship between client and client's customers.

Invoice discounting

The service is a modern form of invoice factoring developed as an attempt to combine all the advantages of invoice factoring with none of the disadvantages. The fundamental arrangement is similar to invoice factoring. Debts are bought by the discounting company, and an advance payment of up to 80% is made to the client by the factoring company as soon as the invoices are issued. The balance is paid over as soon as the debt is paid. The vital distinction is that the debt is collected by the client, not the invoice discounter. In this way, confidentiality may be preserved. Unless the client wishes it so, the customer need never know that debts are being financed. The sales ledger maintenance service is not supplied, but in today's circumstances, it is not so attractive, since modern micro-computers are cheap, and inexpensive reliable accounting software for them abounds.

Advantages
- Permanence — the service is normally continuous as long as the terms of the contract are complied with.
- Confidentiality — automatic increase as sales increase.
- Flexible — only the amount of finance currently required is drawn down.

Disadvantages
- The amount of finance, although very substantial, may not prove adequate for rapidly expanding companies.

Packaged lending

The foregoing sources of working capital all have their adherents but sources are prone to becoming inadequate when expansion is really rapid. A gap develops between requirements and finance which must be bridged if expansion is not to be constrained. Hill Samuel Commercial Finance has examined this problem and designed a new product to combat it. Called Packaged Lending, the new product is modular in construction. Built on a core of Invoice Discounting, it offers additional modules of finance secured on a variety of assets. These may include land, buildings, plant and machinery and stocks. The amount of the advance available against each item will depend on the nature and value of the assets concerned. General purpose assets suitable for use in a whole variety of businesses will attract a larger advance than those of a very specialised nature. Modules available include a variety of aids to foreign trade.

Advantages
- Provides for all the working capital requirements both current and foreseeable in the future.
- No intrusion in the relationship between client and the client's customers.
- Permanent, provided the terms of the contract are complied with.
- Total facility expands as sales and consequently debtors expand.
- Total facility often proves to be more substantial than clearing bankers can provide.

Disadvantages
- None.

Modules for inclusion in Packaged Lending

Currency Discounting
This product enables clients to obtain a prepayment of up to 80 per cent against debts in the currency of the customer's country. This facility removes UK bank charges on incoming funds and enables the client to adopt a flexible approach to the foreign exchange risk. Discount is calculated using currency LIBOR rates which are often lower than UK sterling Bank Base Rates.

Export Finance
Up to 95% prepayment may be advanced against Documentary Credits which are issued and guaranteed by a recognised bank. Finance is provided for the credit term i.e. from presentation of documents to the eventual payment date.

Discounting Bills of Exchange
Up to 90% may be advanced against clean accepted Bills of Exchange.

Trade Finance
A back-to-back purchase and sale agreement for import of goods and onwards within the UK. A prepayment to the initial supplier may be made of up to 85% of the purchase price.

Stock Finance
Up to 45% advance against eligible stock.

Import Finance
This enables the client to purchase goods from overseas on Letter of Credit terms.

Deferment Bonds
The providing of a bond to HM Customs & Excise enabling a client to enjoy credit terms on import liabilities such as VAT and Duty payment.

Property Loans
A medium-term loan of up to 70% of current market valuation is made, secured against freehold property.

CONTACTS

Association of British Factors and Discounters (ABFD)
Information Office
24-28 Bloomsbury Way
London WC1A 2PX
Tel: (071) 831 4268
Fax: (071) 430 1033

ABFD members[1]

Alex Lawrie Factors Limited
Beaumont House
Beaumont Road
Banbury, Oxfordshire OX16 7RN
Tel: (0295) 272272
Fax: (0295) 271634
Telex: 83627
(Also at Basingstoke, Birmingham, Bristol, Cambridge, Coventry, Edinburgh, Hatfield, Leeds, London, Maidstone, Manchester, Newcastle upon Tyne, Newport, Stockport)

Barclays Commercial Services Limited
Aquila House
Breeds Place
Hastings, East Sussex TN34 3DG
Tel: (0424) 430824
Fax: (0424) 427322
Telex: 95450
(Also at Birmingham, Bristol, Leeds, London, Manchester, Newcastle upon Tyne, Northampton)

Century Factors Limited
Southbrook House
25 Bartholomew Street
Newbury, Berkshire RG14 5LL
Tel: (0635) 31517
Tel: (0635) 31703
Telex: 846567
(Also at London, Manchester)

Griffin Factors Limited
21 Farncombe Road
Worthing
West Sussex BN11 2BW
Tel: (0903) 205181
Fax: (0903) 24101
Telex: 87102
(Also at Birmingham, Bristol, Leeds, London, Manchester)

Hill Samuel Commercial Finance Limited
Boston House
The Little Green
Richmond
Surrey TW9 1QE
Tel: (081) 940 4646
Fax: (081) 940 6051
Telex: 8952444
(Also at Birmingham, Manchester)

International Factors Limited
PO Box 240
Sovereign House
Church Street
Brighton
Sussex BN1 3WX
Tel: (0273) 21211
Fax: (0273) 771501
Telex: 87382
(Also at Birmingham, Bristol, Cambridge, Glasgow, Leeds, London, Manchester, Nottingham, Poole, Reading)

Kellock Limited
Abbey Gardens
Reading
Berkshire RG1 3BA
Tel: (0734) 585511
Fax: (0734) 502480
(Also at Birmingham, Edinburgh, Glasgow, Leeds, London, Manchester)

Lombard NatWest Commercial Services Limited
Smith House
PO Box 50
Elmwood Avenue
Feltham, Middlesex TW13 7QD
Tel: (081) 890 1390
Fax: (081) 751 3367
Telex: 22593
(Also at Bedford, Birmingham, Bristol, East Grinstead, Leeds, Manchester, Nottingham)

RoyScot Factors Limited
Exchange Court
3 Bedford Park
Croydon, Surrey CR0 2AQ
Tel: (081) 686 9988
Fax: (081) 680 1799
Telex: 932211
(Also at Birmingham, Edinburgh, Glasgow, Manchester)

Security Pacific Business Finance (Europe) Limited
126 Dyke Road
Brighton, Sussex BN1 3TE
Tel: (0273) 21177
Fax: (0273) 26914
Telex: 877020
(Also at Bristol, Leeds, London)

Trade Indemnity-Heller Commercial
Finance Limited
Park House
22 Park Street
Croydon
Surrey CR9 1RD
Tel: (081) 681 2641
Fax: (081) 681 8072
Telex: 27348

1 At the time of going to press the ABDF was in discussion with potential new members.

4 Export Credit Insurance

Insurance against non-payment

Charles McCartan

All exporting companies know that basically export credit insurance is taken out to secure against bad debts. But by no means all exporters appreciate the full measure of the role of credit insurers in good financial management. Traditionally, the main disincentive to companies in failing to secure against non-payment has not been the cost of cover, which is small, but complacency, or misplaced belief that a company can stand the occasional loss. Things are changing. In the emergent European marketplace it is predicted that the risk of loss will be greater than in the worst recessions of recent times, as the battle between potential losers and winners gets underway. Contrary to popular assumption, the need for export credit insurance will actually increase, the risk being even greater where one believes, erroneously, that it does not exist. This chapter sets out the range of practical benefits of credit insurance against the background of profound change, predictable and unpredictable, in the Europe of the 1990s.

The key year in the making of the Single Market for export credit insurance is not 1992, but 1990, when the EC Directive on cross-border insurance came into effect. The Directive lays down that the marketing of insurance should be liberalised throughout the twelve member states of the Community. This means that a British credit insurer can market its products in any country within the Single Market. Likewise, insurers in other Single Market countries can market their products in the UK. The increase in competition between insurers is expected to encourage them to improve the services they offer and devise new products. For insurers and customers alike, liberalisation is welcomed as good news, and underwriters are investing with confidence, believing that the demand for credit insurance will increase as barriers to trade in Europe are lifted.

More important for companies, however, are the reasons *why* they should obtain credit insurance cover on their European business when all the 1992 publicity suggests that Europe will be a better place for business in the future. It may be a better place, but it will not necessarily be a safer place. Credit insurance has clear attractions for companies adapting to trading across all Europe, where a struggle for a permanent position in the marketplace is, for many companies, inevitable.

To begin with a basic point, the Single Market comprises only part of the larger European Economic Space, which embraces the twelve EC member states, the European Free Trade Association countries and the newly opened Eastern European markets. But even if one confines one's attention to the Single Market, harmonisation of the trading environment encourages companies to view the

Single Market as an enlarged domestic market, not an export market. There is now growing appreciation of the fact that, whether or not one regards selling in the Single Market itself as exporting, the principle attraction of export credit insurance remains the same — insuring against non-payment. In risk terms, therefore, there is little difference in principle between European business, domestic business and third country business. Bad debts occur anywhere.

In the Single Market, as the barriers to trade are eliminated, competition will increase. The forecast, as competition intensifies in all sectors, is that the number of insolvencies is also likely to increase. This being the case, a company's exposure to losses from bad debts becomes greater. Sir John Harvey-Jones, former Chairman of ICI, has forecast that after 1992, half of the companies in Europe will either be bought or merged, or go out of business. In 1989 alone, 80,000 companies in the EC went bust. Inevitably, any substantial increase on this figure will result in higher risk of non-payment for companies selling into Europe, especially when dealing with new customers about whom little is known.

It is easy to fall in with received opinion which says that, in a Single Market in which companies trade on equal terms, selling across European frontiers will be no different to selling in the domestic market. While the popular view of Europe as one big trouble-free domestic market is in many senses accurate, it is also convenient shorthand for projecting the concept of the Single Market itself in easily understandable terminology which can be misleading. In fact, exporters suffer more losses from insolvencies in the developed world, including Europe, than they do from trading with companies in the debt-ridden Third World. The explanation is simple; trade with customers in riskier countries is usually secured as a matter of course. By comparison, trade in Europe is more often left at risk.

Another common misconception is that in strong Western economies individual companies are much less likely to go bust as a result of poor management or downturns in their particular sectors. But experience in the UK during the period of high interest rates has brought home the reality that the number of liquidations increases very substantially when business is hit by adverse economic factors. The wider European Economic Space, despite much welcomed moves towards uniformity in the trading environment, becomes less predictably safe when viewed as a cluster of separate countries, each with a distinct economic identity, vulnerable to fluctuations in economic policies.

Benefits of risk cover

Certainty of payment: Credit insurance assures payment of up to 90 per cent of the losses arising from bad debts. Cover can be provided for almost any type of business, ranging from the whole of a company's turnover to one-off contracts. This form of security allows companies to trade confidently in new markets, knowing that they will not suffer unduly, should one or several customers go bust owing money. The risk of loss increases, of course, if a company's business is spread across only a few customers or, as is sometimes the case, the company derives the bulk of its income from a single major customer. In simple mathematical terms, if a company is working on a profit margin of ten per cent, for every £10,000 lost in bad debts a further £100,000 in new business has to be found to make up the shortfall; and that new business again carries risk if not insured.

Low cost: The cost of insurance is usually a fraction of one per cent of turnover, a sum less than the amount normally held in contingency funds to cover bad debts.

Viewed in this light, the cost of insurance to protect profits and avoid disasters represents real value for money, not just peace of mind.

Accurate credit checks: Credit insurers also assist with other aspects of credit management. Many companies trading in Europe for the first time find it harder to assess the creditworthiness of foreign-based customers, due to language barriers, or the distances involved, all compounded by differing business practices and trading conditions. It is not easy, for example, to judge a company's ability to pay, or obtain its past record on payment from direct contact with a foreign bank which offers glowing references as a matter of course, probably in a foreign language. Underwriters, however, use specialist skills and better access to data to assess clients' potential and existing customers. Most underwriters have immediate access to financial information on millions of UK and foreign companies. Some insurers also have specialist underwriters covering particular industry sectors, each with an insight into the risks inherent in a company's field of activity. After checks have been made, credit limits are then supplied to the policy-holder, indicating a customer's creditworthiness. Though it goes without saying that if one obtains a good credit reference *before* one starts trading there is a much better chance of avoiding losses, many companies still do not obtain risk cover. Yet among those who do insure, experience shows that working with an insurer over a period of time usually reduces the number of bad debts.

Long-term planning: An important long-term benefit to policy-holders is increased confidence to plan ahead and expand, using credit limits supplied by insurers. An underwriter's research may also reveal positive facts about a customer, whose financial strength may be greater than the supplier originally imagined. In such circumstances, more credit can be extended to cover larger orders, knowledge which is also very useful to the supplier's salesforce.

Safer open account trading

In Europe there is a strong tradition of open account trading. Whereas open account trading in a high risk Third World country would be unthinkable, the opposite applies in Europe where suppliers are reluctant to refuse open account terms, even when they feel uncertain about payment. The core of the problem is intense competition in Europe, a factor which will gain in importance in the Single Market, and perhaps even more so when operating across the entire European Economic Space. The level of competition is already such that foreign suppliers seek to avoid imposing extra burdens on customers, such as documentary letters of credit, especially when competing against local suppliers who invariably trade on an open account basis. The fear is that if suppliers force customers to go through the complexities of opening a letter of credit, the best known alternative to credit insurance for securing payment, they may lose the business altogether.

Company managers may consider that such fears are exaggerated, particularly if the product in question has strong credibility in the market place, or in situations where customers demand highly favourable credit terms. But the fact remains that regular customers expect favourable treatment and relations are improved when the formalities and burdens are reduced and an atmosphere of trust is established. Insistence on using letters of credit may undermine a relationship based on trust, but trust is not the problem when a customer gets into financial difficulties.

Letters of credit are also becoming increasingly expensive, since banks are reluctant to increase their exposures and need to achieve higher profits to match the increase in reserves that has been imposed upon them. Moreover, *Just in Time* manufacturing methods result in a greater number of smaller shipments to customers, instead of bulk orders, and a proportionate increase in paperwork. To open letters of credit for each shipment is time-consuming for the supplier, and it is generally easier to invoice normally, thus incurring risk. Credit insurance is a painless way of circumventing these problems and avoiding cash losses in open account situations where there is no inherent security and where the element of trust in the relationship needs to be maintained.

Financial discipline

Large corporations use credit insurance as a means of imposing financial discipline on their subsidiaries. By making each subsidiary take out whole turnover cover, all customers are vetted by the underwriter who sets the credit limits. Subsidiaries can, of course, be given discretionary power to trade uninsured beyond these limits. In such cases, at least the subsidiary is doing so consciously and with accountability. As companies expand into the European marketplace, through a network of subsidiaries, greater emphasis will be given to the control of these subsidiaries. The credit insurer is a useful ally.

Some large exporting companies have their own sophisticated credit management capability, but they too can benefit from using credit insurance. They may not need help to assess the creditworthiness of overseas customers, and they may not need protection against small losses. But they are still vulnerable to a string of unforeseeable losses, or one large unexpected loss. The risk is particularly great when operating a number of European subsidiaries in fluctuating economies, as pointed out earlier. In Europe's competitive environment, the combined minor losses of a group's subsidiaries may add up to a major group loss.

Insurance cover should be obtained for such exceptional losses, if observers are correct in their assumptions that the deregulation of the Single Market will lead to a 'shakeout' in industry. An 'exceptional loss' policy protects against cumulative losses above a preset threshold, with or without assistance in their credit control procedures. Some large companies still use ground-up whole turnover policies, however, in order to protect their short-term profits and thus steady their share price.

Credibility with the bank

Traditionally, export finance has been linked to credit insurance, the banks playing a key role in advancing funds which enable an exporter to meet the initial cost of fulfilling overseas orders or bridge the cashflow gap which may exist up until the date payment is received. Most bank finance schemes require exporters to take out credit insurance policies, as a safeguard for the bank as well as the exporter. However, an important benefit to exporters of taking out credit insurance is a bank's willingness to extend more finance at preferential rates. A company intent on rapid growth to seize any advantages created by the liberalisation of the European marketplace is much more likely to obtain the necessary finance if its sales are insured. Relationships with banks are not always at their best when the economic climate is tough. The private sector understandably baulks at high interest rates which, say many companies, erode confidence in investment in expansion or modernisation. In turn, the banks are inclined at such times to be more cautious about lending, especially when dealing with little known overseas customers. In this situation the credit insurers again play a most useful role in strengthening a borrower's status with the bank, helping to maintain the flow of business activity at potentially difficult times.

The credit insurer also boosts a company's standing with the bank when things are going well! A successful company may suddenly receive much larger orders from overseas customers, or from intermediaries who have stimulated demand for the product. To meet these orders, the supplier has to invest in raising production capacity, perhaps by purchasing equipment, extending the premises or employing more staff. If bank finance is required, increasing the supplier's exposure, albeit temporarily and in a good cause, then insured payment for the overseas orders is bound to weigh substantially in a bank's response to a request for finance.

Pan-European cover

One of the most positive new trends in credit insurance stems from the liberalisation of the European market which has created more demand for combined domestic/export policies. Pan-European policies covering all of a company's sales both in its domestic market and Europe, are now increasingly available. Until recently, pan-European cover has only been supplied by certain niche players in the credit insurance market, such as AIU, Pan Financial and Namur. ECGD (Export Credits Guarantee Department), the government insurer, will be privatised after 1991 and may offer domestic as well as export cover. Meanwhile, Trade Indemnity, the largest UK privately owned insurer has launched its own domestic/export market policy, *Multi-Market*. This combines cover for all business in Europe and with Britain's major trading partners, including the United States, Japan and Australia. A combined domestic/export policy has several advantages:

☐ It is simple to document and operate. Only one policy need be negotiated with underwriters.

☐ A larger, comprehensive policy carries better terms.

☐ Small export orders, not thought to be worth insuring separately, can be tacked onto domestic turnover.

☐ Companies whose main activity is exporting include small domestic orders in their export turnover for credit insurance purposes.

Psychologically speaking, a combined policy is helpful to companies determined to grasp opportunities in the European marketplace, since it breaks down the mental distinctions one makes between the home and export markets. Treating domestic and export markets as one helps to inculcate a pan-European outlook at all levels in a company's administration. Trade Indemnity has endeavoured to combine the best aspects of domestic and export policies for *Multi-Market*. Traditionally, export policies have included a lower first loss clause, but domestic cover could be extended to a larger portion of a company's business. *Multi-Market* offers the option of no first loss at all and reimburses up to 90 per cent of each debt, whether it occurs in the domestic or in an export market. The tailoring of policies by insurers to meet the needs of internationally-minded companies and genuinely transnational companies includes in-house pooling of underwriters combined skills. Export underwriters work closely with domestic underwriters to build a closer client relationship, one underwiter being responsible for the client and providing the sole point of contact.

Projected growth in demand

One outcome of the Single Market programme for the credit insurance industry, has been a sharpening perception of the benefits of credit insurance in the minds of exporters, though many still picture credit insurance as a future, rather than present necessity. Trade Indemnity launched *Multi-Market* after conducting research into the way British companies have been operating prior to the introduction of the EC's Single Market programme, and how they expect to modify their operation to meet the changes in their trading environment for which the Single Market programme is such a bold catalyst. In a survey conducted amongst exporters at the end of 1989, some 65 per cent of respondents said they expected their exports to Europe to increase. Almost all of them said they expected to be using credit insurance in the future, even though many were not using credit insurance at the time. The survey also revealed that in 75 per cent of respondents the same company executive was responsible for covering the company's risk in both domestic and export markets. A single domestic/export policy is, therefore, easily recognised as one which reduces the workload of excutives, without calling for a reorganisation of a company's administrative procedures.

Changes are also occuring on the Continent where private and government insurers are jockeying for position in anticipation of the free market in insurance, on which the EC's competition rules will be brought to bear. The advent of cross-border insurance has naturally provoked much debate over the future of the national export credit insurance agencies, such as ECGD, in the Single Market. Some argue that, technically, trade within Europe should be classed as domestic business, rather than exports. But if this were the case, national credit insurance agencies would not be allowed to cover trade within the Single Market under their existing constitutions. Others argue that the backing a national credit insurance agency receives from government is unfair under EC competition law.

To resolve the problems, most national agencies are seeking amendments to their operating rules. Some are narrowing down their areas of responsibility by handing over insurance of European business to the private insurance sector. Others, including the ECGD, may expand their existing services to offer domestic and export cover in all European markets. Certain more expansionist Continental credit insurance agencies are already producing policies in the English language, but policy wordings are complicated and certain terms are interpreted differently. Generally, the UK credit insurance market is still the most sophisticated in Europe, but there will increasingly be opportunities to get better deals across the Channel.

Whatever the future holds for the credit insurance market, the message for exporters remains the same; it is wise to insure both European and non-European businesses. The range of attractive, custom-made insurance products on offer means that any company can protect itself from losses, or risk financial ruin, as a result of bad debts occuring in a volatile European marketplace.

CONTACTS

Sources of credit insurance in the UK

The following list of credit insurers and credit insurance brokers operating in the UK has been compiled by the leading monthly export magazine, *Export Times*. The magazine regularly publishes news, supplements and features on export finance services, in addition to its coverage of international trade news and developments. For further information contact: *Export Times*, 4 New Bridge Street, Fleet Street, London EC4V 6AA. Tel: (071) 583 0077, Fax: (071) 583 8754.

Credit insurers

AIU (American International Underwriters)
120 Fenchurch Street
London EC3M 5BP
Tel: (071) 626 7866
Fax: (071) 280 8972
(Branch offices at Croydon, Birmingham, Bristol, Glasgow, Leeds, Manchester, Norwich, Southampton, Watford)

Export Credits Guarantee Department (ECGD)
Publicity and Public Relations Branch
Export House
50 Ludgate Hill, London EC4M 7AY
Tel: (071) 382 7777
Fax: (071) 382 7649
(Regional offices at City of London, Croydon, Belfast, Birmingham, Bristol, Cambridge, Glasgow, Leeds, Manchester)

Lloyds of London
(Contacts should be made through a specialist broker)

Namur
Park House
22 Park Street, Croydon
Tel: (081) 680 1565
Fax: (081) 688 4953

Pan Financial
International House
World Trade Centre
1 St. Katherine's Way
London E1 9UN
Tel: (071) 481 3122
Fax: (071) 488 3070

Sun Alliance
Financial Risks Office
Leadenhall Court
1 Leadenhall Street
London EC3V 1PP
Tel: (071) 588 2345
Fax: (071) 826 1135

Trade Indemnity
12-34 Great Eastern Street
London EC2A 3AX
Tel: (071) 739 4311
Fax: (071) 729 7682
(Regional offices at Birmingham, Bristol, Glasgow, Leeds, Manchester, Reading)

Credit insurance brokers

Bain Clarkson Credit and Political Risks
15 Minories,
London EC3N 1NJ
Tel: (071) 481 3232
Fax: (071) 480 6137
(Branch offices at Birmingham, Leeds)

Bowring Credit
Bowring (UK) Ltd
The Bowring Building
Tower Place, London EC3P 3BE
Tel: (071) 283 3100
Fax: (071) 929 2705
(Branch offices at Birmingham, Bristol, Glasgow, Leeds, Manchester, Sidcup)

CAD Consultants
797 London Road
Thornton Heath
Surrey CR4 6XA
Tel: (081) 684 2521
Fax: (081) 684 7554

Credit Insurance Association (CIA)
13 Grosvenor Place
London SW1X 7HH
Tel: (071) 235 3550
Fax: (071) 235 4397
(Branch offices at Birmingham, Glasgow, Leeds, Manchester, Reading)

Credit Insurance Services
Fenchurch House
89 High Road
South Woodford
London E18 2RH
Tel: (081) 505 3333
Fax: (081) 505 5014
(Branches at Birmingham, Manchester)

Credit Management Resources
3 Butter Hill
Carshalton
Surrey SM5 2TW
Tel: (081) 647 3833
Fax: (081) 669 8266

Jardine Credit Insurance
Jardine House
6 Crutched Friars
London EC3N 2HT
Tel: (071) 528 4444
Fax: (071) 528 4437
(Branches at Birmingham, Bradford, Gloucester, Manchester, Woking)

Willis Wrightson Credit
Willis Wrightson House
Wood Street
Kingston-upon-Thames
Surrey KT1 1UG
Tel: (081) 787 6000
Fax: (081) 943 4297
(Branches at Birmingham, Leeds, London)

Unexis
Equitable House
Lyon Road
Harrow
HA1 2EW
Tel: (081) 861 6551
Fax: (081) 861 6313

5 Banking Services

The impact of deregulation

Barclays Bank Plc

Deregulation and the removal of artificial barriers to trade will have a major impact on most financial services in Europe. The impact of the Single Market on banks and their services to business will be considerable. As in other sectors, banks in one country will be able to conduct business more freely in the eleven other Single Market member states. The European Commission aims to create a legal framework to remove barriers and promote a free market in financial services, while ensuring that customers and shareholders of banks and other financial institutions are protected.

The trend towards a Single Market in banking does not mean, however, that banking services will be identical throughout the EC. Differences in taste, culture and custom will remain. Financial products will still have to be packaged in different ways to reflect local requirements in European markets. Nevertheless, technology, economies of scale and the Single Market legislative programme on banking encourage the shift from traditional branch banking, insurance and investment service networks towards centralised delivery systems with minimal investments in bricks and mortar. To keep abreast of the changes in banking style and format companies should keep in close touch with their bank as the Single Market moves towards completion.

For the time being, existing barriers in some states limit the number of branches a foreign bank can establish in a member state, restrict the takeover of domestic banks of other countries and also restrict, by means of exchange controls, the free flow of capital from one state to another. Such restrictions will not be permitted in the completed Single Market. The EC is committed to removing all exchange controls and adopting measures to allow banks to operate freely anywhere in the Single Market.

The guiding principal in creating a free market in banking is a degree of harmonisation to secure mutual recognition of banking services in each member country. This will allow for the introduction of a single EC licence for banks, while retaining supervisory control of individual banks in their home country.

To summarise the general benefits of cross-border banking, bank customers will benefit from an increase in investment opportunities, an increase in the range of banking products, better price competition between banks and credit institutions, and increased rates of return for depositors' funds. There will also be a wider choice of institutions offering them trade financing, deposit taking, leasing, factoring, consumer credit and other financial services. Borrowers are likely to benefit from keener rates as banks compete for a market share. The dismantling of exchange controls will in itself present more borrowing opportunities. The use of electronic payments and electronic funds transfers (EFT) will become more widespread. Progress towards paperless trading, through EDI (Electronic Data Interchange), will accelerate.

In the small and medium-sized enterprises (SMEs) sector, companies will be seeking to increase profits by expanding in Europe in a variety of ways (See *Corporate Structures*, Part Five, Chapter 1). Undoubtedly many companies will adopt one or more of the following strategies:

☐　Establish branches in other European countries

☐　Acquire businesses in other member states

☐　Acquire enterprises in the home market to improve their market position and defend themselves against new competitive forces.

☐　Increase the home product range with new products from elsewhere in Europe

☐　Export to other European countries

Banks will have a part to play in all these activities. Increased trade between EC member states means that many SME's require additional banking finance, more banking advice, and may need to use more sophisticated banking services if they are to make the most of new intra-EC business opportunities.

Although the Single Market will not be completed in every detail immediately, it is only a matter of time before the measures designed to create a homogenous trading environment throughout the EC member states are implemented. The development of the Single Market is and has been a gradual process since the signing of the Treaty of Rome in 1957, via many other steps towards integration including the merger in 1965 of the European Economic Community (EEC), the European Coal and Steel Community (ECSC) and the European Atomic Energy Community (EURATOM) into the European Community (EC). The European Commission's 1985 White Paper *Completing the Internal Market* and the 1986 Single European Act which came into force in 1987 mark the most recent political initiatives in the European integration process. Since then the development of the Single Market has gathered momentum and, step by step, the measures to remove the barriers to trade are falling into place. The creation of the Single Market is not an event which makes a dramatic debut at the end of 1992. The Single Administrative Document (SAD), for example, was a conspicuous step forward in clearing the red tape at intra-EC frontiers.

Impact of changes in the European banking system

Changes in the Single Market banking system will affect companies of all sizes, whether they do business in another EC member state or not. Developments in domestic banking systems will not take place in isolation from the overall Single Market banking trends. New banking technology and systems developed for use in the Single Market and globally will also have applications with national banking systems, however, just as technology developed to put man into Space has subsequently been applied in many ways on earth.

The impact of new banking technology aside, the European Commission's legislation affecting banks is lengthy and complex. In general, however, the legislative programme on banking in the Single Market pursues further the original aims of the 1957 EEC Treaty. Article 2 of the Treaty states that 'by establishing a common market and progressively approximating the economic positions of member states, to promote throughout the Community a harmonious development of economic activities, a continuous and balanced expansion, an increase in stability, an accelerated raising of the standard of living, and closer relationships between the states belonging to it.' The Single European Act added article 8(a) to the EEC Treaty which provides for the completion of the process of creating an internal market in the EC, to be progressively established 'over a period expiring on 31 December, 1992.' It defines the internal market as 'an area without internal frontiers in which the free movement of goods, persons, services and capital is ensured in accordance with provisions of this Treaty.'

When the European Economic Community was set up barriers between member states included customs duties, import and export quotas, immigratiom controls, monetary controls on the flow of capital between member states, and restrictive rules on the establishment of companies. For many years, banks wishing to do business in other member states have been constrained by the need to satisfy differing rules of the twelve banking supervisory authorities of the twelve member states. They have also been bound by rules preventing banks from providing services across intra-Community frontiers, without having to set up local branches or subsidiaries. There have also been limitations on the range of services which a branch or subsidiary of a foreign bank may offer, plus restrictions on local retail banking and bank advertising.

First Banking Co-ordination Directive: Full title: *The First Council Directive on the Co-ordination of Laws, Regulations and Administrative Provisions Relating to the Taking up and Pursuit of Credit Institutions*, of 12 December, 1977. The Directive had two main objectives:

☐ To introduce a degree of harmonisation of the law of the various states for the licensing of banks.

☐ To induce co-operation among banking supervisory authorities of the member states.

Second Banking Co-ordination Directive: This Directive aims to implement the concepts of freedom of establishment (developed by Articles 52 to 58) and that of freedom of services (Article 59). It legislates for a single European banking licence, based on home country control, enabling a bank to engage in a range of permitted activities without the need to comply further with host country rules. Broadly speaking, the single banking licence is designed to allow banks and other credit institutions which are nationals of a member state, to expand their activities anywhere in the Community. They may do so by establishing branches in other member states, or by offering cross-border services, or both. The activities permitted under the single banking licence include:

☐ Deposit taking and other forms of borrowing

☐ Lending (consumer credit, mortgages, factoring, trade finance)

☐ Money transmission

☐ Issuing and administering means of payment (credit cards, travellers' cheques, bank drafts).

☐   Trading in the money market instruments for the bank's own account, or for the account of customers (cheques, bills, certificates of deposit).

☐   Foreign exchange, financial futures and options, exchange and interest rate instruments, securities.

☐   Participation in share issues and the provision of services to such issues.

☐   Money broking.

☐   Portfolio management and advice.

☐   Safekeeping of securities.

☐   Credit reference services.

The list of permitted services may be subsequently extended to take account of any new financial services.

Electronic banking

The use of electronic banking will increase in the Single Market and will continue to develop globally. The European Commission wants to standardise electronic payment systems within Europe and to develop a Single Market payments industry which can compete in world markets, particularly against the US and Japanese banking industries. One principal aim of the Commission is to promote 'interoperability' of electronic payment cards. Interoperability would ensure that payment cards issued in one member state are compatible with the systems in use in other member states, so that cards can be used to obtain cash from automatic dispensers anywhere in the Community.

Electronic banking and Electronic Funds Transfers (EFT) being of such global importance, the Commission liaises closely with other organisations interested in cross-border electronic banking developments. These include UNICTRAL, the United Nations Commission for International Trade Law, and the OECD (Organisation for Economic Co-operation and Development). UNICTRAL has sought to establish 'Model Rules for EFT', primarily concerned with international credit transfers between banks; while the OECD is engaged on a study of consumer related areas, *EFT Systems and the Consumer*.

The use of Electronic Data Interchange (EDI) is likely to grow rapidly. Using modern computer technology to simplify the trading cycle is accelerating the move towards the totally electronic commercial transaction, consisting of the order, invoice, transport details, payment, cash management, reconciliation. All these stages, if completed accurately and promptly, will improve corporate performance all round. However, banks have consistently pointed to the extra cost, and sometimes cash losses, incurred by faulty documentation. EDI should at least eliminate some of the problems, if only by speeding up the reparations. The existence of recently agreed international message standards for the required data transfer means that growth of EDI will, according to conservative predictions, run at 35 per cent per annum throughout the 1990s.

When exchange controls are abolished throughout the entire Community, possibly not until the mid-1990s, and all customs barriers lifted (recently joined member countries still have transitional arrangements to phase out duties) automated links could easily achieve an invoice generated in the seller's currency, say Lira, but debited to the buyer in England in Sterling, with a bank generating an automated foreign exchange contract.

This in turn leads to scope for building automatic stop-loss foreign exchange deals, or option cover, into payment or receipt cashflow programmes, thus minimising currency losses. Currency exchange risks will be minimised by Sterling joining the EC's Exchange Rate Mechanism of the European Monetary System (EMS). It is conceivable that major corporate treasurers will agree among themselves to invoice in European Currency Units (Ecus), thus minimising exposure to currency fluctuations until such time as a common European currency is introduced.

Free movement of capital

The freeing of capital movements is a key element in liberalising financial services. Developments in the European Monetary System, increased use of Ecus, cross-frontier payment systems and the use of plastic cards, plus banking co-ordination, are also crucial, but it is the free movement of capital itself which appeals most directly to business. The Single Market could not function efficiently without a free market in banking services and without freedom of capital movements. In May 1986 the European Commission announced details of a two phase plan to liberalise capital movements and complete removal of exchange controls. The Directive introducing Phase One was adopted in 1986 and covered long-term credits related to commercial transactions, the acquisition by residents of foreign securities and by non-residents of domestic securities, and the admission of securities to stock markets. Most member states have completely or partly liberalised their capital transactions. The rest are expected to do so in the near future. Phase Two, presented in 1987, aims to complete the process of liberalisation, so that what we know as the European Financial Area will become a reality.

Monetary union

Many believe that the completion of the Single Market and freedom of capital movement must ultimately lead to a single currency and full monetary union. Supporters regard monetary union as necessary to cement the success of the Single Market in the free movement of goods, services, people and capital. Although this argument is not universally accepted, the Committee for the Study of Economic and Monetary Union, comprised of central bank governors and outside experts, under the chairmanship of EC Commission President Jacques Delors, was appointed to invesigate a route towards economic and monetary union. The Delors Committee reported in 1989 (*Report on Economic and Monetary Union in the European Community*). Its findings, which did not find favour in its entirety with the British government, were discussed at the European Council summit in Madrid that year. Heads of government agreed, however, to proceed with stage one of the Delors plan.

Delors plan
Stage One is aimed at achieving greater convergence of economic performances via stronger co-ordination of economic and monetary policy. Preparations require amendments to the EEC Treaty. Central bank governors, meeting as a

committee, will take a more prominent role in shaping national monetary, exchange rate and banking policy. All Community currencies, including Sterling, were deemed to participate in the EMS exchange rate mechanism from July 1990.

Stage Two also requires amendments to the EEC Treaty to effect the transfer of decisions, particularly on monetary policy, from national governments to a European System of Central Banks (ESCB), which will establish monetary policy for the Community as a whole. Exchange rate realignments will be made only in exceptional circumstances, and margins of fluctuations would be narrowed.

Stage Three proposes irrevocably fixed Community exchange rates and the transfer to Community institutions of full monetary and economic powers.

Implementation of the Delors Committee report will be dictated by political choice and no overall timetable has been established. Heads of EC governments voted unanimously for Stage One to begin on 1 July, 1990, to coincide with the abolition of all residual exchange controls on capital in France and Italy, which will complete the removal of capital controls in the eight richest member states. No deadline has been established for the completion of Stage One.

Besides capital liberalisation, Stage One will contribute substantially to the completion of the Single Market, as well as seeing the entry of Sterling into the exchange rate mechanism, subject to a number of conditions specified by the UK government. Apart from a reduced level of UK inflation, these relate to ensuring that the Single Market is not diverted from its goal of freeing market forces.

The British government has stated that full monetary union is not essential for the success of the Single Market, and it is certainly the case that the Delors report proposes more than is strictly necessary for monetary integration. Indeed, the UK Treasury has launched a proposal for 'competing currencies' as an alternative, which would allow the markets to dictate which currency would eventually be used throughout Europe. More discussion on monetary union is needed before the final stages of Delors can be accepted enthusiastically by the banks.

Banking services and profits

The international business managers of banks provide companies with specialist support, with access to local experts who are aware of the problems of trading and investing in the European marketplace. They can also provide first-hand knowledge and up-to-date information that companies, particularly smaller companies, might otherwise not be able to obtain. Against the background of legislative change taking place in Europe, small to medium-sized enterprises may need help from their banks to deal with problems of fluctuation in exchange rates, buyer demands for extended credit terms, markets where open account terms are the norm, and unfamiliar customers. Some banks also undertake research to identify suitable trading partners in Europe for smaller companies, in confidence, without disclosing their client's identity. Background trading information on markets is also available to help companies prepare for visits to the marketplace.

Credit insurance: Companies new to trading in European markets will soon grasp that a customer, say, in Portugal can go bust as easily as customers in the domestic market (see *Export credit insurance*, Part Four, Chapter 4). It is expected that sellers who wish to reduce their credit risks in Europe will increasingly turn to four traditional means of minimising exposure: insurance cover, forfaiting, factoring and avalisation. Banks will advise on all these methods of reducing risk and ensuring payment and will provide highly recommended contacts, if they do not offer the full range of services themselves.

To overcome cashflow problems between the date of shipment and the receipt of payment, banks arrange finance linked to credit insurance, worth up to 100 per cent of the value of sales upon evidence of shipment. Provided contractual obligations are met, finance is essentially without recourse.

Forfaiting: In forfaiting, the bank takes over the exporter's receivables for a discount on a non-recourse basis. Again the benefit to the seller is avoidance of disrupting cashflow and, of course, the administrative work in chasing debts.

Factoring: Factoring helps smaller companies sell on open account terms, enabling the business to simplify its trade in Europe and compete on equal terms with local suppliers. Up to 80 per cent of claims on debtors can be advanced, thereby giving the enterprise access to an additional source of working capital which can be used to supplement normal banking facilities. This method of financing is covered in more detail in *Money for Business*, Part Four, Chapter 3.

Avalising: Avalising guarantees that a trade bill will be met at maturity. The guarantee cost has to be met, usually by the buyer. Holding avalised bills means that the exporter can later sell bills without recourse on the forfaiting market and use them as a source of liquidity, or as security against borrowing.

International leasing: If a company's business is capital goods or semi-capital goods related, advice may be sought from banks on all aspects of contract bidding, negotiation and drafting, as well as limited recourse financing. International leasing is one method of providing medium-term finance for sales of capital goods. Local currency domestic leasing can be arranged throughout the EC by way of a variety of direct tax and non-tax financial services. Cross-border leasing is also available in a variety of currencies. International leasing obviates the need for working capital to be tied up, since immediate funds can be made available for 100 per cent of the cost of the seller's equipment.

Foreign currency accounts: Companies which frequently receive or pay out sums in the same European currency may benefit from a foreign currency account demoninated in that currency. This avoids repeated need to convert the currency and it eliminates any exchange risk. Using a foreign currency account, companies do not have to buy and sell currency each time a transaction takes place. Being able to invoice in the local currency adds competitive edge to their business.

Further reading
Report on Economic and Monetary Union in the European Economy, European Community, 1989.
The Cost of Non-Europe in Financial Services European Community, Volume 9 of Cecchini report.
The Role of Money in the European Community, text of Roy Bridge memorial lecture, Sir Leon Brittan, 1989.
The EMS: Ten Years of Progress in European Monetary Co-operation, European Community, 1989.
The exchange rate question in Europe, European Community paper, F Giavazzi, 1989

1992 + Fixed Exchange Rates = Monetary Union, European Community, Target 92 series No. 5, May 1989.

Banking 1992, Clifford Chance, London, 1989.

Investment Services 1992, Clifford Chance, 1989.

The Single European Market: Survey of the UK Financial Services Industry, Bank of England, 1989.

Towards a Big Internal Market in Financial Service, European Community, European File series 17/88.

Towards a European Market for the Undertakings for Collective Investment in Transferable Securities, European Community, Document Public, 1988.

The Single Financial Market, European Community, D. Servais, 1988.

A European Financial Area: the Liberalization of Capital Movements, European Community, European File series 12/88.

1992: Completion of the Single Market in Financial Services, background report, European Commission, London office.

The ECU, European Community, European Documentation series No. 5/1987.

Compendium of Community Monetary Texts, European Community, legal texts of importance to the Monetary Committee, 1986

Periodicals

The Banker, Financial Times, London, monthly.

Bank of England Quarterly Bulletin, Bank of England.

ECU-EMS Information, Statistical Office of the European Communities, monthly.

Money and Finance, Statistical Office of the European Communities, quarterly.

6 Investment Incentives

Inward Investment and Development Agencies

Monica Brebner and James Hogan

In a free European market, relocating businesses or setting up new operations closer to main markets may be an attractive option for companies seeking to expand their operations within Europe. Areas designated as 'assisted areas' in many parts of Europe are attracting new businesses with incentive packages. The main criterion, apart from the broad intention to promote economic growth, is the creation of jobs.

Industrial restructuring is an economic priority for regions throughout the European Community which have either been hit by the decline in traditional industries or have not yet been fully developed. Poorer regions of European Community countries receive substantial sums in EC Funds (see *EC Grants and Loans*, Part Four, Chapter 7). Incentive packages include a variety of benefits to investors, some of them hidden in the sense that,while EC legislation prohibits direct cash subsidies, economic development agencies are often flexible in their interpretation of what an incentive package can include. From the investor's point of view, the objective is to assist companies to expand and develop strategically. From the economic development authority's point of view, investment is encouraged in less developed or assisted regions.

Specific investment incentives provided by national, regional government and city authorities through inward investment and economic development programmes are often generous, each region competing heavily to attract investors. Cash incentives in the form of soft loans and tax concessions are available but, of course, no investor relocates or starts a new plant in a region solely on the basis of availability of cash. But, where a regional development authority cannot match financial incentives offered by other regions, it may place greater emphasis on other advantages which, nevertheless, are of crucial financial significance to an investor. Benefits may include close proximity to the investor's main market, lower labour costs, availability of a skilled workforce and access to research and development facilities. The type of incentives available across Europe in various mixes include:

☐ Loans, interest free or at favourable interest rates, or with interest and repayments 'holidays'.

☐ Grants under assisted area schemes for training, land purchase, equipment purchase, interest relief, marketing development.

☐ Tax credits or exemptions.

☐   Access to enterprise zones and other modern industrial sites at reduced cost or rent.

☐   Location assistance, including the provision of premises

Inward investment promotion frequently involves government and industry organisations in a joint commitment to running investment programmes. Of the major EC economies, France, Germany and the United Kingdom offer a wide range of incentives to industry. Certain regions of Spain — Catalonia, the Basque Country and Valencia — are also actively promoting their inward investment programmes.

Officials at national, regional or local municipal level will guide investors into the 'system' and help them to become part of the business community in which they intend to locate a new operation. Therefore, local contacts in chambers of commerce, city or local authorities will be indispensable sources of information and advice to newcomers in any region. Such people influence the economic development of the regions in which they operate and the development of policies to encourage investors, and will introduce potential investors to those who can assemble an incentive package.

In some European countries chambers of commerce sometimes play a key role in bringing investors into their region. In France, Germany and the Netherlands the role of chambers of commerce and other trade organisations is of key importance. Membership is compulsory and the chambers receive regular income from subscriptions. In the UK, some chambers, mainly the larger ones, have the experience and resources needed to advise and support industrial growth in their areas. But, the chamber movement in the UK is not as well integrated with regional and national investment agencies as in other European countries. For further information on chambers of commerce activities see *Chambers of Commerce*, Part Seven, Chapter 4).

Throughout Europe, regional economic development authorities play a major role in promoting economic growth and strengthening the industrial base of their region. Regional authorities may operate independently as development agencies or as an arm of an autonomous state government, as in Germany, or regional governments as in Spain. Many of them are represented in other EC countries through bilateral chambers of commerce or their own branch offices, as in the case of DATAR, the French regional industrial development agency.

Municipal authorities also play a key part in economic development, administering local incentive programmes in conjunction with regional and national policies.

CONTACTS

Potential investors can obtain information on incentives by contacting national, regional and local industrial development bodies in any EC country. Most inward investment agencies produce detailed economic, industrial and cultural guides. Useful contacts will be located in:

☐   National government; ministries concerned with industrial and economic development; economic development or inward investment agencies.

☐   Regional government: economic development ministries; economic development corporations or inward investment agencies.

☐   Municipal authorities; city or urban development corporations.

- ☐ Representative offices of foreign development agencies in the UK
- ☐ Foreign chambers of commerce in the UK
- ☐ Bilateral chambers of commerce
- ☐ Local chambers of commerce in Europe
- ☐ British chambers of commerce in Europe
- ☐ Embassies and consulates (commercial sections)

Belgium

Belgo-Luxembourg Chamber of Commerce in Great Britain
6 John Street, London WC1N 2ES
Tel: (071) 831 3508
Fax: (071) 831 9151
Telex: 23467 TANLON G

Brussels region

Ministry of the Brussels Region
Foreign Investment Department
Rue Royale 2
B-1000 Brussels
Tel: (32) 2 518 1711
Fax: (32) 2 518 1739

Brussels Regional Development Board (SDRB)
Avenue des Arts 39, Bte 8
B-1040 Brussels
Tel: (32) 2 510 3911
Fax: (32) 2 514 2970

Brussels Regional Investment Board (SRIB)
Avenue Marnix 13
B-1050 Brussels
Tel: (32) 2 511 6483
Fax: (32) 2 511 9074

National Investment Company (NIM)
Montoyerstraat 63
B-1040 Brussels
Tel: (32) 2 230 1180

Flanders

Flanders Investment Opportunities Council (FIOC)
Trierstraat 100
B-1040 Brussels
Tel: (32) 2 230 1225
Fax: (32) 2 230 9834
Telex: 62073

Regional Investment Company for Flanders (GIMV)
Anneessensstraat 1-3, Box 1
B-2000 Antwerp
Tel: (32) 3 233 7576

Regional Development Authority of Antwerp
Desguinlei 102, Box 13
B-2018 Antwerp
Tel: (32) 3 237 7994

Regional Development Authority of Oost-Vlaanderen
ICC Floraliapaleis, Box 6
B-9000 Gent
Tel: (32) 91 21 55 11

Regional Development Authority of Vlaams-Brabant
Toekomststraat 36-38
B-1800 Vilvorde
Tel: (32) 2 251 5171

Regional Development Authority of West-Vlaanderen
Baron Ruzettelaan 33
B-8320 Bruges
Tel: (32) 50 35 81 31

Wallonia

Wallon Regional Executive
Avenue des Arts 13-14
B-1040 Brussels
Tel: (32) 2 211 5511
Fax: (32) 2 211 5570
Telex: 62094 REGWAL B

Denmark

Ministry of Industry
Information Office for Foreign Investment
25 Sondergade
DK-8600 Silkeborg
Tel: (45) 86 825655
Fax: (45) 86 801629
Telex: 0366255 danreg

Ministry of Foreign Affairs
Investment Secretariat
2 Asiatisk Plads
DK-1448 Copenhagen K
Tel: (45) 33 920000
Fax: (45) 31 540533
Telex: 31292 etr dk

Royal Danish Embassy
Economic Counsellor
55 Sloane Street
London SW1X 9SR
Tel: (071) 235 1255
Fax: (071) 235 9321
Telex: 28103

France

DATAR

Delegation a l'Armenagement du Territoire et a l'Action Regionale (DATAR)
1 Avenue Charles Floquet
F-75007 Paris
Tel: (33) 1 47 83 61 20
Fax: (33) 1 43 06 99 01
Telex: 200970

French Industrial Development Board (FIDB)
21-24 Grosvenor Place
London SW1X 7HU
Tel: (071) 823 1895
Fax: (071) 235 8598
Telex: 28657

Regional development agencies

APEILOR
1 Place du Font a Seille
F-57000 Metz
Tel: (33) 87 75 36 18
Fax: (33) 87 75 21 99
Telex: 860047

BDIA
64 rue Voltaire
F-08000 Charleville Mezieres
Tel: (33) 24 57 47 08
Fax: (33) 24 37 55 69
Telex: 840391

Nord pas De Calais Development Agency
16 Residence Breteuil
le Parc Saint-Maur
F-59000 Lille
Tel: (33) 20 55 98 82
Fax: (33) 20 55 39 15
Telex: 120936

Normandie Development
57 Avenue Bretagne
F-76100 Rouen
Tel: (33) 35 03 06 04
Fax: (33) 35 03 94 11
Telex: 771430

ADIMAC
39 rue Georges Clemenceau
BP 491
F-63013 Clermont-Ferrand
Tel: (33) 73 35 20 05
Fax: (33) 73 35 06 90

ADIL
2 rue du Coin
F-42000 Saint Etienne
Tel: (33) 77 33 21 90
Fax: (33) 77 41 99 60
Telex: 307187

Languedoc-Roussillon Prospection
254 rue Michel Teule
F-34080 Montpelier
Tel: (33) 67 61 01 81
Fax: (33) 67 52 69 37
Telex: 485462

Ouest-Atlantic
Immeuble Neptune
F-44000 Nantes
Tel: (33) 40 89 35 00
Fax: (33) 40 48 01 54
Telex: 711416

Enterprise zones

Ministere de l'Industrie des P & T et du Tourisme
101 rue de Grenelle
F-75700 Paris
Tel: (33) 1 45 56 45 45

Delegation a l'Armenagement du Territoire et a l'Action Regionale (DATAR)
1 Avenue Charles Floquet
F-75007 Paris
Tel: (33) 1 47 83 61 20
Fax: (33) 1 43 06 99 01
Telex: 200970

Germany

German state and municipal authorities, alongside chambers of commerce, are strongly committed to economic and industrial development, working together to vigorously promote locally available incentives and advantages. For information on East German investment opportunities see *Doing Business in Eastern Europe,* Part Five, Chapter 2.

Baden-Wurtemberg

Freiburg, Karlsruhe, Heidelberg, Heilbronn, Mannheim, Singen, Stuttgart (state capital), Tubingen, Ulm

Ministry of Economic Affairs and Technology
Postfach 10 34 51
Theodor-Heuss-Strasse 4
D-7000 Stuttgart 1
Tel: (49) 711 20201
Fax: (49) 123 2126
Telex: 723931 WMBWS D

Baden-Wurtemberg Trade and Investment Office
PO Box 104334
Schloss-Strasse 25
D-7000 Stuttgart 10
Tel: (49) 711 227870
Fax: (49) 711 2278722

Bavaria

Augsburg, Bamberg, Bayreuth, Munchen (Munich — state capital), Nurnberg, Regensburg, Schweinfurt, Wurzburg

199

Bavarian Ministry of Economic Affairs and Transport
Industry Location Advisory Service
Prinzregentenstrasse 28
D-8000 Munich 22
Tel: (49) 89 21 62 26 42
Fax: (49) 89 21 62 27 60
Telex: 523759 BYWVM D

Berlin Economic Development Corporation
Budapester Strasse 1
D-1000 Berlin 30
Tel: (49) 30 26 48 80
Fax: (49) 30 26 48 82 39

Bremen (city state)

Economic Development Corporation of the Free Hanseatic City of Bremen
Hanseatenhof 8
D-2800 Bremen 1
Tel: (49) 421 308850
Fax: (49) 421 30885 44
Telex: 245079 BREWI D

Hamburg (city state)

Hamburg Business Development Corporation
Hamburger Strasse 11
D-2000 Hamburg 76
Tel: (49) 40 22 70 19 0
Fax: (49) 40 22 70 19 29
Telex: 2165210 HWF D

Hamburg Business Development Corporation
(UK Representative's Office)
19 Ashley Close, Earley
Reading RG6 2QY
Tel: (0734) 861496
Fax: (0734) 500511
Telex: 847423 COCR G

Hessen

Darmstadt, Fulda, Frankfurt, Kassel, Wiesbaden (state capital)

The HLT Group (Development Company Hessen)
Abraham-Lincoln-Strasse 38-42
D-6200 Wiesbaden
Tel: (49) 6121 774-0
Fax: (49) 6121 774-265
Telex: 4186127 HLT D

Lower Saxony

Celle, Delmenhorst, Emden, Hannover (state capital), Luneburg, Oldenburg, Braunscheig (Brunswick), Gottingen, Hildesheim, Osnabruck, Salzgitter, Wilmshaven

Lower Saxony Ministry of Economic Affairs, Technology and Transport
Postfach 101
Friedrichswall 1
D-3000 Hannover 1
Tel: (49) 511 120-1/120-6520/120-2661
Fax: (49) 511 120 6430
Telex: 923414-35 NL D

North Rhine-Westphalia

Aachen, Bielefeld, Bochum, Bonn, Koln (Cologne), Dortmund, Duisburg, Duren, Dusselforf, Essen, Krefeld, Monchengladbach, Mulheim/Ruhr, Munster, Remschied, Solingen, Wuppertal

Economic Development Corporation for
North Rhine-Westphalia
Kavalleriestr. 8-10
D-4000 Dusseldorf 1
Tel: (49) 211 13 00 00
Fax: (49) 211 13 00 054
Telex: 8587830 GEWI D

Rhineland Palatinate

Kaiserslautern, Koblenz, Ludwigshafen, Mainz (state capital), Rockenhausen, Trier

Rhineland Palatinate Economic
Development Corporation
Erthalstrasse 1
D-6500 Mainz
Tel: (49) 6131 63 20 66/67
Fax: (49) 6131 67 07 25
Telex: 6131/986 RPW

Saarland

Homburg, Merzig, Neunkirchen, Saarbrucken (State Capital), Saarlouis, St Wendel

Saarland Economic Development
Corporation
Bismarckstrasse 39-41
D-6600 Saarbrucken 3
Tel: (49) 681 687990
Fax: (49) 681 65758
Telex: 4421219 GWSA D

Schleswig-Holstein

Flensburg, Kiel (state capital), Luebeck, Neumunster, Pinneberg, Schleswig

Economic Development Corporation of
Schleswig-Holstein
Sophienblatt 60
2300 Kiel 1
Tel: (49) 431 63091

Eastern Germany

See *Doing Business in Eastern Europe*, Part Five, Chapter 2.

East European Trade Council
Suite 10
Westminster Palace Gardens
Artillery Row
London SW1P 1RL
Tel: (071) 222 7622
Fax: (071) 222 5359

UK contact for German inward investment agencies

German Chamber of Commerce and Industry
12-13 Suffolk Street
St. James's, London SW1Y 4HG
Tel: (071) 930 7251
Fax: (071) 930 2726
Telex 919442 GERMAN G

Greece

Hellenic Business Development and Investment Company (HBDIC)
32 Kisfisias Avenue
151 25 Paradisos Amarousiou
Athens
Tel: (30) 1 6833108/6833111
Fax: (30) 1 6820970

Greek Embassy
Commercial Counsellor
1A Holland Park
London W11 3TP
Tel: (071) 727 8040
Fax: (071) 229 7221
Telex: 266751 GREEMB G

Hellenic Industrial Development Bank (ETBA)
18 Panepistimiou Str.
GR-106-72 Athens
Tel: (30) 1 323 7981/7381
Fax: (30) 1 362 1023
Telex: 215203 ETVA GR

British-Hellenic Chamber of Commerce
25 Vas. Sofias Avenue
1064 Athens
Tel: (30) 1 72 10 361
Fax: (30) 1 72 18 751
Telex: 214716 ELBR GR

Ireland

Industrial Development Authority (IDA)
Wilton Park House
Wilton Place, Dublin 2
Tel: (353) 1 686633
   (From UK: 0001 686633)
Fax: (353) 1 603703 (From UK: 0001 603703)
Telex: 93431

Shannon Free Airport Development Company
Town Centre
Shannon, County Clare
Tel: (353) 61 361555
Fax: (353) 61 361903
Telex: 26282

Udaras na Gaeltechta
Na Forbacha
Gaillimh
Tel: (353) 91 92011
Fax: (353) 91 92037
Telex: 50159

Italy

The bulk of government investment incentives relate to new investment in the South of Italy and the islands. The development agency for this part of the country is ISVEMER. In the north, limited incentives are available on a regional basis through regional government offices. Contacts in regional government should be obtainable from the Italian Embassy or the Italian Chamber of Commerce in Great Britain. However, reliable information is difficult to obtain.

Agencia per la Promozione dello Sviluppo del Mezzogiorno
Piazza Kennedy 20
00144 Rome
Tel: (39) 6 59911

British Chamber of Commerce in Italy
Via Agnello 8
20121 Milan
Tel: (39) 2 876981
Fax: (39) 2 28100.262
Telex: 332490

ISVEMER
65/66 Queen Street
London EC4R 1EH
Tel: (071) 283 9981
Fax: (071) 283 9712

Italian Chamber of Commerce in Great Britain
Walmar House
296 Regent Street
London W1R 6AE
Tel: (071) 637 3153
Fax: (071) 436 6037
Telex: 269096 ITACAM G

Luxembourg

Luxdevelopment
Rue Alcide de Gasperi 7
1615 Luxembourg
Tel: (352) 433968
Fax: (352) 433808

Belgo-Luxembourg Chamber of Commerce in Great Britain
6 John Street
London WC1N 2ES
Tel: (071) 831 3508
Fax: (071) 831 9151
Telex: 23467 TANLON G

Netherlands

The Dutch authorities and the Netherlands-British Chamber of Commerce are particularly active in promoting two-way trade and investment between Britain and the Netherlands.

Netherlands Foreign Investment Agency
Ministry of Economic Affairs
PO Box 20101
2500 EC The Hague
Tel: (31) 703 798819/797233
Fax: (31) 703 796322
Telex: 31099 ECZA NL

Netherlands British Chamber of Commerce
Holland Trade House
Bezuidenhoutseweg 181
2594 AH The Hague
Tel: (31) 703 478881
Telex: 33112

Peter Biddlecombe Associates
6th Floor, Vigo Street
London W1X 1AH
Tel: (071) 437 5927
Fax: (071) 491 7971
Telex: 27950

(UK representative of the Netherlands
Foreign Investment Agency)

Netherlands British Chamber of Commerce
The Dutch House
307-308 High Holborn
London WC1V 7LS
Tel: (071) 405 1358
Telex: 23211

Portugal

Instituto de Comercio de Portugal (ICEP)
Avenida da Liberdade 258
1200 Lisbon
Tel: (351) 1 570607
Fax: (351) 1 578543
Telex: 14712 ICEP P

British-Portugese Chamber of Commerce
Rua da Estrela 8
1200 Lisbon
Tel: (351) 1 661586
Telex: 12787

**Portuguese Chamber of Commerce and
Industry in the UK**
4th Floor
New Bond Street House
1-5 New Bond Street
London W1Y ODB
Tel: (071) 493 9973

Spain

All of the autonomous regional authorites throughout Spain run investment and business promotion programmes. The industrial and economic development authorities in the principal centres of industry are listed below. Investment agencies in Catalonia and the Basque Country have, since Spain joined the EC, been notably active in promoting inward investment incentives internationally.

Directorate-General for Regional Economic Incentives
Ministry of Economy and Industry
Castellana 147
28046 Madrid
Tel: (34) 1 571 5836

Spanish Chamber of Commerce in Great Britain
5 Cavendish Square
London W1M 0DP
Tel: (071) 637 9061
Telex: 8811583 CAMCOE G

Cataluna (Catalonia)

Information & Development Management Centre (CIDEM)
Avenida Diagonal 403
08008 Barcelona
Tel: (34) 3 217 2008
Fax: (34) 3 238 2031

Madrid

Consejeria de Economia
Principe de Vergara 132
Madrid
Tel: (34) 1 580 2200

Instituto Madrileno de Desarrollo (IMADE)
Garcia de Paredes 92
2810 Madrid
Tel: (34) 1 410 2063
Fax: (34) 1 319 4290

Pais Vasco (Basque Country)

Sociedad para la Promocion y Reconversion
Industrial (SPRI)
Gran Via 35-3
48009 Bilbao
Tel: (34) 4 415 8288
Fax: (34) 4 416 9623

Valencia

IMPIVA
Plaza Ayuntamento 6
46002 Valencia
Tel: (34) 6 351 0100
Fax: (34) 6 351 4064

Consejeria de Industria Comercio y
Turismo
Isabel la Catolica 8-10
46004 Valencia
Tel: (34) 6 352 6177

United Kingdom

The main agencies are the Department of Trade and Industry's Investment in Britain Bureau, the Scottish Development Agency, the Welsh Development Agency and the Industrial Development Board for Northern ireland. Urban Development Corporations also run local incentive programmes.

Invest in Britain Bureau
Department of Trade and Industry
Kingsgate House
66-74 Victoria Street
London SW1E 6SW
Tel: (071) 215 8439/8438
Fax: (071) 215 8451
Telex: 936069 DTI KH G

Northern Ireland

Industrial Development Board for Northern
Ireland
IDB House
64 Chichester Street
Belfast BT1 4JX
Tel: (0232) 233233
Fax: (0232) 231328
Telex: 747025

Northern Ireland Business Centre
11 Berkeley Street
London W1X 6BU
Tel: (071) 493 0601
Fax: (071) 499 3731

Scotland

Scottish Development Agency
Locate in Scotland
120 Bothwell Street
Glasgow G2 7JP
Tel: (041) 248 2700
Fax: (041) 221 5129

Wales

Welsh Development Agency
Welsh Development International
15th Floor
Pearl Assurance House
Greyfriars Road
Cardiff CF1 3XX
Tel: (0222) 371641
Fax: (0222) 223243

You may be interested to know that the following titles are also available in the Macmillan Dictionary Series:

Macmillan Dictionary of Accounting, 2nd ed (Parker)	hc £29.50	pb £10.95
Macmillan Dictionary of Anthropology (Seymour–Smith)	hc £25.00	pb £10.95
Macmillan Dictionary of Archaeology (Whitehouse)	hc £27.50	pb £9.95
Macmillan Dictionary of Astronomy, 2nd ed (Illingworth)	hc £27.50	pb £10.95
Macmillan Dictionary of Biotechnology (Coombs)	hc £25.00	pb £10.95
Macmillan Dictionary of Building (McMullan)	hc £25.00	pb £7.95
Macmillan Dictionary of Business and Management (Lamming and Bessant)	hc £25.00	pb £10.95
Macmillan Dictionary of Chemistry (Hibbert and James)	hc £45.00	pb £14.95
Macmillan Dictionary of Data Communications, 2nd ed (Sippl)	hc £29.99	pb £9.95
Macmillan Dictionary of Electrochemistry (Hibbert and James)	hc £29.50	
Macmillan Dictionary of Energy, 2nd ed (ed. Slesser)	hc £29.95	pb £10.95
Macmillan Dictionary of the Environment, 3rd ed (ed. Allaby)	hc £29.95	pb £10.95
Macmillan Dictionary of Genetics and Cell Biology (Maclean)		pb £10.95
Macmillan Dictionary of Historical Terms, 2nd ed (Cook)	hc £25.00	pb £8.95
Macmillan Dictionary of the History of Science (Bynum, Browne and Porter)		pb £10.95
Macmillan Dictionary of Immunology (Rosen, Steiner and Unanue)	hc £25.00	pb £9.95
Macmillan Dictionary of Information Technology, 3rd ed (Longley and Shain)	hc £29.99	pb £10.99
Macmillan Dictionary of International Finance, 2nd ed (Walmsley)	hc £9.95	
Macmillan Dictionary of Life Sciences, 2nd ed (Martin)	hc £27.50	pb £10.95
Macmillan Dictionary of Marketing and Advertising, 2nd ed (ed. Baker)	hc £30.00	pb £10.95
Macmillan Dictionary of Materials and Manufacturing (ed. John)	hc £ 29.95	
Macmillan Dictionary of Microcomputing, 3rd ed (Sippl)	hc £27.50	
Macmillan Dictionary of Modern Economics, 3rd ed (Pearce)	hc £25.00	pb £10.99
Macmillan Dictionary of Personal Computing and Communications (Longley and Shain)	hc £27.50	pb £9.99
Macmillan Dictionary of Physics (Lord)	hc £29.95	pb £9.95
Macmillan Dictionary of Production Management and Technology (Lamming and Bessant)	hc £29.50	
Macmillan Dictionary of Psychology (Sutherland)	hc £29.95	
Macmillan Dictionary of Toxicology (Hodgson, Mailman and Chambers)	hc £39.50	
Macmillan Dictionary of Women's Biography, 2nd ed (Uglow)	hc £29.95	
Macmillan Student Encyclopedia of Sociology (ed. Mann)		pb £9.95

All titles are available from your local bookseller. In case of difficulty, please contact Helen Brown, Macmillan Academic and Professional Ltd, Houndmills, Basingstoke, Hampshire RG21 2XS.

(June 1990 – All prices are correct at time of going to press but are subject to change)

7 EC Grants and Loans

Structural funds
Research and development programmes

Mishka Bienkowski

The activities of the European Commission extend into most aspects of our social and economic environment and, as we proceed towards a fully realised Single Market, and beyond, the Commission's role will become even more influential. Knowledge of the financial programmes administered by the Commission is not only an economic priority for companies, but also a source of valuable intelligence about current policy priorities and future directions which the EC might take. Any corporate strategy ignoring EC policy and developments would be deficient in its assessment of opportunities and threats in the future.

The programme to complete the Single Market or Internal Market is an important milestone in the evolution of the European Community and, accordingly, affects all European Commission activities, the various funds and programmes offering financial assistance being no exception. The adoption of the Single European Act, in addition to providing the legislative framework for the Single Market programme, has invigorated and given new impetus to many of the Commission's areas of responsibility. The Act was central to agreement on the concentration of the EC's so-called Structural Funds — the European Regional Development Fund (ERDF), the European Social Fund (ESF) and the European Agriculture Guidance and Guarantee Fund (Guidance Section) (EAGGF) — on the poorest regions of the Community, and a doubling in their budget by 1993. It also enabled the Commission to amend the original EEC Treaty of Rome to give specific reference to research and technological development.

This chapter is concerned with the wide range of funds and programmes administered by the Commission which are designed to promote economic and industrial development within the EC. The programmes fall broadly into two groups:

☐ Programmes concerned with economic development and improvements in living and working conditions.

☐ Programmes concerned with strategic issues which aim to safeguard the commercial competitiveness of European industry and protect the environment.

Most of the Commission's activities are closely linked with parallel or complementary supportive activities within each EC member state. In R & D, for example, national R & D schemes frequently fund areas of R & D or stages of a research project which are not covered under a Community scheme. In the area of private sector investment, such as start-ups or expansion, the ERDF is a major source of funding but, as a rule, is channelled through national investment incentive programmes in 'assisted areas'. The ERDF contribution is calculated as a proportion of the total public sector contribution to the project and subsequently reimbursed to the public authority which is part funding the investment. Although the decision to award assistance is at the discretion of the particular public authority concerned, in most cases such awards would not be made, or could be significantly lower in value, in the absence of an EC contribution. This type of reinforcing link operates to a greater or lesser extent in relation to all of the Structural Funds. Therefore, to understand the framework within which financial incentives operate, it is necessary to become familiar with both the spectrum of Commission activities as well as the national aid regime operated within any particular member state.

Part I of this chapter covers the Community's socio-economic objectives through a review of the activities of each of the Structural Funds, with particular reference to the reforming legislation introduced since the start of 1989, as well as summarising the activities of the Community's loan instruments. Part II covers the strategic and environmental objectives being addressed through the diverse range of Commission funded programmes in scientific and industrial research and technological development.

PART I — STRUCTURAL FUNDS

Central to the Commission's primary objective of achieving more even economic and social development among the regions of the Community are the three structural funds:

☐ European Regional Development Fund (ERDF)

☐ European Social Fund (ESF)

☐ European Agricultural Guidance and Guarantee Fund (EAGGF) (Guidance Section)

Taken as a group, the structural funds have been allocated a total budget of approximately 9 billion Ecus in 1989, rising to 14 billion Ecus in 1992, accounting for roughly 20 per cent of the total Community budget. At this level, the structural funds are second in importance within the Community budget only to the Common Agricultural Policy.

The structural funds are supported in their activities by several Community financial instruments: the European Investment Bank, the New Community Instrument and European Coal and Steel Community. All three instruments have financial resources available for the purposes of providing loan finance on attractive terms to projects promoting Community interests and objectives and, like the Funds, have a strong regional development orientation. With the passing of the Single European Act in 1986, the structural funds were elevated in status as the Community's key instruments for promoting economic welfare and reducing regional disparities. Horizontal Regulation (EEC) 2052/88 (*Official Journal* L185 15.7.89) redefines the tasks of the three structural funds in line with the five priority objectives set out in the Single Act. Regulation 2052/88 assigns the three structural funds to contribute to the specific objectives with which each is broadly concerned:

☐ **Objective 1:** Promoting the development and structural adjustment of the regions whose development is lagging behind [ERDF, ESF, EAGGF Guidance Section].

☐ **Objective 2:** Converting the regions, frontier regions or parts of regions, including employment areas and urban communities, seriously affected by industrial decline (ERDF, ESF).

☐ **Objective 3:** Combatting long-term unemployment (ESF).

☐ **Objective 4:** Facilitating the occupational integration of young people (ESF).

☐ **Objective 5:** With a view to reform of the Common Agricultural Policy; (a) speeding up the adjustment of agricultural structures; (b) promoting the development of rural areas (EAGGF Guidance Section ESF, ERDF)

Assistance offered under Objectives 1, 2 and 5(b) is restricted to particular regions of the Community, proposed by individual member states and agreed by the Commission. Objective 1 regions (structurally backward) are generally designated at NUTS level II (Nomenclature of Statistical Territorial Units — equivalent to regions in the UK) and are targetted to receive 80 per cent of the total Structural Fund budget. Regions designated under Objective 1 remain in force for a five year period. Those designated for 1989-93 are Northern Ireland, Ireland, southern Italy, southern Spain, Portugal, Greece, the French overseas departments and Corsica.

Objective 2 (industrial decline) and 5(b) (rural regions) are designated at NUTS level III (county or district in the UK) and are agreed for a three year period. The Commission Decision establishing an initial list of areas eligible under Objective 2 for the period 1989-91 is published in *Official Journal* No. L 112 25.4.89. In the UK, these correspond roughly with the present Assisted Areas map which determines eligibility for UK regional assistance. With respect to Objective 5 (b), the Commission Decision selecting rural areas eligible to receive assistance is published in *Official Journal* No. L 198 12.7.89. In the UK, Objective 5 (b) regions have been designated in the Highlands and Border regions of Scotland, rural Wales and parts of Devon and Cornwall.

Objectives 3 and 4 are to be advanced on a Community-wide basis taking into account the particular problems of each individual member state. Objective 5(a), to be implemented from 1990, will not be regionally restricted but intervention mechanisms will be tailored to suit national economic circumstances.

The following shows the 1989 budget breakdown for the application of each of the structural funds to each of the Single Act objectives.

Structural Fund 1989 budget breakdown by objective (million Ecus)

Objective	ERDF	ESF	EAGGF
1	3,373	1,533	553
2	721	283	—
3/4	—	1,343	—
5(a)	—	—	541
5(b)	140	90	71

Source: O'Hagan M, Guide to the 1989 General Budget of the Commission of the European Communities, Dartmouth, 1989.

In addition to specifying the objectives to which each of the Funds are to be addressed, Regulation 2052/88 stipulates that the three Funds are to be co-ordinated in their activities, both with each other, and with the other Community financial instruments — the European Investment Bank, European Coal and Steel Community and New Community Instrument.

European Regional Development Fund

The European Regional Development Fund (ERDF) was established in 1975 and is the largest of the three structural funds, accounting for roughly half of the total Structural Fund budget. It is largely responsible for promoting regional economic development through the funding of infrastructure and productive investment. The total ERDF budget allocation for 1989 (including administrative costs) is 4,495 million Ecus, of which 75 per cent (3,373 million Ecus) has been assigned for Objective 1 regions. Of the remaining 25 per cent, 16 per cent is to be spent in Objective 2 regions and just 3 per cent in Objective 5 (b) regions. Roughly 5 per cent (261 million Ecus) has been set aside to fund transitional measures and innovative operations. In addition to direct funding for projects, approximately 0.5 per cent of the annual budget is available to fund technical assistance or feasibility studies in preparation for a full project submission. Such studies may receive funding of up to 100 per cent of eligible expenditure.

ERDF financing is disbursed primarily through existing national aid schemes or through public sector intermediaries. Individual projects are generally proposed by regional authorities, though direct proposals from the private sector may also be submitted. Project proposals must attract a contribution (generally ranging from 30-50 per cent of project costs) from the relevant public authority in the beneficiary state.

Assistance for private sector investment projects is generally awarded through the relevant national aid scheme and, provided the conditions for ERDF co-financing are met, the member state concerned is subsequently reimbursed for part of its contribution to the project. Highest rates of award are available through the regional assistance packages available in the designated problem regions of each member state. Designated problem regions concur largely with those designated under the ERDF; indeed Commission approval is required in any redesignation exercise. Moreover, as it is generally in each member state's interest to maximise receipts from the Commission, the assistance available under the national regional aid packages conforms largely to the objectives and criteria laid down by the Commission in the operation of the structural funds. An understanding of Commission objectives and criteria therefore provides a useful insight into the operation of national assistance schemes.

Under the new reforms to the structural funds, ERDF financing is restricted to areas designated under Objectives 1,2 and 5 (b) of the Single Act. In the UK, however, separate provision has been made for ERDF financing to be available in several inner London boroughs which did not qualify under the criteria used to determine the Objective 1, 2 and 5 (b) regions.

Member state regional aid packages

COUNTRY	INCENTIVE	COMMISSION CEILINGS
Belgium	Interest subsidy/capital grant	20% after tax
Denmark	Regional development grant Municipal soft loan	25% before tax
France	Regional policy grant Local tax concession	25% before tax
Germany	Investment grant Depreciation allowance ERP regional soft loan	23% before tax
Greece	Investment grant/interest rate subsidy. Increased depreciation allowance Tax allowance	75% after tax
Ireland	New industry programme Small industry programme International services programme	75% after tax
Italy	Capital grant National fund loan Tax concession	75% after tax
Luxembourg	Capital grant/interest subsidy Tax concession Equipment loan	25% before tax
Netherlands	Investment premium	25% before tax
Portugal	SIBR regional incentive system SIPE business environment development. SIFIT tourism incentives	75% after tax
Spain	Regional investment grant	75% after tax
UK	Regional selective assistance Regional enterprise grant	30% after tax
N. Ireland	Selective assistance	75% after tax

1 The maxima refer to incentives awarded alone or in combination, and in priority development areas. Lower rates apply in standard development areas. Actual rates awarded are generally significantly lower than the Commission ceilings.

Sources: Yuill,D. et al (eds), *European Regional Incentives*, 1989 Edition, Bowker-Saur, 1989. Commission communication on the method for the application of Article 92 (3) (a) and (c) to regional aid, *Official Journal* No. C 212, 12.08.88.

Since its inception, the bulk of ERDF spending has been used to fund infrastructure investment (accounting, for example, for 91.1 per cent of total ERDF appropriations in 1987). Under the new reforming legislation, however, more restrictive criteria are to be applied in determining eligible infrastructure investment (see below) and it is expected that more funding will be directed towards productive investment.

ERDF implementing Regulation (EEC) No 4254/88 specifies the types of activities which the ERDF can co-finance:

(a) Productive investment linked to the creation or maintenance of permanent jobs.

(b) Infrastructure investment: in Objective 1 regions, eligible investment must increase economic potential, development or structural adjustment although, where a need is demonstrated, certain non-economic facilities (eg. health and education) may also be supported; in Objective 2 regions, eligible investment must relate to the regeneration of the area concerned or provide the basis for the creation or development of economic activity; in Objective 5(b) regions, investment must be linked directly to economic activity which creates jobs other than in agriculture.

(c) Indigenous potential: Services for small and medium-sized enterprises (SMEs), technology transfer, improving access to the capital market (through guarantees and equity participation), direct investment aid (where no aid scheme exists), the provision of small-scale infrastructure.

(d) Operations planned in the context of regional development at Community level.

(e) Preparatory, accompanying and assessment measures.

(f) Productive investment and infrastructure investment aimed at environmental protection where such investment is linked to regional development.

The trend in ERDF funding during the past few years has been away from individual project financing towards 'programme' financing, a concept which was first introduced under Regulation (EEC) 1787/84, now superseded by Regulation (EEC) 4254/88. In addition to funding individual projects, Regulation 1787/84, provided for ERDF financing to be made available for so-called 'Community programmes', instituted by the Commission to advance Community-wide objectives, and also for national programmes of Community Interest (NPCIs) — multi-annual measures devised by individual member states which would contribute to both national and Community objectives. Reflecting the shift in emphasis towards 'programme' financing, priority in the disbursement of ERDF funds is given to programmes which can be classed as 'Integrated Development Operations' (IDOs). IDOs generally combine a range of different economic development measures and attract funding from several Community sources; eg. ERDF, European Social Fund and European Investment Bank. Since Regulation 1787/84 came into force in 1985, several Community Programmes, and a large number of Integrated Development Operations (some classified as NPCIs and others as simple IDOs) have been approved, many of which will continue to run into the 1990's. The following table provides a list of agreed Community Programmes.

European Regional Development: Community Programmes

Programme & Regulation	Description	Budget	Duration
RENAVAL (EEC 2506/88)	Conversion of ship-building closure areas; infrastructure and industrial investment	200 M Ecus	1988-90
RESIDER (EEC 328/88)	Conversion of steel closure areas; infrastructure and industrial investment	300 M Ecus	1988-90
STAR (EEC 3300/86)	Telecommunications investment in poorest regions	778 M Ecus	1986-91
VALOREN (EEC 3301/86)	Exploitation of local energy resources in poorest regions	398 M Ecus	1986-91
RECHAR (EEC 4253/88) (EEC 4254/88)	Economic conversion of coalmining areas.	300 M Ecus	1990-94

The trend towards 'programme' financing continues to be advanced under the provisions introduced in Regulation 4254/88. Under this new Regulation, each member state is required to submit regional development plans of three to five years' duration in respect of one or more regions covered by each Objective. These regional plans then form the basis of a Community Support Framework, agreed with the Commission and specifying the measures eligible for ERDF financing. Operational programmes, including integrated operations involving funding from several Community sources, must fall within the agreed Community Support Framework in order to attract ERDF financing. Individual projects which conform to the relevant Community Support Framework can also be eligible for support. The majority of ERDF financing is, however, expected to be channelled through operational programmes, with integrated operations receiving priority. NPCIs and IDOs approved prior to the entry into force of the new Regulation were designed to tackle the same problems as those set out in any more recently submitted regional plans (and subsequently reflected in the Community Support Frameworks) and as such will continue to be funded under the new arrangements.

Also administered by the Regional Policy Directorate of the Commission (DG XVI) and closely associated with the activities of the ERDF are two other types of programme which have been established to deal with two specific regional problems. These are the Integrated Mediterranean Programmes (IMPs) and the Programme for the Development of Portuguese Industry (PEDIP).

IMPs have been running for a number of years and were set up to improve the competitive position of the Mediterranean regions prior to the accession of Spain and Portugal. IMPs cover Greece and parts of Italy and France. Through the IMPs, special funding has been made available to support investment in the productive sector and in infrastructure. An additional 250 million Ecus was made available to support investment in the productive sector and infrastructure. An additional 250 million Ecus was made available to support IMP projects in 1989. PEDIP has been set up to help Portugal prepare for the completion of the internal market in 1992. PEDIP has been agreed to run from 1988-92 with an overall budget of 2 billion Ecus, covering grants from the ERDF and the Social Fund together with Community loans made available through the European Investment Bank and the New Community Instrument, alongside a top-up grant available through a special PEDIP budget line of 100 million Ecus. PEDIP will contribute to investment in infrastructure, productive investment, vocational training measures and a variety of supportive activities designed to modernise Portugese industry.

European Social Fund

The European Social Fund (ESF) has been operating since 1957 as an instrument by which financial assistance is available to public authorities, private firms or voluntary bodies to support the cost of vocational training and job creation schemes. Projects must be wholly or partly financed by public funds in the beneficiary state. Activities financed by the ESF can be undertaken as part of operational programmes (ie. covering groups of individual projects), can involve global grant schemes administered by designated intermediaries within each member state or can consist of direct support for studies and other supporting measures. As already mentioned, under Framework Regulation (EEC) 2052/88, governing the activities of the three structural funds, the Social Fund has been assigned to contribute to all five Objectives specified in the Single Act. The total Social Fund budget allocation for 1989, including administrative costs, was 3,387 million Ecus.

Priority use of Social Fund assistance is to be directed towards Objectives 3 and 4 relating to long-term unemployment and occupational integration of young people, respectively. In 1989, these two Objectives were ear-marked to receive 1,343 million Ecus of the total ESF budget. Neither of these Objectives are subject to regional restriction. Measures qualifying for funding under each of these Objectives will be set out in broad terms in a Community Support Framework agreed with the Commission in relation to a national plan of three to five years' duration submitted by each member state. Guidelines, outlining in detail the specific actions eligible under Objectives 3 and 4, are periodically reviewed by the Commission. The most recent Guidelines, published in *Official Journal* No C45 24.02.89 took effect from 1 January 1990 and remain in force for three years. All applications for Fund assistance, whether for individual projects or operational programmes, must conform to these Guidelines and to the agreed Community Support Framework.

In the case of Objectives 1, 2 and 5[b], the Social Fund is expected to act in co-ordination with both the ERDF and the EAGGF [Guidance Section] to support qualifying employment and training measures. Almost half of the 1989 ESF budget (1,533 million Ecus) was ear-marked for Objective 1 regions.

Up to 5 per cent of the total ESF budget can be directed towards innovatory training and employment operations, studies and technical assistance, information exchange in relation to technology transfer and guidance counselling for the long-term unemployed.

Under Social Fund implementing Regulation (EEC) 4255/88, ESF part-financing is available towards:

(a) the income of persons receiving vocational training.

(b) the costs of preparing, operating, managing and assessing training operations including vocational guidance, costs of training teaching staff and subsistence and travel costs of those covered by vocational training operations.

(c) the cost of granting recruitment subsidies for a maximum period of 12 months and costs associated with the creation of self-employed activities; the cost of recruitment subsidies of at least six months' duration per person associated with non- productive projects which fulfil a public need and are located in Objective 1 regions.

(d) the cost of technical assistance and studies related to the implementation of the ESF Regulation; the cost of transnational exchange of information between undertakings related to the modernisation of production technology; the cost of guidance counselling for the reintegration of the long-term unemployed.

In Objective 1 regions eligible activities qualify for an ESF contribution of up to 75 per cent of total costs and, as a general rule, at least 50 per cent of the amount of public expenditure committed to the project. Elsewhere, the maximum ESF contribution is 50 per cent of total costs and, as a general rule, at least 25 per cent of public expenditure. In the case of recruitment subsidies, the maximum eligible amount per person and per week is determined each year at a rate equal to 30 per cent of the average gross earnings of workers in the relevant member state. Preparatory studies and technical assistance measures may receive 100 per cent financing in exceptional cases.

Applications are submitted to the Commission on an annual basis through the appropriate Ministry in the member state (Employment Department in the UK) and must conform to the criteria set out in the relevant Community Support Framework agreed in respect of the particular Objective and region concerned.

European Agricultural Guidance and Guarantee Fund

The European Agricultural Guidance and Guarantee Fund (Guidance Section) is the smallest of the three structural funds, representing a total budget in 1989 of 1,165 million Ecus [roughly 13 per cent of the total Structural Fund budget]. Guidance Section funding is primarily concerned with improving agricultural incomes and productivity, particularly to ease the adjustment process made necessary by the reform of the Common Agricultural Policy (CAP).

Like the other structural funds, Guidance Section funding is disbursed primarily through national aid schemes. The main exception to this has been in respect of support relating to the marketing and processing of agriculture and fishery products. Commonly known by its French acronym, FEOGA , this particular assistance is of wider applicability than strictly the farming community since it relates to all stages of food preparation following production and includes market preparation, preservation, treatment and processing, in addition to improvements in marketing channels. Under Regulation 355/77, FEOGA projects in the UK qualify for grants of up to 25 per cent of total expenditure provided they fall within the terms of an investment programme drawn up in agreement with the Commission and attract a contribution from the UK Government. Grant applications are submitted through the relevant agriculture ministry/department.

Under the new Regulations reforming the activities of the structural funds, Guidance Section support will continue to be available for marketing and processing projects in the agriculture and fisheries sectors and has been extended to cover forestry.

Framework Regulation 2052/88, governing the activities of the three structural funds, assigns EAGGF Guidance Section funding to contribute to Single Act Objectives 1 (structural adjustment of underdeveloped regions), 5(a) — speeding up the adjustment of agricultural structures in line with reforms to the CAP, and 5 (b) — development of rural areas. In 1989, approximately 94 per cent of the total Guidance Section budget was allocated to Objectives 1 and 5 (a) on a roughly equal basis; the remaining 6 per cent goes towards spending under Objective 5 (b).

EAGGF (Guidance Section) implementing Regulation 4256/88 sets out the types of measures which can be supported, in relation to each of the Objectives for which Guidance Section funding is available. Within Objective 1 regions support will be directed towards dealing with the backwardness of agricultural structures through the following: encouraging early retirement and supporting 'young' farmers; converting/adjusting production; improving rural infrastructure and encouraging diversification (except where already financed by the ERDF); pasture improvement; irrigation; tourist and craft investment; environmental protection; resumption of production following a natural disaster; afforestation and exploitation of woodland; promotion of alternative activites for farmers; development of advisory services and training.

With respect to Objective 5[a] qualifying activities will not be subject to regional restriction and were expected to be adopted by the European Council by the end of 1989. The legislation provides for activities funded under Objective 5(a) to include: measures to adjust/convert production, including promotion of quality products; afforestation of farmland; early retirement support; farm income support (particularly as compensation for natural handicaps, eg. hill areas); environmental protection measures; encouragement for young farmers; efficiency improvements; improving marketing and processing of agricultural, forestry and fishery products.

Under Objective 5(b) measures qualifying for assistance will be agreed in the form of operational programmes which are drawn up in accordance with the relevant .Community Support Framework for the region concerned. Such programmes could include support for marketing and processing activities.

EAGGF implementing Regulation 4256/88 took effect from 31 December 1989 (31 December 1990 in respect of fishery support) and replaces Regulation 355/77 under which projects relating to the marketing and processing of agriculture and fishery products receive assistance. Regulation 4256/88 extends Guidance Section assistance to the forestry sector; provisional measures have been introduced under Regulation 1612/89 to cover the marketing and processing of forestry products. Studies, preparatory studies and pilot and demonstration projects may also be financed under the new EAGGF Regulation.

As with the other Funds, most Guidance Section funding will be disbursed through operational programmes, ie. multi-annual programmes approved by the Commission and administered by the beneficiary member state, and is expected to complement the activities of the other structural funds.

217

Information sources

For sources of information on grants available from the Structural Funds see the *Contacts* section at the end of this chapter.

COMMUNITY FINANCIAL INSTRUMENTS

Community financial instruments include the European Coal and Steel Community (ECSC), the European Investment Bank (EIB) and the New Community Instrument (NCI). Each of these work to promote particular Community objectives (eg. ECSC to assist the restructuring of coal and steel areas) through the provision of loan finance on favourable terms. Under Framework Regulation 2052/88, Community financial instruments are expected to complement the activities of the structural funds through the financing of individual projects and through their participation in "integrated programmes".

European Coal and Steel Community

The European Coal and Steel Community (ECSC), established by the Treaty of Paris in 1951, was set up to promote the interests of the coal and steel producing nations, initially through the creation of a common market for these products. Under Articles 49, 54 and 56 of the Treaty, the Commission is empowered to raise funds and disburse loans for investment projects which are eligible for support under the terms of the Treaty. ECSC resources available for onlending are raised through the levy it imposes on coal and steel production, through borrowing on international capital markets and through any earnings raised from the placement of funds awaiting disbursement. ECSC loan financing is implemented through two types of loan schemes — conversion loans available under Article 56 for capital investment projects and loans for projects promoting the consumption of European Community coal and steel (available under Article 54). These are described in the sections that follow.

Conversion loans (Article 56)

Under Article 56 of the Treaty, the ECSC makes available so-called "conversion loans". These are intended to assist with the conversion of areas adversely affected by the restructuring of the coal or steel industries. For the purposes of targetting loan assistance, the ECSC designates areas adversely affected by the restructuring process as priority and non-priority ECSC areas. Priority areas are those where ECSC conversion operations have not yet resulted in the creation of new jobs equal to 50 per cent of the ECSC jobs lost between 1 January 1978 and the end of the restructuring process in the relevant area. Non-priority areas are those where the 50 per cent threshold has been reached.

Conversion loans may be granted to undertakings and to public bodies either in the form of direct loans, or in the form of sub-loans through financial intermediaries to which the ECSC has granted a global loan. Loans are available to cover up to 50 per cent of the fixed capital investment associated with approved job creation projects, subject to the following criteria:

(a) Economically sound investment projects in any industrial or service sector will be considered, subject to the restrictions set out in (b), (c) and (d) below.

218

(b) Projects concerning products which, under Article 92 of the EEC Treaty, are prohibited State aids for sectoral reasons are not eligible.

(c) In industries whose activities relate to the coal and steel industries, projects are eligible only if they substantially modify the activity of the undertaking concerned by providing an entirely new employment-creating activity.

(d) The establishment of industrial estates with advance factories and the redevelopment of industrial sites, particularly those formerly occupied by ECSC industries, may be eligible provided they can be shown to be closely related to the creation of new activities and employment opportunities.

The proposed investment for which an ECSC loan is sought must permit the expansion or creation of new economic activities leading to the creation of additional jobs. Eligible investment costs may include intangibles such as patents, licences, know-how and R & D expenditure directly linked to the investment concerned. Working capital is not eligible.

The interest rate on the loan is fixed by the Commission on the basis of the cost of the resources borrowed; in the UK this has generally been below the broadly commercial rate. Subject to the availability of budgetary resources, an interest rebate of 3 per cent for small firms (ie. net fixed assets less than 75 million Ecus and employing fewer than 500) and 2 per cent for larger firms may be awarded during the first five years of the loan. The proportion of loan eligible for rebate is determined on the following basis:

(a) In priority ECSC areas, the amount of loan eligible for rebate is calculated as follows:

(i) applications up to 1 million Ecus — 20,000 Ecus per job created, calculated on two-thirds of the number of jobs created by the project.

(ii) applications over 1 million Ecus — 20,000 Ecus per job created, calculated on two-thirds of the number of jobs created up to 75, plus one-half of jobs created thereafter.

(b) In non-priority ECSC areas, the amount of loan eligible for rebate is calculated as follows:

(i) applications up to 1 million Ecus — 20,000 Ecus per job created, calculated on one-half of the total number of jobs created by the project.

(ii) applications over 1 million Ecus — 20,000 Ecus per job created, calculated on one-half of the total number of jobs created up to 100, plus one-third of jobs created thereafter.

(c) Outside designated ECSC areas, the interest rebate is calculated on the basis of the number of former ECSC workers effectively re-employed by the project.

Loans are disbursed in a mixture of European currencies. In the UK, exchange risk cover is available through the DTI's Exchange Risk Guarantee Scheme for private sector loan applications of up to FILL concerning projects located within the Assisted Areas. For projects located outside the Assisted Areas, or for larger loans, funds not eligible for exchange risk cover may be borrowed from a sterling drawdown.

Article 54 loans
Under Article 54(2) of the Treaty, the Commission is empowered to provide loans for investment projects aimed at increasing or maintaining the consumption of European Community coal or steel.

With respect to investments aimed at promoting the consumption of European Community steel, the following types of industrial projects may qualify for support- those aimed at introducing new applications for steel or at improving the competitiveness of steel in relation to other products — projects by undertakings for which the cost of steel purchased reflected in the price of the finished product accounts for:-

☐ At least 50 per cent of the total cost of raw materials [including steel] or, if this provision cannot be applied for technical reasons,

☐ At least 20 per cent of the total cost of the constituents (including raw materials) of the finished product,

☐ Or, if this provision cannot be applied for technical reasons, at least 5 per cent of the selling price of the finished product.

Only expenditure on installations directly connected with the continuous use of steel will be considered for loan funding. The loan may cover up to 50 per cent of the investment value of the project (excluding working capital).

Separate provision exists under this facility to offer loans to infrastructure projects of European interest. For these, the loan covers up to 20 per cent of the investment cost of the project. The condition relating to the continuous use of steel is waived.

With respect to loans promoting the consumption of Community coal, investments in installations and equipment relating to the combustion, transformation, handling and preparation of coal, and to the treatment and disposal of effluents, which will maintain or increase the consumption of Community coal, all qualify. The maximum loan is set at 50 per cent of the investment value of the project and is reduced proportionately if any non-Community coal is used in the five year period following completion of the project. An interest rebate of 3 per cent may be granted for a five year period and is calculated on the total amount of the loan expressed in Ecus; projects relating to power stations and coking plants do not qualify for rebate.

Interest rates are at favourable market rates reflecting the rate paid by the ECSC on the borrowed funds. Loans of up to 15 million Ecus may be granted through a financial intermediary with which the ECSC has concluded a global loan facility.

European Investment Bank

The European Investment Bank (EIB) was created by the Treaty of Rome establishing the European Economic Community in 1958. Serving both as a bank and as a Community institution, the EIB provides loans for projects promoting the balanced development of the Community, drawing largely on resources raised on the capital markets and operating on a non-profit making basis.

Investments which may be considered for financing by the EIB must contribute to one of the following objectives:

☐ Economic development of the Community's less-developed regions.

☐ Improved transport and telecommunications infrastructure serving the Community's interest.

☐ Protection of the environment and conservation of the Community's architectural and natural heritage.

☐ Urban development.

☐ Attainment of the Community's energy policy objectives

☐ Strengthening the international competitive position of Community industry and furthering its integration at European level.

☐ Supporting the activities of SMEs .

☐ Co-operation with a large number of developing countries.

The EIB grants loans from its own resources, essentially the proceeds of borrowings on the capital markets. It also deploys the proceeds of issues floated by the EEC in conjunction with the New Community Instrument as well as, outside the EEC, budgetary resources provided by the Community or member states.

Loans, available for up to 50 per cent of the gross investment cost of a project or group of schemes, including related working capital increases, intangible assets and expenditure already incurred on current capital programmes, are generally from 7 to 12 years for industrial projects, extending to up to 20 years for infrastructure schemes and projects in the energy sector. Interest rates can be fixed or floating and are at close to the EIB's cost of borrowing; other interest rate formulae can be considered. Rates are the same for all countries and for all sectors. Funds are disbursed at par in a single currency or in a mixture of currencies.

EIB loans may be granted direct to the promoter or through a regional or national financial intermediary with which the EIB has concluded an agreement for a global loan facility. In the UK, Agency loans have ceased to operate since the withdrawal of exchange risk cover in 1985 and as a result, only larger direct loans (minimum loan value — £1 million) are currently available. For private sector loans, industrial projects costing up to £12 million undertaken by SMEs (ie. net fixed assets less than £50 million and employing fewer than 500) are eligible for an EIB loan irrespective of location. Public or private sector projects costing in excess of £12 million are eligible if they are helping regional development or if they help to achieve another Community objective, eg. communications; energy production or saving; innovative or advanced technology; European industrial co-operation; environmental protection or improvement.

Under the recent reforms to the structural funds, provision has been made for the EIB to be co-ordinated in its activities with the activities of the structural funds and to contribute to the part-financing of investments approved for Structural Fund support where these are eligible for EIB financing in accordance with its own Statute, Regulation 4253/88.

New Community Instrument (Ortoli Facility)

Initially under Council Decision 78/870 EEC of 16 October 1978 and subsequently under Council Decision 82/169 EEC of 24 March 1982, the Commission is empowered to raise funds on the capital markets for on-lending. Although the Commission establishes the guidelines for lending NCI money, loans are administered through the European Investment Bank (see above).

NCI loans are intended to promote investment projects contributing to a greater convergence and integration of the economic policies of the member states and projects which help attain the priority Community objectives in the energy, infrastructure and industrial sectors, taking account inter alia of the regional impact of the projects and the need to combat unemployment.

Under the most recent tranche of funding authorised in 1987 under the NCI facility — NCI IV — loans are available to support investment projects undertaken by small and medium-sized enterprises in industry and other productive sectors, in particular with a view to the application of new technologies and innovation and to improving the rational use of energy; with smaller enterprises attracting priority.

NCI loans may be used to finance intangible assets such as patents, licences, know-how, and R & D expenditure directly linked to the investment concerned. Both capital and interest payments may be deferred. Lending terms as regards the reimbursement of the principal and the rate and payment of interest are those applied by the EIB, in accordance with its Statute in respect of loans from its own resources.

NCI loans are generally granted through the agency of a financial intermediary, although in certain limited cases, they may be granted directly to recipients. In the UK, no agency agreement exists for the granting of loans from either NCI or EIB own- resources. NCI funds may, however, be used to finance direct loan applications in respect of projects costing between £2 million and £12 million irrespective of location provided the applicant firm has fewer than 500 employees and net fixed assets of less than £50 million. Loans are at a fixed rate of interest.

European Atomic Energy Community (EURATOM) loans

Under Council Decision 77/270 (EURATOM) the Commission is empowered to issue loans for the purpose of contributing to the financing of nuclear power stations. The objective of the loan scheme is to promote the use of nuclear energy and reduce the Community's dependence on external energy supplies. Loans can be up to a maximum of 20 per cent of project costs. The terms and rates reflect market conditions.

Information sources

For sources of information on grants and loans available under the Community Financial Instruments see the *Contacts* section at the end of this chapter.

PART II — RESEARCH AND DEVELOPMENT PROGRAMMES

Grants and loans for precompetitive research and development programmes are available across a wide range of fields of innovation and technology. However, Community research programmes are not only important in terms of the monetary value of the Commission's contribution to individual research projects, but also in terms of the potential commercial benefits of collaborating with other partners in the development of new technologies. Many firms, sadly, do not take advantage of the support on offer. Sources of information on possible collaborative partners are listed in the *Contacts* section at the end of this chapter.

Technological advance is, of course, fundamental to the competitiveness of European industry. Research and development programmes offer a means of ensuring that technological advancement is funded and promoted in the interests of the European Community economy as a whole. To this end the European Commission has devised Framework Programmes, approved by the Council of Ministers, which run for five years, within which individual R & D programmes are undertaken across many fields of science and technology. The current Framework Programmes are Framework Programme 2 (1987-91) and Framework Programme 3 (1990-94). The basic characteristics of Community research programmes are:

☐ Pluri-annual: Generally agreed to run for 4 to 5 years. Application is made direct to the Commission and not through intermediaries.

☐ Programmes primarily used for funding pre-competitive R & D, between basic fundamental research and commercial development.

☐ Transnational collaboration is usually required or assigned priority.

☐ University/industry partnerships are encouraged by special funding arrangements.

Funding is usually referred to as 'shared cost', with the Commission contributing 50 per cent of industrial partner project costs and 100 per cent of marginal costs incurred by university or higher education institutes. Applications must usually be made within a strict deadline in response to an invitation for proposals published in the *Official Journal*.

Applications are judged on a competitive basis in relation to the perceived importance of the proposed work and the extent to which the project satisfies Community objectives. For example, projects involving collaboration between large and small firms, or projects involving participants from member states which are poorly represented in Community R & D programmes, are treated preferentially.

Activities under the Framework Programme 1987-91

The areas in which Community R & D programmes operate are already agreed in the current Community Framework Programmes for Research and Development. Calls for proposals are, in some cases, still being issued, though in many cases the deadline for applications has passed. Most activities, however, will be continued in the new Framework Programme 1990-94. The total budget for the two Framework Programmes is 11,317 billion Ecus (£8.4 billion). The details of specific programmes set out below demonstrate the scope and value of the Community's R & D activities, much of the information being 'new' to companies which have not yet Europeanised themselves, whether for the purpose of breaking into the European market-place or for strengthening their competitive position in the home market.

Sources of information on research and technological development programmes are generally available within the particular country in which a research programme is being run, and may be in hard copy form or on-line. Information is also available from the relevant Directorates-General within the Commission. An important aspect in the quality of such information is the frequency of updating. New programmes, and new calls for proposals within existing programmes, are announced frequently. In the UK, there is currently only one on-line facility providing standardised, comparative details for all of the national aid schemes available in each of the Community countries, including the European Commission's activities. This is the EUROLOC database operated by the European Policies Research Centre at the University of Strathclyde. Details of EUROLOC and other on-line information services are given in the *Contacts* section at the end of this chapter. Sources of information on individual programmes are given under the separate entries for the programmes in the following pages. Space does not allow for every programme to be listed here. Therefore, potential applicants are advised to obtain further information. In this respect, the Commission itself has set out the objectives, priorities and scope of Community activity in R & D in the medium term in a paper entitled *European Community Research and Development Programmes*, and in a 188-page review of R & D programmes, *EC Research Funding: A Guide for Applicants* prepared by the Commission's Directorate-General for Science, Research and Technology (DGXII).

The broad Action Lines agreed under the framework programmes are:

Framework Programme 1987-91

Quality of Life
Health
Radiation protection
Environment

Towards a large market and information and communications society
Information Technologies
Telecommunications
New services of common interest (including transport)

Modernisation of industrial sectors
Science and technology for manufacturing industry
Science and technology for advanced materials
Raw materials and recycling
Technical standards, measurement methods and reference materials

Exploitation and optimum use of biological resources
Biotechnology
Agro-industrial technologies
Competitiveness of agriculture and management of agricultural resources.

Energy
Fission: nuclear safety
Controlled thermonuclear fusion
Non-nuclear energies and rational use of energy

Science and technology for development

Exploitation of the sea bed and use of marine resources
Marine science technology
Fisheries

Improvement of European scientific and technological co-operation
Stimulation, enhancement and use of human resources
Use of major installations
Forecasting and assessment and other back-up measures (including statistics)
Distribution and exploitation of scientific and technological results.

Quality of Life

This heading covers Community research in the areas of health and environment. The relevant research programmes are listed below:

Medical Research Programme

A research and development co-ordination programme in the field of medical and health research. Projects relating to this programme are carried out by means of concerted actions (ie. funding met wholly by participants or national governments with the Commission meeting the co-ordination costs). The programme covers two subprogrammes relating to major health problems, including cancer and AIDS , and health resources, respectively.

Budget: 65 million Ecus, to cover co-ordination costs

Duration: 1987-91

Calls for proposals: Not relevant

Official Journal **reference:** Council Decision 87/551 EEC *OJ* L334, 24.11.87, p20

Information:

Department of Education and Science
Elizabeth House
York Road
London SE1 7PH
Tel: (071) 934 9376/9000
Fax: (071) 934 9389
Telex: 23171

European Commission Directorate-General for Science Research and Development (DGXII)
Rue de la Loi 200
B-1049 Brussels
Tel: (32) 2 235 0032/1111
Telex: 21877 COMEU B

Medical Research Council
20 Park Crescent
London W1N 4AL
Tel: (071) 636 5422
Fax: (071) 436 6179
Telex: 2489 MRCHQ G

Human Genome Analysis

A programme to cover precompetitive research relating to the application of modern biotechnologies for the improvement of risk forecasting, early diagnosis, prevention, prognosis and treatment of some human diseases. Areas to be covered are: improvement of the human genetic map, setting up of an ordered clone library of human DNA, research on the improvement of advanced genetic technologies, training. Funding is available to support research contracts, centralised facilities and networks, training contracts and grants, courses, consultations with national experts, meetings, seminars, symposia and publications. Formal adoption of the programme is awaiting agreement on Community-wide ethical guidelines to control the uses of biotechnology.

Budget: 15 million Ecus

Duration: 1989-91 [proposed]

Calls for proposals: No application procedure specified

Official Journal **reference:** Proposal, COM(88)424 final *OJ* C27, 1989.

Information:

Department of Education and Science
Elizabeth House
York Road
London SE1 7PH
Tel: (071) 934 9376/9000
Fax: (071) 934 0389
Telex: 23171

European Commission Directorate-
General for Science Research and
Development (DGXII)
Rue de la Loi 200
B-1049 Brussels
Tel: (32) 2 235 0032/1111
Telex: 21877 COMEU B

Medical Research Council
20 Park Crescent
London W1N 4AL
Tel: (071) 636 5422
Fax: (071) 436 6179
Telex: 2489 MRCHQ G

EPOCH (European Programme on Climatology and Natural Hazards)
A research and technological development programme to be implemented
through research contracts, concerted actions, co-ordination activities, education
and training activities and studies and assessments. EPOCH research areas are as
follows: past climates and climate change; climatic processes and models; climatic
impacts and climate-related hazards; seismic hazard.

Budget: 40 million Ecus

Duration: 1989-92

Calls for proposals: Two calls issued in 1989: one general call, deadline 30
November 1989; one specific call in repect of data analysis and modelling in the
field of climate-ozone interactions, deadline 15 September 1989.

Official Journal **reference:** Decision 87/516 (EURATOM) *OJ* C327, 1988.

Information:

Department of the Environment
Chief Scientists Group
Romney House
Marsham Street
London SW1P 3PY
Tel: (071) 276 8460/8365/3000
Fax: (071) 276 4123
Telex: 22221

European Commission
Directorate-General for Science Research
and Development (DGXII)
Rue de la Loi 200
B-1049 Brussels
Tel: (32) 2 235 5735/1111
Telex: 21877 COMEU B

Meteorogical Office
Dr David Carson
Climate Centre
London Road
Bracknell
Berks RG12 2SZ
Tel: (0344) 420242
Fax: (0344) 55034/51719
Telex: 849801

Radiation Protection Research Programme

A research and training programme to support projects relating to the protection of people against ionising radiation and to the regulatory obligations of the Commission. The programme stresses research into countermeasures to prevent or reduce exposure in normal situations and after accidents, and will provide advanced training to young scientists.

Budget: 21.2 million Ecus

Duration: 1990-91

Calls for proposals: One call in 1989

Official Journal **reference:** Council Decision 89/416 (EURATOM) *OJ* L200, 1989.

Information:

Department of Health
Environmental Health and Food Division
Room 918 Hannibal House
Elephant and Castle
London SE1 6TE
Tel: (071) 972 2125/2000
Fax: (071) 703 9565

European Commission
Directorate-General for Science
Research and Development (DGXII)
Rue de la Loi 200
B-1049 Brussels
Tel: (32) 2 235 4045/1111
Telex: 21877 COMEU B

Department of Education and Science
Elizabeth House
York Road
London SE1 7PH
Tel: (071) 934 9376/9000
Fax: (071) 934 0389
Telex: 23171

STEP (Science and Technology for Environmental Protection)

A research programme to be implemented by means of research contracts, concerted actions, co-ordination activities, education and training activities and studies and assessments in the following areas: environment and human health; assessment of risk associated with chemicals; atmospheric processes and air quality; water quality; soil and groundwater protection; ecosystem research; protection and conservation of the European cultural heritage; technologies for environmental protection; major technological hazards and fire safety.

Budget: 75 million Ecus

Duration: 1989-92

Calls for proposals: First call, deadline 15 September 1989, in respect of tropospheric and stratospheric chemistry and ozone depletion. Second call, deadline 30 March 1990 in respect of European cultural heritage, technologies for environmental protection and major technological hazards. Third call, deadline 15 June 1990, in respect of environment and human health and assessment of risk associated with chemicals.

Official Journal **reference:** Decision 87/516 (EURATOM) *OJ* C327, 1988.

Information:

Department of the Environment
Chief Scientists Group
Romney House
Marsham Street
London SW1P 3PY
Tel: (071) 276 8365/3000
Fax: (071) 276 4123
Telex: 22221

European Commission
Directorate-General for Science Research
and Development (DGXII)
Rue de la Loi 200
B-1049 Brussels
Tel: (32) 2 235 1182/1111
Telex: 21877 COMEU B

Information and communications market

Programmes being run in the information and communications market category
include research in information technologies and telecommunications

ESPRIT II (European Strategic Programme for Research and Development in Information Technologies)
A programme promoting precompetitive, collaborative R & D in information
technologies in the following three sectors: Microelectronics and Peripheral
Technologies; Information Processing Systems; IT Application Technologies.

Budget: 1600 million Ecus

Duration: 1987-92

Calls for proposals: Main call issued in 1987. Further calls issued in 1988 relating
to basic research actions and to the promotion of VLSI skills. Two calls issued in
1989: the first relating to Microelectronics and Peripheral Technologies, deadline
4 September 1989; the second relating to Information Processing Systems,
Computer Integrated Manufacturing and Office and Business Systems, deadline
10 January 1990.

Official Journal reference: Decision 88/279 (EEC) *OJ* L118, 6.5.88.

Information:

Department of Trade and Industry
Information Technology Division
Room 927
Kingsgate House
66-74 Victoria Street
London SW1E 6SW
Tel: (071) 215 8577/5000
Fax: (071) 828 1503
Telex: 936069 DTI KHG

European Commission Directorate-
General for Telecommunications,
Information Industries and Innovation
(DGXIII)
ESPRIT Operations Office
Rue de la Loi 200
B-1049 Brussels
Tel: (32) 2 235 7666/235 1111
Fax: (32) 2 235 0655
Telex: 21877 COMEU B

RACE (R & D in Advanced Communications Technologies)
A programme promoting prenormative and precompetitive R & D in advanced
communications technologies designed to bring about the Community-wide
introduction of Integrated Broadband Communications (IBC) by 1995. The
programme is subdivided into the following three areas: IBC Development and
Implementation Strategies; IBC Technologies; Prenormative Functional
Integration.

Budget: 550 million Ecus

Duration: 1 June 1987 — 31 May 1992

Calls for proposals: The first call under the programme closed on 1 October 1987. A second call issued in 1988 related mainly to the launching of Part III work, Prenormative Functional Integration; deadline 3 October 1988. A third call is planned for 1991.

Official Journal **reference:** Council Decision 88/28 (EEC) *OJ* L16, 21.1.88.

Information:

Department of Trade and Industry
TP3B
Room 449
Kingsgate House
66-74 Victoria Street
London SW1E 6SW
Tel: (071) 215 8193/5000
Fax: (071) 931 7194
Telex: 936069 DTI KHG

European Commission Directorate-General for Telcommunications Information Industries and Innovation (DGXIII)
RACE Central Office
Rue de la Loi 200
B-1049 Brussels
Tel: (32) 2 236 3443/235 1111
Fax: (32) 2 235 0575
Telex: 21877 COMEU B

UK RACE Co-ordinator
Business Systems Group
GEC Plessey Telecommunications Ltd
Abbeyfield Road
Lenton Industrial Estate
Nottingham NG7 2SZ
Tel: (0602) 866522 Ext 2428
Fax: (0602) 865555

DELTA *(Developing European Learning through Technological Advance)*

A two year Exploratory Action funding prenormative and precompetitive research related to the exploitation of advanced information and telecommunications technologies for the development of techniques, tools and infrastructures required to support advanced learning, particularly open and distance learning. Areas covered under the exploratory action are as follows: Learning Systems Research; Collaborative Development of Advanced Learning Technology; Testing and Validation; Interoperability; Investigation of Related Factors. Support is available to cover studies, audit contracts, research contracts, provision of facilities, seminars and contracts with experts. Exploratory Actions are frequently used to define priority areas for further research funding under larger-scale five year programmes.

Budget: 20 million Ecus

Duration: 1 June 1988 to 31 May 1990

Calls for proposals: A first call was issued in 1988, deadline 31 October 1988.

Official Journal **reference:** Council Decision 88/417 (EEC) *OJ* L206 30.7.88.

Information:

Department of Employment
Caxton House
Tothill Street
London SW1
Tel: (071) 273 5397
Fax: (071) 273 5475

Department of Trade and Industry
Enterprise Initiative Division 5B
Room 406
Ashdown House
123 Victoria Street
London SW1E 6RB
Tel: (071) 215 6393/5000
Fax: (071) 828 3258
Telex: 8813148 DIHQ G

European Commission
Directorate-General for
Telecommunications, Information
Industries and Information (DGXIII)
DELTA Central Office
Rue de la Loi 200
B-1049 Brussels
Tel: (32) 2 235 7963/1111
Telex: 21877 COMEU B

DRIVE (Dedicated Road Infrastructure for Vehicle Safety)

A programme funding precompetitive R & D in the field of information technology and telecommunications applied to road transport (Road Transport Informatics or RTI). DRIVE entails research, development and assessment of RTI technologies; evaluation of strategic options; and specifications, protocols and standardisation proposals.

Budget: 60 million Ecus

Duration: 1 June 1988 — 31 May 1991

Calls for proposals: A first call was issued in 1988, deadline 17 October 1988. Supplementary call issued in 1989.

Official Journal **reference:** Council Decision 88/416 (EEC) *OJ* L206, 30.7.88.

Information:

Department of Transport
Science Research and Policy Programming
Division
Room P2/040
2 Marsham Street
London SW1P 3EB
Tel: (071) 276 5878/3000
Fax: (071) 276 0818

Department of Trade and Industry
Information Technology Division
Room 747
Kingsgate House
66-74 Victoria Street
SW1E 6SW
Tel: (071) 215 2789/5000
Fax: (071) 931 0397

European Commission
Directorate-General for
Telecommunications Information
Industries
and Innovation (DGXIII)
DRIVE Central Office
Rue de la Loi 200
B-1049 Brussels
Tel: (32) 2 236 3456/235 1111
Fax: (32) 2 235 0654/236 2980
Telex: 21877 COMEU B

EURET

EURET is a proposed new programme to develop a Community transport system capable of responding to the increase in demand resulting from the completion of the internal market. Research areas include optimum network exploitation, logistics, and reduction of harmful externalities.

Budget: 25 million Ecus **Duration:** 1990-93 **Calls for proposals:** First call July 1990

Official Journal **reference**: COM(89)557 final. *OJ* C318, 1989 (proposal).

Information

Department of Transport
2 Marsham Street
London SW1
Tel: (071) 276 5909

AIM (Advanced Informatics in Medicine)

A two year Exploratory Action designed to promote the application of recent developments in advanced information and communications technologies to health care. The programme covers the development of a common conceptual framework for co-operation, prenormative work and technology exploration and the investigation of non-technological factors as required for the objective of concerting European efforts in improving health care by exploiting the potential of medical and bio-informatics (MBI). The Exploratory Action will be used to define priorities for a larger-scale programme of funding.

Budget: 20 million Ecus

Duration: 1 June 1988 — 31 May 1991

Calls for proposals: One call issued in 1988, deadline 14 February 1989. Unlikely to be any further calls during the exploratory phase.

Official Journal **reference:** Council Decision 88/577 (EEC) *OJ* L314, 22.11.88.

Information:

Department of Trade and Industry
Manufacturing Technologies Division
Room 739
Kingsgate House
66-74 Victoria Street
London SW1E 6SW
Tel: (071) 215 2719/5000
Fax: (071) 931 0397
Telex: 936069 DTI KHG

Department of Health and Social Security
Room 813
Market Towers
1 Nine Elms Lane
London SW8 5NQ
Tel: (071) 720 2188 Ext. 3541
Fax: (071) 720 5647

European Commission
AIM Project
Directorate-General for
Telecommunications, Information
Industries and Innovation (DGXIII)
AIM Project
Rue de la Loi 200
B-1049 Brussels
Tel: (32) 2 235 5383/0594/1111
Fax: (32) 2 235 0654
Telex: 21877 COMEU B

Industrial technologies and advanced materials

This heading relates to the modernisation of industrial technologies, covering the application of new technologies to industry as well as the development of new materials and more efficient use of raw materials.

BRITE/EURAM (Basic Research in Industrial Technologies for Europe/ European Research in Advanced Materials)

BRITE/EURAM supports research and technological development projects in the fields of industrial manufacturing technologies and advanced materials applications. The programme covers the following areas: advanced materials technologies, design methodology and quality assurance for products and processes; application of manufacturing technologies; technologies for manufacturing processes; specific activities relating to aeronautics. Projects may be of the following types: industrial applied research, attracting over 90 per cent of the budget; focussed fundamental research, attracting 7 to 10 per cent of the budget; co-ordinated activities, feasibility awards for SME's and demonstration projects, attracting the remainder of the budget.

Budget: 499.5 million Ecus

Duration: 1989-92

Calls for proposals: Second general call made in February 1990 for industrial applied research and focused fundamental research proposals, deadline 14 September 1990. Aeronautics subprogramme call issued in March 1989, deadline 9 June 1989. Other projects, eg. co-ordinated activities, are without strict deadline but should be submitted as early as possible.

Official Journal **reference:** Council Decision 89/237 (EEC) *OJ* L98, 1989.

Information:

Department of Trade and Industry
Manufacturing Technologies Division
Ashdown House
123 Victoria Street
London SW1E 6RB
Tel: (071) 215 6336/5000
Fax: (071) 828 3258
Telex: 8813148 DIHQ G

Department of Trade and Industry
Business Task Force 2
Ashdown House
123 Victoria Street
London SW1E 6RB
Tel: (071) 215 6248
Fax: (071) 828 3258
Telex: 8813148 DIHQ G

European Commission Directorate-General for Science, Research and Development (DGXII)
Rue de la Loi 200
B-1049 Brussels
Tel: (32) 2 235 2345 (General), 235 5960 (Technology), 235 5290 (Materials research), 235 4055 (Aeronautical), 235 1111 (Main switchboard)
Fax: (32) 2 235 8046
Telex: 21877 COMEU B

Raw Materials and Recycling Programme

A research and technological development programme designed to provide the technological base required for strategic, innovative developments in support of the supply and processing of raw materials, both minerals and renewables, and recycling. The programme covers the following areas: primary raw materials; recycling of non-ferrous materials and strategic metals; renewable raw materials, forestry and wood products (FOREST); recycling of waste (REWARD). The programme is being implemented through research contracts, co-ordinated activites and training activities.

Budget: 45 million Ecus [proposed]

Duration: 1990-92

Calls for proposals: Three calls issued in 1989: one concerning primary raw materials and recycling of non-ferrous and strategic metals, deadline was 30 November 1989; a second in respect of forestry and wood products, deadline was 15 December 1989.

Official Journal **reference:** Council Decision 626/89 (EEC). *OJ* L359, 1989.

Information:

Department of Trade and Industry
Manufacturing Technologies Division
Ashdown House
123 Victoria Street
London SW1E 6RB
Tel: (071) 215 6617/5000
Fax: (071) 931 0397
Telex: 8813148 DIHQ G

European Commission Directorate-General for Science, Research and Development (DGXII)
Rue de la Loi 200
B-1049 Brussels
Tel: (32) 2 235 3955/1182/1111
Telex: 21877 COMEU B

BCR (Community Bureau of Reference Programme)

BCR is an applied metrology and chemical analysis programme which provides support for intercomparisons and R & D projects related to the study and improvement of measurement methods and the development of reference materials and transfer standards. The aim of the programme is to improve the reliability of chemical analyses and physical measurements within the Community with a view to eliminating certain obstacles to the operation of the Single Market which originate from the measurements themselves. Topics receiving priority are: foodstuff and agricultural analyses; environmental analyses; biomedical analyses; analyses of metals and surface analyses of materials; applied metrology.

Budget: 59.2 million Ecus

Duration: 1988-92

Calls for proposals: First general call issued in 1988, requesting in particular, proposals relating to measurement and analytical methods necessary for the control of fabrication processes and the quality of products to be marketed with a view to the completion of the Single Market; deadline 31 August 1988. A second specific call relating to the development of co-ordinated activity on metrology for use in automated manufacturing processes was issued in 1989; deadline 15 April 1989. A third specific call relating to sub-micron and macro-metre metrology as applied to manufacturing industries and metrology for automated manufacturing processes was issued in 1990, deadline 30 June. Following the initial calls for proposals, further applications can be submitted at any time.

Official Journal **reference:** Council Decision 88/418 (EEC) *OJ* L206, 30.7.88.

Information:

Department of Trade and Industry
Manufacturing Technologies Division 5
Room 616, Kingsgate House
123 Victoria Street
London SW1E 6SW
Tel: (071) 215 8685/5000
Fax: (071) 931 0397
Telex: 8813148 DIHQ G

European Commission
Directorate-General for Science, Research
and Development (DGXII)
Rue de la Loi 200
B-1049 Brussels
Tel: (32) 2 235 5014/1111
Telex: 21877 COMEU B

Chemical analysis

Laboratory of the Government Chemist
Queens Road, Teddington
Middlesex TW11 0LW
Tel: (081) 943 6270
Fax: (081) 943 2767

Applied metrology

National Physical Laboratory
Building 95
Teddington
Middlesex TW11 0LW
Tel: (081) 943 6039
Fax: (081) 943 6755

Biological resources

Framework Programme Action Line 4, relating to the exploitation and commercialisation of biological resources, covers support for research in the following areas: biotechnology; agro-industrial research; and food-linked research.

BRIDGE (Biotechnology Research for Innovation, Development and Growth in Europe)

The BRIDGE programme offers support for two types of transnational projects in the field of biotechnology: Network-type projects for the integration of research efforts in areas where the main bottlenecks result from gaps in basic knowledge [information infrastructure, enabling technologies, cellular biology, prenormative research]; Targeted-type projects covering initially, sequencing of the yeast genome and molecular identification of the new plant genes. The programme supports research and training actions, and concertation actions to develop the work already started under the previous Biotechnology Research Action Programme.

Budget: 100 million Ecus

Duration: 1990-94

Calls for proposals: First call issued in 1989; deadline 15 December 1989. Second call expected in 1990.

Official Journal **reference:** Proposal COM(88)806 final *OJ* C70, 1989.

Information:

Laboratory of the Government Chemist
Queens Road
Teddington
Middlesex TW11 0LW
Tel: (081) 943 7338/7000
Fax: (081) 943 2767

European Commission
Directorate-General for Science, Research
and Development (DGXII)
Rue de la Loi 200
B-1049 Brussels
Tel: (32) 2 235 4044/1111
Fax: (32) 2 235 0145
Telex: 21877 COMEU B

ECLAIR (European Collaborative Linkage of Agriculture and Industry through Research)

A programme supporting research and technological development projects in biotechnology and other advanced technologies. The aim of the programme is to improve the interface of agriculture and industry by exploiting existing expertise in biotechnology and the life sciences. Though not supporting the development of marketable products or processes, ECLAIR will support projects involving clear-cut agricultural and/or industrial applications or objectives. Separate grants are available for training and mobility costs.

Budget: 80 million Ecus

Duration: 1 July 1988-30 June 1993

Calls for proposals: First call issued in December 1988, deadline 31 March 1989. Second call expected in early 1990.

Official Journal **reference:** Council Decision 89/160 (EEC) *OJ* L60, 1989.

Information:

Laboratory of the Government Chemist
Queens Road
Teddington
Middlesex TW11 0LW
Tel: (081) 943 7343/7000
Fax: (081) 943 2767

European Commission
Directorate-General for Economic and
Financial Affairs (DGII)
Rue de la Loi 200
B-1049 Brussels
Tel: (32) 2 236 8145/235 1111
Telex: 21877 COMEU B

FLAIR (Food-Linked Agro-Industrial Research)

FLAIR is intended to complement existing initiatives in member states through the promotion of further collaborative linkages between research and industrial groups in research and technological development projects concerned with food quality, hygiene, safety, toxicology, nutritional and wholesomeness values. The objectives of the programme are to contribute to Europe's competitiveness in the food industry, to improve food safety and quality for the consumer, and to strengthen the food science and technology infrastructures in Europe. The programme is to be implemented by means of research contracts, concerted actions [research carried out in Commission establishments] and by training/ mobility grants.

235

Budget: 25 million Ecus

Duration: 1 July 1989-30 June 1993

Calls for proposals: First call issued in 1989, deadline 2 October 1989.

Official Journal **reference:** Council Decision 89/411 (EEC) *OJ* L200, 1989.

Information:

Laboratory of the Government Chemist
Queens Road
Teddington
Middlesex TW11 0LW
Tel: (081) 943 7343
Fax: (081) 943 2767

European Commission
Directorate-General for Economic and
Financial Affairs (DGII)
Rue de la Loi 200
B-1049 Brussels
Tel: (32) 2 236 8145/235 1111
Telex: 21877 COMEU B

Agricultural Research Programme

A new research programme designed to help Community farmers adapt to the new situation created by over production and the restrictive prices and markets policy, to improve farming conditions in regions that have been slow to develop, to encourage environmental protection and land conservation, to develop agricultural information services and to improve the dissemination of research results. The programme embraces the following objectives: the promotion and development of products in short supply in the Community; to improve quality of agricultural products and find new uses for traditional products; to reduce economic and social disparities between regions; to reduce costs of agricultural production systems; to prepare long term plans for new systems of water and soil management; develop information dissemination services to help farmers adjust to changes brought about by new developments in the Common Agricultural Policy. The programme is to be implemented by means of research contracts, pilot activities and co-ordination activities.

Budget: 55 million Ecus

Duration: 1989-93

Calls for proposals: A single call covering all areas was issued in 1989, deadline 31 December, 1991.

Official Journal **reference:** Council Decision 90/89 (EEC). *OJ* L58, 1990

Information:

Ministry of Agriculture and Fisheries
Ergon-Nobel House
17 Smith Square
London SW1P 3HX
Tel: (071) 238 5601
Fax: (071) 238 5597

European Commission
Directorate-General for Agriculture
(DGVI)
Rue de la Loi 200
B-1049 Brussels
Tel: (32) 2 235 2418/1111
Telex: 22037 AGREC B

Energy

Within the energy field, the Commission runs a range of research programmes concerning both nuclear energy and all forms of non-nuclear energy.

Controlled Thermonuclear Fusion
A programme supporting research and training in the field of controlled thermonuclear fusion for priority projects, running expenditure for participating organisations, certain industrial contracts, administration costs and expenditure on staff working in organisations co-operating in the programme and the NET (Next European Torus) team, and on a fellowship scheme. The programme forms part of a long term project embracing all activities undertaken in the member states in the field of controlled thermonuclear fusion and is designed to lead in due course to the joint production of prototypes with a view to their industrial production and marketing. The programme also covers the work of the Joint European Torus (JET), a joint undertaking set up to construct, operate and exploit a large facility for the purpose of conducting controlled thermonuclear fusion experiments.

Budget: General Programme: 406 million Ecus. Joint European Torus (JET): 329 million Ecus.

Duration: 1988-92

Calls for proposals: No general calls are issued. The programme is implemented by means of contracts of association between EURATOM and the national organisations active in fusion, and by JET.

Official Journal **reference:** Council Decision 88/522 (EURATOM) *OJ* L222, 20.10.88.

Information:

Department of Energy
1 Palace Street
London SW1 5HE
Tel: (071) 238 3010/3778/3000
Fax: (071) 828 7969

European Commission
Directorate-General for Science, Research and Development (DGXII)
Rue de la Loi 200
B-1049 Brussels
Tel: (32) 2 235 7315/1111
Telex: 21877 COMEU B

Decommissioning of Nuclear Installations
The decommissioning programme offers financial support for selected R & D projects, projects concerned with the identification of guiding principles concerning the design of nuclear installations and their subsequent decommissioning and for a number of selected pilot dismantling projects. The aim of the programme is to promote the joint development of a system of management of decommissioned nuclear installations and of the radioactive wastes produced in their dismantling. The programme is being implemented through research contracts, concerted actions [research undertaken in Commission establishments], studies, co-ordination activities, and secondment, training and mobility support.

Budget: 31.5 million Ecus

Duration: 1989-93

Calls for proposals: First call issued in 1989, deadline 30 September 1989.

Official Journal **reference:** Council Decision 89/239 (EURATOM) *OJ* L98, 1989.

Information:

Department of Energy
1 Palace Street
London SW1 5HE
Tel: (071) 238 3010/3778/3000
Fax: (071) 828 7969

European Commission
Directorate-General for Science, Research
and Development (DGXII)
Rue de la Loi 200
B-1049 Brussels
Tel: (32) 2 235 4080/1111
Telex: 21877 COMEU B

JOULE (Joint Opportunities for Unconventional or Long Term Energy Supply)

JOULE is a research and technological development programme concerning non-nuclear energies and the rational use of energy. The following sub-programmes are covered:

☐ Models for energy and environment.

☐ Rational use of energy.

☐ Energy from fossil sources.

☐ Renewable energy.

Implementation of JOULE is by means of research contracts, study contracts, co-ordination projects and training and mobility grants.

Budget: 122 million Ecus

Duration: 1 January 1989-31 March 1992

Calls for proposals: First call concerning areas 2, 3 and 4 issued in 1989, deadline 30 April 1989.

Official Journal **reference:** Council Decision 89/236 (EEC) *OJ* L98, 1989.

Information:

Department of Energy
1 Palace Street
London SW1 5HE
Tel: (071) 238 3010/3778/3000
Fax: (071) 828 7969

European Commission
Directorate-General for Science, Research
and Development (DGXII)
Rue de la Loi 200
B-1049 Brussels
Tel: (32) 2 235 3978 (Co-ordination), 235
3700 (Energy Systems Analysis), 235 6922
(Renewable Energies), 235 5845 (Rational
Use of Energy), 235 6919 (Fossil Fuels),
235 6962 (Geothermal Energy), 235 1111
(Main switchboard)
Telex: 21877 COMEU B

Management and Storage of Radioactive Waste

A new programme following on from the 1985-89 radioactive waste programme is expected to begin in 1990. The programme will cover waste management and associated R & D actions and the construction and/or operation of underground facilities open to Community joint activities. Implementation will be through research contracts, study contracts, co-ordination activities and training and mobility grants.

Budget: 79.6 million Ecus [proposed]

Duration: 1990-94

Calls for proposals: First call expected in early 1990

Official Journal **reference:** COM(89)226 final *OJ* C144, 1989.

Information:

HM Inspectorate of Polution
Research and Assessments Branch
Room A539 Romney House
43 Marsham Street
London SW1P 3EB
Tel: (071) 276 8080
Fax: (071) 276 8800

European Commission
Directorate-General for Science, Research
and Development (DGXII)
Rue de la Loi 200
B-1049 Brussels
Tel: (32) 2 235 7936/1111
Telex: 21877 COMEU B

TELEMAN (Remote Handling in Nuclear Hazardous and Disordered Environments)

TELEMAN is designed to help the nuclear industry to handle growing quantities of radioactive material, to monitor and replace components of reactors and other nuclear facilities without increasing the radiation dose received by workers and to mitigate the consequences of major accidents. The programme covers: tele-operator component and sub-system development; environmental tolerance; research machine projects; product evaluation and studies. The programme is to be implemented by means of research contracts, concerted actions, studies and co-ordination activities.

Budget: 19 million Ecus

Duration: 18 July 1989-31 December 1993

Calls for proposals: First call published in 1989, deadline 30 November 1989.

Official Journal **reference:** Council Decision 464/89 (EURATOM) *OJ* L226, 1989.

Information:

Department of Energy
1 Palace Street
London SW1 5HE
Tel: (071) 238 3010/3778/3000
Fax: (071) 828 7969

European Commission
Directorate-General for Science, Research
and Development (DGXII)
Rue de la Loi 200
B-1049 Brussels
Tel: (32) 2 235 5355/1111
Telex: 21877 COMEU B

Science and Technology for Development

Under Action Line 6 concerning science and technology for development, the Commission administers a research programme which specialises in the application of science and technology to the problems of the less-developed countries.

Science and Technology for Development

This programme is aimed at promoting increased scientific co-operation between the European Community and developing countries to their mutual benefit. The programme consists of two subprogrammes: Tropical and subtropical agriculture; medicine, health and nutrition in tropical and subtropical areas.

Budget: Tropical and subtropical agriculture: 55 million Ecus. Medicine, health and nutrition: 25 million Ecus.

Duration: 1987-91

Calls for proposals: Deadline December 1989

Official Journal **reference:** Council Decision 87/590 (EEC) *OJ* L355, 17.12.87.

Information:

Overseas Development Administration
Eland House
Stag Place
London SW1E 5DH
Tel: (071) 273 0249
Fax: (071) 273 0219

European Commission
Directorate-General for Science, Research
and Development (DGXII)
Rue de la Loi 200
B-1049 Brussels
Tel: (32) 2 236 2081/235 1111
Telex: 21877 COMEU B

Marine resources

Under Action Line 7 concerning the exploitation of the sea and the commercialisation of marine resources, the Community operates two research programmes.

MAST (Marine Science and Technology Programme)

MAST offers support for research and technology development projects in the field of marine science and technology. The aim of the programme is to contribute to establishing a scientific and technological basis for the exploration, exploitation, management and protection of European coastal and regional seas, through the co-ordination of on-going activities in the member states and the support of transnational R & D activities. MAST embraces four main areas: basic and applied marine science; coastal science and engineering; marine technology; supporting initiatives. Implementation is by means of research contracts, co-ordination activities, supporting initiatives, study contracts and training and exchange of staff.

Budget: 50 million Ecus

Duration: 1989-92

Calls for proposals: A first call was issued in 1989, deadline 30 June 1989. No further calls are expected before mid-1992.

Official Journal **reference:** Council Decision 89/413 (EEC) *OJ* L200, 1989.

Information:

Department of Trade and Industry
Manufacturing Technologies Division
Kingsgate House
66-74 Victoria Street
London SW1E 6SW
Tel: (071) 215 6707/6713/5000
Fax: (071) 828 3258
Telex: 936069 DTI KHG

Department of Education and Science
Elizabeth House
York Road
London SE1 7PH
Tel: (071) 934 9376/9000
Fax: (071) 934 0389
Telex: 23171

European Commission
Directorate-General for Science, Research
and Development (DGXII)
Rue de la Loi 200
B-1049 Brussels
Tel: (32) 2 235 6787/1111
Telex: 21877 COMEU B

Fisheries Research Programme

A research and co-ordination programme in the fisheries sector designed to support and supplement work done by member states. Individual research and co-ordination programmes within the general programme are in the following fields: fisheries management, fishing methods, aquaculture, upgrading of fishery products.

Budget: 30 million Ecus

Duration: 1988-92

Calls for proposals: First call issued in 1988. Second call issued in 1989.

Official Journal reference: Council Decision 87/534 (EEC) *OJ* L314, 4.11.87.

Information:

Ministry of Agriculture and Fisheries
17 Smith Square
London SW1P 3HX
Tel: (071) 238 5601
Fax: (071) 238 5597

European Commission
Directorate General for Fisheries (DGXIV)
Rue de la Loi 200
B-1049 Brussels
Tel: (32) 2 235 7433
Telex: 21877 COMEU B

European Scientific and Technical Cooperation

The eighth Action Line of the Framework programme covers a number of activities designed to improve European co-operation in science and technology. Individual programmes under this heading cover areas ranging from utilising both human and physical resources on a European scale through to improved dissemination of results of scientific and technological research.

SCIENCE

SCIENCE [plan to stimulate the international co-operation and interchange needed by European research scientists] is a programme of funding with the objective of improving the overall scientific and technical quality of R & D throughout the European Community, thereby contributing to the reduction of scientific and technical development disparities between different member states. All fields of science and technology (exact and natural sciences) are covered. Specific objectives of SCIENCE are to promote training through research, to improve the mobility of scientists throughout the Community, to develop and support intra-European scientific and technical co-operation on high-quality projects, and to promote the establishment of intra-European co-operation and interchange networks. Incentives available under SCIENCE include research bursaries, research grants, grants for high level courses, contracts encouraging the twinning of laboratories, and operations contracts including equipment and accompanying measures where appropriate.

Budget: 167 million Ecus

Duration: 1988-92

Calls for proposals: The programme is open to application on a continuous basis.

Official Journal **reference:** Council Decision 88/419 (EEC) *OJ* L206, 30.7.88.

Information:

Department of Education and Science
Elizabeth House
York Road
London SE1 7PH
Tel: (071) 934 9376/9000
Fax: (071) 934 0389
Telex: 23171

European Commission
Directorate-General for Science, Research
and Development (DGXII)
Rue de la Loi 200
B-1049 Brussels
Tel: (32) 2 235 3696/1111
Telex: 21877 COMEU B

SPES (Stimulation Plan for Economic Science)
A programme designed to stimulate co-operation between and the interchange of researchers in economic science. Implementation of the programme is by means of scholarships, research grants, grants for multinational networks or research projects, and subsidies for high level training courses.

Budget: 6 million Ecus

Duration: 1989-92

Calls for proposals: The programme is open to application on a continuous basis.

Official Journal **reference:** Council Decision 89/118 (EEC) *OJ* L44, 1989.

Information:

Department of Education and Science
Elizabeth House
York Road
London SE1 7PH
Tel: (071) 934 9376/9000
Fax: (071) 934 0389
Telex: 23171

European Commission
Directorate-General for Science, Research
and Development (DGXII)
Rue de la Loi 200
B-1049 Brussels
Tel: (32) 2 235 3696/1111
Telex: 21877 COMEU B

Access to Large-Scale Scientific and Technical Facilities
An experimental Community plan to support and facilitate access to large-scale scientific and technical facilities and installations situated in the European Community. Under the plan, support is available to operators of large-scale scientific and/or technical facilities to allow free access and provide technical support to European researchers over a one to four year period. The plan covers all fields of the exact and natural sciences, research and precompetitive technological development.

Budget: 30 million Ecus

Duration: 1989-92

Calls for proposals: Call issued in 1989 inviting preliminary applications from operators of large-scale facilities.

Official Journal **reference:** Council Decision 89/238 (EEC) *OJ* L98, 1989.

Information:

Department of Education and Science
Elizabeth House
York Road
London SE1 7PH
Tel: (071) 934 9376/9000
Fax: (071) 934 0389
Telex: 23171

European Commission
Directorate-General for Science, Research and Development (DGXII)
Rue de la Loi 200
B-1049 Brussels
Tel: (32) 2 235 3696/1111
Telex: 21877 COMEU B

DOSES (Development of Statistical Expert Systems)

DOSES addresses the exploitation of advanced information technologies in the field of statistics , particularly the application of expert systems technology to the whole chain of statistical data processing. DOSES consists of two parts:

☐   Organisation of co-ordinated projects.

☐   R & D projects meriting priority in the field of official statistics.

Budget: 4 million Ecus
Duration: 1989-92
Calls for proposals: Contracts under Part 1 of the programme are awarded by means of restricted invitation to tender. A call for expressions of interest in relation to Part 2 was issued in April 1989. A formal call for proposals is planned to follow.

Official Journal **reference:** *OJ* C184, 1988, C27, 1989: Council Decision 89/415 (EEC), *OJ* L200 1989.

Information:

Central Statistical Office
Millbank Tower
Millbank
London SW1
Tel: (071) 217 4209
Fax: (071) 217 4338

Statistical Office of the European Communities
Batiment Jean Monnet
Rue Alcide de Gasperi
L-2920 Luxembourg
Tel: (352) 43011
Telex: 3423 COMEUR LU

EUROTRA (Machine Translation System of Advanced Design)

EUROTRA is a Community research and development programme aimed at the creation of a machine translation system of advanced design capable of dealing with all the official languages of the Community. The programme entered its third and final phase on 1 July 1988 with the adoption of a specific one year programme to complete supplementary tasks, including the incorporation of Spanish and Portuguese, and to reinforce software development and prepare for industrial involvement. A follow up programme leading towards a practical, commercially viable EUROTRA system and a number of possible industrial applications is now in preparation. In 1989 the Commission awarded a number of feasibility and design study contracts in preparation for the industrial implementation of EUROTRA.

Budget: Completion phase, 7 million Ecus

Duration: 1 July 1988-30 June 1990

Calls for proposals: Two invitations were issued in 1989 following the adoption of the final one year phase of the programme. One, an advanced notice of a call for tenders concerned a feasibility and project definition study on the re-usability of lexical resources in computerised applications and standards for lexical and terminological data. A second invitation requested organisations interested in conducting design and feasibility studies in preparation for the industrial implementation of EUROTRA to state their interest. Studies being carried out in accordance with budgetary appropriations.

Official Journal **reference:** Council Decision 89/410 (EEC) *OJ* L200, 1989.

Information:

Department of Trade and Industry
Room 803
Information Technology Division
Kingsgate House
66-74 Victoria Street
London SW1E 6SW
Tel: (071) 215 8317/2540/5000
Fax: (071) 828 1503
Telex: 936069 DTI KHG

European Commission
Directorate-General for
Telecommunications Information
Industries and Innovation (DGXIII)
Batiment Jean Monnet
Plateau de Kirchberg
L-2920 Luxembourg
Tel: (352) 40311

MONITOR *(Strategic Analysis, Forecasting and Evaluation)*

MONITOR supports strategic analysis, forecasting and evaluation projects concerned with new developments in the area of research and technology. The aim of the programme is to identify new directions and priorities for Community research and technological development policy and to help highlight the relationship between R & D and other common policies. The programme embraces three areas:

□ Strategic and Impact Analysis (SAST)

□ Forecasting and Assessment of Science and Technology (FAST)

□ Activities in support of the evaluation of Community R & D programmes (SPEAR)

Budget: 22 million Ecus

Duration: 1988-92

Calls for proposals: A call for expressions of interest was published in 1989. On the basis of this call, activities funded under the programme were expected to begin in mid-1989. There is no formal deadline by which proposals must be submitted.

Official Journal **reference:** Council Decision 89/414 (EEC) *OJ* L200, 1989

Information:

Department of Trade and Industry
UK MONITOR Co-ordinator
Room 213a, Ashdown House
123 Victoria Street
London SW1E 6RB
Tel: (071) 215 6679/5000
Fax: (071) 828 0931
Telex: 8813148 DIHQ G

European Commission
Directorate-General for Science, Research
and Development (DGXII)
Rue de la Loi 200
B-1049 Brussels
Tel: (32) 2 235 4055/1111
Telex: 21877 COMEU B

UK MONITOR National Network Node
PREST Office
The University
Manchester M13 9PL
Tel: (061) 275 5921
Fax: (061) 273 1123

VALUE (Research Dissemination and Utilisation)

VALUE supports the dissemination and utilisation of results from scientific and technological research. The first part of the programme is to be implemented through two subprogrammes covering:

☐ Dissemination and utilisation of the results of Community research and technological development activities.

☐ Computer communications networks.

The programme will be implemented primarily through calls for tender (restricted and public), contracts for studies and services to be carried out on behalf of the Commission, subsidies and research contracts, and support for European co-operation networks.

Budget: 38 million Ecus

Duration: 27 June 1989-26 June 1993

Calls for proposals: A call for tenders was issued in 1989. A further call is scheduled for 1990.

Official Journal **reference:** Council Decision 89/412 (EEC) *OJ* L200, 1989.

Information:

Department of Trade and Industry
Research and Technology Policy Division
Room 202, Ashdown House
123 Victoria Street
London SW1E 6RB
Tel: (071) 215 6621/5000
Fax: (071) 821 1298
Telex: 8813148 DIHQ G

European Commission
Directorate-General for
Telecommunications Information
Industries and Innovation (DGXIII)
Batiment Jean Monnet
Plateau de Kirchberg
L-2920 Luxembourg
Tel: (352) 40311

Other European Community funding opportunities

Within the overall context of Community activities, the Framework programme for R & D fits into a wider system of programmes supporting training, research, demonstration and innovation projects. Most of these are European Community programmes. In a limited number of specialised areas there are, in addition, funding opportunities available from the European Atomic Community (EURATOM), and from the European Coal and Steel Community (ECSC). The main programmes which form part of the overall Community support available are described below.

ACE (Action by the Community Relating to the Environment)

A programme to support demonstration projects aimed at developing:

☐ New clean technologies.

☐ Techniques for recycling and re-using waste.

☐ Techniques for locating and restoring sites contaminated by hazardous waste and/or substances.

☐ Techniques and methods for measuring and monitoring the quality of the natural environment.

☐ Seriously threatened biotopes which are the habitat of endangered bird species.

☐ Projects for the protection or re-establishment of land threatened or damaged by fire, erosion or desertification.

☐ Other nature conservation techniques.

Budget: 24 million Ecus

Duration: Running from 30 July 1987 to 29 July 1991

Calls for proposals: Most calls issued in 1989, except for the land re-establishment and threatened biotopes projects for which calls can be submitted at any time.

Official Journal **reference:** Council Regulation 2242/87 (EEC) *OJ* L207, 29.7.87.

Information:

Department of the Environment
Room A 304
Romney House
43 Marsham Street
London SW1P 3PY
Tel: (071) 276 8388
Fax: (071) 276 8861

European Commission
Directorate-General for the Environment, Consumer Protection and Nuclear Safety (DGXI)
Rue de la Loi 200
B-1049 Brussels
Tel: (32) 2 236 1388/235 1111
Telex: 21877 COMEU B

COMETT II (Education and Training for Technology)

The second phase of the European Community's COMETT action programme in education and training for technology provides grants for a range of transnational measures designed to strengthen and encourage co-operation between universities and industry in developing training programmes within the European framework. COMETT covers both initial and continuing training programmes, in particular in advanced technology areas. The programme embraces the following broad headings:

☐ Promotion of European networks (university-industry training partnerships).

☐ Transnational exchanges

☐ Joint projects for continuing training

☐ Complementary promotion and back-up measures.

Budget: 200 million Ecus

Duration: Approved for the period 1990-94

Calls for proposals: Issued 1989. Deadline was 28 February 1990.

Official Journal **reference:** Council Decision 89/27 (EEC) *OJ* L13, 1989.

Information:

Department of Education and Science
Further and Higher Education 2
Elizabeth House
York Road
London SE1 7PH
Tel: (071) 934 9654/9000
Fax: (071) 934 0389
Telex: 23171

Department of Trade and Industry
Enterprise Initiative Division
Room 406
Ashdown House
123 Victoria Street
London SW1E 6RB
Tel: (071) 215 6393
Fax: (071) 828 3258
Telex: 8813148 DIHQ G

European Commission
Directorate-General for
Employment, Social Affairs and
Youth (DGV) Task Force Human
Resources Education, Training and
Youth
Rue de la Loi 200
B-1049 Brussels
Tel: (32) 2 235 1111
Telex: 21877 COMEU B

Conservation and promotion of the Community's architectural heritage

A European Commission action to support pilot projects which conserve and promote the Community's architectural heritage. Support in relation to this action was first introduced in 1983 and is allocated on the basis of an annual call for tenders issued at the beginning of each year. In order to prioritise support in the programme, which has been heavily oversubscribed, the Commission has devised a four year plan to run from 1989 to 1992 with a special theme being highlighted for each year as follows:

☐ 1989: Emerging civil and religious monuments.

☐ 1990: Settings of historical buildings which form the urban or rural pattern.

☐ 1991: Testimonies of industrial, agricultural and artisan productive activities of mankind.

☐ 1992: The integrated revaluation of public spaces in historic centres.

The level of support available under the programme depends on the size of the project submitted, ranging from 1 to 10 per cent for very large projects (over 5 million Ecus) through to 20 to 40 per cent for projects below 3 million Ecus. In 1988 a total allocation of 2.7 million Ecus was awarded to 30 out of the 444 projects submitted.

Information:

Historic Buildings and Monuments Commission
Fortress House
23 Saville Row
London W1X 2HE
Tel: (071) 973 3000

European Commission
Cultural Action Division
Office JECL 2/116
200 Rue del la Loi
B-1049 Brussels
Tel: (32) 2 235 9095
Telex: 21877 COMEU B

COST (European Co-operation in the Field of Scientific and Technical Research)

COST is an ongoing programme for European scientific and technological collaboration which extends beyond the EC to include Austria, Finland, Norway, Sweden, Switzerland, Turkey and Yugoslavia. Collaboration is by agreement between participating organisations and not under any formal EC arrangements or programmes. The areas of science and technology covered by the programme include:

Agriculture
Biotechnology
Environmental protection
Food technology
Health and medical research
Informatics
Oceanography
Metallurgy and materials science
Metrology
Socio-technologies
Telecommunications
Transport

Information

COST Co-ordination Office
Department of Trade & Industry
Room 201
Ashdown House
123 Victoria Street
London SW1E 6RB
Tel: (071) 215 6618
Fax: (071) 821 1298
Telex: 8813148 DIHQ G

COST Secretariat
Cabinet Office
Room 421
70 Whitehall
London SW1A 2AS
Tel: (071) 270 0081
Fax: (071) 270 0462

European Coal and Steel Community (ECSC)

In addition to the general loan schemes administered by the European Coal and Steel Community (ECSC) [see page 218], under Article 55 of the ECSC Treaty, the Commission is empowered to grant financial support to promote research in relation to the coal and steel industries. Two separate programmes exist to fund technical research projects in respect of coal and steel, respectively. The Commission issues guidelines periodically specifying the particular areas under each programme in respect of which support is available. In a separate initiative, the Commission also funds pilot and/or demonstration projects in the iron and steel industry.

The European Coal and Steel Community also offers loans at favourable rates of interest towards the cost of converting gas or oil fired boiler systems to coal. Loan coverage is up to 50 per cent of total project costs.

Information:

Department of Trade and Industry
Investment Development and Accountancy
Services Division (IDA)
Kingsgate House
66-74 Victoria Street
London SW1E 6SW
Tel: (071) 215 2604/2545
Fax: (071) 931 0397

European Commission
Directorate-General for Science, Research
and Development (DGXII)
Rue de la Loi 200
B-1049 Brussels
Tel: (32) 2 235 1111
Telex: 21877 COMEU B

ERASMUS (European Community Action Scheme for the Mobility of University Students)

ERASMUS is a Community programme designed to promote greater co-operation between universities, including all post-secondary educational institutions, throughout the Community. The following measures are included under the programme:

☐ Establishment and operation of a European university network.

☐ Grants to enable students to carry out a period of study in another member state.

☐ Measures to promote mobility through the academic recognition of diplomas and periods of study.

☐ Complementary measures to promote student mobility in the Community.

Budget: 85 million Ecus

Duration: Running from 1 July 1987 until 30 June 1990

Official Journal **reference:** Council Decision 87/327 (EEC) *OJ* L166, 25.6.87.

Information:

Department of Education and Science
Elizabeth House
York Road
London SE1 7PH
Tel: (071) 934 9351/9000
Fax: (071) 934 0389
Telex: 23171

ERASMUS Bureau
Rue d'Arlon 15
B-1040 Brussels
Tel: (32) 2 233 0111

EUREKA

EUREKA is a Europe-wide framework agreed between 19 European countries and the European Commission for encouraging further collaboration on advanced technology projects. It encourages cross-border collaborative civilian projects between firms and research institutes from different EUREKA member countries. The aim of EUREKA is to improve European competitiveness in world markets in civil applications of new technologies by encouraging industrial and technological collaboration within Europe. EUREKA projects benefit from the information exchange process provided through the framework and from the commitment to the development of an integrated market by EUREKA-participating countries. Although EUREKA does not directly fund R & D, participants in EUREKA projects usually qualify for financial assistance through the particular funding mechanism adopted by their own national governments.

Information:

Department of Trade and Industry
EUREKA Projects Office
Room 203, Ashdown House
123 Victoria Street
London SW1E 6RB
Tel: (071) 215 6612/5000
Fax: (071) 821 1298
Telex: 8813148 DIHQ G

EUREKA Secretariat
19H Avenue des Arts Bte 3
B-1040 Brussels
Tel: (32) 2 217 0030

IMPACT (Information Services Market)

IMPACT, the European Commission's plan of action for setting up an information services market, supports a range of measures relevant to the promotion and development of European-wide information services. The programme includes support for collaborative pilot and demonstration projects intended to develop new, advanced information services, together with other supportive activities, eg. setting up a European information market observatory (IMO); the elimination of technical, administrative and legal barriers; improvement of conditions of transmission and access to information services; promotional measures; etc.

Budget: 36 million Ecus

Duration: Current IMPACT programme runs to 31 December 1990.

Calls for proposals: No further calls to be issued under the current programme. A follow-on IMPACT 2 programme, expected to cover 1991-92 is in preparation.

Official Journal **reference:** Council Decision 88/524 (EEC) *OJ* L288, 21.10.88.

Information:

Department of Trade and Industry
Information Technology Division
Kingsgate House
66-74 Victoria Street
London SW1E 6SW
Tel: (071) 215 2655/2632/5000
Fax: (071) 828 1503
Telex: 936069 DTI KHG

European Commission
Directorate-General for
Telecommunications Information
Industries and Innovation (DGXIII)
Batiment Jean Monnet
Plateau de Kirchberg, L-2920 Luxembourg
Tel: (352) 40311

LINGUA *(foreign language training)*

LINGUA is a new programme to promote training in the official languages of the European Community. In particular LINGUA will embrace the following lines of action:

☐ Measures to promote training of foreign language teachers.

☐ Development of the network for university co-operation.

☐ Measures to promote the development of foreign language teaching in the business community.

☐ Complementary measures.

Budget: 200 million Ecus

Duration: To run from 1990-94

Official Journal **reference:** LINGUA proposal COM(88)841 final *OJ* C51, 1989.

Information:

UK LINGUA Unit
Seymour House
Seymour Mews
London W1H 9PE
Tel: (071) 224 1477
Fax: (071) 224 1906

European Commission
Directorate-General for Employment,
Social Affairs and Youth (DGV) Task
Force Human Resources Education,
Training and Youth
Rue de la Loi 200
B-1049 Brussels
Tel: (32) 2 235 1111
Telex: 21877 COMEU B

Professional Training in Japan

The Commission sponsors two training programmes in Japan. One programme offers grants to sponsor executives from export-oriented firms to spend eighteen months training in Japan. A second programme sponsors 15 to 21 month placements in Japan of research scientists from universities and public sector laboratories in the Community. Applicants must generally be aged 25 to 35. The programmes are open to application on an annual basis.

Information:

Executive training

KPMG Peat Marwick McLintock
P.O. Box 486
1 Puddle Dock
London EC4V 3PD
Tel: (071) 236 8000
Fax: (071) 248 6552

251

Scientific training

European Commission
Directorate-General for Science, Research
and Development (DGXII)
Rue de la Loi 200
B-1049 Brussels
Tel: (32) 2 235 3990/1111
Telex: 21877 COMEU B

SCA-RS (Action Research Programme on Reactor Safety)

The Commission's action research programme on reactor safety (SCA-RS) addresses problems related to the safe operation of light water reactors (LWR) and liquid metal fast breeder reactors (LMFBR). The programme is one of a number of specific research programmes being implemented by the Joint Research Centre (JRC) and is intended to stimulate collaboration between national organisations and to promote the integration of research performed in national laboratories with that carried out in the Joint Research Centre.

Budget: 147.9 million Ecus

Duration 1988-91

Calls for proposals: A call for participation in relation to Light Water Reactor source term analysis was issued in 1990.

Official Journal **reference:** Council Decision 88/521 (EEC) *OJ* L286, 20.20.88.

Information:

Department of Energy
Atomic Energy Division
Tel: (071) 238 3778

Joint Research Centre
Ispra Establishment
I-21020 Ispra (VA)
Italy
Tel: (39) 789111
Telex: 324878/324880 EUR 1

SPRINT (Strategic Programme for Innovation and Technology Transfer)

The SPRINT programme for promoting innovation and technology transfer throughout the Community covers three broad action lines:

☐ Strengthening the innovation services infrastructure in Europe.

☐ Supporting intra-Community pilot projects for information transfer.

☐ Improving the innovation environment.

The programme funds: the establishment of networks between organisations involved in the promotion of technology transfer; conferences and workshops; specific pilot projects relating to innovation transfer; and a variety of supportive measures designed to ease barriers and promote innovation and technology transfer.

Budget: 90m Ecus

Duration: 1989-93

Calls for proposals: 1989

Official Journal **reference:** Council Decision 89/286 (EEC) *OJ* L112, 1989.

Information:

Department of Trade and Industry
Research and Technology Policy Division
Room 235
Ashdown House
123 Victoria Street
London SW1E 6RB
Tel: (071) 215 6626/6638/5000
Fax: (071) 821 1298
Telex: 8813148 DIHQ G

European Commission
Directorate-General for
Telecommunications Information
Industries and Innovation (DGXIII)
Batiment Jean Monnet
Plateau de Kirchberg
L-2920 Luxembourg
Tel: (352) 40311

THERMIE *(energy technology)*

THERMIE is a proposed Community programme to support projects promoting energy technology. The following fields of application will be covered by the programme:

☐   Rational use of energy.

☐   Renewable energy sources.

☐   Coal and other solid fuels.

Support will be available for innovatory projects, dissemination projects, land targetted projects instigated by the Commission. Priority will be given to projects located in Objective 1 regions (designated under the European Regional Development Fund). The programme is expected to become fully operational in 1990 and will run until 31 December 1994. A first call for proposals was issued in 1990 with a deadline of 20 June 1990.

Information:

Department of Energy
1 Palace Street
London SW1 5HE
Tel: (071) 238 3010/3778/3000
Fax: (071) 828 7969

European Commission
Directorate-General for Energy (DGXVII)
Rue de la Loi 200
B-1049 Brussels
Tel: (32) 2 235 1111
Telex: 21877 COMEU B

Activities under framework programme 1990-94

In the new Framework Programme the share of resources devoted to environmental research, biotechnology and human capital and mobility is to rise "significantly" according to the European Commission. The total proposed budget for the new programme is 5.7bn Ecus. The Commission proposes to overlap the two programmes, extending the concept of rolling programmes which takes account of the speed of technological advance. The overall aims are to accelerate the pace of technological progress, strengthen the competitiveness of European industry globally, and to establish research specifically in the context of the Single European Act.

In its background note on the 1990-94 Framework Programme[2] the Commission sets out several 'important findings' which emerged from its mid-term review[3] of the 1987-91 Framework Programme. Now, in order to optimise European R & D efforts, the Commission wants to:

☐ Ensure a basis for technological progress in less-favoured regions.

☐ Exploit to a greater extent the scope for collaboration.

☐ Encourage further spread of technological skills.

The Commission states in the background report that work undertaken in the 1987-91 programme will continue but there will be a shift in priorities in the structure of the 1990-94 programme. In information and communications technology there is a reduction in traditional research and an increase in new lines of research such as microelectronics. However, there is no change in the weighting of funds assigned to industrial and materials technologies. In the field of natural resources management more money goes towards research into environmental protection and the life and science technologies. But funds for the energy sector are reduced. A 'major boost' in funding is given to the mobility of young researchers. The Commission's concern in environmental issues and the harmonisation of standards is reflected in the programme as both these areas are directly related to the programmme to complete the Single Market.

Information technologies: Priority is given to microelectronics — to contribute to the creation of a European manufacturing capability for advanced products; peripherals, — to produce new generations which are reliable, low-cost and mass produced; software systems and tools to increase software production; and IT applied to industrial engineering, in particular CAD/CAM (computer aided design/computer aided manufacturing).

Communications technologies: Priority is given to the development of 'intelligent, reliable and secure networks' and 'new value-added, profitable services' requiring research in mobile communications, image communications and service engineering amongst others.

Development of telematic systems in areas of general interest: The development of telematics systems combining information technologies, communications and audio-visual techniques.

Industrial and materials technologies: Emerging market requirements and more severe constraints will be considerations in the development of European manufacturing industry's science base and advanced technologies, according to the Commission[2]. Priority is, therefore, given to major integrated projects emphasising materials with specific properties for use in unusual conditions plus life cycle aspects; and design advances in the scientific and technical base.

Energy: Promotion of clean, safe energy technologies by research into fossil, renewable energy sources, energy utilisation; nuclear fission safety; controlled nuclear fusion.

Management of intellectual resources, human capital and mobility: The Commission maintains that in response to the need for trained researchers in Europe the Community will provide for a major project of mobility of young post-graduate researchers in the area of the exact and natural sciences, technologies and economic science. This project may be complemented by support measures for networks of research training centres.

1 COM(89)397 final *OJ* C242, 1989. 2 Background report ISEC/B29/89.
3 *First report on the state of science and technology (December 1988) — evaluation report (June 1989).*

CONTACTS

Structural Funds

As with any area of government policy, the financial programmes are subject to rapid change. This changeability makes it difficult to keep abreast of new developments without ongoing access to updated information sources. For companies with a direct interest in any of the Commission's programmes (ie. as a potential participant), direct dialogue with the relevant national or Commission representative is the best mechanism for keeping informed of any new developments within a specific programme. Secondary information sources are useful for scanning the whole field of Commission activities and developments more generally, provided they are updated frequently.

European Regional Development Fund

The bulk of ERDF funds allocated to the UK go to local authority projects in assisted areas. Applications for industrial assistance and enquiries about eligibility from the ERDF should be addressed to the appropriate Department of Trade and Industry Regional Office.

Department of Trade and Industry
Investment Development Accountancy
Services Division
Room 228
Kingsgate House
66-74 Victoria Street
London SW1E 6SW
Tel: (071) 215 2558/5000
Fax: (071) 931 0397
Telex: 936069 DTI KHG

European Social Fund

Applications for assistance or enquiries about eligibility should be addressed to local authorities, higher education establishments, industrial training organisations and voluntary organisations.

Department of Employment
European Social Fund Unit
11 Belgrave Road
London SW1V 1RB
Tel: (071) 834 6644
Fax: (071) 828 7081

Department of Economic Development
European Communities Branch
The Arches Centre
11-13 Bloomfield Avenue
Belfast BT5 5HD
Tel: (0232) 732411
Fax: (0232) 732835

European Agricultural Guidance and Guarantee Fund: Guidance Section

Ministry of Agriculture Fisheries and Food
Marketing Policy Division
Ergon-Nobel House
17 Smith Square
London SW1P 3HX
Tel: (071) 238 6316

Department of Agriculture and Fisheries for Scotland
Pentland House
47 Robb's Loan
Edinburgh EH14 1TW
Tel: (031) 556 8400
Fax: (031) 244 6453/6014

Welsh Office Agriculture Department
Floor 2
Crown Offices
Cathays Park
Cardiff CF1 3NQ
Tel: (0222) 825111
Fax: (0222) 823036

Department of Agriculture for Northern Ireland
EC Division
Dundonald House
Upper Newtonards Road
Belfast BT4 3SB
Tel: (0232) 650111
Fax: (0232) 659856

European Coal and Steel Community

Applications for assistance from ECSC funds or enquiries about eligibility should be addressed to

European Commission
Directorate General for Regional Policy
C-3
Rue de la Loi 200
B-1049 Brussels
Tel: (32) 2 235 8468/1111
Telex: 21877 COMEU B

Department of Trade and Industry
Investment Development and Accountancy Services Division (IDA)
Kingsgate House
66-74 Victoria Street
London SW1E 6SW
Tel: (071) 215 2604/2545
Fax: (071) 931 0397

European Commission
Directorate-General for Credit and Investment (DGXVIII)
Batiment Jean Monnet
L-2920 Luxembourg
Tel: (352) 43011

European Investment Bank and New Community Instrument

European Investment Bank
100 Boulevard Konrad Adenauer
L-2950
Luxembourg
Tel: (352) 4379-1
Fax: (352) 437704
Telex: 3530 BNKEU LU

European Investment Bank
68 Pall Mall
London SW1Y 5ES
Tel (071) 839 3351
Fax: (071) 930 9929
Telex: 919159 BANKEU G

Published information

The European Policies Research Centre publishes two directories of EC grants and loans and operates the EUROLOC and AIMS databases. (see under *European Policies Research Centre*). The *Official Journal of the European Communties* (L, C and S Series) also publishes regular information (see *European Community Publications*, Part Eight, Chapter 1).

Government Support for British Business, Bienkowski, Walker and Allen, published by EPRC Ltd, Glasgow. (1988).

Guide to European Community Grants and Loans, (now continuously updated) published by Eurofi (UK) Ltd, Newbury.

Guide to the 1989 General Budget of the Commission of the European Communities, M. O'Hagan, published by Dartmouth Publishing Company.

European Regional Incentives (1989 edition), Yuill, Allen et al, published by Bowker-Saur Ltd, London.

Research & Development programmes

Information on specific R & D programmes is available from European Commission and UK government contacts listed under the entry for each separate programme in this chapter. When calls for proposals are announced, the relevant Directorate-General of the European Commission usually issues an information pack to accompany application forms for participation. There are two general guides to EC R & D funding published, which may be regularly updated, both listing information contacts in the Commission and in the UK.

EC Research Funding: A Guide for Applicants: This is a 188-page introduction to EC research and technological development programmes for which EC funding is available. The guide includes details of each programme, essential contacts in Brussels and in member states, and information on eligibility and how to make applications. It is obtainable from European Commission Information Offices (see *The Brussels Connection*, Part Seven, Chapter 1), or from the European Commission, Directorate-General for Science, Research and Development (DGXII), 200 Rue de La Loi, B-1049 Brussels.

A Guide to European Community Industrial Research and Development Programmes is an information pack, published by the Department of Trade and Industry (DTI), containing factsheets on major EC R & D programmes and general information on EC research and technological development. It lists contacts in Brussels and in the UK. However, while the information pack itself is well presented, the 1990 edition suffers because it was published shortly before considerable internal reorganisation within the DTI which rendered some of the contacts out of date. The pack is obtainable free of charge from the DTI's Research and Technology Policy Division (see below), DTI/RTP4a, Freepost, London SW1V 6YU.

Finding collaborative partners

As the European Commission states in the above mentioned review of EC R & D programmes, *EC Research Funding; A Guide for Applicants*, 'small and medium-sized enterprises often have problems finding a suitable partner. It is known that many small and medium-sized enterprises do not participate in publicly supported technology and research programmes for this reason'. Commission R & D contacts for certain programmes may be able to put a company in touch with a prospective partner. Otherwise, potential partners can be located via the Business Co-operation Network (BC-Net) and various on-line databases. For details of BC-Net, which has representatives throughout EC member states, see *The Brussels Connection*, Part Seven, Chapter 1.

As a legal vehicle for a collaborative venture, companies can make use of the EEIG (European Economic Interest Grouping) which has been introduced to facilitate cross-frontier co-operation between groups of companies, while each retains its economic independence. For further comment on the EEIG, see the Joint Venture section of *Corporate Structures*, Part Five, Chapter 1, and *EC Company Law*, Part Six, Chapter 2.

The European Community itself can be considered as a partner in contracted research through its Joint Research Centre (JRC). Initially, the JRC was concerned mainly with nuclear research but its terms of reference are to include other areas of research covered by the EC's Framework Programme in preparation for the Single Market.

257

European Commission
Joint Research Centre
Directorate-General for Science, Research
and Development (DGXII)
200 Rue de la Loi
B-1049 Brussels
Tel: (32) 2 235 0187/1111
Telex: 21877 COMEU B

Germany
Joint Research Centre
PO Box 2266
Linkenheim
D-7550 Karlsruhe
Tel: (49) 721 07247/841
Telex: 7825483 EU D

Italy
Joint Research Centre
I-21020 Ispra, Varese
Tel: (39) 78 91 11
Telex: 324878/324880 EUR I

Netherlands
Joint Research Centre
PO Box 2
Westerduinweg 3
NL-1755 ZG-Petten NH
Tel: (31) 22 46 5656
Telex: 57211 REACP N

Belgium
Joint Research Centre
Steenweg op Retie
B-2440 Geel
Tel: (32) 14 57 12 11
Telex: 33589 EURAT B

Research contracts

The European Commission has developed a 'model contract' for particpants in
EC R & D projects in the interests of 'promoting greater transparency and
homogeneity' in the terms and conditions of contracts as they apply throughout
member states. A guide, *Model Contracts for Community Activities in the Field of
Research and Technological Development* is available from:

European Commission
Directorate-General for Science, Research
and Development (DGXII-B-2)
200 Rue de la Loi
B-1049 Brussels
Tel: (32) 2 236 1094/235 1111
Fax: (32) 2 235 8294
Telex: 21877 COMEU B

Official information sources

Department of Trade and Industry
Research and Technology Policy Division
Ashdown House
123 Victoria Street
London SW1E 6RB
Tel: (071) 215 6686/5000
Fax: (071) 828 3258
Telex: 8813148 DIHQ G

Cabinet Office
Science and Technology Secretariat
Room 421
70 Whitehall
London SW1A 2AS
Tel: (071) 270 0367
Fax: (071) 270 0462

European Commission
Rue de la Loi
B-1049 Brussels
Tel: (32) 2 235 1111
Telex: 21877 COMEU B

**Department of Trade and Industry Regional
Offices**
(See separate page)

(Information contacts on specific programmes are listed throughout this chapter under individual programme entries)

Euro-Info-Centres
(See *The Brussels Connection*, Part Seven, Chapter 1)

European Commission Offices in the UK
(See *The Brussels Connection*, Part Seven, Chapter 1)

On-line databases

ECHO-HOST
The ECHO-HOST service of the European Commission provides access to various databases providing information on calls for research proposals and details of research and development programmes. Some of them are specialist databases dealing with energy, biotechnology, EC law and other subjects. The following selection of databases providing access to information on EC research and development programmes will be useful to companies seeking new opportunities in the European marketplace. Details of other European Community on-line databases are contained in *On-line Databases*, Part Eight, Chapter 3.

ECHO Customer Service
BP 2372
177 Route d'Esch
L-1023 Luxembourg
Tel: (352) 48 80 41 (help line)
Fax: (352) 48 84 40
Telex: 2181 EURO LU

CORDIS (Common Research and Development Information Service)
This is a new one-stop service providing information on EC research and technological development activities from a number of other databases in the field. Access is through ECHO-HOST (above).

TED (Tenders Electronic Daily)
This European Community database corresponds to the printed Supplement to the *Official Journal of the European Communities* which contains information about public tenders and contracts and calls for research proposals. The host organisation is ECHO-HOST above. However, certain trade organisations in the UK may be subscribers on behalf of their membership. (see *On-line Databases*, Part Eight, Chapter 3 for further details).

Export Network Ltd
Regency House
1-4 Warwick Street
London W1R 5WA
Tel: (071) 494 4030
Fax: (071) 494 1245

(UK host organisation)

AIMS

AIMS is produced by the European Policies Research Centre (EPRC Ltd) which is affiliated with the University of Strathclyde. Its purpose is to provide information about the 300 plus financial assistance and incentive schemes for businesses in the UK. Both British and European Community sources are included. For EPRC Ltd see below. For further details of AIMS see *On-line Databases*, Part Eight, Chapter 3.

EUROLOC

EUROLOC (Locate in Europe Information Retrieval System) is similar to AIMS in that it provides information about financial incentives to business but it covers other European countries. The producer is the European Policies Reserach Centre (EPRC Ltd) at the University of Strathclyde. For further details see *On-line Databases*, Part Eight, Chapter 3.

European Policies Research Centre (EPRC Ltd)

EPRC Ltd is a company associated with the University of Strathclyde and has been in the forefront of monitoring and analysing industrial policy in the EC for more than a decade. Recognised as the authoritative UK source of comprehensive information on financial incentives, EPRC Ltd provides a range of information services for location, investment and other business development decisions.

On-line information services

EPRC information services include on-line databases, publications and direct consultancy services.

EUROLOC: This database covers financial incentives available in each of the EC countries from national public sector sources and from the EC Commission.

AIMS: A database covering financial incentives from UK public sources and from the European Commission.

STARS: On-line data on the business legislative environment and sources of business information in the UK.

All three databases are updated on a daily basis. Both direct access and remote search services are available. Principal users include international accountancy and consultancy practices, government departments and agencies and individual companies.

Directories

EPRC publishes two comprehensive directories on financial incentives:

European Regional Incentives. An annual directory providing details of all regional incentives available in each of the European Community countries.

Government Support for British Business (Bienkowski, Walker and Allen). A biennial directory covering all UK and EC financial incentives available in the UK (drawn from the AIMS database).

In addition to hard copy and on-line services EPRC provides specialist consultancy services on financial incentives available for specific investment projects based anywhere in Europe.

EPRC Ltd
University of Strathclyde
Livingstone Tower
26 Richmond Street
Glasgow G1 1XH
Tel: (041) 552 4400
Fax: (041) 552 0775
Telex: 77472

PART FIVE

THE
ECONOMIC
AND
TRADING
ENVIRONMENT

1 Corporate Structures

Options for expanding trade in Europe

John Brebner

In the multi-national Europe that we have been used to, as distinct from the Single Market in the making, an enterprise expanding its activities abroad would probably establish separate, vertically implanted organisations in each country in which it decides to operate. The tendency for companies to 'clone' their operations in this way is encouraged by national restrictions on cross-border business, plus cultural, legal and language differences. Such immovable barriers imposed strong psychological barriers, discouraging domestic management from exerting direct control over the day-to-day running of foreign subsidiaries; hence the duplication of vertically implanted structures, complete with their own suppliers, professional advisers and management hierarchies. Where the cost of setting up such a structure abroad is not affordable or justified, the only real alternative for many companies has been to engage intermediaries — agents, distributors, licensees — as local representives. The Single Market changes all that. The dismantling of barriers restricting the free movement of goods, services, capital and persons, plus the adoption of a much needed common tax policy may obviate the need to establish costly and cumbersome vertical structures, the inevitable subsidiary, operating both legally and psychologically as a self-contained, largely autonomous local organisation. The subsidiary will give way to secondary or branch offices perceived as a mere extension of the domestic company, each directly accountable to central domestic management.

In the aftermath to 1992 the trend will be to grow horizontally anywhere in the Single Market by setting up branches, secondary offices, local sales centres, production units, distribution outlets, warehouses, demonstration centres or any other 'limb' a company chooses. Businesses will operate in the wider European environment in much the same way as they always have in national market. Ideally, in the Single Market scenario, growing companies, or even those trimming down their operation, will move all or part of their activities beyond domestic boundaries, not exclusively in search of a profitable local market, but in pursuit of cheaper premises, labour skills, convenient and cost-effective transport, political stability, local administrative efficiency, flexible financial services, more competent professional services, quality of life and even a preferred climate. All these benefits become easily accessible in a frontier-free Europe.

Free movement of goods, services, capital and people

The main objective of the European Community programme to complete the Single Market is to remove the administrative and legal barriers which fragment business resources throughout the member states. It is expected that the removal

265

of barriers will create a stronger economic group of countries, able to compete favourably with other major economic blocs and world powers. The completion of the Single Market will also establish an expanded internal market in the EC in which business is expected to thrive. Forecasts vary as to how long it will take the Community to implement these ideas and establish a genuinely homogenous Single Market. The original target date, 31 December 1992, is more of a catalyst than a deadline but, by that date, many practical, legal measures will have been adopted, even if the full benefits of the 'new Europe' are to take longer to emerge. The unknown element in all this is how well business will perform. Larger corporations will rationalise their activities to take advantage of the favourable trading conditions, improved access to markets, access to alternative sources of supply, and the speedier transport of goods. Service companies will be able to operate cross-border operations once the legislative restrictions are removed. Europe's economy will be revitalised in every way. The question for individual companies, however, particularly smaller and medium-sized companies (under 500 employees), is whether they should, or should not, expand into Europe. This chapter discusses options at the disposal of businesses which do decide to 'Europeanise' their activities.

Within the frontiers of the Single Market, enterprises will enjoy freedom to move goods, services, people and capital across national frontiers as easily as they do today across domestic regional boundaries. This will not herald change for the regional operator, who has little ambition to expand current activities, and whose domestic market share is unlikely to be much affected by foreign competition. For the medium-sized, or even small business with wider horizons in its sights, the Single Market could provide a spectacular opportunity for breaking new ground.

Commercial and financial reasons which normally induce an enterprise to re-locate will be much the same after 1992 as before. Lower manufacturing costs, developing a local market, cheaper offices, improved transport facilities, better working conditions, all commanding the same urge to improve the efficiency of the business. What will change dramatically is the legal and administrative environment. An enterprise will be able to re-locate its activities anywhere in the Community without having to surmount numerous administrative, legal and psychological barriers which make it difficult, risky and costly to do business abroad today. It is feasible that a business could manufacture, say, in Portugal, while operating its financial and legal services from England, and controlling its sales operations from France, uninhibited by distances and national boundaries.

Advanced communications technology also plays a key role in operating over long distances. Pan-European expansion is made easier by speedy electronic communications, particularly video conferencing and document transmission. Without this technology, great distances in the Single Market could still impede expansion, almost as much as bureaucratic procedures.

Commissioning a business study

Despite the removal of barriers, and even with advanced communications technology, certain obstacles will remain. Language, culture and business practices differ from one Community country to another, though Single Market arrangements will permit and encourage all EC nationals to come to tackle the differences, enabling them to one day do business anywhere in the EC on equal terms. The process of 'harmonising' business practices in Europe is under way but, in the meantime, each member state will preserve a multitude of different laws regulating the conduct of business on a day-to-day basis. Any company hoping to make the most of tomorrow's Single Market should begin mastering the differences now.

As a positive first step, a study should be commissioned, but not a bland study of the business landscape. It should tie in closely with the aims, resources and capabilities of the enterprise, and contain facts which advance the company in its pursuit of new business[1]. There are, however, obvious broad categories of information which should be obtained:

☐ **Market survey**
  Main competitors, EC based and non-EC

☐ **Legal structure for extending domestic operations**
  Agent
  Distributor
  Franchisee
  Licensee
  Joint venture
  European Economic Interest Grouping (EEIG)
  Subsidiary
  Branch office

☐ **Legal requirements**
  Protection of name/trade mark/patent
  Relevant EC laws
  National laws

☐ **Selling direct**
  Marketing and sales staff
  Export formalities — licences or special permits
  Standards, technical and quality assurance
  Labelling and packaging requirements
  Product liability and statutory insurances
  Documentation

☐ **Setting up locally**
  Renting or buying premises
  Setting-up costs
  Labour laws
  Local laws and regulations

☐ **Finance**
  Tax implications
  Export finance
  Exchange controls
  Export credit insurance
  Debt collection

Detailed information confirms management views as to whether, where and how to expand into Europe, at the same time familiarising management with local business practices. Information prepares management for negotiations with local business contacts and potential Euro-partners. It is a generalisation, but nevertheless true, that success in winning a place in the Single Market depends on how well and how quickly a company develops European expertise at the centre of its own organisation. Management must transform itself from being purely domestic in outlook to becoming pan-European in its mentality and skills. Appointing a European marketing director to shoulder the burden may not be enough.

OPTIONS FOR EXPANDING ACTIVITIES

Although the traditional routes into Europe via agents, distributors, or joint ventures, will not disappear, many companies, encouraged by the deregulated trading environment, will be coming to such intermediaries for the first time. This section outlines the function of intermediaries, or representatives, particularly for the benefit of smaller and medium-sized companies seeking new business in Europe.

Appointing an agent

An agent's basic function is to procure business for the supplier and promote the product. Earning commission of around 10 to 15 per cent, most agents expect to be appointed on an exclusivity basis, acting as sole agent for the product in a particular territory. The territory defined in an agency agreement may be a region, a country, or even the whole of Europe. It is not unusual for a principal to appoint several agents in one country.

This simplified, though commonly held view of the agent's role can be deceptive, encouraging the belief that all that an exporter need do to establish a presence in a foreign market is appoint an agent and sit back and wait for the orders to come in. In the Single Market, publicised as an open, deregulated European marketplace, this incomplete vision of an agent's role could persist. But the reverse is true. In a more competitive market agents must also sharpen up their act. They will continue to need constant support from their central management at home across many facets of sales, marketing and after sales service.

The advantages of appointing an independent agent to promote sales locally should be compared to the advantages of employing sales staff directly, or through a local branch or subsidiary. In the long run, a supplier will probably substitute a successful agent with a wholly owned branch or subsidiary. However, the free movement of capital and other benefits of the Single Market may create conditions in which a branch office may prosper from the outset.

First-time exporters should approach a potential agent with a seeking mind. Leading agents with a range of well-established products can afford to be choosy about who they take on. But such agents may not necessarily be the best agents to pursue. Others may make claims that they can never fulfill. These questions can only be answered by careful scrutiny of an agent's operation over a period of time. There are, however, certain legal points which can be settled at an early stage.

Taxation

A careful study should be made of any local rules which determine the extent to which, and under what conditions, an agent's actions bind the domestic supplier. Where a local agent has the power to bind the domestic supplier, the supplier could be regarded by the local tax authorities as having set up a permanent establishment, incurring liability for income tax on profits generated locally. Normally, in such circumstances, the supplier benefits from relief under a double taxation convention between the countries involved, but extra accounting and other professional costs will accrue. One way of avoiding such problems is to use a local branch or subsidiary to employ the agent's services from the outset.

Terminating agreements

Terminating an agency agreement can be expensive. Before appointing an agent, the supplier should clarify to what extent, if at all, it will be possible to contract out of local termination obligations. In some countries, an agent will be deemed to have developed goodwill for the supplier which on termination of the agreement has to be compensated. Different rules may apply depending upon whether the agency agreement is for a fixed duration or an indefinite duration, and upon the the circumstances in which termination of the agency agreement takes place.

Special social security payments

The appointment of a local agent may involve contributions to a special social security fund in proportion to the commission paid to the agent. There are moves to develop a uniform agency agreement for use within the Single Market, but agency relationships continue to present important differences from country to country. For the time being, each agency appointment should be considered separately.

EC law

In EC competition law, an agent is perceived as an ancillary arm of the supplier. The agent's activities will therefore be looked upon as being the activities of the supplier himself. Any controls exercised by the domestic supplier over the conduct of his local agent will not amount to an agreement between two or more enterprises which adversely affects trade between member states.

This should certainly be the case where the local agent is operating merely as a procurer of business for the supplier. However, the relationship should not confer rights on the agent which effectively permit him to develop his own business through selling the supplier's products. If the agent is effectively acting as a licensee or distributor for the supplier, any clauses in the agency agreement restricting his freedom to operate freely throughout the Single Market could be in breach of EC law (see *Distributor* below).

Appointing a distributor

A distributor purchases products from the domestic supplier and has the right to sell them to local customers. The grant of an exclusive right, which the local distributor will normally require, means that the supplier is prohibited from selling to anyone within the distributor's territory. If the supplier wishes to preserve long-standing clients whom he has served directly in the past, or seeks to reserve the right to develop certain relationships in the future (eg. where special support is provided on a continuing basis), provision should be made for this in the agreement with the distributor. The distributor's gain is the difference between the price paid to the supplier and the price at which the goods are sold on. Clearly this has implications for price competitiveness in the marketplace if the distributor's mark-up is high, as does the loss of control over sales and promotion of the product once it has reached the distributor.

In the past, an enterprise unable to sustain the high cost and complexity of setting up and maintaining a local subsidiary would appoint a local distributor as the next best vehicle to expand foreign sales. But many of the reasons which normally induce a supplier to leave local matters to local operators, will disappear as the Single Market transforms business habits and domestic management develops a more global European perception of its business strategy.

In the future, the role of a local distributor will change. The distributor will no longer be essentially a local sales organisation. The trend will be to develop professional distribution organisations with the capacity to penetrate markets at the chain store level, ultimately throughout the Single Market. The ideal distributor may well be an enterprise based in the supplier's own country, able to co-ordinate the marketing throughout the Single Market. In a Single Market scenario, manufacturers will favour Euro-distributors. They will be less inclined to take on a variety of local distributors.

In the meantime, where an enterprise is looking to develop its sales on a regional basis, it may be advisable to take direct action, employing a local sales force, rather than delegating this vital function to a distributor. The distributor's role may become restrictive, rather than beneficial to the Single Market strategy being developed by the domestic supplier, if the distributor is given distributorship rights, but fails to fulfill expectations.

Termination of distributorships
Termination of a distributorship does not normally incur compensation for goodwill. Reasonable notice (six months) of termination should be given to the distributor, and provision made for the withdrawal or transfer of left over stock at an agreed price (eg. cost).

Brand names and trade marks
The use of the supplier's brand names, logos and trade marks is invariably a vital component of the distributor's agreement as these are likely to be important for the successful sale of the product. It is therefore advisable to secure the local registration of trade marks and designs prior to entering into an agreement with the distributor The use of the supplier's trademarks and other distinguishing signs by the distributor should be carefully regulated. (see *Intellectual Property*, Part Six, Chapter 4).

After sales service
After-sales service is normally supplied by the distributor. A distributorship agreement should establish controls to protect the reputation of the supplier's name and product. It may be advantageous for the domestic supplier to set up an independent after-sales service locally where this function is sensitive or requires special technical expertise.

Joint ventures with distributors
In the spirit of 1992 and a free market atmosphere, a supplier may be attracted to the idea of setting up a joint-venture company with a local distributor. There are

several drawbacks to such arrangements. The distributor may be unwilling or unable to put cash into the joint-venture, instead offering goodwill and contacts by way of a contribution for a share in the new business. The danger is that the supplier gets locked into spiral investments to keep an expensive operation afloat; an operation which the distributor cannot maintain alone on existing margins. A better way is to offer the distributor the opportunity of acquiring shares in the joint-venture company at a later stage (based on the company's performance), or to set up a local branch employing the distributor as sales director or marketing manager with appropriate incentives.

Another drawback to forming a joint venture with a distributor is the likely inclusion of an exclusive supply agreement which cannot readily be terminated or enforced. The supplier is understandably reluctant to put the new company under excessive pressure, and is further inhibited by the need to protect the original investment. There could be further complications if the joint venture is terminated and if, as is likely, the supplier's brand name and company name are involved in licensing arrangements with the new company

Minority stakes

It is not recommended that a supplier participates in a joint venture with a minority stake in the new company or accepts a minority on the board. The purpose of a joint-venture is to increase the supplier's sales abroad, a goal which could be frustrated if the new company, under the control of the distributor, is able to capture the local market with the help of the domestic supplier's product, only to find an alternative supplier at a later date.

Local full-time working directors of the new company (eg. the ex-distributor) should be employed, wherever possible, with an arm's length service contract. This costs the new company more in social security payments and leaving indemnities (applicable in many EC countries), but avoids the dangers inherent in using the services of such persons allegedly on a consultancy or free-lance basis. If 'consultants' are actually employed full time, the company may be in breach of local labour law and social security regulations.

EC law

Exclusive distribution agreements can be undermined by the insertion of clauses which are contrary to EC competition policy (Article 85(1) of the EEC Treaty). Legal advice should be sought. The classic situation is one in which a supplier prohibits a local distributor from selling on to customers in another member state to protect another local distributor or the supplier's own freedom of action. This clause would be contrary to EC competition law and, therefore, invalid. A supplier can, however, restrict the distributor's territory in the agreement, without setting down any form of positive prohibition, relying on the fact that distributors do not normally operate outside their own area. The supplier cannot rely on local trade marks, patents, copyright or registered designs to give territorial protection to a local distributor against the introduction of products which are lawfully marketed by a distributor in another EC country. This means that the local registration of intellectual and industrial property rights, under national law, cannot be invoked to prevent goods which are lawfully marketed in one part of the Community from moving to another part of the Community. For small and medium sized enterprises, however, EC law does not, in practice, pose a serious problem.

Under article 85(3) of the EEC Treaty, agreements with a distributor which, in principle, affect competition within the European Community, are exempted if the overall effect of the agreement is such as to improve the production or the distribution of the goods, or to promote technical or commercial progress. If an enterprise intends to invoke this proviso, it is obliged to notify the Commission first (see *The Competition Rules*, Part Six, Chapter 3).

The European Commission has issued a number of block exemption regulations governing certain types of agreements which will be automatically exempted without the need for notification (eg. an agreement between no more than two parties which restricts only the freedom of one of the parties to fix the resale price of the goods supplied by the other).

Block exemptions apply to distribution agreements (exclusive sale and exclusive purchase agreements), certain types of licensing agreements , know-how agreements , franchise agreements (goods and services, but not manufacturing franchises involving the use of patents), agreements for research and development (in the context of joint-ventures), and specialisation agreements between enterprises relating to the separate or joint manufacture of products for economy of scale.

Finally, and of considerable relevance to small and medium sized enterprises, there is a *Commission Notice* relating to agreements of 'minor importance' whose effects on trade between EC member states are considered to be negligible and, therefore, unaffected by the ban on restrictive agreements . In other words, where the agreement is not likely to have any appreciable effect on free trade within the Community, any clauses of a restrictive nature contained in that agreement, which might otherwise have been null and void under Article 85(1), will not be prohibited.

Whether an agreement is one of 'minor importance' or not depends essentially on a quantitive test. By way of guidance, an agreement will be deemed to have a negligible effect where the goods or services of the participating enterprises do not represent more than 5 per cent of the total market (increasingly with reference to the Single Market) for such goods or services, *and* where the annual turnover of the participating enterprises does not exceed 200 million Ecus (approximately US$180 million). In practice, therefore, most agreements with local distributors are not unduly affected by EC law which aims, above all, to prevent those agreements which would have a macro effect in distorting trade within the Community. For most enterprises there would indeed be little sense and virtually no advantage in entering into an agreement with a local distributor if it were not possible to limit the distributor's territory and to insist on other constraints in the interests of the supplier.

Franchising

There are different views as to what, in the strict sense, constitutes a true franchise. In a typical franchise agreement, however, the franchisee purchases certain products, packaging and other materials from the franchisor for an initial fee or 'front money', followed by further payments or royalties. Ideally, the franchisee acquires a replica of a tried and tested profitable business format, plus guaranteed supplies and back-up. The franchisor benefits from a high market profile and a string of dependable outlets for products or services, each run by an enthusiastic owner-manager, linked to the franchisor by the terms of the franchise agreement.

Many familiar high street retail shops are franchises, fast food outlets being the most common. Other franchised businesses include car rental services, computer and clothes shops, and various services. During the 1970s and 80s there was a franchise explosion in the UK, along the lines of the American franchise system. Many familiar retail names turned to franchising as a means of securing a bigger market spread, snapping up numerous prime sites, a rapid form of market penetration that, without the franchisees' investment, might otherwise have proved too expensive. Other familiar UK businesses have established franchised outlets in Europe. As the completion of the Single Market becomes a reality, franchising could become an attractive route to European markets for British companies.

The best known franchises are among the biggest high street chains in existence, but franchising can also be an exciting way for small and medium-sized enterprises to exploit a foreign market. Obviously, it is more difficult for a smaller business to achieve credibility for a new business format, special know-how, and a new product or service. Although the franchise industry is dominated by household names, sales outlets for virtually any type of goods or services can be 'cloned', in theory, guaranteeing the franchisee a ready return on a reliable product; for which, of course, there is an established demand. A business with several identical branches in the domestic market is, therefore, in a strong position to develop a franchise network. Attempts to sell a franchise which is anything less than a blue-print for commercial success (as long as instructions are followed), can amount to fraud, or at least provide a dissatisfied franchisee with grounds for a claim for damages.

Bearing in mind that a franchise agreement is not the same as a simple licensing agreement, a franchisee *always* expects to receive much more than the right to sell goods, even if the licence involves exploitation of the supplier's trade marks. A franchisee pays for a 'ready-made business' without the costs and risks of having to develop the business. The total dependence on the franchisor to deliver a proven way of making money is the chief characteristic of any franchise. For this reason the franchisee is prepared to pay a substantial sum of money up front to acquire a blue-chip franchise.

Franchise agreements

Some European countries have introduced laws applicable to franchises, and standard contract forms can usually be found. The locally accepted form of agreement for setting up a franchise should be followed wherever possible. In civil law countries, in particular, the law recognises certain standard or typical contract forms. This means that some local legal systems have difficulty in accepting new types of contract and fitting them into suitable categories. Most EC countries have adopted special laws which confer formal legal recognition on the status of franchise agreements, and these formats must be followed. If they are not, an agreement may be differently classed, creating different legal obligations and even local tax liabilities for the franchisor. As pointed out in the section dealing with agents (see above), wherever a domestic enterprise sets up a 'permanent establishment', conducting local business on a continuing basis, it becomes liable for payment of local taxes on profits generated locally. This is clearly not the wish of a franchisor who expects, at most, to have to pay only such taxes as may be charged locally (witholding tax), in respect of remittances (down-payment, royalties, etc) from the franchisee.

National franchise associations can advise on the principles of franchising, as can franchise consultants and law firms experienced in franchise agreements. There are certain basic points, however, that a potential franchisor can consider before approaching experts. The franchisor is expected to:

- ☐ Show concrete proof of the viability of the business in a tried and tested format.

- ☐ Be selective in appointing franchisees, offering training and support to ensure success (ie. franchisees will not be abandoned once they have paid the up-front costs).

- ☐ Ensure that trade marks are registered locally before entering into franchise agreements.

- ☐ Guarantee regular supplies of the product, or service, at reasonable cost, permitting franchisees to make a profit and be in a position to pay continuing royalties.

- ☐ Exert strict controls and motivate franchisees to ensure that the business continues to operate within the succesful, identifiable format. It is vital that the whole franchise network has a recognisable corporate identity which is itself perceived as a mark of value by consumers.

- ☐ Promote the business in the marketplace, with or without the participation of franchisees, though a franchisee will usually contribute to the funding of major promotion campaigns or refurbishment projects.

EC law

Appreciation of the interaction of EC law and national laws is needed when planning to extend a franchise network into EC countries. As noted above, most EC countries have their own standard forms of contract, though EC law can apply, particularly where a large corporation is subject to the Community's competition rules. There are also aspects of civil law which should be watched. Some jurisdictions have ruled, for example, that damages should be paid to a franchisee whose contract is terminated without just cause. There may also be difficulties if the cancellation of the head or master franchise agreement in a country adversely affects sub-franchisees.

The rules governing restrictions on competition should be considered at an early stage so that prohibited clauses are not unintenionally written into the franchise agreement (see *The Competition Rules*, Part Six, Chapter 3).

As pointed out in the section dealing with distributors (above), EC competition law will not normally affect the small and medium sized enterprise. But the franchisor should be aware of the general principles of competition law and seek advice concerning restrictions imposed on franchisees which could adversely affect a franchisee's freedom to trade within the Community. The group exemption on franchising agreements (in force from 1 February 1989) exempts from the competition rules all franchising agreements falling within its terms from the requirements of Article 85(1) of EEC Treaty. Therefore, the contracting parties do not need to obtain a specific exemption under Article 85(3) in those cases where the agreement could be potentially anti-competitive. The most important advantage is that an enterprise can set up a network of franchises throughout the Single Market, yet restrict the activities of a local franchisee to an agreed area.

Licensing a product or know-how

A licensee grants permission to manufacture and/or sell a product which incorporates special-know and/or patents belonging to the licensor which the licensee, without that permission, could be legally prevented from manufacturing and/or selling. The prime purpose of granting a license is to develop a market for a technical product which the licensor does not have the resources or the inclination to develop alone. The licensor could be an inventor, for example, without any manufacturing capacity, or a manufacturer in need of a foreign sales network. Each party to a licensing agreement needs protection which can be upheld by the Courts. There is little point in trying to license anything (at least not for very long) that cannot be adequately protected. Once the knowledge is released, use by third parties cannot be controlled. This is the position, for example, with 'know-how' which cannot be protected by patents.

The attraction to smaller businesses of licensing is that a promising product can be licensed to a larger, foreign-based organisation seeking to maximise manufacturing capacity or sales force, or seeking to complement a range of its own products. In the Single Market, a company seeking to expand its European business by granting licences should view licensing as part of a global European strategy, before proceeding piece-meal with individual agreements. One ill-considered licensing agreement, which unwisely eliminates a particular territory, could compromise a licensor's plans to develop a well co-ordinated pan-European policy at a later date.

As the Single Market programme proceeds, differences of law, language and culture become less of a deterrent to expansion. As domestic enterprises increase their European experience, they will depend less on independent local organisations, traditionally perceived to be better equipped to handle local conditions. Similarly, reasons for appointing a licensee will be influenced more by technical and financial, rather than geographical and cultural, factors. Just as we anticipate the emergence of the Euro-distributor, so we may anticipate the emergence of the Euro-licensee, one who deals with the whole of the Single Market. This possibility means that a decision to license a product or know-how need not involve the appointment of multiple licencees, each with territorial rights, when a single license could suffice. This begs the question: why license at all, if the national barriers have been removed? The attraction of licensing is that the potential Euro-licensee has an established position in the marketplace, whereas the licensor has only the know-how or the product, but lacks the means to exploit it to the full without a collaborator.

In anticipation of changes in the trading environment, resulting from the completion of the Single Market, a business which expects to develop technical know-how could set up a holding company to own any patents, designs and trade marks. Safeguarding the rights in this way, a holding company has the choice of either appointing one or more licensees directly, or granting a limited right to a domestic or foreign subsidiary to appoint a sub-licensee. Such a scheme is especially beneficial where the domestic supplier or a foreign subsidiary is providing technical support.

One advantage of using a holding company is that Euro-partners can be included in a joint-venture to further develop and market technology without involving partners in the licensor's domestic activities. In any event, in the run up to 1992, companies should be wary of taking action, such as granting long term local licences, which they may come to regret later.

Licensing agreements

Although licensing is, on the surface, a relatively simple concept, it is important to seek legal advice. A smaller operator may be easily caught out by a larger predator. On the good side, a small enterprise, in possession of a valuable and patentable technical product, will find that the grant of a license to a serious enterprise offers considerable rewards, eliminating risks and anxiety when seeking to build up its domestic manufacturing and marketing resources. Licensing agreements, however, if not carefully drawn up, can lead to serious repercussions.

A licensee generally requires a licensor to warrant ownership and freedom to dispose of the technology under licence. To be certain of possession, the licensor must ensure that patentable rights in the technology are registered locally in the licensor's own name before entering into a licensing agreement. Failure to do so may render a licensee vulnerable to serious damage, for which the licensor can be held to account, should one or more third parties compete against a licensee who has no legal protection. Insurance is obtainable, however, to cover the high costs of defending actions brought by local competitors claiming prior rights, and of bringing actions to defend a licensor's patent against infringement.

The licensor's remuneration normally takes the form of a royalty payment, related to sales. It is not uncommon for an initial fee to be paid in addition. Payments made to the licensor may be subject to a witholding tax, depending upon the terms of any applicable double taxation convention. Liability for tax differs from country to country since, as yet, there is no harmonised system of business taxation applying throughout the EC. Where a witholding tax is payable, it is usually credited by the licensor's domestic tax authority, so that the licensor does not pay twice in respect of the same revenue. A licensing agreement must establish a business structure which is not liable to full local taxation.

A licensor could incur on-going costs for future development and technical support. The small enterprise, therefore, should beware of undertaking obligations in this respect which it may not be able to perform. Agreements should be carefully read and their implications for the parties fully understood.

Licensees expect to be granted exclusive rights to ensure that the licensor, or any other licensee, does not enter into competition. But if the licensor intends to operate alongside the licensee, or wishes to reserve the right to do so in the future, a licence should be granted on a non-exclusive basis.

In certain circumstances, the owner of technology may be content to assign all rights to a third party in exchange for a substantial down-payment, plus some continuing royalties. In such cases, all rights in the technology pass to the assignee, and will not be possible for the original owner of the technology to grant licenses to others.

It is not advisable to fix royalty payments which are unrelated to the volume of sales. Instead, offer sensible market incentives for the licensee. Where high volume sales are expected, fixing royalty payments on a sliding scale, so that the more the licensee sells the less royalties are payable, is an incentive to achieve higher sales targets.

EC law

EC competition law should be taken into account when a licensing agreement is drawn up. Agreements can be particularly complex. However, there are two block exemptions of interest to license operators relating to patent licensing and know-how licensing. In most cases block exemptions permit a licensor to include restrictions which, but for the block exemptions, would be contrary to EC competition policy. Thus, it is acceptable for a licensor to restrict a licensee's territorial freedom and prohibit the licensee, for the duration of the patent or 10 years in the case of know-how, from actively selling into another territory. Protection against 'passive' competition is also possible, prohibiting the licensee from selling to a customer from outside the agreed territory.

Joint venture

The expression joint-venture is a becoming a fashionable term in 'Euro-speak' today. Joint-ventures create a vehicle for domestic enterprises to win new business in the Single Market by pooling resources with foreign-based companies. In some cases, the degree of collaboration is such that, as soon as a joint-venture acquires a direction of its own, the individual aims of its participants are overshadowed. Where this is likely, it may be opportune for partners to merge their enterprises from the start, or lay plans to phase out their individual operations.

The prevalence of joint-venture initiatives has led to the emergence of the European Economic Interest Grouping (EEIG). This is a new form of legal entity set up by Council Regulation 2137/85 for use by companies, firms and individuals seeking to establish a joint-venture. Still in its early stages, the EEIG provides a corporate identity, but not limited liability; a suitable vehicle recognised throughout the Single Market for essentially non-profit making joint-venture initiatives (see *Company Law*, Part Six, Chapter 2). Bringing together professional firms under the mantle of an EEIG will not permit the participating firms to undertake activities which their local rules prohibit in their domestic trading environment.

Tax treatment of the EEIG is still unclear, but the most likely solution is that members will be taxed individually on the portion of any profits to which they become entitled under the partnership agreement and there will be no business or corporation tax as such.

In a joint venture the parties join forces to combine resources and achieve market penetration collectively. However, the identification of immediate benefits in the international arena may prove illusory, unless both parties know each other well and each has committed capital to the venture. There have been many instances where the culture gap between joint-venture partners from different countries has proved fatal to a 'marriage'. In time, this may be less of a problem as operators from different countries share experiences and develop a more common business philosophy and methodology. Nevertheless, the problem should not be overlooked, particularly when one party has a common law background with anglo-saxon instincts, and the other has a civil law background and follows continental European traditions. As in any budding partnership, enthusiasm for starting a new business may blind one to dangers which could inadvertantly be permanently built in, only to surface at some future date. More joint business ventures fail because the partners fall out, letting their differences get the better of their judgement, than for any other reason.

These considerations aside, since it is often difficult to see the downside of partnerships in advance, before entering into a joint venture arrangement with a partner abroad, about whom one may know little, one safeguard is to assess whether the arrangement would be necessary, or desirable, in the domestic market. If the answer is 'no', in the Single Market scenario it is doubtful that any long term advantage will be gained by taking on a Euro-partner merely to acquire an immediate European dimension. It might be less risky to embark on a gradual process of self-introduction to the European marketplace, setting up subsidiaries, or registering branches. This strategy enables domestic management to acquire a European perspective and experience during the crucial early years without the fetters and risks of partnership.

The normal vehicle for setting up a joint venture is a newly formed company in which the partners take shares. The partners' own domestic operations continue independently of the joint venture. The parties may pool resources for research and development purposes, the fulfilment of a specific project or promotion campaign, or to combine resources for the joint production of components or to buy in bulk. The ultimate purpose of such a joint venture is to produce a conspicuous benefit for the individual partners, through their concerted efforts, but in the interests of their individual operations.

EC law

There are occasions where partners to a joint-venture regulate their affairs with adverse effects on competition within the Community, typically where a group of undertakings enjoys an important market share and agrees to produce and sell a given product only through the joint-venture company, significantly at a price intended to break the competition. However, where a joint-venture company is not involved in conducting a commercial activity itself — for example, where it is set up by the partners for joint research and development — there is unlikely to be any infringement of EC law.

To encourage innovation, the European Commission has introduced a block exemption for certain classes of joint-venture which might, but for this exemption, be construed as an infringement of Article 85(1) of the EEC Treaty. Block exemptions apply, for example, where the joint venture involves collaborative research, innovation, or co-production, where the results are also pooled.

Setting up a subsidiary

Establishing a wholly-owned subsidiary has traditionally been viewed as the ultimate, and thereby the best method of expansion into a foreign market. Working through its subsidiary, a principal can proceed with any form of local activity, the purpose being to generate a profit out of the local market. For no other reason, the subsidiary is accepted as the most appropriate company structure for doing business in the target market, meeting all the requirements of the authorities, in particular the tax authorities. A subsidiary, operating as a 'naturalised' business, is obviously better placed to argue its case with local tax assessors. The alternative, one is often told, is to fall prey to an unfavourable tax assessment, based on the global earnings of the parent company, to arrive at an apportionment of the revenue attributable to the local business establishment.

Other local factors, such as labour laws, may be more easily managed by a subsidiary. On the financial side, local exchange control requirements sometimes make it easier to transfer dividends than to remit the profits of a branch operation.

In the Single Market, however, where many of the differences between the laws of member states will be eliminated, the role of management itself is brought into sharper focus. At management level, there is always psychological pressure to set up corporate structures under local management, relieving the parent, or holding company managers, from becoming involved in local issues about which they may have little knowledge or understanding. The drawback, of course, is that derogation of senior management functions to local staff produces higher overall running costs, plus duplication of expertise. The duplication of costs and expertise, though previously justifiable on practical and legal grounds, might in a Single Market scenario hinge simply on one glaring fact; that management and staff at home cannot work in foreign languages and have no form of European training. Once management has mastered this problem, however, the long-held view that the local subsidiary is the best means of maintaining a presence in a foreign market becomes questionable. As the physical, legal and psychological barriers to trade within the Community disappear, domestic companies will not have to depend on vertical structures in the form of subsidiaries for the conduct of business abroad.

Holding company

A pan-European strategy highlights the attraction of operating a holding company, through which a UK domestic company can operate in Europe and:

☐ Acquire participations in local companies

☐ Establish joint ventures

☐ Appoint agents and licensees

☐ Hold patents

☐ Co-ordinate buying and marketing activities

☐ Manage multiple local interests

For the moment, however, there is no formal European-wide company vehicle for this purpose. National company structures still apply, a factor which emphasises the need to choose the most advantageous location for holding operations, always remembering that, when the Single Market has been completed, a suitable European company vehicle may be created.

Naturally, the most suitable location is the spot which offers the most favourable conditions for a European management team to operate. Some of the conspicuous benefits are:

☐ Proximity to prime markets/outlets

☐ Communications

☐ Transport/travel

☐ Availability of skilled labour

- Access to technology/research

- Investment incentives

- Taxation

- Financial and professional services

- Quality of life

By instinct, one may be driven to seek out a residence for the holding company where income from subsidiaries is not taxed. But a 'tax haven' is of no use where the ultimate beneficiaries must declare profits generated abroad. This will always be the case where shareholders of a holding company are EC residents. It is unlikely, and illogical, that any EC country in a Single Market scenario should tolerate a situation which allowed its own residents to evade domestic fiscal obligations by hiding behind non-trading off-shore companies or trusts, operating under the umbrella of the law of another EC country.

There being no European Company vehicle for the time being, and no integrated company tax system (without which European company vehicles could not operate), an enterprise setting up a holding company, whether to effect its Single European strategy or join forces with others, cannot avoid using a company located in an EC country. A decision to locate a holding company in any part of the Single Market should take account of the route by which profits earned in local jurisdictions must pass before reaching domestic shareholders. In theory, profits could be five times taxed:

- As tax on the revenue of the local subsidiary

- As witholding tax on payment of dividends by the local subsidiary to the holding company

- As tax on holding company business revenue

- As witholding tax on dividends by the holding company to domestic shareholders

- As tax on revenue paid to domestic shareholders

In practice, double taxation agreements between EC countries mitigate the effect of multiple cross-border taxation. With careful routing, particularly important where shareholders are scattered throughout Europe, their respective interests can be successfully co-ordinated through a holding company which, in turn, owns the shares in the subsidiaries.

In Luxembourg a special holding company structure is permitted to hold participations in or make loans to foreign subsidiary companies. A Luxembourg-based holding company can also hold patents and grant licenses, but not engage in direct trading activity, nor re-bill or charge commission in respect of its subsidiaries' activities. A Luxembourg holding company is exempt from business tax in Luxembourg on revenue in the form of dividends, interest or royalties from the subsidiaries, and no witholding tax is levied on dividends remitted out of Luxembourg to foreign shareholders. Because business taxes in these circumstances are not levied in Luxembourg, it will be possible for the recipients of dividends to use double taxation agreements to their advantage. Shares can be issued to the bearer, and anonymity preserved for lawful purposes.

A Luxembourg Holding Company is, in other respects, subject to Luxembourg company law and to EC disclosure of accounts requirements under the *Fourth EC Directive on Company Law*. But, in view of the fact that such companies do not have turnover of their own, and are very unlikely to employ over 50 employees, they are invariably regarded as small companies, eligible to abide by the reduced reporting and publication of accounts requirements.

Limited liability

The principle of limited liability exists in every EC country, but the formalities and substantive requirements for setting up and managing a limited liability company vary from one country to another[2]. Exporters seeking to expand into Europe by setting up a wholly owned subsidiary should take professional advice from lawyers with experience of setting up businesses who are familiar with the documentation, procedures and the full significance of local legal requirements.

Limited liability affords shareholders protection against liability for company debts only to the extent of their capital contribution. If the capital of the company falls below the legal minimum, shareholders must either inject more capital, or put the company into liquidation. In many countries it is possible to pay in a lower amount than the issued share capital, though a shareholder can be called upon to pay the balance.

In practice, it is unlikely that a company operating on a pan-European scale will view limited liability as an important consideration. In most cases, a parent company expects to stand by its subsidiary, rather than risk damage to its reputation by allowing a local operation to collapse. There is, too, a growing tendency on the part of national courts in Europe to pierce the corporate veil and make a parent company responsible where it has adopted a dominant role in the running of its subsidiary. Another point to watch is that, to varying degrees, Community countries are adopting stricter controls over the activities of directors. Directors and shareholders alike should, therefore, note carefully what their legal obligations are and what level of local liability applies. The transfer of mandatory minimum capital sums, possibly affected by exchange control regulations, is another aspect of setting up a subsidiary on which specialist advice can be obtained.

Taxation

Corporation tax is charged in the country where the subsidiary is set up. Again, different rules apply to the repatriation of dividends and their taxation. Double taxation conventions apply between EC countries which determine how locally generated profits and dividends, payable to the parent company, will be treated. Double taxation conventions exist to avoid being taxed twice on the same profits, and to ensure that profits are taxed at least once. Exchange of information provisions assists the authorities to combat evasion. These provisions will assume greater importance in the Single Market when increased cross-border business activity promotes co-operation between national tax authorities.

EC law

There has been some progress towards the harmonisation of company law throughout the Community, but there remains much to be done on important aspects of company activity, such as taxation and insolvency. The harmonisation process will accelerate, if the consolidation of Single Market policies goes according to plan, and if the need for a European company legal structure becomes more pressing (see *Company Law*, Part Six, Chapter 2).

Measures taken so far include a proposal for an EC Directive on the structure and management of larger companies and a more recent proposal for a measure allowing two or more companies, based in two or more member states, to form a European company by merging their activities, or forming a joint-holding company or a subsidiary.

A European company, coupled with a European company tax regime, would be an appropriate vehicle for operating in a fully formed Single Market, allowing a business freedom to expand its activities horizontally across Europe, without the need to set up locally autonomous structures. The European Commission is investigating this possibility, though with the interests of multi-national corporations in mind. Widespread disagreement over such matters as workers' rights may delay progress. Certain aspects of the Commission's so-called Social Charter, for example, concerning worker participation at board level have caused dissatisfaction throughout the business community in the UK, particularly among small and medium-sized enteprises who see the statutory presence of workers on the board as a serious, and probably costly threat to management efficiency.

Another obstacle to introducing a European company structure is local tax authority and treasury reluctance to abandon national financial interests. However, a common approach may develop in time, whereby the shareholder is deemed to be the taxable subject, rather than the company itself. In that event, tax offices dealing with the company would collect taxes on behalf of the other tax offices dealing with the shareholders, wherever they may be. Where a shareholder is not resident in the EC, the role of the company's local tax office could be to collect taxes on behalf of the Community as a whole, subject to the application of special tax conventions with the non-EC country concerned.

Currently, every subsidiary is taxed locally on profits. Local tax law further regulates the treatment of dividends payable after that tax has been charged.

Consolidation of accounts directive

Enterprises intending to operate in Europe should study the EC's *Seventh Directive of Company Law* on consolidation of the accounts of subsidiaries. The Directive ensures that a true and fair picture of the whole of the group's activities is presented. Small and medium-sized enterprises should check the extent to which current derogations exempt them from compliance with this directive.

Establishing a branch office[3]

A branch is simply a structural extension of its parent company. The main difference between the branch office and a subsidiary is that a branch need not be a separate legal entity. It will not require its own capital and local statutory management structure. An exception is the local branch of a bank or insurance company, having a sensitive and fiduciary relationship with the public, where local rules require a branch to be supported with its own funds.

For expanding companies, a branch office is usually the most cost effective and, in the long term, the most compatible structure for the multi-point development of a domestic enterprise. Its relevance to expansion into the large Single Market, characterised by cross-border trading and the minimum of formalities, is clear. However, if more than one company is involved in a local venture, a branch needs as its parent a holding company in which the interests of all the parties are represented (see above). In practice, the majority of foreign subsidiaries are owned by one parent, enabling the parent company to dispense with the need for a holding company and establish local branches directly.

In terms of liability, the fact that the parent of a subsidiary enjoys limited liability, where the same company faces unlimited liability in respect of local branch activities, is not normally a primary factor in the choice between using a branch or a subsidiary. Except in rare instances, a company with a good domestic reputation is unlikely to want to commence business abroad through a subsidiary because it wants to escape its responsibilities by hiding behind a subsidiary's corporate veil.

Traditionally a branch activity has always been regarded as a 'microcosm' of the parent (particularly for local tax purposes), rather than as a mere business appendage. Hence, in practice, a local branch is almost always managed in much the same way as a subsidiary company, operating in its own right. For practical purposes, there are numerous activities, including sales, publicity, research and development, which can be set apart from the main company operation for internal organisational purposes, but do not justify the formal establishment of a separately identifiable legal structure.

Taxation
A branch is normally taxed locally, like a subsidiary, and is invariably required to disclose its own accounts (and usually those of the parent) for this purpose. In some cases the domestic tax authority also taxes the profits generated by the local branch, but when it does, the relevant double taxation convention offsets the local tax paid. In other cases, once local taxes have been paid on the branch's profits, there is no further liability for domestic tax on profits.

Witholding tax is not payable on profits remitted cross-border by a branch to its parent, since these profits are not treated as dividends for distribution.

Through a branch, the principal is permitted to employ local staff directly, yet remit salaries from home. Local social security contributions and witholding tax on salaries, however, are payable locally. Within the EC, it is permissible to transfer domestic staff for up to one year, while continuing to make social security payments to the domestic authorities. Social security payments made in one EC country normally count as payments made under domestic schemes, so that statutory pension rights are not affected by short-term foreign postings.

As for tax routing, a company which depends on a network of foreign branches finds it easier to establish the ultimate tax position than by operating through a network of subsidiaries. For the subsidiary, the position is more complicated by local witholding taxes on dividends and the various effects of imputation systems.

Registering a branch
Registration is usually straightforward, involving little more than form filling. Copies of the Memorandum, Articles or Statute with accompanying translations must be deposited at local registration offices. Any changes in the domestic company's Memorandum, Articles or Statutes, (eg. increase of capital, change of address) must also be notified.

On the Continent, registration with the local chamber of commerce is a compulsory formality. The appointment of a local manager is important but, in most cases, it is not necessary for the manager to reside locally. A branch is invariably required, however, to provide a local address, plus the name of a representative for the service of notices by the local tax authorities.

EC law

A proposal for an EC Directive to harmonise the requirements for the local branch to disclose information about the parent organisation is in its final stages of preparation. It is expected that when the Community harmonises taxation throughout the member states, for taxation purposes branches will be put on the same footing as subsidiaries. This holds out the promise of taxation of the parent company alone on global profits.

1 Brebner & Co. (071-489 0215) produce *European Boarding Card*, a tailor made package of information to meet the specific requirements of the customer. A panel session with experts to discuss matters arising out of the written presentation is included in the price. *European Boarding Card* can be commissioned through many chambers of commerce and business centres. The London Chamber of Commerce and industry (071-248 4444) through its *Export Now* programme produces a *First Stage Action Checklist* to help smaller companies enter overseas markets.

2/3 *Setting Up a Company in the European Community*, John Brebner, published by Kogan Page (1989).

2 Doing Business in Eastern Europe

Six countries in search of prosperity

Edward Dolling
Neil Payne
Susanne Schalk

From the point of view of Western observers the history of Europe has, since World War II, been dominated by efforts by the independent states of Eastern Europe to gain their political freedom and determine the development of their own economies. In the cases of Hungary in 1958 and Czechoslovakia in 1968, efforts to change were forcibly put down by military intervention from the Soviet Union. When Mikhail Gorbachev came to power, his efforts to reform the Soviet economy and the introduction of Perestroika (restructuring) heralded a change in attitude towards the Eastern European satellite countries. Unqualified support for the communist leaders and their parties in Eastern Europe was no longer forthcoming from the Soviet Union. Therefore, real change has been allowed to take place without interference.

The need for political and economic reform began to result in changes, once it was clear that Communism and its economic system was not working. The year 1989 saw an acceleration of these changes with the Communist party in each of the Eastern European countries (with the exception of Albania) finally relinquishing its monopoly on political power and great efforts have been made to move rapidly towards a free market economy. Each country concerned has made these moves in its own particular manner. News of fresh political developments reaches us every day as the mood of independence spreads to Soviet satellite states.

For the Western companies these changes are creating opportunities. But it must be remembered that economic change and moves towards political liberty are still taking place, and that economic opportunities must be balanced against the varying degrees of political and economic instability currently found in the Eastern European countries. Inevitably this creates risk for business.

Opportunities and advantages

The changes in Eastern Europe are creating new opportunities, as well as making others, which have always existed, easier to exploit. As with any change, some advantages will only exist in the shorter term, for example high level of aid funding. Other opportunities are only applicable to the long term investor. In general the opportunities can be summarised as follows:

Geographic location: Geographically all Eastern European countries are relatively near the highly developed markets of Westen Europe. Poland, Czechoslovakia, Yugoslavia and Hungary all share borders with free market Western European countries.

Education: General education standards are relatively high and a reasonably well trained work force already exists in most of the Eastern European countries.

Industrialisation: An industrial infrastructure of a reasonably high standard already exists to varying degrees in each of the Eastern European countries.

Labour costs: Wage costs are relatively low even in comparison with European countries previously considered low, such as Spain and Portugal. (For instance, Hungary's monthly average wage is approximately $150).

High level of potential demand: Eastern Europe is one of the few unexploited markets remaining in the world. The large populations (see table), are hungry for the consumer products, services and technology available in the West.

	Population (millions)
Czechoslovakia	15.6
Eastern Germany (now part of Germany)	14.0
Hungary	10.6
Poland	38.0
Bulgaria	9.0
Yugoslavia	23.6
Romania	23.0

Provision of aid and grant funds: A high level of aid is being made available by the developed Western nations for the economic regeneration of the Eastern European countries.

Privatisation: A number of Eastern European nations are undertaking privatisation programmes. Foreign investors are seen as a major source of the hard currency required to develop the previously state-owned industries.

Problems and cultural barriers

The problems and difficulties that may be encountered by Western companies are often of a general nature and as such may be extremely difficult to overcome.

Political and social instability: All the East European countries are, to a differing extent, undergoing a period of economic and political change. Such change may in some cases lead to instability in the short term.

Profit motive is not well understood: Traditionally, enterprises have endeavoured to fulfil their part in a central plan. This has led to many enterprises operating inefficiently with no regard for profit. Therefore, the change to a system where organisations are operating for profit will not be easy. The concept of the management being responsible for a business rather than the State is a new one. Inevitably, Eastern Europeans will find such responsibilites difficult to take on.

Lack of motivation: Effort and achievement were not rewarded with increased economic benefits under the centrally planned system. Therefore, efficiency was low and the work force poorly motivated.

Poor accounting and business administration: Training and experience in accounting, business administration and information technology is very poor or non-existent. Any Western company operating in Eastern Europe will have difficulties in managing and monitoring its operations. Even the basis of accounting differs, and consequently the determination of profits and the book values of assets will not be familiar to the Western companies. These differences will also be relevant for determining profit in relation to such matters as taxation or currency repatriation.

Lack of a legal framework: The statutes and laws to enable free enterprise to flourish are currenly being put in place. The legal structures allowing such things as ownership of land and buildings at best are rudimentary and sometimes non-existent.

Currency convertibility: All Eastern European countries operate some form of currency exchange control and, at best, payments in foreign currency or repatriation of profits will be difficult and in some cases significantly restricted.

Poor state of economies: The economies of the Easern European countries are in a very poor state, most of them, other than Romania and possibly Czechoslovakia, being burdened with high levels of foreign debt, and many suffering from extremely high levels of inflation.

Poor infrastructure: Both in terms of economic infrastructure and physical infrastructure the Eastern European countries are in a poor condition. Banking facilities, stock exchanges, and accounting professions either do not exist or have only recently been created and are in a state of infancy. Communications are poor, and the waiting period for telephone lines is usually measured in years rather than weeks.

Bureaucracy very slow: Governments are moving away from their Communist party domination, but changing a system which has been in operation for over forty years is a slow process. Long delays and excessive paperwork normally accompany many business transactions.

Lack of investment in industry: Industry has suffered for many years from a lack of investment leaving it, in many cases, with outdated working methods and a lack of modern technology.

Lack of English Language capability: English is not spoken widely in Eastern Europe especially in some of the more remote areas.

Joint ventures

Until relatively recently the customary and, often the only way to do business in an Eastern European country, was through methods such as licensing agreements, exchanges of technology, or local assembly. These methods of business co-operation may well be efficient in some cases and should not be overlooked, but they only give very limited rights and little investment opportunity. More recently virtually every Eastern European country has drawn up joint venture or foreign investment legislation, allowing foreign firms to take a share in the business and participate in its management. Legislation continues to evolve throughout Eastern Europe into more general and less restrictive investment legislation. This legislation will continue to change and anyone intending to invest in a joint venture should seek professional advice to ensure that they fully understand the most up to date statutory requirements.

In most cases the process of establishing a joint venture will entail some form of authorisation and registration with the central authorities, which may be involved and bureaucratic. Another aspect that must be considered very carefully is the joint venture agreement made with the Eastern European partner. Such an agreement must cover a wide range of subjects, as many areas of the operation of private enterprise will not be covered by the legislation of the host country.

The joint venture agreement will need to cover areas such as equity, investment, protection, management, employment rules, pay, marketing, areas of activity, export, resolution of disputes, ownership of land and buildings and much more. Establishing a joint venture will inevitably take a great deal of time, research, professional advice and expense, all of which should be taken into account when assessing the eventual return to be made on an investment.

EASTERN EUROPEAN STATES

The following reviews of Eastern European economies are intended to be basic and should be treated as no more than a starting point for considering the possibility of investment in Eastern Europe, not as an investment guide.

To cover Eastern Europe in any greater detail risks misguiding the reader as changes in government, economic situation and the law continue to occur on an almost daily basis. These changes are inevitably to the advantage of Western companies but make anything written in detail almost immediately out of date. Anyone seriously considering investment in Eastern Europe is strongly advised to seek advice from experts known to have the resources to keep up to date and informed of the changes.

Hungary

Political
Hungary has been undergoing reform and moving towards a free market economy for many years. The Communist Party's monopoly on power has gradually come to an end and has finally been made history with the first free elections for forty years in March 1990. A right of centre party is now in government.

Economy
Hungary's total population is 10.6 million, of which 2.1 million live in the capital, Budapest. Gross national product is currently estimated at US$69 billion, giving a gross national product per capita of about 30 per cent of that of the USA. Inflation is currently very high, and is running at 20 per cent to 25 per cent per annum, and is expected to increase further in the near future. Foreign debt is the highest per head of population in Eastern Europe and totals in excess of US$19 billion. Interest payments on this debt accounted for approximately 17 per cent of hard currency outgoings in 1988.

Business aspects
Joint ventures with foreign investors have been allowed in Hungary for 18 years and are currently determined under three laws enacted since 1988.

Minority foreign investors may take up to a 49 per cent share in a joint venture company without permission from the State. Foreign majority owned, or even wholly owned companies can now be established with State authorisation.

Repatriation of earnings: Western investors are guaranteed the right to repatriate dividends and royalty payments in hard currency whether or not the enterprise has generated hard or soft currency. No withholding taxes are deducted from dividend payments abroad. Royalties, which are subject to withholding tax at a rate of 20 per cent are, however, deductible for profits tax purposes. Investors are also guaranteed the right to repatriate the proceeds of selling all or part of their investment, including the case of a forced sale in the event of nationalisation of the enterprise.

Taxation: The standard rate of tax on profits is 50 per cent but joint ventures with an excess of at least 20 per cent foreign participation are entitled to substantial reductions. All such joint ventures have this basic rate reduced to 40 per cent, a rate which continues indefinitely. In addition, manufacturing joint ventures normally receive a reduction to 20 per cent for the first five years and a reduction to a 30 per cent rate indefinitely thereafter. In the case of certain favoured industries, the reduction is even greater and a complete tax holiday for the first five years, followed by an indefinite reduction of 60 per cent of the standard rate may be available. At the current tax level, this gives a long term rate of only 20 per cent of profits. These tax reductions apply to a company, not just to the joint venture partner, and therefore also benefit the Hungarian partner. This strongly motivates Hungarian firms to take in foreign joint venture partners.

Grants: Grants are very limited, and are normally only available in very obscure locations.

Foreign currency: A joint venture is permitted to hold the Western investor's capital contributions in hard currency, provided it is used for the purchase of 'means of production'. Any imports of capital goods required to set up a company are not subject to import licensing or customs duty.

Captial contributions: Capital may be paid in as cash or in kind. Payments in kind may include equipment, intellectual property rights (patents, trade marks, production know-how), and capitalised property rents.

Currency convertibility: Under the present law, capital or profits may be freely transferred abroad to the country making the investment. However, the company will have to purchase the foreign exchange necessary and, although the country's trade balance has improved dramatically in recent years, the availability of foreign currency still remains restrictive.

Labour laws: Joint ventures with an excess of 20 per cent foreign participation worth over Fts 5 million are exempt from local wage regulations.

Poland

Political

About two years ago the Communist Party began to realise that it no longer had sufficient support from the Polish people to continue in government. Elections were held in June 1989 for the Senate which resulted in a Solidarity led government sharing power with the Communists and the smaller Peasants and Democratic parties. Parliamentary elections were postponed for one year. Politically Poland now seems reasonably settled and appears to have embraced the concept of a free market economy and its reforms in a determined manner. The reforms which, in many cases, seem to be causing hardship, apparently have the full support of the Polish people.

Economy

Poland's total population is in excess of 38 million people and, with a gross national product estimated at US$211 billion, it is by far the largest economy in Eastern Europe. However, the current economic problems are of an equally large magnitude. Foreign debt is over twice that of Hungary at slightly more than US$40 billion and inflation is running in excess of 20 per cent per month; it was as high as 78 per cent per month in January 1990. However, a radical economic reform programme is underway as part of an IMF loan facility package. This involves running a balanced budget, cutting subsidies, dismantling of price controls, a squeeze on wages, and an increase in interest rates allowing full currency convertibility. Wage costs are extremely low and are currently estimated at an average of approximately US$100 per month.

Business aspects

Joint ventures with foreign investors are governed by the Polish Foreign Investment law of December 1988. Under this law a Foreign Investment Agency was established to control and deal with foreign investment efficiently. Nearly all sectors of the economy are open for foreign investors by means of an investment through a limited liability type company. Permission to set up any joint venture has to be obtained from the Foreign Investment Agency and under recent law 100 per cent foreign ownership of Polish companies is now allowed.

Repatriation of earnings: All foreign currency profits can be freely transferred and profits in excess of the foreign currency available can be transferred in certain cases with the approval of government. A foreign shareholder also has the right, after tax, to repatriate the proceeds of the sale of his investment. However, certain restrictions will apply if the proceeds are in Zloty.

Management control: The management aspects of the joint venture are left to be determined by the partners in the joint venture.

Taxation: The importation of capital as an 'in kind' investment and the purchase of capital goods from outside Poland are exempt of duty within certain time limits of establishing the joint venture. Profits or income tax is at a basic rate of 40 per cent but is subject to certain variations and incentives. If a joint venture generates income from exports it gains a 0.4 per cent reduction in the 40 per cent basic rate of tax for every 1 per cent of total income that is accounted for by exports. This is subject to a minimum basic rate of 10 per cent. Tax holidays are also available to

Polish companies with foreign shareholders. If tax holidays are obtained, the foreign joint venture is completely exempt from tax for the first three years of operation which may be extended by another three years in so called 'preferred areas' such as agriculture, high technology and the manufacture of construction materials. A tax of 30 per cent is levied on dividends but is the subject of a double taxation treaty with the United Kingdom.

Labour laws: No specific regulations apply to foreign joint ventures other than that the principles for remuneration have to be set out in the company's founding articles. Therefore, all matters relating to employment, benefits and social security are governed by local law.

Czechoslovakia

Political
During 1989 Czechoslovakia appeared to be extremely unstable. Large scale demonstrations were seen on the streets of Prague. These demonstrations were forcibly put down by the Communist authorities. However, a new government was formed at the end of 1989 and economic reform appears to have started in earnest.

Economy
In Eastern European terms, Czechoslovakia has a strong economy. The population is approximatley 16 million, generating a gross national product of US$119 billion. After East Germany, this is the highest gross national product per capita in Eastern Europe. The level of foreign debt, in Eastern European terms, is relatively low at US$6.9 billion. Inflation appears to be under control and is running at approximately 3 per cent per annum. The country has a well-developed industrial infrastructure and a reasonably skilled workforce. However, as with other Eastern European countries, it does not have a convertible currency and faces the same potential problems of high inflation and unemployment as part of the restructuring and privatisation process.

Business aspects
Joint ventures: Czechoslovakia has allowed foreign investment by way of joint ventures since 1986. However, the latest law governing such investment was only introduced in January 1989. This is likely to be amended following the recent elections in June 1990. Currently, joint ventures with foreign participation are only allowed to operate in export orientated sectors, earning hard currency. The law also presumes an element of Czech participation although the maximum foreign interest is not specified. The Czech partner cannot be an individual; only a company (body corporate) can take on this role. A Czech company wishing to take part in a foreign joint venture must have State authorisation. Authorisation has to be obtained for any foreign joint venture but this is assisted by a special government department created for this purpose, the Federal Secretariat on Foreign Economic Relations.

Repatriation of Earnings and Capital: A foreign joint venture has the right to maintain its own foreign exchange bank account and is exempt from the normal requirement of surrendering any foreign currency earnings. The repatriation of foreign currency profits is permitted but is limited to the joint venture's own foreign currency reserves. However, the law does guarantee repatriation of the original investment regardless of foreign exchange resources and of any share of reserves in excess of this if the joint venture has sufficient foreign exchange reserves.

Taxation: The basic rate of tax on profits is 40 per cent. The availability of tax holidays for enterprises with an element of foreign investment is currently under review, as is all Czech legislation relating to taxation. Czechoslovakia operates a 25 per cent withholding tax on dividends paid to a foreign investor but this may be subject to a double taxation treaty which is currently being negotiated.

Labour laws: Foreign joint ventures have no exemption from local labour laws relating to conditions, pay, social security etc.

Yugoslavia

Political
Yugoslavia has a long history of being a relatively liberal Communist regime and, unlike the other countries in the Eastern European region, has not undergone the destabilising changes of the last year. Yugoslavia has been undergoing economic, but not political, reform for a number of years. However, the country is not wholly stable due to major economic problems and unrest between its constituent Republics, which each have strong nationalistic tendencies.

Economy
Yugoslavia has a population of approximately 24 million people and a gross national product of about US$116 billion. The government and the central bank seem unable to control the economy and deep economic problems exist including hyper inflation.

Business aspects
Joint ventures: The first foreign investment was authorised in 1967. However, 1989 saw the introduction of new foreign investment law allowing fully owned foreign enterprises although they are prohibited from operating in certain areas of the economy. All foreign joint ventures have to obtain state authorisation from a special agency set up for the purpose.

Taxation: The basis of taxation in Yugoslavia is currently the subject of intense debate which will probably result in significant changes in legislation.

Repatriation of Earnings and Capital: Yugoslavia is endeavouring to rely on its national foreign exchange market in this area. Any enterprise with sufficient Dinars is allowed to purchase the convertible currency it requires for its foreign exchange needs.

Romania

Political
Romania's revolution was perhaps the most unexpected and rapid. In the space of a few days over Christmas 1989 the dictator Ceausescu was overthrown in a violent uprising. The country is still undergoing some political turmoil but the Communist party has been formally dissoved.

Economy
Romania has a population of 23 million and a gross national product of US$95 billion giving it possibly the lowest gross national product per capita in the whole of Eastern Europe. However, it also has the lowest foreign debt of all Eastern Europe, amounted to only US$1 billion.

Business aspects
New foreign joint venture legislation was introduced in March 1990. Joint ventures can be majority owned by a foreign partner. Authorisation has to be obtained from both the ministries of finance and foreign trade. Repatriation of all foreign currency profits is expected to be allowed soon.

Bulgaria

The Bulgarian Communist party is still in power but a significant number of reformists are present on its central committee. Foreign joint ventures are allowed but the Council of Ministers has to decide on the branches of the economy open for foreign investment. The opportunities for western business are still considered to be limited.

Germany (re-unified)

Despite uncertainty about the pace of reunification of East and West Germany, many West German and foreign companies have taken the first steps to invest in East German enterprises and expand into the new market. Business experts agree that conditions in the GDR for foreign investment are not adequate, but improvements are expected to follow hard on the collapse of the Communist regime and continue during the transitional process of reunification. Non-European investors, encouraged by lower wage rates, also see an opportunity to enter the Single Market by setting up business in the GDR as it becomes part of the European Community. In the meantime, the Community and the GDR have concluded a trade and co-operation agreement similar to agreements with Poland and Hungary. According to this treaty, trade restrictions will be eliminated by 1995. Until then, joint ventures of any kind will be welcomed.

After World War II, the two German nations could not have developed more differently. Based on a liberal democratic constitution and its social market economy, the Federal Republic of Germany (FRG) boomed and achieved one of the highest standards of living in the world. In sharp contrast, the Communist-governed German Democratic Republic (GDR) has been characterised by a dictatorial one-party system and a planned economy. State-owned enterprises and co-operatives produced goods and offered services according to a five-year plan. Investment had been controlled by the State. Private enterprises could exist only as small units without economic power. The system satisfied the basic needs of the people and provided a certain level of wealth and social security, but the economy has not worked efficiently. Outdated means of production, high labour costs and mismanagement resulted in a permanent shortage of goods and productivity of about one third of West German figures. The country's industrial problems included environmental pollution, impairing health, but the GDR still achieved a standard of living which outperformed the other Eastern-bloc countries.

In late 1989, the reformatory movement in the Eastern bloc which swept away hard-line dictatorial regimes in Rumania, Czechoslavakia, Bulgaria and Poland reached the GDR. Before the eyes of the world, the hated Berlin wall was demolished and the process of reunification of the two Germanies began. Briefly, the emotion generated by this historic event swept through Europe but, as it subsided, the economic realities, plus fears that the balance of economic power in Europe would shift further towards a re-united Germany began to surface.

Under pressure from mass emigrations and mass demonstrations the Communist government of the GDR was forced to resign. The transitional government which took its place could rule only under the control of opposition groups. In March, 1990, the first free general elections were held and the winner, with nearly 50 per cent of the vote, was the *Alliance for Germany*, an association of conservative parties, closely related to the Christian democrats in the FRG.

The FRG never gave up its aim of reuniting the two Germanies, an aim which was fixed in the basic constitutional law of the FRG. The people of the GDR also strongly advocated the reunification of the two countries as a guarantee for democracy and wealth. Negotiations between both states and the four victorious powers, whose consent reunification depended on, supported German endeavours in principle. The governments of both Germanies were anxious to achieve full unification as quickly as possible. More than 10,000 people were leaving the GDR each week to begin a new life in the West. Due to this loss of labour, the economy of the GDR was deteriorating.

Details of unification could not be agreed on at an early stage, due to the gap between both economic systems. Different standards of living, relatively backward industries in the GDR, and the difficulties of monetary convergence meant that unification could not be easily achieved. The GDR government seems to be willing to assume the legal system of the FRG in a large part. However, transitional regulations will be found in the interim. Presumably the first step will be a currency union under the control of the powerful German Federal Bank on an agreed exchange rate between the Deutschmark and the Ostmark.

Future economic and political conditions in the GDR are not clearly predictable, largely depending on the attitude and actions of the new GDR government. Political uncertainty underlines the risks for investors in GDR enterprises. Nevertheless, the recovery of the GDR economy requires high public and private investment. Inefficient enterprises may have to close, resulting in a temporary increase in unemployment and a decline in living standards. In a way, these problems mirror the problems of economic convergence throughout the European Community which, though not as acute, still involve the integration of poorer countries with stronger European economies. As in the Community, aid for industrial restructuring and foreign investment will play a significant part in economic recovery. In the GDR, the adjustment of the legal system will be accompanied by adjustment in salaries, the cost of living and levels of social security, to mention just a few of the socio-economic issues to be worked through. Initially, therefore, GDR enterprises may not be in a position to afford FRG wage rates and social security contributions.

CONTACTS

Department of Trade and Industry
East European Branch
1 Victoria Street
London SW1H 0ET
Tel: (071) 215 5152/5267 (Czechoslovakia,
GDR, Romania, Yugoslavia) (071) 215
4734 (Albania, Bulgaria, Hungary, Poland)
Fax: (071) 215 5269

**London Chamber of Commerce and
Industry (LCCI)**
East Europe Section
69 Cannon Street
London EC4N 5AB
Tel: (071) 248 4444
Fax: (071) 489 0391
Telex: 888941

Anglo-Yugoslav Trade Council
(Administered jointly by the East Europe
Section of the LCCI and the Confederation
of British Industry (CBI). For information
on CBI services see *Representing Industry*,
Part Seven, Chapter 3).

**German Chamber of Industry and
Commerce in the United Kingdom**
12-13 Suffolk Street
St. James's
London SW1Y 4HG
Tel: (071) 930 7251
Fax: (071) 930 2726
Telex 919442 GERMAN G

British Chamber of Commerce in Germany
Heumarkt 14
D-5000 Cologne 1
Tel: (49) 221 234284
Telex: 8883400 FIBL D

East European Trade Council
Suite 10
Westminster Palace Gardens
Artillery Row
London SW1P 1RL
Tel: (071) 222 7622
Fax: (071) 222 5359

3 Western European Economies

Economic profiles of EC and EFTA countries

Craig Thomson

Full economic convergence between member states of the European Community, until recent political events in Eastern Europe, was a goal which seemed a long way off. Certain member states, not least the UK, have been less enthusiastic than others about throwing their economic lot in with the rest of the Community, at least in the short term. But the unexpected collapse of the rigid Communist system in Eastern Europe may do more to encourage member states to pursue a cohesive economic policy in the Community than any of the political initiatives taken in Europe since World War II, including the Single Market initiative.

Getting the Community's own house in order has become a renewed political and economic priority, in the sense that it is a priority which is becoming widely accepted by the people and governments of Europe. Almost overnight, Western Europe has grown bigger. One Europe, one economy now seems to be a realistic target for this century.

All this political activity aside, for the time being, cross-border trade in the Community continues to be affected by the familiar fluctuations in EC national economies, since the economic identities of member states are not about to disappear. This chapter contains brief summaries of the economies of each of the twelve member states, serving as an economic backdrop against which companies can weigh any decisions about expanding their business into Europe.

EUROPEAN COMMUNITY

Belgium
Population: 9.88m (1989) GDP: BFr6,133 bn

Belgium is a highly diversified economy which exploits its geographically favourable position at the heart of Europe by acting as a pole for foreign investment and forging intimate trade links with neighbouring countries. Exports and imports each account for over 60 per cent of Gross Domestic Product (GDP). It has a stable currency (Belgian Franc) in the European Monetary System and an inflation rate very close to that of West Germany's.

Successive Belgian governments in the 1980s, almost all under the leadership of Wilfred Martens, have not had an easy time. Their major economic policy problem has been the attempt to bring down Belgium's high public sector deficit. In the period 1975-80 the deficit more than doubled and, as a proportion of GDP, the figure continued to grow until 1982 when it reached a high of 12.3 per cent. Since then attempts to reduce the deficit have met with mixed fortunes. It fell as a percentage of GDP in 1983 and 1984, only to rise again in 1985. In 1986 expenditure other than interest payments, fell in real terms but receipts also declined. Only in 1987 was there a significant fall in the figure as expenditure was cut and receipts rose, a trend which continued in 1988 when the deficit fell to 7.7 per cent of GDP.

Public debt reached Bfr1,013 bn in 1984, falling in 1985 as borrowing slowed and repayments began, but rising again in the period 1986-88 to reach Bfr6,362 bn by the end of 1988, which at 130 per cent of GDP was the highest figure in the European Community.

The government's austerity programme, aimed at cutting public expenditure and controlling wages, resulted in public consumption falling from 19.4 per cent of GDP in 1981 to 16.7 per cent in 1987. Falling real wages led to a decline in wages' share of national income from a peak of 74.4 per cent in 1981 to 66.9 per cent in 1987. The Belgian economy has grown only slowly during the 1980s. In common with the rest of the European Community, GDP growth was low between 1980 and 1983, although Belgium remained slightly above the EC average. Between 1984 and 1987, however, Belgium's average annual GDP growth rate of 1.8 per cent was below that of many of its European partners. In 1988 the country achieved its highest growth rate since 1980 at 4.1 per cent.

Like most industrialised countries, Belgium has seen a decline in its traditional industries including iron and steel, heavy engineering, textiles and non-ferrous metals. These sectors form less than 20 per cent of total industrial output which is now dominated by chemicals, food and drink and light engineering. Industrial performance during the 1980s has been erratic. There was a general recession in 1981 and 1982, followed by an upturn in the next few years. Iron and steel production, however, declined sharply in the period 1985-86, although there has since been a modest recovery. The chemicals and rubber sector which, in 1987, accounted for 12.4 per cent of manufacturing output, performed strongly, helped by firm demand in Europe. Other sectors, particularly textiles, have seen production stagnate.

The Belgian economy is dominated by a small number of holding companies, which have interests in most sectors of industry. The largest company, Societe Generale, was the subject of a major international takeover bid by the Italian financier, Carlo De Benedetti in 1988. Eventually, 'La Generale', which has holdings in around 30 per cent of the Belgian corporate sector, fell under the control of the French company Indo-Suez which owned 50 per cent of its shares, while Belgian interests retained 35 per cent, the rest being in Italian hands. Groupe Bruxelles Lambert is also a major holding group in Belgium.

Exports
The most important improvement in the economy during the 1980s has been in the export sector. In real terms exports of goods and services grew by 3.3 per cent annually, helped by the growing competitiveness of Belgian industry. Imports in the same period grew at an annual rate of 2.9 per cent. Export growth has been helped by Belgium's greater competitiveness following the government's austerity policy. Real wages fell in the period 1982-85 when the previous policy of wage indexation was suspended (fully in 1982-83 and partially in 1984-86). The

share of wages in national income fell from 74.4 per cent in 1981 to 66.9 per cent in 1987.

Belgium's foreign trade is linked with that of Luxembourg in an economic and customs union (BLEU) and foreign trade and balance of payments accounts are issued jointly for the two countries. The faster growth of exports mentioned above led to a fall in BLEU's trade deficit from Bfr260 bn in 1982 to a surplus of Bfr5 bn in 1986, although this was reversed in 1987 when a small deficit of Bfr10 bn was recorded. In 1988 the deficit was cut to Bfr5.4 bn, although this was mainly due to a decreasing energy products deficit. Other goods showed a falling surplus partly caused by a worsening deficit in investment goods. Import growth was slower in the 1980's, due to weak domestic demand, although by 1989 this had begun to improve.

Denmark
Population: 5.13m (1989) GDP: DKr768 bn

The industrial development of Denmark did not really begin until the 1930s, and even afterwards agriculture remained the predominant export sector until the 1960s when the process of industrialisation began to accelerate. At the beginning of that decade agriculture still accounted for nearly two thirds of total exports, but by the early 1970s it had fallen to just a quarter.

This belated, but rapid industrialisation goes some way to explaining Denmark's perennial current account deficits. The growth of manufacturing led to a heavy dependence on imported equipment and energy sources, principally oil, which accounted for 88.4 per cent of total fuel consumption in 1973. The oil price crisis of that year therefore hit the Danish economy hard. A current account deficit equivalent to 3 per cent of GDP was recorded in 1974. By 1976 this had risen to 4.6 per cent of GDP.

At the same time, Denmark was going through a period of high inflation and excessive demand for imports while the export sector stagnated. The government had some success in bringing down the current account deficit by 1978 by pursuing a restrictive incomes policy and a tight fiscal policy. The second oil price crisis, however, led to a record deficit. The current account deficit continued to be unacceptably large. Matters were not helped by the rise in imports, triggered by a boom in domestic demand which continued until the government's attempts to reduce demand led to a decline in GDP in 1987 and 1988. By 1989 recovery had begun. Denmark's economic growth now appears to be more export led. Borrowing abroad by the government to finance the balance of payments deficit means that Denmark's gross foreign debt by the end of 1988 stood at DKr710 bn, equivalent to 57.4 per cent of GDP, compared with 26 per cent in 1980.

On the public finance side, the Danish government has been sucessful in bringing down the public sector deficit, which by 1983 had reached 9 per cent of GDP. In 1985 the deficit had been cut to DKr9.7 bn, which was 1.6 per cent of GDP and in 1986 a surplus was recorded of DKr7.9 bn, aided partly by spending cuts but principally by increases in taxation. In 1988, however, a deficit was recorded.

Manufacturing
The Danish manufacturing sector is dominated by reprocessing and light industry because of the shortage of raw materials in Denmark. The most important

industries are chemicals, food processing, engineering and furniture manufacturing. In 1988 manufactured goods dominated merchandise exports, accounting for 71 per cent of the total. Within this sector, engineering products accounted for 24.3 per cent of total exports and over a third of manufactured exports. Imports are dominated by materials for Danish manufacturing industry, with chemicals and machines among the most important items.

Energy production and consumption
In the energy sector Denmark has been in the forefront of the search to reduce energy consumption, and managed in the period 1972-85 to reduce final energy consumption from 16.32 m tons of oil equivalent (toe) to 15.14 toe. During this period Denmark's energy production also rose considerably. Encouraged by the international rise in oil prices in the 1970s the Danish government has aimed for self-sufficiency in the energy sector. In 1986 oil and gas production was 1,905 mn m3 and in 1988 65 per cent of consumption was satisfied by domestic production, a ratio which it is planned should rise to 80-95 per cent by the 1990s.

France
Population: 55.9m (1988) GDP: Fr6,133 bn

France is the second largest economy in Western Europe. Despite some weaknesses, it has great organisational strengths and has been a driving force behind various forms of European co-operation. Until the first oil price shock of 1973, French GDP grew faster than the West European average. It slowed to an average annual increase of 3.2 per cent in the period 1973-79 and then slowed further to 1.5 per cent in the period 1980-88. However, in 1988 the GDP growth rate was the highest in ten years, helped by a rise in public consumption due to a boom in consumer credit, plus lower oil and energy prices.

Inflation
One of the major problems of the French economy since the World War II has been inflation, which was exacerbated by the oil price rises of the 1970s, leading to periods of high inflation in 1974-75 and 1979-82. Since then, however, there has been a major slowing in the rate of inflation, helped by a tough incomes policy and a firm exchange rate. The rate fell from 9.6 per cent in 1983 to 2.5 per cent in 1986, remaining at around 3 per cent in 1987 and 1988, only marginally above the West German rate.

Industry
France, in common with the rest of Western Europe, experienced a decline in its traditional heavy industries such as steel, coal and textiles. This has resulted in economic activity moving from the old industrial regions, such as Nord-pas-de-Calais and Lorraine, towards the southern half of the country, where many of France's new, high technology industries are located.

Agriculture
Agriculture is still a significant feature of the French economy, compared with other industrialised economies. This sector accounts for around 7 per cent of GDP. Basic and processed agricultural products represented 16.9 per cent of merchandise exports in 1988. France is second only to the USA in size as an agricultural exporter, and is especially strong in dairy products, cereals and wine. Exports in this sector have been aided by the EC's Common Agricultural Policy

(CAP), which has maintained high prices and opened up other EC markets. It is feared that the entry of Spain into the Community in 1986 may become the cause of problems in France, especially to growers of Mediterranean products such as fruit and vegetables who now face competition from Spanish produce imported duty free.

Trade deficit

The trade deficit in the 1980s has fluctuated in line both with changing government economic policy and the fortunes of oil prices. After the second oil price shock in 1979 and the initial expansionary policies of the socialist government in 1981 and 1982, the deficit widened. It began to fall again in the period 1983-84 after the 1983 austerity budget, only for volume imports to rise sharply again in 1985-87, while exports growth was poor. The drop in international oil prices in 1986, however, led to an improvement in the terms of trade and in 1988 export volume rose considerably.

Successive governments since the 1970s have aimed to reduce France's dependence on energy imports. France is the world's highest per capita producer of nuclear power (whose capacity rose by over four times between 1980 and 1986). Nuclear power is now a far more significant energy source than conventional thermal power. However, limited coal, gas and oil reserves mean that France is still heavily dependent on foreign imports. Consequently the French balance of trade is significantly affected by international oil prices. In 1985 the energy deficit was some 4 per cent of GDP, while in 1988 it was just over 1 per cent.

Manufacturing

The French manufacturing sector is a mix of great strengths and weaknesses. France has been the driving force in Europe's aerospace industry, notably the Airbus commercial airliner and the European Space Agency's Ariane programme. It is also very strong in advanced railway and metro equipment, and still a force in automobiles. France is a leader in some aspects of computers and telecommunications, and remains paramount in a wide range of luxury goods and light kitchen equipment. It is, however, notably weak in some engineering goods, particularly machine tools and consumer durables. French prowess in defence equipment may prove of declining value in present circumstances.

In the services sector, by contrast, exports comfortably exceed imports. In franc terms, two of the strongest areas of growth in the 1980s have been in tourism and in engineering and consultancy.

Germany (West)
Population: 61.2m (1989) GDP: DM2,260 bn

The West German economy, in ruins at the end of World War II, has emerged, initially with the help of generous United States aid, to become the third largest in the Western world, after the USA itself and Japan. In dollar terms, the West German economy overtook that of France and the United Kingdom in the 1960s and GNP growth was strong until the second oil price shock and the period of global recession in the early 1980s. The upturn in the economy came in 1983 but growth continued to be hesitant until 1988 when real GNP growth reached 3.4 per cent.

Trade balance

West German growth has been export led during most of the last 30 years. West Germany is the world's largest exporter and ranks behind only the USA as an importer. In 1988 there was a record trade surplus of DM128 bn, beating the record of the previous year by some DM10 bn. The largest contributer to exports, which in 1988 was responsible for $58 bn, or 18.8 per cent, of the total, is the road vehicles sector. In all, capital goods accounted for over 50 per cent of total exports in 1988, with smaller contributions from other sectors. On the imports side, capital goods are again the largest sector, although raw materials and producer goods, including petroleum products and agricultural goods also account for a significant part of the total.

The large trade surplus is usually offset by a deficit on invisible trade. This amounted to DM30 bn on transfers and DM10.5 bn on services in 1988, but a current acount deficit is highly unusual (following the second oil crisis, the three years from 1979 to 1981 saw a cumulative deficit of $27 bn). In 1988 the current account surplus was a record $48 bn, improving on the three previous years' record surpluses.

The West German economy usually runs a deficit on the services account, mainly due to large net outgoings on tourism and travel. Since 1979 the net annual deficit has been at least DM23 bn. There is also a deficit in the transfers account, caused in part by transfers to the EC to which West Germany is a net contributor.

Agriculture

Agriculture accounts for a very small proportion of GNP (1.5 per cent in 1988), although there were 887,000 farms in the country at the 1983 census. 378,000 of them were under two hectares, and of these, 339,000 earned less than DM4,000 that year. The number of farms means that the farming lobby is very strong, a fact that has contributed to the strength of the government's support for the present EC Common Agricultural Policy.

Industry

In the industrial sector, although West Germany has seen a decline in the contribution of manufactures to GNP to the benefit of the growing services sector, in common with other EC states, industry still dominates the economy. There has been a shift in importance in recent years away from the iron and steel industries concentrated in the Ruhr Valley, to the high technology companies based in the south of the country where the automobile industry is also situated. Industry is, however, spread throughout West Germany and there is no north-south divide as is apparent in Italy and the United Kingdom, for example. The government's role in industry is confined mainly to directing research and development budgets towards smaller companies and to subsidising certain industries facing difficulties. It does however have a stake in about 900 companies in all, including Volkswagen. In 1988 industrial output rose by 3.5 per cent, compared with 0.3 per cent in 1987.

Greece
Population: 9.99m (1988) GDP: Dr7,664 bn

Greece is classifed as a developed economy, although in 1988 the manufacturing sector accounted for only 17.2 per cent of GDP. The services sector, including tourism and shipping, two strengths of the economy, accounted for 55.6 per cent of GDP in 1988.

After World War II and the subsequent bitter civil war which ended in 1949, the Greek economy grew at a remarkable rate. In the period 1950-79 average annual GDP growth of 6 per cent was second only to Japan in the OECD. In the 1980's, however, the Greek economy has run into severe problems. Manufacturing output declined and GDP growth was stagnant. The rate of inflation, which reached a high of 24.8 per cent in 1980, remained around 20 per cent until 1986. In 1988 index inflation was still 14 per cent.

Manufacturing

The Greek manufacturing sector is dominated by small companies. In 1984 there were only around 1,000 companies employing more than 50 people, with around 94 per cent employing fewer than ten. The major manufacturing industries are food processing and textiles which, along with cement, are among the principal Greek export earners. In the early 1980s profitability was severely damaged by wages rising faster than prices and many companies became heavily indebted, although the austerity programme of 1986-87 led to some improvements. In 1988 manufacturing output rose by 5.2 per cent as the government relaxed its incomes policy and demand grew. This was from a low base, however, and the index was only marginally up on its 1980 level.

Agriculture

The agricultual sector is handicapped by the small size of the average Greek holding, which leads to inefficient production. In 1988 the agricultural sector employed almost one third of the workforce but contributed only 16.2 per cent of GDP, compared with 33 per cent in 1953. Agriculture is a major contributer to Greece's exports, however, accounting for 28.4 per cent of the total in 1988. The principal export crops are fresh fruit and vegetables, tobacco, olives and olive oil. The EC's Integrated Mediterranean Programme is intended to help upgrade the agricultural infrastructure, including improved irrigation and land reclamation. It has, however, been criticised for failing to take account of the environmental implications of these measures.

Imports

On the import side the major items are manufactured consumer goods and machinery. Demand was reduced by the 1986-87 austerity programme taking effect, but these sectors still constituted 45 per cent of the total in 1987. Tourism remains a significant earner, particular in the islands where the local economy may be almost entirely dependent on tourist spending.

Shipping

Invisibles are an important part of the total balance of payments current account. However, the shipping sector has been weakened in the 1980s, as the number of Greek registered ships has fallen. Tonnnage declined from 42.5 mn grt in 1982 to 21.4 mn grt in 1988 as a result of the international decline in shipping, following the 1979 oil price rises. This rationalisation has led to improved profits for the remaining companies. In 1988 total shipping receipts accounted for $1,382 m.

Overall, the Greek current account deficit has improved considerably since 1985, falling below $1 bn in 1988. There has been no corresponding improvement, however, in the public sector deficit, which fell marginally from 17.9 per cent of GDP in 1985 to 16.1 per cent in in 1988, but is expected to rise. As Greece looks to the 1990s, it is strongly in need of firm government to cope with the challenge of the Single Market.

Ireland
Population: 3.5m (1989) GDP: I£23.4 bn

A major feature of the Irish economy in the past two decades has been the high level of public debt. Much of it is foreign debt, which has built up as successive governments have borrowed to finance the public spending, deemed to be politically necessary to solve Ireland's other economic problems, most notably unemployment. Foreign debt was equivalent to 46 per cent of GDP in 1988. However, net external borrowing in that year was negative as government repayments exceeded new borrowings by I£443 m.

Despite high levels of investment in the decade 1973-82, at an average annual rate of about 24 per cent of GDP, there was no subsequent rise in the number of jobs. Much of the investment went into protecting loss making state enterprises or into social projects including hospitals and schools. Subsequently, the high rate of growth of the Irish labour force has meant that, even given the improvements in GDP, the economy has been unable to create sufficient jobs. Unemployment reached a high of 17.7 per cent of the labour force in 1987 and although this figure declined in 1988 to 16.6 per cent, this was due, at least in part, to the increase in emigration of the workforce.

Agriculture
The agricultural sector remains an important contributor to Irish exports but its share of the total has dropped in recent years, from 34 per cent in 1980 to 18 per cent in 1988. This is in line with the general decline in the agricultural sector as a whole, with the agricultural workforce having declined by almost 100,000 since 1973 to a figure of 162,000 in 1988. The main agricultural category by output value is livestock and livestock produce, which accounted for some 88 per cent of total output value in 1988. Over 50 per cent of the total value of agricultural output is exported.

Industry
As the agricultural sector has declined in relative importance, so the industrial sector has grown strongly. Many of the most successful enterprises in this sector are foreign-owned, attracted to Ireland by government investment incentives. This is done mainly through the Industrial Development Authority (IDA), which administers investment incentives, including research and development grants, interest subsidies and loan guarantees. There is no witholding tax on dividends. Low corporation tax is available to all manufacturing companies and to companies in the data processing and software industries which have been approved for grant aid by the IDA.

Unemployment
The growth of overseas companies in Ireland has not been matched by a comparable increase in employment. In 1987 manufacturing industry employed 18 per cent of the workforce, a fall of 3 per cent compared with 1980. Although foreign companies were responsible for the creation of around 5,000 new jobs between 1986 and 1988, indirect job creation has not been substantial due to these companies' lack of links with the domestic economy. However, foreign owned high-tech industries in the pharmaceutical, electronic engineering and computer sectors have produced the greatest export growth in the 1980s.

Trade balance

Foreign trade is of major importance to the economy. In 1988, exports of goods and services accounted for 72 per cent of GDP, with a merchandise trade surplus of I£2.1 bn, equivalent to some 10 per cent of GDP. This figure represents a remarkable turnaround. The first surplus came in 1985, following a long period of deficits, which reached a high of 15 per cent of GDP in 1981. The current account has also improved, although held back by high interest payments on foreign debt and an outflow of profits from foreign companies in Ireland. However, net international transfers have risen during the 1980s, most notably from the EC. Since 1986, tourism receipts have also risen. The result was a current account surplus in 1987 of I£239 m and I£437 m in 1988. Ireland, unlike the UK, has been a full member of the European Monetary System since 1979. It can claim to be well prepared for the post 1992 Single Market, although it still has a major task in providing jobs, particularly for its young.

Italy
Population: 57.5m (1989) GDP: L19,000 bn

In the years following World War II Italy has witnessed an economic 'miracle'. From a small industrial base the economy has grown until Italy now rivals France, and at least equals the UK as an industrial power in Europe. There are, however, still a number of structural problems in the Italian economy including high unemployment and major regional imbalances, with much of the south of the country remaining an area of deprivation even by southern European standards.

GDP growth in the 1950s averaged over 6 per cent, falling back slightly in the following decade to 5.6 per cent before declining further in the period 1970 to 1979 to 3 per cent. Italy was harder hit by the oil price rises of the 1970's than other EC countries because of its very high dependence on energy imports, above all oil. Inflation was also a major problem. Following the first oil price shock, inflation remained in double figures for a decade. By 1984 it fell to 9.2 per cent and, helped by a firm exchange rate policy within the Exchange Rate Mechanism of the EMS, the annual rise in the consumer price index in the period 1986-88 was under 6 per cent. Despite an acceleration in 1989, inflation seems likely to remain under control. Recent GDP growth figures have also been encouraging, following a period of stagnation in the early 1980s, reaching 3.9 per cent in 1988.

One of the main worries of the Italian economy is the continuing high public sector borrowing requirement (PSBR). This has been a major feature of the economy for decades but has become even more serious in the 1980s, after a period of recovery in the late 1970's. In 1982 the PSBR was L63,800 bn, rising to L109,000 bn in 1988, although it has fallen as a percentage of GDP from 14.8 in 1985 to 11.6 per cent in 1988. Public debt now exceeds annual GDP.

Trade balance

Italy normally has a substantial manufacturing trade surplus, but the overall trade balance is negative, due to Italy's heavy dependence on energy imports and a net deficit in agricultural and food products. The size of the deficit, however, fluctuates enormously. It reached over L20,000 bn in 1984 and remained high the following year, but fell back to under L3,000 bn in 1986 following the collapse in oil prices and the fall in the value of the dollar. It has since climbed back again, however, after poor export figures in 1987 and a boom in imports. In common with other EC countries, there has been a rise in the EC share of total trade. In

1988 exports to the EC accounted for 57.2 per cent of the total, compared with 43.2 per cent in 1981 and imports from the EC accounted for 57.5 per cent compared with 40.7 per cent in 1981.

The agricultural deficit is mainly due to the Italian terrain, which is unable to support large scale grain or livestock cultivation. There is a fertile area in the Po valley in the north of the country, but large areas are mountainous and unproductive. Consequently, Italy has to import large quantities of its meat and dairy product needs. The cereal crop is mainly used in the production of pasta and, recently, imports have been necessary in order to supplement the domestic supply.

Manufacturing

Major areas of export strength include machinery and transport equipment, which in 1988 accounted for over 40 per cent of total exports, and textiles, which accounted for almost 19 per cent of the total in the same year. Italy is a world leader in office machinery through Olivetti, and Fiat, Italy's largest company, is the European leader in car production.

There are few giant private sector companies- Fiat, Olivetti and Feruzzi-Montedison. Fiat produces aeroplane engines, railway rolling stock, machine tools and medical equipment and a wide range of other industrial products in addition to automobiles. Most of the private sector, however, consists of relatively small companies, although many are highly competitive. Foreign direct investment in Italy is also low compared with other EC countries. The role of the state in the economy remains important. This it plays largely through giant holding companies, Iri and Eni, which operate in conjunction with private investors and, in virtually all respects other than the appointment of top managers, as though they were private companies. The Instituto per la Reconstruzione Industriale (Iri), one of the three leading state holding companies, has major stakes in around 140 companies ranging from electronics and telecommunications to aerospace and shipbuilding, plus three major banks. Ente Nazionale Idrocarburi (Eni) is a major world force in petroleum and natural gas and related activities.

Luxembourg
Population: 0.37m (1989) GDP: LFr261 bn

Despite its small size, Luxembourg is one of the richest countries in the world, with GNP per capita the highest in the EC in 1985, behind only the USA, Canada, Switzerland and Norway. This prosperity has been based on Luxembourg's important iron and steel industries, although in recent years, as this has declined, the growing financial services sector, keenly encouraged by the government, has become much more important. There has been a trend towards diversification in the industrial sector in recent years. Iron and steel production has been in decline since the mid 1970s, and in 1975 Luxembourg lost 9 per cent of its national income. Overall output declined from a 25 per cent share of GDP output in 1974 to 11 per cent in 1986, although it rose again in 1988 and is still an important sector of the economy. Engineering is increasing in importance, with 24 per cent of industrial output in 1986, with chemicals accounting for 17 per cent.

Investment

In the past, Luxembourg has had problems in attracting foreign investment because it does not offer the same range of incentives, including grants and tax holidays, as other EC states seeking to improve employment. In April 1989, however, Luxembourg revealed a Lfr5 bn investment programme by the Japanese TDK company, the first such deal by a Japanese company in Luxembourg. Overseas companies are beginning to be attracted by Luxembourg's central geographical position, particularly convenient for selling in West Germany, France, and Belgium, and its economic neutrality, which allows investors to target both the French and the West German markets more effectively.

Services
The services sector continues to grow strongly, with banking and investment finance assuming major importance. The financial sector now accounts for some 20 per cent of Luxembourg's tax revenue. Banks are 'attracted by Luxembourg's favourable regulatory system, including its banking secrecy laws which were strengthened in 1989, although the European Commission and some EC member states are known to be concerned both about these laws and Luxembourg's strong opposition to a harmonised EC witholding tax. Luxembourg's resistance to necessary change in these areas suggests that it underestimates its own skills and suitability as a location for financial services, irrespective of tax advantages.

Netherlands
Population: 14.85m (1989) GDP: G474.3 bn

The Dutch economy picked up in the late 1980's after a difficult period of stagnation and high unemployment as the economy became uncompetitive. GDP showed negative growth in 1981 and 1982 and average annual growth in the period 1981-87 at 1.2 per cent was below the OECD average. In 1988, however, growth was stronger at 3 per cent after a period of low inflation and wage restraint. The Dutch economy is characterised by a very high level of public spending. The consequent public sector deficit was 6.5 per cent of national income in 1988, although this represents a fall from a high of 10.7 per cent in 1983 as a result of government attempts to curb spending. Politically, however, this may not be altogether easy. A long term environmental plan has called for a massive increase in spending on the environment, which is already a comparatively high 1.3 per cent of GDP. The government, therefore, faces the difficult task of reconciling its desire to cut the level of taxation which, combined with welfare premiums make the Dutch the most heavily taxed nation in the EC, with its concern for the environment. This concern has been influenced not only by substantial gains made by the Green Alliance in the 1989 general election, but also by the Netherlands' vulnerability as a densely populated, low lying country, centred on the Rhine delta.

Total public debt is already the highest in the European Community after Italy and Belgium and has more than doubled as a percentage of GDP since 1980. The government is, however, able to borrow primarily on the domestic capital market. There is, therefore, no public foreign debt, although funding is obtained through the sale of government bonds to overseas residents.

Trade
Trade has been central to the Dutch economy throughout its history. Imports and exports each now account for over 50 per cent of GDP. Between 1982 and 1985 export growth was strong, following a period in the late 1970s when the Netherlands experienced a period of trade deficits. 1986 and 1987 saw a fall

in export revenues, mainly due to the substantial decline in world energy prices. The Netherlands is Europe's largest producer of natural gas and is led by only the USSR, the United States and Canada in the world production league. The decline in energy prices also affected imports. Imports and exports have tended in the 1980s to be fairly close. In value terms, energy exports fell from 23 per cent of all exports in 1985 to 11 per cent of the total in 1987 after the 1986 collapse in energy prices, while imports of energy fell to 11 per cent from 22 per cent. In 1988 the trade surplus rose to G7.4 bn from G3.1 bn as export values rose faster than import values.

Industry
Manufactures, however, lie at the heart of the Netherlands' trade and its economy as a whole. Industry has recently experienced a substantial upturn in its fortunes following a decline in output in 1981 and 1982 when a period of rationalisation was taking place. Now, increasing output, coupled with wage costs which are growing less fast than those of the country's major competitors, have led to growing market shares and increasing profit levels. In turn, this has allowed rapid growth in investment. The chemicals, rubber, paper and food and drink sectors have all achieved significant rates of growth. Exports of chemicals rose by 17 per cent in 1988, just behind the rises recorded for machinery and transport equipment (17.6 per cent) and raw materials (17.3 per cent)

The Netherlands is home to a number of multinational industrial companies, including Philips, Royal Dutch Shell and Unilever, which are all in the top 25 European companies in terms of total employment. The Dutch market represents only a small proportion of these companies' total business, with West Germany traditionally the most important overseas market. There is concern, however, that these companies may not have adequate representation in countries with fast growing markets, principally in the south of the EC.

Agriculture
Agriculture also plays a significant role in the economy. Despite its small size, the Netherlands is the third largest farm exporter in the world after the USA and France, and runs a substantial trade surplus in this sector. Fruit, vegetables, dairy and meat products are all important. About 60 per cent of production is exported and agriculture and fishing accounted for 4 per cent of GDP in 1986, compared with 3.6 per cent in 1980.

Portugal
Population: 10.49m (1989) GDP: Esc7,200 bn

The principal feature of the Portuguese economy for the greater part of this century was its stagnation under the authoritarian and conservative Salazar regime. By the 1960's, however, it had become impossible for what was in many ways an anti-capitalist regime to ignore the growing prosperity of the rest of other European countries, and the modernisation and subsequent growth of the poorest economy in western Europe began. The 1974 revolution brought a period of political and economic instability when increasing public expenditure and the subsequent consumer boom caused rising current account deficits and foreign debt, necessitating recourse to the IMF in 1978 and again in 1983. Since 1985, with the easing of the austerity programme imposed by the IMF, a new period of expansion has begun, with GDP growth in the period 1986-88 among the highest in the OECD. This has been helped by a boom in domestic expenditure and a more favourable international economic climate for Portuguese exports.

Strong export growth during this period has also been aided by Portugal's accession to the European Community in 1986. This has led to a rapid increase in much needed foreign investment in industry, which is still highly protected and inefficient in many sectors, as well as a net inflow of Community funds in the form of grants and loans. The importance of foreign investment to the economy has been belatedly realised in the 1980s. Investment legislation was introduced in 1965, but was undermined by bureaucratic delays and lack of incentives as well as the Salazar regime's general wariness of foreigners. Not until 1982, and again in 1986, was the law relaxed. In 1988 an extended system of incentives was introduced, and in the first half of 1989 foreign investment more than doubled over the same period in 1988. The major sectors to have won foreign backing are banking and finance and the hotel industry. Investment in industry has been less strong, but the automotive sector has begun to see a rise in the money received from the major multinational companies.

Trade
Despite increasing exports Portugal consistently runs a trade deficit because of its heavy reliance on food, energy and machinery imports. Agriculture is, in fact, a major problem area for the economy. Yields per hectare are very low, less than a third of the European average, due to the poor quality of the soil, very small farms and inefficient use of the land. Thus the country, which still has one of the most rural economies in Europe, accounting for almost a quarter of total employment in 1983, runs a heavy trade deficit in agricultural produce.

Stronger areas of the economy, where Portugal is a net exporter, include forestry products and textiles. In the textiles sector exports have been helped by increasing EC quotas boosting sales. Export income in this sector more than doubled in the period 1983-87, but it is now facing tougher competition as the EC is forced to increase quotas to non-EC members. In the forestry sector, large areas are being planted with eucalyptus, which is used to produce high quality paper. The Portuguese climate is especially favourable to the fast growing tree, and producers would like to increase the area under plant. The growth in the forestry sector has not, however, been universally welcomed. In what the press has called the 'eucalyptus war', farm workers have resorted to uprooting seedlings, claiming the eucalyptus consumes too much water and ruins the soil for other crops. Their claims have been supported by Portugal's fledgling environmental lobby, which has begun to make its mark on the electorate. Tough new environmental laws are being introduced following the *Basic Law of the Environment* which was passed in 1987, laying down the broad objectives in this field. It remains to be seen whether the legislation will be stringently enforced, given that the government has not appeared willing to help fund the high investment necessary to implement the law's provisions.

As exports have grown, Portugal's import demand has recently increased considerably, particularly in the consumer goods and machinery and vehicles sectors in which domestic industry is very weak. After the years of austerity, imports (excluding food, agricultural and mineral products) in the period 1986-88 almost doubled. The rate of growth will slow down, but should remain healthy.

Spain
Population: 39.2m (1989) GDP: Pta44,690 bn

The Spanish economic 'miracle' began in the 1950s when the country underwent a period of rapid economic growth and industrialisation. The boom was financed by earnings from Spain's fledgling tourism industry and investment from multinational companies, attracted to Spain by low labour costs. The boom came to an end, however, with the oil price shock of 1974 which exposed the weaknesses in the economy. In the period 1975-85 GDP growth slowed markedly. During the years of the economic miracle, GDP growth had been almost 3 per cent above the OECD average. In the decade to 1985, however, growth was around 1 per cent below the average. At the same time inflation was high, reaching a peak of 26 per cent in 1977. After a long period of restraint (and rising unemployment) recovery came in 1986 when GDP growth was 3.5 per cent, followed by higher than average OECD growth in both 1987 and 1988, supported by increased investment and consumer demand. Inflation fell to 3.9 per cent in the year to May 1988 but had risen to above 6 per cent by 1989.

Trade
Higher growth over this period has been encouraged by a consumer boom, and an upsurge in investment — much of it financed from abroad. Coming at a time when tariff barriers are being phased out, a requirement of membership of the European Community, this has led to a surge in imports, especially in the consumer goods sector, in which the share of total imports rose from 10 to 20 per cent in the five years to 1987. Import volume as a whole rose by 42 per cent in 1986-87 leading to a much increased trade deficit.

On the export side the Spanish current account is dominated by a few key sectors, notably tourism, agriculture and the automobile industry. The share of cars, trucks and tractors in total exports doubled in the period 1975-87. In the tourism sector, where foreign tourist receipts account for around 5 per cent of GDP, the number of tourist arrivals has grown from 4.2 m in 1959 to 54.2 m in 1988. It has been estimated that Spanish foreign currency earnings from tourism in 1985 accounted for 8 per cent of world income from international tourism.

Spain's traditional links with South America, viewed in conjunction with the collective strength of the EC, are considered to be factors which may benefit suppliers who have hitherto found South American markets difficult to penetrate. Spain also has a substantial defence manufacturing industry, and export middle-technology 'platform' equipment incorporating sophisticated high-tech components.

Investment
The industrialisation of Spain, including the growth of the automobile sector, has been aided by the important role of foreign investment throughout the period of modernisation. However, after remaining at around $1 bn in the first half of the 1980s, foreign direct investment more than doubled in 1986, rising again in 1987 to over $2.5 bn. Growth in portfolio investment has been even more spectacular, rising from $8 m in 1980 to over $3.5 bn in 1987. This growth has been helped by more liberal capital markets as well as by EC accession and the advantages of labour market costs which are still below most other OECD states. The importance of foreign investment in Spain, especially in the industrial sector, can be seen in the fact that in 1985 the top 26 foreign industrial subsidiaries in Spain,

including 7 car manufacturers, accounted for over 25 per cent of all manufactured exports. Although many of these companies are export oriented, some, notably in the food, domestic appliances and chemical sectors, sell mainly to the domestic market.

Industry

The role of the state in Spanish industry, which goes back to the formation of the Instituto Nacional de Industria, the state holding company, in 1941, continues today, with government involvement in many sectors ranging from energy and steel making through to tobacco and fertilisers. There is, however, a programme of semi-privatisation under way by the government which includes Endesa, the electricity generating company, of which 20 per cent of the shares were floated in 1988. Telefonica, the telephone monopoly is also partly owned by the state, partly by the private sector.

Regional differences in economic output in Spain are evident, with Catalonia, the Basque Country and Madrid leading the industrial output table and gaining the greatest share of foreign direct investment. There is evidence, however, of a shift in emphasis in the areas of growth, with Andalusia, which lost a large number of residents in the period 1950-75. The area of fastest growth was Catalonia in the period 1975-86, as the agriculture and tourism sectors continued to grow. However this region still trails below the Spanish average in both economic output and income terms. The interior of Spain, with the exception of Madrid, looks set to continue to remain a relatively poor area of Spain. For example with backward agricultural methods and a lack of industry, the per capita of the Extremadura region in 1981 was only 63 per cent of the Spanish average and per capita income only 61.6 per cent.

United Kingdom
Population: 57.1m (1989) GDP: £506.4 bn

The UK economy, which, depending on the criteria used, is the fifth or sixth largest in the OECD, has been through a series of important changes in the past decade. There has been, in common with most other industrialised countries but to a greater extent, a decline in the manufacturing sector of the economy as traditional industry has been rationalised. The result has been a widening gap in the relative prosperity of the various regions of the UK. Areas, principally in the north of the country, which have traditionally been dominated by heavy industry, have seen their prosperity decline as the economic centre of the country has moved ever more to the south, where the growing service sector is mainly located.

At the beginning of the decade inflation was a major problem, exacerbated by the second oil price shock of 1979. In May 1980 the annual rate of inflation reached 22 per cent. As a consequence of this, and because of the general world recession, UK GDP fell by 2.7 per cent in the period 1980-81. Unemployment reached record post-war levels.

Since this trough, the economy has returned to growth and GDP grew at an average annual rate of 2.9 per cent in the period 1982-88. During this time, manufacturing output declined as a percentage of total GDP, while the services sector grew, as did energy, boosted by the increase in oil production. The share of government consumption in GDP rose from 19.7 per cent in 1979 to 20.2 per cent in 1988, although the government has aimed to curb public sector expenditure.

The decline of the British manufacturing sector came about at a time when many industries, such as steel, shipbuilding, textiles and metal manufacturing, which have been at the heart of the economy, became uncompetitive in the international market. During the 1981-82 recession, manufacturing output declined by over 14 per cent, and this fall was mirrored by the employment figures for this sector. Despite the rationalisation of industry, output has not risen substantially. In the fourth quarter of 1988, manufacturing output was 5.9 per cent above the level of 1973. The slimming of the manufacturing sector also meant that for the first time in recent history, the United Kingdom became a net importer of manufactured goods in 1983, and has remained so since then.

Foreign trade
The recovery in growth has been accompanied by a worsening in the UK's trade deficit. A major reason for the growing deficit was the 1986 drop in oil prices. By 1985 petroleum exports had reached 20.6 per cent of total exports, compared with 3.7 per cent in 1975, but this figure declined drastically to 6.8 per cent in 1988. At the same time, however, there was a worsening of the position of exports of manufactured goods in relation to imports. In 1988 machinery and transport goods exports, the largest component of trade, accounted for 39.1 per cent of the total, while imports accounted for 37.6 per cent. This compares with 42.3 per cent and 20.4 per cent respectively in 1975. Overall, in the period 1982-88, import volume increased by 61 per cent while export growth was only 26.6 per cent.

The UK's principal trading partners are the USA, West Germany, France and the Netherlands. Trade with the EC has increased considerably in the past decade, with exports rising from 40.6 per cent of the total to 50.2 per cent in 1988.

In contrast to manufacturing trade, the services sector has expanded. Earnings from invisibles accounted for over half of the UK's total foreign earnings in 1987. The two principal components are tourism and financial services. In 1987 banking, finance and insurance accounted for 18 per cent of GDP.

However, even the services sector, which along with oil exports, gave the UK a current account surplus in the period 1980-86, has not been enough to prevent the current account from slipping back into deficit in 1987 and 1988. The 1988 current account revealed a record deficit of £14.7 bn.

Membership of the EC since 1973 has resulted in a marked shift in UK trade towards EC countries. It has been offset by a decline in the UK's export performance in traditional, preferential markets in the Commonwealth. This decline would, however, have occured, irrespective of EC membership as long-established trading partners in the Commonwealth became heavily industrialised and formed their own ties with other markets.

EUROPEAN FREE TRADE ASSOCIATION

Austria
Population: 7.58m (1989) GDP: Sch1,670 bn

The structure of the Austrian economy is based on its resources of raw materials and its small skilled labour force. Historically mining and mineral and metal processing have been the base of the Austrian economy but after the Second World War the manufactures sector was developed with special emphasis on high value added finished goods for export. Manufacturing and mining currently account for around 30 per cent of Austria's GDP. The services sector is also strong, accounting for over 50 per cent of GDP in 1988 with an increasing emphasis on high technology services.

Economic growth in the 1980s was better than neighbouring countries although the world wide recession of the early part of the decade resulted in a year of negative growth in 1981 when GDP fell by 0.2 per cent. After private consumption recovered in 1982-83 GDP rose at an average annual rate of 1.5 per cent, held back by the strong demand for imports but an increase in the rate of VAT caused a slowdown in the rate of growth in 1984. Growth was also weak in 1986 and 1987 as exports slipped back. By the end of the decade, however, rising imports and booming investment led to highest growth figures of the 1980s with GDP rising by 4.2 per cent in both 1988 and 1989.

Manufacturing

As in neighbouring Switzerland the Austrian manufacturing sector is dominated by smaller concerns with around 40 per cent of companies employing fewer than five workers. Only 178 companies employ more than 500 workers, mainly in heavy industry which is dominated by state owned companies. Into this category comes most of the iron and steel industry and the chemical and petro-chemical industries. Traditional basic industries were nationalised after the Second World War and a state holding company was set up in 1970. Towards the end of the 1980s, however, the holding company was split and the workforce rationalised in an attempt to make the state sector less of a burden on public finances. The state sector, however, still employs almost one sixth of the Austrian labour force.

The major employer in the manufacturing sector is the engineering and vehicle industry which is also the most important export sector particularly textiles, wood processing and agricultural machinery.

Finland
Population: 4.93m (1989) GDP: FMk494 bn

In the years since the Second World War the Finnish economy has undergone a rapid transformation, the agriculture sector has declined in importance as the manufacturing sector has grown and the once dominant forestry sector now accounts for only 3 per cent of GDP. During the same period the economy has also become increasingly dependent on foreign trade — export earnings accounted for almost 30 per cent of GDP in 1987 and the expansion in foreign trade has been a significant force behind Finland's economic growth. In 1950 the export market was dominated by the forest industry with around 80 per cent of the total value of exports while the share of the metal and engineering industries was only around 5 per cent. By 1988 the forestry sector had declined to around one third of total merchandise exports with the metal and engineering industries accounting for a comparable figure. However, importing the raw materials, intermediate goods and investment goods on a large scale necessary for this growth has resulted in an almost constant current account deficit since the 1960s although the merchandise trade account has been in surplus since 1980.

Economic growth was stable throughout the 1980s with 3.5 per cent real GDP growth on average in the period 1980-88. The high level of investment coupled with an emphasis on specialisation in industry, growth in export markets and Finland's stable trade relationship with the USSR help explain why the recession of the early 1980s which hit most Western economies did not effect Finland to the same extent. Domestic demand grew as real earnings increased markedly in 1988. However high pay awards coupled with increases in food prices, indirect taxes, public tariffs and charges as well as rises in housing costs (via higher interest rates) contributed to the annual rate of inflation accelerating in 1987 and 1988, after having fallen every year in 1981-86. This trend continued in 1989 with inflation reaching 6.6 per cent.

Industry
In the 1980s extensive modernisation programmes took place in the forestry industry and industrial co-operation and integration took place in order to cut costs and improve international competitiveness. In 1985-87 several major mergers between forestry companies took place and were further evidence of the need to restructure this important export sector. In manufacturing industry engineering has also become a major export earner accounting for 31 per cent of the total in 1988.

Foreign trade
Although the total trade account (fob) has rendered a surplus since 1980, the net debit on the services and income account has traditionally resulted in a current account deficit for Finland (Fmk9,200 mn, $2 bn, in 1987). Capital imports have financed the current deficit, which has led to increased net interest paid abroad. Payments of interest and dividends to foreign investors on their portfolio and direct investments in Finland have also risen in recent years.

Iceland
Population: 0.25m (1989) GDP: IKr309.2 bn

With an economy dominated by the fishing sector which accounts for around 75 per cent of merchandise exports and few other local production sectors, the Icelandic economy is heavily reliant on imports which met over 36 per cent of domestic demand in 1987. This has meant that the economy has in the past been acutely susceptible to inflation due to external factors. After the first oil price shock inflation reached 43 per cent in 1974 and in 1980 after the second rise it climbed to 58.5 per cent. From 1980 to 1985 inflation was running at an average annual rate of 50 per cent fuelled by automatic wage indexation and a labour shortage. Although wage indexation was suspended in mid-1983 and there was a slowdown in the rate of inflation, the consumer prices index only fell below 20 per cent once in the 1980s. In the mid-1980s the economy boomed as fish catches rose and Iceland recorded record growth of 8.7 per cent in 1987, the highest rate of growth in OECD. Recession set in, however, in 1988 as a decline in fishing incomes took place.

Industry
Iceland has attempted to diversify its economy in recent years and although there are few exploitable resources, the country's abundant hydroelectric and geo-thermal suppliers make it attractive as a processing area. Aluminium processing and the production of ferro-silicone and diatomite are now responsible for a major part of the limited industrial sector. The fish processing and knitwear industries are the most important light industries.

Foreign trade
On the imports side, consumer goods make up around 40 per cent of total merchandise imports and capital goods about 30 per cent. The European

Community has steadily become Iceland's most important trading partner. In 1988 the EC accounted for some 58 per cent of Iceland's total trade.

Norway

Population: 4.21m (1989) GDP: NKr630.3 bn

In the 1980s Norway achieved almost full employment with GDP and employment growth among the highest and unemployment among the lowest in the OECD area. However this has been accompanied by inflationary tendencies which have helped to erode the competitiveness of the non-oil sectors of the economy. Investment demand from the oil and oil-related industries stimulated Norwegian manufacturing industry considerably most notably the shipbuilding industry during the 1970s but total manufacturing output showed clear signs of stagnation towards the end of the decade as the strength of the currency due to oil held back the export potential of older industries. There was a recovery in the 1980s until the recession of 1988.

There have been difficulties since the mid 1970s in achieving the twin aims of full employment and maintaining price competitiveness. Apart from a wage and price freeze from mid-1978 to the end of 1979, which was followed by a burst of inflation in 1980 and 1981, strong domestic cost and price pressures have resulted from policies designed to shelter the economy from world recession. Inflation fell from 15 per cent in early 1981 to under 6 per cent by mid-1986 but unit labour costs continued to erode competitiveness.

The 1973/74 oil price crisis had little effect on the economy and real GDP continued to grow rapidly until it slowed down to under 1 per cent in 1981. By mid-1983 a growth in exports helped GDP to rise by 4.6 per cent in that year. Rising private consumption helped growth rates to rise above 5 per cent in 1984 and 1985. Private consumption fell back in 1987 causing a slowdown in the rate of growth to 1.1 per cent by 1988.

Foreign trade

Norway has one of highest per capita foreign trade accounts in the world. In 1987 exports of goods and services accounted for 36 per cent of GDP. However, for most of the post-war period Norway ran substantial deficits on its trade account which worsened in the mid-1970s when imports for the offshore oil industry grew.

The rapid expansion of oil and gas exports drastically altered the structure of the trade account from the mid-1970s. By 1985 exports of fuels accounted for around half of all merchandise exports while manufactured exports accounted for only a third. However, falling oil prices in 1986 reduced fuel exports to only 39 per cent of merchandise exports falling still further in 1987 to 30 per cent. In the manufactured goods sector metals and metal goods are still the most important component of total exports.

Norway now runs a substantial deficit on manufactures trade. In 1988 this amounted to over Nkr45 bn. In krone terms, the most important category of manufactured imports is machinery and equipment, amounting to Nkr34.0 bn in 1987, or 22 per cent of all merchandise imports. Road vehicle imports rose strongly in 1986 to Nkr15.2 bn, over ten per cent of total manufactures imports although they declined again in 1988 to Nkr8.7 bn.

Sweden
Population: 8.53m (1989) GDP: SKr1,190 bn

The Swedish economy is a highly developed, mixed industrial economy based on its natural resources. Growth was strong in the 1950s and 1960s as Swedish exports including motor vehicles, pulp and paper, engineering and high technology products helped GDP to grow by an average 3.4 and 4.6 per cent per annum respectively. In the 1970s, however, annual average GDP growth was only 2 per cent, lower than the OECD average. Growing international competition also revealed Sweden's high unit labour costs although unemployment remained low because of Sweden's labour market schemes and industrial subsidies.

The second oil crisis in 1979 slowed down the economy further, to 1.7 per cent growth in 1980 and the ensuing world recession caused a 0.3 per cent fall in GDP in 1981. Export recovery due to currency devaluations in 1981 and 1982, helped GDP to rise in the years 1981-1984 reaching 4 per cent in 1984. The glut in the oil market and the fall of the dollar, together with strong private consumption, helped to sustain 2.1 per cent growth in 1985. However, in 1986 GDP growth fell back to 1.1 per cent as total demand feel despite buoyant private consumption. At the end of the decade GDP increased by an average 2.1 per cent in the years 1987-1989 although this was still below the OECD average. A labour shortage held back output growth in industry which damaged export expansion and encouraged imports.

Industry
Throughout the century the trend in Swedish industry has been away from raw material production, despite the country's rich natural resources, to high technology engineering and metal products. Like other industrialised countries, however, Sweden went through substantial rationalisation of its traditional industries in the 1980s, including the closure of its last shipyard in 1987.

Foreign trade
Exports and imports account for around one third each of Swedish GDP emphasising the importance of free trade to the Swedish economy. In the early 1950s almost half of Sweden's exports consisted of raw materials, however by 1988 manufactured goods accounted for 79 per cent of total merchandise exports. In this time the importance of raw materials imports has also diminished with fuels representing 8 per cent of the total imports value in 1988. After a period of trade deficits following the world recession in the early part of the 1980s, Sweden returned to surplus in 1983 aided by devaluation in 1981 and 1982. The recovery of the OECD economies also helped to boost Swedish exports and the 1986 oil price fall helped to offset high wage costs in Sweden. Sizeable trade continued until the end of the decade.

Switzerland
Population: 6.64m (1989) GDP: SwFr286.6 bn

The Swiss economy is highly diversified and Switzerland has one of the highest per capita incomes in the world. Because of a relatively small domestic sector, however, Switzerland is dependent on exports for over one third of GDP. The economy is also dependent on foreign labour to supplement its own labour force and Switzerland has a record of low unemployment figures compared with other developed countries.

After experiencing strong GDP growth in the 1960s and early 1970s the Swiss economy with its dependence on foreign trade was hit by the worldwide recession in 1974-75 and GDP fell in both 1975 and 1976. There was a recovery in 1977 but the second oil price shock and an appreciation in the franc led to a second recessionary phase. Recovery began in 1983 and GDP rose throughout the rest of the 1980s, helped both by a weakening of the franc in 1987 which encouraged exports and a rise in domestic consumption.

Inflation in Switzerland, although generally low compared with OECD countries, is influenced by exchange rate movements and world commodity prices. Thus the decline in the level of the dollar and the fall in oil prices in 1986 led to zero inflation at the end of that year. However, the rate of inflation rose in 1987-1989 because of the stronger dollar and higher commodity prices.

Foreign trade
Despite the importance of exports to the economy Switzerland traditionally runs a trade deficit. Most of its energy and industrial raw materials needs are met by imports and Switzerland is a net importer in the food sector. The majority of exports are in the highly specialised manufactures sector which underwent radical restructuring in the 1970s. Since 1970 the number of establishments has declined by a third and the industrial sector now employs 20 per cent fewer workers. There are still many small companies in Switzerland, with most companies employing fewer than 100 people. The engineering and chemical industries, however, contain several multinationals and these sectors were responsible for nearly half of Switzerland's merchandise exports in 1988.

PART SIX

THE
LEGAL
ENVIRONMENT

1 European Community Law

Leathes Prior

Bird Semple Fyfe Ireland WS

The creation of the European Community is realised through the implementation of EC legislation throughout all member states. Likewise, the completion of the Single Market can only be effected by the implementation of legal measures which apply across the whole Community, measures which are adopted at Community level, mostly by the Council of Ministers, and are subsequently implemented in each member state through national legal systems. The European Commission can introduce certain Regulations on its own initiative which are directly binding on member states, but only in limited agreed areas where basic framework laws are already in existence. Over the thirty or so years of its history, the Community has gradually built up a framework of primary legislation. There is also a great body of secondary legislation (see *Sources of European Community Law*, page 329). In the past, it has sometimes taken the Community many years to agree and adopt new laws. The product liability Directive is a notable example, where protracted intra-Community consultations on the draft Directive were spread over a period of more than ten years. The Single Market programme was introduced to revitalise the process of completing the Community's internal market by reducing the likelihood of a stalemate in legislative process and by strengthening the political will to achieve the aims of the Community.

The end of 1992 has been fixed as the target date by which the Community hopes to introduce a large number of new measures. The overall objective is to eliminate the differences in national laws, which have led to disharmony in the European trading environment, and to remove obstacles to the free flow of trade in goods and services between member states.

To understand how best to operate in the Single Market, corporations and individuals alike are looking to the legal profession to gain a better appreciation of the Community's body of law and the specific laws which affect their commercial activities. For example, UK companies have since 1973, the year Britain joined the EC, operated within the legal framework of Articles 85 and 86 of the Treaty of Rome (the competition rules). The purpose of the competition rules is to outlaw anti-competitive practices and the abuse of dominant market positions. The European Commission, the Community institution charged by the European Community Treaties to propose legislation and police it, has stated its intention to apply the competition rules more vigorously in many areas of commercial activity as the Single Market draws nearer to completion. Inevitably more and more companies will be affected by strict application of the competition rules. This factor, plus the introduction of a fresh wave of legislative steps, will have repercussions on a great variety of commercial operations in the coming years.

This chapter points to some of the major areas of legislation which companies must consider as they prepare to do business in the Single Market. However, the comments in this chapter should not be taken as finite legal advice. Companies intending to expand their operations into the European market are strongly advised to take legal advice. Indeed it may be indispensable in many instances. But not only companies operating on a European scale are involved. Many EC laws affect general commercial practice as it applies in a company's domestic market.

General principles of Community law

The principles emanate from the constitutions and laws of the member states or from international agreements, such as the European Convention on Human Rights to which EC member states are a part, though the Community itself is not. The general principles include:

☐ Principle of proportionality: The means used must be proportionate to the ends to be achieved.

☐ Principle of legal certainty: The law applied to a given situation must be predictable.

☐ Fundamental human rights.

☐ Natural justice.

☐ Principle of non-discrimination: Equal situations should be treated equally.

Interaction of national and Community law

As discussed later in this chapter (see *The European Community legal system*), the case law of the European Court of Justice demonstrates that it considers that Community law takes supremacy over national law where the two conflict. UK Courts are bound by both the Treaty obligations and by previous Decisions of the European Court of Justice, one of which is the Supremacy Rule. UK Courts are, therefore, bound to accept the supremacy of Community legislation. Individuals and corporations need to take account of, and seek advice on, the effect of national and Community law across the whole ambit of their commercial operations, both within their own country and within the Community as a whole.

As harmonisation of national law within the EC progresses, the distinction between different types of business medium within the member states should diminish. Much depends on the pace at which harmonisation proceeds, but already the changes that have been implemented by existing EC Directives, incorporated into the national legal systems of member states, have begun to ensure that more homogenous legislative rules and protections for business will apply throughout the Community. However, for the foreseeable future, separate advice on domestic law will continue to be necessary for those companies trading across national boundaries within the Single Market. For a business considering expanding its operations within the Single Market, legal advice is crucial to ensure that the most appropriate legal structure is adopted for the company's specific purposes.

EC Regulations, Directives and Decisions, relating to some or all of the following areas of trading activity will enter national legislation and impact on most companies.

Company law

Existing EC Directives have already been implemented. Greater harmonisation will be introduced when further measures are implemented, such as the proposed European Company Statute, the Fifth Directive on Company Law, containing proposals for worker participation, and the Twelfth Directive concerning single member companies. (See also *EC Company law*, Part Six, Chapter 2)

European Economic Interest Grouping (EEIG)

This new legal company structure has been implemented throughout the EC, providing a vehicle for cross-border co-operation between companies. The measure is intended to promote economic activity. (See *EC Company law*, Part Six, Chapter 2 and *Corporate Structures*, Part Five, Chapter 1).

Intellectual or industrial property

The term covers patents, registered trademarks, copyright, registered designs, know-how and confidential information. The European Patent Convention, when it comes into effect, will unify a system which, at present, requires registration in each individual EC country. It is intended that this will be administered by a Community Patents Court (COPAC). Proposals have also been tabled for a Community Trademark, to be administered centrally from its own office within the next two years. The proposed location for the office is Madrid. (See also *Intellectual Property*, Part Six, Chapter 4)

Customs formalities

The Community proposes to introduce a harmonised system of commodity description and coding, subject to a new Community Tariff (TARIC). The Single Administrative Document (SAD) will be used in the new Community Transit Procedure.

Public procurement

The Community objective is to open up the public procurement sector to free and fair competition. The European Commission is seeking to make existing Directives governing public supply and public works contracts more effective. The Commission also proposes to make it easier for aggrieved parties to enforce public procurement procedures in national Courts.

Competition law

This has already been identified in the Treaty of Rome as an area of primary importance to the Community. Free and fair competition is considered to be fundamental to the maintenance of a healthy competitive environment throughout the Single Market. The competition laws seek to prevent businesses from distorting trade rules or abusing their position in the marketplace in various ways which include price fixing, production quotas or tie-in clauses . They also enable action to be taken against national governments which favour particular firms by grants or tax advantages.

For small businesses, the *de minimis* rules may apply. Specific block exemptions in relation to written arrangements for example, franchising and exclusive distribution agreements are relevant to businesses considering how best to expand their operations in the Single Market. Commercial contracts and joint ventures will, of course, have to take account of the Community's competition policy and legislation (see *The Competition Rules*, Part Six, Chapter 3)

Technical and safety standards

Mutual recognition between member states of national technical and safety standards has become the Community's objective in this area of legislation under the Single European Act 'new approach' concept. This replaces, or enhances, the previously held rigid objective of actually harmonising the different EC country standards which was found to be an unwieldy, difficult and slow moving process. Companies will have to meet Community health and safety standards in any event. The best known legal precedent concerning the mutual recognition of national standards is the decision of the European Court of Justice in the now celebrated *Cassis de Dijon* case which, in 1979, laid down that products legally made and marketed in any one member state must be allowed to circulate freely throughout the entire Community. Member states are required to implement the case law derived from the *Cassis de Dijon* ruling. All businesses must be aware of legal requirements concerning Community standards and the remedies available in case the sale of their products is unfairly prejudiced by the national rules of individual member states.

Other trading practices affected by EC law

The range of company activities affected by laws is binding, either through direct enforcement from Brussels or, as is mainly the case, by EC laws absorbed into the national legal framework. The range is very wide. In addition to the major areas of legislation listed above, many companies will be affected by EC laws governing:

□   Financial services: (See *EC Grants and Loans*, Part Four, Chapter 7; *Banking Services*, Part Four, Chapter 5; *Export Credit Insurance*, Part Four, Chapter 4).

□   Consumer protection

□   Labelling

□   Insurance

ROLE OF THE LEGAL PROFESSION

The ever increasing volume of legislation originating in Brussels places the legal profession in a position of special responsibility. Until the advent of the Single Market, businesses - particularly smaller businesses — turned to the legal profession at key points in their development or growth. The merger, the joint venture, and the listing, say, on the Unlisted Securities Market (USM), these are moments in the life of a business when legal guidance is indispensable. The scope for advice from the legal profession in the context of the Single Market, however, is much wider. Companies are likely to find themselves operating in unknown, untried legal territory. During the period of completion of the Single Market, law firms will be called upon by individuals and corporate clients to advise on a great many aspects of national and Community law. Corporate clients, if they are to comply with the rules and regulations of the Single Market and secure the benefits of it, will obviously gain from advice on the possible impact of forthcoming legislation during the period between the adoption of a new Directive in Brussels and its implementation by member states some time later.

Most commercial law firms can advise on European Community law and its effect on domestic or national law. The larger City law firms, with offices in other European countries, can extend their competence to matters relating to the jurisdiction within which their European offices are situated. Smaller law firms, affiliated to European networks of law firms, have extensive contacts in Europe, enabling them to provide equally broad advice across a number of jurisdictions. Already emerging in response to the increasing interrelation between Community and national law, are specialist Chambers within the Bar, based in London, Brussels and Luxembourg to provide specialist advice and representation.

Suprisingly, the mutual recognition of professional qualifications throughout the Community, in compliance with Article 57 of the EEC Treaty, is unlikely to produce a new breed of Euro-lawyer with true expertise in a number of European jurisdictions. There are two reasons why the all-round Euro-lawyer is unlikely to appear on the scene. First, the lawyer with many years experience of practice within a jurisdiction, plus a wide range of contacts with other professionals, is able to provide better advice than one who, while familiar with the law of the country, does not have the same wealth of experience, or cultural and linguistic ability. Second, via the European networks of law firms, lawyers based in one country can even now advise across a wide range of jurisdictions, offering clients access to the commercial contacts known to their associate law firms. These contacts play a key part in advising clients in one jurisdiction on matters which apply in another. Another reason why contact with European-based lawyers is essential is that, for the time being, UK lawyers may be restricted in the activities they can undertake. At present lawyers attempting to act in another European country for clients in the UK may find that they may only be allowed to practise in matters not reserved for locally established lawyers. This is an unsatisfactory situation which is not in the spirit of 1992. Speaking at a 1989 symposium organised by the Council of the Bars and Law Societies of Europe (CCBE), the leader of the UK delegation, John Toulmin QC, called for an end to monopolies enjoyed by local legal professions: "In my view it is essential in the spirit of 1992 that a common view must emerge as to what activities such lawyers may undertake and whether these activities can be undertaken in multi-national or multi-disciplinary partnerships." Mr Toulmin also recommended that law firms form associations, not necessarily formal partnerships, with lawyers from other European Community member states to 'obtain access to the necessary expertise to enable us to provide a proper service to our clients'.

One unique advantage which UK lawyers pass on to clients is that, practising under more liberal rules than those under which most European lawyers must practise, they can advise across a broader range of commercial activity. The role of many European lawyers is more closely defined since, for the most part, they operate under more restrictive professional rules.

The change in the legal environment is already apparent. In the UK there has been a quiet revolution in the legal profession in recent years, mostly in the field of commercial law, where lawyers themselves are becoming used to advising clients on a far wider spectrum of company activity than ever before. Of all the professions, the legal profession is best placed to *advise* clients on the effect of Community and national legislation and to *represent* clients when they either contravene it or wish to avoid any such difficulty arising. The larger management and accounting consultancies often refer to their own in-house legal experts on behalf of clients.

Legal advice

In its advisory capacity, the legal profession provides clients with information on the latest developments in Community and national law and interprets developments so that clients understand the impact of new laws on their businesses. As stated above, Community law will affect an increasing number of areas of commercial activity, changes which companies must take account of when preparing agreements. Lawyers advising clients on European matters are familiar with the workings of the Community's institutions and can point to other valuable sources of information within the Community. Some law firms have their own offices in Brussels and elsewhere in the Community; or, as is the case with Eu-lex, a group of separate law firms may form an affiliated network of legal practices throughout Europe to provide expertise on general and specialised areas of Community law, as well as domestic law applying in different parts of Europe. Not least, the availability of language expertise which is crucial in the negotiation of contracts and agreements with parties in other member states, is guaranteed when lawyers with established contacts or branches in Europe are consulted. Many individual law firms, however, are employing multilingual legal staff to enable them to represent a client's interests in other member states.

Businesses seeking to expand their operations into the Single Market need advice on the choice of legal structures which best enables them to achieve objectives. This too may involve advice on laws applying within different European jurisdictions, not just advice on UK national law and general Community law. Tax law, for example, varies from one jurisdiction to another. Tax law is a specialised area of law. Specialists on most aspects of international, national and Community law are to be found throughout the legal profession.

Legal represention

The legal profession's representative role falls into two parts:

☐ Assisting clients to lobby government and the Community when their interests may be threatened by proposed legislation.

☐ Representing clients before national Courts, the European Court of Justice, or in commercial arbitrations where disputes arise and require resolution by judicial process.

A growing number of businesses now consult their lawyers as a priority. This is often the first step to be taken in an effort to ensure that company plans to operate in the Single Market are compatible with the legal framework. Companies also seek to take full advantage of a variety of legal structures available to them for the conduct of Single Market market operations [See below and *Company Structures*, Part Five, Chapter 1).

Small and medium-sized enterprises (SMEs)

The Community has established a policy for the benefit small and medium-sized enterprises [broadly speaking, companies with up to 500 employees]. The legal profession can advise smaller companies on legal aspects of the Single Market. Legal advice is not a luxury for rich, giant corporations. Located throughout the Community, many information sources for smaller companies provide basic facts and can direct enquirers to experts in government and Community institutions. Law firms, however, also provide preliminary verbal and written briefings, sometimes free of charge initially to serious, prospective clients. This advice is not always confined to matters of legal interpretation and understanding. It may extend to general commercial considerations such as the availability of EC grants and loans, sources of venture capital, public procurement procedures and, not infrequently, summaries of Community policy, seen from a company point of view. One advantage of this type of advice is that it is free of Community or government propaganda and is easily updated. Certain major law firms publish in-depth reports on areas of Community law and commercial practise, such as competition policy or banking. These reports often represent good value for money, serving as background briefing, offering at reasonable cost an overview of the legal framework, and drawing together the many strands of law applying in a given area of activity.

Legal structures when marketing in the EC

The appropriate structure for any business can be determined by a number of factors particular to the business itself. The options are also covered in a trading context in *Corporate Structures*, Part Five, Chapter 1. The options include:

☐ Licensing: The terms of a licensing agreement may include a combination of the following: Nature and extent of rights; Title to property; Territory; Payments and royalties; Marking of articles; Sub-licensing

   Note: A company considering an offer of a licensing agreement by a foreign interest should ensure that the draft agreement is vetted by their own appointed legal representative

☐ Franchising: Franchising is subject to UK and EC competition laws (Articles 85 and 86 of the Treaty), though a block exemption may apply (see *The Competition Rules*, Part Six, Chapter 3).

☐ Agency or distribution agreements

☐ Subsidiary company

☐ Branch office

☐ European Economic Interest Grouping (EEIG): See *Corporate Structures*, Part Five, Chapter 1, and *EC Company Law*, Part Six, Chapter 2

☐ Acquisition: See *Corporate Strategy*, Part One, Chapter 3

☐ Merger: See *The Competition Rules*, Part Six, Chapter 3

☐ Joint venture

THE EUROPEAN COMMUNITY'S LEGAL SYSTEM

Basic European Community law is set down in the Treaties establishing the three European Communities. The Treaties established the European Economic Community (EEC), the European Coal and Steel Community (ECSC), and the European Atomic Energy Community (EURATOM). The law created by or under these Treaties, together with a number of subsequent Treaties, conventions and agreements, is known as European Community law.

The application of EC law in the United Kingdom was made possible by the passing in the British Parliament of the European Communities Act of 1972. Part I of the Act states that EC law is part of the law of the UK.

It is important to distinguish Community laws from those created under the auspices of other European organisations, such as the Council of Europe, the most well known being the European Convention on Human Rights (ECHR). The Council has its own European Court and a Commission on Human Rights. Confusion arises when these two separate and distinct bodies of law are referred to as European law. Great care should be taken in this respect because, whereas EC law is part of the law of the UK, that of the European Convention on Human Rights is not.

This section gives a brief account of the Community's legal system only, covering the objectives of the Treaties and their institutional framework, the European Courts, sources and status of EC law, methods of interpretation and application, and the nature and enforcement of EC law.

The Treaties

The Treaty of Paris, 1951 establishing the European Coal and Steel Community

The European Coal and Steel Community (ECSC) was established under the Treaty of Paris on 18 April, 1951, the first of the European Communities to be set up. It had an international 'personality' from the outset and was supported by four institutions to which member states transferred sovereign rights, albeit in the limited sphere of the regulation of production and consumption of the coal and steel industries [See *Key events in uniting Europe*, page 16). Production and consumption of coal and steel was placed under the control of the supra-national High Authority with powers to adopt legally binding Decisions and Recommendations. The ECSC also had a supervisory Common Assembly, representing the peoples; a Council of Ministers, the role of which was both consultative and legislative, representing the national interests of all member states; and a Court of Justice. The function of the Court was to 'ensure that in the interpretation and application of this Treaty...the law was observed' (Articles 7-45 contain the provisions regarding the institutions of the ECSC).

The Treaty of Rome, 1957, establishing the European Economic Community

The European Economic Community (EEC) was established under the Treaty of Rome on 25 March, 1957. The immediate purpose of the EEC was to establish a Common Market, initially by way of objectives set out in Article 3, Clauses [a] to [k]:

[a] the elimination, as between member states, of customs duties and of quantitative restrictions on the import and export of goods and all other measures having equivalent effect;

[b] the establishment of a Common Customs Tariff and of a Common Commercial Policy towards third countries;

[c] the abolition, as between member states, of obstacles to freedom of movement of persons, services and capital;

[d] the adoption of a common policy in the sphere of agriculture;

[e] the adoption of a common policy in the sphere of transport;

[f] the institution of a system ensuring that competition in the common market is not distorted;

[g] the application of procedures by which the economic policies of Member States can be co-ordinated and disequilibria in their balance of payments remedied;

[h] the approximation of laws of Member States to the extent required for the proper functioning of the common market;

[i] the creation of a European Social Fund in order to improve employment opportunities for workers and to contribute to the raising of their standard of living;

[j] the establishment of a European Investment Bank to facilitate the economic expansion of the Community by opening up fresh resources;

[k] the association of the overseas countries and territories in order to increase trade and to promote jointly economic and social development.

Throughout the Treaty there is an emphasis on the four freedoms, namely goods, persons, capital and services. The Treaty, however, calls for the implementation of common policies; for example, the Common Agricultural Policy (CAP) (Articles 38-47), the Common Commercial Policy (CCP) (Articles 110-116), and the Social Policy (Articles 117-128). The Treaty lays down a foundation of rules concerning nearly all areas of economic and social life. This can be clearly seen from the preamble to the Treaty and from the broadly worded clauses of Article 3, listed above.

Like the ECSC Treaty, the EEC Treaty provided the Community with a legal personality and four autonomous institutions to carry out the tasks entrusted to them. It used an institutional structure similar to that of the ECSC Treaty. The institutions include an Assembly (since renamed the European Parliament), representing the peoples, again with largely supervisory powers; the Council of Ministers with power to adopt legislation, representing the national interests of member states; and the Court of Justice. This time the High Authority of the ECSC was replaced by the European Commission. The Commission's functions and powers are more limited, its major task being the initiation and supervision of Community objectives (Articles 137-198 relating to the EEC institutions).

The second Treaty of Rome, 1957, establishing the European Atomic Energy Community

The European Atomic Energy Community (EURATOM) was set up by a second Treaty of Rome, also signed on 25 March, 1957. Its aim is to regulate the development and production of nuclear energy for peaceful purposes and the marketing of that energy within and outside the Community. Like the EEC, EURATOM has legal personality and originally had its own four autonomous institutions; an Assembly, a Council of Ministers, a Commission and a Court of Justice (Article 3, EURATOM Treaty).

Merging of the EC's institutions

A convention signed at the same time as the EEC and EURATOM Treaties established a single Assembly and a single Court of Justice for all three Communities. It was not until the Merger Treaty, signed on 8 April, 1965, but not coming into force until 1 July 1967, that the three Communities had a single Council and a Commission. The Commission came into being as a result of the merging of the ECSC High Authority and the EEC and EURATOM Commissions. Although the institutions are common to all three Communities, they remain legally distinct with their powers and functions dependent upon whichever Treaty they are acting under. In all three Treaties the European Parliament is officially referred to as 'the Assembly'. In 1962 it adopted the title of European Parliament. But it was not until the passing of the Single European Act that this title was officially recognised (Article 3 [1]).

Single European Act

The Single European Act was the outcome of a rolling governmental conference convened at Luxembourg on 9 September, 1985, thereafter continuing its discussions at Brussels and Luxembourg, culminating in further meetings at The Hague (17 February 1986) and Luxembourg (28 February, 1986). At these meetings representatives of the governments of member states met to discuss Lord Cockfield 's White Paper, *Completing the Internal Market*[1], and the Dooge Committee's recommendations for a draft Treaty on European Union[2]. The Act came into force on 1 July 1987[3], after some delay as a result of problems with Irish ratification.

1 COM(85)310.
2 Interim and final reports can be found in the House of Lords Select Committee on the European Communities report on European Union (HL 226 Session 1984-5, 14th Report, pp21 and 1 xvi).
3 For the text see *OJL*169/1 1987. The Single European Act was incoporated into UK law by the European Communities (Amendment) Act, 1986.

Treaty amendment and political co-operation

The Single European Act amended the founding Treaties in a number of respects, and at the same time gave Political Co-operation in the field of foreign policy an institutional framework. European Political Co-operation (EPC) runs parallel to the institutional machinery of the Community but it is separate and distinct from it. The Single European Act has become known as the 'Single Act' because it deals with these two separate matters in one Treaty.

European Council

The Single European Act also formally recognised the existence of the European Council without giving it powers or functions, but laying down that it should meet at least twice a year. The six-monthly meetings of EC heads of government are usually the most widely publicised events in the EC calendar.

Majority voting under the Single European Act

Under a new 'co-operation procedure', the European Parliament has been granted a greater role in the legislative process in certain areas of Community activity. More significantly, the Single European Act has widened the scope for legislative decisions to be taken by qualified majority vote in the Council of

Ministers. There is no reference to the Luxembourg Compromise or any machinery for exercising a right of veto. The Treaty permits, for the first time, Community law to be applied differently or at different times, as between the member states, thereby reducing the right of veto, if such a right ever existed.

Completing the Internal Market: the implementation of the Cockfield White Paper

The Single European Act provided for amendments to the EEC Treaty in order to establish the legislative machinery necessary to complete the EC Internal Market — Articles 8(a), 100 (a), 100(b). The White Paper lists some 300 measures designed to remove barriers to trade in goods and services between member states. Some of the measures are listed at the end of relevant sections in this guide.

SOURCES OF EUROPEAN COMMUNITY LAW

Primary sources

The primary source of Community law are the founding Treaties plus the Treaties of Accession of new member states, protocols, conventions and Acts ancillary to the founding Treaties and the Treaties of Accession. The full list is as follows:

☐ Treaty of Paris, 1951 (ECSC); Treaty of Rome, 1957 (EEC); second Treaty of Rome, 1957 (EURATOM)

☐ First Treaty of Accession, 1972 concerning the accession of the United Kingdom, Ireland and Denmark.

☐ Second Treaty of Accession, 1972, concerning the accession of Greece.

☐ Third Treaty of Accession, 1986, concerning the accession of Spain and Portugal.

☐ Protocols, Conventions and Acts ancillary to the founding Treaties and the Treaties of Accession.

☐ Treaties amending, modifying, or extending the founding treaties — the Merger Treaty and the Single European Act.

☐ Conventions between member states concluded within the context of the Treaties, such as the Convention on Jurisdiction and on the Enforcement of Judgments in Civil and Commercial Matters.

☐ Agreements between the Community and third countries. Free Trade Agreements between the Community and some European Free Trade Association (EFTA) countries.

☐ Other international agreements to which the Community is a signatory.

Secondary sources

Measures adopted by the Council of Ministers and the European Commission under the Treaties form the most important secondary source of Community law. Article 189 of the EEC Treaty provides that in order to carry out their tasks, the Council of Ministers and the European Commission shall, in accordance with the provisions of the Treaty 'make Regulations, issue Directives, take Decisions, make Recommendations, or deliver Opinions'. The list of measures detailed in Article 189 is not exhaustive. Community institutions may create legally binding Acts by means other than those mentioned in Article 189.

Regulations: 'A Regulation shall have general application. It shall be binding in its entirety and directly applicable in all member states'. A member state cannot, therefore, pick and choose the provisions of a Regulation it wishes to obey and ignore the rest. Regulations become part of the national legal order without the need for any Act of incorporation. It does not necessarily follow, however, that they will be directly effective, ie. that the Regulation confers rights on the individual which can be enforced in a national Court.

Directives: 'A Directive shall be binding, as to the result to be achieved, upon each member state to which it is addressed, but shall leave to the national authorities the choice of form and method'.

Directives, unlike Regulations, are not directly applicable. They require implementation by member states, leaving the method of attaining this to their discretion. Directives usually contain time limits within which a member state is bound to have implemented it. Failure to do so, or failure to implement a Directive properly, may give rise to proceedings under Article 169. An individual may also raise an action in the national Court if the provisions of a Directive are intended to be directly effective.

Decisions: 'A Decision shall be binding in its entirety upon those to whom it is addressed'. A Decision, unlike a Regulation, is not directly applicable and, unlike a Directive, it can be addressed to individuals as well as to member states. It is binding in its entirety and not merely as to the result to be achieved.

Recommendations and Opinions: 'Recommendations and Opinions shall have binding force'. Recommendations and Opinions are of persuasive value only.

Jurisprudence of the European Court of Justice
The decisions of the European Court of Justice have to be regarded as a major source of Community law. Some of the most important principles of Community law emanate, not from the Treaties, but from the Court's jurisprudence. The doctrine of primacy of Community law was first laid down in Costa v ENEL (Case 6/64 (1984) ECR 585) and has been reiterated in many cases since then. Likewise the Court has developed the concept of direct effect, first discussed in the landmark case of Van Gend en Loos (Case 26/62 (1963) ECR1), thereby increasing the effectiveness of Community law.

THE EUROPEAN COURTS

European Court of Justice

Function and jurisdiction
The function of the European Court of Justice (ECJ or Court of Justice) is to 'ensure that in the interpretation and application of this Treaty the law is observed' (Article 164, EEC Treaty). The extent of the Court's jurisdiction and the conditions for its exercise are laid down by the Treaties. The statutes of the Court (one for each Treaty), the Rules of Procedure and certain other supplementary statutes, protocols and regulations provide further provisions.

Composition
There are 13 Judges and 6 Advocates-General. The Judges and Advocates are of equal status. The role of the Advocate-General is to deliver an opinion in open Court in order to assist the judges, with complete impartiality and independence.

The judges are appointed by common accord of the member states. There is no nationality requirement though, in practice, there is one judge from each member state. The additional judge is appointed by the five larger member states in rotation. The reason for the appointment of an additional judge is that the Court always acts as a college. All judgments are published as the judgment of the Court and there is no dissenting judgment.

Out of six Advocates-General, four come from the four largest member states (France, Italy, West Germany and the United Kingdom). The other two are nominated by the other member states in rotation.

All members of the Court must possess the qualifications required for appointment to the highest judicial office in their respective countries. Members of the Court are appointed for a term of six years.

When a case is brought by a member state or a Community institution, the Court has to sit in plenary session with a quorum of seven judges. In all other cases it usually sits in Chambers. There are three Chambers of three judges and two Chambers of five judges.

Procedure

The procedure is simple, informal and is primarily written. It differs, depending upon whether an action is brought directly before the Court, or indirectly via an Article 177 reference.

In a direct action, the action is stated by an application. This contains a statement of the subject matter of the dispute, the ground upon which the action is based and the order which the applicant seeks. There are no Court fees. The Court registry will make all the necessary translations and notify the defendant and other interested parties. The defence must be lodged within one month of service of the application, although this period can be extended. There may be a reply and a rejoinder. The case will be conducted in the language chosen by the applicant (except where the defendant is a member state or a national of a member state when that member state's language is used). Whatever language is used in the case, member states are also entitled to use their own language.

In an indirect action, no particular form or wording is laid down for the reference from the national Court. The registrar notifies the parties to the proceedings in the national Court, all member states, the European Commission and, where appropriate, the Council of Ministers, who then have two months in which to submit written observations, if they wish. This period cannot be extended.

In all cases, one of the judges is known as the *Juge- Rapporteur*. His task is to present a preliminary report suggesting how the case should be handled. Expert opinions, specialist reports and other documents may be obtained and witnesses can be summoned for examination. This will take place in the presence of the parties. Usually the presiding judge will be asked to put questions to the witnesses. The next stage is known as oral procedure. The *Juge-Rapporteur* will have produced a report summarising the facts and the parties' arguments. The oral stage is brief (the hearing is not for the parties to present their whole case and argument). The written pleadings will have been translated into the Court's working language, which is French, and the parties will be familiar with it. After the hearing the Advocate-General will deliver his opinion. It is more usual for this to be delivered two to three weeks later. Thereafter, the Court deliberates on its judgment in secret. There is only one judgment.

Actions brought before the Court

Proceedings may be brought by a member state natural or legal person or, in some circumstances, by a Community institution on a number of grounds. Reference is made only to the EEC Treaty. The principal forms of action before the Court (and the new Court of First Instance where it has jurisdiction) are:

Direct actions:

1 *Articles 169 and 170 — failure to fulfill an obligation*: An action can be brought by the Commission under Article 169 or by a member state under Article 170 where a member state has failed to fulfill its obligations under the Treaty or is acting in a way which is incompatible with Community law. Article 171 provides that 'if the Court of Justice finds that a member state has failed to fulfill its obligations under this Treaty the state shall be required to take the necessary measures to comply with the judgment of the Court of Justice'. The Court, unfortunately, has no further sanctions at its disposal. There has not been a situation to date where a member state has refused to comply with a judgment, though there have been long delays in some cases. In a recent case, however, the Court has held that even if the national authorities do not take the action required, the national courts must enforce the Court's judgment and not the incompatible national laws.

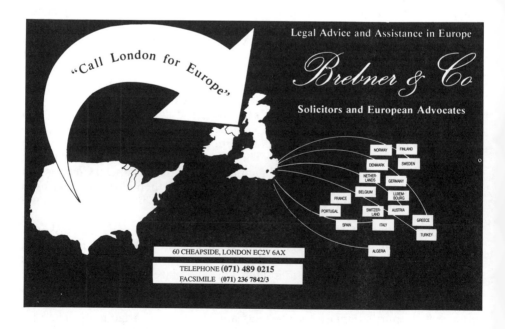

2 *Article 173 — action for annulment:* Article 173 allows the Court of Justice to annul or declare void certain acts of the European Commission and the Council of Ministers found to be incompatible with Community law. The action may be brought by another Community institution or by a member state. Article 173(2) also permits a natural or legal person or corporation in certain limited situations to challenge specific kinds of acts of the Council or the Commission. The grounds are:

☐   Lack of competence

☐   Infringement of an essential procedural requirement

☐   Infringement of the Treaty or any rule of law relating to its application. This has been held by the Court to include the general principles of Community law

☐   Misuse of powers

3 *Article 184 — plea of illegality*: This is a plea which is ancillary to a direct action. It would normally be invoked by a natural or legal person in proceedings before the ECJ where a Regulation or other general Act is in issue and where that natural or legal person is affected by virtue of an individual Act emanating from that Regulation or general Act.

4 *Article 175 — the action for failure to act:* Article 175 permits the Court to review those circumstances where a Community institution has failed to act under Community law where it was legally bound to do so. By virtue of Article 176, the offending institution, if it is found to have failed in its duty, is required to take the necessary measures to comply with that judgment.

5 *Articles 178 and 215(2) — action for damages:* An action brought by an aggrieved party on the grounds that it has suffered loss or damage as a result of a wrongful act on the part of the Community institutions or its officials.

6 *Article 179 — staff cases:* As the name suggests, any dispute involving the Community institutions and their servants can be dealt with by the two Courts. Staff cases are now to be transferred to the new Court of First Instance.

Indirect actions:

Article 177 — reference for a preliminary ruling. The procedure under Article 177 enables any national court or tribunal to request a ruling from the Court of Justice on the interpretation and/or validity of a Community Act which arises in the proceedings before it. The national Court can make such a reference when it considers that such a Ruling is necessary in order to enable it to come to a decision. The role of the ECJ is to give a Ruling or interpretation on the validity of the measure in question and not to apply it to the facts. This latter function is exclusively within the jurisdiction of the national Court.

Opinions
Article 228 provides that the Court of Justice may be called upon to give an opinion on the compatibility with the Treaty of a proposed agreement between the Community and one or more states or an international organisation.

Court of First Instance (CFI)

To ease the increasing workload of the European Court of Justice, the Single European Act amended the Treaties to give the Council of Ministers power, if asked by the Court of Justice, to 'attach to the Court of Justice a Court with jurisdiction to hear and determine at first instance subject to a right of appeal to the Court of Justice on points of law only…certain classes of action or proceedings brought by natural or legal persons'. (In 1988, the number of cases brought before the European Court of Justice was 372. The number of cases pending before the Court was 599)

Such a Court has been created and is to be known as the Court of First Instance (CFI). There are twelve judges. The Court of First Instance sits in Chambers (normally in Chambers of three or five) and may, in certain cases, sit in plenary session. The Court's Rules of Procedure permit it to do so. It is concerned with ascertaining the facts and applying the law as determined by the European Court of Justice. It is bound to follow the decisions of the European Court of Justice, but it is not bound in subsequent cases by its own decisions. The Court has jurisdiction to hear the following cases:

☐ Staff cases. Here the Court acts in effect as an employment tribunal.

☐ Actions by individuals against an EC institution, challenging the institution's omissions or commissions with regard to the implementation of the EC Competition Rules.

☐ Certain proceedings relating to the operation of the European Coal and Steel Community.

The Court of First Instance also has power to entertain an action for damages but *only* where such an action is connected with any of the above.

Appeals

There is a right of appeal to the European Court of Justice, but only on points of law. The grounds of appeal are lack of competence, procedural defects which adversely affect the position of the appellant, and incorrect application of Community law. Mistakes of fact do not constitute a ground of appeal. The ECJ can either sustain the decision of the CFI or can quash it. In the latter situation it can decide the case itself or it can remit it to the CFI for judgment.

Further information

See *Company Structures*, Part Five, Chapter 1; *EC Company Law*, Part Six, Chapter 2; *The Competition Rules*, Part Six, Chapter 3; *Intellectual Property*, Part Six, Chapter 4; *European Community Publications*, Part Eight, Chapter 1; *EC On-line Databases*, Part Eight, Chapter 2; *Libraries* (European Documentation Centres), Part Eight, Chapter 3.

Legislative texts

Copies of legislative texts can be purchased from Alan Armstrong Limited (below), and from Government (HMSO) bookshops, quoting the *OJ* reference which consists of the number of the legal instrument and the date of issue in the *Official Journal (OJ)*, ie. Regulation 4021/87, *OJ* L378, 31.12 87. Texts appear in hard copy and on microfiche. For details of the series published in the *Official Journal* see *European Community Publications*, Part Eight, Chapter 1. Texts can also be examined at European Documentation Centres and other libraries (see *Libraries*, Part Eight, Chapter 3), and accessed through on-line databases (Part Eight, Chapter 2).

HMSO Books
PO Box 276
London SW8 5DT
Tel: (071) 873 0011 (enquiries); (071) 873 9090 (telephone orders).
Fax: (071) 873 8463
Telex: 297138

(HMSO Bookshops: Belfast, Birmingham, Bristol, Edinburgh, London and Manchester, plus 40 bookshops acting as agents for HMSO throughout the UK)

Alan Armstrong Limited
2 Arkwright Road
Reading RG2 0SQ
Tel: (0734) 751855
Fax: (0734) 755164
Telex: 849937 AAATD G

Office for Official Publications of the European Communities
5 rue de Commerce
L-2985 Luxembourg
Tel: (352) 490081/490191
Telex: 1324/1322 PUBOF LU

(Publications on EC law and the EC's legal system, subscriptions to the *Official Journal*. UK agents: HMSO and Alan Armstrong Limited)

CONTACTS

The following contacts provide general information, publications or texts of Community Company Law Regulations and Proposals. However, advice on taking actions under EC law or on the interpretation of EC law as it applies to a company's operation should be sought from legal experts. Many leading law firms practise in EC law and have branches in Brussels and elsewhere in the EC. A number of smaller law firms have joined consortia to enable them to represent clients' interests through associates located throughout the EC. It is important to understand, when considering extending company activities in Europe, that any interaction of EC law and national law should be taken into account and that contact with legal experts in other EC countries may be necessary.

European Court of Justice

European Court of Justice
Information Service
L-2925 Luxembourg
Tel: (352) 43031
Fax: (352) 4303-2600
Telex: 2771 CJINFO L

Published information can be obtained more quickly if it is in the language in which the proceedings were heard by the Court. Texts available include:
Court judgements
Conclusions of Advocates-General
Proceedings of the Court (regular bulletin)
Weekly timetable
Digest of case law
(See also *European Community Publications*, Part Eight, Chapter 1)

European Commission

European Commission
Legal Service
200 Rue de la Loi
B-1049 Brussels
Tel: (32) 2 235 1111
Telex: 21877 COMEU B

General Community law developments.
Does not advise on specific cases or provide
professional legal advice to individuals.

UK offices

The Commission's library and information service provides access to a wide range
of Community publications and texts including new proposals. Many publications
are free. Others can be purchased from the Office for Official Publications of the
European Communities.

European Commission Information Office
8 Storey's Gate
London SW1P 3AT
Tel: (071) 222 8122
Fax: (071) 222 0900
Telex: 23208 EURUK G

European Commission Information Office
4 Cathedral Road
Cardiff CF1 9SG
Tel: (0222) 371631
Fax: (0222) 395489
Telex: 497727 EUROPA G

European Commission Information Office
Windsor House, 9-15 Bedford Street
Belfast BT2 7EG
Tel: (0232) 240708
Fax: (0232) 248241
Telex: 74117 CECBEL G

European Commission Information Office
7 Alva Street
Edinburgh EH2 4PH
Tel: (031) 225 2058
Fax: (031) 226 4105
Telex: 727420 EUEDIN G

2 EC Company Law

Creating a common legal environment

Philip Goldenberg

As the Single Market develops, the distinct national markets which have for so long characterised trade in Europe will be progressively integrated. Part of this process of integration consists in the freedom of establishment of cross-frontier enterprises. Freedom to set up a business in the European Community wherever one chooses may, however, create market distortions if the rules in one member state, in terms of corporate regulation, taxation, or social policy, are more lax than in others. This is known in the United States as the 'Delaware' effect.

Single Market legislation will make important and, in some cases, radical changes to company law, as we know it. Companies can only take advantage of this liberalisation if there are agreed minimum standards. Such a degree of international co-operation can best be achieved on the basis of common structures and requirements. Those concerned with company activities should not be able to shop around the member states in the hope of finding a less regulated environment. So far as company law is concerned, the completion of the Single Market means that there must be substantial changes in attitude and understanding. There is a clear and understandable policy behind the proposed changes; national company law must not hinder the development of a Single Market. It must help to establish a level playing field throughout the Community, and it must provide the corporate structures which will enable the advantages and opportunities offered by the Single Market to be realised.

Accordingly, the programme of EC company law harmonisation is designed to avoid market distortions by creating a homogeneous legal environment for business and investment in the Community. In this respect the Treaty of Rome provides for:

☐ Co-ordinating the legal safeguards available for the protection of shareholders and others, with a view to making such safeguards equivalent throughout the Community — Article 54(3)(g).

☐ Co-ordinating the laws of the member states regulating the conduct of business activities in the member states — Article 57(2).

☐ Approximating those laws of member states which directly affect the establishment or functioning of the Common Market — Article 100.

The Community has adopted two distinct approaches to give effect to these objectives. First, minimum standards being laid down on key aspects of domestic company law. Second, new EC corporate structures are being put in place. This chapter reviews this process in more detail. Set out at the end of this chapter is a list of the Directives and Proposals which constitute the EC company law harmonisation programme. Where these have already been implemented in UK

337

law, they are not further discussed. The principal aim of this chapter is to indicate what is in the pipeline.

Board structures and employee representation

At present, in the UK, each company has a Board of Directors which manages the company's affairs. Directors are elected and may be removed by shareholders in general meeting. Employees have no statutory rights of management or even (with limited exceptions) consultation. But the Board is entitled to have regard to their interests. Radical changes to this pattern are contained in the proposal for a Fifth Company Law Directive , in terms of both board structure and employee participation. This proposal was originally issued in 1972. The lack of progress in reaching agreement on it reflects its controversial nature, and its future advance is unlikely to be rapid. The smaller business lobby has been particularly active in making representations to the European Commission about the employee participation aspect of the proposal (see the *Contacts* section of *The National Wealth*, Part One, Chapter 5). However, the Directive could be adopted by a qualified voting procedure in the Council of Ministers.

Under the proposal, a distinction would be drawn in public companies between directors respectively responsible for 'supervision', on the one hand, and 'management', on the other. This could be defined in one of two ways; a two-tier board consisting of separate management and supervisory boards (on the West German model), or a one-tier board (as in the UK), but with a formal division of management and supervisory functions. In addition, a public company with 1,000 or more employees would have to install a system of employee participation. The precise system would depend on whether the company operated a two-tier or one-tier board structure but, in essence, there are three options:

BOARD STRUCTURES AND EMPLOYEE REPRESENTATION

Present UK Structure

Shareholders
|
Board

Proposed Structure under Fifth Directive

EITHER   OR

Shareholders   Employees or   Shareholders
                      Trade Union(s)
        \   / |
         \   / |
          \   / |
Supervisory Board (or, if one-tier   Supervisory Board (or, if one-tier _ _ _ _ Works Council
board, supervisory element)   board, supervisory element)   or Trade Union(s)
        | |
Managing Board   Managing Board

_____ control/accountability
- - - - - - - - - - - - - - - - - consultation/information

☐ Board representation for employees through election of (at the option of the company) one third to one half of the supervisory directors.

☐ A Works Council (a body which is representative of all employees entitled to regular information and consultation).

☐ A collective agreement (ie. with one or more trades unions) effectively giving employee election rights to the members of those trades unions (but not, it would seem, to all employees).

Employee information and consultation

Since 1980, a proposal has been under discussion for a Directive compelling companies to introduce procedures for informing and consulting employees. It became known as the *Vredeling Directive*, after its author. Two principal difficulties arose: the belief of the governments in some member states (including the UK) that any such procedure should be voluntary; and the fact that *Vredeling* was not limited to collective representation of employees through trades unions.

Vredeling would apply to employers with 1,000 or more employees. Information relating to the business as a whole, and to particular subsidiaries and establishments, would have to be supplied annually to employees' representatives. Such information would include the economic condition of the business, its forecast development, the present and anticipated pattern of employment and its investment prospects.

Management would also be obliged to consult employees' representatives on matters likely to have serious consequences for their interests, with a view to attempting to reach agreement. In the 1983 draft, such matters included major closures and relocations, substantial reductions or alterations in the business, major organisational changes (including those arising from the introduction of new technologies), joint ventures, and health and safety. There may be exceptions on grounds of commercial confidentiality.

Branches and subsidiaries

In the European pipeline there is a draft *Ninth Company Law Directive* which has not yet reached the stage of a formal proposal, and indeed has not progressed since 1984. In effect, the proposal seeks to establish a formal group structure where an undertaking has a dominant influence over a public company, even if that company is not its subsidiary. The objective of the proposal is to protect minority shareholders against abuses of power. The dominant undertaking will be liable for any damage suffered by the public company and, more radically, for any debts incurred by the public company, as a result of the latter acting at the discretion of the dominant undertaking; but this will seemingly not be the case if the dominant undertaking's influence is, in fact, exercised in the best interests of the public company.

A different form of liability will, however, apply if the dominant undertaking — whether or not a shareholder — has formalised its relationships with the public company concerned by a 'control contract' which provides for it to manage the company, and in which it offers the minority shareholders a buy-out or, at the shareholders' option, a 'protected dividend'. Once a control contract has been entered into, the dominant undertaking will be able to give binding directions to the public company in the light of the group's overall interest, rather than that of the public company alone, so overriding the present UK approach of treating companies as separate entities, even if they are in a group. Conversely, the dominant undertaking will be liable for the obligations of the public company, if that company defaults, unless it claims relief on the basis that it did not itself cause the default.

Already adopted is an Eleventh Company Law Directive, which dispenses with any requirement for separate accounts for branches of companies incorporated in other EC member states, and substitutes provisions compelling disclosure in the member states in which a branch operates the affairs of the company or, where it is a subsidiary of the group of which it is a part. From a UK standpoint, this may be helpful. Similar disclosure provisions already operate in the UK in relation to overseas companies having a place of business in the UK, although the requirement to file group accounts would be new. But, in other member states, additional information may currently be required relating to that branch (eg. branch accounts which could effectively reveal dealings between the branch and the rest of the company).

The stated intention of the Eleventh Directive is to harmonise the laws relating to subsidiaries. At the moment, the establishment of a branch tends to require less documentation, formality and cost, while a subsidiary has the advantage of being a separate legal personality, with the result that disclosure requirements may not apply to the parent, and the subsidiary's debts will not necessarily become obligations of its parent in the event of insolvency. However, under the Eleventh Directive, this non-disclosure advantage may disappear and, similarly, if the Ninth Directive is put in place and, in due course, extends to all subsidiaries, whether public or private companies, then this non-recourse advantage may also disappear.

Insider dealing

In November 1989, the Council of Ministers adopted a Directive to make insider dealing unlawful throughout the Community. The related national legislation will have to be enacted before June 1992. For the UK, however, there will be no significant effect. UK company law already incorporates most of the requirements.

The proposed Directive applies to all transferable securities traded on a stock exchange in a member state. As is already the case in the UK, it will render unlawful (although not necessarily in criminal law — the penalties may only be civil) the misuse of unpublished price-sensitive information, either by insiders or by those who obtain the information from insiders. Under English law, 'obtain' in this context can be passive, following a recent Court of Appeal decision. To prevent insider dealing, companies whose securities are publicly traded will be obliged promptly to announce price-sensitive information; similar obligations are already in place in the UK by reason of the Rules of the Stock Exchange and the City Code on Takeovers and Mergers.

Finally, the proposed Directive will contain provisions on co-operation between the competent authorities in the various member states and, in particular, for the exchange of information.

Free movement of capital

Article 67 of the Treaty of Rome (EEC) provided for the abolition of restrictions on the movement of capital within the Community during the first 12 years of the Community's existence (ie. by 1969!). Provision for complete liberalisation was achieved much later, following the adoption of the Single European Act (SEA) of

1986, by the Article 67 Directive. This Directive requires the abolition of any national restrictions on movements of capital between persons resident in member states, and was scheduled to be implemented by mid-1990 in some member states; Greece, Ireland, Portugal and Spain were given transitional relief until the end of 1992. Belgium and Luxembourg may temporarily continue to operate their existing dual exchange market.

The Directive is not significant in terms of inward investment in the UK. UK exchange control was suspended in 1979 and abolished in 1987, although the Directive will prevent its re-introduction in relation to other member states. But outward investment from the UK into other member states will be derestricted in terms of national legislation of those member states.

Disclosure of information

In December 1988, the EC adopted a Directive which requires the acquisition or disposal of 'major holdings' in listed companies to be publicly notified. The Directive lays down minimum disclosure requirements throughout the EC and is aimed at improving the transparency of the securities markets. As an important by-product, it will also make it difficult for prospective bidders to build up stakes in secret. The related national legislation was scheduled to be enacted during 1990.

The Disclosure Directive applies to holdings in a company which is incorporated in a member state and whose shares are officially listed on a stock exchange in that or any other member state. It provides that anyone who acquires a holding (or increases an existing holding) in such a company, above a series of specified thresholds, must notify the company accordingly. Disposals reducing holdings below any of these thresholds also have to be notified.

The notification requirement applies at certain threshold levels, namely 10 per cent, 20 per cent, one third, 50 per cent and two thirds. But member states are given the option of different thresholds in certain cases — for example, a 25 per cent threshold instead of the 20 per cent and one third thresholds. This is a different approach from present UK practice which requires notification of any percentage increase or decrease at levels at or above the single threshold level of 3 per cent. The Directive allows more stringent requirements and, therefore, it would seem that the present UK practice (and its lower initial threshold) can be continued, a fact which may help UK companies fearful of predators.

Enforcement of disclosure of information
One dissimilarity between member states concerning the disclosure of financial information in general is not only the type of disclosure on the statute books, but also the varying degrees of enforcement in the Community. The UK business Community feels that enforcement in the UK of disclosure of annual turnover figures, for example, is strict, whereas in other European countries, notably Germany and France, enforcement is rare. It is believed that foreign companies may gain a competitive advantage over UK companies from the disclosure of UK company 'sensitive' financial information while remaining 'immune' from enforcement themselves. UK government policy, however, is not to relax UK enforcement procedures, but to seek to ensure that disclosure of information provisions are fully and evenly enforced throughout the Community. UK independent companies in the smaller to medium-sized range, however, would prefer not to impose enforcement of sensitive financial information, since it is feared that disclosure encourages agressive takeovers in any event.

Takeovers

In December 1988, the European Commission adopted a proposal on takeovers. The proposed Directive aims to harmonise the laws of member states on the conduct of takeovers in the case of public companies (whether or not quoted). The Commission considers takeovers as a positive phenomenon, through which market forces identify the more competitive businesses and 'Community' businesses which are structured to match international competition. The Commission, by establishing a regime which promotes transparency, also wants to ensure that takeovers which are purely speculative in financial terms must be disclosed as such.

Although some member states have specific rules in this area, others have no system of regulation because takeovers are almost unknown in their countries (Denmark and Greece). Among the member states which do have specific regulations, the types of regulation vary. In Spain, France and Portugal the rules have legal force. Belgium and Luxembourg follow decisions issued by their competent authorities. Other member states (Germany, Italy, Ireland, the Netherlands and the UK) have a voluntary code of conduct. The UK Takeover Code, while voluntary in theory, is in practical terms binding in the UK, albeit less so in Ireland, even though there is a unified stock exchange.

The essence of the proposed Directive is to set out rules with two aims: to ensure equality of treatment of shareholders in the target company, and to obtain full disclosure. So far as the UK is concerned, the proposed Directive contains little that is new in substance and, indeed, it shows clear signs of actually being based on the City Code on Takeovers and Mergers, the present UK rulebook for takeovers. Adoption and implementation of the Directive throughout the Community would, therefore, go a long way towards levelling the takeover playing field for UK investors looking at opportunities in other member states.

Corporate structures

The European Economic Interest Grouping (EEIG)

The EEIG is a flexible company vehicle, permitting companies and others to co-operate within the Community on a cross-border basis. It was originally inspired by a French invention, the *Groupement d'Interet Economique*, allowing an association of companies, seeking to pool office and other resources, to pursue a particular activity without affecting their individual independence and without creating separate liability or a new profit centre.

In essence, the EEIG is a joint venture-type vehicle which has the mixed characteristics of an unlimited company and a partnership. It cannot be an enterprise on its own, but it enables its members to facilitate or develop their economic activities through a vehicle (which may have a legal personality), while the members remain jointly and severally liable for the debts of the combined enterprise and are taxed on a look-through basis.

Potential uses for an EEIG include cross-frontier research and development (particularly data processing), joint manufacturing or purchasing, marketing and professional services (particularly with a joint database), and distribution arrangements, where the manufacturer provides the goods and the agent contributes the legwork.

The EEIG can also be used to co-ordinate the activities of its participants, or to extend their range. Accordingly, an EEIG could come together as a multi-disciplinary vehicle to tender for, say, a construction engineering or high-technology project taking place within or outside of the Community. In such circumstances, if the tender was accepted, the various obligations could be divided among EEIG members, while the EEIG itself would effectively become the project manager with a co-ordinating role. This could, for example, provide a convenient structure for multi-national aircraft or defence projects.

EC competition rules, as they apply to joint ventures, still apply to EEIG operations. A joint venture between competitors or potential competitors would infringe Article 85 of the EEC Treaty, if the participants could reasonably have been expected to enter the market individually.

The European Company (SE)

In October 1989, the European Commission formally published proposals for establishing a European Company (*Societas Europea* or SE) by means of a Regulation dealing with company law and taxation, and a Directive dealing with employee participation. The intended role of the SE is to facilitate cross-border co-operation by means of large-scale mergers and associations. The Commission regards such mergers as imperative for the benefit of the Community, in order to enable European business to compete more efficiently in world markets against, say, US and Japanese megaliths. For this reasons the proposed Regulation provides that, where an SE is superimposed on two or more other companies as a new holding company, there will be an easy mechanism for the resultant merger, with the original companies being automatically dissolved and their former shareholders automatically becoming members of the SE — similar to a British Scheme of Arrangement approved by the High Court.

The SE will be a hybrid structure, incorporated in a particular member state, and the member state's national laws will govern certain aspects of the SE's operation (eg. insolvency). The SE will be subject to tax in the member state of incorporation, but with a limited offset for losses of permanent establishments (branches, but not subsidiaries) in other member states. A system of employee participation in an SE will also be mandatory, a requirement which mirrors the Fifth Directive, but with an additional option based on the most advanced practices in the member state of incorporation.

It is too early to forecast the extent to which use will be made of the SE. It is intended that the Commission's proposal should be adopted and implemented by the end of 1992, but the employee participation element, in particular, is controversial. Moreover, advantages in using an SE in terms of mergers, while real in terms of cross-border merger procedure, are not so overwhelming as to guarantee its use (as opposed to opting, say, for a company in a country such as Luxembourg, the Netherlands, or some other tax haven), particularly if there are perceived concomitant disadvantages; for example, in board structure and in employee representation.

1 Union of Independent Companies policy on enforcement of the disclosure of certain types of financial information.

EC Directives and Proposals

In the following lists *Official Journal* references are given which identify a source of the text of a proposal or measure. The *Official Journal* — full title *Official Journal of the European Communities* — can be obtained on subscription, or by purchasing individual copies from HMSO government bookshops, or can be consulted at European Documentation Centres and other business libraries (see *Libraries*, Part Eight, Chapter 3). The text of measures may also be published as European Commission documents in the COM or SEC series. The *Bulletin of the European Communities* also carries texts. These can be obtained from various sources including the European Commission's information offices in the UK (see *European Communication Publications*, Part Eight, Chapter 1).

First Directive (68/151) on the Mandatory Publication of Specified Company Documents and Information

Adopted 1968

In force in all member states, except Spain (UK: Companies Act 1985).

Official Journal reference: *OJ* Special Edition, 1968 (1), p41-45

Second Directive (77/91) Dealing with the Formation and Capital of Public Companies Adopted 1976

In force in all member states, except Spain. (UK: Companies Act 1985).

Official Journal reference: *OJ* L26, 31.01.77

Third Directive (78/855) on Mergers Between Two Public Companies Subject to the Laws of the Same Member State Adopted 1978

In force in all member states, except Italy, Spain and Belgium. (UK: Companies (Mergers and Divisions) Regulations 1987).

Official Journal reference: *OJ* L295, 20.10.78

Fourth Directive (78/660) on Annual Accounts

Adopted 1978

In force in all member states, except Spain, Italy and Portugal. (UK: Companies Act 1985).

Official Journal reference: *OJ* L222, 14.08.78

Directive to Revise the Amounts Expressed in ECU Within the Fourth Directive

Adopted 1984

Official Journal reference: *OJ* L314, 04.12.84

Proposal for a Fifth Company Law Directive on the Structure of Public Limited Companies and Employee Participation

Amended proposal 1989

Annexed to DTI Consultative Memorandum of January 1990

Official Journal reference: *OJ* C240, 09.09.83

Sixth Directive (82/891) on the Splitting Up of Public Limited Companies (Scissions)

Adopted 1982

In force in all member states, except Spain, Italy and Belgium — scissions are not permitted in West Germany, Denmark or the Netherlands, where the Directive is accordingly inapplicable. (UK: Companies (Mergers and Divisions) Regulations 1987).

Official Journal reference: *OJ* L378, 31.12.83

Seventh Directive (83/349) on Consolidated Accounts

Adopted 1983

Partially implemented in member states. (UK: Companies Act 1989)

Official Journal reference: *OJ* L193, 18.07.83

Eighth Directive (84/253) on the Professional Qualifications of Statutory Auditors

Adopted 1984

Currently in force in Belgium, Luxembourg, West Germany, Spain and the UK. (UK: Companies Act 1989)

Official Journal reference: *OJ* L126, 12.05.84

Proposal for a Ninth Directive on the Conduct of Groups Containing a Public Limited Company as a Subsidiary
No formal proposal — informal draft 1984
No reference
Draft Tenth Directive on International Mergers of Public Companies
Current draft 1985
Official Journal reference: *OJ* C23, 25.01.85
Eleventh Directive (89/666) on the Disclosure Requirements of Branches of Certain Types of Company Adopted 1989
To be implemented by January 1992
Official Journal reference: *OJ* L395, 30.12.89
Twelfth Directive (89/667) Concerning Single Member Private Limited Companies
Adopted 1989
To be implemented by January 1992
Official Journal reference: *OJ* L395, 30.12.89
Proposed Directive on the Information and Consultation of Workers in Groups of Companies (Vredeling Directive)
Amended draft of 1983 withdrawn by the European Commission and revised proposal being prepared.
Official Journal reference: *OJ* C217, 12.08.83
Council conclusions of 21 July 1987 on procedures for informing and consulting the employees of undertakings with complex structures.
Official Journal reference: *OJ* C203, 12.08.86
Directive (86/635) on the Accounts of Banks
Adopted 1986
To be implemented by 31 December 1990. (UK: DTI is preparing a consultative document).
Official Journal reference: *OJ* L372, 31.12.86
Regulation (85/2137) on the European Economic Interest Grouping (EEIG)
Adopted 1985
Effective from 1 July 1989 (UK: European Economic Interest Grouping Regulations 1989)
Official Journal reference: *OJ* L199, 31.07.85
Proposed Regulation on the Statute for a European Company
Formal Proposal
Official Journal reference: *OJ* C263, 16.10.89
Proposed Directive Complementing the Statute for a European Company
Formal Proposal
Official Journal reference: *OJ* C263, 16.10.89
Proposed Directive on the Annual Accounts of Insurance Undertakings
Amended Proposal submitted to the Council on 30 October 1989
Official Journal reference: *OJ* C30, 08.02.90
Proposed Directive on Compulsory Winding Up of Direct Insurance Undertakings
Amended Proposal submitted to the Council on 18 September 1989
Official Journal reference: *OJ* C253, 06.10.89
Directive (89/117) on the Accounts of Branches of Overseas Banks
Adopted 1989
In the UK implementation will take place at the same time as the Directive on the accounts of banks.
Official Journal reference: *OJ* L44, 16.02.89

Proposal for a Thirteenth Directive on Takeovers and Other General Bids
    Current draft COM(88)823
    Official Journal reference: *OJ* C64, 1988
Proposed Directive on the Accounts of Certain Partnerships
    Draft Proposal
    Official Journal reference: *OJ* C144, 11.06.86
Directive (88/627) on the Information to be Published When a Major Holding in a Listed Company is Acquired or Disposed of
    Adopted 1988
    Member states must implement by 1 January 1991
    Official Journal reference: *OJ* L348, 17.12.88
Directive (89/298) Co-ordinating the Requirements for the Drawing-up and Distribution of the Prospectus to be Published When Transferable Securities are Offered to the Public
    Adopted 1989
    Member states must implement by 17 April 1991
    Official Journal reference: *OJ* L124, 05.12.89
Directive Co-ordinating Regulations on Insider Dealing
    Adopted 1989
    Member states must implement by 1 June 1992
    Official Journal reference: *OJ* L334, 18.11.89
Directive (79/279) on Admission of Securities to Listing
    Adopted 1979
    Implemented by member states. (UK: Stock Exchange (Listing) Regulations 1984).
    Official Journal reference: *OJ* L66, 16.03.79
Directive (80/390) on Prospectuses
    Adopted 1980
    Implemented by member states. (UK: Stock Exchange (Listing) Regulations 1984).
    Official Journal reference: *OJ* L100, 17.04.80
Directive (87/345) on the Mutual Recognition of Listing Particulars
    Adopted 1987
    Implemented by member states (UK: Stock Exchange (Listing) Regulations 1984).
    Official Journal reference: *OJ* L185, 04.07.87
Directive (90/211) Amending Directive (80/390) in Respect of Mutual Recognition of Stock Exchange Listing Particulars
    Adopted 1990
    Member states must implement by 17 April 1991
    Official Journal reference: *OJ* L112, 03.05.90
Directive (82/121) on Continuing Disclosure of Information
    Adopted 1982
    Implemented by member states. (UK: Stock Exchange (Listing) Regulations 1984).
    Official Journal reference: *OJ* L48, 20.02.82
Directive (85/611) on Unit Trusts
    Adopted 1984
    Implemented by member states. (UK: Financial Services Act 1986)
    Official Journal reference: *OJ* L375, 31.12.85

Draft Proposal for a Directive on the Reorganisation and Winding Up of Credit Institutions and Deposit Guarantee Schemes
  Amended Proposal 1988
  Official Journal reference: *OJ C36, 08.02.88*
Proposal to Amend the Fourth Company Directive on Annual Accounts and the Seventh Company Law Directive on Consolidated Accounts with Respect to the Exemptions for Small and Medium-Sized Companies and to the Drawing Up and Publication of Accounts in ECU
  Amended Proposal submitted to the Council on 4 December 1989
  Offical Journal reference: *OJ C318, 20.12.89*
Proposed Directive Amending Requirements in Respect of Mutual Recognition of Stock Exchange Listing Particulars
  Commission proposal 3 April 1989
  Official Journal reference: *OJ C101, 22.04.89*
Proposal on Obstacles to Takeovers and Other General Bids
  Commission Proposal May 1990
  Commission Communication SEC(90)901 Final

CONTACTS

Legislative texts
Copies of legislative texts can be purchased from Alan Armstrong Limited (below), and from Government (HMSO) bookshops, quoting the *OJ* reference which consists of the number of the legal instrument and the date of issue in the *Official Journal* (*OJ*), ie. Regulation 4021/87, *OJ* L378, 31.12 87. Texts appear in hard copy and on microfiche. For details of the series published in the *Official Journal* see *European Community Publications*, Part Eight, Chapter 1. Texts can also be examined at European Documentation Centres and other libraries (see *Libraries*, Part Eight, Chapter 3), and accessed through on-line databases (Part Eight, Chapter 2).

HMSO Books
PO Box 276
London SW8 5DT
Tel: (071) 873 0011 (enquiries); (071) 873 9090 (telephone orders).
Fax: (071) 873 8463
Telex: 297138

(HMSO Bookshops: Belfast, Birmingham, Bristol, Edinburgh, London and Manchester, plus 40 bookshops acting as agents for HMSO throughout the UK)

Alan Armstrong Limited
2 Arkwright Road
Reading RG2 0SQ
Tel: (0734) 751855
Fax: (0734) 755164
Telex: 849937 AAATD G

Further information
The Department of Trade and Industry (DTI) publishes a booklet, *The Single Market: Company Law Harmonisation* containing details of developments on company law and related Proposals within the EC. *The Companies Acts Annual Report* contains details of progress on EC Company Law harmonisation and

is prepared and distributed by their Companies Division and interested parties can obtain these on a regular basis by registering on a mailing list (see below).

Companies Division contacts provide information on those EC Company Law measures which have not yet been incorporated into UK national law. However, in view of the frequency with which the DTI undertakes internal reorganisations, the individual telephone extensions of contacts dealing with specific Directives have not been listed here. They are listed in the publications mentioned above and in the DTI's *The Single Market: The Facts* (Factsheet 15). These publications are updated from time to time. *The Single Market: The Facts* and *Single Market: Company Law Harmonisation* are published as part of the DTI's Single Market information and awareness campaign and can be obtained by ringing the *1992 Hotline* which also provides contacts within Whitehall. Other enquiries should be directed to:

Department of Trade and Industry
Companies Division
10-18 Victoria Street
London SW1H 0NN
Tel: (071) 215 3204/5000
Fax: (071) 215 3323

(Mailing list enquiries and requests for
Companies Division publications)

DTI 1992 Hotline Tel: (081) 200 1992

Or write to:

DTI 1992
PO Box 1992
Cirencester
Gloucestershire GL7 1RN

3 The Competition Rules

Edward Pitt

The European Community's competition rules apply in all sectors of the economy, in manufacturing and service sectors alike, though special rules apply in the transport and coal and steel industries. Competition policy therefore occupies an important position in the development of the internal market programme and the completion of the Single Market. For the full benefits of the Single Market to be realised, regulation of anti-competitive activities is essential.

The substantive EC competition rules, designed to provide that regulation, are set out in Articles 85, 86 and 92 of the Treaty establishing the European Economic Community. Articles 85 and 86 deal with market practices prohibited to commercial undertakings. Article 92 lays down rules under which member states may grant state aids. The rules apply directly to all companies and member states and are enforced by the European Commission, with recourse to the European Court of Justice, if need be. The competition rules serve two economic objectives:

☐ To ensure that companies do not frustrate the development of a common market — particularly the economic benefits resulting from the removal of customs and other barriers to trade — by entering into agreements to protect national markets from competing goods or services originating in other Community member states.

☐ The promotion of free and unfettered competition being a stimulus to economic growth and efficiency, competition policy is an instrument of Community economic policy in its own right. This objective has assumed an increasingly important role.

Article 85: Agreements and concerted practices

Article 85 prohibits 'All agreements between undertakings, decisions by associations of undertakings, and concerted practices which may affect trade between member states and which have as their object or effect the prevention, restriction or distortion of competition within the common market'.

The wording of Article 85(1) is wide. The EC Commission, which has primary responsibility for enforcing the competition rules, supported by the European Court of Justice, has given the Article a wide scope of application. What matters is the economic effect of an agreement, rather than its legal form. Thus the term 'undertakings' includes any company, individual, partnership or other form of business organisation. 'Agreements and concerted practices' extends to unwritten agreements and informal understandings, and an agreement may still have 'an effect on trade between member states' when both undertakings are in the same member state, or when one or even both undertakings involved are outside the Community.

Article 85(1) applies to so-called 'horizontal' agreements; that is, agreements between two manufacturers or agreements between two distributors. Such agreements may contain terms fixing prices or other supply terms. For example, Article 85(1) would be infringed by an arrangement between two or more competing undertakings designed to maintain prices of a particular product at an artificially high level, or seeking to divide up the marketplace by allocating particular territories or customers to the parties to the agreement. Other prohibited practices include less obvious forms of co-operation, such as the exchange between competitors of pricing and other commercially sensitive information.

Article 85(1) can also apply to so-called 'vertical' agreements; that is, agreements between undertakings at different stages in the same product chain. For example, an agreement between a manufacturer and a wholesaler, or an agreement between a wholesaler and a dealer. Typically, many exclusive distribution agreements, patent licences, copyright licences or know-how licences may infringe Article 85(1). Long term exclusive supply agreements for raw materials may also be caught by Article 85(1). Apart from the exclusivity, such agreements may often contain other restrictions, such as seeking to control the price at which, or the customers to whom, the product may be resold by the purchaser.

The competition rules do not, however, apply to agreements of minor economic importance. In the European Commission's view, set out in a Commission notice on agreements of minor importance, reissued in 1986, agreements between small companies (those having a combined turnover of less than 200 million Ecus and a combined market share which in no part of the EC exceeds 5 per cent) meet this test. However:

☐ The Commission's notice should be treated with caution; it is not legally binding, and the Commission has departed from it in a number of cases.

☐ A practice or agreement which falls outside the EC rules may still fall within the national competition rules of an individual member state. France, Greece and Spain have recently passed legislation similar in scope to Articles 85 and 86. Other member states, in particular the UK and West Germany, have comprehensive laws to control anti-competitive agreements.

Exemptions to Article 85(1)
Since the wording of the prohibition of Article 85(1) is broad, it can catch many agreements which, although restrictive, have overall economic benefits and can be allowed to operate. There is therefore provision in Article 85(3) of the Treaty for the EC Commission to grant exemption from the effects of the prohibition in Article 85(1) to agreements showing benefits. Exemption is normally available for agreements which, although restrictive, offer counterbalancing benefits, such as improved efficiency in production or distribution, or technical research and development, while allowing consumers a fair share of those benefits.

Given the very large number of agreements potentially falling within the basic prohibition in Article 85(1), the Community has adopted a number of 'block' exemptions under Article 85(3) to various categories of common agreements fulfilling certain conditions. These exemptions codify the approach of the Commission to the relevant agreements. Their purpose is to give guidance to the companies concerned and to prevent notifications of agreements which do not usually pose any serious anti-competitive problems. These block exemption regulations cover:

□ Exclusive distribution agreements

□ Exclusive purchasing agreements

□ Patent licensing agreements

□ Motor vehicle distribution agreements

□ Specialisation agreements

□ Research and development agreements

□ Franchise agreements

□ Know-how licensing agreements

If a restrictive agreement cannot be brought within a block exemption, it can be notified to the Commission with a view to individual exemption. By way of example, this will often be the case where a joint venture is set up, particularly where it is between actual or potential competitors. Detailed Community legislation thus needs to be taken into account before it can be determined whether or not a particular agreement falls within Article 85(1) and, if it does, whether or not it is acceptable under Article 85(3).

Article 86 : Abuse of a dominant position

Article 86 provides that: 'Any abuse by one or more undertakings of a dominant position within the common market, or in a substantial part of it, shall be prohibited as incompatible with the common market insofar as it may affect trade between member states'. A company may be dominant in one or two member states, or part of a single member state. A company enjoys a dominant position where it possesses such market strength that it can act to an appreciable extent independently of its competitors and customers.

Article 86 prohibits the abuse by a company of its dominant position in the marketplace by, for example, driving competitors out of the market. Article 86 essentially strikes at unilateral behaviour by a dominant company when there is no agreement or concerted practice to which Article 85(1) can attach.

For the assessment of dominance the definition of what constitutes the relevant market is of capital importance. The Commission has in a number of cases adopted a narrow definition of what constitutes a relevant market. Consequently, Article 86 as implemented by the EC authorities, does not have regard solely to absolute financial power; it is not only big companies which may be dominant.

Dominance, however, is not itself unlawful. Only the *abuse* of a dominant position is prohibited by Article 86. Nevertheless, a company which is dominant in any product sector needs to be especially vigilant to ensure observance of the competition rules. For example, an abuse may consist of:

□ Unfair prices

□ Discriminatory pricing (selling to customers at significantly different prices)

☐ Refusals to supply without objective justifications (particularly to a creditworthy or cash customer on regular terms).

☐ Tie-in provisions, or provisions obliging a customer to take additional goods or services with the product supplied.

☐ Exclusive supply agreements or predatory pricing known to be likely to injure a competitor.

Merger control

For many years merger control has existed in the individual member states. With the increasing integration of the common market the Commission has sought the adoption of an EC Merger Control Regulation which it has now succeeded in obtaining. The Regulation was adopted by the Council of Ministers on 21 December, 1989, and took effect from 21 September, 1990.

Scope of the Community Merger Control Regulation

Under the Regulation, consent by the Commission to mergers will be necessary whenever a merger meets the regulation's threshold requirements:

☐ The aggregate worldwide turnover of all the undertakings concerned is more than 5 billion Ecus.

☐ The aggregate Community-wide turnover of each of at least two of the undertakings concerned is more than 250 million Ecus.

If the two above threshold requirements are met, the merger has to be notified to the Commission. There is one exception; the regulation does not apply where both undertakings concerned achieved more than two-thirds of their aggregate Community-wide turnover in the same member state. These thresholds are to be revised by qualified majority by the Council of Ministers after four years from 21 December, 1989.

The Merger Control Regulation allows member states to apply their own competition rules even to mergers falling under the regulation when necessary, in order to protect their legitimate interests. For example, a member state will be able to scrutinize a merger on grounds of national security or defence. However, it is not clear, as yet, what constitutes a 'legitimate interest'.

Appraisal of mergers

A merger that falls within the Regulation will only be permitted if it is 'compatible with the common market'. Mergers which 'would not create or strengthen a dominant position as a result of which effective competition would be impeded in the common market or in a substantial part thereof' will be permitted. Further, even if a merger is deemed to be incompatible with the common market, it could still be exempted upon grounds that it ultimately benefits the market, ie., through improving production or distribution.

In general, the criteria to be used for appraisal of mergers are those presently used under Articles 85 and 86, as developed by the European Commission and the European Court of Justice. There is one particularly controversial point; that is, whether in assessing a merger the Commission can take account of matters other than competition issues, such as regional development, loss of employment, balance of trade, or strategic issues. The Commission's public position is that it will only consider competition issues.

Procedure

Undertakings must notify the Commission within one week of taking the decision to merge (by, for example, signing a protocol agreement). The Commission then has one month within which to decide whether formally to investigate the merger. The Commission may at this stage authorise the merger.

If the Commission decides to initiate an investigation of the merger, it has a further four months from the date of initiation to decide whether the merger is compatible with the Common Market. In practice, therefore, the Commission might take up to five months to assess that a proposed merger is compatible with the Common Market and that it can be allowed to proceed. This could have serious implications for national timetable rules on takeovers. Moreover, it is likely that an attempt to encourage an investigation by the Commission will become a common defensive strategy for unwilling target companies.

Merger control of smaller transactions under the EEC Treaty

Even if the Merger Control Regulation does not apply to a takeover or merger (because the turnover limits in the Regulation are not met), some mergers may still fall within Articles 85 and 86, or under the merger provisions of Article 66 of the European Coal and Steel Treaty. Certain mergers between undertakings in the coal and steel industries require authorisation from the Commission.

In announcing the adoption of the Merger Control Regulation, the Commissioner for competition policy, Sir Leon Brittan, said that the Commission intends to apply the regulation to cases above the threshold and to leave national law exclusive jurisdiction in cases below the threshold. He has even suggested that Articles 85 and 86 will no longer apply in any cases. It is, however, almost certain that, as a matter of law, neither the Commission nor the Council of Ministers could limit the application of Articles 85 and 86 without amendment of the Treaty. Accordingly, Articles 85 and 86 will continue to apply to mergers in the four distinct situations set out below:

Acquisition by a dominant undertaking: In the *Continental Can* case the European Court held that an abuse within the meaning of Article 86 'may occur if an undertaking in a dominant position strengthens such a position in such a way that the degree of dominance reached substantially fetters competition, ie., that only undertakings remain in the market whose behaviour depends on the dominant one'. In practice, however, Article 86 has rarely been used by the Commission in adopting a formal decision prohibiting a merger. Its use has been threatened by the Commission, so that some proposed mergers have been abandoned, and its existence has possibly prevented some merger proposals from being consummated.

Acquisition of minority holdings in competing undertakings: The EC Commission initially took the view that Article 85 did not apply to mergers at all. However, the European Court has confirmed that whereas Article 85 may not apply to a full merger, eg., where 51 per cent control of the board is achieved, Article 85 will or may apply where one company acquires a minority holding in a competitor. In effect a minority holding in a competitor raises a presumption (which may be rebutted) that there will or may be co-ordination between the companies.

Holdings in joint ventures : Where actual or potential competitors hold a common interest in a third undertaking, the very existence of that structure may have the effect of restraining competition between each company or between either company and the joint entity. Consequently, Article 85 may apply to the structure, as well as to the precise terms contained in any agreement between the parties in a joint venture.

Consortium bids: Consortium bids organised by competitors may contravene Article 85. For example, in *Irish Distillers* the EC prevented a consortium bid by three competitors for a controlling interest in another competitor, Irish Distillers, in the spirits market.

Article 92: State aids

An integral part of the EC competition rules are the state aid rules contained in Article 92 of the EEC Treaty. Article 92 lays down rules determining the circumstances in which member states may grant financial support to their national industries. Many forms of government financial assistance must be notified to the Commission for approval before such assistance may be granted. The Commission has enforced the state aid rules with increasing severity over recent years. In some cases illegally granted aid has been ordered to be repaid. Those intending to make significant investment should ensure that any financial support given by a national government has been cleared by the EC Commission.

Enforcement

Powers and role of the EC Commission
The EC's competition rules are enforced by the EC Commission. In certain circumstances they can also be enforced by anti-trust enforcement agencies of the member states. The Commission's Directorate-General for Competition (DGIV) is based in Brussels, staffed by some 200 officials.

The procedural powers of the Commission to enforce Articles 85 and 86 are set out in three principal EC Regulations. Regulation 17 sets out the Commission's power in investigations into alleged breaches of the competition rules and applications for exemption under Article 85(3) (or 'negative clearance'; a declaration by the Commission that Article 85(1) does not apply). Regulations 19/65 and 2821/71 deal with block exemptions and associated procedural requirements.

Regulation 17 also sets out a procedure under which third parties adversely affected through agreements entered into by, or unfair commercial practices of, other companies, which infringe Article 85 or 86, may complain to the Commission. Where the Commission accepts a complaint, it may investigate the company complained against and issue a Decision against such a company, forcing it to end the practice in question. The Commission may also impose heavy fines.

Policy of enforcement
The practical implementation by the EC Commission of Community competition policy over recent years has focused on the following main issues:

1. The need to complete, in the interests of certainty for companies, the range of block exemptions available under Article 85(3) for agreements in common form, such as distribution, patent licensing, research and development, or know-how licensing agreements, and to issue notices or guidelines for agreements not

susceptible to block exemption. These include subcontracting, joint ventures and agreements of minor economic importance.

2. The more effective observance of the existing competition rules, firstly through raising the overall level of fines to a deterrent level for 'classic' anti-trust infringements, such as price fixing cartels or export bans, and secondly through encouraging private actions before national courts to enforce the EC rules.

3. The extension of the practical enforcement of the rules to certain areas of the economy not previously the subject of particular attention, such as insurance, banking, air transport and telecommunications.

Consequences of infringement

An infringement of the EC competition rules may have serious consequences for the undertakings concerned. There may be a full scale investigation by the Commission involving time, expense, management disruption and possibly bad publicity. If an undertaking is found to have infringed the competition rules, then it is exposed to the risk of heavy fines. Fines can amount to the higher of 1 million Ecus or 10 per cent of the undertaking's turnover in the preceding year. Fines as high as 15 million Ecus have been imposed on some companies.

Any anti-competitive provisions contained in an agreement infringing Article 85 or 86 are automatically void and cannot be enforced in national courts of member states. Articles 85 and 86 are directly applicable in the courts of member states and take precedence over national laws. Therefore, even if an agreement is valid under national law, it may still be caught by Article 85 or 86. Civil actions for damages can also be brought in the courts of member states by third parties who are harmed by a violation of the competition rules; for example a dissatisfied customer, distributor or competitor.

Anti-trust compliance programmes (to ensure that sales and management executives understand the impact of the EC competition rules through seminars and compliance manuals) play an important role in preventing breaches of the competition rules.

Scope of the competition rules

Overlap with national competition rules of member states
Companies will also have to ensure that they are operating within the ambit of any relevant national competition rules. Such rules are increasingly emerging in the member states in parallel with the development of EC competition law; for example, in France, Italy, Greece and Spain. It is therefore necessary to consider the operation of Articles 85 and 86 within the context of the national competition laws.

Proceedings before national courts

The Commission increasingly seeks to encourage undertakings to invoke the competition rules before the national courts, often at the same time as filing a complaint to the Commission.

355

Extra-territorial application of EC competition law

The European Court of Justice's recent judgement in the *Wood Pulp* case has serious implications for companies carrying on business within the Community, but whose head offices or main businesses are situated outside the Community (and even those with no place of business within the Community). Whenever a company or companies engage in anti-competitive conduct which is implemented within the EC, such conduct is subject to the Community's competition rules.

Main competition law Regulations and Notices

Substantive
Regulation (19/65) on the Application of Article 85(3) of the EEC Treaty to Certain Categories of Agreements and Concerted Practices
    Enabling Regulation
    Official Journal reference: *OJ* L36, 6.3.65 *OJ* Second edition 1965-6
Regulation (2821/71) on the Application of Article 85(3) of the EEC Treaty to Categories of Agreements, Decisions and Concerted Practices
    Enabling Regulation
    Official Journal reference: *OJ* L285, 29.12.71
Regulation (1983/83) on the Application of Article 85(3) of the EEC Treaty to Categories of Exclusive Distribution Agreements
    Official Journal reference: *OJ* L173, 30.6.83 and L281, 13.10.83.
Regulation (1984/83) on the Application of Article 85(3) of the EEC Treaty to Categories of Exclusive Purchasing Agreements
    Official Journal reference: *OJ* L173, 30.6.83
Explanatory Notice on Regulations 1983/83 and 1984/83
    Official Journal reference: *OJ* C101, 1984
Regulation (2349/84) on the Application of Article 85(3) of the EEC Treaty to Certain Categories of Patent Licensing Agreements
    Official Journal reference: *OJ* L219, 16.8.84 and L113 26.4.85
Regulation (123/85) on the Application of Article 85(3) of the EEC Treaty to Certain Categories of Motor Vehicle Distribution and Servicing Agreements
    Official Journal reference: *OJ* L15, 18.1.85
Explanatory Notice on Regulation 123/85
    Official Journal reference: *OJ* C17 1985
Regulation (417/85) on the Application of Article 85(3) of the EEC Treaty to
    Categories of Specialisation Agreement
    Official Journal reference: *OJ* L53, 22.2.85
Regulation (418/85) on the Application of Article 83(3) of the EEC Treaty to Categories of Research and Development Agreements
    Official Journal reference: *OJ* L53, 22.2.85
Regulation (4087/88) on the Application of Article 85(3) of the EEC Treaty to Categories of Franchising Agreements
    Official Journal reference: *OJ* L359, 28.12.88
Regulation (556/89) on the Application of Article 85(3) to Categories of Know-How Licensing Agreements: Official Journal reference: *OJ* L61, 1989
Notice on Exclusive Agency Contracts
    Official Journal reference: *OJ* 2921 1962

Notice on Co-operation Agreements
　Official Journal reference: *OJ* C75 1968
Notice on Agreements of Minor Importance
　Official Journal reference: *OJ* C231 1986
Notice on Sub-contracting Agreements
　Official Journal reference: *OJ* C1 1979
Council Regulation (4064/89)
　Merger Control Regulation
　Official Journal reference: *OJ* L395/89
Regulation (2367/90)
　Procedure under Merger Control Regulation
　Official Journal reference: *OJ* L219/90
Commission Notice regarding concentrative and co-operative operations under Council Regulation 4064/89.
　Official Journal reference: *OJ* C203/90
Commission Notice regarding restrictions ancillary to concentrations
　Official Journal reference: *OJ* C203/90

Procedural
Regulation (17/62)
　Setting out the Commission's basic powers
　Official Journal reference: *OJ* L13 21.2.62
Regulation (27/62) as amended by Regulation 2526/85
　Implementing Reg. 17/62
　Official Journal reference: *OJ* L35 11.5.62 and L240 7.9.85.
Regulation (99/63)
　Hearings provided for in Reg. 17/62
　Official Journal reference: *OJ* L127 20.8.63

Legislative texts
Copies of legislative texts can be purchased from Alan Armstrong Limited (below), and from Government (HMSO) bookshops, quoting the *OJ* reference which consists of the number of the legal instrument and the date of issue in the *Official Journal (OJ)*, ie. Regulation 4021/87, *OJ* L378, 31.12 87. Texts appear in hard copy and on microfiche. For details of the series published in the *Official Journal* see *European Community Publications*, Part Eight, Chapter 1. Texts can also be examined at European Documentation Centres and other libraries (see *Libraries*, Part Eight, Chapter 3), and accessed through on-line databases (Part Eight, Chapter 2).

HMSO Books
PO Box 276
London SW8 5DT
Tel: (071) 873 0011 (enquiries); (071) 873 9090 (telephone orders).
Fax: (071) 873 8463
Telex: 297138

(HMSO Bookshops: Belfast, Birmingham, Bristol, Edinburgh, London and Manchester, plus 40 bookshops acting as agents for HMSO throughout the UK)

Alan Armstrong Limited
2 Arkwright Road
Reading RG2 0SQ
Tel: (0734) 751855
Fax: (0734) 755164
Telex: 849937 AAATD G

CONTACTS

Complaints about unfair competition practices within the scope of the Community's competition rules are investigated by the European Commission. Advice on the procedure for lodging complaints and on the application of the competition rules to specific situations is available from national competition authorities (UK: The Office of Fair Trading). The Department of Trade and Industry (DTI) provides information on EC Competition Policy. General information is also published by the European Commission and can be obtained from the Commission's information offices in member states or from the Office for European Community Publications in Luxembourg. (see *European Community Publications*, Part Eight, Chapter 1)

European Commission
Directorate-General for Competition
Policy (DGIV)
200 Rue de la Loi
B-1049 Brussels
Tel: (32) 2 235 1111
Telex: 21877 COMEU B

Office of Fair Trading
Competition Policy Division
Field House
15-25 Bream's Buildings
London EC4A 1PR
Tel: (071) 269 8824
Fax: (071) 269 8960

Department of Trade and Industry
Competition Policy Division
1-19 Victoria Street
London SW1H 0ET
Tel: (071) 215 5337
Fax: (071) 215 5016/222 2629

(DTI regional offices: See *UK Official Sources of Information*, Part Eight, Chapter 2)

4 Intellectual Property

Ian Starr

Intellectual property is a form of intangible property right involving the ownership and exercise of legal monopolies or quasi-monopolies for the commercial application and exploitation of ideas and inventions. There are four main species of intellectual property right — patents, industrial designs, copyright and trade marks. Confidential information/trade secrets, whilst generally not considered to fall within the definition of intellectual property rights, are often regarded as a fifth species commonly termed 'know-how'.

The advent of the Community Trade Mark and, to a lesser extent, the Community Patent signals a fundamental change in the means of protection and of enforcement of intellectual property rights in the European Community. It is important that companies understand how the changes will affect them and what they should be doing now to place themselves in the most advantageous position. They should also be aware of the problems and possibilities raised by the Brussels Convention when contemplating litigation.

For example, many companies (both within and outside Europe) are developing and registering pan-European brands, whereas previously they registered separate brands for each European country. Furthermore, many companies are applying for trade marks in some jurisdictions that, although not registrable in some countries, may well give them a head start over competitors, once the Community Trade Mark Regulation comes into effect. One notable example is the 3-dimensional trade marks which are registrable in the Benelux countries but not generally in the UK and West Germany.

Monopoly or free competition?

The philosophy behind the granting of monopoly rights is to encourage invention and to reward intellectual effort by giving the "inventors" a head start in exploitation. Obviously, too broad or too long a monopoly could be counter-productive in that it can stifle development and free competition. A balance must be struck between incentive and restriction. Within the EC there is a further problem as intellectual property rights, having been historically national/territorial are capable of restricting the free movement of goods between member states and of being used to segregate markets along national boundaries. In addition, differing national laws have resulted in numerous anomalies and restrictions on trade between EC countries.

Both the European Commission and the European Court of Justice have tried to limit the effects of such restrictions by emphasising that, although the existence of a national right is not *per se* anti-competitive (nor unduly restrictive of freedom of movement), it is how the right is actually *exercised* that is important from the "freedom of movement" perspective. And in that respect the "specific subject-matter" (ie. the essential function of the intellectual property right in question) is taken into account. For example, products sold by a trade mark or patent owner in one member state can freely circulate within the whole of the EC and national trade marks or patents cannot be used by that owner to prevent this (the so-called "exhaustion of rights" doctrine). In less clear-cut cases the result may differ depending on whether one is dealing with patented or trade-marked goods.

The member states realised at an early stage that uniform intellectual property laws were vital to the creation of a single uniform internal market. Uniformity could be achieved via two complementary methods. Firstly, by harmonising existing national rules, so as to achieve similar solutions in every member state; and, secondly, by introducing Community-wide intellectual property rights which could, at least initially, co-exist with the harmonised national ones. A Community Patent and a Community Trade Mark have been under consideration for several years, but progress has been slow. The Community Patent Convention is in an agreed form, but awaiting ratification. Much progress has been made on the trade mark front, and there has been a recent Green Paper on copyright which aims to provide a basis on which future measures aiming at the creation of minimum standards for copyright laws in certain areas could be relied on. It is expected that substantial progress will have been made on trade marks and probably patents by 1992, although this is more unlikely in respect of the various copyright aspects.

Community institutions are also actively considering a number of related intellectual property matters. They include unfair competition laws, counterfeiting, patent term restoration, genetic engineering and plant varieties. A proposal for a Directive on legal protection of biotechnological inventions and a proposal for Regulations providing for a patent term restoration certificate have already been issued while other Community measures are under consideration.

Another area of intellectual property which has attracted the Commission's attention is the licensing of such rights and the obvious competition law implications. There is a lot of case law on this subject already. The Commission has also adopted "block exemptions" which, in a sense, codify the current Commission approach on this issue. These exemptions itemise a list of acceptable and unacceptable provisions relating to the licensing of patents (Regulation 2349/84 *OJ* L219 of 16.8.84), know-how licensing (Regulation 556/89 *OJ* L61 of 4.3.89), and on franchise agreements (Regulation 4087/88 *OJ* L359 of 28.12.88). Provided any particular agreement contains no unacceptable provisions, agreements need not be notified under Article 85 of the EEC Treaty (competition Rules). These exemptions are important, not least because the Commission can levy very substantial fines for failure to notify, or continuing to operate unlawful licence agreements.

PATENTS

There are two multi-lateral conventions relevant to patents — the European Patent Convention and the Community Patent Convention. The European Patent Convention came into force on 7 October 1977 and on 1 January 1990 it had 14 members (all the EC member states, except Portugal, Denmark — due to join on 1st January 1990 — and Ireland, plus Switzerland, Austria, Sweden and Liechtenstein). The Community Patent Convention is not yet in force.

European Patent Convention (EPC)

The European Patent Convention provides for a centralised method of applying for national patents. One application is made by an authorised European Patent Attorney to the European Patent Office (EPO) in Munich. If the application is deemed to be patentable, a bundle of individual national patents is then granted as designated by the patentee (ie. there is not one patent covering the whole Community).

An application can be in any one of the three official languages — English, French or German. The language then becomes the language of the proceedings. Upon grant the claims must be translated into the other two official languages. The designated member countries may, and usually do, demand that a full translation of the whole patent is made.

Any opposition to the grant of the patent(s) must be heard before the EPO within 9 months of grant. If this is successful the patent is revoked for *all* the designated countries. A European patent lasts for 20 years from the date of filing of the application, not from the priority date. For other purposes the granted patents are treated just as if they were local patents granted by the national patent offices.

National patents are still available from national patent offices. They are less expensive to obtain, if a company simply wants local protection, but a European patent is generally more cost-effective if protection is sought in three or more countries. Most local patent laws have already been harmonised so that they broadly equate with the European Patent Convention. Issues of infringement and validity should theoretically be dealt with in a similar way.

The Community Patent Convention

The Community Patent Convention (CPC) is intended to produce a single Community-wide right rather than the bundle of national patents provided for by the European Patent Convention. The CPC was signed on 15 December 1975 (and amended in December, 1989 — Commission Decision 89/695 *OJ* L401 of 30.12.89), but it only comes into force once all the member states have ratified it. To date, all of them except Denmark and Ireland, have ratified the Convention. It is uncertain when these two countries will do so, if at all.

A compromise to overcome non-ratification by these two member states has been reached in an intergovernmental conference, held at Luxembourg in December 1989. Twelve member states have decided that, if on 31 December 1991, these two countries have not ratified the Convention, a new intergovernmental conference will decide, unanimously, the number of member states which will have to ratify the convention to allow it to enter force as between those member states. It is therefore likely that the Convention will enter into force at least between ten member states in the forseeable future and possibly by the end of 1992.

The aim of the Community Patent Convention is that any European patent application which designates a member state will automatically become a Community Patent application, unless a contrary intention is expressed. When granted, the patent will extend to every member state. Questions of invalidity will be handled centrally in the European Patent Office, but infringement actions will be dealt with by local national courts in the first instance. It is possible for member states to decide that, in respect of actions for infringement relating to their territory, their courts can decide on both infringement and validity for their country. Once again, translations of the patent into the language of the individual member states will be required.

The patent can only be transferred, or revoked in exceptional circumstances, or allowed to lapse in respect of the whole Community. It will, however, be possible to license for only part of the Community and indeed to obtain national compulsory licences in some circumstances, although patentees must be aware of the principle of exhaustion of rights. There are provisions to prevent protection under both national and Community patents. There will be one common appeal court, COPAC, which will hear all appeals from national courts and the European Patent Office on matters involving the infringement or validity of Community patents.

Advantages of the Community Patent

The Community Patent will not only help to cement the internal market. It will also mean that a patentee's administration of his patent portfolio will be substantially simplified and cheapened. The advantages are:

☐ Only one set of renewal fees need be paid.

☐ An assignment need only be made once, rather than in several countries and in several languages.

☐ Reduced cost of obtaining and maintaining patent protection. The cost of a Community Patent should be less than the bundle of national patents of the European Patent Convention.

☐ Infringement action would be possible which would have Community-wide effect.

☐ Only one revocation action [in the European Patent Office] need be brought. It would also have Community-wide effect.

There are also disadvantages with a single patent, the most obvious being that a non-specialist court in another country could make a decision with serious ramifications across the whole Community. This could lead to a measure of forum shopping, within the restraints of the Brussels Convention, 1968 on Jurisdiction and the Enforcement of Judgements in Civil and Commercial Matters, as enacted in the UK by the Civil Jurisdiction and Judgements Act 1982. If COPAC hears appeals by way of a full re-examination of the case, this should become less of a risk.

Brussels Convention

Although not directly part of the EC's 1992 programme, the Brussels Convention on Jurisdiction and the Enforcement of Judgments in Civil and Commercial Matters is in keeping with the Single Market philosophy. It lays down rules regulating in which countries suits should be brought and the rules as to the reciprocal enforcement of judgments. The basic principle is that proceedings may be commenced in the home country of the Defendant. There are a number of exceptions. Claims based in tort, including infringement of intellectual property rights, can be made in the country where the tort occurred. Claims concerning the validity of registered rights, such as patents or trade marks, must be brought in the country of registration.

However, it is clear that considerable scope still exists for forum shopping. It is now probably more necessary than ever to ensure that the first set of proceedings are brought in the most appropriate jurisdiction. One must think 'European' when considering major litigation and not country by country, particularly as much interim relief granted, such as the preservation of property, can have Community-wide implications.

Patent Term Restoration Certificate

Another area which has attracted attention is the duration of the term of patent protection in cases where the marketing of a product depends on an administrative authorisation. It is well known that the marketing of certain patented products, such as pharmaceuticals, is often dependent on prior marketing approval by the competent national authorities. Such approval is normally given well after the product gets patent protection and is usually a lengthy process. This normally results in effective patent protection being eroded since the period during which the patent owner may benefit from his inventive efforts is considerably shortened.

To tackle this problem, the Commission has tabled a proposal for a Regulation introducing a 'Restoration Certificate' (N 90 *OJ* C114 of 8.5.90). Under the proposed system, the restoration Certificate will extend protection for the product after the end of the basic patent for a period equal to the period which elapsed between the date on which the patent application for the basic patent was lodged and the date of the first authorisation to place the product on the market in the Community, less four years. For example:

Application made on 1.5.90
Product Licence given on 1.5.99
Patent expires on 30.4.2010
Restoration Certificate extends protection to 30.4.2015

The period of four years has been deducted because the Commission took the view that in all patent applications (irrespective of whether a further approval will be needed) four years normally elapse between the filing of a patent application and putting the patented product on the market. Since the restoration certificate is designed to deal only with additional delays imposed on, in particular, pharmaceutical products and not to provide a more favourable treatment for these products, the Commission thought it appropriate to exclude the four-year period from the protection under the certificate.

The certificate should extend the life of protection so that such a patented product should get a 16 year protection overall, although the duration of the certificate cannot exceed 10 years from the date on which it has taken effect.

The certificate will confer the same rights and shall be subject to the same limitations as the basic patent. It will not, however, protect the expired patent in its entirety, but only the authorised product.

The Commission opted for such a certificate, rather than for the amendment of national laws on patent protection, since that latter course would also have made necessary the partial revision of the European Patent Convention, which, the Commission acknowledged, was not possible, at least in the short term.

The proposal is that this certificate will initially cover only proprietary medicinal products. However, the Commission has taken the view that the scope of the Regulation might be extended, at a later stage, to any product protected by patent which is also subject to an administrative authorisation procedure, for reasons of public safety and environmental protection, prior to being sold for public use.

COMMUNITY TRADE MARK

The European Commission is aware that the removal of restrictions caused by the existence of national trade marks, by means of total harmonisation of national trade mark laws, is unrealistic. The Commission's solution has, therefore, been to introduce the concept of a Community Trade Mark (CTM) which is comparable to that of a Community Patent. It has chosen to do this through the medium of a Regulation, which would be directly effective and immediately form part of the legal systems of the member states without the need for separate, national implementation.

The current draft of the Regulation is lengthy and fairly detailed. It provides that Community nationals, and other nationals from countries which currently co-operate with Community countries in trade mark protection may apply to a Community Trade Mark Office (CTMO) for a Community Trade Mark. The Community Trade Mark will be valid and have identical effects throughout the whole Community.

Registration

The proposed Community Trade Mark will be obtained by registration with the register being open to public inspection. Registration can be refused on the grounds of non- distinctiveness, as being contrary to public policy, or because there is a conflicting Community Trade Mark or a national trade mark, although it seems likely that the latter two grounds of refusal will require an application to be made by the holder of the conflicting trade mark.

The Community Trade Mark will be subject to an almost totally separate legal regime set out in the Regulation. There is a system of appeals from the decisions of the Community Trade Mark Office to a Board of Appeal and then to the European Court of Justice. National law will only come into play with respect to infringement proceedings, civil actions for damages and competition law. Once a Community Trade Mark is registered, the equivalent national trade mark will be suspended.

Effect of a Community Trade Mark

The Community Trade Mark will constitute an item of property in the same way as a national trade mark. It will, therefore, be possible to transfer, licence, or mortgage it. As with the Community Patent Convention, assignments must be for the whole Community, but licensing can be for part of the Community. Once the trade mark has been registered, the holder can prevent anyone else from using the same, or a similar mark, with respect to the same, or similar, goods or services; or in circumstances where its use would constitute an unwarranted exploitation of the commercial value of the trade mark. The Community Trade Mark will have a duration of ten years from the date of filing and will be renewable. A Community Trade Mark will be revocable on grounds of:

☐ Non-use for five years.

☐ Having fallen into generic use due to the acts or omissions of the proprietor.

☐ If its use is liable to mislead the public.

A third party will be able to apply to the Community Trade Mark Office for revocation, or make a counterclaim for revocation in infringement proceedings before a national court.

Technical and legal problems

The form of the Regulation has, in large part, been agreed, but major political obstacles to its implementation remain. These include:

☐ Disagreement as to whether an applicant for an existing Community Trade Mark should be obliged to make a full search of not only all existing Community trade marks but also national trade marks which could constitute earlier rights disentitling registration.

☐ Official Language. The European Commission prefers English as the sole language on grounds of costs of administration. Some member states advocate at least a three language system like that of the European Patent Convention. The solution most recently under consideration was that the CTM should adopt all nine languages, but each applicant would be obliged to file in two languages — presumably their own, along with a translation in another language. Although there is not restriction on which two languages an applicant chooses, it was expected that at least the second language would be English, French or German. This solution has not yet been approved by some of the member states.

☐ Location of the Community Trade Mark Office: Current contenders for the site are Luxembourg, the Hague, Munich, London and Madrid.

☐ Whether it is appropriate for the Community Trade Mark to be introduced by Regulation or by Convention. If by Convention, constitutional changes by Denmark and the Republic of Ireland would be necessary to achieve implementation.

Advantages and disadvantages of the CTM

The Community Trade Mark will enhance the benefits of a Community-wide market by providing trade marks which are effective throughout all Community countries. This should provide savings in:

☐ Time; subject to the problem of searches for prior rights and the swiftness of the application procedure by the Community Trade Mark Office.

☐ Cost; subject to the level of fees and the official language problem.

National trade marks systems will continue and co-exist alongside the Community system. Hence, businesses may instead continue to apply for national trade marks. Some businesses will not consider it worthwhile applying for the new Community Trade Mark, if they operate mainly within the boundaries of one member state. In any event, after the adoption of the Trade Mark Approximation Directive the various national systems will be brought into line with each other, as far as their essential features are concerned by the end of 1991 or possibly, if an extension is provided, by the end of 1992.

Madrid Arrangement

The possible future introduction of the CTM already has wider effects. Of particular importance is its relation with the Madrid Arrangement for trade marks. The Madrid Arrangement, which became effective in 1982, provides a system whereby, once trade mark owners have achieved registration in their home country, they can apply to the World Intellectual Property Organisation (WIPO) in Geneva to extend the cover of that mark into some or all of the 27 Member Countries. Every application for extension is then sent by the World Intellectual Property Organisation to the national trade mark offices concerned, where the application(s) are processed in accordance with national laws. The successful applicant gets a bundle of national rights, but the process is cheaper than a series of local filings.

Most of the EC member states, with the exception of the UK, Ireland, Greece and Denmark, are parties to the Madrid Arrangement. The expected introduction of the CTM which raised the question of a possible link between the two systems along with the hope of making the Arrangement more attractive to non-member countries, such as the four EC member states mentioned above, the United States, Japan, Korea, Sweden and others led to the adoption of a Protocol signed in Madrid in June 1988 (WIPO MM/DC/27 of 27.7.90)

The primary objective of the Protocol, which is, in fact, a new Treaty, was to broaden the Madrid system to allow greater participation of countries and other intergovernmental bodies which have expressed an interest in joining an international registration system, but whose national practices and laws prevented their participation in the Madrid Arrangement (there were a number of features of the Madrid System which were unacceptable to the UK and other countries). The second goal was to provide a method for eventual linking with the European Community Trade Mark system.

The Protocol creates a 'Special Union' (the Madrid Arrangement being called a 'General Union'). By virtue of a safeguard provision, the Madrid Arrangement will continue to govern relations between original members for a minimum of ten years, even if these countries decide to join the Protocol. A revision will be possible in order to allow member countries to denounce their membership in Madrid if they find that the Protocol is a more favourable system.

Under the terms of the Protocol, any intergovernmental organisation which has at least one member state belonging to the Paris Union may join, and providing that the organisation has a regional office for registering trade marks in the territory. Thus the EC may become a member.

The Protocol thus paves the way for eventual linking with the CTM when it comes into effect, assuming that the EC joins the Protocol. This will mean that, once a trade mark owner succeeds in obtaining a CTM registration, he may file for an international registration and obtain extension to the other non-EC members of the Protocol, whether or not his home country is a Protocol member. This may be interesting to companies coming from countries which may choose not to join the Protocol.

The Protocol has now been signed by 28 countries including all EC member states, but it is not expected to enter into force for one or two years. It still has to be ratified and the necessary regulations for its implentation are in the process of being drafted.

Trade Mark Approximation Directive

The Council of Ministers has adopted a Directive to approximate national trade mark laws (Regulation 89/104 *OJ* L40 of 11.2.89). Its objective is to approximate those national provisions which most directly affect free movement of goods and services, not full harmonisation. The new laws will be national and enforced by national courts and Trade Mark Registries. It goes hand in hand with the proposal for a Community Trade Mark. In many respects it is similar to the proposed Regulation on the Community Trade Mark, so that the conditions for obtaining and keeping a mark are broadly similar.

As with all EC Directives, it is up to individual member states to pass implementing legislation. France and Spain have already done so. The rest must do so by the end of 1992. The Directive sets out certain mandatory provisions as well as others which are optional. The principal mandatory provisions include:

☐ A wide definition of the term, 'trade mark'.

☐ Protection for service marks as well as trade marks.

☐ Protection where reputation is acquired through extensive use.

☐ Removal from the register of a trade mark after five years non-use.

INDUSTRIAL DESIGNS

The member states have widely differing laws concerning the degree and extent of protection for industrial designs, designs of products meant for industrial application and/or commercial use. For example, in the UK the Copyright Designs and Patents Act, 1988, has created a new unregistered Design Right, which has no counterpart in the rest of the EC.

The European Commission is now examining this situation, but its deliberations are at an early stage and no firm proposals have yet emerged. A current favourite is some form of inexpensive registration system, but it is far from certain that this will be accepted (at least not before the problems over the Community Patent and CTM are resolved).

There has been a Council Directive (Directive 87/54 *OJ* L24 of 27.1.87) on the protection of the topography of semi-conductor chips, also a form of industrial design, and this Directive has been implemented in some member states by the passing of national laws. Unfortunately not all laws are identical; the UK and Belgium do not require registration, whilst Spain and Italy are opting for compulsory marking of a suitable symbol as well as registration.

Biotechnical inventions

Another area of growing importance is biotechnology. In order to provide for a common approach in the twelve member states, the Commission has issued a draft Directive (Directive 89/C10/03 *OJ* C10 of 13.1.89) to ensure that all member states should, subject to the fulfilment of the appropriate conditions, grant patent protection to biotechnological inventions. The Commission believes that the adoption of the Directive will enable European companies to compete on an equal footing with their US and Japanese counterparts which enjoy such protection in their home markets.

The proposed Directive will not introduce a new system of protection; it will adapt the existing legal framework. The Commission proposes that all living matter except plant or animal varieties should be patentable. Such patented inventions should still be patentable, even if they are incorporated into a variety. Also, processes for the production and use of plant and animal varieties and microbiological processes should be patentable, as well as any processes involving human intervention with biological matter, except conventional breeding activities.

Under the proposed Directive a patented product or improvement which includes genetic information for its multiplication (ie. is self-replicable) should only be multiplied by a third party for experimental purposes. Multiplication for commercial purposes should be an infringement unless it is unavoidable in commercial procedures (other than procedures for propagation).

The proposal contains some controversial provisions such as that under which, if a holder of a plant variety right can only exploit his rights by infringing an existing patent, he should be entitled, after a certain period, to a non-exclusive royalty-paying licence as of right under the patent, provided that the new variety is a genuine technical achievement.

Where a patent covers an invention involving self-reproducing biological material, which is not available to the public and cannot sufficiently be disclosed in writing, the Commission recommends that a deposit of a sample of the material should be made. Implementation of the Directive should be in the forseeable future.

COPYRIGHT

Initially, the Community institutions were not concerned with copyright. They considered that copyright was not really part of industrial or commercial property. However, this assessment has changed as a result of various cases involving cable TV, and it has been decided that copyright does fall within the remit of the Community institutions.

Green paper

In June 1988 a Green Paper (COM(88)172 Final) was issued by the European Commission on *Copyright and the Challenge of Technology* after several years in the drafting. The stated aim of the discussion document is to bring copyright law into the modern electronic age and to deal with various multi-national issues.

The Green Paper was *not* intended to be a comprehensive review of copyright law, nor was it intended to harmonise the laws of member states. It simply sought to focus on certain areas which were thought to be of importance, and to suggest minimum standards of legal protection and enforcement. Some areas which were *not* discussed were industrial design copyright, infringement of copyright by photocopying, and public performances of satellite or cable TV, all of which are very important.

Specific proposals

Piracy

The European Commission views commercial counterfeiting as a major problem and one which requires urgent action. The Commission proposes a Directive requiring all member states to:

☐ provide for rights for producers of films, videos and sound recordings, allowing them to authorise their reproduction for commercial purposes.

☐ provide for similar rights for performing artists, broadcasters and cable TV operators.

☐ provide for a licensing scheme for all digital audio tape commercial duplicating equipment and to keep a register of everyone so licensed.

The Commission proposes to extend the Council Regulation No. 3842/86 (*OJ* L357 of 18.12.86) prohibiting the free circulation of counterfeit goods to cover copyright infringements as well as trade mark infringements.

The Commission also proposes minimum standards of legal protection, such as the availability of search and seizure orders, criminal sanctions, seizure and destruction of counterfeit goods. Another Commission proposal is for a central register of rights holders in sound and video recordings and films.

Home taping

There are no proposals concerning the home taping of sound and video recordings, even though producers are at a disadvantage, because it is virtually impossible to police. The Commission views the advent of digital technology as a great worry and proposes that all DAT recorders carry a device to prevent or at least limit the scope of copying by such machines.

Rental rights

The Commission propose that copyright owners be given a rental right for sound and video recordings.

Computer software programmes

The Commission is firmly of the view that copyright is the appropriate form of legal protection for software programmes. It has proposed a Directive (COM(88)816 *OJ* C91 of 12.4.89) which includes the following provisions:

☐ Software programmes should be protected where they are original, in the sense that they are the result of their creator's own intellectual effort and are not commonplace in the industry.

☐ There should be no protection for the specification of interfaces which constitute ideas and principles underlying the program. This is a very contentious issue.

☐ There should be a right to prevent unauthorised use. It will be an infringement to network a programme amongst several computers unless this is specifically licensed.

☐ The duration of the term of protection should be 50 years.

☐ Protection should extend to programs fixed in any form.

The proposal has generated animated discussions within the software industry, especially on two issues — reverse engineering and copyright protection of interface information. It is not yet clear whether the Directive will be adopted in the near future and/or whether the present text will be amended.

Databases

The Commission recognises that the provision of computer databases is now a substantial industry, and that is and likely to become more so when memory discs can carry sufficient capacity. It recommends that the mode of compilation of the database be protectable — that there is a separate right, owned by the database operator [over and above the underlying literary copyright of what is in the database] which is either a copyright or a *sui generis* right. The Commission planned that a draft Directive would be put forward before the end of 1990.

As copyright issues impinge more directly on the general public than the more commercially-based patents and trade marks, it is likely that there will be intensive lobbying to garner public sympathy and politics may well play a very significant role in any final decision.

EXTERNAL POLICY

Apart from the so-called 'internal' developments on intellectual property rights in the EC, the Community is also increasingly involved in the world intellectual property scene. In addition to the Regulation on counterfeit goods which deals with imports of such products from third countries, the Community is also very active in GATT (General Agreement on Tariffs and Trade) negotiations on TRIPS (Trade Related Intellectual Property Rights). It has recently submitted a draft agreement for consideration by the other GATT members which deals, *inter alia*, with worldwide standards of protection and enforcement of intellectual property rights.

In 1984 the Council also passed a new trade policy instrument, *The New Commercial Policy Instrument* (NCPI) (No. 2641/84 *OJ* L252 of 20.09.84) which enables the Community to take action, ranging from the initiation of international consultation procedures to the adoption of import quotas into the EC, in response to what it sees as illicit commercial practices of another country. Three of the four cases under the NCPI which have received publicity concerned intellectual property.

In March 1987 the International Federation of Phonogram and Videogram Producers complained that Indonesia allowed unauthorised reproduction of sound recordings by not giving protection to works of Community nationals. After discussions, Indonesia agreed (on the basis of reciprocity) to grant copyright protection to Community nationals. If it had not done so, it may well have had sanctions taken against it (eg. raising of customs dues, trade barriers, withdrawals of GSP (Generalised Scheme of Preferences) benefits etc).

In another case the Commission has used its powers against an allegedly discriminatory application of Section 337 of the US Táriff Act of 1930. The case was initiated by a complaint made by Akzo that its products were banned from the US market on the grounds that they infringed Dupont's US patents. The complaint was based on the fact that the ban was issued by the US International Trade Commission (ITC) and, according to the complaint, the procedures followed by the ITC were different (ie. less favourable to foreign respondents) from those governing patent litigation in the US Federal Courts. The Commission referred the matter to a GATT panel which concluded that the US legislation accords less favourable treatment to imported patented products than that to products of US origin.

The Commission also suggests the signing of more bilateral treaties and agreements in the intellectual property field. Korea has already been subjected to a tough stand as the Council has agreed to suspend generalised tariff preferences for goods of Korean origin, as it was felt that Korea was procrastinating over a bilateral agreement concerning intellectual property rights.

LEGISLATION

Convention for the European Patent for the Common Market (Community Patent Convention)
   Council Decision 76/76 — *OJ* L17, 23.1.76.
   Regulation (2349/84) on the Application of the EEC Treaty to Article 85(3) to Certain Categories of Patent Licensing Agreements
   Official Journal reference: *OJ* L219, 16.8.84
Proposal for a Regulation on Community Trade Marks
   Commission documents COM(80)635 and COM(84)470, *OJ* C230, 31.8.84.
Regulation (2641/84) on the Strengthening of the Common Commercial Policy with regard in Particular to Protection Against Illicit Commercial Practices
   New Commercial Policy Instrument (NCPI)
   Official Journal reference: *OJ* L252, 20.9.84
Proposal for a Regulation of the Rules Needed for Implementing the Community Trade Mark Regulation
   Commission document COM(85)844
Regulation (3842/86) Laying Down Measures to Prohibit the Release for Free Circulation of Counterfeit Goods
   Official Journal reference: *OJ* L357, 18.12.86
Proposal for a Regulation on Rules of Procedure for the Boards of Appeal of the Community's Trade Mark Office
   Commission document COM(86)731
Directive (87/54) on Legal Protection of Topographies of Semiconductor Products
   Official Journal reference: *OJ* L24, 27.1.87
Proposal for a Regulation on Fees Payable to the Community Trade Mark Office
   Commission document COM(86)742, *OJ* C67, 14.3.87
Proposal for a Directive on Legal Protection of Computer Programmes
   Commission document COM(88)816
Draft Regulation on the Community Trade Mark
   5865/88 of 11.5.88
Decision (88/311) on the Extension of Legal Protection of Topographies of Semiconductor Products in Respect of Persons from Certain Countries and Territories
   Official Journal reference: *OJ* L140, 7.6.88
Regulation (4084/88) on the Application of Article 85(3) of the EC Treaty to Categories of Franchising Agreements
   Official Journal reference: *OJ* L359, 28.12.88
Proposal for a Directive on Legal Protection of Biotechnical Inventions
   Commission document COM(88)496, *OJ* C10, 13.1.89

First Directive on the Approximation of the Laws of Member States Relating to Trade Marks
    Directive 89/104 *OJ* L40, 11.2.89
Regulation (556/89) on the Application of Article 85(3) of the EEC Treaty to Know-How Licensing Agreements
    Official Journal reference: *OJ* L61, 4.3.89
Commission Proposal for a Directive Protecting the Copyright of Computer Programmes
    Commission document COM(88)816. *OJ* C91, 12.4.89
    Community Patent Convention Amending Regulation
    Regulation 89/695, *OJ* L401, 30.12.89
Commission Proposal for a Regulation Introducing a Patent Term Restoration Certificate
    Commission Proposal N90 *OJ* C114, 1990

Legislative texts
Copies of legislative texts can be purchased from Alan Armstrong Limited (below), and from Government (HMSO) bookshops, quoting the *OJ* reference which consists of the number of the legal instrument and the date of issue in the *Official Journal (OJ)*, ie. Regulation 4021/87, *OJ* L378, 31.12 87. Texts appear in hard copy and on microfiche. For details of the series published in the *Official Journal* see *European Community Publications*, Part Eight, Chapter 1. Texts can also be examined at European Documentation Centres and other libraries (see *Libraries*, Part Eight, Chapter 3), and accessed through on-line databases (Part Eight, Chapter 2).

HMSO Books
PO Box 276
London SW8 5DT
Tel: (071) 873 0011 (enquiries); (071) 873 9090 (telephone orders).
Fax: (071) 873 8463
Telex: 297138

(HMSO Bookshops: Belfast, Birmingham, Bristol, Edinburgh, London and Manchester, plus 40 bookshops acting as agents for HMSO throughout the UK)

Alan Armstrong Limited
2 Arkwright Road
Reading RG2 0SQ
Tel: (0734) 751855
Fax: (0734) 755164
Telex: 849937 AAATD G

CONTACTS

European Commission

Commission of the European Communities
Directorate-General III/D/4
Internal Market and Industrial Affairs
Rue de la Loi 200
1049 Brussels
Tel: (32) 2 235 1111
Telex: 21877 COMEU B

Patent Offices

European Patent Office
Erhardtstrasse 27
D-8000 Munich 2
Tel: (49) 89 2399-0

Patent Office
Industrial Property and Copyright
Department
State House
66-71 High Holborn
London WC1R 4TP
Tel: (071) 829 6134/831 2525
Fax: (071) 405 0292

Representative organisations

Confederation of British Industry (CBI)
Company and Commercial Law Group
Centre Point
103 New Oxford Street
London WC1A 1DU
Tel: (071) 379 7400
Fax: (071) 240 1578
Telex: 21332

**Common Law Institute of Intellectual
Property (CLIP)**
Charles Clore House
17 Russell Square
London WC1B 5DR
Tel: (071) 637 1721

**Association of Trade Mark Proprietors
(MARQUES)**
852 Melton Road
Thurmaston
Leicester LE4 8BN
Tel: (0533) 640080
Fax: (0533) 640141

Chartered Institute of Patent Agents (CIPA)
Staple Inn
High Holborn
London WC1V 7PZ
Tel: (071) 405 9450
Fax: (071) 430 0471

**Institute of International Licensing
Practitioners (IILP)**
78 Kent House
87 Regent Street
London W1
Tel: (071) 439 7091

Institute of Trade Mark Agents
4th Floor, Canterbury House
2-6 Sydenham Road
Croydon
Surrey CR0 9XE
Tel: (081) 686 2052

PART SEVEN

THE
INFORMATION
NETWORK

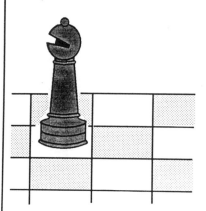

1 The Brussels Connection

Institutions of the European Community

Roland King

The European Community (EC) comprises three Communities which share the same institutions. Through interaction between the institutions, Community legislation and policy is formed and adopted. The European Commission, for example, is the institution which administers the activities of the European Economic Community (EEC), the European Coal and Steel Community (ECSC) and the European Atomic Energy Community (EURATOM). All three Communities were established in the 1950's, as explained in the introduction to this book which charts the steps towards European unity taken since World War II. In one important step, the 1965 Treaty of Brussels merged all the administrative bodies of the three Communities into unified institutions to co-ordinate the activities of the EC as a whole. The primary objective of the Single European Act, signed in 1986, is to establish significant further progress towards European economic, monetary and political union by the end of 1992. The institutions of the Community are thus committed to bringing measures to complete the Single Market into being by this date. This chapter outlines the work of the main institutions as well as lesser known institutions, such as the European Court of Auditors, whose activities have a bearing on business. Further details of the work of the Community's institutions are given in a range of publications (See *European Community Publications*, Part Eight, Chapter 1)

Each of the EC's institutions fulfills an important function, and together they are responsible for all aspects of EC affairs. Most people are acquainted only with the activities of the following main institutions:

□   European Commission (Full title — The Commission of the European Communities)

□   Council of Ministers

□   European Parliament

□   Economic and Social Committee

□   European Court of Justice

□   European Investment Bank

□   Court of Auditors

EUROPEAN COMMISSION

The European Commission is headed by 17 Commissioners, appointed for four year renewable terms of office by the Council of Ministers on nomination by their national governments. Each of the twelve EC member states has either one or two Commissioners:

Belgium	1
Denmark	1
France	2
Germany	2
Greece	1
Ireland	1
Italy	2
Luxembourg	1
Netherlands	1
Portugal	1
Spain	2
United Kingdom	2

Although Commissioners are nominated by their national governments, they swear an oath renouncing the defence of national interests while in office. This is not an empty gesture. The Commissioners are invariably Community-minded, as demonstrated by the fact that they sometimes have no choice but to incur the displeasure of national politicians by adhering firmly to Community aims. This is what is meant by 'going native', an unfair accusation since national governments are in no doubt about the role of the Commissioners they nominate. The Commissioners are supported by an administrative staff of 12,000 EC civil servants. Some 9,000 Commission employees are translators, assistants, secretaries and drivers, etc. This leaves 3,000 actual administrators running the daily activities. Community civil servants are not, however, nominated by national governments, though in some cases they may serve the Commission for a few years on 'secondment' from a national government department. The degree of interest taken by national governments in attaching civil servants to Community institutions varies. It is a distinct policy of the French government, for example, to encourage its civil servants to work in Community institutions and then return to work in France. By contrast, the British government has not so far favoured such a concerted policy of attachment. However, the staff of the Commission is naturally comprised of nationals from all Community member states, whether or not on a tour of duty from national administrations.

The Commission has a President (currently Jacques Delors) and five Vice-presidents, initially chosen from among the 17 Commissioners for two-year terms of office. But, in practice, this has been extended to four years almost automatically.

Each Commissioner is responsible for several portfolios and has a Cabinet to advise and assist. Cabinet staff are political appointees and work closely with their Commissioner. The *Chef de Cabinet* is considered to be the Commissioner's deputy. Commissioners head at least one of the 23 Directorates-General (DG) within the Commission covering broad areas of EC activity as follows:

DGI	External Relations
DGII	Economic and Financial Affairs
DGIII	Internal Market and Industrial Affairs
DGIV	Competition
DGV	Employment, Social Affairs and Education
DGVI	Agriculture
DGVII	Transport
DGVIII	Development
DGIX	Personnel and Administration
DGX	Information, Communication and Culture
DGXI	Environment, Consumer Protection and Nuclear Safety
DGXII	Science, Research and Development
DGXIII	Telecommunications, Information Industries and Innovation
DGXIV	Fisheries
DGXV	Financial Institutions and Company Law
DGXVI	Regional policy
DGXVII	Energy
DGXVIII	Credit and Investments
DGXIX	Budgets
DGXX	Financial Control
DGXXI	Customs Union and Indirect Taxation
DGXXII	Co-ordination of Structural Instruments
DGXXIII	Company Policy, Commerce, Tourism and Employment Relations, Small and Medium-Sized Enterprises (SMEs), SME Task Force.

Function of the European Commission

The Commission is the executive arm of the Community. It conceives and drafts proposals for new legislation for consideration by other Community institutions and eventual adoption by the Council of Ministers. It is the only EC institution with the right to initiate this kind of action, as laid down in the constitution of the EC established by the founding Treaties. However, the Council of Ministers and the European Parliament can also request the Commission to review certain issues and draft proposals. The Commission is also responsible for:

Administering EC expenditure
Implementing Community policies
Enforcing the provisions of the Treaties
Monitoring the implementation and application of EC legislation

Before presenting a draft proposal to the Council for consideration, various interest groups may, and in certain cases must, be consulted for their opinion on how proposed legislation will affect them directly or those they represent. For example, since 1986 all proposals must be accompanied by a report discussing the impact legislation will have on small and medium-sized enterprises (SMEs). The interests of SME's are also monitored by the EC's Economic and Social Committee which meets in Brussels and has a right to be consulted for an opinion.

The Commission's weekly meeting is chaired by the President. Individual Commissioners submit first drafts of proposed measures for discussion. Most proposals will have already been discussed in technical meetings as well as by the *Chefs de Cabinet*. Voting by the Commission is based on the simple principle, one Commissioner, one vote. Once accepted by the Commission, a proposal is submitted for further scrutiny, perhaps over a period of some years, at each stage of the legislative process, now amended by the New Co-operation Procedure.

In its capacity as the enforcement arm of the Community, the Commission monitors the progress of legislation through all stages of the procedure and it issues implementing instructions and ensures compliance by member states. (For a detailed description of Community law see *European Community Law*, Part Six, Chapter 1). Any EC-based business or individual has the right to file a complaint with the Commission if it is believed that an infringement of Community law has taken place. Complaints should be addressed to the Secretariat-General of the European Commission, Brussels.

General complaints about EC proposals may be sent to the Commission but companies with grounds to be concerned about the impact of legislation on their operation are advised to seek the support of interest groups, such as trade associations, and other representative bodies including government departments. Local MEP's may also be prepared to intervene in the interests of companies in their constituencies, as will members of the Economic and Social Committee, especially where the interests of a wider or vulnerable industrial sector are at risk. There are many avenues of protest and inquiry. In some cases, British government departments issue detailed consultative documents setting out the terms of proposed legislation and inviting comment from interested parties. These helpful memoranda are sometimes distributed automatically to interested parties on a mailing list. Where EC proposals attract widespread opposition, as in the case of the Social Charter, national government ministers are likely to voice their protest at meetings of the Council of Ministers, often having taken the views of interest groups such as small firms organisations, trade federations or professional bodies.

The European Commission and business

As initiator as well as enforcer of legislation, the Commission influences and shapes the practical working environment for European business, setting the pace and extent of European integration. The overall aim, of course, is to establish a barrier-free European market complete with homogenised rules and practices in which businesses can operate in an atmosphere of free and fair competition. The competition rules are to be extended to cover other areas of business life as the Single Market programme continues and, as has been the case in the past, the rules will be rigidly enforced.

Aside from this overall task, the Commission is engaged in closer liaison with business than most people realise. Virtually as a way of life Commission officials are in contact with national government departments, special interest groups, and even individual companies. It is of strategic importance for companies to know the key players in the Commission involved in their sector, or at least be in touch with any representative body, such as a trade association, which may be involved in discussions with the Commission about proposed legislation. Most trade organisations, including chambers of commerce, publish newsletters which serve as pointers to forthcoming Single Market developments. Where direct contact with the Commission or trade bodies is not necessary, companies can keep up to date with events by obtaining copies of the many free booklets and explanatory documents published by the EC. The Commission, however, makes a determined effort to inform business through its publishing activities, mainly through the Office for Official Publications of the European Community (See *European Community Publications*, Part Eight, Chapter 1), and through a network of information offices and libraries which extends throughout all member states.

European Information Centres

Sometimes known as Euro-Info-Centres, this network of business contact points was launched in 1987. There are now well over 150 centres located throughout the twelve EC countries to aid in decentralising information on Community activities. One of the main goals is to inform industry about Community affairs and to provide contacts for further information. The project is administered by the Directorate-General for Company policy, Commerce, Tourism and Employment Relations (DGXXIII). Company managers can direct their enquiries about the facts of EC legislation and policy to local Euro-Info-Centres. Enquiries about the impact on their business or sector should also be addressed to interest groups and/ or contacts in the relevant national government department who will be aware of any perceived disadvantages. On the whole, however, EC legislation has positive benefits for business without incurring serious disadvantages, despite the publicity given to contentious issues such as the proposal for a Social Charter. (For a list of UK-based Euro-Info-Centres see *CONTACTS* at the end of this chapter).

Business Co-operation Centre (BCC)

The BCC was established by the Commission in 1973. The BCC assists businesses, particularly SME's, to enter collaboration agreements. The basis for joint activities ranges from technology sharing to finance. The BCC, sometimes referred to as the 'marriage bureau' of the Community, has initiated several schemes to encourage SME's:

Business Co-operation Network (BC-Net): A computerised system linking hundreds of business contacts throughout the EC. These contacts, sometimes consultants, can access the BC-Net system to search for companies which match the request. So far, more than 10,000 company profiles have been transmitted through the system. Indications are that there is at least one potential technical match per profile, although the usable rate is around 15 per cent. BC-Net is co-ordinated by the Business Co-operation Centre, Brussels (address at end of chapter).

Euro-partnership programmes: These programmes are designed to encourage co-operation with companies in underdeveloped or declining regions in the EC. A listing of companies, describing their activities and the type of agreement being sought, is available. Interested companies may attend regional meetings to obtain details or enter negotiations with other companies. Programmes have involved more than 200 companies and had more than 300 participants.

Promotion of transnational subcontracting: In 1988 the Commission organised a conference in Brussels on sub-contracting in Europe. The programme included workshops to discuss 'relations between main contractors and sub-contractors' and 'the search for partners', among other topics. The Commission is developing programmes and publications to promote the growth of sub-contracting business throughout the EC.

INFO 92

This database provides information in all Community languages on Single Market developments (See *EC On-line Databases*, Part Eight, Chapter 2). A Commission publication describing data banks is available, listing them by economic sector with details on the type of information held, price and means of access. The booklet can be obtained from the Office for Official Publications in Luxembourg or Commission Information Offices in the EC (See *European Community Publications*, Part Eight, Chapter 1 and *EC On-line Databases*, Part Eight, Chapter 2).

COUNCIL OF MINISTERS

The Council is the Community's highest authority, agreeing policy and adopting new legislation at Council meetings which take place about 80 times a year. The composition of the Council varies according to the topic on the agenda. Each member state is represented by one minister at any Council meeting, usually the minister whose portfolio parallels the subject being discussed by the Council. The Foreign Affairs Council will be attended by foreign ministers of the EC. Likewise the Social Affairs Council is attended by employment ministers. All main areas of government activity are covered. The Council's schedule of meetings includes the much publicised, twice-yearly meetings attended by heads of government known as the European Council or European Summit . At these meetings policy options and guidelines for Community activities are emphasised or laid down.

The presidency of the Council is held by each member state in alphabetical rotation, using the vernacular spelling of a country's name (Deutschland, Espana etc.), for a period of six months. Thus the order of presidencies is:

Belgium (Belgie)
Denmark (Danmark)
Germany (Deutschland)
Greece (Ellas)
Spain (Espana)
France
Ireland
Italy (Italia)
Luxembourg (Luxemburg)
Netherlands (Nederland)
Portugal
United Kingdom

Procedure

The examination of proposals is carried out by working parties made up of national officials. Commission representatives also attend to defend the Commission's views. The number of working parties varies according to needs. They are set up and disbanded by the Committee of Permanent Representatives

(COREPER — the French acronym for the Committee), but the supervision of proceedings is handled by the President of the Council. COREPER is the secretariat of the Council and is made up of senior ambassadors and their staff appointed by member states. The UK 'ambassador' to Brussels is know as the UK Permanent Representative to the European Communities. The Permanent Representative's office, close to the the main Commission building, is known as UKREP.

The role of COREPER is to prepare the Council meetings, reviewing the agenda, discussing proposed legislation and aiming to reach informal agreement prior to Council meetings when ministers take the final decision on whether or not to adopt a proposal. COREPER also negotiates with the Commission, serving as the direct representatives of the member states in Brussels. COREPER's workload is such that the Committee has been split. The ambassadors sit on COREPER II which deals with the most politically sensitive issues. The Deputy Permanent Representatives sit on COREPER I which deals with all other issues. A third committee, composed of agricultural experts, works on agri-business matters.

When a proposal is sent to the Council, after consultations with the European Parliament and the Economic and Social Committee (ECOSOC), the first stage of review is carried out by a Council Working Party. The Working Party submits its opinions to COREPER and COREPER decides whether or not to confirm the Working Party's opinion. If confirmed, the proposal is put before the Council. Proposals are categorsied as A or B items. Type A items are those on which Council approval is likely to be given without controversy. Type B items are those likely to need discussion on points of disagreement uncovered at Working Party or COREPER level.

Voting

The Single European Act introduced the principle of majority voting as a means of avoiding deadlock on proposals if one member state exercises a veto. Previously, delays in adopting new legislation had sometimes frustrated progress. A vote may be taken by simple majority or qualified majority. Qualified majority has become the most frequently used method of voting. However, the majority voting system does not apply in every case. Some measures still require a unanimous vote. They include fiscal matters, enlargement of the Community and environmental action. Abstentions do not preclude the adoption of decisions which require unanimity. Under qualified majority ballot, each member state has a weighted vote, roughly proportionate to the size of its economy, as follows:

Belgium: 5 votes
Denmark: 3 votes
Germany: 10 votes
Greece: 5 votes
France: 10 votes
Ireland: 3 votes
Italy: 10 votes
Luxembourg: 2 votes
Netherlands: 5 votes
Portugal: 5 votes
Spain: 8 votes
United Kingdom: 10 votes

Co-operation procedure

The co-operation procedure is a development arising from the Single European Act, and the procedure gives the European Parliament the opportunity to read a proposal twice. The second reading takes place when the Council reaches a 'common position'. In other words, after the first reading in the Parliament, the Council reviews a proposal for the second time and reaches a common position, taking into account the views of all member states. This amended proposal is then resubmitted to the Parliament for a second review. If the Parliament rejects the common position or proposes changes, it must do so by absolute majority of its members. At this point a proposal may be referred back to the Commission for review, and the Commission may incorporate some or all of the proposed amendments. The Council then has three options:

□   In a qualified majority vote, the Council can adopt the Commission's proposal.

□   In a unanimous vote, the Council may amend the proposal.

□   In a unanimous vote, the Council can adopt any amendments proposed by the Parliament not accepted by the Commission.

Every stage in the co-operation procedure has a set time limit to ensure that the decision-making process is not brought to a halt.

Council Acts: There are four types of measure, varying in the degree to which they may be binding on member states or individuals and in the method of implementation. For a detailed survey of Community law refer to *European Community Law*, Part Six, Chapter 1. The four categories of Act or measure are:

Regulations: Legally binding on member states, applied and enforced directly by the Commission. In any conflict with national law, EC Regulations prevail. Regulations are published in the *Official Journal of the European Communities* and, unless otherwise noted, take effect 20 days after publication.

Directives: Legally binding, but require national authorities to pass enabling legislation. It is up to member states to ensure that EC Directives are fully implemented to become part of their national law. Directives are effective upon publication in the *Official Journal*.

Decisions: Decisions are taken on specific issues and are directly binding on the parties named in the Decision. They are effective upon notification.

Recommendations and Opinions: Not legally binding, but should be monitored by interested parties since they may indicate developments in current and future policy.

The European Council and business

The Council is relatively closed to public access except via the national political process. The best means of obtaining information on Council business is through the Permanent Representatives of member states, who have knowledge of the scheduling of meetings on any particular proposal and its current status. It is important to grasp that, although the Council is the decision-making authority for EC legislation, it can only act on proposals drafted by the Commission, and consults many interested parties prior to finally adopting a proposal. Lobbying

EC LEGISLATIVE PROCESS

CO-OPERATION PROCEDURE

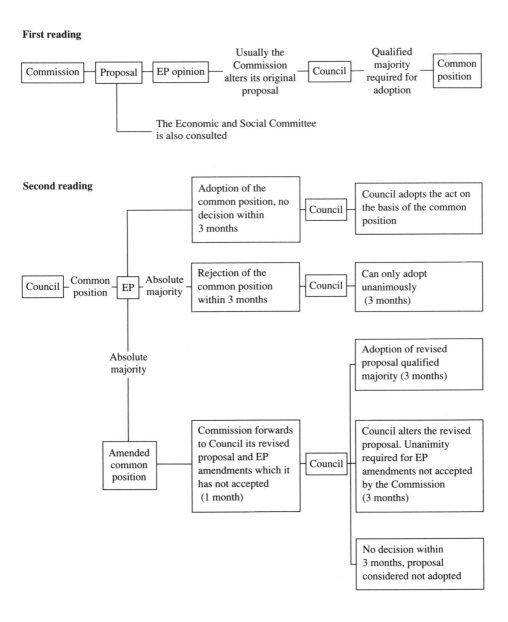

First reading

Commission — Proposal — EP opinion — Usually the Commission alters its original proposal — Council — Qualified majority required for adoption — Common position

The Economic and Social Committee is also consulted

Second reading

Council — Common position — EP

Absolute majority — Adoption of the common position, no decision within 3 months — Council — Council adopts the act on the basis of the common position

Absolute majority — Rejection of the common position within 3 months — Council — Can only adopt unanimously (3 months)

Absolute majority — Amended common position — Commission forwards to Council its revised proposal and EP amendments which it has not accepted (1 month) — Council

Adoption of revised proposal qualified majority (3 months)

Council alters the revised proposal. Unanimity required for EP amendments not accepted by the Commission (3 months)

No decision within 3 months, proposal considered not adopted

Source: The European Parliament: *Ten Years that Changed Europe*

385

efforts can be most effective in influencing the Commission if channelled through both the member state mission to the EC and the national governments themselves.

Council directory
The directory contains a list of the Permanent Representatives to the EC, plus their addresses and telephone numbers in Brussels, and lists current members of working parties and committees. Copies are available from the Office for Official Publications of the European Communities, Luxembourg.

EUROPEAN PARLIAMENT

The European Parliament represents the interests of the citizens of the European Community in the development of EC policy and legislation. The Parliament has 518 directly elected members (MEPs), elected for a five year term. The most recent elections were held in June 1989. The President of the European Parliament is elected by the MEPs for a two and a half year term. There are also 14 Vice-Presidents, elected for the duration of the Presidential term. The number of MEPs representing constituencies in each member state is fixed according to the size of the country:

Belgium: 24
Denmark: 16
Germany: 81
Greece: 24
France: 81
Ireland: 15
Italy: 81
Luxembourg: 6
Netherlands: 25
Portugal: 24
Spain: 60
United Kingdom: 81

MEPs do not, however, sit in national groups, but in political groups, the largest after the 1989 Euro-elections being the Socialist Group with 180 members. Next comes the European People's Party with 121 members. There are nine other political groups representing the remaining 217 members. As one would expect, various political alignments between groups take place, especially where small parties feel they can extend their influence by informal alliances. Of the 81 British MEPs, the majority are Socialists following the 1989 Euro-elections in which the European Democrats (Conservatives) lost their majority. This means that in the current term, Britain is represented at Strasbourg by a stronger Socialist faction, even though Conservatives hold a large majority at Westminster.

Function of the European Parliament

The European Parliament does not have the power to enact legislation, though its influence has been gradually extending since the first Euro-elections in 1979. Plenary sessions are held in Strasbourg during one week per month, except August. Other sessions may be scheduled for important issues. Committee meetings take place in Brussels at other times in the month. Political groups meet in Brussels and other venues as they decide. The Parliament's secretariat is in Luxembourg. Despite its limited formal powers, the Parliament wields significant influence in the performance of several important functions. The main powers of the Parliament are:

□   To give opinions and submit amendments to proposals for Community legislation, under its constitutional rights as laid down in the founding Treaties.

□   To adopt or reject the Community's annual budget.

□   To exercise control over implementation of the budget.

□   To submit questions to the Commission and the Council. The Commission is obliged to answer, but the Council is not.

□   To dismiss the Commission, though to date this has never occurred.

As with all EC institutions, since all EC nationalities are represented, debates and meetings are co-ordinated with simultaneous translation/interpretation into the nine official languages of the Community. Minutes of proceedings are published in different languages in various forms, including a series nicknamed the 'Rainbow' because it bears the document colour representing each member state. Britain's colour is purple. Details of published proceedings are given in *European Community Publications*, Part Eight, Chapter 1.

In accordance with the Treaty of Rome establishing the European Economic Community (EEC), the Council of Ministers is obliged to consult the European Parliament on European Commission proposals relating to certain types of Community activity, including the Common Agricultural Policy, the free movement of goods, and the completion of the Community's internal market (1992 programme). When the Parliament receives a request for an opinion, the President of the Parliament refers the request to the appropriate committee (see below). The committee reviews the proposal to determine its legal validity and then either amends it, accepts it as it stands, or rejects it.

During parliamentary plenary sessions, debates are held on committee reports, special issues and statements received from the Commission, the Council, political groups and individual MEPs. After a debate, the Parliament votes first on the amendments to the proposal and then on the draft legislative resolution. If a proposal does not attract a majority vote, the President of the Parliament may ask the Commission to withdraw the proposal. In such instances, a proposal may be redrafted and resubmitted.

There are exceptions to this basic procedure. Under the "Urgent Procedure" a debate is limited to one speaker in favour and one against. The chairman of the committee, or the rapporteur, is usually responsible and may be heard before the Parliament votes. On certain less urgent matters, Commission proposals can be approved without report or debate.

Parliamentary committees

Committees prepare reports on matters referred to them for an opinion. In each case a 'rapporteur' is appointed to draft the report and present it to the committee and to the Parliament during plenary sessions. Committee meetings are closed to the public, except in special situations when a committee may request a public hearing. In such cases, a committee can invite experts and interest groups to give evidence. There are 18 committees:

      Political Affairs
      Agriculture, Fisheries and Rural Development
      Budgets
      Economic and Monetary Affairs and Industrial Policy
      Energy, Research and Technology
      External Economic Relations
      Legal Affairs and Citizens' Rights
      Social Affairs, Employment and the Working Environment
      Regional Policy and Regional Planning
      Transport and Tourism
      Environment, Public Health and Consumers
      Development and Co-operation
      Youth Culture, Education, the Media and Sport
      Budgetary Control
      Institutional Affairs
      Rules of Procedure, the Verification of Credentials and Immunities
      Women's Rights
      Petitions

The European Parliament and business

Petitions
Individually or collectively, every EC citizen, company or organisation has the right to file a petition and defend personal or group interests at Community level. Although the European Parliament is not a judicial body, it offers a means of resolving Problems through consultation with Community authorities. Petitions are often filed when unfair treatment or loss is suffered as a result of a conflict between national law and Community law. The types of problem giving rise to petitions include customs or VAT questions, the provision of services in different member states, capital movement and transport of goods. It is important for business to know that petitions may be filed with the Parliament on any matter relating to EC law, Decisions and Communications from EC institutions, and international agreements to which the EC is a party.

Petitions are referred by the President of the Parliament to the parliamentary committee dealing with the subject matter. However, the admissibility of a petition is determined by the petition Committee, made up of 25 members with proportional national and political representation. Once a petition is admitted, the committee investigates the laws which apply to determine if they are adequate and have been correctly applied. This stage in the procedure may be followed by a hearing and contact with the Commission before a parliamentary Resolution is drawn up. If the results are not satisfactory to the petitioner, the matter can be referred to the European Court of Justice (See *European Community Law*, Part Six, Chapter 1). To file a petition:

☐   A complaint must be in writing, in any EC language.

☐   A complaint must be signed and include the name, address, nationality, and occupation of the petitioner(s).

Petitions and any supporting documentation should be sent to the President of the European Parliament, L-2929 Luxembourg.

Any company or individual considering filing a petition is advised to contact their local MEP. MEPs have been extremely helpful in securing benefits for constituents, despite having a comparatively low political profile. They are also, of course, acquainted with the petition procedure, and may know of similar petitions; and they may be prepared to advise on the content and presentation of a petition. It is, in any case, useful for MEPs to be apprised of problems occurring in the areas they represent, especially when important industrial or commercial interests are at stake. The Parliament publishes a list of members, sometimes known as the *Grey List* (See *European Community Publications*, Part Eight, Chapter 1). European Parliament offices in the UK may also provide the name and address of MEPs.

ECONOMIC AND SOCIAL COMMITTEE

The Economic and Social Committee (ECOSOC) is an advisory body comprised of representatives of employees, trades unions, the professions and other interest groups in the European Community. An alternative, formal title — Economic and Social Consultative Assembly — is still retained on documents. Plenary sessions are held in Brussels every month and, as in other EC institutions, the detailed work is allocated to committees. ECOSOC is important to business as a forum for discussion which directly represents the interests of industry and commerce, generally any economic grouping, in the EC's decision-making and law-making processes. The 189 members of ECOSOC serve for four year terms and are nominated by national governments of the member states:

Belgium: 12 members
Denmark: 9 members
France: 24 members
Germany: 24 members
Greece: 12 members
Ireland: 9 members
Italy: 24 members
Luxembourg: 6 members
Netherlands: 12 members
Portugal: 12 members
Spain: 21 members
United Kingdom: 24 members

ECOSOC has eight sections dealing with broad sectors of industrial and social interest:

- Agriculture and fisheries
- Industry, commerce, crafts and services
- Economic, financial and monetary questions
- Social, family, educational and cultural affairs
- Transport and communications
- External relations, trade and development
- Energy, nuclear questions and research
- Regional development and town and country planning
- Protection of the environment, public health and consumer affairs

THE ECONOMIC AND SOCIAL COMMITTEE

Genesis of opinions

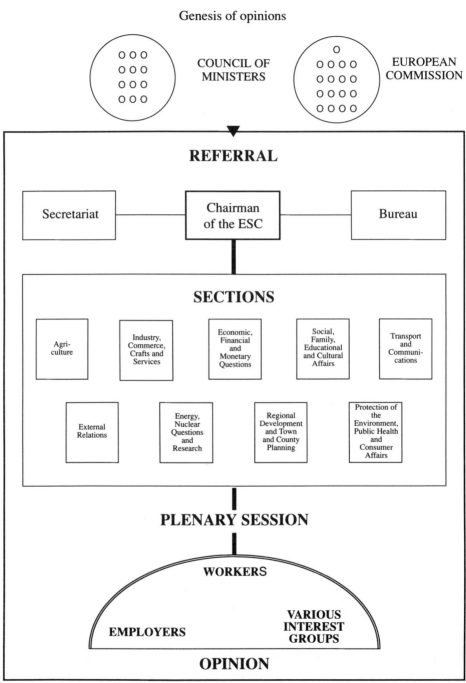

COUNCIL OF
MINISTERS

EUROPEAN
COMMISSION

REFERRAL

| Secretariat | Chairman of the ESC | Bureau |

SECTIONS

| Agri-culture | Industry, Commerce, Crafts and Services | Economic, Financial and Monetary Questions | Social, Family, Educational and Cultural Affairs | Transport and Communi-cations |

| External Relations | Energy, Nuclear Questions and Research | Regional Development and Town and County Planning | Protection of the Environment, Public Health and Consumer Affairs |

PLENARY SESSION

WORKERS

EMPLOYERS

VARIOUS
INTEREST
GROUPS

OPINION

Source: Economic and Social Committee

The committee's chief practical function on behalf of business is to scrutinise EC proposals and suggest amendments. Members are in close touch with the Commission, the Council and officials in their own countries. In certain circumstances ECOSOC is asked for its opinion on Commission proposals, the ECOSOC reading taking place simultaneously with the European Parliament's first reading. The committee may also pass opinions on its own initiative. Although ECOSOC's opinions are not binding on the other institutions, they are taken into consideration as representing the views of employers, trades unions, professions or other interested parties affected by a proposal. Many Commission proposals have been amended, or even dropped, as a result of ECOSOC's intervention.

Any company which feels strongly about possible adverse affects of proposals under discussion should, if they intend to make representation, approach the ECOSOC committee involved and the UK member or members representing the interests affected. A list of members may be held by various libraries or other sources mentioned in this guide. It is also obtainable direct from ECOSOC.

In a booklet *The Other European Assembly*, published by the Committee's Public Relations, Press and Information Division, ECOSOC's role is described as representing those 'active in economic and social life'. The Single European Act confirms the role of ECOSOC in the co-operation procedure by which EC legislation is formulated and discussed between the EC institutions, prior to final adoption by the Council of Ministers. Much as the work of ECOSOC goes unnoticed by ordinary EC citizens. It is hard to imagine how a legislative process could work efficiently without the direct input from an institution representing everyone in the workplace. ECOSOC is, however, concerned with the overall shaping and development of EC policy, in particular the completion of the Single Market, issuing opinions and reports urging the Commission and other institutions to press ahead with reforms. *The Economic and Social Committee Supports the Removal of Fiscal Frontiers*, published in 1988, is one example of an ECOSOC study which focuses on key areas of reform. This 75-page document, subtitled *Horizon 1992* states: 'The Committee fully endorses the aim of removing all frontiers and all border checks by 1 January 1993, including those checks now made for the collection of indirect taxes (VAT and excise duties).' Unfortunately, in October 1989, the Council of Ministers postponed a decision to adopt measures to restructure the VAT collection system throughout the Community which would have eased the burden of formalities at frontiers.

As a source of information for business. ECOSOC studies and briefing material are useful surveys of policies and proposals under discussion and an indication of the way that the three main ECOSOC groups — the Employers' Group, the Workers' Group and the Various Interests Group — expect to see the Community develop. A selection of ECOSOC publications is listed in *European Community Publications*, Part Eight, Chapter 1.

EUROPEAN COURT OF JUSTICE

The Court of Justice, based in Luxembourg, is the supreme judicial body of the European Community. The Court interprets the Treaties establishing the Communities, rules on legal disputes, and resolves disputes involving other EC institutions. The President of the Court Directs the work of the Court, fixing schedules and assigning cases to the 13 Judges. The Court of First Instance handles cases involving competition, and disputes between EC civil servants and their employers. For a full description of the Court, its jurisdiction and procedures, see *European Community Law*, Part Six, Chapter 1.

The European Court and business

The court assists industry and commerce by effectively banning measures, through case law, which restrict or prohibit trade between EC member states. Although competition complaints are usually handled by the EC Commission's Directorate-General for Competition (DGIV), companies have the right to appeal to the Court against Commission decisions and fines. Some decisions have been upheld by the Court, some have been annulled and others altered.

When complaints are dealt with by national Courts of member states, the European Court can issue preliminary rulings interpreting Community law, if a national Court so requests. The case is then referred to the national Court for a final decision. In circumstances where a company or individual considers that national laws infringe upon their rights as EC citizens (or businesses), national Courts will refer the case to the European Court. If the Court finds that a member state has not complied with its Treaty obligations, the Court ruling is likely to lead to national comformity to EC law. The principal is that EC law takes precedence where national and EC laws conflict and, in practice, national law is made to conform with EC law when the European Court passes judgement upholding EC law. However, it has been argued that, in a strict legal sense, the sovereignty of national Parliaments remains intact, that the supremacy of EC law is accepted by member states insofar as it relates to a country's EC Treaty obligations, and that member states have not abandoned the ultimate sanction, that of withdrawal from the Community by means of a referendum[1]. It is generally accepted that, in the present political climate in Europe, such an eventuality is unlikely.

1 *Why the state is subject to the will of the people*, John Barnes, The Guardian, 3 January 1990.

European Investment Bank

The European Investment Bank (EIB) was established in 1958 as an autonomous organisation owned by the member states of the Community. The bank finances capital investment to encourage balanced regional development in the EC. Operating on a non-profit basis, the bank provides loans for both public and private sector organisations. To find out if a project qualifies for an EIB loan, potential borrowers should contact the EIB directly or an intermediary bank, handling EC loans. Details of EC grants and loans are given in *EC Grants and Loans*, Part Four, Chapter 7.

COURT OF AUDITORS

The Court of Auditors produces annual reports examining the financial position of the Community and its institutions. The Court also assists the European Parliament and the Council of Ministers to implement the EC budget. It is entitled to make observations at any time and submit opinions at the request of any of the EC's institutions. Based in Luxembourg, the Court of Auditors has twelve members, one from each member state.

CONTACTS

European Community Institutions

European Commission

European Commission
200 Rue de la Loi
B-1049 Brussels
Tel: (32) 2 235 1111
Telex: 21877 COMEU B

Statistical Office of the European Commission
Batiment Jean Monnet,
Rue Alcide de Gasperi
L-2920 Luxembourg
Tel: (352) 43001
Telex: 3423/3446 COMEUR LU

UK Information Offices

European Commission Information Office
8 Storey's Gate, London SW1P 3AT
Tel: (071) 222 8122
Fax: (071) 222 0900
Telex: 23208 EURUK G

European Commission Information Office
4 Cathedral Road, Cardiff CF1 9SG
Tel: (0222) 371631
Fax: (0222) 395489
Telex: 497727 EUROPA G

European Commission Information Office
Windsor House, 9-15 Bedford Street
Belfast BT2 7EG
Tel: (0232) 240708
Fax: (0232) 248241
Telex: 74117 CECBEL G

European Commission Information Office
7 Alva Street
Edinburgh EH2 4PH
Tel: (031) 225 2058
Fax: (031) 226 4105
Telex: 727420 EUEDIN G

Council of Ministers

Council of the European Communities
Secretariat for Information, Publications
and Documentation
170 rue de la Loi
B-1048 Brussels
Tel: (32) 2 234 6111
Telex: 21711 CONSIL B

European Parliament

European Parliament
Secretariat
PO Box 1601
Centre Europeen
Plateau du Kirchberg
L-2920 Luxembourg
Tel: (352) 43001
Telex: 2894/3494 EUPARL LU

European Parliament
Information Bureau
Rue Belliard 97-113
B-1040 Brussels
Tel: (32) 2 234 1111

European Parliament
Directorate-General for Information and
Public Relations
Publications and Briefings Division
L-2929 Luxembourg
Tel: (352) 43001

European Parliament Information Office
2 Queen Anne's Gate
London SW1H 9AA
Tel: (071) 222 0411
Fax: (071) 222 2713
Telex: 894160 EPLDN G

European Democratic Group
2 Queen Anne's Gate
London SW1H 9AA
Tel: (071) 222 0411
Fax: (071) 222 2713
Telex: 894160 EPLDN G

British Labour Group
2 Queen Anne's Gate
London SW1H 9AA
Tel: (071) 222 0411
Fax: (071) 222 2713
Telex: 894160 EPLDN G

Economic and Social Committee (ESC)

A list of members of the ESC is available from its Press, Information and Public Relations Division. For ESC publications see *European Community Publications*, Part Eight, Chapter 1.

Economic and Social Committee
Press, Information and Public Relations
Division
2 Rue Ravenstein
B-1000 Brussels
Tel: (32) 2 519 9011
Telex: 25983 CESEUR B

European Court of Justice

European Court of Justice
Information Service
L-2925 Luxembourg
Tel: (352) 43031
Fax: (352) 4303-2600
Telex: 2771 CJINFO L

(See also *European Community Law*, Part Six, Chapter 1)

European Investment Bank (EIB)

For details of grants and loans available through the EIB see *EC Grants and Loans*, Part Four, Chapter 7.

European Investment Bank
100 Boulevard Konrad Adenauer
L-2950
Luxembourg
Tel: (352) 4379-1
Fax: (352) 437704
Telex: 3530 BNKEU LU

European Investment Bank
68 Pall Mall
London SW1Y 5ES
Tel (071) 839 3351
Fax: (071) 930 9929
Telex: 919159 BANKEU G

European Court of Auditors

Court of Auditors
29 Rue Aldringen
L-1118 Luxembourg
Tel: (352) 47731
Telex: 3512 EURAUD LU

European Centre for the Development of Vocational Training (CEDEFOP)
For details of vocational training initiatives and information available from CEDEFOP see *Creating a Workforce*, Part Three, Chapter 7.

European Centre for the Development of
Vocational Training (CEDEFOP)
Bundesallee 22
1000 Berlin 15
Tel: (49) 30 88 41 20
Fax: (49) 30 884 12 222
Telex: 184163 EUCEN D

European Foundation for the Improvement of Living and Working Conditions

European Foundation for the Improvement
of Living and Working Conditions
Loughlinstown House
Shankill
Co. Dublin
Ireland
Tel: (0001) 826888/(353) 826888

(Headquarters)

Small and Medium-Sized Enterprises (SME Task Force)

SME Task Force
European Commission
Directorate-General for Enterprise Policy,
Commerce, Tourism and Social Economy
(DGXXIII)
80 Rue d'Arlon
B-1040 Brussels
Tel: (32) 2 230 3949/4091
Fax: (32) 2 236 2572
Telex: 61655 BURAP B

Business Co-operation Network (BC-Net)
An initiative of the European Commission's Small and Medium-Sized Enterprises Task Force (DGXXIII) to assist SMEs to locate collaborative partners within Europe. BC-Net contacts are located in certain banks, chambers of commerce, development agencies, local authorities and other specialist advice centres. To make contact with potential EC partners, companies send details of their offer or request for collaboration to a BC-Net contact who contacts other advisers in the network in search of potential partners. A list of over 400 business advisors, including many in the UK, within the BC-Net computerised European network is available from the Buiness Co-operation Centre:

Business Co-operation Centre
80 Rue d'Arlon
B-1040 Brussels
Tel: (32) 2 230 3949/4091
Fax: (32) 2 236 2572
Telex: 61655 BURAP B

European Business and Innovation Centre Network (EBN)

EBN promotes the exchange of technical information and experience between member Business Innovation Centres (BICs) throughout the EC and their associated companies. BIC's, locally based in industrial areas, are professionally managed organisations, operating systems for encouraging entrepeneurs and innovative business opportunities, leading to the development of new business. BIC services include:

Entrepreneurial training
Technology research, assessment and transfer
Management, marketing advice
Provision of finance
Preparation of business plans
Provision of premises with shared services

There are numerous BICs throughout the UK. For further information contact:

European Business and Innovation Centre
Network
205 Rue Belliard (Box 3)
B-1040 Brussels
Tel: (32) 2 231 0747
Fax: (32) 2 231 1016
Telex: 65138 EISA B

Centre for the Development of Industry (ACP-EC)

Set up in 1977 under the first ACP (African, Caribbean and Pacific States)/EC Lome Convention , the CDI's function is to 'help to establish and strengthen industrial enterprises in the ACP states, particularly by encouraging joint initiatives by economic operators of the European Community and the ACP states'. As far as EC companies are concerned, what this means in practice is that it is possible to gain opportunities to participate in joint ventures or supply industrial projects in ACP countries which may be receiving EC financial assistance. Companies registering with the CDI are automatically informed of ACP projects for which they could become suitable technical, marketing or investment partners.

Centre for the Development of Industry
(ACP-EC Lome Convention)
28 Rue de l'Industrie
B-1040 Brussels
Tel: (32) 2 513 4100
Telex: 61427

Euro-Info-Centres

The Community has set up Euro-Info-Centres throughout the member states to advise business, especially smaller companies, on developments in the Single Market and guide them to information sources. They are mainly located in chambers of commerce and other business organisations. They are now widely used as general information sources by local businesses. No two Euro-Info-Centres are alike, however, as both the host organisations and services may differ considerably. There are some 150 centres throughout the EC but more are coming on stream:

UK Euro-Info-Centres[1]

Local Enterprise Development Unit
Ledu House
Upper Galwally
Belfast
BT8 4TB
Tel: 0232 491031

Chamber of Commerce
75 Harborne Road
Birmingham
B15 3DH
Tel: 021 454 6171

Federation of Sussex Industries
Seven Dials
Brighton
BN1 3JS
Tel: 0273 268282/5

Chamber of Commerce
16 Clifton Park
Bristol
BS8 3BY
Tel: 0272 737373

Wales Euro Info Centre
University of Wales
PO Box 430
College of Cardiff
CF1 3XT
Tel: 0222 229525

North Wales Office
Library & Information Centre
County Civic Centre
Mold
Clywd
CH7 6NW
Tel: 0352 2121 Ext 2494

Exeter Enterprises Limited
University of Exeter
Hailey Wing
Reed Hall
Exeter
EX4 4QR
Tel: 0392 214085

Scottish Development Agency
21 Bothwell Street
Glasgow
G2 6NR
Tel: 041 221 0999

Highland Opportunity Limited
Highland Regional Council
Regional Buildings
Glenurquhart Road
Inverness
IV3 5NX
Tel: 0463 234121

Yorkshire and Humberside Development Association
Westgate House
Wellington Street
Leeds
LS1 4LT
Tel: 0532 439222

Euro Team
University of Leicester
Leicester
LE1 5RH

North West Euro Services Limited
Liverpool Central Libraries
William Brown Street
Liverpool
L3 8EW
Tel: 051 298 1928

Small Firms Service
11 Belgrave Square
London
SW1V 1RB
Tel: 071 828 6201

Kent County Council
Springfield
Maidstone
Kent
ME14 2LL
Tel: 0622 671411

Chamber of Commerce
56 Oxford Street
Manchester
M60 7HJ
Tel: 061 236 3210

Northern Development Company
Great North House
Sandyford Road
Newcastle upon Tyne
NE1 8ND
Tel: 091 261 0026

Chamber of Commerce
112 Barrack Street
Norwich
NR3 1UB
Tel: 0603 625 977

Chamber of Commerce
60 Station Road
Sutton in Ashfield
Nottingham
Tel: 0623 551111

**Thames Chiltern
Chamber of Commerce**
2-6 Bath Road
Slough
SL1 3SB
Tel: 0753 77877

Southern Area Euro Info Centre
Central Library
Civic Centre
Southampton
SO9 4XP
Tel: 0703 832462

Shropshire Chamber of Commerce
Industry House
16 Halesford
Telford TF7 4TA
Tel: 0952 588766

1 In operation in 1990. More EICs are expected to open.

EC on-line databases

Details of a selection of EC on-line databases are given in *EC On-line Databases*, Part Eight, Chapter 3.

United Kingdom Permanent Representative (UKREP)

**United Kingdom Permanent Representative
to the European Communities (UKREP)**
6 Rond-Point Robert Schuman
B-1040 Brussels
Tel: (32) 2 230 6205
Fax: (32) 2 230 8379/4680
Telex: 25681 UKECBR B

2 UK Official Sources of Information

Department of Trade and Industry

Preparing to do business in the Single Market is primarily a matter for individual companies. The aim of the Government is to encourage the process of wealth creation through a competitive and open economy; not just in the UK, but throughout the European Community. Nonetheless, there are ways in which the Government helps business in practical ways to meet the opportunities and challenges of the 1990's. The main channel of this help is the Department of Trade and Industry (DTI). Relevant government departments have specific responsibility for matters such as education, environment, health and safety and transport policy, in which they take the lead.

The DTI offers a comprehensive source of information and expert help to British business from its own resources and, in certain categories of information and advice, in association with outside bodies, such as chambers of commerce. The Department's information service on the legal and procedural changes taking place in Europe to complete the Single Market, for example, is widely used by industry and commerce and the 1992 Hotline receives a regular stream of calls from business. A range of Single Market publications covering important areas of change, such as mutual recognition of standards, is also available. Practical schemes, in particular the consultancy initiative which forms part of the DTI's Enterprise Initiative, help companies in two key aims; to make the most of opportunities being created in the enlarged 'home' market of 320 million people, and to deal with competition from other European businesses.

Another important area of DTI support is that which assists companies to take advantage of EC programmes to encourage collaborative research and development; and the range of DTI export services continues under the guidance of the British Overseas Trade Board, providing further practical help for companies doing business, or planning to do business in other European countries.

EUROPE OPEN FOR BUSINESS

The DTI's *Europe Open for Business* campaign was launched in April, 1988. Research had shown that only one in six British businesses were aware of the end of 1992 deadline for completing the Single Market. The Department set out to raise the awareness level to above 90 per cent by the end of 1988. This target was reached ahead of schedule and the new, high level of awareness remains constant among companies of all sizes. But awareness is not enough on its own and the Department recognises that awareness must be translated into action; indeed, action which must be taken now, since no-one in business should assume that the changes taking place in the Single Market will not affect them in some way.

Although not every company has to make radical changes to its operation as a result of Single Market developments, the DTI is concerned by the fact that too many companies, especially in the smaller firms sector, are dismissing 1992 as being irrelevant or too distant a deadline to give much thought to taking immediate action.

In making any decision to take action and the form that action should take, companies need to keep up to date on changes taking place in the Single Market and assess the impact of these changes on their business. Already around 60 per cent of the measures in the European Commission's White Paper, *Completing the Internal Market*, have been agreed at Community level and are now being implemented in each EC member state. Central to the DTI's *Europe Open for Business Campaign* is the Department's regularly updated and expanded information service which provides details of changes in the business environment as the Single Market programme unfolds.

The launch of the *Europe Open for Business* campaign was followed by a series of regional seminars, primarily organised by the private sector including trade associations and chambers of commerce. The DTI has a database with details of nearly 3,000 conferences and seminars which have been held or are planned. DTI ministers and officials regularly speak at these events.

The demand for authoritative information on the Single Market programme from the DTI remains high. By the end of 1989 some 375,000 requests for information had been recorded since the campaign began. Of these, 185,000 were received by the 1992 Hotline. More than 900,000 copies of the DTI's information pack have been distributed; 700,000 copies of *1992 for You — An Action Guide for Smaller Firms* and well over 500,000 standards booklets have been supplied on request. The print run of *Single Market News* has reached 250,000. The main features of information service are:

1992 Hotline

The 24-hour telephone Hotline (081-200 1992), through which orders can be placed for Single Market material published by the DTI. The Hotline also puts callers in touch with officials dealing with specific Single Market measures and, increasingly, private sector and other organisations offering detailed information and advice.

SPEARHEAD on-line database

The Spearhead on-line database provides named Government Department contacts plus summaries of all current and prospective EC measures in the Single Market programme and in other areas of EC activity which raise implications for business including:

□ EC Research and Development programmes

□ Measures on Health and safety at work

□ Environmental measures

Spearhead is accessed through Profile Information (Financial Times Group), British Telecom Gold, One to One, Mercurylink Electronic Mail Services, the European Space Agency Information Retrieval System (IRS/Dialtech) and the JUSTIS on-line database, operated by Context Ltd. See *EC On-line Databases*, Part Eight, Chapter 2).

FT PROFILE
PO Box 12
Sunbury on Thames
Middlesex TW16 7UD
Tel: (0932) 761444
Fax: (0932) 781425

Single Market publications and videos[1]

The DTI has undertaken a major publication programme to enable companies to obtain information, free of charge, in the form of concise introductions to a range of Single Market topics. Publications (as well as videos) can be obtained by ringing the 1992 Hotline on (081) 200 1992, or by writing to:

DTI 1992
PO Box 1992
Cirencester
Gloucestershire GL7 1RN

1992 information pack
The information pack provides an introduction to Single Market developments plus essential contacts:

☐ *The Facts* — a series of factsheets explaining the main elements of the Single Market programme and Community activity in areas such as research and development and deregulation. The information is updated every six months up to the end of each EC Presidency.

☐ *An Action Checklist for Business:* A working document to help companies examine the impact of the Single Market on their business.

☐ *Single Market News:* A quarterly newsletter covering Single Market developments, examples of ways in which companies are meeting the challenge of 1992, conference and seminar dates, new publications.

1992 for You
An Action Guide for Smaller Firms, *1992 for You* is specifically designed to help smaller businesses address key Single Market issues which affect them.

Progress on the Commission White Paper
This publication sets out the up-to-date position on the measures listed in the White Paper, *Completing the Internal Market*. It is updated bi-monthly.

Standards booklets series
A series of booklets on the harmonisation or the mutual recognition of standards and the removal of barriers to trade includes *Standards Action Plan* for business, booklets on the New Approach to technical harmonisation and standards and on EC Directives affecting a wide range of products. Titles include:

Action Plan for Business
Construction Products
Directives Under Discussion
Electromagnetic Compatibility

401

> *Machinery Safety*
> *Mobile Machinery and Lifting Equipment*
> *The New Approach to Technical Harmonisation and Standards*
> *Personal Protective Equipment*
> *Simple Pressure Vessels*
> *Testing and Certification*
> *Toy Safety*
> *Standards Testing and Certification Round-up*

Other Single Market publications

The series includes detailed booklets concerning the professions, public purchasing, company law harmonisation and financial services. Titles include:

> *A Guide to Public Purchasing*
> *Avoiding New Barriers to Trade*
> *Brussels Can you Hear Me?*
> *Company Law Harmonisation*
> *Financial Services*
> *Why You Need to Know More About the Single Market*
> *Guide to Practical Advice for Business (National Edition)*
> *Guide to Practical Advice for Business (South East Region)*
> *Guide to Practical Advice for Business (South West Region)*
> *Guide to Practical Advice for Business (East Region)*
> *Guide to Practical Advice for Business (East Midlands)*
> *Guide to Practical Advice for Business (West Midlands)*
> *Guide to Practical Advice for Business (Yorkshire and Humberside Region)*
> *Guide to Practical Advice for Business (North West Region)*
> *Guide to Practical Advice for Business (Northern Ireland)*
> *Guide to Practical Advice for Business (Scotland)*
> *Guide to Practical Advice for Business (Wales)*
> *Help for Representative Organisations*

Videos

Titles include:

> *Brussels Can you Hear Me?*
> A guide to influencing the EC decision-making process plus a handbook and speaking notes.
> *Signposts to 1992*
> Explains the main Single Market changes *Europe Open for Business/Europe What's That?* Compilation video available from CFL Vision. Tel: (0937) 541010.

1 Check with DTI for additions to list.

Your voice in the Community

Government officials maintain intensive contacts with Community institutions to represent British industry's interests, playing a full part in influencing decisions taken in Brussels. But the DTI also encourages businesses to liaise on their own behalf with and seek the support of counterparts in other member states. There are five key points to grasp:

☐ Get in early. Businesses should make their views known in Brussels before the Commission has reached decisions and produced formal drafts of proposals. The Commission welcomes informed advice.

☐ Work with others. A spread of opinion carries more weight than a lone voice.

☐ Think European. Member states and Community institutions are committed to making the Single Market work. Much can be gained by working with the grain of Community policy. Defending narrow, protective interests can be counter-productive.

☐ Be prepared. In particular, find out what businesses in the same sector in other member states think about EC proposals in question.

☐ Get involved. It is important to remain in close contact with the Brussels network and react quickly to developments as soon as they arise.

The DTI's *Brussels Can you Hear Me?*, produced in video and booklet form, provides further advice on the Community's institutions and how they can be influenced (see also *The Brussels Connection*, Part Seven, Chapter 1).

The DTI also actively encourages trade associations, professional bodies, chambers of commerce, consultants, banks and similar sources of professional advice to provide information on Single Market matters to their members or clients. Companies and members of the professions should themselves encourage their representative organisations to provide a service to help prepare for the Single Market.

Compliance with EC measures

Once a Community measure has been adopted there is, in most cases, a set time limit within which member states must implement it through national legislation (see *European Community Law*, Part Six, Chapter 1). Britain's record on implementing Community legislation, and on compliance, is second to none in the Community, reflecting the Government's determination to ensure that artificial barriers to trade within the EC are removed in practice and that a genuine Single Market is created. A Compliance Unit has been established in the DTI to analyse complaints from business about unfair barriers to trade which remain. The onus, however, is on business to bring problems to the attention of the Compliance Unit so that it can assist in taking any complaints further with the Commission and the member states concerned.

Single Market Compliance Unit
Department of Trade and Industry
Room 405
1-19 Victoria Street
London SW1H 0ET
Tel: (071) 215 4648

CONSULTANCY INITIATIVES

The information available through the *Europe's Open for Business* campaign helps companies to identify Single Market opportunities and challenges. The crucial factor is the ability to compete. Even companies which do not do business in other member states, and have no plans to do so, may still be affected, directly or indirectly, in the UK market by Single Market developments. For example, if you supply a local business, your customer may find more competitive suppliers across the Channel. Similarly, if you normally buy in from local UK suppliers, there may be more competitive suppliers in other member states. It is important to identify any such areas of competitive weakness and take steps to strengthen their position (see *Winners and Losers*, Part One, Chapter 4).

Assisted consultancies

The Consultancy Initiative is the most visible component of the DTI's Enterprise Initiative. Independent, private sector expertise is made available through this service to help companies improve their competitiveness by focussing on detailed elements of its management operation. The service is available to companies whether or not they intend to do business in the Single Market. The DTI pays half the costs between five and fifteen consultant days; two thirds if a company is located in an Assisted Area or Urban Programme Area.

Details of the consultancy advice available can be obtained from DTI Regional Offices. Applicants receive a free business review lasting up to two days with one of the DTI's Enterprise Counsellors , experienced business people who help applicants to analyse strengths and weaknesses and direct them to sources of help and advice. A company employing fewer than 500 people can apply for a consultancy in any two of the following:

□ Marketing (including export marketing)

□ Design

□ Manufacturing systems

□ Business planning

□ Financial and information systems

COLLABORATIVE RESEARCH AND DEVELOPMENT

Companies in the Single Market are increasingly recognising the advantages of working together on research and development. It is expected that the importance of collaborative research projects will grow as more companies seek to exploit the benefits of completing the Single Market, enabling them to compete more strongly both in Europe and in the rest of the world. The DTI offers guidance and information to companies wishing to take advantage of EC research and development programmes. Two major programmes are designed to encourage research and development:

Framework programmes: The two current Community research and development Framework Programmes cover a wide range of projects. The combined funding of the two programmes exceeds 11mEcus. More than half is allocated to pre-competitive industry-related work.

EUREKA: Collaboration on advanced technology projects under a Europe-wide framework involving 19 countries in cross-border civilian projects. DTI funding for UK participants in EUREKA projects continues to be available under the Department's Research and Technology Initiative .

Further information
Details of most of the EC's research and development programmes are given in *EC Grants and Loans*, Part Four, Chapter 7. General information on the programmes plus an information pack, *Guide to European Community Research and Development Programmes* describing individual programmes and giving UK and Brussels contacts is available from:

Department of Trade and Industry
Research and Technology Division
Ashdown House
123 Victoria Street
London SW1E 6RB
Tel: (071) 215 6686/5000
Fax: (071) 828 3258
Telex: 8813148 DIHQ G

THE EXPORT INITIATIVE

Although the DTI's Export Initiative is designed to help companies export to any country in the world, most of the Department's export services are relevant to selling in the Single market. The removal of barriers to trade within the EC, while technically making it as easy to sell in other member states as it is in the UK, does not remove the need for companies to adopt the same strategic approach that they may use when selling outside the Community.

Companies should regard the Single Market of twelve countries as their home market. However, selling in other member states is still regarded as 'exporting' since it brings into focus the strategic approach to selling anywhere outside the UK and the need to look on exporting as an integral part of a whole business operation. Exporting beyond the Community is also a key element in preparations for the completion of the Single Market. Selling in overseas markets sharpens a company's competitive edge; and export sales themselves help to spread production costs and reduce the unit cost of the product. Many products with the cachet of a proven sales record in overseas markets have more immediate appeal to customers in the home market.

The British Overseas Trade Board (BOTB) export services

The DTI provides export services under the guidance of the British Overseas Trade Board , which consists mainly of business people with extensive experience of exporting. Working with the Board itself there are 17 Area Advisory Groups, also comprised of people in business with experience of trading in particular areas of the world. In total, some 200 experienced exporters are involved in ensuring that the DTI's export promotion activities firstly meet the needs of industry and commerce and, secondly, that they are based on a sound understanding of international markets.

In its Forward Plan, the BOTB has identified markets where outstanding opportunities exist for Britain's exporters. Resources are concentrated on publicising these targeted opportunies in particular. European countries are at the top of the Board's priorities. Assisting exporters is also a priority task for Britain's Diplomatic   Posts   overseas.   With   Diplomatic   Service   Commercial

Officers and locally-recruited market experts in key posts throughout the world, and with its Regional Office network, plus the Scottish, Welsh and Northern Ireland offices, the DTI provides a comprehensive and integrated export service to British business.

Guide to exporting

The object of the Export Initiative is to encourage potential exporters to think seriously about selling overseas and existing exporters to sell more. A *Guide to Exporting* outlines the available export services and explains how they are best incorporated into an export strategy. The guide's step by step approach takes potential exporters through the export process and encourages them to look more closely and realistically at their readiness and commitment to export. The guide also explains how the DTI's Export Initiative helps all exporters, not necessarily large companies, to export profitably; indeed, the Export Initiative takes special account of the needs of small and medium-sized companies.

For the experienced exporter, the guide provides information and advice on how the DTI's export services help improve export performance. For companies competing for major projects overseas, it explains how the Department can support their efforts. Also included in the guide is an 'Exporters Checklist' which highlights the benefits of exporting as well as pitfalls which can be avoided, and helps companies to identify key issues which arise at each stage of the exporting process.

Export Development Advisers

For help at any stage of the exporting process, companies should contact Export Initiative staff at the nearest DTI Regional Office for advice on entering the European marketplace and using official export services. However, potential exporters can benefit from practical advice from others who have had exporting experience. To meet this need, the DTI, in collaboration with the Chamber of Commerce movement, has set up a national network of Export Development Advisers under the *Into Active Exporting* scheme. Other forms of expert consultancy are also available under the *Enterprise Initiative*. Export Development Advisers are listed in *Chambers of Commerce*, Part Seven, Chapter 4.

Researching markets

There are no short cuts in conducting marketing research. The DTI's Export Initiative offers comprehensive information and practical advice at every stage of this fundamental process. Initially, companies should contact their nearest DTI Regional Office which has direct access to the DTI's computerised export intelligence and product information services, as well as to the UK's diplomatic service commercial posts in Europe.

Export Market Information Centre (EMIC)
Based at the DTI's headquarters, the Export Market Information Centre houses a large selection of research material. The database of the DTI's own British Overseas Trade Information Service (BOTIS) can be accessed for information on

products, markets, overseas agents, distributors and importers, export opportunities, promotional events and for an index of other published market information. Information available for reference in the library section includes:

Statistics
Market research reports
Directories
Mail order catalogues
Development plans
On-line databases

The EMIC is easy to use and trained staff are on hand to assist. It is advisable to confirm that the information needed is available before visiting the centre.

Export Market Information Centre
Department of Trade and Industry
1-19 Victoria Street
London SW1 0ET
Tel: (071) 215 8444/5

Export Intelligence Service (EIS)

The EIS is a computerised system designed primarily to give firms advance notice on trade opportunities in overseas markets for their products. A service for subscribers, EIS gathers information from diplomatic commercial posts and other sources worldwide, including tender opportunities accessed through TED (Tenders Electronic Daily), the Community's database containing details of calls for tender by public purchasing organisations in member states and the EC itself (see *EC On-line databases*, Part Eight, Chapter 2).

Specific EIS information is targeted to customer needs by matching it to their profiles. Delivery can be on-line, by fax or by post. There is also rapid access to information received over the previous three years, providing exporters with a valuable market research tool. More than 5,500 exporting companies already subscribe to the EIS. Responsibility for selling and delivering the service has been contracted out to Export Opportunities Ltd (EOL). For further information contact a DTI Regional Office or EOL direct:

Export Opportunities Ltd
87a Wembley Hill Road
Wembley
Middlesex HA9 8BU
Tel: (081) 900 1313

(See also Export Network, *EC On-line Databases*, Part Eight, Chapter 2)

Specialist market knowledge

When researching a market there may be a need for specialist knowledge. If so, DTI Regional Offices put companies in touch with the DTI market branches in London. For European business, the contact point is a 'country desk' in the Exports to Europe Branch. Enquirers may also be put in touch with a commercial specialist at a diplomatic post in Europe for on-the-spot guidance. Having first hand knowledge of the local market the commercial departments at Embassies and Consulates can advise on product suitability, marketing methods and local competition. They can test a local response to a product and help to publicise products and services in the marketplace. Country profiles and pocket guides in the *Hints to Exporters* series are also published by the DTI (see page 416).

Export Marketing Research Scheme (EMRS)

For more structured market research, the DTI puts companies in touch with professional export marketing research advisers. EMRS provides free professional advice to enable exporters to decide whether specific market surveys are needed, advises on how to initiate market surveys, and offers financial support, often in the form of grants for market research studies undertaken overseas. Financial support covers:

□ Use of a professional consultancy

□ Use of a company's own staff

□ Purchase of published market research

□ Research commissioned by a trade association

Companies intending to investigate an overseas market should contact the Export Marketing Research Team via a DTI Regional Office, or EMRS direct at:

The Association of British Chambers of
Commerce
4 Westwood House
Westwood Business Park
Coventry CV4 8HS
Tel: (0203) 694484

Tariffs, regulations and licences

Exporters need details of tariffs and customs regulations, though tariffs do not, of course, apply in countries with which the UK has free trade arrangements, such as the EFTA (European Free Trade Association) countries, and the Single Market, except during transitional periods when new EC members have dismantled tariffs over a period of a few years. The DTI provides an information services covering duties, local taxes, exchange controls and legislation affecting UK exporters. Contact DTI Regional offices or the appropriate market branch at the DTI headquarters in London.

Certain goods are subject to export licencing. For information on export licence requirements contact:

Export Licencing Unit
Kingsgate House
66-74 Victoria Street
London SW1E 6SW
Tel: (071) 2158070/8376

Standards

Under its 'New Approach to Technical Harmonisation and Standards' system the EC is accelerating its programme of eliminating technical barriers to trade. Under the New Approach EC Directives set out 'essential requirements' relating to safety and other requirements which must be met before products may be sold anywhere in the Community. All products must satisfy the 'essential requirements', even if there is no intention to sell them across national boundaries. Products meeting these requirements are to bear the 'CE' mark. Many local standards requirements are still in operation, however, since all member states impose a wide range of legal obligations on business in the interests of safety and consumer protection, often in the form of mandatory standards. No matter how well justified they may be, they may give rise to technical barriers to trade because of differing requirements and procedures in different member states. The DTI's range of Single Market publications includes several on standards (see page 401) and information on various aspects of the EC standards harmonisation programme can be obtained via the 1992 Hotline — Tel: (081) 200 1992.

Technical Help to Exporters (THE)

THE is a service operated by the British Standards Institution (BSI) and BSI's staff of engineers and information specialists, providing practical asistance with compliance with foreign standards and details of foreign standards requirements including:

> National laws (particularly safety and environmental protection requirements).
> Technical standards
> Certification procedures

THE services include:

> Technical enquiry service
> Updating service
> Consultancy
> Technical research
> Library of over 500,000 standards

For further information contact DTI Regional Offices or THE direct.

Technical Help to Exporters
British Standards Institution
Linford Wood
Milton Keynes MK14 6LE
Tel: (0908) 220022
Fax: (0908) 320856

Single Market standards information

The DTI publishes a range of publications on EC standards harmonisation Directives being implemented in various industry sectors. Contacts on specific standards measures are given in the booklets. The publications form part of the DTI's *Europe Open for Business* publicity campaign. A selection of titles is listed under *Standards Publications* page 401). Copies can be obtained by ringing the 1992 Hotline ((081) 200 1992). Further information is available from the British Standards Institution or government contacts dealing with specific items of EC standards legislation. Names can be also obtained by ringing the 1992 Hotline. An on-line database, *Standardline*, accessed through Pergamon Financial Data Services, covers all current *British* standards including codes of practice, drafts for development, automobile, marine and aerospace series.

BSI Standardline
Pergamon Financial Data Services
Paulton House
8 Shepherdess Walk
London N1 7LB
Tel: (071) 490 0049
Fax: (071) 490 2979

Quality standards
Product quality standards are becoming increasingly important in the Single Market. Quality assurance certification procedures are described in *The Mark of Quality*, (Part Two, Chapter 5)

New Products from Britain

The principal aim of this service is to test market reactions to new products and services on a targeted basis. Companies seeking to assess the viability of new products in the European marketplace can use this service to secure publicity for their producers in the technical and trade press, business journals and newspapers. Articles are prepared with the exporter's co-operation by specialist journalists employed by the Central Office of Information . There is a charge for the service (see page 424) For details contact a DTI Regional Office.

Appointing agents and distributors

Many companies consider finding and appointing an agent or distributor as their top priority. The DTI helps companies to identify representatives in Europe through diplomatic commerial posts. Staff at these posts have extensive knowledge of individual markets and posts have many years experience in providing reliable information and advice on local agents and distributors. The DTI maintains records on computer of potential business contacts in overseas markets, regularly updated by diplomatic posts. Contact DTI Regional Offices or Exports to Europe Branch (see page 429).

Export Representative Service
The DTI carries out investigations on behalf of exporters through diplomatic posts. Drawing on local contacts and expertise, and armed with product or service information, inclusing trade literature and prices, posts can determine which representatives would be interested in handling the product. They can advise on the suitability of likely candidates and report on their trading interests, capabilities, scope of activities, other agencies held, territory covered, warehousing and distribution facilities, salesforce details, technical know-how and after sales service. **Contact:** DTI Regional Offices.

Overseas Status Reports Service
The DTI, through diplomatic posts, can check the suitability of organisations which have been identified in Europe or have approached a UK supplier. However, neither the DTI nor diplomatic posts can advise on creditworthiness. This advice should be sought from banks or a commercial agency. **Contact:** DTI Regional Offices.

Trade Missions

Outward missions

Participation in outward missions enables companies to explore at first hand prospects for their products and services, or to reinforce existing marketing efforts. A variety of trade bodies run missions to most parts of the world including chambers of commerce and trade associations (See *A Shop Window in Europe*, Part Two, Chapter 2, for a list of BOTB approved sponsors). New exporters, or exporters new to a particular market, joining such a mission, make contact with more experienced exporters. The DTI helps financially in the case of missions *outside* of Western Europe. **Contact:** DTI Regional Offices or:

Department of Trade and Industry
Fairs and Promotions Branch
Dean Bradley House
Horseferry Road
London SW1P 2AG
Tel: (071) 276 3000

Inward missions

DTI financially supported inward missions bring to the UK key people from foreign markets who influence the purchase of goods and services by overseas organisations, such as government departments. Journalists are included in the various categories of visitors coming to the UK to visit companies under this scheme. To qualify, mission participants must have a real interest in a UK company's products. Inward missions must be sponsored by a trade association or other approved non-profit making bodies (See *A Shop Window in Europe*, Part Two, Chapter 2 for a list of approved bodies). The DTI pays a significant share of the costs of travel to and from the UK, travel and accommodation within the UK, and interpeter's fees. **Contact:** DTI Regional Offices or:

Department of Trade and Industry
Fairs and Promotions Branch
Dean Bradley House
Horseferry Road
London SW1P 2AG
Tel: (071) 276 3000

European trade fairs

Exhibiting at European trade fairs is one of the most effective forms of export promotion. Many major trade fairs attract buyers from all over the world enabling exhibitors at one event to sample the possibilities of making sales in many different markets (See *A Shop Window in Europe*, Part Two, Chapter 2). By taking part in a trade show companies meet a variety of marketing objectives including:

☐ Attracting customers

☐ Appointing agents or distributors

☐ Contacting wholesalers

☐ Conducting market research

☐ Making immediate sales

411

Each year, the DTI supports over 7,000 participants in British groups at selected trade fairs throughout the world. Financial support is available to companies making their first three appearances at such events. The support takes the form of stand provision at subsidised rates. For some events, mainly outside of Europe, a contribution towards travel costs may be available.

The DTI arranges for space booking and stand construction, thus relieving group participants of much of the organisational burden associated with trade fair participation. Advice is available on how to make the most effective use of participation and, at the fair itself, the DTI's Installation Officer and overseas Commercial Officer, Embassy or Consulate based, are on hand to deal with any problems which may arise. **Contact:** DTI Regional Offices or:

Department of Trade and Industry
Fairs and Promotions Branch
Dean Bradley House
Horseferry Road
London SW1P 2AG
Tel: (071) 276 3000

EXPO 92
Department of Trade and Industry
Overseas Trade Division 3
20 Victoria Street
SW1H 0NF
Tel: (071) 215 3192/5000
Fax: (071) 222 2602

Overseas seminars
Seminars offer companies a means of increasing awareness of their products in European markets. The DTI helps trade associations and other representative organisations to mount events which allow British companies to take their goods and services to specific audiences. Financial assistance covers:

☐   Hire of venue

☐   Interpreters, projectionists

☐   Printing and distribution

☐   Local publicity

☐   Graphics display material

☐   Local staff

☐   Hospitality

☐   Associated small exhibition

☐   Travel grants (for seminars outside Western Europe)

Contact:

Department of Trade and Industry
Fairs and Promotions Branch
Dean Bradley House
Horseferry Road
London SW1P 2AG
Tel: (071) 276 3000

Store promotions

British 'theme' promotions at retail outlets in European cities offer an ideal showcase for a company's products. Again, this is a highly effective way of introducing products to the marketplace. The DTI assists in staging this type of promotion which is aimed at boosting sales of British made goods. **Contact:** DTI Regional Offices or:

Department of Trade and Industry
Fairs and Promotions Branch
Dean Bradley House
Horseferry Road
London SW1P 2AG
Tel: (071) 215 4923

Simplification of Trade Procedures Board (SITPRO)

Help with processing documentation and cutting down the red tape and paperwork involved in exporting is provided by the Simplification of Trade Procedures Board (SITPRO). SITPRO provides a list of specialists in export documentation and has developed a range of systems for processing export documentation inexpensively and accurately, without the need for repetitive typing. SITPRO's distributors will discuss systems suited to a company's individual needs.

SITPRO leads in developing techniques for transmitting documentations via Electronic Data Interchange (EDI), or paperless trading (see *Electronic Data Interchange*, Part Two, Chapter 3). EDI facilitates quicker, less expensive and more secure communication than paper documents, giving traders more scope for reducing stock holdings (Just in Time inventory control) and improving customer service at the same time. The new method is available to anyone with an ordinary desk-top micro-computer and a telephone connection, or access to a dedicated computer link or value-added network. The principal SITPRO products are:

☐   Spex software (document processing)

☐   Interbridge software (EDI)

☐   EDIFACT Service (EDI)

☐   Export Stationery (Exportsets, Postpacks)

☐   Copier systems (overlays)

Contact: For further information on SITPRO products:

Simplification of Trade Procedures Board
Venture House
29 Glasshouse Street
London W1R 5RG
Tel: (071) 287 3525
Fax: (071) 287 5751

SPEX 3 software distributors

ESL Computer Services Ltd
Beckenham
Tel: (081) 658 7821

Export Trade Connections Ltd
Milton Keynes
Tel: (0908) 221172

International Software Marketing
East Grinstead
Tel: (0342) 324117

Nord Systems Ltd
Leeds
Tel: (0532) 444577

The Software Connection Ltd
Chichester
Tel: (0243) 531984

Xerox Design Technology
Uxbridge
Tel: (0895) 51133

SPEX 3 sub-agents

Export Analysis Ltd
Leamington Spa
Tel: (0926) 311537

Export Development Services Ltd
Southampton
Tel: (0703) 332787

Export Paperwork Services Ltd
Stansted
Tel: (0279) 871010

Interbridge 4 (Sitpro's EDIFACT translator) distributors

Scicon Industry
Cheadle
Tel: (061) 491 3683

ESL Computer Services Ltd
Beckenham
Tel: (081) 658 7821

The Software Connection Ltd
Chichester
Tel: (0243) 531984

Hoskyns Group Plc
Birmingham
Tel: (021) 333 3536

Overlay systems distributors

Export Analysis Ltd
Leamington Spa
Tel: (0926) 311537

Export Development Associates
Blackburn
Tel: (0254) 883529

Export Development Services
Southampton
Tel: (0703) 332787

Export Paperwork Services Ltd
Stansted
Tel: (0279) 871010

Export Trade Connections Ltd
Milton Keynes
Tel: (0908) 221172

LS Printing Ltd
Birkenhead
Tel: (051) 647 8006

Maxwell Terence Ltd
Hereford
Tel: (0432) 277711

Newman White Ltd
Southwick, Wiltshire
Tel: (0225) 762337

Northern Export Systems Suppliers Ltd
South Wirral
Tel: (051) 336 7080

P & H Export Services Ltd
Ashton-under-Lyne
Tel: (061) 339 0821

SITPRO Postpack and Exportset Distributors

Formecon Services Ltd#
Crewe
Tel: (0270) 500800

Tate Freight Forms#
Milton Keynes
Tel: (0908) 221162

Burnley District Chamber of Commerce
Tel: (0282) 36555

Anglia Export Services Ltd
Beccles, Suffolk
Tel: (0502) 717877

Export Analysis Ltd
Leamington Spa
Tel: (0926) 311537

Export Development Services Ltd
Southampton
Tel: (0703) 332787

Export Paperwork Services Ltd
Stansted
Tel: (0279) 871010

Export Trade Connections Ltd
Milton Keynes
Tel: (0908) 221172

Luton Chamber of Commerce
Tel: (0582) 695011

Exportset distributors

Maxwell Terence Ltd
Hereford
Tel: (0432) 277711

Medway and Gillingham Chamber of Commerce
Chatham
Tel: (0624) 44178

Newman White Ltd
Southwick, Wiltshire
Tel: (0225) 762337

Northern Export Systems Supplies Ltd
South Wirral
Tel: (051) 336 7080

P & H Export Services Ltd
Ashton-under-Lyne
Tel: (061) 339 0821

Printers (SSN, DGN, RO/RO)

Formecon Services Ltd
Crewe
Tel: (0270) 500800

Lonsdale Business Forms Ltd
Wellingborough
Tel: (0933) 228855

LT Printing Ltd
Birkenhead
Tel: (051) 647 8006

Regent Print Group
Huddersfield
Tel: (0484) 530789

Systemforms Ltd
Woodford
Tel: (081) 505 6125

Tate Freight Forms Ltd
Milton Keynes
Tel: (0908) 221162

Printers (aligned documents)

Export Development Services Ltd
Southampton
Tel: (0703) 332787

Export Paperwork Services Ltd
Stansted
Tel: (0279) 871010

Export Trade Connections Ltd
Milton Keynes
Tel: (0908) 221172

Formecon Services Ltd
Crewe
Tel: (0270) 500800

H Hocking & Son Ltd
St Austell
Tel: (0726) 72548

LT Printing Ltd
Birkenhead
Tel: (051) 647 8006

Newman White Ltd
Southwick, Wiltshire
Tel: (0225) 762337

Northern Export Systems Supplies Ltd
South Wirral
Tel: (051) 336 7080

P & H Export Services Ltd
Ashton-under-Lyme
Tel: (061) 339 0821

Reedform Ltd
Berkshire
Tel: (0344) 55155

Standard Forms Ltd
Hampshire
Tel: (0794) 517206

Tate Freight Forms Ltd
Milton Keynes
Tel: (0908) 221162

Laser systems

Dataficiency Ltd
Worthing
Tel: (0903) 214916

Document Technology Ltd
Newbury
Tel: (0635) 37773

ESL Computer Services Ltd
Beckenham
Tel: (081) 658 7821

Export Trade Connections Ltd
Milton Keynes
Tel: (0908) 221172

International Software Marketing
East Grinstead
Tel: (0342) 324117

Laserlogic Ltd
Shepton Mallet
Tel: (0794) 3116

Rank Xerox (UK) Ltd
Uxbridge
Tel: (0895) 51133

The Software Connection Ltd
Chichester
Tel: (0243) 531984

Vistec Business Systems Ltd
Belper
Tel: (0773) 826811

WS Systems Ltd
Bruton, Somerset
Tel: (0749) 813581

Export publications and handouts

Various publications and handouts are distributed by the DTI for the benefit of exporters visiting overseas markets or keeping up to date with international trade developments. The main publications are:

☐ *Hints to Exporters:* A series of booklets containing basic factual, economic and travel information (£5.00 each).

☐ *Country Profiles*

☐ *Sector Reports*

☐ *Guide to Exporting*

☐ *British Overseas Trade Board Annual Report*

Overseas Trade
Overseas Trade is the DTI's monthly magazine for exporters carrying a range of news and features of interest to new and established exporters.

Overseas Trade
Department of Trade and Industry
29 Bressenden Place
London SW1 5DD
Tel: (071) 215 4860

Export Publications Catalogue
The following list of titles of publications and hand-outs comprises the Western European list in the DTI's *Export Publications Catalogue* (September 1990 edition).

		PRICE CODE	PUBLICATION NUMBER
AUSTRIA			
Hints to Exporters (pp53)	1988/89	A	5004
Country Profile (pp60)	June 88	C	5121
Barter Trade Companies with East Europe (pp12)	Oct 89	C	5369
Sector reports			
Automotive Components (pp10)	Sept 89	E	5201
Clothing Market (pp34)	Jul 89	E	5202
Computer Educational Software (pp20)	Nov 89	E	5203
Electronic Components (pp24)	Oct 89	E	5204
Environmental Technology (pp18)	Oct 89	E	5205
Medical Equipment (pp64)	Oct 89	E	5206
Office Equipment (Including Computers) (pp38)	Oct 89	E	5207
Security Equipment (pp18)	Mar 90	E	5370
Telecommunications Equipment (pp23)	Oct 89	E	5208
BELGIUM			
Hints to Exporters — Belgium and Luxembourg (pp73)	1989/90	A	5009
Country Profile (pp79)	Nov 89	C	5122
Export Strategy. Document for Belgium and Luxembourg (pp37)	Jul 89	E	5371
Sector reports			
Agriculture (pp38)	Jul 89	E	5209
Construction Industry (pp40)	Oct 89	E	5210
DIY Products (pp30)	Dec 87	F	5212
Electronic Components		E	5398
Light Aircraft (pp20)	Jul 89	C	5213
Marketing Consumer Goods in Belgium (pp62)	May 90	F	5211
CYPRUS			
Hints to Exporters (pp64)	1989	A	5023
Goods Subject to an Import Licence (pp11)	Mar 89	C	5372
Sector reports			
Agricultural Sector (pp75)	Jan 87	F	5214
Food Processing and Packaging Industry (pp96)	Feb 89	E	5215
Medical Equipment (pp17)	May 87	F	5216

		PRICE CODE	PUBLICATION NUMBER
DENMARK			
Hints to Exporters (pp51)	1989/90	A	5025
Country Profile (pp78)	Apr 88	C	5123
Agency Legislation (pp23)	1989	C	5373
Finding a Collaboration Partner		E	5402
How to Sell to the State (part translation of booklet issued by the Danish Government's Purchasing Department) (pp13)	Jan 89	C	5374
Sector reports			
Banking (pp14 + pp3 enclosure)	Nov 89	E	5217
Energy Scene (pp34)	1987	E	5218
Environmental Policy and Technology (pp10)	Feb 88	E	5219
Faroe Islands (pp13)	Nov 89	E	5220
Sportsgoods (pp13)	Oct 87	E	5221
FINLAND			
Hints to Exporters (pp52)	1989/90	A	5031
Country Profile (pp51)	Mar 87	F	5124
Sector reports			
Machine Tools (pp28)	Oct 88	E	5223
Medical Equipment and Supplies (pp14)	Oct 88	E	5224
Pumps (pp16)	Oct 88	E	5225
FRANCE			
Hints to Exporters (pp75)	Jan 90	A	5032
Country Profile (pp73)	1989	C	5125
Marketing Consumer Goods		E	5376
Overcoming the Language Barrier (pp10)	1989	C	5375
Sector reports			
Agricultural Machinery (pp31)	Feb 87	F	5226
Amateur Gardening Market (pp16)	Feb 89	E	5227
Building Industry (pp12)		F	5228
Business and Promotional Giftware (pp15)		F	5229
CAD Market (pp19)	Dec 88	F	5230
Clothing (pp13)		F	5231
DIY Products (pp11)		F	5232
Electrical Appliances, Domestic (pp25)	Nov 89	E	5233
Electronic Components (pp18)	May 87	F	5234
Electronic Equipment (pp15)	Mar 87	F	5235
Equipment for the Handicapped (pp14)	May 89	E	5236
Fertilisers (pp54)		F	5237
Garden Sheds (pp11)	Jul 87	F	5238
Giftware Market: Background and Trends (pp34)	Mar 88	E	5239
Giftware Products (short guide) (pp10)	Jun 89	E	5240
Grinding Mills (pp12)	Jul 89	F	5241
Healthcare in France (pp40)	Sep 89	F	5242
Lubricants (pp10)	May 89	F	5243
Mail Order Houses in France (pp120)	June 88	F	5378
Marketing Consumer Goods in France (pp83)	1989	E	5376
Pharmaceutical Processing and Packaging Machinery (pp29)		F	5245
Plastic Machinery (pp20)	Jun 87	F	5246
Positioning Systems (pp13)	Feb 87	F	5247
Public Sector Purchasing in France (pp10)	Jan 90	E	5377

		PRICE CODE	PUBLICATION NUMBER
Register of Companies Involved in National and Third Country Projects (pp65)	Jan 87	E	5379
Scientific Instruments (pp13)	Feb 89	E	5248
Security Equipment (pp31)	Jun 89	E	5249
Software Market (pp19)	Oct 87	F	5250
Sportswear (pp80)	Nov 89	E	5251
Tableware (pp24)	Feb 87	F	5252
Water Industry (pp11)	Apr 89	E	5253

GERMANY (FEDERAL REPUBLIC)

Hints to Exporters (pp88)	Mar 90	A	5035
Country Profile (pp48)	Dec 89	C	5126
Exporters' Guide to Technical Requirements in the Federal Republic of Germany (pp12)	1988	C	5380
Solicitors Conversant with German Law (pp21)	Jun 89	C	5381
Export Marketing Consultants with Experience in the West German Market		C	5408

Sector reports

Bicycles and Accessories (pp10)	Oct 87	F	5254
Building and Construction Industry (pp28)		F	5255
Clothing and Textiles (pp12)	Mar 87	F	5271
Consumer Goods (pp87)	Aug 87	F	5256
DIY (pp18)	Jun 89	E	5257
Domestic Electrical Appliances (pp24)	Sep 88	F	5258
Electronic and Electrical Industry ('Focus Germany') (pp50)	Jan 87	F	5259
Food Marketing in Germany (pp37)	May 87	F	5260
Footwear (pp13)	Aug 89	E	5261
Heating and Ventilating/Air Conditioning (pp20)	Nov 87	F	5262
High Tech Products (Marketing) (pp11)	Jun 88	E	5263
Medical Supplies and Equipment (pp73)	Apr 87	F	5264
Pet Foods and Supplies (Market Survey) (p22)	1988	E	5265
Register of Companies in 3rd Country Projects (pp101)	Jun 89	E	5266
Security Systems (pp57)	Nov 87	F	5267
Selling in the Single Market (pp60)	Jun 89	E	5268
Sports Goods (pp17)	Oct 88	E	5269

GREECE

Hints to Exporters (pp52)	1988	A	5037
Country Profile (pp65)	Apr 89	C	5128
Marking and Labelling Requirements (pp20)	May 88	C	5388

Sector reports

Automotive Parts and Accessories (pp65)	Feb 88	E	5272
Health and Medical Equipment (pp64)	Jan 88	E	5275
Register of Consulting Firms Involved in National and Third Country Projects (pp49)	Dec 89	E	5386
Register of Contracting Firms Involved in National and Third Country Projects (pp39)	Oct 89	E	5387
The Passenger Car in Greece (pp20)	1989	E	5273
The Energy Situation in Greece (pp10)	May 89	E	5274

ICELAND

Hints to Exporters (pp48)	1989/90	A	5044
Country Profile (pp40)	Aug 86	F	5129

		PRICE CODE	PUBLICATION NUMBER
Sector reports			
Fish Farming (pp11)	Oct 89	E	5369
Shipping, Shipbuilding and Ship Repair (pp13)	Aug 87	F	5276
IRELAND			
Hints to Exporters (pp51)	1989	A	5048
Country Profile (pp57)	Jul 88	C	5130
Sector reports			
Chilled Foods (pp22)	Jun 87	F	5277
Component Supplies and Services to the Electrical and Electronic Manufacturing Industry (pp23)	Apr 88	E	5278
Electronic Components (pp97)	Aug 89	F	5279
Food Processing (pp25)	Jul 87	F	5280
Gardening and Horticultural Sectors: Market Prospects		E	5400
Hospitals and Healthcare (pp29)	1987	F	5281
Plant and Equipment Supplies to the Chemical and Pharmaceutical Industry		E	5401
Plastics Industry (pp16)	Jul 87	F	5282
Sports and Leisure Goods (pp79)	Mar 89	E	5283
ITALY			
Hints to Exporters (pp64)	Dec 89	A	5050
Country Profile (pp72)	Dec 89	C	5131
Sector reports			
Aerospace (pp20)	Mar 89	E	5284
Automotive Market in Italy (pp14)	May 87	F	5285
Chemical Industry (pp53)	Oct 87	F	5286
Clothing Report (pp85) *with Clothing: Brief Report* (pp16)	Jul 89	E	5288
Clothing and Textile Industries (p11)	Sep 88	E	5289
Construction Industry (pp31)	Dec 88	E	5290
Doing Business in Italy: Focus on Rome (pp23)	1989	E	5384
Environment (pp28)	Aug 89	E	5291
European Preview of Sports Articles for Winter 1990 (pp10)	Jan 90	E	5382
Food Report Italy (pp54)	Jun 87	F	5292
Hospital and Medical Equipment (pp57)	Dec 88	E	5293
Industrial Ceramics Industry (pp10)	Jun 89	E	5294
Iron and Steel Industry (pp10)	1988	E	5295
Oil and Gas Industry (pp28)	Sep 88	E	5296
Optical Glass Industry (pp13)	Jun 89	E	5297
Ornamental, Horticultural and Gardening Products (pp18)	May 89	E	5383
Register of Companies Involved in National and Third Country Projects (pp104)	Aug 88	E	5385
Swimwear (pp11)	Jun 89	E	5298
Television and Broadcasting (pp32)	Dec 88	E	5299
LUXEMBOURG			
Hints to Exporters		A	5009
Country Profile (pp52)	Jul 89	C	5132
MALTA			
Hints to Exporters (pp40)	1989/90	A	5062

		PRICE CODE	PUBLICATION NUMBER
NETHERLANDS			
Hints to Exporters (pp60)	1989/90	A	5067
Country Profile (pp105)	Aug 89	C	5133
Marketing Consumer Goods in the Netherlands	Mar 90	E	5307
Public Purchasing in the Netherlands	May 90	E	5399
Sector reports			
Advanced Business Systems (pp29)	Feb 90	E	5301
Automotive Parts and Accessories in the			
Netherlands (pp54)	May 89	E	5302
Caravans (pp25)	Apr 88	E	5303
Catering Equipment (pp36)	Dec 89	E	5304
Clothing (Men's and Ladies' Outwear) (pp16)	Jun 87	F	5305
Construction (pp31)	Feb 88	E	5306
Data and Telecoms (pp49)	Feb 87	F	5308
DIY Market in the Netherlands (pp43)	Mar 89	E	5309
Domestic Footwear (pp20)	Aug 89	E	5370
Electricity Generating Industry (pp40)	May 89	E	5310
Equipment for the Disabled (pp18)	Oct 89	E	5311
Gardening Equipment (pp13)	Mar 87	F	5312
Golf in The Netherlands (pp13)	Oct 88	E	5313
Horse Riding Equipment and Clothing (pp21)	Sep 89	E	5314
Marketing Consumer Goods in the Netherlands (pp48)	Mar 90	E	5307
Mechanical Handling	May 90	E	5395
Medical Instruments and Equipment (pp73)	Jun 88	E	5315
Oil and Gas Reserves (Offshore) (pp20)	Jun 88	E	5316
Packaging Machinery (pp18)	May 88	E	5317
Pleasure Craft (pp26)	Aug 87	F	5318
Security Equipment (pp63)	Dec 89	E	5319
Underwear and Nightware (pp41)	Oct 88	E	5322
NORWAY			
Hints to Exporters (pp45)	1988/89	A	5071
Country Profile (pp62)	1989	C	5134
Sector reports			
Agriculture (pp11)	1989	E	5323
Building Articles (pp29)	Jul 88	E	5324
Fish Farming (pp10)	1989	E	5325
Machine Tools (pp12)	Jun 87	E	5326
Motor Vehicles (pp24)	Apr 88	E	5327
Offshore Industry (pp20)	Nov 89	E	5328
PORTUGAL			
Hints to Exporters (pp80)	1989/90	A	5080
Country Profile (pp68)	1987	F	5135
Sector reports			
Banking and Financial Services (pp18)	Dec 88	E	5329
Books (pp13)	Sep 89	E	5330
Cigarettes, Cigars, Tobacco and Pipe Tobacco (pp12)	Jul 89	E	5331
Civil Construction (pp12)	Dec 88	E	5332
Condoms (pp13)	Feb 90	E	5333
EC Funding For Agricultural Projects (pp12)	Sep 88	E	5334
EC Structural Funds In Portugal (pp31)	Feb 89	E	5335

		PRICE CODE	PUBLICATION NUMBER
Fish and Shellfish (p11)	Sep 88	E	5336
Hospital, Medical and Surgical (pp20)	Aug 88	E	5337
Information Technology (pp20)	Jan 89	E	5338
Laboratory Ware (pp24)	Aug 88	E	5339
Machine Tools (pp20)	Apr 88	E	5340
Milk Production (pp14)	Feb 88	E	5341
Optical Trade (pp25)	Jan 88	E	5342
Pharmaceuticals (pp24)	Aug 88	E	5343
Pulp Production (pp11)	Jan 88	E	5344
Toys and Games (pp14)	Jul 87	F	5345

SPAIN
Hints to Exporters (pp88)	1990/91	A	5088
Regional Developments in Spain (pp26)	Oct 89	E	5371

Sector reports
Agricultural Machinery (pp12)	Dec 89	E	5346
Construction Industry (pp71)	Feb 90	E	5347

SWEDEN
Hints to Exporters (pp58)	1989/90	A	5091
Country Profile (pp59)	Aug 88	C	5137
Public Procurement	June 90	E	5404

Sector reports
Chemical Industry (pp26)	Dec 89	E	5348
Clothing and Knitwear Market (pp28)	Feb 88	E	5349
Electronic Components (pp38)	Jun 89	E	5350
Floor Coverings (pp18)	Jun 89	E	5351
Food and Beverages (pp48)	Jan 90	E	5373
Furniture (pp12)	Jan 89	E	5353
Garden Equipment and Supplies	June 90	E	5403
Health Food and Health Products (pp10)	Jan 88	E	5355
Pets and Pet Food (pp11)	Jan 90	E	5374
Pharmaceutical Market (pp44)	Jan 90	E	5357
Security Equipment (pp46)	Jun 89	E	5358
Sports Equipment and Clothing (pp51)	Jun 89	E	5359
Textile Market (pp23)	Apr 88	E	5360
Water Distribution Network (pp13)	Feb 90	E	5375

SWITZERLAND
Hints to Exporters (pp80)	1989/90	A	5092
Country Profile (pp83)	Jun 89	C	5138

Sector reports
Broadcasting Equipment (pp22)	Jun 89	E	5361
Medical Scene (pp36)	Jul 89	E	5364
Pet Products (pp17)	Mar 89	E	5365
Scientific Instruments (pp36)	Sep 88	E	5366
Telecommunications (pp33)	Mar 90	E	5367

MISCELLANEOUS PUBLICATIONS
Marketing Consumer Goods in Western Europe	May 90	E	5368

Eastern Europe

	PRICE CODE	PUBLICATION NUMBER
BULGARIA			
Hints to Exporters (pp52)	1989/90	A	5014
CZECHOSLOVAKIA			
Hints to Exporters (pp54)	1989	A	5024
GERMAN DEMOCRATIC REPUBLIC			
Hints to Exporters (pp56)	1988	A	5034
HUNGARY			
Hints to Exporters (pp56)	Nov 89	A	5043
POLAND			
Hints to Exporters (pp60)	1990/91	A	5079
ROMANIA			
Hints to Exporters (pp56)	1989/90	A	5081
USSR			
Hints to Exporters (pp80)	1990/91	A	5103
Guide to the Soviet Market (pp22)	Dec 88	C	5432
Sector reports			
Soviet Chemical Industry (pp10)	Oct 89	E	5425
Soviet Enterprises with Direct Foreign Trading Rights (pp25)	Jun 89	E	5426
Soviet Organisations Concerned with the Oil, Gas, Petrochemical and Coal Industries (pp11)	May 88	E	5428
Soviet Pharmaceuticals and Medical Equipment: The Outlook for Foreign Trade (pp19)	Aug 87	F	5429
YUGOSLAVIA			
Hints to Exporters (pp60)	1988/89	A	5106
Trading with Yugoslavia (pp19)	Feb 87	F	5433
Sector reports			
Automotive Industry (pp30)	*circa 1988*	E	5430
The Pharmaceutical Industry (pp16)	Jul 89	E	5430

Source: (i) Export Publications Catalogue (1990) Department of Trade and Industry.

Cost codes
All publications listed are given letter codes, the corresponding prices for which are given below:

A = £5	C = £10	E = £30
B = £8	D = £20	F = Free

Contact: DTI Regional Offices, Exports to Europe Branch (see page 425), or:

DTI Export Publications
PO Box 55
Stratford upon Avon
Warwickshire CV37 9GE
Tel: (0789) 296212
Fax: (0789) 292341
(Fax and telephone orders DTI Service Card holders only)

Charges for export services

The DTI has introduced a Service Card, to be used like a charge card, as a convenient way of paying for export services. Before the introduction of the Service Card companies had to pay for services cash in advance. Increasingly, the card will become the means by which companies pay for export services such as the Export Representative Service, Overseas Status Reports, market information which involves specific work by overseas diplomatic commercial posts. The Service Card is available free of charge to any company exporting from the UK and can be used at all government export service outlets in the UK as well as at the 192 diplomatic posts throughout the world. Companies can nominate individuals to be card holders, each having a personal account number.

Credit is not available through the use of the Service Card. Users are billed monthly in arrears in the UK in Sterling, regardless of where in the world the services were bought. Statements or invoices cover all chargeable export services purchased during the period for which the user is billed. Normally the balance, which should be paid in full, is collected by direct debit 25 days after the receipt of the invoice. The charges listed below are inclusive of VAT at 15 per cent.

Export Representative Service

Up to 24 hours work, £300
Over 24 hours work, £600

Overseas Status Reports Service

Up to four hours, £60
Four to eight hours, £120
Over eight hours, £180

Fairs and promotions

50 per cent of DTI costs for a maximum of three participations in each market (five in Japan). Thereafter, payment is on the basis of the DTI's full costs.

Publications

Hints to Exporters visitors guides, £5
Country Profiles, £10
Sector Reports, from £30

Market Information enquiries

Readily available, free
Held by posts, £30
Up to four hours, £60
Four to eight hours, £120
Over eight hours, £180

New Products from Britain

£60 per article in up to 15 markets.

CONTACTS

The following is a list of key Single Market and Western European contacts within the official information network. Some contacts listed also appear in the body of the chapter. The DTI's brochure, *A Guide for Business*, and other brochures list contacts in many areas of business activity within the DTI organisation itself and elsewhere.

Department of Trade and Industry (DTI)

DTI headquarters

Department of Trade and Industry
1 Victoria Street
London SW1H 0ET
Tel: (071) 215 5000
Fax: (071) 222 2629

Regional organisation

DTI North East
Stanegate House
2 Groat Market
Newcastle upon Tyne NE1 1YN
Tel: (091) 232 4722.
Fax: (091) 232 6742
Telex: 53178

Single Market enquiries: Ext. 2273/2279

Cleveland Office
Tel: (0642) 23220

DTI North West
Sunley Tower
Piccadilly Plaza
Manchester M1 4BA
Tel: (061) 236 2171
Fax: (061) 228 3740
Telex: 667104

Single Market enquiries: (061) 838 5227

Liverpool Office
Graeme House
Derby Square
Liverpool L2 7UP
Tel: (051) 224 6300

Crewe Office
Tel: (0270) 500706

Preston Office
Tel: (0772) 653000

Kendall Office
Tel: (0539) 723067

DTI Yorkshire and Humberside
Priestly House
Park Row
Leeds LS1 5LF
Tel: (0532) 443171
Fax: (0532) 421038
Telex: 557925

Single Market enquiries: (0532) 338254

Hull Office
Tel: (0482) 465741

Sheffield Office
Tel: (0742) 729849

DTI West Midlands
Ladywood House
Stephenson Street
Birmingham BS1 4DT
Tel: (021) 631 6181
Fax: (021) 643 5500
Telex: 337919

Single Market enquiries: (021) 631 6180

Droitwich Office
Tel: (0905) 794056

Stoke on Trent Office
Tel: (0782) 285171

Telford Office
Tel: (0952) 290422

DTI East Midlands
Severns House
20 Middle Pavement
Nottingham NG1 7DW
Tel: (0602) 506181
Fax: (0602) 587074/2221496
Telex: 37143

Single Market enquiries: (0602) 596381/ 596384

Derby Office
Tel: (0332) 290487

Chesterfield Office
Tel: (0246) 239905

Leicester Office
Tel: (0533) 531245

Lincoln Office
Tel: (0522) 512002

Northampton Office
Tel: (0604) 21051

DTI East
Area Office
Building A
Westbrook Research Centre
Milton Road
Cambridge CB1 1YG
Tel: (0223) 461939
Fax: (0223) 461941
Telex: 81582

Single Market enquiries: (0223) 346705/ 346710

Chelmsford Office
Tel: (0245) 492385

Ipswich Office
Tel: (0473) 212313

Norwich Office
Tel: (0603) 761294

DTI South East
Bridge Place
88/89 Eccleston Square
London SW1V 1PT
Tel: (071) 215 5000
Fax: (071) 828 1109
Telex: 297124

Single Market enquiries: (071) 215 0573

DTI South East
Area Office
40 Caversham Road
Berkshire RG1 7EB
Tel: (0734) 395600
Fax: (0734) 502818
Telex: 847799

Single Market enquiries: (0734) 395603/ 395605

DTI South East
Douglas House
London Road
Reigate, Surrey RH2 9QP
Tel: (0737) 226900
Fax: (0737) 223491
Telex: 918364

Single Market enquiries: (0737) 226917/ 226918

Chatham Office
Tel: (0634) 828688

Margate Office
Tel: (0843) 290511

Portsmouth Office
Tel: (0705) 294111

DTI South West
The Pithay
Bristol BS1 2PB
Tel: (0272) 272666
Fax: (0272) 299494
Telex: 44214

Single Market enquiries: Ext. 450

Industrial Development Board for Northern Ireland
IDB House
64 Chichester Street
Belfast BT1 4JX
Tel: (0232) 233233
Fax: (0232) 231328
Telex: 747025

Industry Department for Scotland
Alhambra House
45 Waterloo Street
Glasgow G2 6AT
Tel: (041) 248 2855
Fax: (041) 242 5404
Telex: 777883

Single Market enquiries: (041) 242 5499

426

Welsh Office
Industry Department
New Crown Building
Cathays Park
Cardiff CF1 3NQ
Tel: (0222) 825111
Fax: (0222) 823088
Telex: 498228

Single Market enquiries: (0222) 823271/823977

1992 Hotline
The 1992 Hotline is a telephone enquiry service only, dealing with requests for information and specialist contacts within Whitehall and elsewhere.

Tel: (081) 200 1992

SPEARHEAD on-line database
See entry in this chapter and *EC On-line Databases*, Part Eight, Chapter 2.

FT PROFILE
PO Box 12
Sunbury on Thames
Middlesex TW16 7UD
Tel: (0932) 761444
Fax: (0932) 781425

Single Market Unit

Single Market Unit
Department of Trade and Industry
Room 420
1 Victoria Street
London SW1H 0ET
Tel: (071) 215 5603/4603/5000
Fax: (071) 222 2531

Single Market seminars and conferences
The Single Market Unit provides details of conferences and seminars being held on Single Market topics and provides the names and addresses of the organisers. A calendar of forthcoming events is published in the DTI's quarterly publication *Single Market News*

Single Market Unit
Department of Trade and Industry
Room 420
1 Victoria Street
London SW1H 0ET
Tel: (071) 215 4647/5000
Fax: (071) 222 2531

Company law

See *Company Law*, Part Six, Chapter 2. The DTI publishes a booklet, *The Single Market: Company Law Harmonisation* containing details of developments on company law and related proposals within the EC. *The Companies Acts Annual Report* contains details of progress on EC Company Law harmonisation is prepared by the DTI's Companies Division. Consultation documents on individual EC proposals are also prepared and distributed by Companies Division and interested parties can obtain these on a regular basis by registering on a mailing list (see below).

Companies Division contacts provide information on those EC Company Law measures which have not yet been incorporated into UK national law. However, in view of the frequency with which the DTI undertakes internal reorganisations, the individual telephone extensions of contacts dealing with specific Directives are listed in the publications mentioned above and in the DTI's *The Single Market: The Facts* (Factsheet 15). These publications are updated from time to time. *The Single Market: The Facts* and *Single Market: Company Law Harmonisation* are published as part of the DTI's Single Market information and awareness campaign and can be obtained by ringing the *1992 Hotline* (081 200 1992) which also provides contacts within Whitehall. Other enquiries should be directed to:

Department of Trade and Industry
Companies Division
10-18 Victoria Street, London SW1H 0NN
Tel: (071) 215 3204/5000
Tel: (071) 215 3323

(Mailing list enquiries and requests for Companies Division publications)

Competition policy

Competition Policy Division
Department of Trade and Industry
1 Victoria Street, London SW1H 0ET
Tel: (071) 215 5337/5000
Fax: (071) 222 2629

Consumer affairs

Consumer Affairs Division
Department of Trade and Industry
10-18 Victoria Street, London SW1H 0NN
Tel: (071) 215 3325/5000
Fax: (071) 222 9280

Enterprise and Deregulation Unit

The unit welcomes views from business on the cost and burdens of complying with EC regulations and procedures.

Enterprise and Deregulation Unit
Department of Trade and Industry
1 Victoria Street, London SW1 0ET
Tel: (071) 215 5271/5000
Fax: (071) 222 2531

Enterprise Initiative

Freefone 0800 500200

Environment

DTI Environmental Enquiry Point
Warren Spring Laboratory
Gunnels Wood Road
Stevenage, Hertfordshire SG1 2BX
Tel: Freefone 0800 585794
Fax: (0438) 360858

Business and Environment Unit
Department of Trade and Industry
Ashdown House
123 Victoria Street, London SW1 6RB
Tel: (071) 215 6082
Fax: (071) 828 3258

EUROENVIRON
Department of Trade and Industry
Ashdown House
123 Victoria Street
London SW1 6RB
Tel: (071) 215 6529
Fax: (071) 828 3258

EC environmental technology rearch programme

Exports to Europe Branch

Exports to Europe Branch
Department of Trade and Industry
1 Victoria Street, London SW1H 0ET
Tel: (071) 215 4786/4782/5000
Fax: (071) 222 2531

Austria: Tel: (071) 215 215 4798
Belgium: Tel: (071) 215 5486
Denmark: Tel: (071) 215 5140
France: Tel: (071) 215 4762 (consumer goods), (071) 215 5197 (capital goods).
Germany: Tel: (071) 215 4796 (consumer goods), (071) 215 5179 (capital goods).
Greece: Tel: (071) 215 5103 (consumer goods), (071) 215 4776 (capital goods).
Ireland: Tel: (071) 215 4783

Italy: Tel: (071) 215 5103 (consumer goods). (071) 215 4776 (capital goods).
Luxembourg: Tel: (071) 215 5486
Netherlands: Tel: (071) 215 4790
Norway: Tel: (071) 215 5341
Portugal: Tel: (071) 215 5307
Spain: Tel: (071) 215 5624 (consumer goods), (071) 215 4284 (capital goods).
Sweden: Tel: (071) 215 5341
Switzerland: Tel: (071) 215 4359

Eastern Europe Branch

East European Branch
Department of Trade and Industry
1 Victoria Street, London SW1H 0ET
Tel: (071) 215 5258/5000
Fax: (071) 215 5269

Albania: Tel: (071) 215 4734
Bulgaria: Tel: (071) 215 4734
Czechoslovakia: Tel: (071) 215 5152/5267
Hungary: Tel: (071) 214 4734
Poland: Tel: (071) 214 4734
Romania: Tel: (071) 215 5152/5267
Yugoslavia: Tel: (071) 215 5152/5267

For details of German unification on liberalisation measures in Eastern Europe countries contact:

The Export Control Organisation
Department of Trade and Industry
Kingsgate House, 66-74 Victoria Street
London SW1E 6SW
Tel: (071) 215 8070

429

Library and Information Centre
Not to be confused with the Export Market Information Centre, the Library and Information Centre is the DTI's in-house library to which there is no personal public access. However, library staff deal with telephone and written requests for information on the Single Market and export activities.

Library and Information Centre
Department of Trade and Industry
1 Victoria Street
London SW1H 0ET
Tel: (071) 215 5444/5445/4245
Telex: 8811074 DTHQ G
Fax: (071) 215 5665

HM Customs and Excise

The Board of Customs and Excise has created a Single Market Unit which has responsibility for co-ordinating Single Market issues, including the implementation of EC regulations, within the department. The Unit is also concerned with the representation of Single Market issues within the UK and Brussels and liaison with interested trade bodies, and provides guidance and publicity within the department. Companies seeking information on compliance with existing regulations should contact their local Customs and Excise offices. General enquiries can be addressed to the HM Customs and Excise General Information Branch.

HM Customs and Excise
General Information Branch
New Kings Beam House
22 Upper Ground
London SE1 9PJ
Tel: (071) 865 3997
Fax: (071) 865 5625
Telex: 917905/886231

HM Customs and Excise
Single Market Unit
11th Floor
New King's Beam House
22 Upper Ground
London SE1 9PJ
Tel: (071) 865 5426 (fiscal), (071) 4787 (frontier controls), (071) 865 4795 (migration), (071) 865 4044 (transitional arrangements).
Fax: (071) 865 4051
Telex: 917905/886231

Department of Employment

Small Firms Information Service
Tel: Freefone 0800 222999

Social Charter
The DoE has published an information pack *Employment in Europe* which sets out the implications for business of the European Community's proposed Social Charter.

3 Representing Industry

Confederation of British Industry

As the nation's business voice, the Confederation of British Industry (CBI) speaks for some 250,000 firms, together employing more than half the nation's workforce. Its prime function is to ensure that its members' problems and requirements are fully understood at Westminster and Whitehall, and also increasingly in Brussels, the seat of the European Commission, and in Strasbourg, where the European Parliament meets. At the same time, the CBI tries to promote "best practice" throughout British business — on every aspect of doing business from management development to employee involvement.

European Community legislation now affects virtually all aspects of economic activity. An essential aspect of the CBI's work on behalf of its member companies is therefore to monitor and increase awareness of developments in the Single Market, and to influence the direction and content of European legislation.

It is a common fallacy, however, that CBI member companies are all industrial giants. Certainly most of the major multi-national companies are to be found within its ranks, but half the members are small firms employing fewer than 200 people. The active and vocal CBI Smaller Firms Council speaks out on their behalf.

Membership is diverse in the sectoral representation, ranging from high street retailers, including most of the big supermarket groups, food production and textiles, through engineering, manufacturing, mining and construction, into the City, where many banks, insurance companies and accountancy firms are in membership. The nationalised industries are also members.

The CBI was founded in 1965, formed by a merger of three older organisations, the biggest of which was the Federation of British Industries, which dates back to 1917. It is a non-profit making organisation, financed mainly by members' subscriptions, although frequent conferences — at its Centre Point headquarters in London, as well as in the regions — provide an additional source of income. These cover a wide range of subjects, including industrial relations, economics, finance, exporting, training and education.

Preparing for the Single Market

The European Commission's deadline for completion of a Single Market by 31st December 1992 has meant British companies, large and small, faced a difficult period of readjustment to the realities of business life in the new Europe. To help firms prepare for and cope with the change, the Confederation of British Industry launched a major private sector initiative. Ten leading British companies were brought together under the Chairmanship of Alan J Lewis, Chairman of the textile company, Illingworth Morris, to create *CBI Initiative 1992*.

The Initiative was intended to build on the success of the Government's *Europe — Open for Business* campaign, which had managed to create among firms a 90 per cent awareness factor of the significance of "1992". However, Alan Lewis warned that awareness of the single market was not enough; businesses had to start to prepare in detail to meet the challenge of an expanded market of 322 million consumers. The CBI is in a unique position to provide the necessary qualities of information by drawing on the knowledge of the best in British business and had assembled an elite task force of ten companies which were all experts in their field.

The ten companies are: Hill Samuel Bank; National Westminster Bank; S J Berwin & Co; Price Waterhouse; D'Arcy Masius Benton & Bowles; Rank Xerox; Edward Erdman Surveyors; PA Consulting Group; TNT Express (UK) and Blue Arrow. They provided specific advice to British firms on the following key areas of corporate strategic planning for the single market:

- Mergers, acquisitions and alternative corporate strategies
- Strategic corporate tax planning
- Finance for growth
- Company law and competition
- Marketing to the consumer
- Information technology
- Marketing to the public sector and industry
- Distribution and transport
- Property
- Employment and training

The CBI Initiative 1992 offered detailed advice to over 12,000 senior executives. Its £7 million programme offered British businesses a total resource in the form of a package of ten seminars, ten books, audio cassettes and an information service. The seminars ran throughout 1989 in each of the CBI's thirteen regions.

A telephone information service, the Eurolink Phoneline answers queries from businesses on practical problems, ranging from possible skill shortages in the construction industry to details of trade fairs for the sale of hunting goods in West Germany.

Eurolink Phoneline
CBI Initiative 1992: (071) 836 1992.

CBI POLICY

Economic and monetary union

The CBI believes that discussions on European economic and monetary union should not delay UK participation in the exchange rate mechanism of the European Monetary System. It considers that exchange rate stability is of fundamental importance to business, and with 1992 drawing closer, stability against other European currencies is particularly crucial.

The CBI believes that there will be significant benefits to business from a single European currency. But discussions to develop the EMS further in this direction cannot sensibly take place until the UK is a full a member of the system.

The CBI does not believe that binding rules for fiscal policy — proposed by the Delors report — will be needed to develop greater exchange rate stability and a move to a common currency. In fact, the reverse is true. Member countries will need more scope to use fiscal measures to pursue national policy objectives as monetary policy will be increasingly determined at a European level.

The social dimension

A Europe that is "open for business" is by definition a "People's Europe". Out of the economic advantages of the single market will flow better performance by EC trade and industry and hence more jobs, more secure jobs, better working conditions and a better quality of life; a Europe which benefits all Europe and allows everyone to share in the resulting prosperity.

To meet the challenges, Europe will have to be able to compete with Brazil, South Korea and Taiwan, for example, where employers have access to workers with skills approaching Northern levels, but where labour costs are much lower.

If the Community is more interested in rights than in duties, preoccupied with the distribution of wealth rather than its creation, the benefits of the Single Market could all too easily be realised in the Pacific Basin and South America, rather than within the Community.

UK employers fully support steps under way to develop social policies in the European Community such as health and safety legislation, training and retraining for the long-term and young unemployed, and measures to improve mobility. But they do not believe that the creation of the market will give rise to specific problems which justify a programme of social or employment legislation.

Commission proposals for measures such as a European Community Charter of Fundamental Social Rights, a European Company Statute or directives on social and employment issues must satisfy a number of criteria before UK employers can support them. Measures must not damage the ability of EC companies, and particularly small firms, to provide secure jobs, to compete in world markets and to generate the wealth needed for the EC's prosperity and improved working conditions.

So there should be a genuine need for a measure and a proper assessment of its cost implications. Issues should be tackled too at the most appropriate level, whether this is EC, national, sectoral, company or plant level, so that national systems are not undermined.

The priority is to create a Europe which is open, free and competitive. Employers would like to reassure employees that there is no distinction between the benefits of the internal market for companies and for employees. Economic growth generated by increased trade in the Single Market will provide for increased employment opportunities and security; for high wages; improved standards and conditions of work. People will have opportunities to develop their skills, and progress their careers, with access to training and retraining. They will have opportunities to contribute fully to the success of the enterprise and share in the financial rewards of that success. They will enjoy highest practicable standards of health and safety. They will have the right to belong or not to belong to a trade union, to be collectively bargained for if they so wish, and the right not to be discriminated against on the basis of race, sex, religion or disability. With time,

433

individuals will be free to move and work anywhere in the EC on equal terms with locals and with full recognition of skills and qualifications and equivalent transferable social security protection.

The real Social Dimension of the Single Market is not regulation on a Europe-wide basis, but our ability to improve the benefits of all aspects of employment to all in the Community, through the creation of globally competitive companies. The message that employees really wish to hear — whether through a Social Charter or some other means — is that their future employment prospects in all senses will be greatly enhanced through the processes of strengthening the EC's economy and trading ability with the world.

CBI ACTIVITIES

Brussels

The CBI maintains an office in Brussels to assist and to support the activities of CBI Committees and headquarters staff. The Office has four main tasks:

☐ To represent the CBI on the spot, keeping channels open, and liaising with the European Commission and other EC institutions as well as with the UK's Permanent Representative (UK REP).

☐ To maintain permanent liaison with UNICE (Union of Industrial and Employers' Confederations of Europe), which is European industry's prime policy representative in contacts with the Community institutions. The Head of the Brussels office is the CBI's Permanent Delegate to UNICE.

☐ To monitor developments in the EC and contribute to the CBI's policy work by providing early warnings to the CBI headquarters at Centre Point.

☐ To help and advise CBI members in their dealings with the EC.

Services to members
Brussels Office staff are available to personal callers, and by telephone or facsimile, to:

☐ Brief on the latest EC developments.

☐ Advise on representational strategy.

☐ Identify contacts in the Commission, UK Permanent Representation.

☐ Help with making appointments.

☐ Arrange visits for groups of CBI members.

CBI's Brussels Office

40 Rue Joseph 11, Bte 14
B - 1040 Brussels
Tel: (32) 2 231 0456
Fax (32) 2 230 9832

Wealth creation

The CBI is a high profile organisation. Its annual conference, which takes place in November each year, has achieved a recognised place in the business calendar. It receives media coverage on a par with that given to annual conferences of the Trades Union Congress and the political parties.

A total of some 2,000 delegates, media representatives and observers attend each year, many of them from organisations with a deep involvement in EC countries, institutions and companies.

The CBI exists to encourage a climate of opinion in which trade and industry can operate efficiently and create the wealth on which the UK's national standard of living depends. The CBI is in politics but it is not a party political organisation. It has no formal links with the Conservative Party (in the way the TUC has with the Labour Party) or indeed with any other party.

CBI officials and office-bearers have frequent discussions with members of all political parties in which they seek to explain the industrial and economic facts of life from the business viewpoint.

Policy making

When the Government seeks views on proposed legislation affecting industry, the CBI is the principal organisation to which it turns. The CBI then sounds out its members' views, making these known to ministers, civil servants, MPs and the media. This consultative process results in a clear statement of policy.

Treasury officials are familiar with the CBI's *Economic Priorities* — which give its views on the budget — and which are sent to the Chancellor of the Exchequer each year. The consultation process with members is much the same on other issues but the *Economic Priorities* presentation can serve as an example of how typically the CBI goes about its work. First, a framework of the CBI's ideas is set out by its Economic and Financial Policy Committee, with separate contributions from the Tax Committee, the Economic Situation Committee, other specialist committees and the Smaller Firms Council. Then there is a "grass roots" input from each of the 13 regional councils. Some 600 business executives are involved in these discussions, improving, adding to and amending the details before the policy suggestions come before the CBI's national Council for discussion and approval.

The Council

The CBI Council is made up of some 400 members, all senior executives from individual member firms, the nationalised industries, trade associations, employers' organisations, and the Smaller Firms and Regional Councils, ensuring that the whole range of members' views is taken into account.

The Director General and the President frequently meet groups of back-bench MP's for discussions on key issues of financial and economic policy and they play a leading role with their European counterparts in the union of industrial and employers' confederations in Europe (UNICE).

When necessary, extensive lobbying takes place, not only at Westminster and in Brussels, but also in the constituencies. Each of the CBI's regional councils has Parliamentary "linkmen", business people who volunteer to acquaint MPs at constituency level of CBI thinking and MEPs frequently attend these constituency meetings.

Surveys

The Confederation also initiates first-class research work. Every month, nearly 2,000 firms take part in the *Industrial Trends Survey*, telling how trading conditions are with them and how they see the future prospects. Sixty per cent of Britain's trade is now with Europe and 50 per cent with the Community. The survey provides a reliable indication of future trends in manufacturing industry. It is respected by economists, politicians, journalists and others, and has achieved a reputation for accuracy over 30 years.

This is now paralleled by a *Distributive Trades Survey*, which measures sales activity and prospects in Britain's high streets, among wholesalers and in the motor trade. Produced in conjunction with the *Financial Times*, and with the collaboration of the Retail Consortium and the Federation of Wholesale and Industrial Distributors, this survey is gaining increasing acceptance as a leading economic indicator.

Publications

CBI news

The CBI's monthly business magazine *CBI News* covers all aspects of business affairs:

☐   Economic trends and analysis.

☐   Exports — Europe and overseas.

☐   Parliamentary legislation and lobbying.

☐   Conferences, meetings and exhibitions.

☐   Industrial and commercial issues.

☐   Grants information.

☐   Personal viewpoints.

☐   Employment and industrial relations matters.

☐   Education, training, technology.

☐   Checklist of CBI activities.

CBI News also carries special reports and supplements on specific business topics such as aviation, property, car fleets, exhibitions, conferences, relocation, pensions and regional developments. *CBI News* is posted free to member companies on request: extra copies are chargeable at £1.50 an issue. Non-members may subscribe at: UK, £25; Western Europe £49; elsewhere, £59.

Europe sans frontiéres

A briefing pack is available covering all aspects of developing European Community policy for the new Single Market at the end of 1992, updated quarterly as new decisions are taken. Each pack contains some 20 briefs covering legislation, for example, on customs, transport, employment, health and safety and financial services. The service is designed to keep business up to date on these critical developments. Prices (1990): One year's subscription £60 for CBI members; £120 for non-members.

Employment Affairs Report

This comprehensive analysis of the employment scene is published six times a year. It regularly considers the implications on the labour market, pay and productivity of developments in the European Community. It includes:

☐ Employment/unemployment trends.

☐ Labour shortages.

☐ Pay settlements and earnings.

One year's subscription, £65 for CBI members; £100 for non-members. Single copies price £20.

Economic Situation Report

This gives a monthly up-to-date picture of recent and expected trends in the UK economy. It covers:
    CBI manufacturing survey and CBI/FT distributive trades survey summaries.
    Analysis of official economic and financial indicators.
    World output and commodity prices.
    Regular CBI forecasts.

One year's subscription £116 for CBI members; £185 for non-members. Single copies price: £9.20 to CBI members; £14.60 to non-members.

CONTACTS

CBI head office

The Confederation of British Industry
Centre Point
103 New Oxford Street
London WC1A 1DU
Tel: (071) 379 7400
Fax: (071) 240 1578
Telex: 21332

CBI regional offices

Belfast (Northern Ireland)
Fanum House
108 Great Victoria Street
Belfast BT2 7PD
Tel: 0232 326658
Fax: 0232 245915

Birmingham (West Midlands)
Hagley House
Hagley Road
Edgbaston
Birmingham B16 8PS
Tel: 021 454 7991
Fax: 021 456 1634

Bristol (South Western)
8-10 Whiteladies Road
Bristol BS8 1NZ
Tel: 0272 737065
Fax: 0272 238457

Cambridge (Eastern)
14 Union Road
Cambridge CB2 1HE
Tel: 0223 65636
Fax: 0223 355101

Cardiff (Wales)
Pearl Assurance House
Greyfriars Road
Cardiff CF1 3JR
Tel: 0222 232536
Fax: 0222 220688

Eccles (North Western)
Emerson House
Albert Street
Eccles
Manchester M30 0LT
Tel: 061 707 2190
Fax: 061 787 7571

Glasgow (Scotland)
Beresford House
5 Claremont Terrace
Glasgow G3 7XT
Tel: 041 332 8661
Fax: 041 333 9135

Henley (Southern)
Bank Chambers
10a Hart Street
Henley-on-Thames
Oxon RG9 2AU
Tel: 0491 576810
Fax: 0491 410382

Leeds (Yorkshire & Humberside)
Arndale House
Station Road
Crossgates
Leeds LS15 8EU
Tel: 0532 644242
Fax: 0532 606937

Newcastle (Northern)
15 Grey Street
Newcastle-upon-Tyne
NE1 6EE
Tel: 091-232 1644
Fax: 091-222 0793

Nottingham (East Midlands)
17 St Wilfrid Square
Calverton
Nottingham NG14 6FP
Tel: 0602 653311
Fax: 0602 655260

Sevenoaks (South Eastern)
Tubs Hill House
London Road
Sevenoaks
Kent TN13 1BX
Tel: 0732 454040
Fax: 0732 456510

4 Chambers of Commerce

A link between national policy and local enterprise

James Hogan

Despite the efforts of many local chambers of commerce, particularly the larger ones, the involvement of the chamber of commerce movement in the conduct of UK industrial and commercial policy and delivering national business support programmes lags behind its counterparts in other European countries. Membership of a chamber is compulsory in some Single Market countries and the chambers are invested with statutory powers and responsibilities. In eight of the twelve EC member states, chambers carry public law status. As a London Chamber of Commerce and Industry survey has shown, this has created a 'solid financial base from which these chambers are able to provide sophisticated and wide ranging services to business'. By comparison with the financial position of UK chambers, other European chambers are generously financed, enabling them to carry out a wide range of support activities for local business. But the role of chambers in these countries is not wholly mundane, or dealing with the detail of putting policies into practice. The heavy reliance on chambers in Germany and France, for example, to nurture local business is more than just a matter of administrative style. It symbolises a profound difference in official attitudes to industry and commerce, showing due regard for the importance of the health of the business sector in the national economy.

In recent years there has been an attempt in the UK to off-load some hitherto government initiatives onto the chambers. They include: Certain British Overseas Trade Board services; the role played by the now disbanded DTI weekly magazine, *British Business*, which has been replaced by the Association of British Chambers of Commerce's *Business Briefing*; and the attachment of Export Development Advisers to some 20 or so chambers. Like many Thatcherite initiatives in the industry sector they carry more publicity value than material gain. They do little, if anything, to strengthen the manufacturing base, particularly among the smaller manufacturing companies which, at the beginning of the 1990s find themselves ill-equipped to invest in modernisation or increased production, invest in training the workforce, having to battle against adverse economic factors arising from industrial policies and fashionable beliefs, operating far above the heads of the average smaller company manager. The chambers, most of which are underfunded, are not yet in a position to form the vital link between local and national activity that is taken for granted in other

European countries. As delivery agents for government programmes, the chambers are ideally placed in theory but, in practice, many are understaffed and underfunded and will remain so for a long time.

Nevertheless, chambers of commerce in the UK provide services of consistent quality for their membership, and for non-members, though at higher rates of charges for the latter. The London Chamber of Commerce and Industry, as well as some of the chambers in larger cities, provide an impressive range of services for local industry. Most produce informative magazines and newsletters to brief local companies on new developments affecting business in Europe. There are many practical services, including help with language training, export promotion, export documentation and Single Market seminars. Companies which have not participated in their local chamber of commerce activities may be pleasantly surprised by the benefits on offer, even under the existing financial constraints within the movement. Typical services may include:

Sponsorship of participation in overseas trade fairs
Inward and outward trade missions
Single Market information
On-line business information services
Export documentation
Export Development Adviser
Export Clubs
BC-Net liaison (see *The Brussels Connection*, Part Seven, Chapter 1).
Contacts in European markets via the international chamber network
Language courses
Translating and interpreting services
Advice of legal requirements
Company search and credit references
Shipping and transport information
ATA carnets
Advice on visa and health requirements
Export finance information
Fax and telex services
Library services
Trade bulletins and Journals

CONTACTS

Association of British Chambers of Commerce

The ABCC is the central co-ordinating body for some 100 chambers of commerce within its membership, ie. most of the active chambers in the UK. The Association provides details of services available from individual chambers and contact names and addresses within the movement. Its publishing activities include the production, editing and distribution of *Business Briefing*, a weekly magazine replacing the Department of Trade and Industry weekly, *British Business* which ceased to be published in 1989. The annual subscription to *Business Briefing* is £78.00. The magazine regularly carries news and information on Single Market developments.

Association of British Chambers of Commerce
Sovereign House
212 Shaftesbury Avenue
London WC2H 8EW
Tel: (071) 240 5831
Fax: (071) 379 6331

Business Briefing (subscriptions)

Business Briefing
Border House
High Street
Farndon
Chester CH3 6PK
Tel: (0829) 270714

Export Services
This is a who-does-what ABCC survey of chamber export services. It also includes a list of export clubs and contacts in the BC-Net chain of use to companies seeking collaborative partners in other European countries. Available from the ABCC's Export and Trade Unit.

Export and Trade Unit
Association of British Chambers of Commerce
4 Westwood House
Westwood Business Park
Coventry CV4 8HS
Tel: (0203) 694484
Fax: (0203) 694690

Export Development Advisers
Export Development Advisers have been attached to the following chambers of commerce and other agencies for an initial period of three years ending in 1992. The scheme is under review and the number of EDAs may vary, according to the ability of chambers to meet the cost. EDAs encourage companies to export and to make use of existing export services.

Aberdeen Chamber of Commerce
15 Union Terrace
Aberdeen AB9 1HF
Tel: (0224) 641222
Fax: (0224) 644326

Northern Ireland Chamber of Commerce & Industry
22 Great Victoria Street
Belfast BT2 7BJ
Tel: (0232) 244113
Fax: (0232) 247024

West Midlands Regional Group
Chamber of Commerce
PO Box 360
Edgbaston
Birmingham B15 3DH
Tel: (021) 454 6171
Fax: (021) 455 8670

Bristol Chamber of Commerce & Industry
16 Clifton Park
Bristol BS8 3BY
Tel:(0272) 737373
Fax: (0272) 745365

Cardiff Chamber of Commerce & Industry
101-108 The Exchange
Mount Stuart Square
Cardiff CF1 6RD
Tel: (0222) 481648
Fax: (0222) 489785

Essex Export Agency Limited
Chelmer Court
Church Street
Chelmsford
Essex CM1 1NH
Tel: (0245) 283030
Fax: (0245) 492486

Edinburgh Chamber of Commerce & Manufacturers
3 Randolph Crescent
Edinburgh EH3 7UD
Tel: (031) 225 5851
Fax: (031) 220 1508

Exeter & District Chamber of Commerce
31 Southernhay East
Exeter EX1 1NS
Tel: (0392) 436641
Fax: (0392) 50402

Gatwick Export Enterprise Centre
Room 120
Timberham House
Cargo Terminal
Gatwick Airport
West Sussex RH6 0EY
Tel: (0293) 560884
Fax: (0293) 549615

Kent Export Centre Limited
The Gatehouse
St George's Centre
Chatham Maritime
Gillingham
Kent ME4 4UH
Tel: (0634) 828688
Fax: (0634) 829425

An EDA is also based at Kent Export
Centre's Dover office Tel: (0304) 241400.

Glasgow Chamber of Commerce & Manufacturers
30 George Street
Glasgow G2 1EQ
Tel: (041) 204 2121
Fax: (041) 221 2336

Thames Chiltern Chamber of Commerce
16 Blenheim Road
High Wycombe
Buckinghamshire HP12 4TU
Tel: (0494) 462370
Fax: (0494) 440156

Association of Yorks & Humberside Chambers of Commerce
Commerce House
2 St. Alban's Place
Wade Lane
Leeds LS2 8HZ
Tel: (0532) 430491
Fax: (0532) 430504

Leicester & County Chamber of Commerce and Industry
4th Floor
York House
91 Granby Street
Leicester LE1 6EA
Tel: (0533) 471237
Fax: (0533) 55048

Merseyside Chamber of Commerce
Number One Old Hall Street
Liverpool L3 9HG
Tel: (051) 227 1234
Fax: (051) 236 0121

London Chamber of Commerce & Industry
69 Cannon Street
London EC4N 5AB
Tel: (071) 248 4444
Fax: (071) 489 0391

Luton, Bedford & District Chamber of Commerce & Industry
Stuart Street
Luton LU1 5AU
Tel: (0582) 450467
Fax: (0582) 419422

Manchester Chamber of Commerce
56 Oxford Street
Manchester M60 7HJ
Tel: (061) 236 3210
Fax: (061) 236 4160

Tees-side Chamber of Commerce
Exchange Square
Middlesbrough
Cleveland TS1 1DW
Tel: (0642) 230023
Fax: (0642) 230105

Tyne and Wear Chamber of Commerce
65 Quayside
Newcastle upon Tyne NE1 3DS
Tel: (091) 261 1142
Fax: (091) 261 4035

Nottinghamshire Chamber of Commerce
Unit 14
Faraday Building
Highfields Science Park
Nottingham NG7 2QP
Tel: (0602) 222414
Fax: (0602) 220312

Norwich & Norfolk Chamber of Commerce
112 Barrack Street
Norwich NR3 1UB
Tel: (0603) 625977
Fax: (0603) 633032

Dorset Chamber of Commerce & Industry
Upton House
Upton Country Park
Poole
Dorset BH17 7BJ
Tel: (0202) 682000
Fax: (0202) 680315

South East Hampshire Chamber of Commerce and Industry
27 Guildhall Walk
Portsmouth PO1 2RP
Tel: (0705) 294111
Fax: (0705) 296829

Reading Chamber of Commerce
43 West Street
Reading
Berkshire RG1 1AT
Tel: (0734) 595049
Fax: (0734) 500511

Wolverhampton Chamber of Commerce
93 Tettenhall Road
Wolverhampton
West Midlands WV3 9PE
Tel: (0902) 29069
Fax: (0902) 26028

PART EIGHT

PUBLICATIONS, LIBRARIES AND DATABASES

Break through into Europe

European Trends keeps you up-to-date with the latest developments and business opportunities in the European Community.

As 1992 approaches, business are increasingly aware of the need to look beyond their national borders into a wider market, offering greater opportunities. But the elimination of trade barriers will expose them to greater competition as well.

European Trends gives you the competitive advantage. Published every quarter by The Economist Intelligence Unit, *European Trends* is designed to keep you informed of the key trends and developments taking place within the European Community.

In over 50 pages, each issue contains coverage on: progress towards the Integrated market; recent cases before the European Court such as judgements on guarantees, franchising etc; external relations with the other major world trading blocks; cross border cooperation and environmental legislation; the development and implementation of new technologies. In addition to the four reports, a subscription includes an annual supplement, the essential background information on events monitored each quarter.

FORTHCOMING TOPICS TO BE COVERED INCLUDE:

- New Horizons for Savings Banks in Spain and Italy
- Council Decision Making After the Single European Act
- New Food Processing Technologies
- Prospects for a European Environmental Protection Agency

- Can Europe Recover in the Chip Race?
- Anti-Dumping Action: a Form of Protectionism?
- Economic and Monetary Union: the Lessons of History
- Banking after 1992

The Economist Intelligence Unit Limited, 40 Duke Street, London W1A 1DW.

ORDER FORM

Please enter _____ annual supscription/s to European Trends (4 issues plus supplement)

Price: £165; US$315 North America (postage included)

☐ I enclose a cheque for £/US$ _____
(payable to The Economist Intelligence Unit Limited)

I wish to pay by ☐ American Express   ☐ Visa

Account No.

Signature _____ Expiry date _____

☐ Please invoice me

☐ Please send details of other European publications.

Name _____

Position _____

Company _____

Address _____

Please send your completed order form to:

The Economist Intelligence Unit

Marketing Department (EHFLA)
40 Duke Street London W1A 1DW
Telephone (01) 493 6711 Telex 266353

Overseas Office:
215 Park Avenue South   Phone: (212) 460-0600
New York, NY 10003   Telex: 175567

Business International
GLOBAL BUSINESS INFORMATION AND ADVICE

The Economist Intelligence Unit Limited Registered Office: 25 St James Street, London SW1A 1HG. Registered in London no 1762617.

1 European Community Publications

EC Treaties, Official Journal, Single Market programme, work of Community institutions, periodicals, series, statistics

Marguerite-Marie Brenchley

To business managers with little time to spend on research, the Single Market is yet another distraction from the all important task of running a business; and to the business adviser, it brings a fresh dimension to counselling and assisting clients, a task which requires them to monitor European Community developments. A major benefit to business managers and business advisers alike, though underused and underrated, is the detailed information which the EC publishes. The range of available information on EC topics is unprecedented in Europe. EC publications include periodicals, studies, reports, documents, statistical analyses, books and booklets touching on virtually every aspect of doing business.

The Office for Official Publications of the European Communities produces the bulk of EC material, describing policies, principles, and workings of the Community. Proposals for new legislation are always well documented and appear in standard, mandatory publications such as the *Official Journal of the European Communities*. The journal, rather like a gazette, records all proposed or adopted Regulations, Directives, Decisions, Opinions and Recommendations, plus notices of tenders for major public supply contracts and calls for proposals for research projects.

Many EC documents and reports take the form of communiques, such as *COM documents*, which set out the background, aims and the terms of proposals for new legislation. These documents pass between the institutions of the Community and between the institutions and interested parties throughout Europe. The reality is, however, that such documents are read mainly at a professional or political level. The average company manager rarely obtains a document, though reports and interpretations of new proposals do, of course, appear in the daily press and trade publications which most company managers read.

EC publications promote Community-wide aims, reflecting the duty of the Community to bring the aims of the Treaties and the Single European Act to fruition. These aims aside, the factual content of EC publications is extremely valuable, even though it is usually framed in a Community context. EC documents and publications are, in any case, intended to be read in conjunction with other material. They are in many instances the first word on a subject, so to speak, rather than the last.

A general misconception is that EC documents and publications only cover new legislation and, as such, make heavy reading. The Community produces many informative and even entertaining publications to meet the need for information. The range is such that no commercial publisher could undertake even a fraction of the required output, let alone meet the demands of a readership of 320 million people in twelve countries, speaking so many different languages. Companies should, of course, monitor new developments as best they can, even if the task seems awesome. Not surprisingly most smaller companies and their advisers are selective in the information they monitor. This chapter cannot include the entire range of publications published by the European Community. But it outlines the main threads of published information and data which exist for the benefit of companies and researchers. Once they have immersed themselves in the Community's information network, however, the task becomes easier. For those coming to this network for the first time, the basic options are to:

☐ Subscribe to a periodical covering EC affairs.

☐ Establish and update a selective library.

Many people, however, will continue to seek information only when questions arise from time to time in the course of doing business. They may find useful material in this Chapter, which lists publications covering most areas of Community activity. For those who, as a result of the 1992 publicity campaign, intend to become part of the informed Community by obtaining a regular flow of information, this survey of EC publications serves as an introduction to the Community's information output.

Catalogue

A general catalogue, *The European Community as a Publisher — 1990* is available free of charge from the European Commission UK Offices and the European Parliament. Most publications are available for sale in the United Kingdom from H.M.S.O. or from Alan Armstrong Ltd (see *Contacts* at the end of the Chapter). Whenever possible the ISBN number is given, plus prices in national currencies and/or Ecus (European Currency Units).

TREATIES OF THE EUROPEAN COMMUNITIES

The Treaties of the European Communities
Treaty of Paris 1951 (ECSC), Treaty of Rome (EEC) 1957, Treaty of Rome 1957 (EURATOM) and amending Treaties. The Treaties constitute the primary legislation of the European Communities whether they are the Founding Treaties, the Treaties amending these Treaties (Volume I) or the later Treaties of Accession (Volume II). The treaties are published in all official languages of the Communities.

Volume I £33.00
Volume II £58.00
Volumes I & II £75.00
Available from HMSO Bookshops

The Single European Act
Text of the Act. Signed in 1986, the SEA came into force in 1987 and is the instrument amending the founding treaties to create a legal basis for

completion of the Internal Market. Important also because, being part of EC law, its provisions have far reaching implications for trade, commerce and industry.

Bulletin of the European Communities, 2/86
ISBN 92-825-5965-3
Price £1.50.

OFFICIAL JOURNAL OF THE EUROPEAN COMMUNITIES

This is the daily, legal gazette of the European Communities recording Regulations, Directives, Decisions, Recommendations, Proposals and other documents. Subscriptions are available from HMSO. Individual copies can also be purchased and the journal is kept in libraries, including European Documentation Centres (See *Libraries*, Part 8, Chapter 3). The journal is published in three series:

L series
The L series, or legislative series, contains mainly secondary legislation, i.e. post-treaties legislation.

☐ Regulations: Binding in their entirety and directly applicable in all member states.

☐ Directives: Binding on member states as to the result to be achieved, but leaving the governments of member states to choose the method of implementation through national legislation.

☐ Decisions: Similar to regulations, directly binding, but addressed to specific parties (one or more member states or individuals).

☐ Recommendations and Opinions: Not binding.

C series
The C series, also known as the Communications series, is sub-divided into three sections:

☐ Information: Daily rate of the Ecu, opinions of the European Parliament, written questions, notices of actions brought before the Court of Justice etc.

☐ Preparatory Acts: Proposals for legislation, opinions of the ESC and of the Court of Auditors.

☐ Notices: Invitations to tender relating to agricultural products or notices of competitions for recruitment in the Community institutions etc.

The L and C series are not available independently. One has to subscribe to both, in hard copy form or on microfiche. Retrospective annual collections of the two series are available on microfiche only. Subscriptions include the bi-annual directory of Community legislation in force. The directory can also be purchased independently, price 75 Ecus. Indices to the L and C series are published monthly. A cumulative index is published annually.

S series

The S series, or supplement to the *Official Journal*, is published daily and contains notices of public works and supply contracts; projects financed by the European Development Fund and supply or works contracts compulsorily published under Community rules; or contracts not required to be published under Community rules. Subscriptions to the S series are obtainable independently from the L and C series, but not available on microfiche. The contents of the Supplement are, however, published electronically on TED (Tenders Electronic Daily) which is updated daily in view of the fact that tender information is required instantly. TED data is available on-line throughout the Community (See *EC On-line Databases*, Part 8, Chapter 2).

Annex (debates of the European Parliament)

This series can be obtained by annual subscription or as separate issues and is available in hard copy or on microfiche. Retrospective collections are only available on microfiche.

SINGLE MARKET TITLES

The completion of the Single Market and the requirement to remove all major barriers to trade by 1992 has generated many useful, if not indispensable, booklets, reports and papers as well as series such as *Target 1992*. Established series such as the *Documentation Series* of booklets also include items prepared with 1992 in mind to meet the information needs of the business community and the general public. The following list includes the main series with a 1992 focus, plus individual publications and titles falling within the general EC series.

The Commission's White Paper and the Single European Act

Completing the Internal Market

European Commission White Paper to the European Council, preceding the Single European Act. Original text published as COM(85)310 final, later reproduced in the *Document* series
Main contents:

PART ONE: THE REMOVAL OF PHYSICAL BARRIERS
I.   Introduction
II. Control of goods
      Commercial and economic policy
      Health
      Transport
      Statistics
      Conclusion and timetable
III. Control of individuals

PART TWO: THE REMOVAL OF TECHNICAL BARRIERS
I.   Free movement of goods
      The need for a new strategy
      The chosen strategy
      Harmonisaton — a new approach
      Preventing creation of new obstacles
      Mutual recognition
      Nuclear materials

II.   Public procurement
III. Free movement for labour and the professions:
      a new initiative in favour of Community Citizens
IV.   Common market for services
         Traditional Services
         Financial services
         Transport
         New technologies and services
V.   Capital movements
VI.   Creation of suitable conditions for
      industrial co-operation
         Creation of a legal framework facilitating
         co-operation between enterprises
         Intellectual and industrial property
         Taxation
VII. Application of Community Law
         Infringements
         Transparency
         Competition policy and state aids

PART THREE: THE REMOVAL OF FISCAL BARRIERS
I.   Introduction
         Commercial Traffic and Value Added Tax
         The Individual Traveller
         Excises
II.   Approximation
         The Broad Picture
         Value Added Tax
         Excises
III. The Commission's proposals
         Value Added Tax
         Excises
         Enforcement
         Derogatons

CONCLUSION

ANNEX: Timetable for completing the Internal Market by 1992
         ISBN 92-825-5436-8
         Price £3.90

The Single European Act
         Text of the Act. Signed in 1986, the SEA came into force in 1987 and is the
         instrument amending the founding Treaties to create a legal basis for
         completion of the Internal Market. Important also because, being part of EC
         law, its provisions have far reaching implications for trade, commerce and
         industry. Text of the Single European Act, Supplement to the *Bulletin of the
         European Communities.*
         No. 2/86
         ISBN 92-825-5965-3
         Price £1.50.

Cecchini Report: Research on the Cost of Non-Europe

The *Cecchini Report* is a preparatory study of the costs of NOT completing the Single Market. It is a highly detailed study based on research into key industrial sectors and other Single Market areas of activity. Probably the largest EC research project of its kind, it serves as a basic study of the benefits of the Single Market but, more important, it comes closest to providing an 'empirical' basis for the economic and industrial aims of the Commission's Single Market programme. Its concentration on industry sectors makes it a particularly valuable source for industries.

Basic Studies: Executive Summaries
    Volume 1
    ISBN 92-825-8605-7
    Price £35.10
Studies on the Economics of Integration
    Volume 2
    ISBN 92-825-8616-2
    Price £38.00
Completion of the Internal Market: A Survey of European Industry's Perception of the Likely Effects.
    Volume 3
    ISBN 92-825-8610-3
    Price £16.80
Border-related Controls and Administrative Formalities: An Illustration in the Road Haulage Sector.
    Volume 4
    ISBN 92-825-8618-9
    Price £15.00
The Cost of Non-Europe in Public Sector Procurement
    Volume 5
    Part A: ISBN 92-825-8646-4
    Part B: ISBN 92-825-8647-2
    Price A+B £78.00
Technical Barriers in the EC
    Volume 6
    An illustration by six industries: Some case studies on technical barriers.
    ISBN 92-825-8649-9
    Price 21 Ecus
Obstacles to Trans-border Business Activity
    Volume 7
    ISBN 92-825-8638-3
    Price £8.50
The Cost of Non-Europe for Business Services
    Volume 8
    ISBN 92-825-8637-5
    Price £9.00
The Cost of Non-Europe in Financial Services
    Volume 9
    ISBN 92-825-8636-7
    Price £78.00

The Benefits of Completing the Internal Market for Telecommunications Services and Equipment in the Community.
Volume 10
ISBN 92-825-8650-2
Price £11.50
The EC 1992 Automobile Sector
Volume 11
ISBN 92-825-8619-7
Price £18.50
The Cost of Non-Europe in the Foodstuffs Industry
Volume 12
Part A: ISBN 92-825-8642-1
Part B: ISBN 92-825-8643-X
Price: A+B £78.00
Le Cout de la Non-Europe des Produits de la Construction
Volume 13
In French. NEDO has its own translation
ISBN 92-825-8631-6
Price £9.40
The Cost of Non-Europe in the Textile/Clothing Industry
Volume 14
ISBN 92-825-8641-3
Price £14.10
The Cost of Non-Europe in the Pharmaceutical Industry
Volume 15
ISBN 92-825-8632-4
Price £9.00
The Internal Markets of North America: Fragmentation and Integration in the USA and Canada.
Volume 16
ISBN 92-825-8630-8
Price £9.00
1992: The European Challenge
An important parallel to the Cecchini report, emerging out of *The Cost of Non-Europe* project, it distils the arguments and evidence of the benefits of a Single Market for general consumption at an economical price.
Paolo Cecchini, with Michel Catinat and Alexis Jaquemin
Published by Wildwood House Limited
Gower House
Croft Road, Aldershot
Hants GU11 3HR
ISBN 0-7045-0613-0
Price £6.95 (127pp)

Completing the Internal Market: Current Status December 1989

Set of brochures, summarizing current problems, the 1992 objectives, and the measures and proposals towards the completion of the Internal Market. The series is to be up-dated regularly until 1992. The format is clear and practical, each publication being sub-divided into specific topics. Situation at December 1989.

A Common Market for Services
ISBN 826-0851-4
A New Community Standards Policy
ISBN 826-0878-6

Conditions for Industrial Co-operation
A Single Procurement Market
ISBN 826-0869-7

Elimination of Frontier Barriers and Fiscal Controls
ISBN 826-0860-3

Veterinary and Plant Health Controls
ISBN 826-0887-5
Price per brochure 15 Ecus, or the set 50 Ecus (excluding VAT)

Target 1992

1992 and Beyond
John Palmer
"Deadline 92" Document
Analysis of the concept of the single market with a view of what it can offer
to the peoples of Europe up to and beyond 1992.
ISBN 92-826-0088-2
Price 8 Ecus.

Summaries of specific developments in the Internal Market, published in a
monthly newsletter on the Single Market, prepared by the European
Commission, Directorate-General for Information, Communication and Culture
(DGX) and Directorate-General for Information Market and Innovation
(DGXXIII).

Back numbers available from the European Commission UK Offices.
Free

A Frontier-Free Europe series

New publications in varied formats under a common *A Frontier-Free Europe* logo,
reporting on different aspects of the Community plan to create a large frontier-
free market by 1992. Examples:

A Guide to Working in a Europe Without Frontiers
Jean-Claude Seche
1988
ISBN 92-825-8067-9
Price £13.00

Common Standards for Enterprises
Florence Nicolas
1988
ISBN 92-825-8554-9
Price £6.20

Other Single Market-related titles

Completing the Internal Market: An Area without Internal Frontiers
Mid-term report required by article 8b of the SEA
COM(88)650 final
ISBN 92-825-8803-3
Price 6 Ecus

Europe Without frontiers: A Review Half-way to 1992
European File series, 10/89
Free

Progress Report by the Commission, Council and European Parliament on the Implementation of the Internal Market.
COM(90)90 final

Communication from the Commission on the Implementation of the Legal Acts Required to Build the Single Market.
COM(89)422 final

The Economics of 1992
Evaluation of the potential economic impact of completing the Internal Market — the insertion of micro-economic information into a coherent picture at macro-economic level.
European Economy series, 35, March 1988

Europe 1992: Developing an Active Approach to the European Market
A 36-page booklet on questions concerning the practical aspects of running a business in an integrated market. Published for the Commission by Whurr Publishers Ltd, 2 Alwyne Road, London N1 2HH.

Europe Without Frontiers: Completing the Internal Market
European Documentation series, 2/1989
Free

Guide to the Reform of the Community Structural Funds 1989
Reform of the structural funds made imperative by the completion of the Internal Market.
ISBN 92-826-0029-7
Price 11.25 Ecus

THE WORK OF THE COMMUNITY AND ITS INSTITUTIONS

The structure and workings of the institutions of the European Communities generate a regular flow of documents. As progress of political and economic integration of the European Communities continues the quantity and range of information and documentation increases. Many documents begin as internal documents, but are later developed into publicly available policy information or communication documents.

When a Community institution's document reaches the public, it may take the form of the broadly known documents such as the Commission *COM documents* or as an entry in the *Official Journal*. These are read by a most professional, commercial or political organisations in the Community which monitor EC developments. Some documents may take the form of specific articles on specialised EC topics. Others update or revise previous reports and proposals. The Office of Official Pubications in Luxembourg is conscious of the increasing importance of meeting the needs of the general public and business for concrete information on specialist topics. The advent of 1992 has given impetus to this task, emphasising the importance of seeking and finding specialist information, be it legal, financial, social or economic in character.

Once a document has been drafted, it acquires new status and the logical, but sometimes painstaking path the document will follow sometimes confuses the information seeker. This may be the case whether the document is a communication from the Commission, or presents the final text of a proposal, marks a further step in a policy making process or is the work of one of the other institutions. The confusion is often compounded by the various channels of distribution. All official publications are ultimately available from the Office of Official Publications Luxembourg. But each member state has its own sales agents. It is also possible to obtain other documents free of charge from European Commission UK offices, European Parliament information offices in member states, and direct from the institutions themselves.

The Office for Official Publications of the European Communities publishes documents, booklets and periodicals in nine community languages covering the activities of Community institutions:

European Parliament
Council of Ministers
European Commission
Economic and Social Committee
European Court of Justice
Court of Auditors
European Centre for the Development of Vocational Training
European Foundation for the Improvement of Living and Working Conditions
Other Community bodies

Bulletin of the European Communities

Published eleven times a year, covering the activities of the Community institutions on a monthly basis. Jointly published with the *Bulletin* is the *Supplement* to the *Bulletin of the European Communities*. The *Supplement* contains reprints of texts of specific and most major documents, eg. the text of the Single European Act. Available separately or on annual subscription, eleven issues plus index and supplements, price £66.00.

Annual reports on Community activities

General Report
Review of all Community activities over the year. The latest edition is the *Twenty-third General Report on the Activities of the European Commmunities, 1989*.
ISBN 92-826-1102-7
Price 12.40 Ecus
The Agricultural Situation in the Community, 1989 Report
ISBN 92-826-0913-8
Price 25.50 Ecus
Report on Social Developments, 1988
ISBN 92-826-0226-5
Price 16.50 Ecus

Eighteenth Report on Competition Policy, 1989
 ISBN 92-826-0623-6
 Price 17.50 Ecus

European Commission

The Commission is the Community's 'think-tank' and executive institution, charged under the Treaties with initiating Community legislation. As the administrative arm of the Single Market the Commission functions as the intermediary in any EC internal agreements. The Commission produces many documents. Some are working documents, not available to the public. The Commission documents are:

Working documents

Prepared by the Commission's Directorates-General, Working documents are prepared by Commission officials for internal purposes. The numerification indicates their provenance, eg. document III/134/89 denotes the 134th document issued by Directorate-General III (Internal Market) in l989. Working documents frequently form the basis of proposals for legislation, but do not represent official Commission policy. Occasionally such documents are reports prepared by independent experts who have been invited to help a Directorate-General formulate policy guidelines.

COM documents

Final working documents are submitted to the Secretariat-General of the Commission for consideration by the seventeen-member Commission. They are re-issued by the Secretariat General bearing a *COM document* number, eg. COM[89]205 — 205th document issued by the Secretariat-General in 1989. Draft documents may be amended several times before they are issued as *COM final* documents.

COM final documents

Once approved by the Commission as a college, *COM documents* are given the suffix, 'final', eg. COM[89] final, an important distinction meaning that the document is now finalised and available to the public from sales agents or the Office for Official Publications in Luxembourg. *COM final* documents are published as proposals for legislation or official communications memoranda. They can be obtained singly, or on an annual subscription basis. Selective subscriptions by subject are also available.

SEC documents

Less formal documents issued by the Commission's Secretariat-General, containing statistical data or information on the implementation of Community decisions, eg. when they reach the 'common position' stage. Not for sale to the public.

C documents

Legislative documents issued by the Commission in its day-to-day role of supervisor and administrator of EC policy, first drafted in the form of C documents. The final text of Commission decisions and regulations is eventually published in the *Official Journal*.

Joint subscription

Selective Commission documents, by topic, can also be obtained through a joint subscription to European Commission, European Parliament and Economic and Social Committee documents. Contact the sales office of Official Publications Office of the European Communities.

European Parliament

Regular series

Official Journal of the European Communities — Annex: Debates of the European Parliament.

> Verbatim reports of the sittings constituting a monthly session of the European Parliament.
>
> Monthly, annual subscription March to February
>
> Price £83.00

Minutes of sittings of the European Parliament

> Record of the business conducted during the sessions of the Parliament. Published in the C series of the *Official Journal.*

Fact sheets on the European Parliament and the activities of the European Community, 1989.

> ISBN 92-823-0163-X
>
> Price 17.50 Ecus

European Parliament News

> Monthly newspaper covering the debates and activities of the European Parliament. Free to mailing list subscribers.

European Parliament

> Briefing diary of items to be discussed during the sessions plus summaries of some reports. Free to mailing list subscribers.

European Parliament: The Week

> Weekly summary of parliamentary activities, published mid-week.Free to mailing list subscribers.

Research and documentation papers

> Series of research studies published by the European Parliament Directorate-General for Research. Free. Titles available in English.

Joint subscription

Selective EP documents, by topic, can also be obtained through a joint subscription to European Commission, European Parliament and Economic and Social Committee documents. Contact the sales office of Official Publications Office of the European Communities.

Other European Parliament titles

Forging Ahead: European Parliament 1952-88

> Published to coincide with the third European Parliament elections, this 230-page guide describes the powers and working methods of the European Parliament, its integration with the other Community institutions and its role in the process of European integration.
>
> ISBN 92-823-0154-0
>
> Price 20 Ecus

The European Parliament
    1987 (20pp)
    AX-47-86-777
    Free
European Parliament: Rules of Procedure
    1989
    Free
European Parliament: List of Members
Also known as the 'Grey List'
    Free
Europe's Parliament and the Single Act
    1989
    Free
Progress Towards European Integration: Survey of the Main Activities of the European Parliament.
    1988
    Free
Ten Years that Changed Europe, 1979/1989
    A survey of all areas of EC policy 1989
    Free

Economic and Social Committee

The Economic and Social Committee (ESC) is the Community body comprised of delegates from employers, trades unions and the professions. It still retains its formal title of Economic and Social Consultative Assembly on documents. As a consultative body, its role in the Community's legislative procedures is to give its opinions on proposals for new legislation on issues of economic and social importance. A range of publications covering the work of the ESC is available:

Annual reports of the Economic and Social Committee
    1988 report: ISBN 92-830-0145-1
    Price 8.50 Ecus
Briefing
    Monthly communique in the form of a diary of events including statements to the ESC, discussions, preparation of opinions and reports, and dates of plenary sessions. Mailing list distribution.
Bulletin of the Economic and Social Committee
    Published monthly. Available on annual subscription
    ISBN 0256-5846
    Price £19.00
Opinions and reports of the Economic and Social Committee
    Published on a day-to-day basis.
    Annual subscription £184.00
    Also published later in the "C" series of the *Official Journal.*

Joint subscription
Selective ESC documents, by topic, can also be obtained through a joint subscription to European Commission, European Parliament and Economic and Social Committee documents. Contact the sales office of Official Publications Office of the European Communities.

459

Other ESC titles

The Other European Assembly
> A 31-page booklet outlining the structure and work of the ESC.
> l989
> Free

Horizon 1992: The ESC Supports the Removal of Fiscal Frontiers
> Contains eight opinions
> 1988

Target Date 1992: The ESC Supports 'the New-frontier Europe'
> Contains seven opinions
> 1988

Europe and the New Technologies
> 1986

Disadvantaged Island Regions
> 1988

Basic Community Social Rights
> Opinion
> 1989

Community Advisory Committee for the Representation of Socio-Economic Interests.
> Gower Publishing Co Ltd
> 1 Westmead
> Farnborough
> Hants GU1 47RU
> Price £8.50

European Interest Groups and their Relationship to the Economic and Social Committee.
> Gower Publishing Co Ltd (address above)
> Price £25.00

Council of Ministers

The Council of Ministers, comprised of ministers of member states, is the EC's principal legislative institution. When the Council adopts a proposal put forward by the Commission, the final text of adoption is published in the *Official Journal of the European Communities*, L series. Other items relating to the work of the Council appear in the series C of the *Official Journal*.

Regular series
Minutes of Council meetings
Extracts from minutes of Council meetings can be obtained from the European Commission UK offices. General publications covering the Council's activities include:
Review of the Council's work
> Published annually

Other titles
Guide to the Council of the European Communities
> Secretariat of the Council, 1988
> ISBN 92-824-0546-X
> Price 6.50 Ecus

European Court of Justice

Regular series
The Community's judicial authority is in matters of compliance with Community law and national law where Community law may take precedence (see *European Community Law*, Part 6, Chapter 1).

Digest of Case Law A Series
> Judgements of the Court relating to the EEC, ECSC, and EURATOM Treaties and secondary law. Loose-leaf with updates.
> Issue 1, 1983 (1,069pp) £40.80
> Issue 2 (1st update), 1985 £20.40
> Issue 3 (2nd update), 1986 £20.80

Digest of Case Law D series
> Case law on the Convention of 27 September 1968 on jurisdiction and enforcement of judgements in civil and commercial matters.
> Issue 1, 1979 (basic edition) £20.80
> Issue 2 (1st update), 1984 £20.40
> Issue 3, December 1985 (basic edition: 1981) £20.80

Reports of cases before the Court
> Published at irregular intervals
> Contains the judgements of Court cases published with an annual index.
> Price £75.00

Proceedings of the Court of Justice of the European Communities
> Published weekly. Available only from the Court of Justice in Luxembourg. Summaries of the judgements, opinions, oral proceedings and new cases. Indispensable to the legal profession.

Other Court of Justice titles
The European Court of Justice
> *European Documentation* series, 5/1986
> Free

Synopsis of the work of the Court of Justice
> Summary of the work of the Court in 1984 and 1985. Information on the administration of the Court plus summaries of important judgements.
> ISBN 92-829-0141-6
> Free

Court of Auditors

The Court of Auditors is the Community institution in charge of external auditing of the Community's general budget and the ECSC's operating budget.

Regular series
Special reports
> Reports by the Court of Auditors on specific aspects of Community spending, published in the C series of the *Official Journal*.

Annual reports of the Court of Auditors
> Annual reports on Community spending. Published in the C series of the *Official Journal*.
> 1987 C316 of 12.12.88.
> 1988 C312 of 12.12.89

Other Court of Auditors titles
The Court of Auditors of the European Communities
> Booklet describing the work of the Court
> 1988
> Free

European Foundation for the Improvement of Living and Working Conditions

The Foundation's role is to plan and establish better living and working conditions by disseminating knowledge.

EF-News
> Newsletter, published five times a year, highlighting the activities of the Foundation, plus other work being done in Europe on themes related to the Foundation's aims.
> Free

European Foundation for the Improvement of Living and Working Conditions: Catalogue of publications 1988.
> Cumulative list of all Foundation publications since its inception.
> ISBN 92-825-8729-0
> Free

Annual reports
European Foundation for the Improvement of Living and Working Conditions: Annual Report 1988
> ISBN 92-825-9544-7
> Price 8.75 Ecus

European Centre for the Development of Vocational Training (CEDEFOP)

The Centre promotes co-operation among Community member states including vocational training through an exchange of information on national vocational training systems.

CEDEFOP News
> Multilingual journal in German, French and English. Free from CEDEFOP.

Vocational Training
> Published three times a year
> ISSN 0378-5068
> Price per single copy 5 Ecus; annual subscription 12 Ecus:
> Main themes include:
> *Wanted: New media for vocational training!* 1/1988
> *The social dialogue: Bridging the divide* 2/1988
> *Selective funding: A regulative instrument for initial and continuing training* 3/1988.

Education and training: The keys to the future 1/1989

Annual reports
CEDEFOP: Annual report l988
    ISBN 92-825-8442-9
    Free

GENERAL EC TITLES

The European Community as a Publisher
    Catalogue of EC publications, mainly sales items
    Free
About Europe
    Illustrated background information booklet on the European Community.
    Free.
Working Together
    Emile Noel
    The European Community institutions and how they work together,
    published in nine languages. Basic reading.
    Reprinted 1988
    English version ISBN 92-825-8526-3
    Free
Political map of the European Community
    Map (42 x 30 cm), incorporating basic statistics
    Free
The European Community and the Third World
    Colour map of the world highlighting the Community and developing
    countries, with graphics on aid and trade. Available in two sizes, 100 x 70 cm
    or 40 x 28 cm.
    Free
Development
    Illustrated booklet on official development assistance obtainable from
    Community and member states. Film list

Films and videos available for free hire

Videos are available for use by schools, professional associations, conference organisers etc.
    To borrow one of the following titles contact the distributor: Guild Sound and Vision Ltd, 6 Royce Road, Peterborough, PE1 5YB. Tel: 0733 315315.

Currently available:

Europe of Opportunities (1982):
    A guide for businessmen on grants and loans from the European Community
Europe Why? (1987):
    A general introduction to the European Community.
ESPRIT (1984):
    A brief outline of the EC's strategic programme for research in information
    technologies.

Europe's Bank
   The work of the European Investment Bank.
Let's Save the Environment (1985)
   The EC's environmental policies.
What has Europe to do with the Third World? (1987)
   The EC's policies towards the developing world.
Women in Partnership (1988)
   The role of women in today's world.
Europe Sans Frontieres (1988)
   What 1992 means for the UK. Aimed at business and general audiences.
Research and Technological Development (1989)
   The EC's research programmes.
A European Journey (1987)
   The EC as seen through the eyes of a boy travelling with his grandfather.
A Day in the Life of the Spokesman's Group (1989)
   Description of the work of the press service in the Commission in Brussels.
EuroInfo Centres (1990)
   A promotional video to describe the work of the EuroInfo Centre network
   and the services available to local small and medium sized enterprises.

Series documents

All purpose series covering all sectors of EC policy or re-print documents no
longer available in their original format. There is no overall index because of the
diversity and frequency of the titles. Some series documents are listed in the EC's
publication catalogue (see above). Others in the series, as and when they are
published, are usually known to librarians involved with EC documentation. The
following selection of recently issued series documents gives an idea of the
character and content of the series.
Completing the Internal Market
   White paper from the Commission to the European Council
   Series document
   ISBN 92-825-5436-8
   Price £3.90
Disharmonies in EC and US Agricultural Policy Measures 1988
   Experts' report on the differences between the agricultural policy of the
   European Community and of the United States of America.
   Series document
   ISBN 92-825-7949-2
   Price £43.00
*Disharmonies in EC and US Agricultural Policies: A Summary of Results and
Major Conclusions 1988.*
   Series document
   ISBN 92-825-8599-9
   Price £5.20

MAILING LIST PUBLICATIONS

The European Commission London Office supplies the following information
sheets to names on its mailing list.
The Week in Europe
   Summary of highlights concerning Community events, issued each Thursday.

Background Reports
> Summaries of Community policies and issues for general consumption with references to source documents.

Periodicals

Target 1992
> Summaries of specific developments in the Internal Market, published in a monthly newsletter on the Single Market, prepared by the European Commission, Directorate-General for Information, Communication and Culture (DGX) and Directorate-General for Company Policy, Commerce, SMEs, etc (DGXXIII).
> Back numbers available from European Commission London Office.
> Free

European Affairs
> Quarterly magazine on European issues and their impact on political and business relations. Strictly, this is a commercial publication. However, many authors are former European officials and back copies are available from the European Commission London Office.
> Published by Elsevier and available on subscription from European Affairs, Subscription Department, PO Box 470, 1000 Al Amsterdam, Netherlands.
> Annual subscription £36.00

Note: Other periodicals concerning specific areas of EC activity are listed under sectoral headings from page 473.

SERIES

European Documentation Series

Series of substantial, informative booklets (average length 50pp) describing the origin and working of EC policies and developments. They are available free of charge from the European Commission London Office and the Office of Official Publications of the European Communities, Luxembourg. They are sometimes obtainable from other sources to personal callers, such as the Commission's headquarters in Brussels. The following list contains some titles which may be out of print, but library copies will be of value to researchers since the booklets explain key Community issues in depth and detail.

The Economy of the European Community 7-8/1984
The European Community's Fishery Policy 1/1985
The European Community and the Mediterranean 3-4/1985
Nuclear Safety in the European Community 5/1985
The European Community's budget 1/1986
The ABC of Community law 2/1986
European Unification 3/1986
Europe as seen by Europeans 4/1986
The Court of Justice of the European Community 5/1986
The Common Agricultural Policy and its Reform 1/1987
The European Community and the Environment 3/1987
The Ecu 5/1987

Wine and the European Community 1/1988
Research and Technological Development Policy 2/1988
The Audio-Visual Media in the Single European Market 4/1988.
Jean Monnet: A grand Design for Europe 5/1988
Public Procurement and Construction — Towards an Integrated Market 1988.
EEC Competition Policy in the Single Market 1/1989
Europe without frontiers: Completing the Internal Market 2/1989.
The European Commission and the Administration of the Community 3/1989.
The European Financial Area
European Unification — Gestation and Growth (third edition)
1992 — The Social Dimension (fourth edition)
Europe — A Fresh Start — the Schuman Declaration

European File Series

Short introductory summaries of EC policies and developments available free from the European Commission London Office. The following selected list includes trade, commerce and industry-related titles. Out of print titles can be consulted at the library of the European Commission's London office. Titles published since 1979 have been included, some still serving as useful introductions, others of historical research interest.

General
The European Community in the 1980's 1/80
The Community of Ten: Welcome to Greece 17-18/80
The 30 May Mandate and the Relaunching of the European Community 16/81.
The European Community: Some Questions and Answers 5-6/84
A Community of Twelve: Welcome to Spain and Portugal 17-18/85.
The Institutions of the European Community 11/86
Europe, Our Future. A European Community — Why? 13/87
The European Community in Diagrams 1-2/88
Jean Monnet: A Message for Europe 9/88
A Community of Twelve: Key Figures 20/88
European File: Catalogue 1979-89 18/89
Health and Safety at Work in the European Community 3/90
The European Community and Environmental Protection 4/90

Agriculture/fisheries
How the European Community is Tackling Dairy Surpluses 4/80.
A Future for Europe's Wine 12/80
Relaunching Europe: Agricultural Policy, Target 1988 4/82
Europe's Common Agricultural Policy 2/86
The Common Fisheries Policy 10/86
The Community's Agricultural Policy on the Threshold of the 1990's 1/90

Budget
European Community Borrowing and Lending 1/85
The European Community Budget 17/86

Competition policy
The European Community and State Aids to Industry 9/82
European Competition Policy 6/85

Consumer protection
The European Community and Consumers 12/87
Civil Protection 8/88

Economy
The Fifth Economic Policy Programme 19/81

Education
The European Community and Culture 10/88

Employment
Microelectronics and Employment 16/80
Management and Reduction of Working Time in the European Community 11/81.
Workers' Rights in Industry 19/84
Migrants in the European Community 13/85
The Social Policy of the European Community: Looking Ahead to 1992 13/86.
The European Social Fund 19/86
Equal Opportunities for Women 10/87
Health & Safety at Work in the European Community 3/90

Energy
Economic Growth and Energy Conservation 16/79
New Energy Sources for the Community 2/80
Investing to Save Energy 17/81
The Nuclear Industries in the European Community 16/85
European Demonstration Projects in the Energy Field 7/86
The European Energy Policy 2/87
Europe and Nuclear Fusion 3/87
Nuclear Energy in the European Community 18/87

Environment
The European Community and Water 6/80
The European Community and Waste Recycling 10/80
The European Community and Environmental protection 4/90

External relations/trade
The Raw Materials Challenge 1/81
The Community and the North-South Dialogue 14/81
The Europe-United States-Japan Trade Controversy 9/83
European Political Co-operation 13/83
The European Community and Latin America 12/86
The External Trade of the European Community 1/87
The European Community and the Third World 15/87
Generalized Preferences for the Third World 16/87
The European Community in the World 16/88

Finance/financial services

European Community Borrowing and Lending 1/85
The Approximation of European Tax Systems 9/86
The European Monetary System 15/86
The Liberalisation of Capital Movements 12/88
Towards a Big Internal Market in Financial Services 17/88

Industry

Europe and the New Information Technology 3/80
Tomorrow's Bio-society 11/80
Microelectronics and Employment 16/80
The Raw Materials Challenge 1/81
Towards the European Patent and Trade Mark 18/81
Relaunching Europe: A New Community for Industry and Employment 3/82.
Euronet-DIANE: Towards a Common Information Market 18/82
The European Community and New Technologies 3/84
The Community and the Car Industry 16/84
The European Steel Policy 2/85
Company Law in the European Community 4/85
The Nuclear Industries in the European Community 16/85
The European Community and the Textile Industry 19/85
An Industrial Strategy for Europe 4/86
The SPRINT Programme 18/86
Europe Without Frontiers: Towards a Large Internal Market 17/87.
The Action Programme for Small and Medium-sized Enterprises 3/88.
Towards a Large Europe Audio-Visual Market 4/88
The European Community and Co-operation among Small and Medium-sized Enterprises 11/88.
The Big European Market: A Trump Card for the Economy and Employment 14/88.
Telecommunications: The New Highways for the Large European Market 15/88.
The Removal of Technical Barriers to Trade 18/88

Professions

Recognition of Diplomas and Professional Qualifications 14/84.

Regional policy

The Community and the Countries and Regions of the Mediterranean 19/82.
The Regions of Europe 15/84
European Community Borrowing and Lending 1/85
The Integrated Mediterranean Programmes 1/86
European Regional Policy 14/87

Research and Technology

Tomorrow's Biosociety 11/80
The Current State of European Research and Development 15/82.
FAST: Where Does Europe's Future Lie? 7/84
The European Community and New Technologies 8/84
Europe and Nuclear Fusion 3/87
Research and Technological Development for Europe 19/87
Towards a Large European Audio-visual Market 4/88
COMETT/ERASMUS, Youth for Europe 7/88

Transport/tourism
A Better Transport Network for Europe 5/81
The Community and Transport Policy 10/85
The European Community and Tourism 9/87
1990, European Tourism Year 2/90

European Economy Series
Series containing important reports and communications from the Commission to the Council and to the European Parliament on the economic situation and developments and on the lending and borrowing activities of the Community.
Quarterly
Subscription, or separate issues
Price 58.00 Ecus

Two supplements accompany the main periodical:

Series A: Economic Trends
Eleven issues per year, with tables and graphs; recent trends of industrial production, consumer prices, unemployment, balance of trade, exchange rates etc. together with Commission staff's microeconomic forecasts and communications to the Council on economic policy.
Annual subscription 23.50 Ecus
Series B: Business and Consumer Survey Results
Eleven issues per year. Results of opinion surveys of industrial chief executives and of consumers in the Community together with other business cycle indicators.
Annual subscription 23.50 Ecus

Both supplements: Annual subscription 37.00 Ecus
Combined subscription (European Economy plus supplements) 87.50 Ecus.

European Economy, issues 1-40
1 *Annual Economic Report 1978-79: Annual Economic Review 1978-79* November 1978.
2 *European Monetary System* (texts of the European Council of 4th and 5th December 1978) March 1979.
3 *Short-term Economic Trends and Prospects: The European Monetary System* (commentary, documents) July 1979.
4 *Annual Economic Report 1979-80: Annual Economic Review 1979-80* November 1979.
Special issue 1979 *Changes in Industrial Structure in the European Economies Since the Oil Crisis 1973-78: Europe — Its Capacity to Change in Question* 1979.
5 *Short-term Economic Trends and Prospects: Adaptation of Working Time* March 1980.
6 *Short-term Economic Trends and Prospects: Borrowing and Lending Instruments Looked at in the Context of the Community's Financial Instruments* July 1980.
7 *Annual Economic Report 1980-81: Annual Economic Review 1980-81* November 1980.
8 *Economic Trends and Prospects: The Community's Borrowing and Lending Operations - Recent Developments* March 1981.

9 *Fifth Medium-term Economic Policy Programme: The Main Medium-term Issues, an Analysis* July 1981.

10 *Annual Economic Report 1981-82: Annual Economic Review 1981-82* November 1981.

11 *Economic Trends and Prospects: Unit Labour Costs in Manufacturing Industry and in the Whole Economy* March 1982.

12 *Documents Relating to the European Monetary System* July 1982.

13 *The Borrowing and Lending Activities of the Community in 1981* September 1982.

14 *Annual Economic Report 1982-83: Annual Economic Review 1982-83* November 1982.

15 *Economic Trends and Prospects: Budgetary Systems and Procedures: Industrial Labour Costs: Greek Capital Markets* March 1983.

16 *Business Investment and the Tax and Financial Environment: Energy and the Economy, a Study of the Main Relationships in the Countries of the European Community: The Foreign Trade of the Community, the United States and Japan* July 1983.

17 *The Borrowing and Lending Activities in the Community in 1982* September 1983.

18 *Annual Economic Report 1983-84: Annual Economic Review 1983-84* November 1983.

19 *Economic Trends and Prospects: Industrial Labour Costs: Medium-term Budget Balance and the Public Debt: The Issue of Protectionism* March 1984.

20 *Some Aspects of Industrial Productive Performance in the European Community, an Appraisal: Profitability, Relative Factor Prices and Capital/ Labour Substitution in the Community, the United States and Japan 1960-83: Convergence and Co-ordination of Macroeconomic Policies, some Basic Issues* July 1984.

21 *Commission Report to the Council and to Parliament on the Borrowing and Lending Activities of the Community in 1983* September 1984.

22 *Annual Economic Report 1984-85: Annual Economic Review 1984-85* November 1984.

23 *Economic Trends and Prospects 1984-85* March 1985

24 *The Borrowing and Lending Activities of the Community in 1984* July 1985.

25 *Competitiveness of European Industry, Situation to Date: The Determinants of Supply in Industry in the Community: The Development of Market Services in the European Community, the United States and Japan: Technical Progress, Structural Change and Employment* September 1985.

26 *Annual Economic Report 1985-86: Annual Economic Review 1985-86* November 1985.

27 *Employment Problems, Views of Businessmen and the Workforce: Compact, a Prototype Macroeconomic Model of the European Community in the World Economy* March 1986

28 *Commission Report to the Council and to Parliament on the Borrowing and Lending Activities of the Community in 1985 May 1986.*

29 *Annual Economic Review 1986-87* July 1986

30 *Annual Economic Report 1986-87* November 1986

31 *The Determinants of Investment: Estimation and Simulation of International Trade Linkages in the Quest Model* March 1987.

32 *Commission Report to the Council and to Parliament on the Borrowing and Lending Activities of the Community in 1986* May 1987.
33 *The Economic Outlook for 1988 and Budgetary Policy in the Member States: Economic Trends in the Community and Member States* July 1987.
34 *Annual Economic Report 1987-88* November 1987
35 *The Economics of 1992* March 1988
36 *Creation of a European Financial Area* May 1988
37 *Commission Report to the Council and to Parliament on the Borrowing and Lending Activities of the Community in 1987* July 1988.
38 *Annual Economic Report 1988-89* November 1988
39 *International Trade of the European Community* March 1989.
40 *Horizontal Mergers and Competition in the European Community* May 1989.
41 *The Borrowing and Lending Activities of the Community in 1988 Economic convergence in the community: a greater effort is needed* June 1989

European Perspectives Series

Series in glossy book format and giving an insight into the main factors involved in making EC policies work. Examples:

Transport and European Integration
    ISBN 92-825-6199-2
    Price £9.60
The European Communities in the International Order
    ISBN 92-825-5137-7
    Price £3.00
Thirty Years of Community Law
    ISBN 92-825-2652-6
    Price £8.50

Studies on Concentration, Competition and Competiveness

Series focussing on concentration of industry in some areas and its effect on the European market. A list of the various studies on concentration of industry is given as an annex to the Annual Report on Competition Policy. Examples:

The Textile Machinery Industry in the EEC
    Study on concentration, competition and competitiveness
    1985
    ISBN 92-825-4780-9
    Price £5.40
The European Consumer Electronics Industry
    Study on concentration, competition and competitiveness
    1985
    ISBN 92-825-5110-5
    Price £11.10

EUR reports

Reports published on completion of research programmes and scientific and technical studies funded by the Commission. The reports may be difficult to trace, being highly technical. They can be ordered easily, however, by quoting the EUR number. The European Commission, Directorate-General for Telecommunications, Information Industries and Innovation (DGXIII), produces a monthly publication, *Euro-abstracts* which lists and gives details of all EUR publications.

Euro Abstracts

> Section I: Euratom and EC R & D and demonstration projects; scientific and technical publications and patents.
> Monthly
> Annual subscription £52.00

> Section II: Coal, steel and related social research
> Monthly, plus annual index
> Annual subscription £69.00

> Combined subscription Sections I & II: Price £101.00

Eurostat (statistics)

The European Community has its own Statistical Office which publishes series of statistics under the general heading of Eurostat. A Eurostat Catalogue of publications and electronic services is available free of charge from the European Commission UK Offices. A free quarterly publication, *Eurostat News* is obtainable from the Statistical Office in Luxembourg. The main themes are:

General statistics (dark blue cover)
Basic statistics: Annual, pocket-size book, covering a large selection of general statistics comparing the EC countries with other industrialised countries.

Eurostat Review
Annual statistical review covering a broad economic overview of the Community on a ten-year comparison with Japan and the USA, identifying economic trends.

Agriculture, forestry and fisheries (green cover)
Agriculture Statistical Yearbook
Statistical vade-mecum containing the most important data published by Eurostat in specialised sections dealing with agriculture, forestry and fisheries.

Regional statistics (dark blue cover)
Published annually, the only statistical review giving all statistical groupings on a regional basis.
Economic Accounts

Economy and finance statistics (violet cover)
National accounts ESA
> Aggregates 1970-86.
> Main national accounts aggregates of the EC countries, the US and Japan.

National Accounts ESA
> Breakdown by branch

National Accounts ESA
> Breakdown by sector

General Government Accounts and Statistics
> Yearbook

Consumer Price Indices
> Published monthly

Energy and industry statistics (pale blue cover)
Industry Statistical Yearbook
   Analysis of the industrial structure of the Community, its member states, Japan and the US.
Industrial Trends
   Monthly data on industrial activity in the EC.
Structure and Activity of Industry
   Co-ordinated annual inquiry into industrial activity, carried out by member states.
Energy Statistical Yearbook
   Statistical data relating to the energy economy of the Community and member states.
Iron and Steel Statistical Yearbook
   Detailed data on the structure and the economic situation of the Community's iron and steel industry.

Foreign trade statistics
External Trade Statistical Yearbook
   Main external trade statistics of the European Communities from 1958 to 1986. Breakdown by country commodity.
Analytical Tables of External Trade: Nimexe
   Breakdown of external trade statistics of the EC and member states according to the NIMEXE nomenclature, including:
   Exports 1987 (13 volumes)
   Imports 1987 (13 volumes)

Population and social conditions (yellow cover)
Demographic Statistics
   Issued yearly, including population projections. Detailed breakdown for each country.
Employment and Unemployment Statistics
   Issued yearly
Unemployment Statistics
   Monthly breakdown of unemployment statistics on a monthly plus basis comparison with previous years.
Labour Force Sample Survey
   Yearly data on the structure of economic activity, employment and unemployment, and working time.

AGRICULTURE, FORESTRY AND FISHERIES

Periodicals, annual reports
Green Europe
   An amalgamation of the former *Green Europe: Newsletter* (analysis and overview of a range of agricultural topics) and *Green Europe: Newsflash* (analysis of a single, current agricultural topic).
   Free from the European Commission, Directorate-General for Information, Communication and Culture, DGX. Separate issues can also be obtained free of charge from the European Commission London Office.

Situation on the Agricultural Markets: Report 1988
> Annual report giving an analysis of the agricultural market organisations and agricultural markets of the European Communities.
> COM(88)796 final 18.01.89

The European Agricultural Guidance and Guarantee Fund (EAGGF): Annual reports.
> 17th financial report
> Guidance Section COM(88)437 final
> 18th Financial Report SEC (89) 1984 final
> Guarantee and Food Aid COM(88)563 final
> 18th Report SEC(89)1343 final

Other agriculture titles

Directory of European Agricultural Organisations
> Handbook describing the structure of European and national agricultural organisations, their decision-making procedures, priority policies and activities.
> Economic & Social Committee
> 1984
> ISBN 92-830-0032-3
> Price £45.00

The Agricultural Situation in the Community: 1989 Report
> Comprehensive report with analyses and statistics on agriculture; factors of production, structures and situation of markets for agricultural products, obstacles to the common agricultural market, the position of consumers and producers, financial aspects, together with an analysis of the general prospects and market outlook for agricultural products.
> 1990
> ISBN 92-826-0913-8
> Price 25.50 Ecus

Economic Situation of Agricultural Holdings in the EEC: Report 1987
> Financial results of farmers throughout the European Community in 1984/85 and 1985/86.
> The Farm Accountancy Data Network
> 1988
> ISBN 92-825-8718-5
> Price £9.20

Green Paper on Perspectives for the CAP
> Available free of charge from the European Commission London Office.
> COM(85) 333 final, later re-printed in *Green Europe: Newsflash* series, 33/1985

A Future for Community Agriculture
> Commission guidelines following the consultations in connection with the Green Paper.
> Available for reference only at the library of the European Commission London Office.
> COM(85)750 final
> Later re-printed in *Green Europe: Newsflash* series, 34/1985

Report from the Commission on the Economic Effects of the Agri-Monetary System.
   Updated 1987
   COM(87)168 14.08.87
Environment and Agriculture
   COM(88)338 final
Completing the Internal Market: Current Status December 1989
   Veterinary and Plant Health Controls
   Issues and problems in creating an Internal Market in veterinary and plant health controls, approach adopted in individual sectors of health controls, summaries of all measures adopted or proposed to achieve the Internal Market in the sector.
   European Commission.
   One of a set of five brochures
   ISBN 92-826-0887-5
   Price 15.00 Ecus
The Common Agricultural Policy and its Reform
   Analysis of the CAP, simply explained
   European Documentation series, 1/1987
The Common Fisheries Policy
   European File series, 10/86
The Community's Agricultural Policy on the Threshold of the 1990's
   European File series, 1/90

COMPETITION

Reports, series, studies

Eighteenth Report on Competition Policy
   Latest in yearly series
   1989
   ISBN 92-826-0623-6
   Price 17.50 Ecus
First Survey on State Aids in the European Community
   Document series, 1989
   ISBN 92-825-9535-8
   Price 7 Ecus
Studies on Concentration, Competition and Competitiveness
   Series looking at the concentration of industries in a competition and competitiveness light. The most recent titles in this series are listed in the annual competition report (see above). Examples:
The EEC Telecommunications Industry: The Adhesion of Spain and Portugal
   1987
   ISBN 92-825-7551-9
   Price £15.10
The Likely Impact of Deregulation on Industrial Structures and Competition in the Community.
   1987
   ISBN 92-825-7594-2
   Price £12.90

Other competition titles

Competition Rules in the EEC and the ECSC Applicable to State Aids
A collection of the basic texts on State aid of different kinds and differing legal status.
1987
ISBN 92-825-6735-4
Price £13.40

Competition Law in the EEC and the ECSC
1986
ISBN 92-825-5832-0
Price £4.00

Recent Trends of Concentration in Selected Industries of the European Community, Japan and the US.
Document series, 1988
ISBN 92-825-8617-0
Price 12.00 Ecu

Innovation in the EC Automotive Industry: An Analysis from the Perspective of State-aid Policy.
Document series, 1988
ISBN 92-825-8776-2
Price £10.50

Community Framework on State-aid to the Motor Vehicle Industry
Official Journal of the European Communities C123 of 18.5.89

The Aid Element in State Participation to Company Capital
Document series, 1989
ISBN 92-825-9510-2
Price 19.50 Ecu

Barriers to Entry and Intensity of Competition in European Markets
Document series, 1989
ISBN 92-825-9625-7
Price 9 Ecu

Horizontal Mergers and Competition Policy in the European Community
European Economy 40, May 1989

EEC Competition Policy in the Single Market
European Documentation series, 1/1989
Explains the objectives and rules of European competition policy applying not only to big companies but also to SME's, showing how they may benefit from cooperation with other firms and thus take full advantage of a unified market.

CONSUMER AFFAIRS

Selected titles

A New Impetus for Consumer Protection Policy
Supplement 6/86 to the *Bulletin of the European Communities*
ISBN 92-825-6649-8
Price £1.70

Individual Choice and Higher Growth: The Task of European Consumer Policy
  E Lawlor
  A Frontier-Free Europe publication
  1989
  ISBN 92-826-0087-4
  Price 8 Ecus
Reports of the Scientific Committee for Food (20th series)
  EUR 11558 EN
  1989
  ISBN 92-825-9680-X
  Price 5 Ecus
The European Community and Consumers
  European File series, 12/87
Three Year Action Plan of Consumer Policy in the EEC (1990-1992)
  COM (90) 98 final

CUSTOMS AND FISCAL CONTROLS

Selected titles

The Customs Union of the European Economic Community
  The mechanism of the customs union, its role in European integration, the
  external Commons Customs Tariff as a commercial instrument with regard to
  non-member countries, the application of the customs regulations and trade
  with the Community.
  European Perspectives, 1985
  ISBN 92-825-1911-2
  Price £2.60
Explanatory Notes to the Combined Nomenclature of the European Communities
  1987
  ISBN 92-825-7813-5
  Price 17.50 Ecu
  Addendum 1988 to the 1987 explanatory notes
  ISBN 92-825-8723-1
  Price 13.25 Ecu
Customs Valuation
  Compendium of European Community legislation relating to customs
  valuation.
  Document series, 1989
  ISBN 92-825-8835-1
  Price 38.25 Ecu
*European Customs Inventory of Chemicals: A Guide to the Tariff Classification of
Chemicals in the Combined Nomenclature.*
  Document series, 1988
  ISBN 92-825-7919-0
  Price £23.50
List of Authorized Customs Offices for Community Transit Operations
  1986
  ISBN 92-825-6575-0
  Price £8.00

Practical Guide to the Use of the European Communities' Scheme of Generalized Tariff Preferences.
  1986
  ISBN 92-825-6139-9
  Price £8.10
Completing the Internal Market: Current Status December 1989
  Elimination of frontier barriers and fiscal controls
  Control of goods
  Control of individuals
  Valued-added tax
  Excise duties
  European Commission
  One of a set of five brochures
  ISBN 92-826-0860-3
  Price 15 Ecus
The Cost of Non-Europe
  Volume 4
  Border-related Controls and Administrative Formalities: An illustration in the road-haulage sector.
  ISBN 92-825-8618-9
  Price £15.00
Generalized Preferences for the Third World
  European File series, 16/87
The Removal of Technical Barriers to Trade
  European File series, 18/88
Europe Without Frontiers: Completing the Internal Market
  European Documentation series, 2/89

ECONOMIC, MONETARY AND FINANCIAL AFFAIRS

Annual reports, series, business surveys, economic papers, EC budget, European Investment Bank, monetary union, Ecu

European Economy
  Series containing important reports and communications from the Commission to the Council and to the European Parliament on the economic situation and developments and on the lending and borrowing activities of the Community.
  Quarterly
  Subscription, or separate issues
  Price 58.00 Ecus
  Two supplements accompany the main periodical:
  Series A: Economic Trends
  Eleven issues per year. Describes with tables and graphs recent trends of industrial production, consumer prices, unemployment, balance of trade, exchange rates etc. together with Commission staff's microeconomic forecasts and communications to the Council on economic policy.
  Annual subscription 23.50 Ecus

Series B: Business and Consumer Survey Results

Eleven issues per year. Results of opinion surveys of industrial chief executives and consumers in the EC, plus other business cycle indicators.

Annual Economic Reports
Annual Economic Report 1988-1989: Preparing for 1992
    First published as COM(88)591 Vol. I & II
    Later published as *European Economy* 38, November 1988
    ISSN 0379-0991
Facing the Challenges of the Early 1990's: Annual Economic Report 1989-1990
    COM(89)497 final
    Later published as EUR Economy 42, November 1989
Twenty-ninth Activity Report of the Monetary Committee
    1988
    ISBN 92-825-8995-1
    Price £3.25
The Community Budget: Facts in Figures
    The full budget is published yearly in the L series of the *Official Journal of the European Communities*. This publication aims at explaining the budget in a more digestible format.
    Annual publication
    1989 edition
    ISBN 92-825-9716-4
    Price 10 Ecu
Financial Report 1987
    Information on the implementation of the budget in an accessible format.
    1988 report is in French.
Financial Report 1988: European Coal and Steel Community
    Financial activity of the European Commission in the field covered by the ECSC Treaty.
    1989
    ISBN 92-826-0693-3
Results of the Business Survey Carried out Among Managements in the Community
    Monthly
    ISSN 0378-4479
    Annual subscription 58.50 Ecus

EURECOM
Monthly bulletin of European Community economic and financial news.
Published by the European Commission, 3 Dag Hammarskjold Plaza, 305 East 47th Street, New York, NY 10017.

DGII: Economic papers
Papers written by officials in European Commission Directorate-General for Economic and Financial Affairs (DGII). Reports on a macro-economic scale. The full collection of the reports is available for reference in the library of the European Commission London Office. Examples:
The completion of the Internal Market: results of macro-economic model simulations.
    M Catinat, E Donni, A Italianer
    1988

66 *Europe after the crash: economic policy in an era of adjustment*
C Bean
1988

67 *A survey of the economies of scale*
C Pratten
1988

74 *The exchange rate question in Europe*
F Giavazzi
1989

76 *Europe's prospects for the 1990's*
H Giersch
March 1989

The European Investment Bank in 1988
Overview of the Bank's activity
European Investment Bank
ISBN 92-861-0181-3
Free from the European Investment Bank, 68 Pall Mall, London SW1Y 5ES,
tel: (071) 839 3351.

The European Investment Bank: Annual Report 1988
EIB activities in 1988 with statistics, in particular loans within and outside the
Community.
European Investment Bank, 1989. Free from the European Investment Bank
(address above)

The European Monetary System: Origins, Operation and Outlook
European Perspectives series
1985
ISBN 92-825-3468-5
Price £3.00

Money, Economic Policy and Europe
T Padoa-Schioppa
European Perspectives 1985
ISBN 92-825-4410-9
Price £5.30

Report on Economic and Monetary Union in the European Community
Known as the *Delors Report*, this document details the stages by which the
complete economic and monetary union will be achieved. A summary of the
report can be obtained free of charge from the European Commission
London Office.
1989
ISBN 92-825-0655-4
Price 10 Ecus

The Ecu
European Documentation series, 5/87
The European Financial Area
European Documentation series, 4/1989

Other economic and monetary titles

Community Public Finance: The European Budget After the 1988 Reform
  The publication is an informative guide on the working of the budgetary and
  financial policy after the reform of the budgetary procedure.
  ISBN 92-825-9830-6
  Price 10.50 Ecu

Efficiency, Stability and Equity: A Strategy for the Evolution of the Economic
System of the European Community.
  Report of a study group appointed by the Commission of the European
  Communities. In-depth analysis of the problems encountered between now
  and 1992 in order to achieve a single Internal Market.
  T Padoa-Schioppa
  1987
  ISBN 0-19-828629-5
  Oxford University Press

The Economics of 1992
  European Economy series, 35 of March 1988
  CB-AR-88-035-EN-C
  Price £11.50

Compendium of Community Monetary Texts
  Legal texts of importance to the Monetary Committee
  Monetary Committee, 1989
  ISBN 92-825-9489-0
  Price 10 Ecus

Inventory of Taxes Levied in Member States of the European Communities
  13th edition
  Analysis of tax law in the member states
  ISBN 92-825-8829-7
  Price 47.50 Ecus

The Single Financial Market
  D Servais
  1988
  ISBN 92-825-8572-7
  Price £4.10

Completion of the Internal Market: Approximation of Indirect Tax Rates and
Harmonization of Indirect Tax Structures.
  COM(87)320 final
  COM(89)260 final

The Approximation of European Tax Systems
  European File series, 9/86

A European Financial Area: The Liberalization of Capital Movements
  European File series, 12/88

The Big European Market: A Trump Card for the Economy and Employment
  European File series, 14/88

Towards a Big Internal Market in Financial Services
  European File series, 17/88

EDUCATION AND CULTURAL POLICY

Education Training Youth Guide to the European Community Programmes.
Free from the London office of the Commission

COMETT, ERASMUS, EURYDICE, PETRA, SPES

ERASMUS (Community programme for the mobility of university students)
Directory of programmes 1987-88
Published for the Commission by the Erasmus Bureau, Rue d'Arlon 15, B-1040 Brussels
Free

ERASMUS Annual Report 1988
COM(89)119 final

ERASMUS Newsletter
Commission newsletter on the joint study programme
Three issues per year
Annual subscription £6.00

COMETT Community programme for co-operation between universities and enterprises in the field of training for technology and its applications: Annual report 1988.
COM(89)171 final

COMETT: The training needs of staff in the Community's higher education sector engaged in co-operation with industry.
Document series 1988
ISBN 92-825-8763-0
Price 47.75 Ecus

SPES (stimulation plan for economic science) 1989-92
Commission document explaining the plan to encourage academic links in the field of economics throughout the countries of the community. A free information pack is available from the European Commission London Office.
COM(88)98 final

PETRA: The European Community action programme for the vocational training of young people and their preparation for adult and working life.
Free information note available from the European Commission London Office.

EURYDICE Info
Published for the European Commission, Directorate-General for Employment, Social Affairs and Education, DGV by the European Unit of EURYDICE, Education information network in the European Community, Rue Archimede 17, Bte 17, B-1040 Brussels.

Other education and culture titles

European Educational Policy Statements
Third edition
Council of the European Communities
1988
ISBN 92-825-0471-4
Price £8.00

The Education Structures in the Member States of the European Communities
    1987
    ISBN 92-825-7543-8
    Price £11.00

Transition Education for the 1990's
    Supplement 1/88 to *Social Europe*
    1988
    Price £3.60

Education in the European Community: Medium-term Perspectives 1989-92
    Communication from the Commission
    COM(88)280 final

Higher Education in the European Community: Student Handbook
    Fifth edition
    Directory of courses and institutions in 12 countries. Basic information needed by those seeking higher education in another member state.
    1988
    ISBN 1-85091-501-6
    Price £11.95

Young Europeans in 1987
    Survey of attitudes of young Europeans towards Europe, including languages.
    Document series
    1989
    ISBN 92-825-9511-0
    Price 14.70 Ecus

Employees' Organisations and their Contribution to the Development of Vocational Training Policy in the European Communities.
    CEDEFOP document
    1988
    ISBN 92-825-7734-1
    Price £3.50

The European Community and Culture
    European File series, 10/88
The European Community and Recognition of Diplomas for Professional Purposes.
    European Files series, 13/89
A Fresh Boost for Culture in the European Community
    Supplement 4/87 to the *Bulletin of the European Communities*
    ISBN 92-825-8241-8
    Price 3.50 Ecus

Public Administration and the Funding of Culture in the European Community.
    Document series
    1989
    ISBN 92-825-6737-0
    Price 16.20 Ecus

Books and Reading: A Cultural Challenge for Europe
    Communication from the Commission
    COM(89)258 final

ENERGY

Periodicals

Energy in Europe
Energy policies and trends in the European Communities
Three issues per year
Annual subscription £24.00

The Internal Energy Market
Energy in Europe special issue. Reprint of COM(88)238 final, together with the inventory of obstacles to an internal energy market and a number of conclusions.
ISBN 92-825-8507-7
Price 12.70 Ecus

Major Themes in Energy
Energy in Europe special issue.
1989
ISBN 92-826-0724-0
Price 12.70 Ecus

Nuclear energy

EURATOM Supply agency: Annual Report 1988
ISBN 92-826-0023-8
Price 5 Ecus

Nuclear Safety in the European Community
European Documentation series, 5/85

Nuclear Energy in the European Community
European File series, 18/87

Other energy titles

Recueil des Textes Legislatifs et des Actes Relatifs au Domaine de l'Energie
Compendium of EC legislation relating to the energy field, available in French only.
Document series
1988
ISBN 92-825-8725-8
Price 58.75 Ecus

Collection of Legislation and Acts Relating to Energy: Situation at 1.1.89
EC legislation relating to the energy field with *Official Journal* references.
Document series
1989
ISBN 92-825-9549-8
Price 5.00 Ecus

The Internal Energy Market
Commission report outlining the expected results of an internal energy market and priorities which should be addressed in order to remove the obstacles to its creation.
COM(88)238 final

Towards a Continuing Policy for Energy Efficiency in the European Community
Commission communication
COM(87)223 final

Accelerating Discrete Energy Efficiency Investments Through Third Party Financing.
    Commission communication
    COM(88)175 final
Commission Communication on Transparency of Consumer Energy Prices
    COM(89)123/2 final
The Market for Solid Fuels in the Community in 1988 and Outlook for 1989
    SEC(89)280
    Official Journal of the European Communities C148 15.6.89
Investment in the European Coal and Steel Community 1988
    Yearly
    ISBN 92-825-9369-X
    Price 19 Ecus
National Laws and Regulations Relating to the Natural Gas Industry
    EUR document 11433
    1988
    ISBN 92-825-8543-3
    Price 8.75 Ecus
Energy and the Environment
    Commission Communicaton
    COM (89) 369 final

ENVIRONMENT

Selected titles

The State of the Environment in the European Community 1986
    EUR 10633
    ISBN 92-825-6973-X
    Price £11.60
European Environment Policy: Air, Water & Waste Management
    Economic and Social Committee
    1987
    ISBN 92-830-0108-7
    Price £2.60
European Community Environmental Legislation 1967-1987
    Vol I General policy and nature protection
    Vol II Air and noise
    Vol III Waste
    Vol IV Water
    Published by the European Commission, Directorate-General for Environment, Consumer Protection and Nuclear Safety (DGXII).
Living conditions in urban Europe
    European Foundation for the Improvement of Living and Working Conditions
    1988
    ISBN 92-825-7054-1
    Price £3.60

The Impact of Biotechnology on the Environment
  European Foundation for the Improvement of Living and Working Conditions
  1987
  ISBN 92-825-7529-2: Price £4.10
  ISBN 92-825-7532-2: Price £5.80
  ISBN 92-825-6767-2: Price £6.60
EINECS (European Inventory of Existing Commercial Chemical Substances)
  1987
  8 volumes
  Also available on magnetic tape
  Price £250.00
Working for a Better Environment: The Role of the Social Partners
  European Foundation for the Improvement of Living and Working Conditions
  1989
  ISBN 92-825-8781-9
  Price £3.30
Fourth Environmental Action Programme 1987-1992
  Official Journal of the European Communities C328 7.12.87
The Greenhouse Effect and the Community
  Commission working programme concerning the evaluation of policy options to deal with the greenhouse effect.
  COM(88)656 final
"1992" The Environmental Dimension
  Report by a task force chaired by a commission official and including independent experts.
  Available for reference in the Library of the London Commission Office.
Energy and the Environment
  Commission Communication
  COM (89) 369 final
The European Community and the Environment's Protection
  European Documentation series, 4/90

EXTERNAL RELATIONS, FOREIGN TRADE, OVERSEAS DEVELOPMENT

Periodicals, series

The Courier
  Magazine published every two months, covering ACP/EEC relations including contract tender information.
  Free subscription available from the European Commission, Directorate-General for Development (DGVIII).
Europe Information: Development
  Publications covering development topics
Lome III: Mid-term Review 1986-88
  European Information series: Development DE61
  ISSN 1012-2184

STABEX
>The STABEX system, EC system of export earnings from agricultural commodities for Third World countries.
>*Europe Information* series: Development DE59
>1988

Europe Information: External relations
>Publications dealing with a country or group of countries' relations with the EC:
>*The European Community and China* 90/88
>*The European Community and the Yemen Arab Republic* 91/88
>*The European Community and ASEAN* 92/88
>*The European Community and Bangladesh* 93/88
>*The European Community and Yugoslavia* 94/88
>*The European Community's relations with COMECON and its East European members* 1/89

Other foreign trade and external relations titles

Corps Diplomatique Accredite Aupres des Communautes Europeennes
>Annual directory, updated at intervals, of the diplomatic corps accredited to the European Community.
>1989 edition
>ISBN 92-826-0896-4
>Price 5.50 Ecus

International Trade of the European Community
>A Review of certain aspects of the external trade of the Community.
>*European Economy* series, 39, March 1989

Thirteen Years of Development Co-operation with the Developing Countries of Latin America and Asia.
>Data and results
>SEC(89)713 final

European Community Report on US Trade Barriers and Unfair Trade Practices
>1990
>Published by the European Commission, Directorate-General for External Relations, DGI. Available for reference at the library of the European Commission London Office.

Report of the European Parliament on Protectionism in Trade Relations Between the European Community and the United States of America.
>Rapporteur: Dame Shelagh Roberts
>Report by the European Parliament committee on external economic relations.
>PE doc A2-89/88

The Internal Market of North America: Fragmentation and Integration in the USA and Canada.
>*The Cost of Non-Europe* Volume 16
>ISBN 92-825-8630-8
>Price 13.50 Ecus

Relations between the Community and Japan
>Commission communication
>COM(88)136 I & II final

Sixth Annual Report of the Commission on the Community's Anti-Dumping and Anti-subsidy Activities.
COM(89) 106 final

Relations Between the European Community and International Organisations
A Frontier-Free Europe publication
1989
ISBN 92-826-0085-8
Price 30.75 Ecus

Europe in the World
European File series, 16/88
Free from the European Commission London Office

The North-South Dialogue in Practice
EC development policy: Rural development, industry and trade, education, training and health, regional co-operation.
1988
ISBN 92-825-8436-4

Economic Transformaiton in Hungary and Poland
European Economy
March 1990
Price 43 Ecus

Lome IV, 1990-2000 — Background, Innovations, Improvements
Europe Information DE 64, March 1990
Free from London Commission Office

INDUSTRY

Selected titles

Completing the Internal Market for Industrial Products
Document series
ISBN 92-825-6481-9
Price £8.30

Panorama of EC Industry
Overview of more than 125 sectors of manufacturing and services industries with some comparisons with the US and Japan.
1989; 1990
ISBN 92-825-8435-6
Price £14.70

Completion of the Internal Market: A Survey of European Industry's Perception of the Likely Effects.
The cost of non-Europe Volume 3
ISBN 92-825-8610-3
Price 25.50 Ecus

Technical Barriers in the EC: An Illustration by Six Industries
The cost of Non-Europe Volume 6
ISBN 92-825-8649-9
Price 21 Ecus

The EC 1992 Automobile Sector
    The Cost of Non-Europe Volume II
    ISBN 92-825-8619-7
    Price 27.75 Ecus

The Cost of Non-Europe in the Foodstuffs Industry
    The Cost of Non-Europe Volume 12
    Part A: ISBN 92-825-8642-1
    Part B: ISBN 92-825-8643-X
    Price: A + B 120 Ecus

Le Cout de la Non-Europe des Produits de la Construction
    The cost of non-Europe Volume 13
    In French. NEDO has its own translation
    ISBN 92-825-8631-6
    Price 14.25 Ecus

The Cost of Non-Europe in the Textile/Clothing Industry
    The Cost of Non-Europe Volume 14
    ISBN 92-825-8641-3
    Price 21.75 Ecus

Rules Governing Medicinal Products in the European Community.
    Volume I
    The Rules Governing Medicinal Products for Human Use in the European Community.
    ISBN 92-825-9563-3
    Price 13.50 Ecus
    Volume II
    Notice to Applicants for Marketing Authorizations for Medicinal Products for Human Use in the Member States of the European Community.
    ISBN 92-825-9503-X
    Price : 16.50 Ecus
    Volume III
    Guidelines on the Quality, Safety and Efficacy of Medicinal Products for Human Use.
    ISBN 92-825-9619-2
    Price 23.25 Ecus
    Volume IV
    Guide to Good Manufacturing Practice for the Manufacture of Medicinal Products.
    ISBN 92-825-9572-2
    Price 9.75 Ecus
    Volume V
    The Rules Governing Medicinal Products for Veterinary Use in the European Community.
    ISBN 92-825-9643-5
    Price 14.25 Ecus

The Community's Pharmaceutical Industry
    Document series, 1985
    ISBN 92-825-5224-1
    Price £8.30

The Cost of Non-Europe in the Pharmaceutical Industry
    The Cost of Non-Europe Volume 15
    ISBN 92-825-8632-4
    Price 13.50 Ecus

The Tourism Sector in the Community
    A study of concentration, competition and competitiveness
    1985
    ISBN 92-825-5276-4
    Price £9.00

ECSC Investments 1988
    Overview of investments in the coal and steel sector
    European Commission
    ISBN 92-825-9369-X
    Price 19 Ecus

The European Aerospace Industry: Trading Position and Figures 1989
    III/4100/89-EN final
    Available from the European Commission, Directorate-General for the
    Internal Market and Industrial Affairs (DGIII).

LAW

Annual reports

Sixth Annual Report to the European Parliament on Commission Monitoring of the Application of Community Law.
    1989
    COM (89) 411 final or *Official Journal* C 330 of 30.12.89
Community Law: Offprint from the 22nd General Report
    Offprint from the Annual General Report on the activities of the European
    Communities, pertaining to legal matters, including summaries of important
    judgements.
    ISBN 92-825-9693-1
    Price 4 Ecus

Other law titles

The ABC of Community Law
    Guide with basic information on Community law, specifically orientated to
    use by the layman.
    European Documentation series, 2/1986

Lawyers in the European Community
    Comparison of the legal profession in 10 of the member states of the
    European Community (not Spain and Portugal — to be covered in a future
    edition).
    S P Laguette and P. Latham
    European Perspectives series, 1987
    ISBN 92-825-6978-0
    Price £9.60

Harmonization of Company Law in the European Communities: Measures Adopted and Proposed — Situation as at 1.1.89.
> *Document* series, 1989
> ISBN 92-825-9578-1
> Price 29.25 Ecus

> *Completing the Internal Market: Current Status December 1989*
> Conditions for industrial co-operation
> Company law
> Intellectual property
> Taxation
> The European Commission
> One of a set of five brochures
> ISBN 92-826-0869-7
> Price 15 Ecus

> *Commission Green Paper on Copyright and the Challenge of Technology*
> Copyright issues requiring immediate action
> COM(88)172 final

The European Economic Interest Grouping (EEIG)
> *European File* series, 6/89

Complaint to the European Commission for Failure to Comply with Community Law.
> Standard complaint form issued by the Commission
> *Official Journal of the European Communties* C26 of 1.2.89

Company Law in the European Community
> *European File* series, 14/89
Patents, Trade Marks and Copyright in the European Community
> *European File* series, 17/89

PUBLIC PROCUREMENT

Selected titles

Public Procurement and Construction: Towards an Integrated Market
> *European Documentation* series, 1988
> ISBN 92-825-8891-2
> Free from the European Commission London Office

The Cost of Non-Europe in Public Procurement
> *The Cost of Non-Europe* Volume 5
> Part A: ISBN 92-825-8646-4
> Part B: ISBN 92-825-8647-2
> Price: A + B 120 Ecus
> *A Single Public Procurement Market*
> Completing the Internal Market: Current status December 1989, part 2.
> European Commission
> One of a set of five brochures
> ISBN 92-826-0869-7
> Price 15.00 Ecus

REGIONAL POLICY, EUROPEAN REGIONAL DEVELOPMENT FUND (ERDF), STRIDE

Annual reports

European Regional Development Fund: Thirteenth Annual Report from the Commission to the Council, the European Parliament and the Economic and Social Committee.
 1989
 ISBN 92-825-9517-X
 Price 12 Ecus

Other regional policy titles

Main Texts Governing the Regional Policy of the European Communities
 Document series, 1985
 ISBN 92-825-5283-7
 Price £5.60

The Regions of the Enlarged Community: Third Periodic Report on the Social and Economic Situation and Development of the Regions of the Community — Summary and Conclusions.
 Document series, 1987
 ISBN 92-825-7526-6
 Price £16.50

Long-term Regional Demographic Developments up to the Beginning of the Next Century and Regional Policy.
 Document series, 1988
 ISBN 92-825-8620-0
 Price £11.50

Peripheral Regions in a Community of 12 Member States
 Document series, 1988
 ISBN 92-825-8640-5
 Price £8.30

Research and Technological Development in the Less-favoured Regions of the Community (STRIDE)
 1988
 ISBN 92-825-7852-6
 Price £19.50

STRIDE: Science and Technology for Regional Innovation and Development in Europe.
 1988
 ISBN 92-825-7858-5
 Price £26.50

Urban Problems and Regional Policy in the European Community
 Document series, 1988
 ISBN 92-825-7871-2
 Price £18.50

Living Conditions in Urban Europe
European Foundation for the Improvement of Living and Working Conditions.
1988
ISBN 92-825-7054-1
Price £3.60
ERDF in Figures 1988 (1975-88)
1989
ISBN 92-826-0055-6
Available for reference at the library of the European Commission London Office.
European Regional Policy
European File series, 14/87
The Integrated Mediterranean Programme
European File series, 7/89

SERVICES

Selected titles

The Cost of Non-Europe: Obstacles to Trans-border Business Activity
The Cost of Non-Europe Volume 7
ISBN 92-825-8638-3
Price £8.50
The Cost of Non-Europe for Business Services
The Cost of Non-Europe Volume 8
ISBN 92-825-8637-5
Price £9.00
The Cost of Non-Europe in Financial Services
The Cost of Non-Europe Volume 9
ISBN 92-825-8636-7
Price £78.00
The Benefits of Completing the Internal Market for Telecommunications Services and Equipment in the Community
The Cost of Non-Europe Volume 10
ISBN 92-825-8650-2
Price £11.50
The Single Financial Market: Liberalization of Capital Movements and Financial Integration.
D Servais
A Frontier-free Europe publication, 1988
ISBN 92-825-8572-7
Price 6 Ecus
Creation of a European Financial Market
European Economy series, 36 of May 1988
Towards a Big Internal Market in Financial Services
European File series, 17/88
The European Financial Area
European Documentation series, 4/1989

The Insurance Industry in the Countries of the EEC: Structure, Conduct and Performance.
    Document series, 1985
    ISBN 92-825-4919-4
    Price £10.80
Completing the Internal Market: Current Status December 1989:
    A Common Market for Services
    Banking, insurance, securities, transport, new technologies and services, capital movements, free movement of labour and the professions
    Commission of the European Communities
    One of a set of five brochures
    ISBN 92-826-0851-4
    Price 15.00 Ecus
Credit Institutions: Community Measures Adopted or Proposed — Situation at January 1989.
    Compendium of texts of EC proposed and existing legislation relating to the banking sector.
    Document series, 1989
    ISBN 92-825-9508-0
    Price 24.75 Ecus
Securities Markets — Community Measures Adopted or Proposed
    Document series, 1989
    ISBN 92-826-0017-3
    Price 15.00 Ecus

SMALL AND MEDIUM-SIZED ENTERPRISES (SMEs)

Periodicals/annuals

Euro-Info
    SME craft industry newsletter for small business and craft trades. Available from the European Commission, Directorate-General for Company Policy, Commerce, Tourism and Social Economy (DG XXIII), 200 Rue de la Loi, B-1049 Brussels.
Operations of the European Community Concerning Small and Medium-sized Enterprises: Practical Handbook.
    Document series
    ISBN 92-825-8741-X
    Price £14.70

Other SME titles

Evaluation of Policy Measures for the Creation and Development of Small and Medium-sized Enterprises: Synthesis Report.
    Part A: Analysis of measures taken by the member states and the Community to create and develop SME's.
    Part B: In-depth analysis of the situation in Portugal
    ISBN 92-826-0104-9
    Price 15.75 Ecus

Practical Guide to Legal Aspects of Industry Sub-contracting within the European Community.
> Volume I: The Sub-contract
> *A Frontier-Free Europe* publication, 1989
> ISBN 92-825-9593-5
> Price 11.25 Ecus

Methods of Promoting the Supply of Risk Capital: Utilizing Innovative Banking to Improve the Equity Capital Resources of SMEs.
> Pilot study designed to look at the existing role of the banks and the role banks could play in the market for risk capital assets.
> *Enterprise Policy Document* series, 1989
> ISBN 92-826-0105-6
> Price 8.25 Ecus

Strengthening Co-operation between European Firms. A Response to the 1992 Internal Market Deadline.
> The BC-net Euro-partnership promoting transnational sub-contracting.
> Commission communication
> COM(88)162 final

SME Task Force: Data Banks of Interest to SME's
> Directory of databases of special interest to SME's
> Produced by the SME Task Force of the European Commission
> 1988
> Available from the SME Task Force, Rue de la Loi 200, ARLN, B-1049 Brussels.

The Action Programme for Small and Medium-sized Enterprises
> *European File* series, 3/88

The European Community and Co-operation among Small and Medium-sized Enterprises.
> *European File* series, 11/88

RESEARCH AND DEVELOPMENT, SCIENCE AND TECHNOLOGY, COMMUNICATIONS

For details of Community Research and Development programmes see (*Grants and Loans from the European Community,* Part Four, Chapter 7).

Periodicals

Innovation and Technology Transfer
> Newsletter, 5-6 issues per year, replacing the *New Technologies and Innovation Policy* newsletter covering the activities and fields of interest of Directorate-General Telecommunications, Information Industries and Innovation (DGXIII).
> Free from DGXIII, C-3 (Exploitation of Research, Technological Development, Technology Transfer and Innovation), European Commission, JMO B4-091, L-2920 Luxembourg.

Eurotec
> Research and Development news periodical, published by the European Commission, Directorate-General for Information, Communication and Culture (DGX).
> Free from DGX.

Eurotec: Technology in Europe
> Special issue of Eurotec, drawing attention to the existence of Community information and provides details of access to its databanks.
> Issue No. S 4/86
> 1986
> Available for reference at the library of the European Commission London Office.

Information Market
> Newsletter published by the European Commission, Directorate-General Telecommunications, Information Industries and Innovation (DGXIII). Research and development activities relating to the information market, covering notices of conferences, etc.
> Free from the European Commission, Directorate-General for Exploitation of Research, Technological Development, Technology Transfer and Innovation (DGXIII), Jean Monnet Building B4-091, L-2920 Luxembourg.

ESRA (European Safety and Reliability Association) Newsletter
> Three times a year
> Published by the Joint Research Centre of the European Commission, Ispra Establishment, I-21020 Ispra, Italy.

Other R & D, technology titles

European Community Research Programmes: Status at 1.9.89
> New published catalogue of research programmes within the Framework Programme of the European Community 1987-1991.
> Published by the European Commission, Directorate-General for Science, Research and Development (DGXII).

EC Research Funding — A Guide for Applicants
> Commission of the European Communities, January 1990
> Free from the European Commission London office.

First Report on the State of Science and Technology in Europe
> First published as COM(88)647 final
> Reprinted and available free of charge from the European Commission London Office.
> No ISBN number

Vade-Mecum of Community Research Promotion 1987 1980-90: A New Development on the European Scientific Policy.
> EUR 7121, 1982
> ISBN 92-825-3111-2
> Price £21.00

Scientific Research and Technological Development in the Community. The Facts in Figures, 1988.
> Short analysis of European Communities R & D presented in statistics.
> EUR 11975
> ISBN 92-825-9286-3

Publications on Science and Technology
　　Booklet issued by the European Commission, Directorate-General for Telecommunications, Information Industries and Innovation (DGXIII). Free from DGXIII/C-3, European Commission, Jean Monnet Building, L-2920 Luxembourg.

Publicly Funded Research and Development in the European Community. Improving the Utilisation of Results
　　EUR 11528, 1988
　　ISBN 92-825-8269-8
　　Price 8.75 Ecus

Utilisation of the Results of Public Research and Development in the UK
　　EUR 11539, 1989
　　ISBN 92-825-9054-2
　　Price 10 Ecus

Directory of Contract Research Organisations in the EEC
　　Directory aiming at furthering the integration of technological progress into the Community industrial structure.
　　EUR 12112, 1989
　　ISBN 92-825-9766-0

The Impact of Biotechnology on Working Conditions
　　European Foundation for the Improvement of Living and Working Conditions, 1988.
　　ISBN 92-825-6767-2
　　Price £6.60

Copyright and the Challenge of Technology: Copyright Issues Requiring Immediate Action
　　Background discussion paper on various issues such as piracy, copyright, home copying, distribution rights, computer programmes, databases, etc.
　　COM(88)172 final

Progress Report on the Implementation of a Community Telecommunications Policy
　　COM(88)240-I

Working towards Telecom 2000 (Launching of the Programme RACE)
　　COM(88)240-II

The Benefits of Completing the Internal Market for Telecommunications Services and Equipment in the Community 1988
　　The Cost of Non-Europe — Volume 10
　　ISBN 92-825-8650-2
　　Price £11.50

Completing the Internal Market: Current Status December 1989
　　Banking, insurance, securities, transport, new technologies and services, capital movements, free movement of labour and the professions
　　Commission of the European Communties
　　One of a set of five brochures
　　ISBN 92-826-0851-4
　　Price 15.00 Ecus

Telecommunications in Europe
> H Ungerer with N P Costello
> Basic objectives ensuring a free choice for the user in Europe's 1992 market.
> The challenge for the European Community.
> *European Perspectives* series, 1988
> ISBN 92-825-8209-4
> Price £7.50

The European Consumer Electronics Industry
> Study on concentration, competition and competitiveness, 1985
> ISBN 92-825-5110-5
> Price £11.10

The MEDIA Programme
> Measures to encourage the development of the industry of audiovisual production.
> 1988

Media Vade Mecum 1990
> Free from London office of the Commission
> ISBN 92-826-1326-7

Action Programme to Promote the Development of the European Audiovisual Industry "Media" 1991-1995.
> Commission Communication
> COM (90) 132 final

TV Broadcasting in Europe and the New Technologies
> Prof. G Locksley
> *Document* series, 1988
> 92-825-8759-2
> Price 31.50 Ecus

Telecommunications: The New Highways for the Single European Market
> *European File* series, 15/88

The Audio-Visual Market in the Single European Market
> *European Documentation* series, 4/1988

TECHNICAL BARRIERS

Selected titles

Technical Barriers
The cost of Non-Europe
> Volume 6
> An illustration by six industries: Some case studies on technical barriers.
> ISBN 92-825-8649-9
> Price 21 Ecus

Catalogue of Community's Legal Acts and Other Texts Relating to the Elimination of Technical Barriers to Trade for Industrial Products.
> *Document* series
> ISBN 92-825-7908-5
> Price 9.00 Ecus

Common Standards for Enterprises
    F Nicolas, with J Repussard
    A Frontier-Free Europe publication
    ISBN 92-825-8554-9
    Price 6.20 Ecus
Completing the Internal Market: A New Community Standards Policy, Current Status December 1989.
    The new approach in harmonization
    Motor vehicles
    Tractors and agricultural machinery
    Food
    Parmaceuticals
    Chemicals
    Construction products
    European Commission, one of a set of 5 brochures
    ISBN 92-826-0878-6
    Price 15 Ecus
The Removal of Technical Barriers to Trade
    European File series, 18/1988
Guide to the Reform of the Structural Funds
    ISBN 92-826-0029-7
    Price 11.25 Ecus

SOCIAL AFFAIRS

Annual reports, special reviews, series

1992: The Single European Market — The Social Dimension
    Series of European Commission pamphlets, 1988
    First four titles:
    Questions and Answers: Workers' Rights in the Single European Market.
    Women's Rights and Equal Opportunities
    Social Security Will Apply to Workers in All Member States in the Single European Market
    Workers' Rights
    Free from the European Commission London Office
Employment in Europe
    First annual report of the series: In-depth analysis of employment developments in the Community, sectoral analysis and other trends in the member states.
    European Commission 1989
    First published as COM(89)399 final
    Later reproduced in book form
    ISBN 92-825-9769-5
    Price 11.25 Ecus
Seventeenth Report on the Activities of the European Social Fund — Financial Year 1988.
    Report from the Commission to the Council and the European Parliament.
    SEC (89) 2200 Final

Social Europe
>   Three part review of social affairs in Europe:
>   1 Overview of current developments in social affairs
>   2 Conferences, studies and other information destined to stimulate the debate on social affairs
>   3 developments in national policies and introduction of new technologies.
>   Plus annual statistics on social trends in the member states
>   Published 3 times a year
>   Annual subscription £21.00

Social Europe Supplements
>   In-depth analysis of specific subjects; technologies of the future, equal treatment for men and women, etc. Up to ten per year
>   Combined annual subscription (Social Europe plus Supplements) £51.00.

Comparative Tables of the Social Security Schemes in the Member States of the European Communities. General Scheme (employees in industry and commerce).
>   15th edition: Situation as at 1 July 1988
>   ISBN 92-825-9523-4
>   Price 12 Ecus

Vocational Training Systems in the Member States of the European Community
>   Published by CEDEFOP - European Centre for the Development of Vocational Training
>   *Vocational Training in Belgium*
>   HX-48-85-252-EN-C 1987
>   Price £2.50
>   *Vocational Training in Denmark*
>   HX-47-86-195-EN-C 1988
>   Price £7.00
>   *Vocational Training in France*
>   HX-49-87-971-EN-C 1988
>   Price £3.50
>   *Vocational Training in the Federal Republic of Germany*
>   HX-48-86-044-EN-C 1987
>   Price £5.00
>   *Vocational Training in Greece*
>   HX-45-86-846-EN-C 1987
>   Price £2.50
>   *Vocational Training in Ireland*
>   HX-46-86-880-EN-C 1987
>   Price £3.50
>   *Vocational Training in Italy*
>   HX-47-86-745-EN-C 1988
>   Price £2.50
>   *Vocational Training in the Luxembourg*
>   New edition being prepared
>   *Vocational Training in the Netherlands*
>   New edition being prepared
>   *Vocational Training in Portugal*
>   HX-45-85-276-EN-C 1987
>   Price £2.50

Vocational Training in Spain
HX-45-85-280-EN-C 1987
Price £2.50
Vocational Training in the United Kingdom
HX-46-86-864-EN-C 1987
Price £2.60

Women of Europe
Twice-monthly information bulletin plus supplements
The effect of Community policies on the daily life of women
Published by the European Commission, Directorate-General for Information, Communication and Culture (DGX), Women's Information Service.
Free from DGX.

Women in Europe
Bi-monthly news-sheet
Published by and available free from the European Commission London Office.

HELIOS Journal
Quarterly
Formerly published as *Interact News*. The work of HELIOS (Handicapped People in the European Community Living Independently in an Open Society) programme.
Available from HELIOS, Information Service, Avenue de Cortenberg, B-1040 Brussels.

Trade Union Information Bulletin
Quarterly
Published by the European Commission, Directorate-General for Information, Communication and Culture (DGX).

InforMISEP
Quarterly bulletin covering activities of MISEP (Mutual Information System on Employment Policies). Changing policies and actions at national level aimed at promoting and improving employment within the European Community.
Published by and available from the European Commission, Directorate-General for Employment, Industrial Relations and Social Affairs.

Other social affairs titles

Report on Social Developments: Year 1988
Review on the development of EC policy together with a review of the current social situation in the member states.
ISBN 92-826-0226-5
Price 16.50 Ecus

Compendium of Community Provisions on Social Security
1988, 3rd edition
ISBN 92-825-7317-6
Price 23.30 Ecus

Commission Report on the Medium-term Projections of Social Protection Expenditure and its Financing.
 1990 projections summary report
 COM(88)655 final

A Guide to Working in a Europe Without Frontiers
 Community policy and legislation about freedom of movement and establishment of professional people within the large Internal Market.
 J C Seche
 A Frontier-free Europe publication, 1988
 ISBN 92-825-8067-9
 Price 18.50 Ecus

Freedom of Movement in the Community: Entry and Residence
 Collection of EC legislative texts relating to the freedom of movement of workers.
 A Frontier-free Europe publication, 1988
 ISBN 92-825-8660-X
 Price 7.50 Ecus

Employment in Europe: Trends and Priorities
 Report posing a set of questions on specific issues analysed in COM(89)399 final
 SEC(89)1880

The Social Dimension of the Internal Market
 Commission Report, known as the *Marin Report* after the member of the Commission who initiated the document.
 SEC(89)1148

The Social Dimension of the Internal Market
 Interim Report of the Interdepartmental Working Party
 Special edition of *Social Europe* 1988
 ISBN 92-825-8256-6
 Price 4.20 Ecus

The Social Aspects of the Internal Market
 Volume I
 Synthesis of 3 seminars held in Brussels in November/December, 1987 and January, 1988. Further seminars to be reported in later volumes.
 Social Europe Supplement 7/1988
 ISBN 92-825-9316-9
 Price 5.10 Ecus

1992: The European Social Dimension
 P Venturini
 A Frontier-free Europe publication, 1989
 ISBN 92-825-8703-7
 Price 9.75 Ecus

Social Europe 1/90
 Essential document with regards to the social dimension of 1992 containing: The Community Charter of Basic Social Rights, The Action Programme Relating to the Implementation of the Charter, and the Social Policy, Progress Review for 1989
 ISSN 0255-0776
 Price 13.50 Ecus

Europe 1992: The Social Dimension
Address by Jacques Delors to the TUC 8.9.88
Free from the European Commission London Office
1992 and Beyond: New Opportunities for Action to Improve Living and Working Conditions in Europe.
European Foundation for the Improvement of Living and Working Conditions, 1989.
Free from the Foundation (see *Contacts* at the end of the Chapter).
People's Europe: Information Handbook
Loose-leaf publication covering all aspects of the People's Europe concept.
Published by the European Commission, Directorate-General for Information, Communication and Culture (DGX).
Free from DGX.
Available for reference only at the European Commission London Office.
The Social Policy of the European Community
European File series, 13/88
The Big European Market: A Trump Card for the Economy and Employment
European File series, 14/88
Health and Safety at Work in the European Communities
European File series, 3/90
The Re-insertion of Women in Working Life Initiatives and Problems
1987
ISBN 92-825-7165-3
Price 10.70 Ecus
The Rights of Working Women in the European Community
E Landau
European Perspectives series, 1986
ISBN 92-825-5341-8
Price £3.00
First Report Concerning the First Three Years of Operation of the First Joint Programme for Exchange of Young Workers, 1985-1987.
COM(88)382 final
Childcare and Equality of Opportunity
Consolidated report to the European Commission
1988
Peter Moss (co-ordinator)
Caring for Children: Services and Policies for Childcare and Equal Opportunities in the United Kingdom.
B Cohen
Published by the European Commission's Childcare Network
1988
Available from Family Policy Studies Centre, 231 Baker Street, London NW1 6XE
Price £8.00
Who Cares for Europe's Children?
Short report of the European Childcare Network
Angela Phillips and Peter Moss
1989
ISBN 92-825-96079
Price 10.50 Ecus

TRANSPORT

Annual reports, series

Europa Transport: Oberservation of the Transport Market
Annual subscription: Four issues, annual report and annual analysis and forecasts, £24.00.

Europa Transport: Observation of the Transport Market
Annual Report 1987
Review of recent developments in the carriage of goods from between member states.
1988
ISBN 92-825-9092-5
Price 7.50 Ecus

Europa Transport: Observation of the Transport Market Analysis and forecasts 1988.
ISBN 92-825-8463-1
Price 6.25 Ecus

Other transport titles

Transport and European Integration
Carlo Degli Abbati
European transport policy of the European Community and other international institutions.
European Perspectives series, 1987
ISBN 92-825-6199-2
Price £9.60

The Cost of Non-Europe: Border-related Controls and Administrative Formalities — An Illustration in the Road Haulage Sector.
The Cost of Non-Europe — Volume 4
ISBN 92-825-8618-9
Price £15.00

Electronics and Traffic on Major Roads: Technical, Regulatory and Ergonomic Aspects.
EUR 9793 EN 1986
Price £24.00

EEC Maritime Transport Policy
Economic and Social Committee, 1986
ESC-86-008-EN
Available from the ESC

Air Transport: ESC Opinion and Report on Civil Aviation
Memorandum No. 2: Progress towards the Development of a Community Air Transport.
Economic and Social Committee, 1985
ESC-85-010-EN
Available from the ESC

Community Rail Policy: Stocktaking and Prospects
　　Economic and Social Committee, 1987
　　ECS-87-007-EN
　　Available from the ESC
Proceedings of the Air Safety Symposium
　　Report on a symposium held in Brussels on 26-27 November, 1987
　　Document series, 1988
　　ISBN 92-825-8788-6
　　Price 15.00 Ecus
Communication on a Community Railway Policy
　　Commission Communication
　　COM (89) 564 final
Air Transport and Aeronautics: Towards a Europe of the Skies
　　European File series, 1/89

CONTACTS

Office for Official Publications of the
European Communities
2 Rue Mercier
L-2985 Luxembourg
Tel: (352) 499281
Telex: 1324 PUBOF LU

European Commission Information Offices

(See page 393).

2 EC On-Line Databases

Terry Hanson

The European Community has been active in the provision and promotion of on-line access to information for many years. Its databases are accessed through its own host organisations, such as ECHO and Eurobases, or through commercial hosts such as WEFA, FT Profile and Context. In the case of statistical databases, magnetic tapes can be supplied direct to users. Where the EC contracts out distribution to others, microcompter diskettes and, more recently, CD-ROM are also used. The databases covered in this chapter fall into four categories — legal, bibliographic, statistical and factual. The overlap between them is sometimes considerable. In such cases, the database is categorised by its principal coverage, though several more specialist databases are listed by host, eg. ECHO.

This survey describes the publicly available databases produced by the EC, certain databases produced by private companies from EC information, and principal database services operated by other companies or organisations covering EC affairs. Much of the information accessed from these databases is of key importance to business, industries and the professions. Non-EC databases, too numerous to list here, may now incorporate EC material impinging on their subject areas, as well as EC information downloaded from the EC's own databases. There are, as exporting companies know, innumerable privately operated databases offering financial information, patents and other types of general business information.

LEGAL AND SINGLE MARKET DATABASES

Celex

Celex is the official database of European Community law[1][2][3]. For many people it is the most important and most useful of all the EC databases. Celex contains the full text of much of the documentation generated by the EC and is, therefore, used as a documentary source as well as an index. In addition to EC legal texts (Directives, Regulations, Decisions etc), Celex carries virtually all documentation arising from the EC's legislative process. It is divided into sectors as follows:

- Sectors 1 & 2: Primary legislation — the Treaties establishing the Communities and amendments, such as those required for the accession of new members, and the Single European Act (full text).

- Sectors 3 & 4: Secondary legislation — Regulations, Directives, Decisions etc., published in the L Series of the *Official Journal of the European Communities* every day (full text).

☐   Sector 5: European Commission legislative proposals in the form of COM Documents, and published Opinions and Resolutions on them from the European Parliament and the Economic and Social Committee (references only).

☐   Sector 6: Reports of cases before the Court of Justice of the European Communities (full text).

☐   Sector 7: National legislative measures implementing EC Directives (references only).

☐   Sector 8: National Court decisions relating to EC provisions.

☐   Sector 9: Parliamentary questions (European Parliament).

☐   Sector 10: Published works on EC law (references).

Substantial improvements to Celex are planned which include the use of the Common Command Language CCL for information retrieval, as well as Mistral; more full texts of documents, such as COM Documents; more coverage of the C Series of the *Official Journal*; and better thesaurus control. The coverage of Celex in French is from 1951 (ECSC Treaty) to date (Sector 5 from 1974). In English, complete coverage dates from 1 July, 1979, though the Treaties are included. Sector 5 coverage dates from 1984. Updating is weekly. Information is available from the host organisation, Eurobases. Single enquiries for documents may be directed to European Documentation Centres (Part Eight, Chapter 3) and Euro-Info-Centres (Part Seven, Chapter 1), which have free access to Celex.

Hosts

Eurobases
European Commission
200, Rue de la Loi
B-1049 Brussels
Tel: (32) 2 235 0001

Context Ltd
Tranley House
Tranley Mews
Fleet Road
London NW3 2QW
Tel: (071) 267 7055
Fax: (071) 267 2745

FT Profile
PO Box 12
Sunbury on Thames
Middlesex TW16 7UD
Tel: (0932) 761444
Fax: (0932) 781425

(Sector 3: Secondary legislation only)

SPEARHEAD

SPEARHEAD is the Department of Trade and Industry's Single Market database, carrying details of Single Market legislation. It is available through FT Profile, or via gateway services — Telecom Gold, Mercurylink, ESA-IRS — and as part of the JUSTIS service available from Context. The database contains short summaries of Single Market-related legislation, Commission proposals (COM Documents), projected Commission proposals, and details of EC sponsored Research and Development programmes. Full texts of legislation can be obtained through FT Profile's limited version of Celex (above).

Host organisation

FT Profile
PO Box 12, Sunbury on Thames
Middlesex TW16 7UD
Tel: (0932) 761444
Fax: (0932) 781425

Context Ltd
Tranley House, Tranley Mews
Fleet Road, London NW3 2QW
Tel: (071) 267 7055
Fax: (071) 267 2745

EUROSCOPE

The EC 1992 database from Deloitte, Haskins & Sells[4][5][6] has now been superceded by EUROSCOPE from Coopers & Lybrand Europe. The database, however, remains substantially the same. It comprises a collection of some 35 reports, each devoted to a particular industrial sector or area of EC activity. Reports run to some 30 pages, on average, and describe the overall strategy and appropriate legislative measures required to achieve the Single Market. Where a user seeks to examine the actual text of EC legislation, it is necessary to refer to other sources, such as Celex (above) or the *Official Journal of the European Communities*.

Access arrangements for the database also remain unchanged. EUROSCOPE is available either through the Belgian host, Infotrade, or FT Profile (and as part of the INVESTEXT service from Thompson Financial Networks which is available on Dialog and Datastar etc.)

Hosts

Infotrade
Gossetlaan 32A
B-1702 Groot-Bijgarden
Tel: (32) 2 466 6480

FT Profile
PO Box 12
Sunbury on Thames
Middlesex TW16 7UD
Tel: (0932) 761444
Fax: (0932) 781425

INFO 92

INFO 92 is one of the newest of the Single Market databases[7]. It comes from the host organisation, Eurobases, and covers legislative progress towards the completion of the Single market in three main categories:

☐ Removal of physical barriers

☐ Removal of technical barriers

☐ Removal of fiscal barriers

Each record gives details of the measures, plus a summary. It is available in either videotext form (though not on Prestel), whereby successive choices are made from hierarchical menus, or as a conventional database using the same retrieval software (Mistral) as Celex and SCAD.

Host

Eurobases
European Commission
200, rue de la Loi
B-1049 Brussels
Tel: (32) 2 235 0001

POLIS

POLIS (Parliamentary On-line Information System) is devoted to British parliamentary activities and information[8]. It is available from UCC Group (formerly Meridian Systems Management). The database includes all European Community Legislation since 1983 and other selected EC documents since 1984 (and, therefore, overlaps into the bibliographical category). Information retrieval is via the BASIS text retrieval system.

Host

UCC Group
Bromley Data Centre
18 Elmfield Road
Bromley, Kent BR1 1LR
Tel: (081) 313 0178
Fax: (081) 313 0813

ABEL

ABEL is a new database enabling users to see a copy of the contents page of the *Official Journal of the European Communities* as soon as it comes out every morning. It is then possible to order, on-line, a copy of the *OJ*, the complete issue or an item within it. Complete issues are sent by mail, extracts by fax. The database is available on the new official publications office host, EUR-OP (also known as OPOCE or OOPEC).

Host

EUR-OP
2 Rue Mercier
L-2985 Luxembourg
Tel: (352) 499282-522
Telex: 1324 PUBOF LU

LEXIS (UK)

This is a comprehensive legal database for English, Scottish and related European and Commonwealth law[9]. In the category of European law, however, only Court of Justice reports are available in English (Library: EUROCOM). The legislation is available in French only. For more information contact Butterworth Telepublishing.

Butterworth Telepublishing Ltd
6 Bell Yard,
London WC2A 2JR
Tel: (071) 405 9691
Fax: (071) 831 1463

JUSletter

JUSletter is produced by the Association pour la Diffusion de l'Information Juridique (ADIJ) in Brussels and is available from ECHO (European Community Host Organisation). It provides information on EC legislation and legal matters generally. The coverage is from 1988 to date. As with most ECHO databases, use of JUSletter is free.

Host

ECHO (European Community Host Organisation)
PO Box 2373
177 Route d'Esch
L-1023 Luxembourg
Tel: (352) 488041
Fax: (352) 488040
Telex: 2181 EURO LU

BIBLIOGRAPHIC DATABASES

SCAD

SCAD is a bibliographic database produced by the European Commission and is available, along with Celex, from the Eurbases host[10]. The database contains four types of information:

□ Type A documents: Principal Community legislation and preparatory legislative documentation (COM Documents, Opinions and Resolutions of the European Parliament and the Economic and Social Committee).

□ Type B documents: All official publications of the European Community.

□ Type C documents: Selected articles from a range of some 1,200 journals covering EC affairs in all official languages.

□ Type D documents: Statements and opinions from European level organisations representing employees and employers.

With SCAD Mistral information retrieval has been enhanced by the addition of a series of so-called Macroprocedures. These facilitate quick retrieval of various categories of Single Market related documents (for example, all Commission proposals) by a simple command.

Host

Eurobases
European Commission
200, Rue de la Loi
B-1049 Brussels
Tel: (32) 2 235 0001

ECLAS

The European Commission's Library Automated System, ECLAS, was launched in 1990 and is accessed through the Eurobases host, along with Celex and SCAD. The database corresponds to the printed publications on the EC — recent EC publications and documents received by the Commission's central library:

EC official publications
Publications of other international organisations (United Nations, OECD etc.)
Books from commercial publishers
Publications from national governments
Articles from periodicals
Theses
Statistical publications

All EC official languages are represented with English and French predominating. Information retrieval is not by the Mistral system, but by the BASIS retrieval language which permits the database to be searched using standard bibliographic database techniques. For controlled vocabulary searching, the OECD Macrothesaurus is used in an enlarged version.

Host

Eurobases
European Commission
200, Rue de la Loi
B-1049 Brussels
Tel: (32) 2 235 0001

EPOQUE

EPOQUE (European Parliament On-line Query) is the database of the European Parliament. In the past, access by the public has been restricted, but recently appears to be less so. The database contains references to all documents produced or discussed by the European Parliament, and it serves as a catalogue of the Parliament's library. The coverage begins in 1979 for Sessions documents and 1983 for Questions and library acquisitions. A new service, OVIDE, is planned for public use, developed by the Parliament and SD-Scicon which is intended as an overall information network for MEPs and their constituents. Among its many features is 'gateway' access to EPOQUE and other important EC databases, such as Celex. For more information contact the European Parliament.

European Parliament
Documentary Databases Division
L-2929 Luxembourg
Tel: (352) 4300-2308

CATEL

CATEL is the main database of the Office for Official Publications of the European Communities. It contains references to all publicly available official publications and documents of the EC institutions. All nine official langage versions are included. The coverage begins in 1985. The EOROVOC thesaurus is used to index the database.

Office for Official Publications of the
European Communities
2 Rue Mercier
L-2985 Luxembourg
Tel: (352) 499281
Telex: 1324 PUBOF LU

EABS

EABS is the on-line version of the printed *European Abstracts* which covers reports from the EC's various science and technology research programmes. Coverage dates from 1962. The database is available from the ECHO host system and is currently free of charge. Updating is monthly.

Host

ECHO (European Community Host Organisation)
PO Box 2373
177 Route d'Esch
L-1023 Luxembourg
Tel: (352) 488041
Fax: (352) 488040
Telex: 2181 EURO LU

EURISTOTE

EURISTOTE is a bibliographical database providing coverage on more than 10,000 studies, mainly theses, on European integration[11]. It corresponds to the printed listing: University Research on European Integration produced by the Catholic University of Louvain. Coverage dates from 1952. The database is available from ECHO and is currently free of charge.

Host
ECHO (European Community Host Organisation)
PO Box 2373
177 Route d'Esch
L-1023 Luxembourg
Tel: (352) 488041
Fax: (352) 488040
Telex: 2181 EURO LU

MISEP

The Mutual Information System on Employment Policies in Europe, MISEP, database provides references to published documents related to the MISEP programme. Coverage dates from 1983. It is available from ECHO free of charge.

Host

ECHO (European Community Host Organisation)
PO Box 2373
177 Route d'Esch
L-1023 Luxembourg
Tel: (352) 488041
Fax: (352) 488040
Telex: 2181 EURO LU

UKOP

UKOP (Catalogue of United Kingdom Official Publications) is a CD-ROM catalogue, produced jointly by HMSO and Chadwyck Healey, of British official publications and those of twelve international organisations including the EC. It corresponds to the annual publications catalogues of HMSO, the *International Organisations Publications Catalogue* (or Agency Catalogue) from HMSO and Chadwyck Healey's *Catalogue of British Official Publications Not Published by HMSO*. Coverage dates from 1980.

Chadwyck Healey Ltd
Cambridge Place
Cambridge CB2 1NR
Tel: (0223) 311479
Fax: (0223) 66440

HMSO Online

HMSO Online is a database equivalent to the printed catalogues of HMSO (Her Majesty's Stationery Office). As these include EC publications, so too does the database. Coverage dates from 1976. The service is offered on BLAISE and *Dialog*.

Hosts

BLAISE Information Services
British Library Bibliographic Services
Boston Spa, Wetherby
West Yorkshire LS23 7BQ
Tel: (0937) 546602/843434
Fax: (0937) 546586

Dialog Information Services
PO Box 188
Oxford OX1 5AX
Tel: (0865) 730725

SIGLE

SIGLE (System for Information on Grey Literature in Europe) is devoted to the bibliographic control of this type of documentation in the member states of the EC and is produced by the European Association for Grey Literature in Europe. The database covers all subject areas and such diverse source material as conference proceedings, theses, reports and other items which would normally be difficult to obtain. SIGLE is available through BLAISE.

Host

BLAISE Information Services
British Library Bibliographic Services
Boston Spa
Wetherby
West Yorkshire LS23 7BQ
Tel: (0937) 546602/843434
Fax: (0937) 546586

STATISTICAL DATABASES

Eurostat, the Statistical Office of the European Communities, is located in Luxembourg and is one of the Directorates-General of the European Commission. Its task is to collect and process statistical data on EC member states and their main trading partners to serve as a basis for the policy decisions taken at Community level. Eurostat has developed a range of databank systems, including CRONOS, EUROSTATUS, REGIO and COMEXT. Data is available to the general public and is disseminated in various forms by Eurostat in printed form via the Office for Official Publications of the EC and electronically by commercial hosts only. In the UK the host is WEFA (See next page).

CRONOS

This database carries a wide range of general statistics including short-term economic indicators and current trends in the twelve EC member states, the USA and Japan. The sectors, or domains, are:

General economic statistics
Economic and financial statistics
Social statistics
Energy and industrial statistics
Agriculture and fisheries statistics
External trade statistics
Statistics on developing countries
Eurostatus (main economic indicators for EC, US and Japan (see separate heading below)

EUROSTATUS

This is a small, but important part of the CRONOS database carrying macroeconomic data covering all sectors of the economy in the form of time series covering, in some cases, periods of over 30 years. The database was created to meet the demands of customers for the latest and most sought after harmonised statistics for the twelve member states, the USA and Japan.

REGIO

This demographic databases carries figures on the regions of the European Community. The range of figures is wide and the main categories are:

Demography
National accounts
Unemployment
Workforce
Industry
Agriculture
Transport
EC grants, loans and incentives

COMEXT

COMEXT is the databank of statistics on intra-Community and external trade. Figures are based on Community legal acts applicable in member states. The methodology (concepts, definition and methods) is laid down in Council Regulations (EEC) Nos. 1736/75 and 2954/85. The goods nomenclature is set out in Council Regulations (EEC) Nos 1445/72 and 3065/75.

Hosts

WEFA Ltd
60-62 Margaret Street
London W1N 7FJ
Tel: (071) 631 0757
Fax: (071) 631 0754

Magnetic tape and CD-ROM products

In addition to an on-line database, Eurostat produces information on magnetic tape and CD-ROM microcumpter diskettes. The CD-ROM products are distributed by DSI (see below). The series available in this form are Eurostatus and Eurostatistics from the CRONOS database. DSI also produce the *World of Macroeconomic Databases on CD-ROM*, a collection of statistics from various sources including Eurostat. Files on magnetic tape include:

□ FSSRS (Farm Structure Retrieval System) contains the results of the EC's surveys on the structure of farm holdings. There have been four such surveys (up to 1990), dating from 1975.

□ Sabine: A database used to store and manage classification schemes, or nomenclatures used in statistical series. Examples include the Nimexe used for product classification in overseas trade statistics, SITC for general industrial product classification and the geonomenclature scheme for geographical information.

□ TES: A database containing the input-output tables of the national accounts of EC member states.

Eurostat enquiries

Eurostat
Statistical Office of the European
Communities
Jean Monnet Building
PO Box 1907
L-2920 Luxembourg
Tel: (352) 4301-2975 (foreign trade), (352)
4301-3220 (on-line dissemination).
Telex: 3423 COMEUR LU

DSI Data Service and Information
PO Box 1127
D-4134 Rheinberg 1
Germany

FACTUAL BUSINESS AND TECHNICAL DATABASES

The databases listed in this section are grouped by host organisation or source. They cover a wide range of business and technical subject areas as well as general EC information. Subscription or general enquiries should be addressed to the host EC organisation itself or to alternative hosts in the UK where listed.

Gateways
Access to many databases is available through various systems, known as gateway services, a useful way for user-beginners to obtain occasional access to databases accessible through the network.

ESA-IRS
European Space Agency Retrieval Services
Via Galileo Galilei
I-00044 Frascati
Italy
Tel: (39) 6 941801
Fax: (39) 6 94180361
Telex: 610637 ESRIN I

Telecom Gold
British Telecom
Units 8-10 Oxgate Centre
Oxgate Lane
London NW2 7JA
Tel: Freefone 0800 200 700

Mercurlylink
Mercury Communications Ltd
1 Brentside Executive Centre
Great West Road, Brentford
Middlesex TW8 9DS
Tel: (081) 914 2500
Fax: (081) 914 2366

ECHO

ECHO is a European Commission host system. Its function is to promote the use of electronic information services and to provide a test bed for new databases[12]. The databases available from ECHO are mostly free of charge. However, with Eurobases firmly established to manage Celex and SCAD and other databases, some ECHO databases will be transferred to Eurobases, possibly incurring charges. The first batch to 'migrate' include THESAURI, ENREP and SESAME. They are listed, therefore, under the Eurobases umbrella. ECHO databases use the Common Command Language for information retrieval.

ECHO (European Community Host Organisation)
PO Box 2373
177 Route d'Esch
L-1023 Luxembourg
Tel: (352) 488041
Fax: (352) 488040
Telex: 2181 EURO LU

TED

TED (Tenders Electronic Daily) is probably the most useful business database for exporting companies, since it provides details of EC tenders and contracts as published in the *Official Journal of the European Communities*. Contracts may be from the EC itself or in the ACP (African, Carribean and Pacific) states where projects are financed by EC development aid. As well as being available on ECHO, the database is offered in various forms in the UK on FT Profile and Export Network and via the gateway systems Telecom Gold and Mercurylink. In addition to conventional database use, TED also allows users to construct a profile describing their subject interests and it will then automatically send appropriate information by telex as soon as it becomes available.

Export Network Ltd
Regency House,
1-4 Warwick St.,
London W1R 5WA
Tel: (071) 494 4030
Fax: (071) 494 1245

FT Profile
PO Box 12
Sunbury on Thames
Middlesex TW16 7UD
Tel: (0932) 761444
Fax: (0932) 781425

Other ECHO databases

ARCOME: Research information exchange
BIOREP: Biotechnical research
BROKERSGUIDE: Information brokers[13]
CCL-TRAIN: Common Command Language training file
CORDIS (RED) (see page 259)
DIANEGUIDE: Database directory (also CD-ROM and printed)

DOMIS: Information services
DUNDIS: Directory of United Nations databases
ELISE: Local employment initiatives
EUREKA: High technology research projects
EURODICAUTOM: Scientific and technical terminology
IES-DC: Information technology and communications
IM: Information Market newsletter (see below)
PABLI: EC development projects
TECNET: Vocational training and new technology projects

Eurobases

In addition to the databases mentioned earlier in this chapter, Eurobases is already the host for other databases (and some planned) including:

ENREP: Environmental research projects
THESAURI: Structural vocabularies
SESAME: Energy technology projects
RAPID: EC press releases, speeches and memos

Eurobases
European Commission
200, Rue de la Loi
B-1049 Brussels
Tel: (32) 2 235 0001

EUROCONTACT

EUROCONTACT is a service for researchers in information technology and telecommunications throughout the EC to enable them to liaise with fruitful contacts. It is currently free of charge. Further information:

EUROKOM
UCD Computer Centre
University College
Belfield
Dublin 4
Tel: (0001) 697890

Joint Research Centre (JRC)

The European Commission's Joint Research Centre at Ispra, in Italy produces three databases:

Ecdin (Environmental Data and Information network): Harmful chemical products. HTM-DB (High Temperature Materials Databank): Engineering materials with high temperature applications. REM (Radio Environmental Monitoring): Radioactivity measurements in member states of the EC.

Joint Research Centre
Ispra Establishment
I-21020 Ispra (VA)
Italy
Tel: (39) 789111
Telex: 324878/324880 EUR 1

Export Network

Export Network is a comprehensive 'one-stop shopping' database service covering most aspects of the export marketing process. The company offers access to around 1000 new export sales leads per day, plus background information on overseas markets and key contacts. The main menu screen offers various options.

☐ Business opportunities: British Overseas Trade Board's Export Intelligence Service, international projects and supplies sales leads, Eastern Europe and China sales and business opportunities, Tenders Electronic Daily (TED), EC aid-funded contracts; agents and buyers; information on development bank financed aid projects; exhibitions and trade fairs.

☐ European Community — 1992: Information on progress towards the Single Market in general and by sector plus information on grants and incentive schemes; Celex legal database.

☐ Finance: Economic and political risk reports worldwide.

☐ Transport and travel: Freight forwarders, export documentation.

Export Network also operates a private electronic mail service linking subscribers with the database's information and service providers, and with other subscribers.

Export Network Ltd
Regency House,
1-4 Warwick St.,
London W1R 5WA
Tel: (071) 494 4030
Fax: (071) 494 1245

BC-NET

The BC-NET, or Business Cooperation Network, database is a European Communities initiative intended to help small and medium-sized enterprises (SMEs) to form links with similar firms in other member states. It works by establishing a network of some 200-250 business advisers (such as chambers of commerce) throughout the Community, through whom interested firms make their enquiries with an application form. The advisers will then arrange for the firm's details to be entered into the BC-NET database in Brussels.

All information on the database is entered in coded form to preserve the confidentiality of the applicant. When a good match is found the two respective business advisers are informed and then contact each other to check the details. If they are satisfied then the firms are contacted. Then direct contact can be made. Information can be obtained from the Commission's SME Taskforce which can provide UK contacts, often located in local chambers of commerce.

SME Task Force
European Commission
Directorate-General XXIII
200 rue de la Loi
B-1049 Brussels
Tel: (32) 2 235 1111
Telex: 21877 COMEU B

Perinorm

Perinorm is a CD-ROM database of references to standards and technical regulations from national standards organisations in Britain (BSI), France (AFNOR), and Germany (DIN). Also included are European and international standards from ISO (International Standards organisation), IEC, CEN and CENELEC. EC technical regulations will eventually be included. For information contact:

British Standards Institution
BSI Database, Linford Wood
Milton keynes MK4 6LE
Tel: (0908) 220022 Ext. 2035
Fax: (0908) 320856

1 Hanson T., Celex. *The Law Librarian* Vol. 20 No.3, December, 1989, pp98-99. 2 Hanson T., Celex on CD-ROM. *The Law Librarian*, Vol. 20 No. 3, December 1989, pp99-100. 3 Hanson T., *An Introduction to Celex: The Database of European Community Law. European Access* No. 3, June, 1989, pp29-32. 4 Hanson T., *EC 1992 Database from Deloitte, Haskins and Sells. European Access*, No. 1, February 1989, pp16-17. 5 Hanson T., *EC 1992 Database from from Deloitte, Haskins and Sells. The Law Librarian*, Vol. 20 No. 3, 20 December, 1989, p101. 6 Oakley-White P., *EC 1992 Database. Brit-Line*, Directory of British Databases. McGraw Hill, 1989, ppx-xii. 7 Hanson T., *Info 92: The EC Commission's 1992 Database. The Law Librarian*, Vol 20. No. 3, December, 1989, pp101-102. 8 Gore J. M., *POLIS. The Law Librarian*, Vol. 20 No. 3, December, 1989, pp99-100. 9 Barringer B., *LEXIS. The Law Librarian*, Vol. 20 No. 3, December, 1989, pp103-104. 10 Hanson T., *An Introduction to SCAD*; The European Community's Bibliographic Database. *European Accesss* No. 4, August, 1989, pp36-39. 11 Bottle D., and Voudouris C. E., *A Bibliometric Critique of the Euristote. Journal of Information Science*, Vol. 14 No. 4, 1988, pp205-220. 12 European Commission: *ECHO Databases and Services.* 13 Cornelius P., *Brokersguide. Infomediary* Vol. 3 No. 1, pp21-28.

INFORMATION SOURCES

Database periodicals

The following selection of periodicals carrying news of databases and information market developments is not exhaustive. Many private database companies issue their own newsletters which make useful reading. *European Access* is particularly recommended for those who wish to receive information on a wide range of news, comment and listings of EC information sources and developments.

European Access
Chadwyck Healey Ltd
Cambridge Place
Cambridge CB2 1NR
Tel: (0223) 311479
(Bi-monthly journal of EC developments and information sources, including a database column. Subscription £90 pa)

Eurobases Bulletin
Eurobases
European Commission
200, rue de la Loi
B-1049 Brussels
Tel: (32) 2 235 0001
(For *Eurobases* users. Issued free at irregular intervals)

ECHO News
ECHO (European Community Host Organisation)
PO Box 2373, 177 Route d'Esch
L-1023 Luxembourg
Tel: (352) 488041
Fax: (352) 488040
Telex: 2181 EURO LU
(For ECHO users, bi-monthly, free)

Information Market (IM)
ECHO (European Communities Host Organisation)
PO Box 2373, 177 Route d'Esch
L-1023 Luxembourg
Tel: (352) 488041
Fax: (352) 488040
Telex: 2181 EURO LU
(Five times a year, free to anyone. EC information market news and developments. Also available from the European Commission)

519

Information World Review
Learned Information Ltd
Woodside
Hinksey Hill
Oxford OX1 5AU
Tel: (0865) 730275
(Monthly newspaper covering the
European information market.
Subscription £30 pa)

Online Review
Learned Information Ltd
Woodside
Hinksey Hill
Oxford OX1 5AU
Tel: (0865) 730275
(Quarterly, covering the EC information
market and database news)

Training

Each of the hosts, EC or otherwise, runs training programmes for users. Training for Eurobases and ECHO usually takes place in Brussels, but occasionally training is offered in Britain for groups of users by special arrangement. The European Information Association (formerly Association of European Documentation Centre Librarians) also runs a training programme for the Celex and SCAD databases, though additional courses relating to other databases are envisaged.

The European Information Association
T. Hanson
Database Training
Portsmouth Polytechnic Library
Cambridge Road,
Portsmouth PO1 2ST
Tel: (0705) 843240

European Association of Information Services (EUSIDIC)
First Floor, 9/9A High Street
Caine, Wiltshire SN11 0BS
Tel: (0249) 814584
Fax: (0249) 813656
(An association of Information professionals with a strong interest in the European information community. It publishes a newsletter, NEWSIDIC)

Representative organisations

ASLIB
Association for Information Management
Information House, 20-24 Old Street
London EC1V 9AP
Tel: (071) 253 4488
Fax: (071) 430 0514
(ASLIB offers advice, training and a range of publications aimed at helping newcomers and experienced researchers)

Note: Sections of this Chapter were first published in *ASLIB Proceedings*, Vol. 42 No. 6 of June 1990.

3 Libraries

Susan Foreman

The advent of 1992 has been widely recognised in the library and information community, and a variety of activities have been undertaken to prepare for it. There is an immense amount of material available: the problem, of course, lies in identifying what is needed and where to find it.

In order to assess which libraries are providing information and at what level, it is necessary first to define the different categories. The usual point of contact for most enquirers will be their nearest business library, whether their local public library, polytechnic or technical college. Many of these have established '1992' collections.

Outside the public sector other sources are organisations, sometimes large companies, with libraries of their own, professional or trade associations and, in particular, the CBI through seminars and a series of Initiative 1992 publications. Chambers of commerce throughout the country are also setting up inquiry points on the Single Market. National or regional centres exist in major business libraries and in business schools, as well as at the British Library.

Specialist collections and information services available to the public may be found in the libraries of the UK offices of the European Commission and European Parliament in London, in the Export Market Information Centre (EMIC), formerly SMIL (Statistics and Market Intelligence Library), and in many government departments, especially DTI. These will often be valuable sources when local contacts have been exhausted. Many government department libraries deal with specific inquiries in their field, and elusive documents may also be traced from such sources if other libraries have failed to find them.

In the private sector many large banks, accountancy and international law firms have made special arrangements to cope with EC literature, and have set up a number of information services specifically targeted to clients. Many produce newsletters and briefings of varying depth for their customers.

The growth of literature on 1992 in the past year or two has been huge, as reflected in the bibliography. Of particular interest to businessmen are the current awareness services such as databases, newsletters, business briefings and looseleaf publications. Until it was closed in September 1989, the DTI's journal *British Business* was an invaluable weekly source of news relevant to businessmen, especially on EC and overseas information. Some of this magazine's ouput has been taken over and incorporated into *Business Briefing*, published by the Association of British Chambers of Commerce.

The British Library's Business Information Service has a range of online databases, market research and industry surveys, trade directories and journals. EMIC is provided by the Department of Trade and Industry and located at DTI headquarters in Victoria Street, London SW1 and is designed to help exporters research overseas markets. It includes the resources of the British Overseas Trade Information System, commercial online databases, statistics, trade directories, market research reports and development plans.

Specifically set up to disseminate EC information, a network of Euro Info-Centres (see Part 7, Chapter 1), has been set up throughout the Community. These have been launched by the EC Commission's task force for small and medium-sized enterprises, and include centres in London, Birmingham, Newcastle and Glasgow. The Centre for European Business Information is the London branch and is part of the Department of Employment's Small Firms Service. By 1992 more centres should be open in the UK. The centres provide an inquiry service and contain a wealth of material relevant to business, including single market legislation, company law, competition policy, details of EC R&D programmes and of grants and loans, and co-operation initiatives.

The most comprehensive collections of EC documents will be found in those libraries granted deposit status by the Commission. The EC depository library network includes three types of collection: European Documentation Centres (EDCs) of which there are 44 in the UK; four Depository Libraries (DEPs), as well as the much more modest European Reference Centres (ERCs). ERCs are small collections of basic EC documents and are based mainly in academic institutions.

The EDCs contain substantial collections of EC documents, legislation, research studies and reports, statistics and background material and are based mainly in university and polytechnic libraries. Many provide a full EC information service while others will allow the public to use the material and will answer or redirect EC-related inquiries, but they are not able to give specialised consultancy-type advice.

Depository libraries are comprehensive collections of EC documentation based in libraries providing a service to the public. UK DEPs are in the British Library Official Publications and Social Sciences Service in London, the Commercial and Social Sciences Library in Liverpool, Westminster Central Reference Library and the British Library Document Supply Centre at Boston Spa. Through the latter, documents should be accessible via their local library's interlending service.

EUROPEAN DOCUMENTATION CENTRES

The Library
University of Aberdeen
Meston Walk
Aberdeen
AB9 2UE
Tel: 0224 40241 Ext 2787

The Library
University of Bath
Claverton Down
Bath
BA2 7AY
Tel:0225 826826 Ext 5594

William Kendrick Library
Birmingham Polytechnic
Perry Barr
Birmingham
B42 2SU
Tel: 021 331 5289

J B Priestley Library
University of Bradford
Bradford
BD1 7DP
Tel: 0274 733466 Ext 8263

The Law Library
University of Bristol
Wills Memorial Building
Bristol
BS8 1RJ
Tel: 0272 303370

The Library
Wye College
Ashford
Kent
TN25 5AH
Tel: 0233 812401 Ext 497

The Library
Queens University
Belfast
BT7 1LS
Tel: 0232 245133 Ext 3605

The Library
University of Birmingham
PO Box 363
Birmingham
B15 2TT
Tel: 021 414 5823

The Library
University of Sussex
Falmer
Brighton
BN1 9QL
Tel: 0273 678159

The Library
University of Cambridge
Cambridge
CB3 9DR
Tel: 0223 333138

Arts and Social Studies Library
University of Wales
College of Cardiff
PO Box 430
Cardiff
CF1 3XT
Tel: 0222 874262

The Library
New University of Ulster
Coleraine
BT52 1SA
Tel: 0265 4141 Ext 257

The Library
University of Warwick
Coventry
CV4 7AL
Tel: 0203 523523 Ext 2041

The Library
University of Durham
Durham
DH1 3LY
Tel: 091 374 3041

Centre for European Legal Studies
University of Exeter
Amory Building
Rennes Drive
Exeter
EX4 4RJ
Tel: 0392 263356

The Library
University of Essex
PO Box 24
Colchester
CD4 3UA
Tel: 0206 862286

The Library
Lanchester Polytechnic
Priory Street
Coventry
CV1 2HF
Tel: 0203 24165/2698

The Library
University of Dundee
Perth Road
Dundee
DD1 4HN
Tel: 0382 23181 Ext 4101

Centre for European Government Studies
University of Edinburgh
Old College
South Bridge
Edinburgh
EH3 9YL
Tel: 031 667 1011 Ext 4292

The University Library
University of Glasgow
Hillhead Street
Glasgow
G12 8QE
Tel: 041 339 8855 Ext 6744

The George Edwards Library
University of Surrey
Guildford
GU2 5XH
Tel: 0483 509233

The Library
University of Keele
Keele
ST5 5RG
Tel: 0782 621111 Ext 3737

The Library
University of Lancaster
Lancaster
LA1 4YX
Tel: 0524 65201 Ext 276

The Library
University of Leeds
20 Lyddon Terrace
Leeds
LS7 9JT
Tel: 0532 31751

The Library
Queen Mary College
Mile End Road
London
E1 4NS
Tel: 081-980 4811 Ext 3307

Brynmor Jones Library
University of Hull
Cottingham Road
Hull
HU6 7RX
Tel: 0482 465441

The Library
University of Kent
Canterbury
CT2 7NU
Tel: 0227 66822

The Library
Leeds Polytechnic
Leeds
LS1 3HE
Tel: 0531 462925

The Library
University of Leicester
Leicester
LE1 7RH
Tel: 0533 522044

The Library
Polytechnic of North London
Prince of Wales Road
London
NW5
Tel: 071-359 0941

The Library
Royal Institute for International Affairs
10 St James Square
London
SW1Y 4LE
Tel: 081-930 2233 Ext 260

The Library
Loughborough University of Technology
Loughborough
LE11 3TU
Tel: 0509 222344

The Library
Newcastle Upon Tyne Polytechnic
Ellison Place
Newcastle Upon Tyne
NE1 8ST
Tel: 091 232 6002

The Library
University of Nottingham
Nottingham
NG7 2RD
Tel: 0602 506101 Ext 3741

Frewen Library
Portsmouth Polytechnic
Cambridge Road
Portsmouth PO1 2ST
Tel: 0705 277201

British Library of Political and Economic Science
10 Portugal Street
London
WC2A 2HD
Tel: 071-405 7686 Ext 2993

John Rylands Library
University of Manchester
Oxford Road
Manchester
M13 9PP
Tel: 061 275 3727

The Library
University of East Anglia
Norwich
NR4 7JT
Tel: 0603 56161 Ext 2412

The Bodleian Library
University of Oxford
Radcliffe Camera
Oxford
OX1 3BG
Tel: 0865 277201

The Library
University of Reading
Whiteknights
Reading
RG6 2AE
Tel: 0734 318782

The Library
University of Salford
Salford
M5 4WT
Tel: 061 736 5843 Ext 7218

Faculty of Law
University of Southampton
Highfield
Southampton
SO9 5NH
Tel: 0703 559122 Ext 3451

The Library
Sheffield City Polytechnic
Pond Street
Sheffield
S1 1WB
Tel: 0742 20911 Ext 2494

Robert Scott Library
Polytechnic of Wolverhampton
St Peter Square
Wolverhampton
WV1 1RH
Tel: 0902 313005 Ext 2300

Depository Libraries

Commercial and Social Sciences Library
Central Libraries
William Brown Street
Liverpool
L3 8EW
Tel: 051 207 2147 Ext 45

Central Reference Library
City of Westminster Library
St Martin's Street
London
WC2 7HP
Tel: 081-758 3131

**British Library Official Publications and
Social Sciences Service**
Great Russell Street
London
WC1B 3DG
Tel: 071-323 7602

British Library Document Supply Centre
Boston Spa
Wetherby
LS23 7BQ
Tel: 0937 843434 Ext 6035

4 Bibliography

Susan Foreman

The literature on the Single Market and doing business in Europe is growing exponentially and it is not possible to be comprehensive. European Community publications are listed in in Part Eight, Chapter 1. Department of Trade and Industry Single Market publications are listed in *UK Official Sources of Information*, Part Seven, Chapter 2.

Most of the entries have been published since the Single European Act (1987), but the amount of literature on the subject generated by publishing houses and trade and professional organisations is still growing rapidly. The variety of subjects covered and the percentage of semi-published or "grey" literature means that tracing certain items is comparatively difficult. A selection of grey literature has been included here since, in certain cases, it may be the only published source available, and is often of good quality.

Information services, such as newsletters continue to grow, all endeavouring to keep readers up to date with developments. Many of these are produced by professional advisers, including international law firms, accountants and management consultancies. They tend to be routinely available only within a limited circulation, although it has been the experience of the compiler that once one knows of the existence of a document, firms are often willing to supply copies to 'outsiders'. The law firms Clifford Chance and Brebner & Co. for example, provide excellent material.

The bibliography is arranged in the following categories. Annotations are provided if the title is not sufficiently descriptive of the contents:

1992, Single Market, European Community

ARBUTHNOT, Hugh & EDWARDS, Geoffrey. *A Common Man's Guide to the Common Market.* 2nd ed. Macmillan, 1989. 236pp. ISBN 0-333-40913-2.

ARTHUR YOUNG INTERNATIONAL. *The Single Internal Market. EEC Brief*, special issue. Prepared with the Brussels Office of McKenna & Co. No. 4, July 1988. 8pp.

BARNES, I & PRESTON, J. *The European Community.* Longman, 1988. 172pp. ISBN 0-582-29716-8. Guide to recent changes in decision making brought about by the Single European Act.

BUDD, Stanley A. *The EEC: A Guide to the Maze.* 3rd ed. Kogan Page, 1989. 260. ISBN 0-7494-0023. Guide to operations, policies and decision making process, grants and loans, sources of information.

BULMER, Simon & WESSELS, Wolfgang. *The European Council: Decision Making in European Politics.* Macmillan, 1987, reprinted 1989. 174pp. ISBN 0-333-36841-X.

BURGESS, Michael. *Federalism and European Union: Political Ideas, Influences and Strategies in the European Community 1972-1986.* Routledge, 1989. 256pp. ISBN 0-415-00498-5. Critique of contrasting theories of Monnet and Spinelli and their proposals for a unified Europe.

BUTT Philip, A. *Implementing the European Internal Market.* Royal Institute of International Affairs, 1988. 20pp (RIIA discussion paper No. 5).

BUTTERWORTH & CO.. *Butterworths Guide to the European Communities.* Butterworths, 1989. 205pp. ISBN 0-406-16999-3. Covers history, institutions and policies, enacted and proposed legislation.

CALINGAERT, Michael. *The 1992 Challenge from Europe: Development of the European Community's Internal Market.* Washington DC. National Planning Association, 1988. 148pp. ISBN 0-89068-096-5. Discusses prospects for action by 1992 and opportunities for US business.

CCH INTERNATIONAL. *Doing Business in Europe.* Looseleaf. 1 vol. Country by country commentary, and discussion on Single Market and progress towards 1992.

CECCHINI, Paolo and others. *The European Challenge. 1992: The Benefits of a Single Market*, English edition by John Robinson. Wildwood House, 1988. 127pp. ISBN 0-7045-0613-0. Study based on research for 'costs of non-Europe' project (for details see *European Community Publications*, Part Eight, Chapter 1). Identifies benefits and opportunities for a number of manufacturing and service sectors, and produces figures showing costs of 'non-Europe'.

CLARKE, William M, (editor). *Planning for Europe.* Waterlow, 1989. ISBN 0-08-036903-0. General introduction, with chapters covering sectors such as banking, transport, etc.

CLIFFORD CHANCE. *Intellectual Property and the EEC: 1992.* 1988. 12pp memorandum.

CLIFFORD CHANCE. *1992: An Introductory Guide.* 1989. 93pp.

COLCHESTER, Nicholas & BUCHAN, David. *Europe Relaunched: Truths and Illusions on the Way to 1992.* The Economist/Hutchinson, 1990. 256pp. ISBN 0-09-174382-6.

CONFEDERATION OF BRITISH INDUSTRY. *Europe Sans Frontieres (1992 — how it affects you).* 1988. Briefing pack with quarterly updates, analysing

527

the many areas within the Single Market: standards, environment, competition and commercial policy, public procurement, financial services, etc.

CONSUMERS IN THE EUROPEAN COMUNITY GROUP. *1992: Border Controls and Consumer Health and Safety*. 1989. (CECG paper 89/10).

CONSUMERS IN THE EUROPEAN COMMUNITY GROUP. *The Participation of Consumers in National and European Community Policy Making in the Run-up to 1992 and Thereafter*. 1989. (CECG paper 89/8)

CRONER PUBLICATIONS. *Croner's Europe*. Looseleaf. 2 vols. ISBN 0-900319-83-6. Reference service with monthly updates on legal developments likely to affect business. Also covers business and tax issues of single market. Includes checklist of directives in pipeline for 1992 and 'Brussels update'.

CURZON PRICE, Victoria. *1992: Europe's Last Chance? From Common Market to Single Market*. 19th Wincott Memorial Lecture (Occasional paper No. 81) Institute of Economic Affairs, 1988. 46pp. ISBN 0-255-36217-X.

CUSACK, Mark & HARTE, Linda, (editors), *Nineteen Ninety Two: An Unworkable Utopia*. Hoare Govett, 1988. 58pp.

CUTLER, Tony, and others. *1992: The Struggle for Europe. A Critical Evaluation of the Single Market*. Berg, 1989. ISBN 0-85496-596-3.

DAHRENDORF, Ralf, and others. *Whose Europe? Competing Visions for 1992*. Institute of Economic Affairs, 1989. 100pp (IEA readings No. 29) ISBN 0-255-36222-6. Collection of essays on Brussels and 1992, banking and monetary control, financial services and company law.

DANKERT, Piet & KOOYMAN, A (editors). *Europe Without Frontiers: Socialists on the Future of the EEC*. Cassell, 1989. 110pp. ISBN 0-304-31842-6. Seven European socialists put forward their vision of Europe in 1992.

DAVIS, Evan, and others. *1992: Myths and Realities*. London Business School, Centre for Business Strategy, 1989. 123pp. ISBN 0-902583-17-4.

DESIGN COUNCIL. *Designs on Europe: The Challenge of the Single Market* 1989. 24pp. Includes case studies on companies featured in the *Designs on Europe* exhibition 1989 that will be affected by harmonised technical standards in European Industry.

ECONOMIST, The. *A Survey of Europe's Internal Market*. Supplement in *The Economist*, 9 July 1988. 52pp.

ECONOMIST, The. *A Survey of Europe's Internal Market. 1992 Under Construction'*. Supplement in *The Economist*, 8 July 1989. 56pp.

EUROMONITOR. *1992: Single European Market*. 1988. 177pp. ISBN 0-86338-341-6. background and major issues, legislative processes involved and accompanying measures, and implications for industry.

EUROMONITOR. *1992: The Single Market Handbook*. 1989. 250pp. Statistical data and essays on 1992 legislation and developments, sources of information and research services.

FEATHERSTONE, Kevin. *European Internal Market Policies*. Routledge 1989. 220pp (Spicers European policy reports) ISBN 0-415-03827-8. Includes information on how policy programme emerged and its implications for European economy in general and specific sectors. Also analyses issues most likely to affect government and businesses outside EC.

GLEED, Richard, and others. *Deloitte's 1992 Guide*. Butterworth & Co., 1989. 126pp. ISBN 0-406-50481-4.

GRAHL, J & TEAGUE, P. *1992 — The Big Market: The Future of the European Community*. Lawrence & Wishart.

HENLEY, the Management College. *The Living Market: The Impact of 1992 on Europe at Work*. A report by Henley — the Management College and Sanders & Sidney Plc in association with *The Observer*, edited by D. Turner. Sanders & Sidney, 1989. 111pp. ISBN 1-87207-500-2.

HESELTINE, Michael. *The Challenge of Europe: Can Britain Win?*. Weidenfeld & Nicolson, 1989. 226pp. ISBN 0-297-79608-9.

HOPKINS, Michael, (editor). *European Communities Information: Its Use and Users*. Mansell, 1985. 304pp. ISBN 0-7201-1701-1. Information on the European Community and parliament, business community, EC law, and statistical sources.

JEFFREYS, Janie. *Pressing Ahead to 1993*. Eibis International, 1989. 12pp.

JOURNAL OF COMMON MARKET STUDIES. *Making the Common Market Work. Journal of Common Market Studies Special issue, March 1987*.

KEY NOTE. *1992: The Single European Market*. Key Note guides. Key Note Publications, 1989. 93pp. ISBN 1-85056-644-5. Briefing on background, EC markets, 1992 proposals and their implications, UK experience.

LEONARD, Dick. *Pocket Guide to the European Community*. Basil Blackwell and The Economist Publications, 1988. 210pp. ISBN 0-631-16284-4. Guide to major economic, political and social issues, institutions and activities of the EC.

LINKLATERS & PAINES. *1992: A General Introduction*. 1988 15pp.

LODGE, Juliet, (editor). *The European Community and the Challenge of the Future*. Pinter, 1989. 334pp. ISBN 0-86187-724-1. Issues and priorities facing EC member states.

MORRIS, Brian, BOEHM, Klaus & GELLER, A. *The European Community 1991/2*, 3rd ed., 1990. ISBN 0-333-39838-6. Detailed guide to the EC institutions and European business organisations. A practical guide for business, industry and trade.

MORRISON, Catherine. *1992: Leading Issues for European Companies*. New York. The Conference Board Inc, 1989. 33pp. Summarises findings of a survey in Europe on public policy issues management.

MYLES, Gregg. *EEC Brief*. Locksley Press, 1979-. 3 looseleaf binders. Handbook of EC law, practice and policy. Regular updates include material on the single market and catalogue acts and proposals relating to 1992.

NICOLL, William & SALMON, Trevor C. *Understanding the European Communities*. Philip Allan. c.288pp. 1990.

NUGENT, Neill. *Government and Politics of the European Community*. Macmillan, 1989. 368pp. ISBN 0-383-42896-X. Origins, historical development, powers, influence and methods of functioning of the main institutions.

OWEN, R & DYNES, M. *The Times Guide to 1992: Britain in a Europe Without Frontiers. A Comprehensive Handbook*. Times Books, 1989. 238pp. ISBN 0-723-0316-5.

PALMER, John. *Trading Places: The Future of the European Community*. Radius, 1988. 203pp. ISBN 0-09-173182-8. Companion to Granada TV series.

POWELL, Enoch, *Enoch Powell on 1992* (Richard Ritchie, Editor). Anaya Publishers Ltd, 1989. 177pp. ISBN 1-85470-008-1. Based on Enoch Powell's speeches and writings, arranged by topic.

PRICE WATERHOUSE. *The European Single Market — Putting 1992 in Perspective*. 1989. 25pp. Overview in plain English for the businessman, and 1992 strategy checklist.

RAJAN, Amin. *1992 A Zero Sum Game*. Industrial Society Press, 1990. 289pp. ISBN 0-85290-594-7. Business know-how and training challenges in an integrated Europe.

REDWOOD, John. *Europe 1992: The Good and the Bad*. Centre for Policy Studies, 1989. 28pp.

RITCHIE, Richard, (editor). *Enoch Powell on 1992*. Anaya Publishers Ltd, 1989. 177pp. ISBN 1-85470-008-1. Based on Enoch Powell's speeches and writings, arranged by topic.

RODGERS, William & RANDALL, Heather, (editors). *Government and Industry: A Business Guide to Westminster, Whitehall and Brussels*. Kluwer, 1986-1989, Longman since 1989. Looseleaf with updating service. ISBN 0-903393-92-1. Practical guide, includes information on lobbying and the EC, role of MEPs, 1992, details of current and planned legislation.

RONEY, Alex. *The European Community Fact Book*. Kogan Page in association with the London Chamber of Commerce and Industry, 1989. 187pp. ISBN 0-7494-0067-6. Question and answer format.

ROOSTER. *1992: The New Europe*. CBI/The Economist conference report. Rooster Books Ltd, 1988. 146pp. ISBN 1-871510-05-8. Papers on progress towards single market, legal aspects, small firms, marketing and training, mergers, etc.

ROYAL BANK OF SCOTLAND. Special 1992 edition *Royal Bank of Scotland Review*, June 1989.

SILVA, Michael & SJOGREN, Bertil. *Europe 1992 and the New Power game*. John Wiley & Sons. ISBN 0-471-51550-7.

SLOT P. J. & VEN DER WOUDE, (editors). *Exploiting the Internal Market: Co-operation and Competition Towards 1992*. Kluwer, 1988. 160pp. ISBN 90-654-4390-8.

SUNDAY TIMES. *1992: are you ready? The Sunday Times Magazine* special issue 23 October 1988.

TAYLOR, Catherine & PRESS, Alison, edited by Gina Marks. *1992: The Facts and Challenges*. Industrial Society, 1988. 61pp. ISBN 0-85290-459-2. Shows how organisations should begin to inform themselves and plan for 1992.

THOMSON, Ian. *The Documentation of the European Communities: A Guide*. Mansell 1989. 304pp. ISBN 0-7201-2022 5. Describes current publicly available printed documentation produced by the EC.

TODD, Jonathan. *The Club de Bruxelles Practical Guide to the European Single Market*. Brussels. European News Agency, (1988). Various paging.

TOUCHE ROSS INTERNATIONAL. *Completing the Internal Market: A Guide to 1992, the Cockfield White Paper*. 1986. 54pp.

TUTT, Nigel. *Europe on the Fiddle; The Common Market Scandal*. Christopher Helm, 1989. 301pp.ISBN 0-7470-3207-6. Assesses progress to date on removal of physical controls, technical barriers and fiscal reform for 1992.

WISTRICH, E. *After 1992: The United States of Europe*. Routledge, 1989. 154pp. ISBN 0-415-04451-0. Examines EC's responsibilities in the monetary, economic, social and cultural spheres and traces progress towards European union.

Databases

HANSON, Terry. *Going Online*. ASLIB (1991).

Directory of European Communities Databases. European Information Association (1991).

Documents of the EC

EUROFI PLC. *Index to Documents of the Commission of the European Communities*. Annual publication originally created by Giancarlo Pau, dating from 1981.

THOMSON, Ian. *The Documentation of the European Communities: A Guide:* Mansell, 1990 ISBN 0-7201-2022-5. A skilled compilation; recommended.

Economy, ECU, European Monetary System

COFFEY, Peter, (editor). *Main Economic Policy Areas of the EEC — Towards 1992: The Challenge to the Community's Economic Policies When the 'Real' Common Market is Created by the End of 1992*. 2nd rev ed. Kluwer, 1988. 166pp. ISBN 90-247-36757.

ECONOMIST INTELLIGENCE UNIT. *European Community: Economic Structure and Analysis*. EIU, 1989. 2 vols. 1: Belgium, Denmark, Ireland, Luxembourg, Netherlands, UK, West Germany. 197pp; 2: France, Greece, Italy, Portugal, Spain. 203pp. ISBN 0-85058-310-1.

EMERSON, Michael, and others. *The Economics of 1992: The EC Commission's Assessment of the Economic Effects of Completing the Internal Market . OUP, 1988. 304pp. ISBN 0-19-877294-7. Study carried out as a contribution to the Cecchini Cost of non-Europe* project, and contains detailed economic analysis of the possible impact of completing the internal market.

EUROCOOP. *The 1993 Internal Market: Effects of the Single European Act on the Economy and Consumers; Current Harmonisation of Food Law; Approximation of Indirect Taxation; Sectoral Problems*. 1989. 25pp + annexes.

EUROMONEY PUBLICATIONS. *ECU: European Currency Unit*. Richard M. Levich (editor). ISBN 0-870031-50-4.

EUROMONITOR. *Retail Structure in Europe: Strategy 2000*. 1990 2 vols, loose leaf. Analyses likely future patterns after 1992 and includes official forecasts.

EUROMONITOR. *West European Economic Handbook*. 1987. 184pp. ISBN 0-86338-142-1.

FERRI, Pierro (editor). *Prospects for the European Monetary System*. Macmillan. ISBN 0-333-52575-2.

HAMILTON, Carl B. & STALVANT, Carl-Einar. *A Swedish View of 1992*. Royal Institute of International Affairs, 1989. 39pp (RIIA discussion paper 13).

HENDERSON, David. *1992: The External Dimension*. Group of Thirty, 1989. 23pp. (Occasional papers No. 25). Effects of completion of Single Market as viewed by countries outside the EC.

HITIRIS, T. *European Community Economics: A Modern Introduction*. Harvester/Wheatsheaf, 1988. 264pp. ISBN 0-7450-0366-4. Student text on objectives, successes and failures of economic policy in the EC.

HOLMES, Peter. *Real and Imaginary Barriers to Trade Within the EEC and Economies of scale*. University of Sussex, 1987. 14pp (discussion paper 87/47).

O'HAGAN, Michael, (editor). *Guide to the 1989 General Budget of the Commission of the European Communities and the Other Community Institutions*. Dartmouth, 1989. 213pp. ISBN 1-85521-043-6.

PELKMANS, Jacques & WINTERS, Alan. *Europe's Domestic Market.* Routledge, 1988. 149pp (Chatham House paper 43). ISBN 0-415-00213-3. Critical analysis of single market objectives and economic benefits that might follow.

RIBOUD, Jacques. *The Case for a New ECU: Towards Another Monetary System.* Translated by Stephen Harrison. Macmillan Press, 1989. 209pp. ISBN 0-333-44810-3.

SWANN, Dennis. *The Economics of the Common Market.* 6th ed. Penguin, 1988. 326pp. ISBN 0-14-022781-4.

WARWICK UNIVERSITY. *Sources of European Economic and Business Information.* 5th ed. Gower/University of Warwick. Business Information Service, 1989. 250pp. ISBN 0-566-02658-9. Lists major sources by country. Publications cover economic conditions, socio-economic data, public finance, industry, business and commerce.

ZIS, George. *The European Monetary System, 1979-89: An Assessment.* Institute of Chartered Accountants in England and Wales, 1989. 20pp. ISBN 1-85355-047-7.

Employment

BLUE ARROW PLC. *Employment and Training.* Mercury Books (W. H. Allen) 1990, CBI Initiative 1992. 224pp. ISBN 1-85251-057-9.

HOMSTEDT, Margareta. *Employment policy.* Routledge, 1990 176pp (Spicers European policy reports). Outlines EC legislative framework for employment rights and practices.

RABAN, A. J. *Working in the European Communities: A Guide For Graduate Recruiters and Job Seekers.* 2nd ed. Hobsons Publishing, 1988. 180pp. ISBN 1-85324-095-8.

Environment

HAIGH, Nigel. *Environmental Policy and 1992.* 2nd ed. Longman, 1987. 380pp. ISBN 0-582-05959-3.

HAIGH, Nigel & BALDOCK, David. *EEC Environmental Policy and 1992.* Institute for European Environmental Policy, 1989. 56pp. Report prepared for the Department of the Environment on the consequences for environmental policy of the completion of the Single Market.

Exporting

See *Marketing, exporting*, page 538.

Financial services, taxation, exchange controls

ACCOUNTANCY. Special report, *Europe 1992.* August 1988, pp 73-90. Overview of important legislative instruments under consideration, harmonisation of indirect taxes, impact of proposed changes on accountancy profession.

BANK OF ENGLAND. *The Single European Market: Survey of the UK Financial Services Industry.* 1989. 33pp + appendices.

BANKING, INSURANCE AND FINANCE UNION. *Beyond 1992.* Conference report, January 1989. 42pp. Implications of single European market on finance industry.

BARRET, Matthew & KING, Paul. *Towards a Single Market.* Supplement to *Euromoney*, September 1988. 172pp. Includes features on 1992 theory and practice, financial services, taxation, industry, and monetary union.

CLIFFORD CHANCE. *Banking 1992.* 1989. 105pp. Introduction to developments in banking, in light of proposal for single European banking licence, and practical implications for EC and non-EC banks.

CLIFFORD CHANCE. *Insurance 1992* 1989.

CLIFFORD CHANCE. *Insurance 1992.* 1990. 106pp. Guide to insurance industry as affected by the 1992 programme.

CLIFFORD CHANCE. *Investment Services 1992.* 1989. 161pp.

CONSUMERS IN THE EUROPEAN COMMUNITY GROUP. *Financial Services After 1992.* 1989 (CECG paper 89/4).

COOPERS & LYBRAND DELOITTE (Eurotax group). *Tax Harmonisation and 1992.*Financial Times Business Information, 1988. 72pp. ISBN 1-85334-021-9.

ERNST & WHINNEY. *Insurance in the European Community: An Industry Overview.* 1988.

EUROFI PLC. *1992 — Planning for Financial Services and the Insurance Sector.* Butterworth & Co., 1989. 261pp. ISBN 0-408-0408-0. Summarises proposed and adopted legislation for completion of Financial Area.

EUROMONITOR. *European Retail Banking.* 1989. 500pp. Analyses major developments in next decade. Examines effects of European harmonisation and liberalisation of banking laws, countries and companies in operation.

HENDRIE, Anne, (editor). *Banking in the EEC, 1988: Structures and Sources of Finance.* Financial Times Business Information, 1988. 370pp. ISBN 1-85334-108-8. Information on current banking systems in member states, details of legal aspects, foreign exchange controls and tax.

HILL SAMUEL BANK LTD. *Mergers, Acquisitions and Alternative Corporate Strategies.* Mercury Books (W. H. Allen), CBI Initiative 1992. 164pp. ISBN 1-85251-012-9. Impact of 1992 on R & D, manufacturing, distribution and pricing. Evaluates options open to companies, such as alliance within EC, vertical or horizontal integration, joint ventures, etc.

IFR PUBLISHING. *1992: The Single European Market.* 1988. 267pp. ISBN 0-946559-45-7. Based on conference. Covers financial sectors country by country.

NATIONAL WESTMINSTER BANK PLC. *Finance for Growth.* Mercury Books (W. H. Allen), CBI Initiative 1992. ISBN 1-85251-022-6. Describes facilities which can support business in the changing environment and analyses likely effects of removal of barriers in provision of financial services.

NOBES, Chistopher. *Interpreting European Financial Statements: Towards 1992.* Butterworth & Co,. ISBN 0-406-51170-5.

PRICE WATERHOUSE. *Tax: Strategic Corporate Tax Planning.* Mercury Books (W. H. Allen), CBI Initiative 1992. 195pp. ISBN 1-85251-017-X. Outlines business tax regimes in EC member states and implications of various options open to companies seeking to expand or develop.

ROOSTER BOOKS. *Restructuring Europe's Financial Services: 1992 and Beyond*. Economist Conference Reports, 1989. 107pp. ISBN 1-871510-10-4. Progress in financial services, life assurance and pensions, banking, investment services, etc.

TOUCHE ROSS. *Accounting for Europe: Success by 2000 AD?*. 1989. Accounting practice in different European countries.

SPICERS CENTRE FOR EUROPE. *Opportunities in European Financial Services*. Paul Quantock (editor) John Wiley & Sons. ISBN 0-471-52213-9.

WALTER, Ingo & SMITH, Roy C. *Investment Banking in Europe After 1992*. Blackwell, 1990. 208pp. ISBN 0-631-17179-z 7.

Grants and incentives

DAVISON, Ann. *Grants from Europe: How to Get Money and Influence Policy*. 4th ed. Bedford Square Press in association with ERICA, 1988. 91pp. ISBN 0-7199-1248-2. Primarily for charities but also relevant for small business and professional bodies.

EUROPEAN COMMISSION. *EC Research Funding: A Guide for Applicants*. Comprehensive guide to EC R & D programmes under the Framework Programmes. 188pp.

MELLORS, Colin & COPPERTHWAITE, Nigel. *Regional Policy*. Routledge, 1990. 240pp (Spicers European policy reports). ISBN 0-415-03828-6. Explains how European Regional Development Fund operates and the way it relates with other EC sources of funding.

NUNN, Hilary, (compiler). *Grants from Europe: A Survey of Current Awareness Services*. Hertis Information & Research, 1989. 37pp. Includes material on published series and databases.

SCOTT, Gay & REID, Tony. *A Guide to European Community Grants and Loans: For Commerce, Industry, Local Authorities, Academic and Research Institutions*. Eurofi Plc. Looseleaf with updates.

YUILL, Douglas and others, (editors). *European Regional Incentives: A Survey of Regional Incentives in the Countries of the European Community and Sweden*. Bowker-Saur Ltd in association with European Policies Research Centre, University of Strathclyde, 1989. ISBN 0-86291-910-X. Annual survey. (See also *EC Grants and Loans*, Part Four, Chapter 7).

Industrial studies by sector (excluding financial services)

CAPEL, James & Co. *Special Report on the Impact of 1992 on European Industrial and Financial Markets*. 1988. 66pp. Covers telecommunications, pharmaceuticals, chemicals, insurance and banking.

CLIFFORD CHANCE. *Information Technology 1992*. 104pp.

CONSUMERS IN THE EUROPEAN COMMUNITY GROUP. *Completion of the Internal Market in Food*. 1989 (CECG paper 89/1).

CONSUMERS IN THE EUROPEAN COMMUNITY GROUP. *Pharmaceuticals and 1992*. 1989 (CECG paper 89/5).

EDWARD SHERMAN SURVEYORS. *Property*. Mercury Books (W. H. Allen), CBI Initiative 1992. 244pp. ISBN 1-85251-052-8. Guide to each property market and different brokerage and conveyancing systems.

EUROFI PLC. *1992 — Planning for Chemicals, Pharmaceuticals and Biotechnology*. Butterworth & Co., 1989. 256pp. ISBN 0-408-04095-5.

EUROFI PLC. *1992 — Planning for the Engineering Industries*. Butterworth & Co., 1989. 256pp. ISBN 0-408-04097-1.

EUROFI PLC. *1992 — Planning for the Food Industry*. Butterworth & Co., 1989. 377pp. ISBN 0-408-0491-2. Summarises legislation for elimination of technical, physical and fiscal barriers to trade in food and drink sector.

EURFOFI PLC. *Planning for the Information Technology Industries*. Butterworth & Co., 1989. 350pp. ISBN 0-408-0493-9. Summarises legislation in IT and telecommunications sectors.

EUROPEAN COMMISSION. *Panorama of EC Industry*, 1989. Describes over 125 sectors of the European Community's industry, including both manufacturing and services, with a macroeconomic outlook and a view of emerging industries. ISBN 92-825-8435-6.

FALLOWS, Stephen. *The Food Sector. Routledge, 1989.208pp (Spicers European Policy Reports). ISBN 0-415-03833-2.* Explains role of EC policy in this area and implications for those involved in business and the public sector. Key EC documents are summarised and relevant official material listed.

FOOD FROM BRITAIN. *1992: Strategic Issues for the Food & Drink Industry*. Transcript of Institute of Directors conference, 1988. 118pp.

HAMILTON, Ken. *Transport Policy*. Routledge, 1989. 160pp (Spicers European Policy Reports). ISBN 0-415-03831-6. Covers channel tunnel, high-speed rail network, improvement of urban transport systems. Summarises key EC policy documents and gives details of relevant official material.

MORGAN STANLEY & CO. *1992: What is it?* 1988. 59pp. Report on Europe 1992 and likely 'winners' in the different industrial sectors.

P. A. CONSULTING GROUP. *Information Technology: The Catalyst for Change*. Mercury Books (W. H. Allen). CBI Initiative 1992. 214pp. ISBN 1-85251-042-0. Sets out conditions for successful investment in IT infrastructure.

PEMBERTON, Max. *Europe's Motor Industry: 1992 and Beyond: A Review of the Impact of Single Market Legislation, the Channel Tunnel and Block Exemption*, by Max Pemberton. Economist Intelligence Unit, 1988. ISBN 0-85058-227-X.

RANK XEROX LTD. *Marketing to the Public Sector and Industry*. Mercury Books (W. H. Allen), CBI Initiative 1992. 224pp. ISBN 1-85251-037-4. Examines marketing strategies appropriate to winning contracts in a multinational single market and how companies should organise sales, distribution and service operations.

ROOSTER BOOKS. *1992: The Implications for Marketing, Advertising, and the Media. The Economist* conference transcript, 1989. 82pp. ISBN 1-871510-06-6.

ROOSTER BOOKS. *The Defence Market You are Missing*. Transcript of CBI conference, 1988. 76pp. ISBN 1-871510-04-X.

TNT EXPRESS. *Transport and Distribution*. Mercury Books (W. H. Allen) CBI Initiative 1992. 224pp. ISBN 1-85251-047-1. Study of future of transport and distribution after liberalisation of transport services and removal of border and other controls.

TOUCHE ROSS. *The Single Market: The Impact on the UK Construction Industry*, 1988. Compares practices in UK, France and West Germany.

UBS PHILLIPS AND DREW. *Europe 1992: Breaking Down the Barriers: Economic and Sector Prospects*, 1988. 94pp. Covers capital goods, consumer goods, transport, financial services, mergers.

Legislation

ADVOKATERNE BREDGRADE 3, and others. *Merger Control in the EEC: A Survey of European Competition.* Kluwer, 1989. 306pp.

BREALEY, Mark & QUIGLEY, Conor. *Completing the Internal Market of the European Community. 1992 Handbook.* Graham & Trotman, 1989. 273pp. ISBN 1-85333-159-7. To be updated annually. Sets out legislative changes which Commission's programme entails and puts in context of law of Single Market as a whole.

BREALEY, Mark & QUIGLEY, Conor. *Completing the Internal Market of the European Community: 1992 Legislation* Graham & Trotman, 1989. ISBN 1-85333-194-5. Looseleaf in 3 vols + 5 individual volumes covering legislation as it affects different sectors of business, commerce and industry. Basic works include legislation on transport, customs and travel; veterinary; technical standards; financial services; business. Volumes to be updated quarterly.

BREBNER, John, (Brebner & Co). *Setting up a Company in the European Community: A Country by Country Guide.* London Chamber of Commerce/Kogan Page, 1988. 251pp. ISBN 1-8509-860-0. Outlines EC company law directives and other important proposals and regulations. Each country section includes documentary and regulatory requirements, tax law, capital required, etc.

BUTTERWORTH & CO.. *Butterworths European Communities Brief.* ISBN 0-406-04004-4. Information service includes 4-page weekly newsletter with summaries of proposals, enacted legislation of EC and UK implementing legislation, Court decisions and Commission documents; lists new publications.

BUTTERWORTH & CO.. *Butterworths European Communities Legislation. Current Status 1952-198-.* 2 vols + index. ISBN 0-406-05609-9. Standard annual guide to all secondary EC legislation published in the *Official Journal of the European Commmunities* since 1952.

BUTTERWORTH & CO.. *Butterworths Guide to the European Communities,* 1989. 205pp. ISBN 0-406-16-999-3. Concise summary of EC legislation, the treaties, events in the formation of the EC, the workings of the EC.

CCH INTERNATIONAL. *Common Market Reporter.* 1987. 4 vols. Looseleaf. Includes texts and commentary, and case law.

CLIFFORD CHANCE. *The CCH Guide to 1993 Changes in EEC Law.* CCH, 1989. 119pp. ISBN 0-86325-206-0. Examines new laws in different practice areas, impact of the Single Market on different business sectors and implications for EEC, EFTA and non-European companies.

CLIFFORD CHANCE. *Takeovers and Mergers in Europe.* 101pp.

FINANCIAL TIMES BUSINESS INFORMATION. *European Tax Law,* 1989. *Financial Times* management report. Details of laws and regulations of EC member states and EFTA countries, EC Directives, proposals and Working Papers on company law as at June 1989.

FINANCIAL TIMES BUSINESS INFORMATION. *European Company Law,* Rev. ed., 1989. *Financial Times* management report. Policy, debates, existing EC legislation, proposed and planned measures. Also gives details of member states' and EFTA countries national laws and regulations.

MONTAGNON, Peter (editor). *European Competition Policy.* Pinter Publishing. ISBN 0-86187-164-2.

S. J. BERWIN & CO. *Company Law and Competition*. Mercury Books (W. H. Allen), CBI Initiative 1992. 210pp. ISBN 1-85251-027-7.
S. J. BERWIN & CO. *The 1988 Businessman's Guide to EEC Legal Developments*. 1988. 2 vols. 1: *1992: The New Business Environment. 87pp; 2: Intellectual Property and Competition*. 58pp. Vol 1 summarises law on public tendering and procurement, consumer protection, financial services, tax, and telecommunications. Vol 2 outlines legal developments in law of intellectual property and competition.
STEWART-CLARKE, Sir Jack & JACOBS, David. *Competition in Law in the European Community*: A Concise Guide for Business. Kogan Page, 1990. 152pp. ISBN 1-85091-972-0.
VAUGHAN, David. *Law of the European Communities*. Two vols. Butterworth & Co. ISBN 0-406-00300-9.
WYLES, Alison. *1992 Food Law Facts*. Food Research Association (BFMIRA) 1989. Looseleaf. Describes EC institutions relevant to food industry, existing and proposed food legislation, full texts of decisions and directives provided.

Management

BANNOCK, Graham & PEACOCK, Alan. *Governments and Small Business*. Paul Chapman Publishing for the David Hume Institute, 1989. 278pp. ISBN 1-85396-035-7. Includes discussion of policies in EC member states, and small firms as exporters.
BRITISH INSTITUTE OF MANAGEMENT. *Managers' Manifesto 1989: Leading in Europe*. 1989. 18pp.
BRITISH INSTITUTE OF MANAGEMENT. *New Business Horizons in Europe: Completion of the Internal Market and its Management Implications*. 1987. 30pp.
BROWN, Richard. *Europe — Update '88*. British Institute of Management, 1988. (Discussion paper No. 10) 47pp.ISBN 0-854946-195-5. Updates BIM's previous discussion papers on completing the internal market.
BUSINESS INTERNATIONAL. *The 1993 Company: Corporate Strategies for Europe's Single Market*. The Economist Group, 1989. 103pp. Part I looks at underlying trends that the internal market programme reflects, and its progress. Part II examines business response from Europe's major companies.
DEWHURST, James. *Your Business in 1992*. Rooster BOOKS, 1989. 304pp. ISBN 0-948032-18-9. Guide to opportunities and pitfalls for British businessmen.
DUDLEY, James W. *1992: Strategies for the Single Market*. Kogan Page/ Chartered Institute of Management Accountants, 1989. 400pp. ISBN 1-85091-240-8. On intensification of competition and intrusion of foreign competitors in the EC since Single European Act. Written for managers who wish to take advantage of opportunities now available.
DYSON, Kenneth. *Small and Medium-Sized Enterprises*. (Spicers European Policy Reports) Routledge, 1989. 192pp. ISBN 0-415-03829-4. Explains how EC policies towards small and medium-sized companies have developed. Guide to policy initiatives and other relevant proposals.
ERNST & WHINNEY. *Europe in 1992*. 1988. 18pp + questionnaire. Discusses awareness of and attitudes to single market by business.

HANCOCK, Colin. *Croner's 1992 Company Audit* Croner Publications, 1989. 141pp. Aims to help companies set up an action plan in the build up to the completion of the Single Market. Audit is presented in worksheet form, and guides the reader through stages of examination required to assess the impact of the Single Market on a business operation.

HOPKINS, Michael & BINGHAM, George. *The Business use of European Communities Information in the UK*. British Library, 1987. 141pp (Library and Information Research Report 59). ISBN 0-7123-3113-1. Detailed, authoritative and much needed study analysing the EC's impact on British business in, both at national and company level. Evaluates suppliers of EC information such as institutions, government, MEPs, chambers of commerce and trade associations.

HSIA, M. *The Role of Small and Medium-Sized Enterprises in a Single European Market*. University of Reading, Graduate School of European and International Studies (Discussion Paper No.32), 1989. 36pp (Discussion paper No. 32)

INSTITUTE OF DIRECTORS. *Business Leaders' Manifesto. 1992: European Parliament Election . 1989. 23pp*. Discusses 1992 lobbying tactics for British business.

LYNCH, Richard. *European Business Strategies: An Analysis of Europe's Top Companies*. Kogan Page. ISBN 0-7494-0217-2.

MCKENNA & CO. *1992 and the Manufacturer: A Practical Plan for Action*. 1988. 15pp. Brief guide to manufacturing, selling, mergers and acqusitions.

RAJAN, Amin. *1992 A Zero Sum Game*. Industrial Society Press, 1990. 289pp. ISBN 0-85290-594-7. Business know-how and training challenges in an integrated Europe.

THURLEY, Keith & WIRDEMIUS, Hans. Towards European Management. Pitman Publishing. ISBN 0-273-03125-2.

Marketing, exporting

BRITISH INTERNATIONAL FREIGHT ASSOCIATION. *Exporter and Forwarder*. 1990. 327pp.

BROOKE, Michael Z. & BUCKLEY, Peter J. *Handbook of International Trade*. 2nd ed. Macmillan, 1988. 460pp.ISBN 0-333-45333-6.

BROOKE, Michael Z. & MILLS, William R. *Profits from Abroad: Managing Foreign Business*. Kogan Page, 1989. 218pp. ISBN 1-85091-481-8. Describes problems which might arise in any international business operation, basics of setting up, marketing, quality control, etc.

CRONER PUBLICATIONS. *Croner's Reference Book for Exporters*. Looseleaf with monthly updates. Includes documentation, import and exchange control regulations, packing, UK provisions and procedures.

D'ARCY, Masius Benton and BOWLES. *Marketing: Communicating with the Consumer*. Mercury Books (W. H. Allen), CBI Initiative 1992.

DANTON DE ROUFFIGNAC, Peter. *How to Sell in Europe*. Pitman, 1990. 260pp. ISBN 0-273-03149-X. Introduction for exporters on the main changes affecting selling operations.

DAVIS, M. A. *The Documentary Credits Handbook*. Woodhead-Faulkner, 1988. 130pp. ISBN 0-85941-372-1. Practical guide from pre-issuance stage until full utilisation or expiry of the credit.

GIBSS, Paul. *Doing Business in the European Community*. Kogan Page, 1990. 250pp. ISBN 1-85091-971-2. Overview of Europe and 1992 with detailed country by country guide to marketing opportunities, consumer bahaviour etc.

HOGAN, James. *The Export Guide to Europe*. Macmillan, 1986. 1026pp. ISBN 0-333-42827-7. Guide to exporting to France, Germany, Italy, The Netherlands, Spain and Portugal with lists of importers.

INTERNATIONAL CHAMBER OF COMMERCE. *1992 Pack*. Contains: *Guide to Incoterms, Keywords in International Trade, Managing Exchange Rate Risks, Commercial Agency, Guide to Drafting International Distribution Agreements.*

JACQUEMIN, Alexis & SAPIR, Andre. *The European Internal Market: Trade and Competition*. Oxford University Press, 1989. ISBN 0-19-829532-4. Readings on structural changes in European trade after 1992.

LANE, Steven. *The Essential Guide to Exporting*. Independent Freight Communique, 1989. 55 leaves.

McMAHON, Richard. *Goods and Persons in the Single European Market*. Croner Publications. ISBN 0-85452-062-8.

OGLEY, Brian. *Exporting: Getting Your Business off the Ground*. Barclays Bank Plc, 1989. 19pp. ISBN 1-85396-091-8.

OLIVER, Peter. *Free Movement of Goods in the EEC*. 2nd ed. European Law Centre, 1988. 350pp. ISBN 1-85091-972-0.

PERRY, Keith. *Business in Europe: Opportunities for British Companies in the EEC*. Heinemann, 1987. 206pp. ISBN 0-434-91544-0. Describes EC policies affecting business and practical steps for exporters, such as payment methods, market research, credit insurance and lobbying.

QUELCH, John A., BUZZELL, Robert D. & SALAMA R. *The Marketing Challenge of 1992*. Addison-Wesley. ISBN 0-201-51562-8.

ROOSTER BOOKS. *1992: The Implications for Marketing, Advertising and the Media*. Rooster Books Ltd, 1989. 83 leaves. ISBN 1-871510-06-6.

SCHMITTHOFF, Clive M. *Schmitthoff's Export Trade: The Law and Practice of International Trade*. 8th ed. Stevens, 1986. 689pp. ISBN 0-420 46640-1.

WALKER, A. G. *Export Practice and Documentation*. 3rd ed. Butterworth & Co., 1987. 279pp. ISBN 0-408-02800-9.

Directories

The following selection of directories is listed by publisher. Individual editions have not been specified since most are published on a regular basis.

CAPITAL PLANNING INFORMATION. *Eurojargon: A Dictionary of EEC Acronyms, Abbreviations and Sobriquets*. 2nd ed. 1989.

CBD RESEARCH. *Directory of European Industrial and Trade Associations*, Richard Leigh (editor). Edition4, 1986. 405pp.

CBD RESEARCH. *Directory of European Professional and Learned Societies*, Robert W. Adams (editor). Edition 4, 1989. 380pp.

CBD RESEARCH. *Statistics Europe: Sources for Social, Economic and Market Research*, Joan M. Harvey

EUROCONFIDENTIAL. *Euroconfidential 1990 directory of EEC Information Sources*. Belgium. Euroconfidential, 1990. Various paging.

EUROMONITOR. *European Directory of Marketing Information Sources*. 2nd ed. Euromonitor, 1988. 400pp. Covers official sources and publications, libraries and information services, market research companies, databases, abstracts, indexes and journals.

EUROMONITOR. *European Directory of Non-Official Statistical Sources.*

EUROMONITOR. *European Directory of Trade and Business Journals.*

EUROMONITOR. *European Marketing Data and Statistics.*

EUROPAGES. *Europages: The European Business Directory.* Paris. Euroedit SA. Annual listing of 140,000 firms in 10 countries with keyword index to products and services.

LONDON CHAMBER OF COMMERCE AND INDUSTRY. *Chambers of Commerce Worldwide: A Selected List 1989.* 167pp.

PIMS European Directory of Public Relations. PIMS International.

PIMS European Media Directory. Three sections covering newspapers, consumers, trade and technical. PIMS International.

VACHER'S PUBLICATIONS *Vacher's European Companion & Consultants' Register.* Updated quarterly on the European Community, sections on all Western European countries, 1992, and a register of consultants in Europe.

Journals

Agence Europe. Agence internationale d'information pour la presse. Daily press and information service.

Consumers and Europe. Consumers in the European Community Group. Quarterly. Newsletter on matters of interest to consumers.

Countdown 1992. American Chamber of Commerce in Belgium, EC Committee. Quarterly. Details of progress of legislation.

EC Brief. Arthur Young Europe. A periodic review.

EC Bulletin. Price Waterhouse. Bi-monthly.

Economist Intelligence Unit Country Report and *Country Profiles.* Country reports are quarterly and include business orientated analysis of latest indicators and important political and economic developments. Country profiles are published annually and provide resumes of politics, economy and industry.

Economist Intelligence Unit Economic Prospects Series. Specially commissioned reports focus on countries of interest to business community. EC countries covered to date include: Ireland to 1992: putting its house in order. 1988; Portugal to 1993: investing in a European future. 1989; Spain to 1992: joining Europe's mainstream.

EEC Information Services. Advisory service for business enquiries about EEC Directives, Regulations, Agreements or Documents. Monitor Press. Quarterly.

EEC Monitor. KPMG. Monthly review of EC affairs.

Europe 2000. Dower House Publications. 10 issues pa. Information service, news and reviews, supplements and special features for business.

European Access. Ian Thomson (editor) Chadwyck-Healey in association with the UK offices of the European Commission. Bi-monthly. Current awareness bulletin on developments, activities and policies of the EC.

European Business. Europe Information Service. Monthly. Covers business law sector at EEC level.

European Business Journal. European Business Journal Ltd, Whurr Publishers. Quarterly. Major business, political, social and technical issues affecting European business.

European Community Law Bulletin. McKenna & Co. Monthly.
European Focus. KPMG, EC Centre. Quarterly review of topical EC affairs.
European Report. Europe Information Service. Twice weekly. Information on institutions and policy co-ordination, economic and monetary affairs, business brief, internal market, external relations.
European Trends. Economist Intelligence Unit. Quarterly with annual supplement. Analysis and discussion of developments in the EC. Topics of importance to European integration and of direct relevance to businesses.
The Kangaroo News. The Movement for Free Movement. The Kangaroo Group of MEPs. Monthly. Newsletter containing features and brief news items.
Marketing in Europe. Economist Intelligence Unit. Monthly. Research bulletin on consumer goods, marketing and distribution in Europe. Now designed to help firms prepare for 1992.
New European. New European Publications Ltd. Quarterly. Review covering major aspects of European development.
1992 European Alert. Infomat. Weekly. Monitors developments in Europe leading up to 1992: industrial, mergers and acquisitions, EC and government initiatives, financial services, etc.
1992 Single Market Monitor. Tolley Publishing. Monthly. Newsletter summarising EC business and market news, legislation, announcements and new developments.
1992: The External Impact of European Unification. Buraff Publications, Washington DC 20037. Bi-weekly. News for business and government.
Open Market 1992. Westminster Publishing House. Annual. Comment and opinion to help companies enhance sales and prestige before advent of Single Market.
The Single Market Report. Eurostrategy Publishing & Communications Ltd in association with London World Trade Centre. Bi-monthly. News, features, special reports.

Bibliographies

BARCLAY, Christopher & EDMOND, Timothy. *The Single European Market in 1992*. House of Commons Library Research Division (Background Paper No. 211), 1988. 41pp.
DTI, Headquarters Library. *Single Market*, by Jane Garner, (Bibliography series No. 10), 1988. 15pp.
THOMSON, I. *Bibliographic Review: European Political Co-operation. European Access*, November 1988, pp 19-24; and *Bibliographic Review: The Single European Market (SEM). European Access*, February 1989, pp 32-42. Each issue of *European Access* also contains 'Recent references', annotated guides to current material arranged under topics such as 'Single Market — competition' and 'business — industry — trade'.

Index